lonely

T0245995

Argentina

Salta & the Andean
Northwest
p168

Iguazú Falls &
the Northeast
p125

Córdoba &
the Central Sierras
p215

Mendoza
& the Central
Andes
p256

⊙ BUENOS AIRES
p54

Pampas & the
Atlantic Coast
p299

Bariloche & the
Lake District
p344

Patagonia
p391

Tierra del Fuego
p440

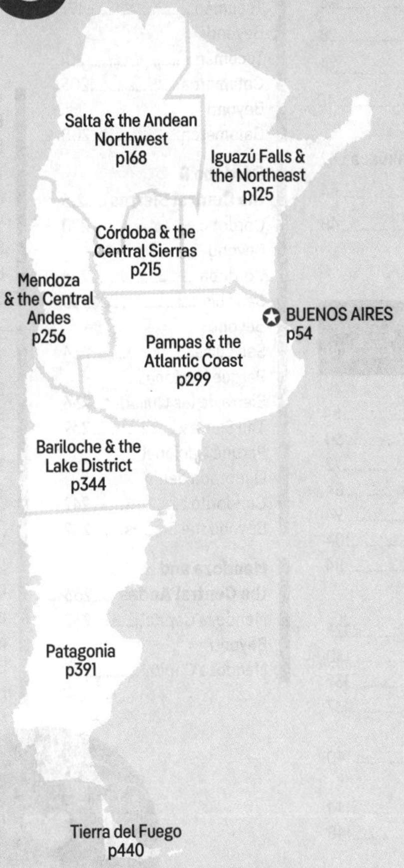

**Isabel Albiston, Ray Bartlett, Christine Gilbert, Victoria
Gill, Diego Jemio, Sorrel Moseley-Williams, Rachel
Tolosa Paz, Federico Perelmuter, Madelaine Triebe**

CONTENTS

Les Eclaireurs
(p448)

Asado (p44)

Perito Moreno Glacier (p421)

Toolkit

Storybook

ANGELA MEIER/SHUTTERSTOCK ©

Iruya (p194)

ARGENTINA
THE JOURNEY BEGINS HERE

When Argentina won the soccer World Cup in 2022, it felt as though the whole world cheered, though perhaps it was just the reverberations of the celebrations in Buenos Aires. This is a place where passion seeps in and wins you over, such that soon you find yourself gunning for Argentina against even your home team. I've always felt enlivened by this colorful land, where dogs wear soccer shirts and septuagenarians dance tango until dawn. It's a country whose cultural riches are ever present; a land of super-latives and such sublime natural wonders it's almost too much to take in. The Andean Northwest is particularly special to me, where the landscapes and culture are be-yond compare. Life in Argentina can be challenging, but everyday absurdities are met with humor, resilience and kindness. From the moment I hear Argentinians chatter in the airport arrivals hall, I feel like I've come home.

Isabel Albiston

@isabel_albiston

Isabel is a writer who lived in Buenos Aires for five years, and never stops returning.

My favorite experience is following the path of the river through a landscape of multicolored mountains on the hike from **Iruya to San Isidro** (p194), with donkeys and condors for company.

WHO GOES WHERE

Our writers and experts choose the places
that, for them, define Argentina

The glacial waters from the Andes seep into **Lago Nahuel Huapi** (p352) and in turn the Río Limay drains the lake and winds through the Patagonia steppe, hugging the highway to Neuquén where it flows to the Atlantic Ocean. The Limay is often overlooked but I am always struck by its beauty – from all that snow, the waters turn to turquoise and are a vision to behold against all that rust steppe landscape.

Rachel Tolosa Paz
@racheltolosapaz

Rachel is a writer and photographer – and the author of The Food of Argentina.

I've been to many places around the world but no place has me like **Patagonia** (p390); the towering Andes and the invigorating smell of the pine trees in Epuyén, the wild horses of Santa Cruz, and the cobalt blue Patagonian coast, with Cabo Raso being my absolute favorite spot – all things that strip me down to my bare bones and remind me what I hold closest to my heart: dramatic landscapes, horses and Argentina.

Madelaine Triebe
@mymaddytravel

Madelaine is a writer with a passion for horses and a love for Argentina and Brazil.

Volcán Galán is one of the most captivating destinations in Argentina. You embark on an eight-hour journey to reach its crater, 4500m above sea level. The road unveils breathtaking vistas of flamingos, lagoons, and the most transparent sky I have seen. Nestled within Puna (p184), it is one of the most inhospitable yet awe-inspiring landscapes.

Diego Jemio
@djemio

Diego is a travel and culture writer and a theater enthusiast.

HEMIS/ALAMY STOCK PHOTO ©

Mendoza (p256) is magical for me because it's where the story of Argentinian winemaking begins. As a sommelier, I'm excited to be able to visit one of the 200 bodegas open to visitors. Framed by the Andes, its foothills, slopes and rivers also create a canvas for outdoor sports and activities such as horseback-riding, rafting and skiing.

Sorrel Moseley-Williams
@sorrelita

Sorrel is a writer about gastronomy, travel and wine.

ERIK COX PHOTOGRAPHY/SHUTTERSTOCK ©

Moisés Ville (p504) was the earliest Jewish settlement in rural Argentina. Founded in the 20th century to house Russian émigrés, it was known as the 'Jerusalem of South America' and remains a testament to the origins of Argentine Jewish culture and one of the largest global Jewish communities.

Federico Perelmuter
Twitter @cementeriocc; Instagram @gorpcore.gaucho

Federico is a writer specializing in culture, history and politics, and is based in Buenos Aires.

GERARDO C.LERNER/SHUTTERSTOCK ©

GEERT SMEY/SHUTTERSTOCK ©

Córdoba and the Sierras (p214) is a wonderfully rich place to explore, filled with all sorts of surprises. Mining towns, beautiful reservoirs, and a youthful vibe in the cities. People rush to the Iguazú Falls, but the other parts have so much to offer, too, especially in the realm of nature.

Ray Bartlett
@kaisoradotcom

A tanguero, novelist and travel writer, Ray has worked on nearly 100 Lonely Planet titles. His next novel will be set in Argentina.

PAULINE LEGAY/GETTY IMAGES ©

Once you start down the road to **Epecuén** (p318), the world changes. Cars and motorcycles make their way past the flamingos feeding in the salt sea. The only sounds you hear are birds in the art-deco slaughterhouse. Passing the ruins, you feel the weight of an avoidable tragedy – one of many in Argentina.

Christine Gilbert
@see_christine_run

Texan by birth and Buenos Aires transplant by choice, Christine is a travel writer, journalist and circus artist.

STEVE BARZE/SHUTTERSTOCK ©

While **Tierra del Fuego**'s (p440) towns and Fuegian Andes are an assault to the senses and unlike anywhere else in the world, if I had to choose a destination it would be the pastoral *estancias* lining the Ruta 3 culminating in the shock of the Desdemona shipwreck. It conveys the wealth and devastation of the terrain in one lesser-explored enclave.

Victoria Gill
@vis4victoria

Victoria is an author of guidebooks, blogs and features on South America's Southern Cone.

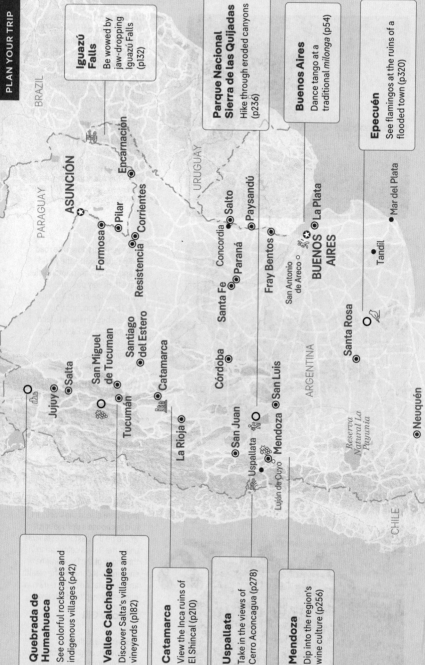

Quebrada de Humahuaca
See colorful rockscapes and indigenous villages (p42)

Valles Calchaquíes
Discover Salta's villages and vineyards (p182)

Catamarca
View the Inca ruins of El Shincal (p210)

Uspallata
Take in the views of Cerro Aconcagua (p278)

Mendoza
Dip into the region's wine culture (p256)

Iguazú Falls
Be wowed by jaw-dropping Iguazú Falls (p132)

Parque Nacional Sierra de las Quijadas
Hike through eroded canyons (p256)

Buenos Aires
Dance tango at a traditional *milonga* (p54)

Epecuén
See flamingos at the ruins of a flooded town (p320)

BRAZIL

PARAGUAY

ASUNCIÓN

Encarnación

Formosa
Pilar
Corrientes
Resistencia

URUGUAY

Salta
Jujuy

San Miguel de Tucuman
Santiago del Estero
Tucumán
Catamarca

La Rioja

San Juan
Uspallata
Mendoza
San Luis
Luján de Cuyo

Córdoba

Santa Fe
Concordia
Paraná
Salto
Paysandú

Fray Bentos
San Antonio de Areco
La Plata
BUENOS AIRES

ARGENTINA

Reserva Natural La Payunia

Santa Rosa

Mar del Plata

Tandil

Neuquén

CHILE

8

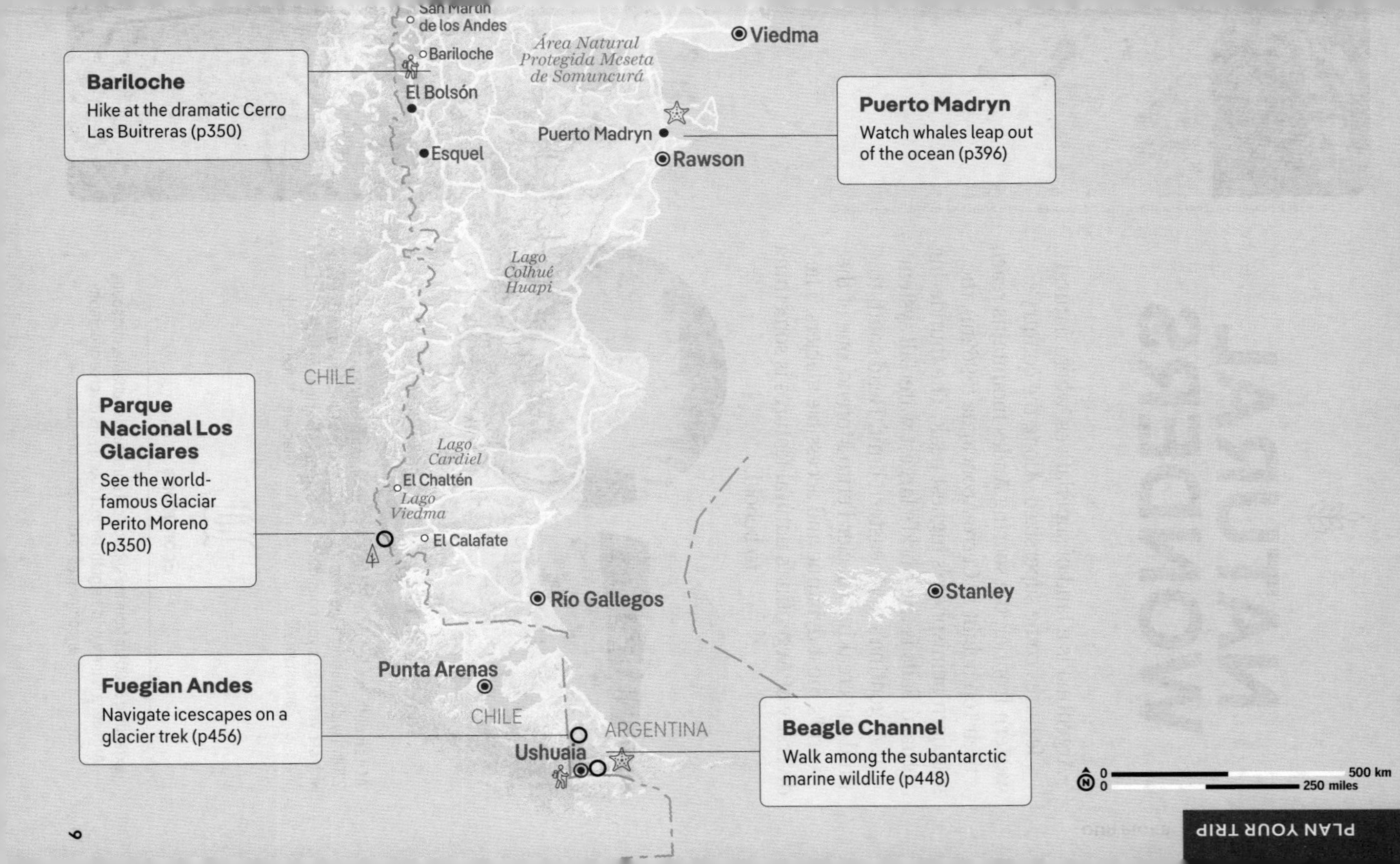

NATURAL
WONDERS

0   250 miles
0   500 km

Bariloche
Hike at the dramatic Cerro Las Buitreras (p350)

Puerto Madryn
Watch whales leap out of the ocean (p396)

Beagle Channel
Walk among the subantarctic marine wildlife (p448)

Parque Nacional Los Glaciares
See the world-famous Glaciar Perito Moreno (p350)

Fuegian Andes
Navigate icescapes on a glacier trek (p456)

San Martín de los Andes
Bariloche
El Bolsón
Esquel
Viedma
Puerto Madryn
Rawson
Stanley

Área Natural Protegida Meseta de Somuncurá

Lago Colhué Huapi

Lago Cardiel
El Chaltén
Lago Viedma
El Calafate

Río Gallegos

Punta Arenas

CHILE

Ushuaia

ARGENTINA

CHILE

9

NATURAL WONDERS

Argentina is a land of superlatives, where natural features come supersized. Along the country's western frontier, the soaring Andes mountains reach their top height at Cerro Aconcagua (6962m), the southern hemisphere's highest peak. The thundering Iguazú Falls is the world's largest waterfall system at Argentina's northeastern limit. Head south to find the creaking Glacier Perito Moreno, one of the world's most dynamic and accessible glaciers. The diversity of Argentina's natural features is something to behold.

Río de la Plata

At its mouth, the Río de la Plata is 220km wide, making it the world's widest river (unless you consider it an estuary).

Unesco Natural Sites

Argentina has five protected natural sites on the Unesco World Heritage list, including Iguazú Falls and Los Glaciares National Park.

Ecoregions

Extending 3800km from the subtropical north to the subantarctic south, Argentina is the world's eighth-largest country. Its diverse geography encompasses 18 different ecoregions.

BEST NATURAL FEATURE EXPERIENCES

Admire one of Argentina's greatest natural wonders, the majestic, slow-moving ❶ **Glacier Perito Moreno** (p421) in El Calafate.

Get wet and go 'Wow!' at ❷ **Iguazú Falls** (p132), the jaw-dropping waterfalls with rainbows and walkways in Misiones.

Take an unforgettable trekking trip through the glaciers, ice caves and the blue and green lagoons of the ❸ **Fuegian Andes** (p456) above Ushuaia.

Hike through the spectacular eroded canyons and dried-out valleys of the ❹ **Sierra de las Quijadas** (p236) in San Luis.

Marvel at the lunar landscape at the ❺ **Valle de la Luna** (p297) in Parque Nacional Ischigualasto in San Juan, then check out the rock formations at nearby Parque Nacional Talampaya in La Rioja.

IN THE WILD

Considering Argentina's vast size, long coastline and extensive mountain ranges, it's no wonder that this varied terrain is home to a variety of flora and fauna. Wildlife-watching opportunities abound, from penguin spotting to whale watching to guanaco glimpsing. Over the past 10 years, a project to reintroduce jaguars to Argentine wetlands has successfully released eight felines in Corrientes; in 2022, cameras captured the births of jaguar cubs in the wild.

Parque Nacional Iberá

This swampy area in Corrientes is home to a variety of wildlife, including swamp deer, capybaras and caimans, along with many migratory birds.

Camelids

Herds of wild guanaco live in the Andean foothills and Patagonian plains. Head to high-altitude areas of Argentina's Andean northwest to see vicuñas.

Coastal Wildlife

In the south, look out for a range of marine wildlife, including Magellanic penguins, sea lions, fur seals, elephant seals, orcas and whales.

BEST WILDLIFE EXPERIENCES

Watch southern right whales leap out of the water just a few meters offshore on ❶ **Playa Las Canteras** (p398), close to Puerto Madryn.

See the world's largest rodent, the docile capybara, at the ❷ **Parque Nacional Iberá** wetlands (p140) in Corrientes.

Hang with the condors on a hike through the other-worldly landscape of ❸ **Cerro Las Buitreras** (p360) near Bariloche.

See one of Argentina's largest flamingo colonies near the ruins of a flooded former spa town at salty ❹ **Lago Epecuén** (p469) in Buenos Aires Province.

Walk among and watch the marine wildlife of the islands and subpolar waters of the ❺ **Beagle Channel** (p448) in Tierra del Fuego.

URBAN DELIGHTS

With a range of museums and galleries to discover, Argentina's cities offer a wealth of cultural experiences. The influence of European immigration can be seen in the Italian- and French-style architecture of buildings constructed in the early 20th century, during Argentina's economic boom, and in the elegant, old-time cafes that are perfect for people-watching. Head to city parks and plazas to see dog walkers, and friends and families sharing *mate* (a local tea).

Museum Tours

Many museums have knowledgeable guides available to show you around. Usually you decide how much to pay the guide; there is no formal charge.

White Headscarf

The emblem of the human rights organization the Mothers of the Plaza de Mayo can be seen in city plazas across Argentina.

Street Art Scene

Argentina's cities are some of the best places to see the country's vibrant street art, including pieces by Martín Ron and El Marian.

❸

❺
   ❷❶

❹

BEST CITY EXPERIENCES

Wander the extensive collection of fossils, giant sloth bones, and Egyptian tomb treasures at the ❶ **Museo de La Plata** (p327), an impressive natural history museum.

Admire the amazing architecture of the ❷ **Palacio Barolo** (p76) in Buenos Aires, which was inspired by *The Divine Comedy*.

See the mummified body of one of three children who died as part of an Inca ritual at Salta's ❸ **Museo de Arqueología de Alta Montaña** (p176).

Visit the ❹ **Museo Paleontológico Egidio Feruglio** (p407) in Trelew, housing one of South America's most important dinosaur collections.

Learn all about the region's wine culture on an immersive tour and tasting at Mendoza's ❺ **La Enoteca** (p264), a thematic wine center.

FOLK CULTURE

Argentine folk culture is personified in the enduring icon of the gaucho, the nomadic cowboys who made a living by taming wild horses. Today gaucho traditions are very much a part of life for rural communities, especially in the Pampas and in areas of Patagonia. Beyond gaucho horsemanship, Argentine folk traditions include a vibrant folk music scene, which is particularly active in the northwest. Other folk traditions center around the stories, music and art of Argentina's indigenous communities.

Feria de Mataderos

Each week, Argentine folk culture comes to the city at this Buenos Aires fair, with horse shows, artisan crafts, music and dancing.

Music & Dance

Argentina's *música folclórica* (folk music) includes *zamba*, a genre which is accompanied by a traditional dance involving waving a handkerchief.

Andean Northwest

In northwest Argentina, traditional spiritual beliefs are reflected in cultural practices and artistic representations, such as the use of carnival masks representing sacred animals.

BEST FOLK EXPERIENCES

Watch a *doma india* (horse whispering) demonstration and give folkloric dancing a whirl at ❶ **Estancia El Ombú de Areco** (p305) in San Antonio de Areco.

Head out on horseback and stop for wine on an expedition with gaucho Nino Masi of ❷ **El Viejo Manzano** (p285) in the Valle de Uco.

Join the festivities at ❸ **Trabún** (p377), a festival in San Martín de los Andes where Chilean and Argentine indigenous communities come together for folk music and dancing.

Spend a week in the mountains at a working ❹ **Patagonian estancia** (p470), riding horses and getting to know sheep-farming culture.

Experience the vibrant culture of the ❺ **Quebrada de Humahuaca's** (p42) indigenous villages during Carnaval.

PARTY TILL DAWN

Argentina's nightlife is legendary, from dancing tango at a *milonga* to hitting the bars and clubs. Crowds converge in urban nightlife areas, where the streets are lined with bars serving craft beer, cocktails and local wine, before the clubs start to warm up from around 2am. And Argentina's cities aren't the only place to party. Across the countryside, you'll find rural *peñas* (folk music venues), restaurants and bars that open late into the night.

Tango Beyond Buenos Aires

For beginners, Córdoba city's *milongas* (tango dance venues) are some of Argentina's most welcoming and accessible. Rosario also has a number of *milongas*.

Late-Night Snack

Argentina's *heladerías* (ice-cream parlors) often stay open past midnight. Stopping for a scoop is the perfect interlude to a steamy summer night.

Theater

Buenos Aires has a thriving theater scene, which includes a packed schedule of *teatro alternativo* (fringe productions) staged in atmospheric art-house theaters and warehouses.

BEST NIGHTLIFE EXPERIENCES

Fuel your night with the locals' favorite tipple, Fernet and cola, and hit the bars and clubs of ❶ **Córdoba's** youthful Güemes district (p225).

Attend an outdoor night circus near the coast in ❷ **Villa Gesell** (p340), when Circo del Aire takes to the stage each summer.

Watch tango being danced in the very streets where the dance form emerged, and take to the floor yourself at a traditional ❸ **Buenos Aires** *milonga* (p56).

Hear the country's best *música folclórica* and learn the traditional dances that accompany each song at ❹ **Salta's** *peñas* (folk music venues; p179).

Discover the restaurants and bars of ❺ **Mendoza's** Calle Arístides (p264), where the party spills out onto the sidewalks.

ARTISAN CRAFTS

If you enjoy shopping for llama wool blankets, hand-woven ponchos, leather bags and silver jewelry, leave space in your suitcase for souvenirs. Across the country, Argentina's skilled artisans produce high-quality textiles and crafts. Whether or not you plan to shop, be sure to spend a Sunday browsing the craft and antique stalls at the Feria de San Telmo in Buenos Aires, where tango dancers and other street performers add to the fun.

Leather Goods

Argentina has a long tradition for producing quality *marroquinería*, hand-crafted leather pieces, including belts, bags and wallets, as well as gaucho paraphernalia.

Ponchos

In July, the streets of Catamarca city fill with artisan stalls selling fine, handwoven tunics as the city celebrates the Fiesta del Poncho.

Fair Trade

Look for artisan cooperatives or shops that offer local craftspeople fair prices (*comercio justo*). Alternatively, buy directly from the artisans at market stalls.

BEST ARTISAN EXPERIENCES

Buy knives, jewelry, or *mate* kits from the silversmith workshops in ❶ **San Antonio de Areco** (p304) in the Pampas.

Take a pottery class at the Municipal Ceramics and Pottery Workshop in Villa Gesell's ❷ **Reserva Pinar del Norte** (p340).

Visit the home workshops of the craftspeople of Tafí del Valle to see handmade textiles and ceramics on the ❸ **Ruta del Artesano** (p203) in Tucumán.

Watch artisans weave ponchos and blankets the traditional way – from sheep and llama fleece to finished product – at their workshops in ❹ **Belén** (p211) in Catamarca.

Spend a day wandering ❺ **El Bolsón's** (p361) sprawling Feria Artesanal beneath the fairy-tale peak of Cerro Piltriquitrón.

ARCHAEOLOGICAL WONDERS

The intriguing remnants of earlier cultures can be seen at the excavated ruins of previous settlements, including the extensive remains of the Ciudad Sagrada de Quilmes in Tucumán. Such sites now have worthwhile museums offering background context, and are managed by the local indigenous community. Elsewhere, local guides offer hikes to see ancient cave paintings and point out stones once used to mark the seasons. Archaeological museums house ancient tools, textiles and ceramics recovered from remote locations.

Cave Paintings

Argentina's early peoples left a number of intriguing cave paintings, most notably the remarkable hand prints at the Cueva de Las Manos Pintadas.

Inca Empire

By the late 15th century, the Inca empire of Tawantinsuyu extended all the way from Colombia to northwestern Argentina, reaching as far south as Mendoza.

Ceramics

Items of pottery found at archaeological sites, such as ceremonial pipes and drinking vessels, offer an insight into the cultures that once lived there.

BEST ARCHAEOLOGICAL EXPERIENCES

Venture into sparsely populated inland Patagonia to marvel at the enchanting rock paintings of **①** **Cueva de Las Manos Pintadas** (p434), believed to be more than 10,000 years old.

Visit the remains of an Inca city at **②** **El Shincal de Quimivil** (p210), including remarkable temples devoted to the sun and moon, near Londres in Catamarca.

Admire the sun-drenched stonework of the atmospheric ruins of the **③** **Jesuit Missions** (p146) in Misiones.

Discover the extensive ruins of a city once occupied by the Quilmes at the **④** **Ciudad Sagrada de Quilmes** (p204) in Tucumán.

Visit the hilltop remains of an Aguada culture settlement at **⑤** **Pueblo Perdido de la Quebrada** (p207) on the outskirts of Catamarca city.

EPIC ROAD TRIPS

Traveling overland through Argentina is a true adventure, whether it be by car, bus, bicycle, horseback or on foot. The destination is hardly the point as you move through memorable multicolored landscapes. The gradually changing scenery gives a sense of Argentina's awesome geography, and you'll pass rural villages that offer a glimpse of regular everyday life. Plus, there's plenty of wildlife to spot en route. So prepare your playlists, download maps and hit the road.

Ruta Nacional 40

Running parallel to the Andes from Jujuy in the north all the way south to Santa Cruz, this highway passes through spectacular mountain scenery.

Argentina by Bike

Many of Argentina's highways are light on traffic and make for memorable adventures on two wheels. Plan for long distances between towns.

The Motorcycle Diaries

In 1952, Ernesto 'Che' Guevara and Alberto Granado set off from Buenos Aires and stopped in Miramar and Bariloche, before crossing into Chile.

BEST ROAD TRIP EXPERIENCES

Access Parque Provincial Aconcagua and the highest summit in the southern hemisphere via the ❶ **Uspallata Pass** (p278) in Mendoza.

Take in the extraordinary beauty of seven lakes and soaring peaks on a journey by car or bike along the ❷ **Ruta de los Siete Lagos** (p378).

Drive past soaring volcanoes and grazing vicuñas on ❸ **Ruta Los Seismiles** (p209) through Catamarca to the Chilean border.

Cycle, drive or hike Bariloche's bite-sized ❹ **Circuito Chico** (p356), the perfect taster for Northern Patagonia.

Gawp at cardon cacti and stop at high-altitude vineyards in Salta's ❺ **Valles Calchaquíes** (p182).

REGIONS & CITIES

Find the places that tick all your boxes.

Salta & the Andean Northwest

MOUNTAINS, INDIGENOUS CULTURE AND FOLKLORE

The Andean culture of Argentina's Northwest can be experienced through folk music and dancing, the flavorsome regional cuisine, artisan textiles, and carnival celebrations that meld indigenous and Spanish traditions. Amid the sun-drenched multicolored mountains and cacti lie the ruins of Inca cities.

p168

Iguazú Falls & the Northeast

WATERFALLS, WILDLIFE AND WONDER

From the jungles of Argentina's northeastern corner emerges one of the world's greatest natural features, the thundering waters of the Iguazú Falls. Nearby, the wetlands of Parque Nacional Iberá offer astonishing wildlife watching. This is a region of natural wonders and Jesuit mission ruins.

p125

Córdoba & the Central Sierras

VIBRANT, AUSTERE, DESOLATE AND CHARMING

Argentina's second city is home to both a youthful student population and some of the country's oldest buildings, including a 17th-century Jesuit church. Beyond the city limits lie rolling hills dotted with little towns, each with their own eccentric character.

p215

Mendoza & the Central Andes

BLENDING WINE COUNTRY WITH THE ANDES

Wine enthusiasts know Mendoza as a world-leading region for Malbec. Grapes take central stage here, but beyond the *bodegas* (wine cellars) the province of Mendoza offers mountain climbing, horseback riding and whitewater rafting adventures, as well as wintertime skiing.

p256

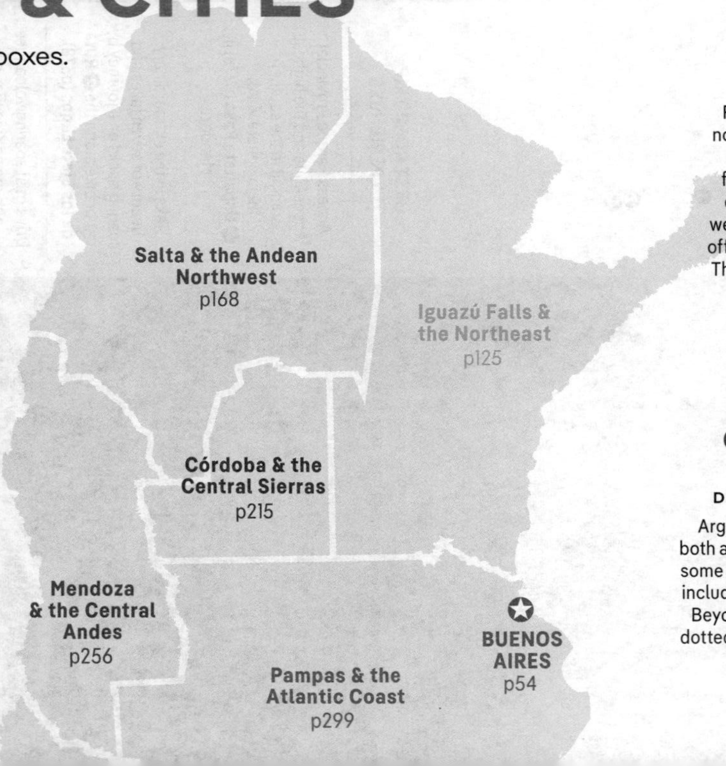

Iguazú Falls & the Northeast p125

BUENOS AIRES p54

Salta & the Andean Northwest p168

Córdoba & the Central Sierras p215

Pampas & the Atlantic Coast p299

Mendoza & the Central Andes p256

Buenos Aires

FASCINATING AND VIBRANT CULTURAL SCENE

Argentina's capital city is a seductive blend of cultural riches and hedonistic fun. Whether your interests lie in literature or *fútbol* (soccer), architecture or tango, politics or street art, or simply enjoying a delectable steak, there is something for everybody here.

p54

Patagonia

JAGGED PEAKS, GLACIERS AND MARINE WILDLIFE

The vast expanse of land that comprises southern Patagonia is both barren and beautiful. From whale watching and penguin spotting in the east to Glacier Perito Moreno and the hiking trails of the west, this awe-inspiring region offers nature and wildlife on a grand scale.

p391

Tierra del Fuego

SOUTHERNMOST ENDS OF THE EARTH

At Argentina's southern tip is an archipelago of windswept islands that are home to marine wildlife, snow-capped mountains and glaciers. At the ends of the earth, the town of Ushuaia offers bountiful seafood and is the jumping-off point for Antarctic adventures.

p440

Bariloche & the
Lake District
p344

Patagonia
p391

Tierra del Fuego
p440

Pampas &
the Atlantic Coast

GAUCHO COUNTRY, ESTANCIAS AND BEACH FORESTS

Buenos Aires Province is a region of fertile grasslands, once roamed by *gauchos* on horseback. Here, rural traditions are kept alive at countryside *estancias* (ranches). Meanwhile, the province's cities are cultural hubs with noteworthy architecture. Come summertime, the Atlantic coast beaches fill with holidaymakers.

p299

Bariloche & the
Lake District

BREATHTAKING LANDSCAPES AND EPIC DRIVES

With forested mountains and glacier-fed lakes, Bariloche attracts hikers, climbers and skiers to its spectacular scenery and fresh climate. Add in Neuquén's Pinot Noirs and dinosaur footprints, and it is no wonder this region tops many traveler to-do lists.

p344

SUNSINGER/SHUTTERSTOCK ©

San Antonio de Areco (p304)

ITINERARIES

East Coast Highlights

Allow: 5 days **Distance:** 1161km

The city of Buenos Aires is the star attraction here, but explore beyond the city limits and you'll discover enchanting rural towns that offer fresh air, artisan produce, and a decidedly high quality of life. This route cuts through the Pampas and then hits the top spots on the coast.

❶ BUENOS AIRES ⏱ **2 DAYS**

You could spend a lifetime in **Buenos Aires** (p54) and still find new things to see, but with two days in the city you'll have time to explore Plaza de Mayo and San Telmo, see the Cementerio de la Recoleta (pictured), hit the shops in Palermo, dine out at the city's excellent restaurants and dance tango at a *milonga* (tango dance venue).

🚗 *1½ hours*

❷ SAN ANTONIO DE ARECO ⏱ **1 DAY**

The Pampas town of **San Antonio de Areco** (p304) can be visited on a day trip from Buenos Aires, but it's worth staying overnight at an *estancia* (ranch) to dip into rural life. Spend a morning horseback riding, then head into town to visit the silversmith workshops and hang out with guachos (cowboys) at old-time bars.

🚗 *5 hours*

❸ TANDIL ⏱ **½ DAY**

On your way to the coast, make a stop in **Tandil** (p312) for hikes in the hills and to sample the city's famous cheeses and salamis, which come sliced on wooden boards to be shared in the form of a *picada*. Then take the chairlift over the pine forests of Cerro El Centinela for walks in the trees and panoramic views.

🚗 *2¼ hours*

4
MAR DEL PLATA – ⏱ 1 DAY

Besides its famous sandy beach, **Mar del Plata** (p334) has museums to visit, interesting architecture to see, as well as craft beer to imbibe and seafood to sample. Allow time to visit the nearby sea lion reserve.

🚌 5¼ hours

🚗 *Detour:* From Tandil, take the coastal route via Villa Gesell, where you can walk through forested dunes and see the circus. ⏱ 7 hours.

5
BAHÍA BLANCA ⏱ ½ DAY

The port city of **Bahía Blanca** (p319) has museums covering the city's shipping and immigrant history, including one housed in a striking former power plant. It is the reputed site of some unnerving paranormal activity.

🚗 *Detour:* Hikers will want to head to Parque Provincial Ernesto Tornquist for walks to the window-shaped Cerro de la Ventana or to nearby waterfalls. ⏱ 5 hours.

Ushuaia (p446)

ITINERARIES

Southern Sights

Allow: 4 days **Distance:** 992km

Argentina's extreme south is a windswept region of breathtaking beauty. This itinerary takes you on an adventure to the country's southernmost tip, where you can walk with penguins and go glacier trekking, before heading to the southern Andes region for more mountain hiking and to gawp at Glacier Perito Moreno.

❶ RIO GRANDE ⏲ ½ DAY

The first stop on the journey to the ends of the earth is **Río Grande** (p412), the northern Tierra del Fuego town that has a thriving cultural scene as well as museums to visit and birds to spot on coastal walks. The town's equestrian centers offer opportunities to explore the area on horseback, or take a polo lesson.

🚌 1 hour 20 minutes

❷ TOLHUIN ⏲ ½ DAY

On the forested banks of Lago Fagnano (pictured), the low-key town of **Tolhuin** (p471) is Tierra del Fuego's spiritual heart. Here you can get out onto the water in a kayak and then sample home cooking in a log cabin, followed by a local craft beer.

🚌 1½ hours

🚶Detour: Explore the Fuegian Andes on foot on a hike between Lago Escondido and Lago Fagnano. ⏲ 3 hours.

❸ USHUAIA ⏲ 1 DAY

The spectacularly located town of **Ushuaia** (p446) is the gateway to Antarctica. From here you can go glacier trekking and explore the snow-capped mountains, valleys and lakes of Tierra del Fuego National Park. Ushuaia also has a number of museums and some of the country's best seafood.

✈ 1¼ hours

🚶Detour: See subpolar wildlife on a boat tour around the Beagle Channel archipelago. ⏲ 3 hours by boat.

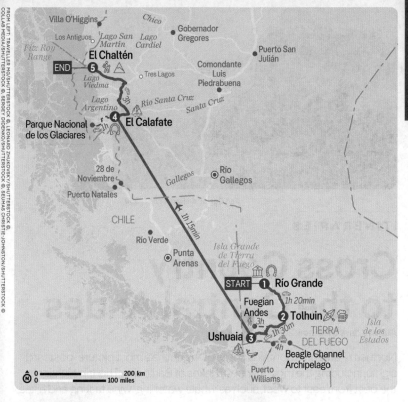

4
EL CALAFATE ⏱ 1 DAY

El Calafate (p419) is the place to go to see one of Argentina's top attractions, the slow-moving Glacier Perito Moreno. Beyond its famous glacier, El Calafate is well-known for mountain hikes and horseback riding at Patagonian *estancias* (ranches).

🚌 *5 hours*

🚗 *Detour: Take a tour, drive or catch the bus to Parque Nacional de los Glaciares to view Glacier Perito Moreno. ⏱ 4 hours.*

5
EL CHALTÉN ⏱ 1 DAY

The main reason to visit the small town of **El Chaltén** (p429) is for adventures in the snow-capped, jagged peaks that surround the town. The trails near town offer hikes ranging from gentle walks to extreme treks. Nearby is the highest mountain in the Patagonian Andes, the pointy granite peaks of Cerro Fitz Roy (3375m, pictured).

JOSE DE JESUS CHURION DEL/SHUTTERSTOCK ©

San Carlos de Bariloche (p350)

ITINERARIES

Cross Country to the Central Andes

Allow: 7 days **Distance:** 2070km

Northern Patagonia contains some of Argentina's most picture-postcard sights, including the mountains and lakes of Bariloche. This trip highlights the best from east to west, such as whale watching, wine tasting and hikes.

❶ PUERTO MADRYN ⏱1 DAY

Start your Patagonian adventure in **Puerto Madryn** (p396) for wildlife watching and platters of fresh-off-the-boat seafood. Head to nearby beaches to see southern right whales, who come here from June to mid-December to breed.

🚗 7 hours

Detour: Puerto Madryn is the gateway to the Península Valdés nature reserve, home to guanacos, rheas, penguins, sea lions and elephant seals.

❷ ESQUEL ⏱1 DAY

In Patagonia's wild west, the town of **Esquel** (p408) offers off-piste skiing and snowboarding in winter and accessible forest hiking in summer. Look out for roadside stalls selling local cheeses and bread on the way to the trailheads and slopes.

🚗 2 hours

Detour: Ride La Trochita railway from Esquel to Nahuelpan, with views over the rolling steppe of northern Chubut. ⏱3 hours.

❸ EL BOLSÓN ⏱½ DAY

Situated roughly halfway between Esquel and Bariloche, **El Bolsón** (p361) makes a scenic place to stop. Here you can visit its hippy artisan market, shop for organic produce grown in the surrounding valley and drink craft beer. If you have more time to spare, you can hit the hiking trails of Cajón del Azul.

🚗 2 hours'

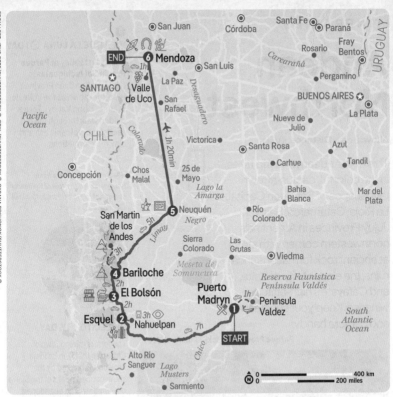

④ BARILOCHE ⏱ 2 DAYS

Sitting on the shores of Lago Nahuel Huapi (pictured) and beautiful year-round, **Bariloche** (p350) is beloved by Argentines and foreign visitors alike. Get a taste of the area's mountains and lakes by driving or cycling the Circuito Chico.

🚗 5 hours

🛤 *Detour:* Drive the Ruta de los Siete Lagos, the 110km stretch of the RN 40 between Villa la Angostura and San Martín de los Andes. ⏱ 3 hours.

⑤ NEUQUÉN ⏱ 1 DAY

Patagonia's largest city is **Neuquén** (p381), the meeting place of the rivers Limay and Neequén. There are a number of galleries and museums to visit and dinosaur-related sights nearby, and you can sample Pinot Noir at *bodegas* located less than an hour's drive from the city. At night, visit the observatory to see the stars of the desert sky.

✈ 1¼ hours

⑥ MENDOZA ⏱ 1½ DAYS

In addition to its world-class wineries and culinary scene, the city of **Mendoza** (p262) is the gateway to whitewater rafting, mountain climbing and horseback riding adventures in the Andes. Wine enthusiasts should base themselves in the Malbec heartland of Luján de Cuyo, south of Mendoza city.

🛤 *Detour:* Spend an afternoon touring and tasting at the wineries of the Valle de Uco. ⏱ 4 hours.

ITINERARIES

Andean Northwest

Allow: 5 days **Distance:** 1075km

This epic Andean road trip takes in the colorful, cactus-strewn landscapes of San Juan Capital, La Rioja, Catamarca, Salta and Jujuy Provinces in Argentina's northwestern corner, with stops at ancient rock formations, Inca ruins, the elegant city of Salta, and Cafayate's high-altitude wineries. Keep your sunglasses and camera handy.

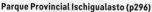

Parque Provincial Ischigualasto (p296)

❶ VALLE DE LA LUNA ⏱ 1 DAY

The desert valley of **Parque Provincial Ischigualasto** (p296), in San Juan Province, is better known as the Valle de la Luna (Moon Valley). Take a guided walk through the red sandstone, volcanic ash and clay rock formations.

🚐 2½ hours

🛤 *Detour:* Combine a trip to Ischigualasto with a tour of the nearby canyons of La Rioja's Parque Nacional Talampaya. ⏱ 4 hours.

❷ CHILECITO ⏱ ½ DAY

The former mining town of **Chilecito** (p213), in La Rioja Province, is backed by the snow-capped peaks of the Sierra de Famatina. The abandoned stations of the cable car (pictured) that once transported minerals from the mines are now museums. Nearby, take a look at the unusual phenomenon of the confluence of two different colored rivers.

🚐 3 hours

❸ BELÉN ⏱ ½ DAY

In Catamarca Province, the town of **Belén** (p211) is home to artisan weavers' workshops and close to the Inca ruins of Shincal de Quimivil, which include hilltop temples to the sun and the moon.

🚐 3½ hours

🛤 *Detour:* Take a drive via the historic buildings of the Ruta de Adobe to Fiambalá, where you can relax in hot springs and sandboard down dunes. ⏱ 7 hours

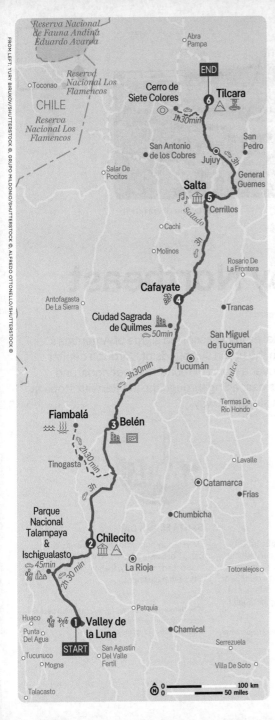

❹
CAFAYATE ⏱ 1 DAY

In the rugged landscapes of the Valles Calchaquíes, **Cafayate** (p183) is a picturesque and laid-back town. Here you can visit the high-altitude wineries that produce Malbec and the region's famous Torrontés, and learn about wine production in the town's Museo de la Vid y El Vino.

🚗 3 hours

🔀Detour: Stop to see the ruins of a pre-Inca city at the Ciudad Sagrada de Quilmes. ⏱ 3 hours.

❺
SALTA ⏱ 1 DAY

Salta's (p174) top sight is the Museo de Arqueología de Alta Montaña, where you can see the Inca mummies of three children, found high in the Andes mountains. Then browse the boutiques, hike (or take the cable car) up Cerro San Bernardo, and catch a performance by some of Argentina's best folk musicians at one of the city's *peñas* (folk music venues).

🚗 3 hours

❻
TILCARA ⏱ 1 DAY

The village of **Tilcara** (p186) makes an ideal base for exploring the mountains and indigenous villages of the Quebrada de Humahuaca in Jujuy (pictured). Hike to a nearby waterfall, visit a mountainside photography museum and take in the views from the Pucará.

🔀Detour: Count the colors of Purmamarca's Cerro de Siete Colores and stage a photo shoot at the Salinas Grandes. ⏱ 5 hours.

Parque Nacional Iberá (p140)

ITINERARIES

North by Northeast

Allow: 4 days **Distance:** 1546km

This steamy trip north takes in the assorted sights of Argentina's northeast. Emerge from the urban surrounds of Córdoba capital and head north to discover a world of fauna-rich wetlands, and awe-inspiring waterfalls cascading through the jungle, with stops at historic Jesuit missions along the way.

1
CÓRDOBA ⏱1 DAY

Begin your trip northeast in **Córdoba** (p220), Argentina's second city. Here you can visit the city's museums, art galleries and Jesuit ruins (pictured). At night, dance tango at a *milonga* or join the students for a Fernet-and-cola-fueled night out in the city's Güemes neighborhood.

🚌 4½ hours

🛣 *Detour: Take a trip to see Che Guevara's former home in Alta Gracia in the Córdoba hills.* ⏱ 4 hours.

2
SANTA FE ⏱½ DAY

On your way north, stop in the provincial capital of **Santa Fe** (p162) to visit the landmark Franciscan monastery, then take your pick of the city's other museums.

🚌 9 hours

🛣 *Detour: Home to cute capybaras and palm trees, the spectacular Parque Nacional El Palmar in Entre Ríos is worth the effort it takes to get there.* ⏱ 9 hours.

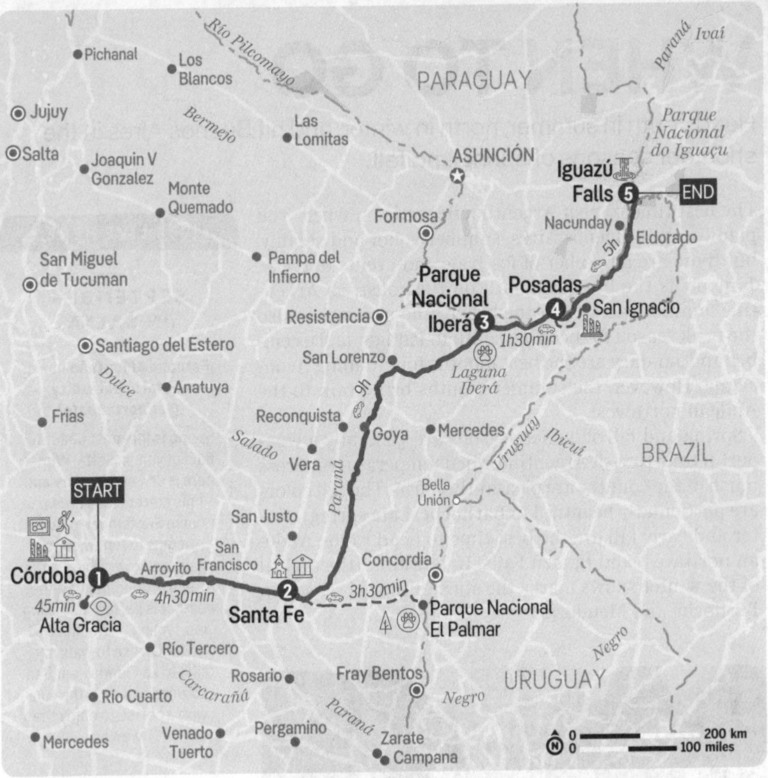

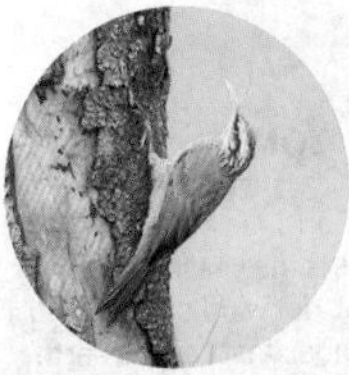

3 PARQUE NACIONAL IBERÁ ⏱ 1 DAY

Nature lovers should be sure to make the trip to the wetlands of **Parque Nacional Iberá** (p140), one of the best places in South America to view wildlife. The shallow lakes and lagoons (esteros) of Iberá are home to caimans, capybaras, marsh deer, howler monkeys, otters and an extraordinary array of birdlife (some 350 species).

1½ hours

4 POSADAS ⏱ ½ DAY

The town of **Posadas** (p145) in Misiones is worth a stop to view the ruins of 17th-century buildings constructed in the area by Jesuit missionaries. The sun-drenched remains are notable for their ornamental carved stonework.

5 hours

***Detour:** Head to San Ignacio to see San Ignacio Miní, the most complete of the area's Jesuit missions. ⏱ 3 hours.*

5 IGUAZÚ FALLS ⏱ 1 DAY

Emerging peacefully from the jungle at the border of Argentina and Brazil, the Río Iguazú plunges over basalt cliffs in a series of cascades known as the **Iguazú Falls** (p132). This thundering spectacular can be embraced from jungle paths on the Argentina side and viewing platforms in Brazil. Be prepared to be awestruck – and sprayed with water.

WHEN **TO GO**

Head south in summer, north in winter, and hit Buenos Aires in the shoulder seasons of spring and fall.

The best time to visit Argentina depends on where you plan to go. In Buenos Aires, summer is hot and steamy, but there are a number of festivals and events to enjoy. January is the busiest month on the coast, as Argentine families vacation at the beach, and summer is also the peak season for heading south to Patagonia. December and January are the best months for climbing Aconcagua. However, the summer months bring rain to the Andean northwest.

Spring and fall shoulder seasons are generally a wonderful time to visit Argentina when temperatures across much of the country are pleasantly warm. The fall colors are particularly beautiful in Bariloche. Late spring, winter and early fall are the best time to head to the Andean northwest and Iguazú Falls. In late June, the arrival of the winter snows marks the start of the ski season in Bariloche and Mendoza.

LEFT: JAVIER ETCHEVERRY/ALAMY STOCK PHOTO ©
FAR RIGHT: LILI RAIJELI/SHUTTERSTOCK ©

Día de la Pachamama

⊗ **I LIVE HERE**

SEPTEMBER IN SALTA

Fernando Montaño has a hostel in Salta city.
@allnortehostel

Spring is the most beautiful time of year in Salta. Winter here is dry, and the city and hills start to look brown, but in September, nature begins to renew once again, and everything turns green. During the day, the weather is perfect for hiking and cycling – around 20°C to 25°C. I like to walk my dogs to La Tienda near San Lorenzo and sit in the sun with a coffee to enjoy the views.

ZONDA

Winter in San Juan and La Rioja Provinces is the season of the *zonda*, a hot, dry wind descending from the Andes that carries earth and dust, reducing visibility, and causes dramatic increases in temperature.

Weather Through The year

JANUARY	FEBRUARY	MARCH	APRIL	MAY	JUNE
Avg daytime max: **20°C–28°C**	Avg daytime max: **20°C–27°C**	Avg daytime max: **18°C–24°C**	Avg daytime max: **15°C–21°C**	Avg daytime max: **12°C–17°C**	Avg daytime max: **9°C–15°C**
Days of rainfall: **5**	Days of rainfall: **6**	Days of rainfall: **6**	Days of rainfall: **7**	Days of rainfall: **5**	Days of rainfall: **6**

EL NIÑO

This weather effect causes soaring temperatures and heavier than normal rainfall in Argentina. It's prompted by the warming of the surface of the central and eastern Pacific Ocean. It usually lasts between nine and 12 months.

Argentina's Biggest Festivals

Festival Nacional del Folklore In January, Argentina's cultural calendar kicks off with the Cosquín Folk Festival near Córdoba city, the country's biggest folk music event. 🌸 **January**

Carnaval de Humahuaca (p192) Carnival is celebrated across Argentina in February or March, with dancing troupes, bands and parades. In the Quebrada de Humahuaca, the celebrations are a fusion of indigenous and Spanish traditions. 🌸 **February**

Tango BA Festival y Mundial (p109) In August, dancers from around the world arrive in Buenos Aires for the tango festival and world cup dancing competition, the world's most important Argentine tango event. 🍂 **August**

Fiesta de la Tradición (p307) In November, gauchos ride into the Pampas town of San Antonio de Areco to compete in displays of horsemanship. The air fills with the smoke of barbecues. 🌸 **November**

Weird & Wonderful Gatherings

Fiesta Nacional de Trekking In March, outdoor enthusiasts converge on El Chaltén in Patagonia for rock-climbing and woodcutting competitions. 🌸 **March**

Guardia Bajo las Estrellas (p179) Thousands of northern gauchos gather on horseback in Salta City to pay their respects to Independence hero General Güemes on the June anniversary of his death. 🍂 **June**

Fiesta del Invierno The most magical event in Tierra del Fuego's Winter Festival, held in July, is the Bajada de Antorchas (torchlit descent) down the slopes of Cerro Castor. 🍂 **July**

Día de la Pachamama (p202) On August 1, communities across the Andean northwest hold ceremonies to make offerings of local foods and coca leaves to the Pachamama (Mother Earth). The tradition is observed across Jujuy, as well as in areas of Salta and Tucumán. 🍂 **August**

Palermo (p60)

RAIN SHADOW ZONE

Argentina has an area of arid eastern coastline, caused by a rain shadow zone. This effect is created when air masses lose their moisture as they pass over the high Andes mountains.

	JULY	AUGUST	SEPTEMBER	OCTOBER	NOVEMBER	DECEMBER
Avg daytime max:	8°C–14°C	9°C–16°C	11°C–18°C	14°C–21°C	16°C–24°C	19°C–27°C
Days of rainfall:	6	5	5	8	6	6

Cerro Fitz Roy (p432)

GET PREPARED FOR ARGENTINA

Useful things to load in your bag, your ears and your brain

Clothes

Hiking boots For the trails in Patagonia.
Windproof jacket Important for the south.
A buff or bandana For hiking and horseback riding.
Hat, sunscreen and sunglasses You'll need them year-round in the Andes.
Umbrella Useful in Buenos Aires, which has rainy days every season.
Casual clothes Tank tops and shorts are fine in most situations.
A smarter outfit Pack for a night out.
Dancing shoes The best shoes for tango have leather or suede soles without too much grip; women often dance in heels, but it's not required.

Manners

Friends greet each other with one kiss on the cheek to say hello and goodbye. In a group, greet each person individually.

Join the line to board buses, and give up your seat to anyone who needs it.

Use the name Islas Malvinas rather than Falkland Islands. Be thoughtful in how you choose to discuss this subject (if at all).

Comfortable walking shoes or sneakers You'll be glad of them.
A cross-body bag or fanny pack For your wallet and documents.

📖 READ

Fictions (Jorge Luis Borges; 1944) An anthology of fantastic tales of dreams within dreams, complex labyrinths and mysterious worlds.

The Tunnel (Ernesto Sabato; 1948) An engrossing, existentialist novel about an obsessed painter's distorted take on reality.

Kiss of the Spider Woman (Manuel Puig; 1976) This novel depicts a series of dialogues between two cellmates in an Argentine prison.

Hopscotch (Julio Cortázar; 1963) Experimental novel prefaced with instructions on how the chapters can be read.

Words

The Spanish spoken is sprinkled with words known as *lunfardo,* a dialect that includes expressions that originally came from Italian. The influence of Italian immigrants can also be seen in communicating with hand gestures.

'Boludo/a' Idiot.
'Bondi' or **'Colectivo'** Bus.
'Buena onda' Someone who is good company. '*¿Qué onda?*' means 'What's up?'
'Chabón' or **'Chabona'** Guy or girl.
'Chamuyero/a' Someone who is charming but loose with the truth. Can be used in verb form ('*chamuyar*').
'Che' Used as an exclamation ('hey!') for mate or buddy.
'Chorro/a' Thief.
'Dale' Depending on the tone of voice, it means either 'Yes, okay' or 'Come on, hurry up'.
'Escabiar' To drink alcohol.

'Fiaca' A feeling of laziness ('*¡Qué fiaca!*'), or 'I can't be bothered' ('*Tengo fiaca.*')
'Guita' or **'Plata'** Money.
'Macanudo/a' A complimentary word to describe a person or situation you like.
'Morfar' To eat. '*Morfi*' means food.
'Mufa' or **'Yeta'** The name given to someone who is believed to bring bad luck; for example, someone whose arrival to watch a football match coincides with the opposing team scoring.
'Posta' Exactly right. Used to show that you are being serious.
'Qué hacés?' or **'Cómo andás?'** 'How are you?'
'Quilombo' A complete mess.
'Trucho' Fake.
'Zapardo/a' Used to describe someone whose behavior is shocking or irresponsible.

📺 WATCH

The Secret of Their Eyes (Juan José Campanella; 2009, pictured) A former prosecutor writes about a murder case he worked on 25 years before.

The Official Story (Luis Puenzo; 1985). During the military dictatorship a woman realizes her complicity in brutality.

Nine Queens (Fabián Belinsky; 2000) Two con artists scam their way around the streets of Buenos Aires in a film full of humor.

The Headless Woman (Lucrecia Martel; 2008) Unsettling film about a woman left confused after hitting something (or someone) with her car.

🎧 LISTEN

Piano Bar (Charly García; 1984) The third album by the prolific father of Argentine rock is rich in intriguing, irreverent lyrics and creative melodies.

Estaciones Porteñas (Daniel Barenboim, Rodolfo Mederes and Héctor Console; 1996). Composer Astor Piazzolla wrote a tango for each Buenos Aires season.

Corazón Valiente (Gilda; 1995) This cumbia album, released the year before Gilda's tragic death in a road accident, includes the hits 'Fuiste' and 'Paisaje'.

Mar Dulce (Bajofondo; 2007) Combines electronica with musical genres from the Río de la Plata region, including tango, *candombe, murga and milonga.*

Cerro de los Siete Colores (p191)

TRIP PLANNER

QUEBRADA DE HUMAHUACA

In the province of Jujuy in Argentina's Andean Northwest, the Quebrada de Humahuaca is an arid valley where the mountains and rockscapes reflect a vast palette of colors, offset by vivid blue skies and dazzling sunshine. Along the Quebrada are a string of villages where local indigenous culture and traditions continue to thrive.

Geography

The Quebrada de Humahuaca is a scenic gorge that forms a narrow valley around the Río Grande, extending south for 155km from near the border with Bolivia to the village of Volcán. There's evidence that the valley has been an important trade route for more than 10,000 years, including during the Inca period. In recognition of its cultural heritage, the Quebrada de Humahuaca is a designated Unesco World Heritage Site.

Indigenous Culture

Indigenous culture is reflected in local clothing and textiles, architecture, music and food, as well as in the community's spiritual beliefs and traditions.

Festivals & Events

The Carnaval de Humahuaca (p192) is one of Argentina's most fascinating celebrations. The use of animal masks reflects the traditional spiritual beliefs of the people of the Quebrada. On the Día de la Pachamama (August 1), communities hold ceremonies in honor of the Pachamama (Mother Earth); offerings of coca leaves, tobacco and local foods are placed in the ground.

Natural Features

The different colors of the landscapes are the result of complex geological processes occurring over the course of millions of years, including tectonic activity, erosion and sedimentation. The effect is most

BEST ACTIVITIES IN THE QUEBRADA DE HUMAHUACA

Llama Trekking
Let a pack-carrying llama take the load as it walks alongside you through the hills.

Hiking
Walk to waterfalls and through rocky canyons, or hire a local guide to show you ancient rock paintings.

Horseback Riding
Locals rent horses for excursions in and around Tilcara.

Photography
The colors of the hillsides of the Serranía de Hornocal are particularly photogenic.

Shopping
Throughout the Quebrada, local artisans sell colorful Andean textiles, including llama wool blankets, scarves and ponchos.

Birdwatching
Spot condors soaring above Iruya and hummingbirds in Tilcara.

notable in the Cerro de los Siete Colores (the Hill of Seven Colors) in Purmamarca, and in the mountains of the Serranía de Hornocal, near Humahuaca. Near the Quebrada are the Salinas Grandes salt flats, an hour's drive over the mountains from Purmamarca.

Flora & Fauna
The Quebrada landscapes are strewn with cardon cacti and algarrobo trees. Near rivers and streams, the leaves of willow trees rustle in the wind. The botanical garden at the Pucará de Tilcara contains local plant species. At higher altitudes, look out for grazing vicuña; you might spot them on the drive from Humahuaca to the Serranía de Hornocal.

Local Specialties
Quebrada specialties include maize, llama meat dishes, quinoa salads and soups, Andean potatoes, and tortillas (flatbreads with various fillings that are cooked in the street on a carbon grill). There are also some vineyards in the area; try local wine at Pachamanka in Humahuaca and La Picadita in Tilcara.

WHERE TO STAY

Tilcara
In an excellent location towards the southern end of the Quebrada, Tilcara has a wide range of accommodation options, including boutique hotels, family-friendly cabins, campsites, guesthouses and hostels. It also has plenty of restaurants and lively nightlife, making it an ideal base for exploring the region.

Purmamarca
Famous for its Cerro de los Siete Colores (Hill of Seven Colors), Purmamarca is a pretty village with a large artisan market in the main square. Several excellent, high-end hotels and lodges are here, but most of the village's accommodation falls into the higher price bracket.

Humahuaca
The Quebrada's largest town is Humahuaca, where there is a strong folk music tradition. Humahuaca has several hostels and a fresh produce market, making it an appealing option for budget travelers.

Iruya
This indigenous village is reached via a long, bumpy drive over a spectacular mountain pass. Since the bus journey takes at least four hours, you'll need to stay overnight in the village. There is a hotel and guesthouse with good facilities, and locals rent rooms in their homes to visitors, too. Alternatively, you can hike to the neighboring village of San Isidro (which is even smaller and more remote than Iruya) and spend a night there before walking back.

Hand-made
dolls, Jujuy (p195)

Asado

THE FOOD SCENE

Argentina is famous for its beef, but beyond steak you'll find a tasty array of dishes to feast on.

Argentina's cuisine reflects its varied geography, indigenous cultures and immigrant history. Regional specialties vary according to the terrain (seafood at the coast and llama meat in the Andes) and the cultural traditions of the people who live there. The large numbers of Italians who emigrated to Argentina during the late 19th century and early 20th century brought their culinary traditions with them, and staples such as pasta and pizza are found throughout the country. Then there are *medialunas,* crescent-shaped pastries (or croissants) whose arrival in Argentina was no doubt thanks to people who emigrated from France. Empanadas are believed to have been brought to Argentina by people from the Spanish region of Galicia.

But the food that continues to define Argentine cuisine is beef, traditionally grazed on Pampas grassland and grilled on the *parrilla* over an open flame. Walk through most Argentine cities on a warm evening, and the air will carry the scent of smoke and grilling meat.

Asados

In Argentina, the practice of grilling meat on the *parrilla* forms part of an important ritual known as an *asado* (barbecue). From selecting the cuts of meat at the butchers to building and managing the carbon- or wood-fueled flames, the person in charge of the grill (the *asador* or *asadora*) takes their responsibilities seriously. Indeed, choosing when and where to place the different

Best Argentine Dishes	STEAK	EMPANADAS	CHORIPÁN	PIZZA
	Generous cuts of beef grilled to perfection on the *parrilla*.	Savory pastries filled with beef, ham and cheese, or chicken.	Sausage cooked on the grill and served in crusty bread.	Argentine pizza is thick and doughy and covered in cheese.

cuts on the *parrilla* is itself something of an art form. Traditionally, an *asado* begins with *chorizo* (pork sausage) and *morcilla* (blood sausage), and continues from there, with an array of cuts brought to the table ready to be sliced on a wooden board to be offered around. The cuts usually increase in quality as the night goes on, so don't fill up on salad and bread and beware of the early evening *picada* (a sharing plate of cold cuts and cheese). There may also be *chimichurri*, a sauce made with parsley, garlic, vinegar and oil, used as a condiment for *choripán*.

Regional Cuisines

Traveling in Argentina means sampling the regional specialties. In the Andean northwest, you'll find dishes made with llama meat and quinoa. The country's best empanadas come from Salta and Tucumán. In La Rioja, San Juan and Mendoza, look out for *chivito* (young goat), while Patagonia is known for its lamb. In the northeast, you'll find river fish, including dorado and surubí. Naturally, the coast is the place to go for seafood, including Ushuaian king crab and mixed seafood platters in Puerto Madryn.

Empanadas

The Italian Influence

Look out for neighborhood stores selling boxes of fresh pasta and ravioli, and ice-cream parlors selling gelato; they are particularly good in Rosario, where many people are Italian descendants. However, thick, doughy Argentine pizza is distinct from its thin-crust Italian cousin. Another Italian favorite is Fernet Branca, a herbal digestive liqueur; in Argentina it is drunk with cola and ice.

FOOD & DRINK FESTIVALS

Fiesta Nacional de Asado (February) Feast on flame-grilled beef and lamb at this festival in Cholila in Chubut.

Fiesta Nacional del Lúpulo (p365, February) Beer flows at this music festival in El Bolsón that celebrates the hops harvest.

Fiesta de la Vendimia (March, pictured) The grape harvest is celebrated in wine-producing regions across the country, including Mendoza, Salta and Neuquén.

Fiesta Nacional de Chocolate (Easter) In Bariloche, this sweet festival includes the creation of what is claimed to be the world's longest chocolate bar.

Bariloche a la Carta (October) Feast on Patagonia's gastronomic specialties during this week-long food festival.

Fiesta Nacional del Chivito (November) This folk festival in Chos Malal in Neuquén involves barbecuing goats.

PATAGONIAN LAMB	LOCRO	MILANESA	ÑOQUIS
Lean, tender grass-fed lamb that is cooked on the grill.	Hearty winter stew made with maize, beans, squash and meat.	Large, flat beef or chicken cutlet covered in breadcrumbs.	Traditionally eaten on the 29th of the month (before pay day).

Local Specialties

Savory Snacks

Fainá Chickpea flatbread sold at pizzerias; usually eaten on top of a slice of pizza.

Humita Andean dish made with seasoned corn.

Picada Sharing boards of cold cuts (cured ham, salami and bondiola), cheese and olives.

Sandwiches de Miga These thin crustless sandwiches are sold in bakeries.

Maní Peanuts in bars; usually brought to the table with drinks.

Morcilla Blood sausage.

Sweet Treats

Dulce de Leche Milk caramel spread; often eaten with pastries or added to desserts.

Alfajor Cookie filled with *dulce de leche* and covered with chocolate or meringue.

Helado Argentina's Italian-style ice cream is some of the best in the world.

Medialuna Croissants; can be sweet (*de manteca*) or savory (*de grasa*).

Facturas Sweet pastries that may be filled with custard and jam or *dulce de leche*.

Dulce de Membrillo Quince jelly, often eaten with cheese.

Alfajor

Milhojas 'Thousand sheets' dessert made with puff pastry, cream and *dulce de leche*.

Cuts of Beef

Bife de Chorizo Sirloin; a thick and juicy cut.

Bife de Costilla T-bone steak.

Bife de Lomo Tenderloin.

Cuadril Rump steak; a thin cut.

Ojo de Bife Rib eye.

Tira de Asado Short ribs.

Vacío Flank steak; textured, chewy and tasty.

MEALS OF A LIFETIME

Alma Yagan (p459) In Puerto Almanza, Diana Méndez offers cooking demonstrations and a seafood feast in her cozy cabin.

Casa Cassis (p359) Chef China Müller offers an intimate, kitchen garden dining experience at this Bariloche restaurant.

Época de Quesos (p316) In Tandil, eat cheese and cured meats on the patio, then head inside to browse the shelves.

Roux (p89) This Buenos Aires restaurant serves dishes prepared with ingredients from all over the country, including suckling pig from Ranchos.

Zonda (p275) At the restaurant at Bodega Lagarde in Mendoza, dining is a hands-on experience that involves picking veg and prepping dishes, then savoring a tasting menu.

THE YEAR IN FOOD

SPRING

The best time of year for hake and Patagonian lamb. Fresh spring greens include spinach, asparagus, lettuce and artichokes. Look out for strawberries from Santa Fe and peaches from Mendoza.

SUMMER

Fruit and veg stalls are a riot of color, stocked with watermelons from Tucumán and melons from San Juan, as well as cherries, plums, tomatoes and blueberries. Families gather around the grill for Christmas *asados*.

FALL

In March, grapes are harvested in Argentina's wine-growing regions. Late fall mushrooms, potatoes, sweet potatoes, carrots, onions and squash are the perfect ingredients for wholesome soups.

WINTER

It begins with bowls of *locro* (stew), eaten on May 25 to celebrate the 1810 Revolution. Citrus fruits are in season – lemons from Tucumán, oranges from Corrientes and grapefruits from Misiones.

Enjoying some *mate*

HOW TO...

Drink Mate

For Argentines, drinking *mate* (pronounced mah-tey) is an intrinsic part of everyday life, but to the uninitiated, it is a custom that requires some explanation. First, there's the confusion of the name itself: the word *mate* is used for both the drinking gourd and the bitter tea infusion it holds. Then there are the complicated tasks of preparing *mate* and knowing how to drink it (through a metal straw with its own strainer, no less), not to mention the subtleties involved in sharing *mate* with friends (a minefield of faux pas). And as for the taste? Well, it takes some getting used to. Read this guide to find out all you need to know.

Mate Equipment

First you'll need a *mate*, a hollow drinking gourd traditionally made from a squash, which holds the *yerba*, the leaves of a plant that is native to northeast Argentina (look for packets of *yerba* in any Argentine supermarket). You'll also need a *bombilla*, a metal straw with a strainer at the end, and a thermos flask to fill with hot water.

How to Prepare Mate

Heat the water to between 75°C and 80°C, but do not allow it to boil (electric kettles in Argentina have a special temperature setting for *mate*). Pour some *yerba* into your *mate* and give it a shake to remove some of the dust. Put the *bombilla* into the *yerba*, so that the strainer is near the bottom of the *mate* and the opening is at the top. Some people add sugar to the *yerba* to sweeten it.

How to Drink Mate

Holding the *mate* with one hand and the thermos in the other, carefully pour hot water into the gourd. Drink it immediately, by sipping the liquid through the *bombilla*. Keep the thermos near you and continue filling and drinking for as long as you like. The first *mates* poured are the strongest; after a while the *yerba* becomes 'washed' (weakened).

When to Drink Mate

Many Argentines start their day with *mate*, but it's also common to drink it in the afternoon, perhaps accompanied by a *merienda* (early evening snack) of cookies.

HOW TO SHARE MATE

When drinking *mate* in a group, one person takes responsibility for serving everybody (the *cebador*). They will serve themselves first (it's polite to take the strongest hit), then pass the *mate* to each person in the group in turn. You should drink all the water in the *mate* (sip gently and avoid noisy slurping) before wordlessly returning it to the cebador. Saying 'gracias' indicates you do not wish to drink any more.

47

MOCHILAOSABATICO/SHUTTERSTOCK ©
OPPOSITE PAGE: CAIO FEDERNERAS/SHUTTERSTOCK ©

Bariloche (p350)

THE OUTDOORS

Argentina's wild rivers, steamy jungles, snowy mountains and open plains can be experienced through a range of activities, from exhilarating extreme sports to gentle hikes.

Go beyond the city limits, and you'll soon see that there is no shortage of space in Argentina. The world's eighth-largest country by area has natural features that invite exploration, be it on foot, by bike, on horseback, or on skis. Indeed, Argentina has a long tradition of outdoor pursuits. The Inca built their trails along existing paths, gauchos have long roamed the Pampas on horseback, and independence hero José de San Martín led his troops across the Andes back in 1817.

WALKING & HIKING

Argentina's beautiful and varied landscapes are traversed by a series of hiking trails. Opportunities for walks range from the Inca trails through the Andean northwest to day hikes through the jungle at Iguazú Falls in the northeast to multiday treks through the lake lands of Bariloche and near San Martín de los Andes. Further south, El Bolsón is an excellent base for spectacular hikes through nearby forests and at Lago Puelo. The Córdoba hills are also a lovely place for walking. In Buenos Aires, you can embrace nature with a walk around the waterside Reserva Ecológica, without leaving the city.

Serious mountain climbers can scale the peaks of Mendoza and San Juan, including an expedition up Aconcagua, the highest mountain in the southern hemisphere.

Then there are the hikes through the remarkable scenery of the Parque Nacional Los Glaciares and around the Fitz Roy range near El Chaltén. For challenging and exhilarating glacier trekking, head to Ushuaia, where you can hike over the ice and see frozen caves.

Bigger Thrills

MOUNTAINEERING
Climb **Cerro Aconcagua** (p279) in Mendoza and enjoy the views from the southern hemisphere's highest summit.

MOUNTAIN BIKING
Take a six-day mountain-biking trip around **Volcán Domuyo** (p389) in Neuquén, including a stop at Lake Varvarco Tapia.

PARAGLIDING
Soar over lush Yungas forests on the outskirts of Tucumán city on a **tandem paragliding flight** (p204).

Horseback Riding

Argentina may be one of the best countries in the world to go horseback riding. Horses here are generally well-cared for and well-behaved, and riding forms part of a long-established cultural tradition rooted in the gauchos who caught and tamed the wild horses let loose by the Spanish. Countryside *estancias* (ranches) offer accommodation and horseback excursions, as well as an insight into traditional rural life.

Horseback trekking is an idyllic way to take in the landscapes of the Tucumán hills, the Pampas grasslands, the Patagonian plains, the mountains of Mendoza or the Córdoba Sierras. Many operators offer tempting packages, including picnics and wine-tasting in scenic spots, but if you have sufficient horseback riding experience, you can hire a horse and head out on your own in places like Tafí del Valle in Tucumán. In San Martín de los Andes, you can even go horseback riding through the mountain snow.

Skiing & Snowboarding

Argentina's mountains offer outstanding skiing and snowboarding, with plenty of quality powder and bright sunny weather. The main ski resorts are in Mendoza, Bariloche and Ushuaia.

Las Leñas in Mendoza generally has the best snow and the longest runs of any Argentine resort, though the views are more beautiful further south, especially at Cerro Catedral near Bariloche and Cerro Chapelco near San Martín de los Andes. In Patagonia, El Hoyo near Esquel is one of Argentina's best-value resorts, with excellent powder. In Ushuaia, you can hit the slopes at Cerro Castor, the only full-scale ski resort this far south.

MORE ACTIVITIES
See our map on page 50

Ushuaia (p446)

GLACIER TREKKING
Trek to the glaciers surrounding Ushuaia and tackle the challenging ascent up to **Alvear Glacier** (p457).

AERIAL DANCING
Don a harness and rappel down the walls of a former railway station in **La Plata** (p326).

KAYAKING
Paddle around Bariloche's lakes in a kayak; one of the best spots is Playa Sin Viento on **Lago Moreno** (p353).

WHITEWATER RAFTING
Get the adrenaline pumping as you ride Andean rapids on a raft near **Potrerillos** (p277) in Mendoza.

ACTION AREAS

Where to find Argentina's
best outdoor activities.

BRAZIL

PARAGUAY

ASUNCIÓN

URUGUAY

Encarnación

Formosa

Pilar

Corrientes

Resistencia

Santiago
del Estero

San Miguel
de Tucuman

Tucumán

Catamarca

Santa Fe

Concordia

Paraná

Salto

Paysandú

Fray Bentos

San Antonio
de Areco

Córdoba

San Luis

La Plata

BUENOS
AIRES

Mar del Plata

Tandil

Jujuy

Salta

La Rioja

San Juan

Uspallata

Luján de Cuyo

Mendoza

Santa Rosa

Reserva
Natural La
Payunia

ARGENTINA

Neuquén

CHILE

Horseriding

1 San Antonio
   de Areco (p304)
2 Tandil (p312)
3 Valle de Uco (p280)
4 Bariloche (p350)
5 San Martin
   de los Andes (p370)
6 Santa Cruz (p419)
7 Rio Grande (p412)

Extreme Adventures

1 Scaling Cerro
   Aconcagua (p279)
2 Aerial dancing
   in La Plata (p328)
3 Rafting near
   Potrerillos (p277)
4 Mountain-biking
   at Volcán Domuyo (p389)
5 Glacier trekking
   near Ushuaia (p278)
6 Paragliding
   in Tucumán (p204)
7 Off-piste skiing
   in Esquel (p410)

Vineyard/Winery

1. Luján de Cuyo (p270)
2. Valles Calchaquíes (p182)
3. Chapadmalal (p341)
4. Neuquén (p381)
5. Mendoza (p256)
6. San Juan (p294)
7. Valle de Uco (p280)

National Parks

1. Parque Nacional Los Glaciares (p421)
2. Parque Nacional Talampaya (p213)
3. Parque Nacional Sierra de las Quijadas (p236)
4. Parque Nacional Iberá (p140)
5. Parque Nacional Nahuel Huapi (p359)
6. Parque Nacional Lanín (p377)
7. Parque Nacional Tierra del Fuego (p450)

Animals/Wildlife

1. Sea lions in Mar del Plata (p344)
2. *Gato montés* in Península Hiroki (p384)
3. Yungas wildlife in Tucumán (p200)
4. Orcas at Península Valdés (p399)
5. Penguins at Isla Martillo (p448)
6. Vicuñas in Catamarca (p205)
7. Flamingos at Epecuén (p321)

500 km
250 miles

ARGENTINA

THE GUIDE

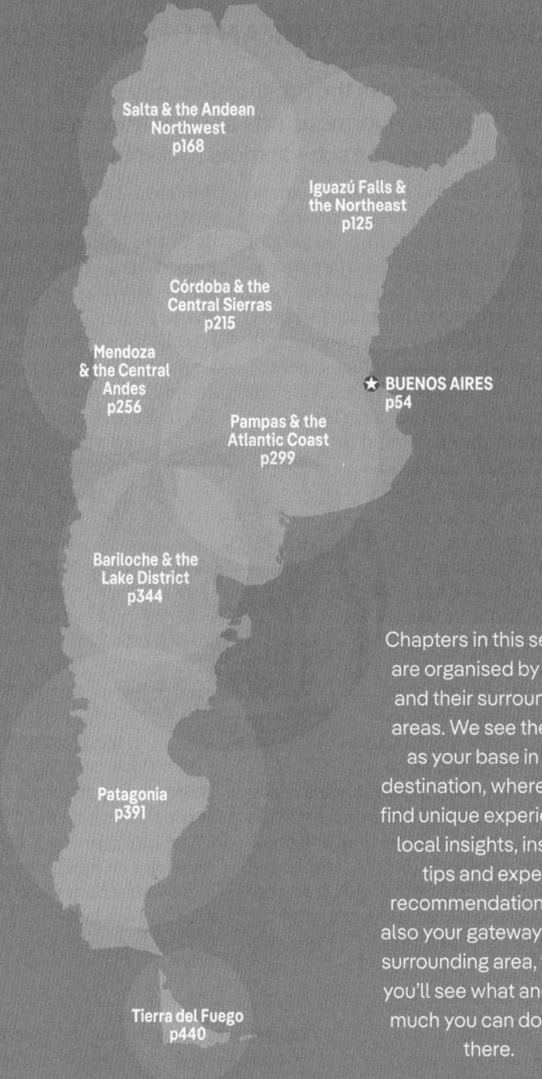
Salta & the Andean Northwest p168
Iguazú Falls & the Northeast p125
Córdoba & the Central Sierras p215
Mendoza & the Central Andes p256
BUENOS AIRES p54
Pampas & the Atlantic Coast p299
Bariloche & the Lake District p344
Patagonia p391
Tierra del Fuego p440

Chapters in this section are organised by hubs and their surrounding areas. We see the hub as your base in the destination, where you'll find unique experiences, local insights, insider tips and expert recommendations. It's also your gateway to the surrounding area, where you'll see what and how much you can do from there.

Traditional blankets, Jujuy (p195)

Buenos Aires

FASCINATING AND VIBRANT CULTURE SCENE

The Argentine capital is the most-visited city in Latin America. There are enormous arts and gastronomic offerings and numerous sub-districts to discover.

Buenos Aires, founded in 1580 by Juan de Garay, has managed to preserve its ancient traditions and the charming corners of yesteryears. Its port served as the gateway for goods and people from all corners of the world who came to populate its lands.

One of the main attractions drawing millions of tourists is tango, which emerged as a fusion of various cultures. This enchanting music and dance form is very much alive in the city, found in every *milonga* (where tango is danced), and at professional shows featuring great dancers, and concerts showcasing a new generation of musicians revitalizing the genre. During your stay, you'll likely take a tango class or visit Caminito, the famous colorful alley just meters from the port in the neighborhood of La Boca.

Tango is just one facet of Buenos Aires' incredibly vibrant cultural and nightlife scene. The city boasts more than 380 bookstores, 287 theaters, 160 museums, and an array of architectural wonders that blend neoclassical, art nouveau, and art deco styles, reflecting the city's European influence. In recent years, a captivating gastronomic scene has emerged, primarily in the neighborhoods of Palermo and Puerto Madero. While there's no shortage of *parrillas*, where you can savor the country's renowned meat, you'll also find establishments that blend Argentina's classic products with culinary influences from around the world.

In Buenos Aires neighborhoods, you can visit the tomb of Eva Perón in the famous Cementerio de la Recoleta, experience soccer enthusiasm at La Bombonera (Boca Juniors Club stadium), and explore its markets and historic cafes.

Despite being a bustling metropolis, Buenos Aires offers green spaces for exploration on foot or by bicycle. The Reserva Ecológica Costanera Sur and Parque Tres de Febrero are must-visit spots for fresh air and a relaxing picnic.

As captivating as it is lively, Buenos Aires leaves an indelible mark on its visitors in just a few hours. You will fall in love, as many others have.

PHILIP LEE HARVEY/LONELY PLANET ©

THE MAIN AREAS

PALERMO	CENTRO HISTÓRICO	RECOLETA & RETIRO
Nightlife, parks, restaurants and shopping. **p60**	Downtown and monumental area. **p72**	Full of history, museums and architecture. **p84**

OLIVERDELAHAYE/SHUTTERSTOCK ©

Above: La Boca (p104); Left: Market, San Telmo (p94)

SAN TELMO
Old district and
antique bargains.
p94

LA BOCA
Famed for its colorful
houses, tango and Caminito.
p104

PUERTO MADERO
The perfect walk
by the river.
p114

Find Your Way

The historic center is the starting point to admire the architecture and European influence of the town. Although it is a big city, the heart of Buenos Aires is easy to get around on foot or by subway.

N
0 ————— 1 mile
0 ————— 2 km

FROM THE AIRPORT

Ministro Pistarini International Airport is located in Ezeiza, 40 minutes from the city center. The Tie'nda Leon shuttle company is hired at the airport and has a stop in the Puerto Madero. Bus number 8 goes to Plaza de Mayo, the city center.

WALK

The best way to explore the neighborhoods of Buenos Aires is on foot. Be careful with the sidewalks, which can be a little neglected, and take care of your cell phone on the street at night.

Río de
la Plata

Dársena A

Dársena

LAS CAÑITAS

PALERMO

COLEGIALES

PALERMO SOHO

VILLA CRESPO

Palermo
p60

🏛 MALBA

Museo Nacional de 🏛
Bellas Artes

RECOLETA

Recoleta & Retiro
p84

RETIRO   Palacio Paz

TRIBUNALES

Teatro Colón ◇

MICROCENTRO

LA CITY

Puerto Madero
pl4

Plaza de Mayo ◎

ONCE

ABASTO

*Cementeria de
la Recoleta* ◎

BALVANERA

*Palacio del
Congreso* ◎

CONGRESO

Centro Histórico
p72

MONTSERRAT

*Mercado de
San Telmo* 🏛

CONSTITUCIÓN

San Telmo
p94

*Museo Histórico
Nacional* 🏛

BARRACAS

LA BOCA

La Boca
pl04

◇ *Caminito*

PUERTO
MADERO

*Canal
Sur*

*Reserva Ecológica
Costanera Sur* △

ALMAGRO

CABALLITO

SAN
CRISTOBAL

BOEDO

PARQUE
PATRICIOS

CHACABUCO
PARK

PUBLIC TRANSPORT

The Buenos Aires subway network, except San Telmo and La Boca, reaches the main tourist attractions. *Colectivos* (buses) are also a good option. To use public transportation systems, buying a SUBE card at a subway station is necessary.

TAXI & RIDESHARES

The number of cabs in Buenos Aires has decreased considerably in recent years. The reason is simply the massive use of apps like Uber and Cabify. Sometimes, cab and app fares are similar.

Plan Your Days

Start the day in an old cafe before touring the city's most traditional and architecturally beautiful avenues. Later, enjoy some nighttime attractions in a city known for its vibrant cultural scene.

Teatro Colón (p77)

Day 1

Morning

● Start the day at **Plaza de Mayo** (p73), where the country's most important historical events occurred. Visit the **Casa Rosada** (p73). Walk west along Av de Mayo. Have lunch or a drink at the historic **Café Tortoni** (p76), the oldest cafe in the city.

Afternoon

● Explore Buenos Aires from above with a tour of **Palacio Barolo** (p76), the *Divine Comedy*–inspired building. Explore the **Congreso de la Nación Argentina** (p78) and enjoy a coffee on **Av Corrientes** (p79), the theater district.

Evening

● End the day with a dinner show at **Tango Porteño** (p81), a few meters from the **Teatro Colón** (p77) and the Obelisco, the city's most emblematic historical monument.

You'll Also Want To...

Walk along the river, attend a *fútbol* (soccer) game and enjoy a day at a fair in a working-class neighborhood.

WALK AROUND PALERMO

Spend the day at **Parque Tres de Febrero**. It is the largest in the city, with lakes, squares and 370 hectares to enjoy.

GO TO A FÚTBOL GAME

Soccer is a great passion in Argentina. Watching a game is an opportunity to see the craze for your favorite team in action.

VISIT SAN TELMO SUNDAY MARKET

Defensa, the famous cobblestone street of the neighborhood, has hundreds of street vendors of handicrafts, leather and antiques.

58

Day 2

Morning

● Visit **Ateneo Grand Splendid** (p86), a former theater currently considered one of the most beautiful bookstores in the world, in Recoleta. Walk along the stately **Av Alvear** (p89), home to aristocratic residences. Grab a bite at **La Biela** (p85), a historic bar and restaurant where writers Jorge Luis Borges and Adolfo Bioy Casares used to go.

Afternoon

● Take a tour of **Cementerio de la Recoleta** (p88), where some of the country's great personalities, such as Eva Perón, rest. Walk through **Plaza Francia** (p89) with its craft fair and visit the **Museo Nacional de Bellas Artes** (p87).

Evening

● End the day with dinner and a walk through **Puerto Madero** (p114), an excellent place to enjoy the river in the city.

Day 3

Morning

● Start in **Caminito** (p108), a set of streets with multicolored buildings reminiscent of how the first immigrants lived. Have lunch in one of its small restaurants watching the couples dancing tango. Visit the **Museo Benito Quinquela Martín** (p106). Continue along Dr del Valle Ibarlucea St until you reach La Bombonera, the Boca Juniors Club's stadium. There, you can visit the **Museo de la Pasión Boquense** (p107).

Afternoon

● Visit **El Zanjón de Granados** (p96) in San Telmo, a journey into Buenos Aires' past, situated within one of the city's oldest areas and featuring subway tunnels.

Evening

● End the day in Palermo, an area full of bars and restaurants, with a **wine tasting** (p67).

SUNSET AT PUERTO MADERO

Find your spot in the youngest neighborhood of the city. One can be **El Puente de la Mujer**.

ATTEND A TANGO CLASS

The *milongas* offer options during the day and at night. **La Viruta** is one of the best known in town.

GO TO THE THEATER DISTRICT

Av Corrientes, between Callao and 9 de Julio, is very busy, especially at night; full of theaters, stores and pizzerias.

SHOP AT PALERMO SOHO

Fashion and object lovers will find dozens of local brands and good restaurants around Gurruchaga St.

Palermo

NIGHTLIFE, PARKS, RESTAURANTS AND SHOPPING

Palermo is the largest and most populated neighborhood in the city. Since the 1990s, the environment and the urban landscape have changed significantly. The city's nightlife, cafes and restaurants began to draw crowds. Tourists and locals chose it as a place to live and spend their free time. Moreover, due to this transformation in the urban landscape, some blocks have adopted names such as Palermo Soho and Palermo Hollywood. Parque Tres de Febrero, also known as Los Bosques de Palermo (The Forests of Palermo), and the Jardín Botánico are great green spaces. The neighborhood also offers an impressive variety of museums and architectural styles, from Casa Chorizo (Standard House) to mansions. In spite of the important changes of the recent decades, Palermo preserves in some corners vestiges of the old Buenos Aires. Today, without a doubt, it stands as the heart of tourism in the city.

☑ **TOP TIP**

Palermo has many cultural activities and fantastic gastronomic offerings, so it is best to take it easy. A great way to get to know it is to visit the parks and museums early in the day (perhaps by bike). Life in Palermo Soho and Hollywood, two of the most visited areas, starts after noon and ends late at night.

NIARKRAD/SHUTTERSTOCK ©

Parque Tres de Febrero (Los Bosques de Palermo, p66)

Tierra Santa
Jerusalem in Buenos Aires

Tierra Santa, located in the area known as Costanera Norte, is the only religious theme park in the country. Pope Francis inaugurated it in 1999 when he was not yet so famous, and everyone knew him as Jorge Bergoglio. The place, which can be visited alone or with a guide, offers a tour of the manger, the Last Supper, the Stations of the Cross and the Wailing Wall. In short, the places Jesus walked during his life more than 2000 years ago. The setting has a touch of kitsch, but it is still a celebration of religion. Open only on weekends and holidays.

Hipódromo Argentino de Palermo

Hipódromo Argentino de Palermo
Experience the Excitement of a Horse Race

Admission to the Hipódromo Argentino de Palermo is free, and it is worth visiting for its beautiful entrance porches, facades and chandelier composition. But if you set foot on what is arguably the most important track in Latin America, where thoroughbred racehorses compete, why not add excitement to the trip and bet a few pesos on one of them? On Mondays, races are held year-round, with the exception of holidays, and additional races are scheduled on other days of the week, which may vary. The place has some restaurants. Events, such as fairs and concerts, are organized in its halls throughout the year. Be sure to check the website for more information.

Tierra Santa

MALBA
Latin American Modern Art

In 2001, philanthropist businessman and collector Eduardo Costantini promoted the opening of the Museo de Arte Latinoamericano de Buenos Aires (MALBA). In a short time, the place became an undisputed reference for the art of the city and the region. The permanent collection has more than 220 significant works of Latin American art by masters such as Frida Kahlo, Diego Rivera and Tarsila do Amaral. Of course, there is also a place for Argentines, such as Xul Solar, Emilio Pettoruti and Antonio Berni. It is open every day except Tuesdays. The site has a cafeteria and restaurant overlooking a park.

PALERMO

1 *Hipódromo Argentino de Palermo*

28

Museo Sívori **5**

LAS CAÑITAS

Av del Libertador

Arce
Ortega Y Gasset
Av Luis María Campos
Av Báez

Av Dorrego

Av Figueroa Alco...

Av Infanta Isabel

Av Pedro Montt

8 *Parque Tres de Febrero*

Av Iraola

Campo Argentina de Polo

Sinclair
Juan Seguí
Demaría
Colombia

Savio
Av Cabildo
Zapata

Estación Ministro Carranza

Ministro Carranza S

PALERMO

Av Int Bullrich
Av Cerviño

Av Sarmiento
República de la India

Av Dorrego
Arévalo
Di Emilio Ravignani
Ángel Justiniano Carranza
Guatemala
Soler
Nicaragua
Bonpland
Costa Rica
El Salvador

Av Santa Fe

Fitz Roy

Estación Palermo S **Palermo**

Juncal
Beruti

La Rural

Plaza Italia S

Museo Evita **3**

JM Gutier...

Jardín Botánico Carlos Thays

Humboldt
Av Juan B Justo

6 *Palermo Hollywood*

19

JSM de Oro
Darrégueyra
Uriarte

Jorge Luis Borges
Guruchaga

Beruti

PALERMO HOLLYWOOD

36

17

29

PALERMO SOHO

Charcas
Malabia

Scalabrini Ortíz S

Salguer...

Nicaragua
Soler
Guatemala

Paraguay
Av Scalabrini Ortíz

24

32
31
38
20
35
34

30

Godoy Cruz
Honduras
El Salvador

27

Plaza Palermo Viejo

21

Niceto Vega
Av Juan B Justo
Av Córdoba
Thames
Serrano

Guruchaga
Armenia
Costa Rica

15

Aráoz
J Álvarez

13

7 *Palermo Soho*

16

18

Aceveda
José Antonio Cabrera
Malabia

El Salvador
Av Medrano
Salguero
Soler

33

Perón Perón

Guruchaga
Juffré
Lerma
Castillo
Loyola
Aguirre
Juan Ramírez de Velasco
Av Scalabrini Ortíz
Malabia
Aráoz
J Álvarez

14

9

22

El Salvador

Honduras
Gorriti

26

José Antonio Cabrera

Av Córdoba

Lavalleja
Gascón
Acuña Figueroa

Lavalle

Malabia S Av Corrientes

Av Estado de Israel
Estado de Palestina

Guardia Vieja

TOP SIGHTS
1. Hipódromo Argentino de Palermo
2. MALBA (Museo de Arte Latinoamericano de Buenos Aires)
3. Museo Evita
4. Museo Nacional de Arte Decorativo
5. Museo Sívori
6. Palermo Hollywood
7. Palermo Soho
8. Parque Tres de Febrero
9. Perón Perón
10. Planetario Galileo Galilei

SIGHTS
11. Biblioteca Nacional
12. La Colorada
13. La Malbequería

ACTIVITIES, COURSES & TOURS
14. Bar de Fondo

SLEEPING
15. Duque Hotel
16. Jardín Escondido
17. Selina Palermo

EATING
18. Gran Dabbang
19. La Pescadorita
20. Picsa
21. Rapanui

DRINKING & NIGHTLIFE
22. Amores Tintos
23. Casa Cavia
24. Club 69
25. Feliza Arcoiris
26. Maricafé
27. Peuteo
28. Rheo
29. Tres monos
30. Varela Varelita

ENTERTAINMENT
31. Bebop
32. Congo Cultural Club
33. La Viruta

SHOPPING
34. Borges 1975
35. Dain Usina Cultural
36. Eterna Cadencia
37. Librería Santa Fe
38. Libros del Pasaje

Museo Evita

Perón Perón
A Bar about an Argentine Passion

Peronismo is more than a political movement. **Perón Perón** is a themed bar that pays tribute to the passion for the political current that emerged from Juan Domingo Perón. As soon as you walk through the door, you will find images of the classic figures of *peronismo*, from the former president to more recent ones, such as Cristina Fernández de Kirchner. There is a small altar to Evita and other objects. The dishes are tasty succulent, and have allegorical names, such as 'La vida por Perón' (Life for Perón).

Planetario Galileo Galilei

Museo Evita
The Most Influential Woman in the Country

Eva Perón was a woman who aroused love and hate in Argentine history. Even today, p*eronismo* and *anti-peronismo* are antagonistic and still very much in force. Museo Evita celebrates the first lady who began her life as an actress and became one of the country's most influential figures. You can see her dresses, objects and family memorabilia in the place. The tour is short (less than an hour). In the courtyard of the large house, there is a bar and restaurant. Admission and guided tours are free. It is closed on Mondays.

Planetario Galileo Galilei
Wonders of the Universe

People walking through Parque Tres de Febrero may see something similar to a flying saucer. The five-story building opened in 1967, and its shape simulates the planet Saturn with its rings. The tour and activities are focused on children and anyone interested in astronomy. Galibot, the host robot, welcomes visitors at the entrance door. Children can learn about the Milky Way and the universe through games, touch screens and virtual reality. The place also has a museum and a circular projection room of about 300 seats, where images of stars, planets and satellites of the universe, obtained thanks to its powerful equipment, are reproduced. Some days a month, it organizes astronomical observation days with the telescopes. The activity is free but has a maximum capacity of 250 observers.

Palermo Soho & Palermo Hollywood

The Area That Has It All

Palermo has numerous unofficial names. In the last 20 years, two have become famous: Palermo Hollywood and Palermo Soho. The former was so named because many movie production companies and TV channels settled there. Palermo Soho is characterized by craft fairs and local designer clothes in renovated chorizo houses. On Gurruchaga St, there are dozens of clothing stores. Some are outlets of well-known brands. Others are small stores of local brands, such as Las Pepas and Las Oreiro, owned by famous actress Natalia Oreiro. Nightlife is concentrated near Plaza Serrano and Plaza Armenia, which are full of breweries and bars. Thames St condenses the diverse spirit of the area: there are steakhouses, Asian and Arabic restaurants and eclectic bars. Palermo Soho and Palermo Hollywood tend to have a hectic nightlife; restaurants and clothing stores usually open from around midday. These two areas are adjacent, separated by Av Juan B Justo, making them easily explorable on foot.

Museo Sívori

Museo Sívori

Argentine Art and a Beautiful Garden

There are several reasons to visit this museum. It has one of the best collections of Argentine art; it was recently remodelled; and the building has a beautiful garden. The museum has an inheritance of about 4000 pieces from the 20th and 21st centuries. In its permanent exhibition, the works of Antonio Berni, Emilio Pettoruti and Lucio Fontana, among others, stand out. The stained-glass windows in the museum's venues are interactive, inviting visitors to approach and engage with the collection. It has a bar and restaurant.

Parque Tres de Febrero

The City's Green Lung

Known by locals as Los Bosques de Palermo, it is a succession of parks, gardens, rose gardens and the new Ecoparque, a former zoo converted into a conservation center. In its 370 hectares, three points stand out: the Jardín Japonés, the Jardín Botánico and El Rosedal (flowering from October to May). The former was built in the mid-1960s for the visit of the Emperor of Japan, Akihito, and his wife, Michiko. It is charming to walk through its small alleys surrounded by bonsais, azaleas, kokedamas, orchids and cement lanterns. If you have a choice, it is best to go during the week. The Jardín Botánico, with free admission, is home to 900 species and some 2000 varieties of trees. Although it is on a busy avenue, it is a haven in the middle of the city. The rose garden is an excellent spectacle of thousands of roses of 93 species along 4 hectares. The white bridge of the rose garden is one of the great photographic highlights of the area.

Parque Tres de Febrero

Museo Nacional de Arte Decorativo

As Beautiful as It Is Solemn

The museum's heritage is as valuable as its magnificent building, which belonged to the aristocratic Errázuriz Alvear family. The lobby, the winter garden, the office and the rooms are decorated in the Louis XVI style. The museum has extensive patrimony, including Roman sculptures and contemporary silverware. Two of its jewels are an oil painting by El Greco and a sculpture by Auguste Rodin. A bar and restaurant called Croque Madame is at the entrance, with good cakes and coffee. It is open from Wednesday to Sunday. Admission is free.

Museo Nacional de Arte Decorativo

JEFFREY ISAAC GREENBERG 7+/ALAMY STOCK PHOTO ©

Animales salvajes

HISTORICAL MONUMENTS

Torso
A sculpture almost 4m high, by Fernando Botero. It was donated by the Colombian artist himself.

Sarmiento
Homage to the father of public education, Domingo Faustino Sarmiento. Created by Auguste Rodin.

Fuente Riqueza Agropecuaria Argentina
The monument, crafted from Carrara marble, bronze and stone, was skilfully created by Gustav Adolf Bredow, and notably, it was donated by the German government.

Caperucita Roja
The legendary Le Petit Chaperon Rouge, or Caperucita Roja, has her marble monument in Buenos Aires. Inaugurated in 1937 during a visit to Argentina, the monument was crafted by the French artist Juan Mario Carlus as a tribute to the classic children's tale.

Animales salvajes
Two imposing lions guard Los Bosques de Palermo in Plaza Holanda.

MORE IN PALERMO

Immersion in the World of Malbec

Tasting the Flagship Variety

Wine production in Argentina has a long and storied history. Historians suggest that the first vine plantations were established in Argentina between 1569 and 1589. However, the wine industry blossomed at the end of the 19th century, with Mendoza and San Juan at their core. Over time, wine production expanded to other regions of the country. Eighteen of the country's 23 provinces are involved in wine production today. Malbec has become the emblematic grape variety, winning numerous international awards. Although this grape variety originates from France, Argentine Malbec is now celebrated as one of the world's best, boasting a unique character and international fame. Chardonnay and Torrontés also receive high praise and recognition despite Argentines consuming less white wine than their European counterparts.

In Palermo, **La Malbequería** pays tribute to wine, particularly Malbec. Combining a wine house with a restaurant, this establishment offers tastings of four labels paired with cheese

---

 WHERE TO STAY IN PALERMO

Selina Palermo
Good design; comfortable single and shared rooms. $

Duque Hotel
Has a romantic atmosphere in an old renovated house. It has a small swimming pool and a spa. $$$

Jardín Escondido
A five-star hotel with a country feel and a garden in the center of Palermo. $$$

BEST LGBTIQ+ BARS IN PALERMO

Club 69
One of the longest-running parties of the community, with more than 20 years of existence. Held on Saturdays and sometimes Thursdays at the Niceto disco, with funk and disco music.

Peuteo
A venue that features music and drinks, typically hosting drag shows.

Feliza Arcoiris
The cultural club has a playful side, with video games, talks and concerts.

Maricafé
A cafe, bar and LGBTIQ+ bookstore. Sells cakes with a rainbow filling.

Rheo
A nightclub with signature drinks. The music is usually pop.

Don Julio

or empanadas. A knowledgeable sommelier guides the tasting, providing extensive insights into different regions and the characteristics of each Argentine terroir. These explanations delve into the country's wine-producing areas, focusing on Mendoza, the star region. Mendoza is the leading player in the national wine industry, with over 70% of the country's vineyards and hosting most of Argentina's wineries. The tasting experience is enjoyable and relaxed, allowing ample time for questions about the wine's history and recommendations for the best labels to consider. Furthermore, the sommelier provides a map to enhance your understanding of the country's wine production.

Tastings typically take place in the afternoon, starting at 4pm. Even if you're not a wine specialist, you'll leave with a greater appreciation for wine and the tools to navigate the vast world of wine more confidently. If you stay for dinner, you can head to La Malbequería or **Lo de Jesús**, which share the same menu. The menu includes delicious options like burrata with prosciutto, *choripán* (a grilled chorizo sausage sandwich), meat empanadas, and succulent *bife de lomo*. One standout dish is the 400g chorizo steak, matured for 21 days and grilled using red and white quebracho, an excellent wood known for its hardness, resilience, and remarkable

 ## WHERE TO EAT IN PALERMO

Gran Dabbang
This tiny, inconspicuous place serves food based on the fusion of flavors from Asia and Latin America. $$$

Picsa
Empanadas and pizzas cooked on a wood fire in Argentine style. $$

La Pescadorita
Specializes in fish and seafood. The star dish is paella. $$$

durability. One thing is sure: you'll have a wide selection of wines, with the menu offering 400 labels, including 100 Malbecs. Walking through the aisles and shelves makes you want to carry several bottles.

In addition to La Malbequería, the rest of the city is home to numerous wine-focused bars, such as **La Cava Jufré**, **Aldo's**, **Cru Deli Wine**, **Vina**, and **Amores Tintos**. Cheers!

Experience Tango in Its Birthplace
La Viruta Tango Club

All Buenos Aires neighborhoods have one thing in common: they all have some *milonga*. La Viruta is one of the city's most popular, where many locals and foreigners learn to dance. The activities begin at 6pm. There are classes, practices and other tango-related activities, such as seminars and concerts. If you have taken courses or are an expert, it is better to go at night. Dancer and entrepreneur Horacio Godoy runs the place and is usually on the dance floor, along with Cecilia Troncoso. The Hoy Milonga page (hoy-milonga.com) updates daily information about *milongas* and classes throughout the city. The activity is incredibly intense every day.

Palermo Old Style
A Coffee at Varela Varelita

When discussing Palermo Soho and Palermo Hollywood, the word trendy is cliché but true. This cafe is just the opposite, perhaps a kind of retreat where Palermo is still a traditional neighborhood. The bar has a bohemian and intellectual spirit. The walls are decorated with old movie posters. The menu, as it could not be otherwise, is classic. The large *sánguche de milanesa* (a sandwich consisting of a baguette-type bread cut in half and filled with a veal schnitzel) is one of the customers' favorites. Other specialties include the raw ham sandwich and coffee (don't expect specialty coffee because they don't have any). Something curious about the place: Carlos 'Chacho' Álvarez, a famous neighbor, used to go there – almost as if it were his office – when he was vice president of Argentina. Although it is open practically all day (from 7am to 2am), the best times are during breakfast, and as the afternoon turns into the evening, when long-time customers begin to order their first drinks. Palermo changes. **Varela Varelita** has remained the same for nearly 70 years.

WHERE TO EAT MEAT IN PALERMO

Don Julio
Perhaps the most famous steakhouse in the city. It deserves it. It takes work to get a table. **$$$**

La Carnicería
The place is small, specializing in exquisite smoked meats. It has an informal atmosphere. **$$$**

Hierro
The classics of the Argentine grill, meats matured for 30 days, and wagyu: modern ambience and chill-out music. **$$**

Niño Gordo
Recently, it has become a classic for young people in Palermo. A grill that mixes Asian and Argentine flavors. **$$**

Club Eros
A club that maintains the old spirit of the neighborhood, with reasonable prices. **$**

WHERE TO HAVE A DRINK IN PALERMO

Tres monos
Small, with a punk aesthetic and lots of colored lights. The drinks have received international awards.

Casa Cavia
A beautiful old house offering sophisticated drinks. It is also a restaurant.

Amores Tintos
It started as a wine store and became a wine and gin bar. Its sidewalk tables are ideal for the summer.

The British Corner
The Unique La Colorada Building

On the corner of Cabello and República Árabe Siria, there is a building that looks like it belongs to another city, another country and another continent. **La Colorada** is so called because of the red-colored exposed bricks. At the time of construction, the building was considered innovative not only because of its color and design but also because of its materials. It was built using iron beams rather than concrete. British engineer Regis Pigeon designed and built the English neoclassical–style building in 1911. The materials came exclusively from England. Early on, it was used for the staff of British-owned railway companies, but in the mid-1950s it became a residential building. There is an identical building, also designed by Pigeon, in Boston. The best time to visit is early in the morning or at sunset. During those hours, the red of the sun complements the red of the building's bricks. While it's primarily a residential building with no guided tours, you can get a sense of the place's spirit by visiting a clothing store located on the 1st floor.

Sexy Chocolat
The Delights of Rapanui

The chocolate shop **Rapanui** was born in Bariloche but soon spread throughout the country. On a walk through Palermo, the advice is simple: take a piece of some of those glorious chocolate blends (the milk chocolate bar with pistachios, salt and caramel is lovely) and continue on your way to the next stop. Chocolate frappé and cheesecake are other specialties. The atmosphere is relaxed and rustic, with lots of plants, ideal for those who want to use it as a workspace. It's in Malabia 2014, and it has other locations in the city.

BEST BOOKSTORES IN PALERMO

Libros del Pasaje
Has a retro style, a cafeteria and an internal patio ideal for quiet reading.
Eterna Cadencia
The ambience is inviting, complete with a terrace that frequently hosts book presentations.
Dain Usina Cultural
More than just a bookstore, it organizes cultural activities all year round and has a lovely terrace to enjoy the sun.
Borges 1975
The atmosphere is like a bookstore, but it also has an exhibition hall, recitals and workshops.
Librería Santa Fe
A well-stocked place inside Alto Palermo, one of the largest shopping malls in the city.

ROBERTO FIADONE, CC BY-SA 4.0, VIA WIKIMEDIA COMMONS ©

La Colorada

 WHERE TO LISTEN TO LIVE MUSIC IN PALERMO

Bebop
Jazz club with low lights, excellent sound and a good wine list. Has shows by local artists and international figures.

Bar de Fondo
Concerts in an old house, with an alternative spirit. Has a varied agenda and a good atmosphere.

Congo Cultural Club
You can drink, listen to indie music and enjoy a beautiful garden during the summer.

STREET ART STROLL

Buenos Aires has a reason to be proud of its neighborhoods and walls. The city has one of Latin America's most active street art movements. Street artists found this city a great workplace, mainly because the laws are more flexible than in other countries. The city even commissioned large-scale works. The Visit Buenos Aires office suggests a good self-guided walking tour in different areas north of the town, such as Coghlan, Villa Urquiza, Colegiales and Palermo. The street art scene is vibrant there, with different techniques and big names arriving in the country.

At El Salvador 5715, there is the mural **Mujer cargando casa** (Woman carrying house) by Australian Fintan Magee. It tells the story of the place which was once usurped. The artist plays with the cement of construction in his artwork. He also offers a critical look at the issue of housing

in the city. Follow Bonpland and turn right on Costa Rica. At Costa Rica 5514, Cabaio, an artist of the Vomito Attack collective, did a magnificent **stencil work** on a restaurant specializing in noodles. Then walk south along Humboldt and Cabrera streets until you reach Malabia and Córdoba. There, on the border with Villa Crespo, there is a giant **mural of a hydra** by Spock and Lean Frizzera, the alter ego of Félix Reboto from Madrid. At **Post Street** (Thames 1885) is a bar with a permanent urban art display (you can visit it daily). If you want to make a stop, the place offers a simple menu with burgers, pizzas and classic and signature cocktails. Also worth a visit is the small **Russel Passage** in Palermo Soho, full of street art.

Free Walks Buenos Aires and Graffiti Mundo are two companies that also organize street art walking tours in Buenos Aires.

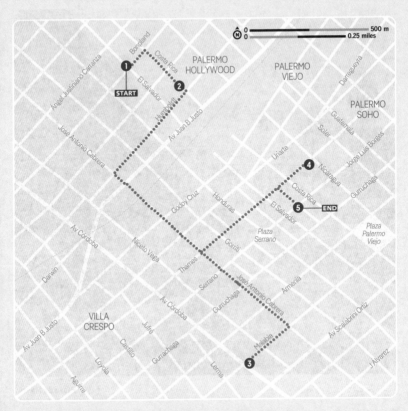

THE GUIDE

PALERMO BUENOS AIRES

71

Centro Histórico

DOWNTOWN AND MONUMENTAL AREA

San Nicolás, Balvanera and Montserrat are the three neighborhoods that form the area that the *porteños* call the 'downtown' of the city. Plaza de Mayo is the central stage where the country's most important historical events occur. The Cabildo, the Catedral Metropolitana and the Casa Rosada (National Government seat) are in its surroundings. The area also has almost a hundred buildings of great cultural and architectural heritage. The styles are diverse. There are buildings and churches from the 1700s and others of brutalist architecture. Others are great city icons, such as the magnificent Teatro Colón and the Obelisco. Av de Mayo, the city's first boulevard, and Av Corrientes stand out as the theater district, full of life and restaurants. The area underwent a reconfiguration after the pandemic and with the increase of remote work, but still offers bars, theaters and architectural heritage that are part of the city's identity.

☑ **TOP TIP**

El Tortoni is the oldest cafe in the city. It was opened in 1858, and many of the country's personalities have passed through its tables. Today it is one of the most visited spots in downtown. The waiters recommend going from 8am to 10am to avoid queues. It is open until 10pm.

GUADALUPE POLITO/SHUTTERSTOCK ©

Plaza de Mayo

Cabildo

The Beginning of Independence

The Cabildo was the scene of the Revolución de Mayo (1810). That event marked the beginning of the construction of Argentina's independence, which took place six years later. The museum retraces the colonial period and the revolutionary process that ended it. In its halls, the museum exhibits everyday items of the time, weapons, furniture and works of art. The story is told through contemporary technological resources, such as augmented reality and 3D.

Cabildo

Casa Rosada

At Evita's Balcony

The seat of government operates on land that was once a fort. It's a great mix of architectural styles and construction changes throughout history. On weekends and holidays, you can visit free from 10am to 6pm (prior registration is required at visitas.casarosada.gob.ar). The tour lasts about an hour, and you can see the patios, halls, the president's office and the most famous balcony in the country, where Eva Perón gave her most emblematic speeches. You can avoid the Salón Eva Perón, which she used and which preserves some of her objects today.

Casa Rosada

Plaza de Mayo

The Most Famous Square

This is the starting point for getting to know the city's center, with the **Pirámide de Mayo** and the **Monumento al General Manuel Belgrano** as central works. Its name is a tribute to the Revolución de Mayo (1810), which took place here, and started the country's independence. Among the trees in the square, there is a special one. It is an olive tree planted by Pope Francisco (Jorge Bergoglio) as Archbishop of Buenos Aires. The buildings that border it are some of the most important in the city. If you go on a Thursday at 3:30pm, you will see the *ronda* of the Madres de Plaza de Mayo. They wear a white handkerchief on their heads, a symbol that identified them over the years to claim the fate of their children who disappeared during the last dictatorship.

CENTRO HISTÓRICO

RETIRO

Plaza San Martín

San Martín

Plaza Libertad

Plaza Rodríguez Peña

MICROCENTRO

Plaza Lavalle

Teatro Colón

Lavalle

TRIBUNALES

Tribunales

Plaza de la República

Carlos Pellegrini

Florida

9 de Julio

Diagonal Norte

Callao

Pasaje Rivarola

Café Tortoni

Congreso

Plaza del Congreso

Plaza Lorea

Palacio Barolo

Palacio del Congreso de la Nación Argentina

CONGRESO

Moreno

Belgrano

MONTSERRAT

Independencia

CONSTITUCIÓN

SAN CRISTÓBAL

San Juan

San José

Entre Ríos

TOP SIGHTS
1 Cabildo
2 Café Tortoni
3 Casa Rosada
4 Centro Cultural Kirchner
5 Feria de an Telmo
6 Mercado de San Telmo
7 Palacio Barolo
8 Palacio del Congreso de la Nación Argentina
9 Pasaje Rivarola
10 Plaza de Mayo
11 Teatro Colón

SIGHTS
12 Catedral Metropolitana de Buenos Aires
13 Colección de Arte Amalia Lacroze de Fortabat
14 El Zanjón de Granados
15 Fragata Sarmiento
16 Librería Ávila
17 Museo de Arte Moderno de Buenos Aires
18 Pasaje de la Defensa
19 Puente de la Mujer

SLEEPING
20 725 Continental Hotel
21 Buenos Aires Marriott
22 Che Juan Hostel
23 Hotel Jousten
24 Hotel NH Latino Buenos Aires
25 Savoy Hotel

EATING
26 Boca de Toro Club
27 Cadore
28 Chungo
29 Confitería La Ideal
30 El Tropezón
31 Freddo
32 Güerrín
33 La Americana
34 La Giralda
35 Las Cuartetas
see 33 Los Inmortales
36 Lucciano's
37 Parrilla Peña
38 Pepito
39 Sattva
40 Scannapieco

DRINKING & NIGHTLIFE
41 36 Billares
42 Café de los Angelitos
see 15 Puerto Rico
43 Paulín

ENTERTAINMENT
44 El Beso
see 35 Opera Theater
45 Rojo Tango
46 Tango Porteño
47 Teatro Gran Rex
48 Teatro San Martín

Café Tortoni

Café Tortoni

Oldest and Most Famous Cafe

Having coffee with friends is a very Argentine custom. Tortoni was the first cafe in town, inaugurated in 1858. Visiting here is to take a journey through time. In addition to the bar and the waiters in suits and bow ties, you can see old coffee cups, black and white photographs of Buenos Aires and even elements of an old hairdresser's shop that used to operate here in the 1940s. There is a basement where jazz and tango concerts are organized.

Centro Cultural Kirchner

Beautiful Post Office

The magnificent French academicism–style building was the headquarters of the Central Post Office. It was then abandoned for many years. In 2015 it was restored and reopened as a cultural center, named after former president Néstor Kirchner. The central balcony looks diagonally to the Casa Rosada because, legend has it, in those years, the job of the postmaster was as crucial as that of the president. From Thursday to Sunday, at 2:30pm and 4pm, the building has guided tours. The place has a full schedule of exhibitions, concerts and lectures. Admission to all activities is free.

Palacio Barolo

Palacio Barolo

Inspired by Dante's *Divine Comedy*

On Av de Mayo 1370 is the building that was described as 'the first skyscraper in Latin America'. That may not be its most outstanding feature. Palacio Barolo was designed more than 100 years ago as a shrine to Dante Alighieri. Its breathtaking architecture contains clues from the *Divine Comedy* and signs of Freemasonry. The guided tour explains the site's history, but perhaps the most fascinating moment of the experience is climbing the small lighthouse, which symbolizes God. It is about 100m high, and from there, you can see the layout of the avenue. You can visit it every day except Tuesdays and Sundays. There are day and night tours; the night ones offer a more impressive view of the city. Reservations are essential.

Teatro Colón

The Country's Most Impressive Theater

The Italian tenor Luciano Pavarotti once said: 'The Teatro Colón has a very great defect: its acoustics are perfect. Imagine what that means for a singer. If you do something wrong, you notice it right away.' The Teatro Colón is a building of which the city of Buenos Aires can be proud. The beauty and luxury of the opera house also tell the story of a country at the time of the theater's construction, which was one of the richest in the world. The guided tour takes place from Monday to Sunday, from 10am, every 15 minutes in Spanish and less frequently in English and Portuguese. The tour explains the history of the construction of the theater. It is also a journey back to the Buenos Aires of the late 19th and early 20th centuries. The magnificent stained-glass windows, ornamentation, and the Palace of Versailles stand out. Tickets can be purchased in advance for the tour and, of course, to see a concert or an opera. An excellent complementary visit is to go to **Colón Fábrica** (p109), the scenery and costumes warehouse of the Teatro Colón, located in La Boca.

DOMES

The interior dome of the Teatro Colón is one of the wonders of the place. Raúl Soldi painted it in the 1960s. In downtown Buenos Aires, many buildings have beautiful domes. This architectural element was used in the late 19th and early 20th centuries to mark corners and signify distinction. Most buildings with domes are downtown (Balvanera, San Nicolás and Montserrat). Green Eat is a chain of restaurants that may not catch your eye. However, the 2nd floor of one of their locations, Florida 102, has a good view of some of the downtown domes.

SHARPTOYOU/SHUTTERSTOCK ©

Teatro Colón

Palacio del Congreso de la Nación Argentina

National Historic Landmark

The Palacio del Congreso de la Nación Argentina is one of the most imposing in the historic center of Buenos Aires. It is the seat of the country's legislative power. The great central dome and the sculptures of Lola Mora, one of the country's great artists, stand out from the outside. It is worth taking a free guided tour, which takes place during the week and goes through the main rooms of the building, including the **Salón de los Pasos Perdidos** and the **Recinto de la Cámara de Diputados**. Depending on the officials' activities, some areas of the building may not be available. The tour lasts one hour, and prior registration is required. In front of the monument is the **Plaza del Congreso**, which stands out for the monuments to transcendent figures of Argentine politics. There is also a sculpture of **The Thinker**, by Auguste Rodin. It was inaugurated in 1907 and cast in the famous sculpture's original mould.

SAIKO3P/SHUTTERSTOCK ©

Palacio del Congreso de la Nación Argentina

Pasaje Rivarola

The Perfect Symmetry

The full name of the street is **Pasaje Dr Rodolfo Rivarola**. It joins Juan Domingo Perón and Bartolomé Mitre streets, parallel to Talcahuano and Uruguay. The small street passage calls for calm in the middle of the city center. It has only eight buildings in perfect symmetry. Each one faces the other, like a mirror that catches the attention of unsuspecting travelers. The buildings were built in the mid-1920s, in a style with domes that evoke some of the narrow streets of Paris. At that time, copying French architecture was considered prestigious.

BUTEO/SHUTTERSTOCK ©

Disney's *The Beauty and the Beast*, Opera Theater

MORE IN CENTRO HISTÓRICO

Theater Along Av Corrientes

Nightlife and Theater District

Buenos Aires has 300 registered theaters, including the commercial, independent and official circuits. Many theaters are excellent examples of art deco architecture. The most emblematic is the **Teatro Gran Rex**, a few meters from the Obelisco. Another emblematic building is the **Opera Theater**, inspired by the Rex Cinema in Paris. The city's drama and arts scene is undoubtedly the most effervescent in Latin America. Av Corrientes, mainly between Callao and Maipú, is home to many theaters and restaurants. The offerings are varied, from stand-up to dramatic works. There are also plays by Argentine and international authors, with tickets at affordable prices. At Av Corrientes 1530 is the Teatro San Martín, an official institution with a vast theater, cinema and dance program.

On the other hand, **Paseo La Plaza** has five theaters. Recently, the place inaugurated a food court, with several restaurants of Argentine and international food. Tickets to see plays in official theaters are usually cheaper than commercial ones.

BEST PLACES FOR PIZZA

Güerrín
Perhaps the most popular pizza in the city. Two Genoese immigrants founded it in the 1930s when the Obelisco had not yet been completed. It serves pizzas with industrial quantities of cheese and grease – a delight. You may have to wait in line.

Banchero
Born in La Boca but became famous downtown. The house specialty is the '*fugazzeta*' with mozzarella cheese and onion.

Las Cuartetas
Next to the Opera Theater, the restaurant specializes in tomato and anchovies pizza.

Los Inmortales
Founded in the 1950s. Neapolitan pizza, with slices of tomato and garlic, is its specialty.

La Americana
A classic of the city. In addition to pizzas, it specializes in meat empanadas.

 WHERE TO EAT IN CENTRO HISTÓRICO

Parrilla Peña
Offers excellent-quality meat in an unpretentious atmosphere. The fried empanadas are an impeccable starter. **$$**

Confitería La Ideal
Recently renovated historic bar and restaurant. Excellent pastry shop; also serves a succulent *bife de chorizo*. **$$**

Boca de Toro Club
Located in the basement of a hotel. Serves Spanish-inspired tapas and cocktails in an intimate atmosphere. **$$**

BEST ICE CREAM

Cadore
It deserves all the awards it has received throughout its history. Its *dulce de leche* flavor is heaven on earth.

Chungo
Has been in the city for more than 40 years, offering ice cream and coffee. The product is creamy, and flavors are rotated according to the season.

Lucciano's
The company was born in Mar del Plata and moved to Buenos Aires a few years ago. The house specialty is ice-pops, which received awards in the city.

Scannapieco
The brand has been in existence since 1938. Its specialty is pistachio ice cream.

Freddo
Italian immigrants founded the company. Its specialty is the *dulce de leche tentación*.

JEFFREY GREENBERG/UNIVERSAL IMAGES GROUP VIA GETTY IMAGES ©

Librería Ávila

The theater is popular in the city: if you attend a performance, you may see everyone from teenagers and young adults to elderly couples enjoying the diverse offerings of the theater. If you travel in February, you can attend the **Festival Internacional de Buenos Aires** (FIBA), which brings together outstanding works from around the world in numerous venues throughout the city.

A Piece of City History

A Visit to Librería Ávila

Buenos Aires has the most bookstores per capita in the world. On Av Corrientes, dozens of bookstores are open until after 10pm. The historical center, very close to Plaza de Mayo, has a unique bookstore because of its history. Librería Ávila is the oldest in the city (1785). The bookstore is 400 sq m in size. The store's two floors have seven display windows holding 150,000 books. Although it was in danger of disappearing at various times, it is still part of one of the city's cultural legacies. It was built in 1785 when Buenos Aires was 205 years old and 25 years before the First Patriotic Government. Miguel Ávila, the current

WHERE TO EAT IN CENTRO HISTÓRICO

Pepito
A classic charcoal grill located in a corner of the theater district. **$$**

El Tropezón
A historical place born in 1869, with dishes of the *porteño* and Spanish cuisines. **$$$**

Sattva
Tasty vegetarian dishes at reasonable prices. **$**

owner, who personally attends to his customers, notes that at one point, the building was going to be bought by a hamburger chain.

The store sells mainly used books and has some ancient ones, which Ávila proudly displays. Some of the fabulous jewels of the place are the first editions of books by writers such as Jorge Luis Borges, Julio Cortázar and Manuel Puig, and an ancient copy of *Billiken* magazine. It is a great pleasure to talk to Miguel, who is always willing to answer your questions. Many of the visitors are young people. Across the street is the Colegio Nacional de Buenos Aires, one of the country's most important schools, where many significant Argentine historical figures studied.

The Art of Tango

A Journey to the Origins of Music

A few meters from the Obelisco and the Teatro Colón, the Tango Porteño show re-creates the '40s, one of the most glorious decades of Buenos Aires music. The space where the show is performed used to be a cinema. The show has more than 20 people on stage, with some of the most critical moments in the musical genre's history. The musicians and dancers are of excellent technical quality and good expressiveness. Throughout the show, the musicians perform songs by famous tango orchestras such as Canaro, Fresedo, De Caro, Gobbi, Biagi, De Angelis, Di Sarli, D'Arienzo, Lomuto, D'Agostino, and, of course, Troilo and Pugliese.

There is also room for the pioneering music of Ástor Piazzolla, who is perhaps the most widely performed tango musician in the world today. Similar shows focused on the so-called stage tango are offered in other parts of the city. These presentations emphasize sensuality and the acrobatic skills of their dancers. On the other hand, in the *milongas*, a much more intimate and

THE ART OF ASKING SOMEONE TO DANCE

If you attend a *milonga*, you should know some local codes, such as the *cabeceo*. What is it? It's a subtle head movement directed toward the person you want to invite to dance. This gesture is used instead of approaching them directly. The sequence works as follows: first, you search for someone you'd like to dance with. When you successfully catch their attention and your gazes meet, it's time to nod. If they maintain eye contact, they've accepted your invitation, and you can walk towards them. However, if they look away, it indicates that your invitation has been declined, and you should restart your search.

THE GREAT COMPETITION

Although tango lives all year round in the city, there is a particular month for lovers of this music. In August, the World Tango Dance Championship is held. There are two categories: Track Tango and Stage Tango. See p519 for more on **tango**.

 WHERE TO STAY IN CENTRO HISTÓRICO

Hotel Jousten
This historic building from the 1920s has all the comforts. It is a few meters from the Casa Rosada. **$$**

Che Juan Hostel
Single and shared rooms, with a youthful atmosphere. Rooms are named after public figures, including Lionel Messi. **$**

725 Continental Hotel
Excellent location, a few meters from the Obelisco and the famous Florida St. Has an outdoor swimming pool. **$$**

closer dance is practiced, though it is less spectacular. Rates vary, depending on whether you attend only for the show or choose the VIP experience with dinner and pickup at the hotel. There is also the possibility of taking tango classes on the same site. Classes start at 7:30pm, before the show, and the teachers are the same dancers participating in the exhibition. They teach the basic movements, the embrace and how to walk on the dance floor. At the end, a certificate is given.

Where Pope Francis Led Mass as Archbishop

The Stories of the Catedral Metropolitana

The city's main Catholic church has five naves and a large dome over 40m high. There is the mausoleum of General José de San Martín, a key figure in the declaration of Argentina's independence. The works of the Via Crucis belong to the Italian Francesco Domenighini. Besides being a National Historic Monument, the cathedral has an additional attraction for Catholics. In this place, Jorge Bergoglio served as Archbishop of Buenos Aires until March 19, 2013, when he became Pope Francis. When entering the site, there is a system of audio guides of the tour 'Del Cardenal Bergoglio al Papa Francisco'. The cathedral also offers guided tours as well as self-guided tours. In both cases, these tours cover various aspects, including the cathedral's history and its significance in the country's history, such as the mausoleum of San Martín. A noteworthy detail to observe is the Venetian mosaic floors, which span over 2600 sq m. The cathedral's grand and impressive golden altar is also a standout feature.

Milonguero-Style Milonga Dance

A Close Embrace

The city is full of tango shows for all budgets. In many cases, the choreographies are spectacular and attract the attention of both locals and tourists. However, there is another way to dance tango, with the most intimate embrace and away from the show. El Beso is a traditional *milonga* that operates from Monday to Sunday. There, *milongas* have different names, depending on the people who organize them, but they are all held in the same place. Unlike the big shows, the *milonguero* style is more intimate and close. Many couples usually dance in the same space (they do it counterclockwise), and the figure of the tango DJ is highly valued. Going to one of these *milongas* is a fascinating, immersive experience, whether you want to learn to dance tango or just watch.

BEST HISTORIC CAFES & BARS

Puerto Rico
A classic cafe with specialties like *medialunas* (croissants) and *dulce de leche* cake.

La Giralda
Located in the theater district. Its churros with chocolate are famous.

Café de los Angelitos
The cafe where singer Carlos Gardel used to go. It organizes tango shows and exhibits a collection of old photographs.

36 Billares
Born in 1894 as a place for poets and intellectuals. It still preserves that spirit. You can play billiards until late at night.

Paulín
An office worker's bar famous for its sandwiches.

WHERE TO STAY IN CENTRO HISTÓRICO

Hotel NH Latino Buenos Aires
Spacious and comfortable rooms close to the Obelisco and Av Corrientes. **$$$**

Savoy Hotel
An emblematic hotel in a neo-baroque building just a few meters from the Congreso Nacional. **$$**

Buenos Aires Marriott
A five-star hotel with a heated swimming pool and a view of the Obelisco. **$$$**

CHACABUCO

TRIUNFO EN SAN LORENZO - 1813
AFIRMÓ LA INDEPENDENCIA ARGENTINA - 1816

Mausoleum of General José de San Martín, Catedral Metropolitana

Recoleta & Retiro

FULL OF HISTORY, MUSEUMS AND ARCHITECTURE

Formerly, these neighborhoods were the northern outskirts of the city. Nowadays, they have the most tourist attractions in the city. Their streets are full of large houses and palaces, built when the city's wealthiest families moved from the south to the north due to yellow fever and cholera epidemics at the end of the 19th century and the beginning of the 20th century. The Cementerio de la Recoleta, with the tomb of Eva Perón, the mansions surrounding the Plaza General San Martín, and the Museo Nacional de Bellas Artes are some of the many attractions. Another highlight is the Ateneo Grand Splendid bookstore, the largest in South America and chosen by several publications as one of the most beautiful in the world. The area also offers an effervescent nightlife scene, with excellent restaurants, cocktail bars and unique coffee shops. Welcome to the most elegant part of this city.

☑ **TOP TIP**

Cementerio de la Recoleta is thronged with tourists. Avoid accepting help from strangers who want to show you 'the best and less known' of the area. It is worth taking a tour of the architecture and the site's stories. Free Walks Buenos Aires organizes one every day at 3:30pm. It lasts two hours. You must first pay your entrance fee and then look for the guides, usually dressed in orange.

MIRALEX/GETTY IMAGES ©

Cementerio de la Recoleta (p88)

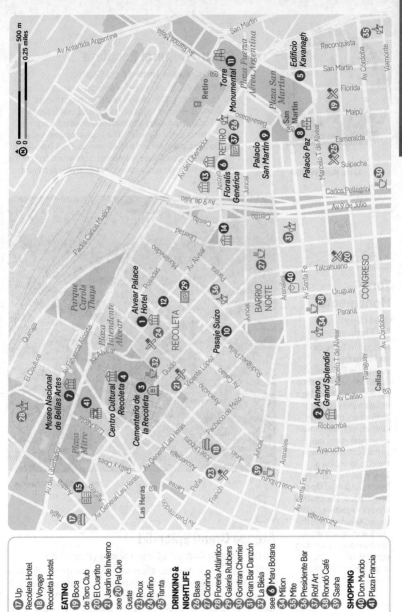

RECOLETA & RETIRO BUENOS AIRES

TOP SIGHTS
1 Alvear Palace Hotel
2 Ateneo Grand Splendid
3 Cementerio de la Recoleta
4 Centro Cultural Recoleta
5 Edificio Kavanagh
6 Floralis Genérica
7 Museo Nacional de Bellas Artes
8 Palacio Paz
9 Palacio San Martín
10 Pasaje Suizo
11 Torre Monumental

SIGHTS
12 Av Alvear
13 Museo de Arte Hispano-americano Isaac Fernández Blanco
14 Pereda Palace

ACTIVITIES, COURSES & TOURS
15 Biblioteca Nacional Mariano Moreno

SLEEPING
16 see 21 Loi Suites Recoleta

17 Up Recoleta Hotel
18 Voyage Recoleta Hostel

EATING
19 Boca de Toro Club
20 El Cuartito
21 Jardín de Invierno
see 20 Pal Que Guste
23 Roux
24 Rufino
25 Tanta

DRINKING & NIGHTLIFE
26 Basa
27 Clorindo
28 Florería Atlántico
29 Galería Rubbers
30 Gontran Cherrier
31 Gran Bar Danzón
32 La Biela
see 6 Maru Botana
34 Million
35 Mite
36 Presidente Bar
37 Rolf Art
38 Rondó Café
39 Sasha

SHOPPING
40 Don Mundo
41 Plaza Francia

85

Torre Monumental

Centro Cultural Recoleta
An Old Convent Turned Arts Center

This 1732 building is a symbol of both the avant-garde and the city's history. The convent of the Recollect monks, who gave their name to the neighborhood, was located here. Today, it is the city's cultural center, which has an effervescent cultural agenda. There are exhibition halls, auditoriums, a theater and a small cinema. From Tuesday to Sunday afternoons, there are guided tours which explore the history of the building and provide an overview of current exhibitions.

Torre Monumental
Great Spot for Pictures

Also called **Torre de los Ingleses**, this building, in Elizabethan Renaissance style, was a gift from British residents to the country on the anniversary of the May Revolution. It was closed for several years, but visitors can now climb the 60m to access a viewpoint. You can see Retiro and part of the port from the top. The coats of arms of Argentina and the United Kingdom, and the clock with its four dials, are the most outstanding elements of the place. It is open every day except Tuesdays and Sundays.

Ateneo Grand Splendid

Ateneo Grand Splendid
An Old Theater Converted into a Modern Bookshop

This bookstore is one of the great tourist attractions of Buenos Aires. The number of people visiting to look around is as high as the number that buy a book. It was built in 1923 as Teatro Grand Splendid, where opera concerts, ballet and the first sound films of Buenos Aires were presented. It has been used as a bookstore since 2000. The decoration and the frescoed dome are intact, and upon entering, one has the impression of entering an imposing theater. It has four floors. The old theater boxes are used as spaces for quiet reading, while a small cafe is on the stage. The basement is devoted to children's literature. It holds book presentations and exhibitions; check online for details.

Pasaje Suizo
Charming Alleyway

The cliché equates Buenos Aires with Paris. But this charming passage is called Swiss (but also known as Pasaje del Correo) and was built by an Italian architect, Felipe Restano – that's the authentic mix of cultures made in Argentina! The place was intended as a set of 21 single-family homes, but over time they were converted into bars and restaurants. The big highlight is **Aramburu**, one of the most awarded restaurants in the country. It still preserves details of the original construction, such as ironwork, doors, canopies and street lamps.

Floralis Genérica

Floralis Genérica
Art Under the Sky

There is no doubt that the Obelisco is the most famous monument in Buenos Aires, but the modern city has another icon: the **Floralis Genérica**. It is a large stainless steel sculpture of a flower, the work of architect Eduardo Catalano. The piece has a peculiarity: the six petals that compose it, which look like the covering of an aeroplane wing, are movable. Thanks to a hydraulic system and photoelectric cells, they close at night and open during the day. The monument is in a 4-hectare park and over a mirror of water. It is halfway between the Museo Nacional de Bellas Artes and the MALBA.

Museo Nacional
de Bellas Artes

Museo Nacional de Bellas Artes
The Biggest Collection of Argentine Art

This museum has the most extensive collection of Argentine art and is one of the most impressive in Latin America. In addition, the building is located on Av Libertador, full of parks and elegant buildings. The focus is on the 19th and early 20th centuries. The museum's management always adds new pieces to its permanent display from its extensive collection, which dates back to 1896. In addition to works by Gauguin, El Greco and Picasso, visitors can tour 200 years of Argentine art in its exhibition halls. Cándido López, Antonio Berni and Xul Solar are some highlights. It is open every day except Mondays. Admission is free. On weekends, try to go in the morning before the crowds arrive.

Cementerio de la Recoleta

Explore the City's History

This is much more than a cemetery. You can travel through the history of the last 200 years of Argentina through its tombs and admire the impressive mausoleums, which turn it into an open-air museum. The city's first public cemetery was inaugurated in 1822 and is one of the most visited in the world, along with Peré Lachaise and Montparnasse (Paris). More than 20 Argentine presidents are buried here, as well as heroes of the country and other great Argentine celebrities, such as Victoria Ocampo, Luis Federico Leloir, Adolfo Bioy Casares and Blanca Podestá. Be amazed by the magnificence of some of the mausoleums and the wide variety of architectural styles of the buildings, such as art deco, art nouveau, baroque and neo-Gothic. The cemetery contains ghosts, myths and legends, such as that of a young woman buried alive. The guides usually tell it gracefully, and it is worth taking a tour to avoid missing anything. The big highlight, of course, is the tomb of Eva Perón.

FINDING EVITA'S GRAVE

Cementerio de la Recoleta has 4780 vaults. Some are in narrow corridors and are not easy to find because no maps are provided at the entrance. Many people go directly to the most famous, the Eva Perón vault, located 200m to the left of the main gate. The first lady from 1946 to 1952 fought for workers' rights and women's suffrage. The vault of the Duarte family – her maiden name – is simple compared to many others. However, it is the only one that always has fresh flowers, which people continue to leave. Guides explain the tortuous journey of her body until it reached the cemetery, 8m underground, to protect it from vandalism.

JAVIER CATANO GONZALEZ/SHUTTERSTOCK ©

Cementerio de la Recoleta

Plaza Francia Market & Craft Fair
A Lazy Weekend Excursion

The market at Plaza Francia unites artisans and skilled crafts-people from 11am onward on weekends. The square, named after France because it was a gift from the community to Argentina on the occasion of the Centenary of Revolución de Mayo, is surrounded by sculptures. It is also a place chosen by young people to spend the day and drink *mate* in the sun. Stalls sell glass, silver and leather objects, and there are small food shops. You can buy handicrafts and enjoy the open-air theater. Throughout the day, the streets inside the square are filled with street performers, such as musicians, jugglers, mimes, clowns, puppeteers and living statues. It is within walking distance of Recoleta's main attractions, such as the cemetery and the Museo Nacional de Bellas Artes. Alongside the San Telmo Fair, it's one of the city's most important markets and an excellent option for enjoying the day outdoors.

The City's Most Aristocratic Avenue
The Charm of Walking Through Alvear

Designed in 1885 by Mayor Torcuato de Alvear, this strip is one of the most elegant avenues in the city. Some aristocratic residences exist, such as the Ortiz Basualdo Palace (French Embassy). Some big-brand stores are also here, although perhaps due to the Argentine economic crisis, it has had more splendorous times. All the large mansions now have other uses except for one. Av Alvear 1683 is the Hume residence, the only one still inhabited, which is a mystery because it is not known who lives there, so much so that it is called the house of the eclectic facade, or Dracula's house, by the locals. Av Alvear and its surroundings are charming because they demonstrate the significant influence of French academicism in Buenos Aires. Nearby, at Arroyo 1130, is the **Pereda Palace**, which now serves as the Brazilian embassy. The sumptuous mansion of the Unzué family is currently the headquarters of the Jockey Club. Stroll through these streets of Buenos Aires, which have a Parisian style.

WHERE TO GET A COFFEE

Maru Botana
The pastry chef is a celebrity in Argentina, with dozens of TV shows. Her specialty is the Rogel cake, with lots of *dulce de leche*.

Rondó Café
Specialty coffee is famous in the city. The flat white is one of the most requested by customers.

Gontran Cherrier
In a winter garden, the place offers French pastry delicacies in an atmosphere with a touch of belle époque.

Clorindo
A hidden cafe in honour of the famous Argentine architect Clorindo Testa.

Sasha
This place specializes in cakes. Its best-known recipe is the brownie with Nutella.

WHERE TO EAT IN RECOLETA & RETIRO

El Cuartito
It isn't quiet and is always busy, but well worth the effort. The pizza *fugazzeta* is the undisputed star of the house. $

Roux
Haute cuisine prepared with ingredients from all over the country. The suckling pig is a tender and crispy delicacy. $$$

Pal que guste
Offers tasty food from the north, with a rural ambience and reasonable prices. Also has folklore shows. $

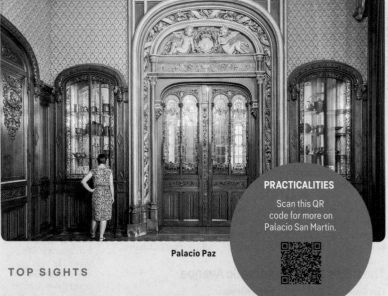

HEMIS/ALAMY STOCK PHOTO ©

Palacio Paz

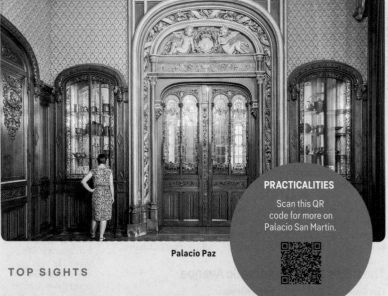

PRACTICALITIES

Scan this QR
code for more on
Palacio San Martín.

TOP SIGHTS

Mansions & Palaces

Retiro and Recoleta contain many of the grand palaces, emblematic buildings and mansions of Buenos Aires. Plaza San Martín and Av Alvear are particularly well endowed. The buildings are part of the living memory of Buenos Aires' history. Some were transformed into hotels, others into institutional headquarters and museums that can be visited. Many of them are French in style, and were built between the end of the 19th century and the beginning of the 20th century when Argentina was a great world power.

DON'T MISS

Palacio Paz

Palacio
San Martín

Edificio
Kavanagh

Alvear
Palace Hotel

Four Seasons
Hotel Buenos Aires

Palacio Paz

Located in front of Plaza San Martín, this is one of the most luxurious mansions in the city. It belonged to José C Paz, a businessman, diplomat and one of the most important figures of 19th-century Argentina. Currently, it houses the Military Circle. Walking through these corridors is like returning to the belle époque but in Buenos Aires. The French influence is notable throughout the building, which has 140 rooms, reminiscent of the Chantilly Palace and the side of the Louvre Palace overlooking the Seine. All the materials are original and brought from Europe, as they used to do when Argentina looked at that continent. The marble floors, stairs and columns were brought from Italy and Spain, the stained-glass windows are French and the oak parquet floors from Slavonia. The house's impressive places are the ballroom, Gothic galleries and the Hall of Honor. Guided tours of the mansion take place on Tuesdays, Thursdays and Fridays. Reservations are essential and can be made by writing to reservaspalaciopaz@gmail.com. The tour is only given in Spanish.

Another way to visit the mansion is to go to **Croque Madame Palacio Paz**. The place has a cafeteria in an outdoor gallery and a restaurant in one of the halls of the old mansion.

Palacio San Martín

This mansion belonged to the Anchorena family. It currently serves as the headquarters of the Argentine Foreign Ministry. The winter gardens, built-in ironwork, and the details of the French eclectic architecture stand out during the visit, along with the beautiful gardens. In addition, the place houses an impressive collection of Argentine art. Getting into the guided tours is difficult because they have limited spaces. To schedule your tour, you must register on the website turnos-palacio.mrecic.gov.ar/palacio (in Spanish). Or you can settle for seeing some parts of the house from the outside.

Edificio Kavanagh

This apartment building in front of Plaza San Martín was, at its inauguration in 1936, one of the first skyscrapers in Buenos Aires. The esplanade of the square offers an extraordinary view of its rationalist and art deco style, which became an emblem of modern architecture in the city. Although it cannot be visited, the city's tourist office offers a self-guided tour of the area and explains its history. One very interesting tale is the love story between Corina Kavanagh, who commissioned the building, and the son of the Anchorena family of the Palacio San Martín.

Alvear Palace Hotel

This building was born as a hotel which sought to emulate the Parisian ones. Throughout history, it hosted presidents, princes, kings and great stars, who chose its luxurious details and Louis XV–style furniture. Although guided tours are not organized, it is possible to experience that atmosphere and walk through its imposing central gallery, which simulates an ocean liner. One way to visit it is to drink in some of its bars or live the whole experience with afternoon tea service in natural light.

ICONIC HOTEL ROOFTOP BAR

From the rooftop bar at the Alvear Palace Hotel you can view Recoleta's sunset and green spaces. It is located on the 11th floor, with light dishes, signature drinks and house music. It is open only from Wednesday to Sunday, and reservations are required. A small gourmet *choripán* and the Malibulísima drink (white rum, Malibú, lime, sugar) are worth it.

TOP TIPS

- Some palaces and mansions have restricted visits a few days a month. Check websites and social networks to sign up for visits.
- Tourists usually visit the Plaza San Martín area during the day. It is advisable to avoid the area at night.
- Visit the palaces and mansions on the weekend and combine with an excursion to the Plaza Francia fair.
- Junin and Vicente Lopez streets, close to the cemetery, are full of bars, breweries and restaurants. The atmosphere is relaxed, and there are options for all tastes. It's a good stop after a walk.

BEST ART GALLERIES

Rolf Art
Rolf Art has been engaged in photography and its boundaries for over a decade. Additionally, it supports the production and promotion of editorial and audiovisual projects, and carries out research and archival work related to modern arts.

Galería Rubbers
Showcasing modern and contemporary Argentine art with over 65 years of history, Rubbers Gallery has honed a keen eye for identifying emerging talents who subsequently attain recognition.

Mite
With a youthful spirit, Mite presents various exhibitions encompassing painting, drawing, photography, sculpture, performance, video and installation. It is dedicated in an independent and self-managed way to the diffusion of new and established artists.

Biblioteca Nacional

The Most Important Library in Town
Books, Views and Good Drinks

This concrete building features a brutalist style, and one of its creators was Clorindo Testa, one of the most prominent figures in Latin America. It houses a collection of almost one million items and a library of spoken word recordings. The Museo del Libro y de la Lengua, inaugurated in 2006, is on the same premises. Visiting any of the nine reading rooms at the Biblioteca Nacional is worthwhile. The one on the 5th floor is highly recommended, with large windows offering remarkable views of Recoleta illuminated by natural light. Admission might involve a bit of paperwork, as identification is requested at the entrance, and then an admission card is necessary to order books. However, the experience is well worth it. Adjacent to the door on Agüero St is Invernadero, a gin and tapas club set in a charming winter garden. Enjoying a drink amid books makes for a perfect escape.

 WHERE TO EAT IN RECOLETA AND RETIRO

Rufino
Classic Argentine grill dishes with some gourmet touches. One highlight is the 750g bone-in beef ribeye. $$$

Tanta
Peruvian food with the seal of Gastón Acurio, one of that country's most famous chefs. $$

Jardín de Invierno
Cuisine from Argentina and around the world is served amid the lush garden setting of a five-star hotel. $$$

The Irresistible Passion for Maps & Globes

Where the World Appears More Beautiful

Don Mundo's slogan is 'The world deserves to look prettier', and it certainly lives up to it. Without any precedent in the city, this unique business is dedicated to selling globes. Some of its products feature classic geographical divisions, while others showcase highly original designs. It offers globes with lights featuring the character Mafalda, and adorned with remarkable drawings of Argentina's flora and fauna. If you visit this store, you might be tempted to take one home, even though they aren't the most convenient to carry around.

The Place of Writers

A Coffee with the Great Borges

It is the most famous bar in Recoleta and one of the most frequented by tourists. At the entrance door, a table has two sculptures of its most famous customers: Adolfo Bioy Casares and Jorge Luis Borges. The writers spent long hours at their table, as did Julio Cortázar. Many of their stories sought inspiration in this typical *porteño* cafe. The hall is enormous, with a capacity for 400 people, and its walls are full of vehicle parts as ornaments. There are also photographs of great motorsport champions. The menu has Argentine classics, such as *bife de chorizo, sánguches* and a wide variety of coffee. Before leaving, don't forget your souvenir: a photo on the table of Borges and Bioy.

Florería
Atlántico

BEST COCKTAIL BARS

Florería Atlántico
The most famous and awarded speakeasy in Buenos Aires. The star drink is the Negroni Balestrini, with an Argentine gin and touches of *yerba mate*.

Gran Bar Danzón
Many of the great bartenders of the country have passed through here. It has a vast cocktail menu and more than 350 wine labels to taste.

Presidente Bar
Small hotel converted into an elegant cocktail club. Try the suggestive Zombie in Buenos Aires, which has a mix of rums and comes in a container that imitates the Obelisco.

Basa
This place, located in a basement, has a large bar and a minimalist style.

Milion
Offers drinks and tapas in a beautiful old house.

WHERE TO STAY IN RECOLETA & RETIRO

Voyage Recoleta Hostel
Shared and single rooms in a perfect location. Sometimes has live music and other shows in the large common areas. $

Loi Suites Recoleta
This boutique hotel has an extraordinary winter garden and a restaurant, plus a gym and a heated swimming pool. $$$

Up Recoleta Hotel
Experience comfort at its finest while near Recoleta and Palermo's renowned attractions. $$

San Telmo

OLD DISTRICT AND ANTIQUE BARGAINS

The ambience of San Telmo is bohemian and nostalgic, making it a captivating destination. This neighborhood stands as one of the city's oldest, boasting a remarkable architectural heritage that unveils itself through its streets and museums. Cobblestone streets, quaint houses, and charming courtyards with cisterns have been preserved. The area's allure is further heightened by its array of bars, restaurants and diverse antique shops. Since 1970, Plaza Dorrego has been the heart of a remarkable event – the city's most significant antique fair, held every Sunday. This fair immerses you in a world of stores (especially along Defensa St), food stalls, and pockets of greenery. Furthermore, Plaza Dorrego is a hub for street artists, offering a vibrant display of artistic expression. The essence of tango saturates every corner. You can engage with tango through captivating performances, dance lessons, and venues resonating with live music.

☑ TOP TIP

The San Telmo Market is popular with both locals and tourists. It is held every Sunday, from 10am to 5pm. Two o'clock in the afternoon is perhaps the busiest; it is best to go in the morning as soon as it opens. The streets are cobblestone, so wear comfortable shoes and avoid high heels.

TRAVELBUENOSAIRES ©

Feria de San Telmo (p97)

TOP SIGHTS
1. Bar Británico
2. El Zanjón de Granados
3. Feria de San Telmo
4. Mercado de San Telmo
5. Museo Histórico Nacional
6. Parque Lezama
7. Pasaje de la Defensa

SIGHTS
8. Casa Mínima

9. Galería Solar de French
10. Iglesia Ortodoxa Rusa de la Santísima Trinidad
11. Museo de Arte Moderno de Buenos Aires
12. Viña San Telmo

ACTIVITIES, COURSES & TOURS
13. La Scala de San Telmo
14. Pista Urbana

15. Teatro Margarita Xirgu
16. Todo Mundo

EATING
17. La Casa del Dulce de Leche
18. Pulpería Quilapán

DRINKING & NIGHTLIFE
19. Bar Sur
20. Bierlife
21. Café Rivas
22. Doppelgänger Bar

23. El Hipopótamo
24. La Poesía
25. La Puerta Roja
26. Margal
27. Punto Café

ENTERTAINMENT
28. Centro Cultural Torquato Tasso

SHOPPING
29. Taller Pallarols

Bar Británico

Bar Británico

Neighborhood Favorite

Bar Británico is an emblem of San Telmo, to the extent that neighbors campaigned to prevent its closure on multiple occasions. Situated on the corner of Parque Lezama, its name originates from English ex-combatants who frequented it after WWI. For years it served as a gathering spot for writers and intellectuals. Choose one of the old tables overlooking the park and watch life go by over a cup of coffee. The cakes are excellent and huge. Time seems not to have passed inside.

El Zanjón de Granados

Parque Lezama

History and Chess Players

Unlike others in the city, this park features an irregular layout; it was created by renowned French landscape designer Carlos Thays, the mind behind the Jardín Botánico. It is distinguished by its amphitheater, extensive wooded areas, and a ravine that stretches towards Avs Martín García and Paseo Colón. Throughout its history, the park served as a center for the sale of enslaved individuals, and is believed by some historians to be the site of the city's initial foundation. Chessboards can be found in the park's northwest corner, adjacent to the theater.

El Zanjón de Granados

Mysterious Tunnels

This site is more than a museum; it condenses a part of the history of Buenos Aires in a house and geological layers. In the 1980s, businessman Jorge Eckstein bought the property to remodel it as a restaurant. As construction began, he discovered that a series of subway passages ran through it, draining rainwater into the Río de la Plata. The restaurant project was forgotten and it became the most important archaeological recovery of the city. The guided tour allows you to visit the subway tunnels and part of the city's past through objects found. The tour lasts an hour, but sometimes Jorge himself is the guide – if that happens, you are fortunate, and you won't know how long the experience will last because he has hundreds of stories to tell.

Pasaje de la Defensa

Charming Old Bourgeois House

If you want to know what an old mansion in San Telmo used to be like, you must visit this building. It has two floors, rooms that converge in a central gallery, and large patios. It belonged to a distinguished family in the city with the surname Ezeiza. Since the beginning of the '80s, it has been used as a commercial gallery, selling antiques, clothes and paintings. It is a great pleasure to walk through its checkerboard tiles, stop at the cistern and see the details of pine roofs.

TOP RIGHT: T PHOTOGRAPHY/SHUTTERSTOCK ©; BOTTOM LEFT: SANDRA MORAES/SHUTTERSTOCK ©

Pasaje de la Defensa

Casa Mínima

Enigmatic Tales of a Historic House

The front of this house spans just over 2m wide, concealing the enigma of its walls and colonial architecture. Who inhabited such a compact space? What lies within its walls? These inquiries find answers during a tour taking just over an hour, revealing a residence that has diligently preserved original materials from the early 18th century. Notably, the walls are constructed from terracotta. Among the narratives woven into the fabric of this house are stories of apparitions and other accounts of the lives of enslaved individuals who once inhabited Buenos Aires during that era.

Feria de San Telmo

Feria de San Telmo

Handicrafts, Antiques and Street Performers

Spending a Sunday basking in the sunshine at the Feria de San Telmo is a beloved pastime for locals and visitors alike. The vibrant heart of this experience lies along Defensa St, where more than 300 antique dealers assemble their enticing stalls. Embarking from Defensa and Yrigoyen (Plaza de Mayo) towards Plaza Dorrego sets the stage for an enriching exploration. While the stalls encircling the square predominantly house antique treasures, many others showcase an array of leather, silver and wooden crafts alongside unique artefacts and clothing. The plaza's periphery transforms into a dynamic tableau, with numerous restaurants arranging alfresco seating. As daylight graces the streets, an engaging spectacle unfolds with street performers adorning the scene – musicians, living statues and, naturally, couples entwined in tango's graceful embrace.

97

Mercado de San Telmo

Antiques and Foodie Spot

This striking marketplace is one of the most emblematic buildings in the neighborhood. Its inauguration dates back to 1897, when it was created to supply provisions to the new wave of European immigrants arriving in the city. As time went by, its use changed. Antique shops were installed, which coexisted with greengrocers and butchers. In 2022 the city government restored the building, respecting its original architecture of beams, arches and metallic columns, which were imported from Germany. The roofs, with a large dome, are made of sheet metal and glass. Today, there are still some antique shops, and many gastronomic stalls have been added, including Argentine and French restaurants, and specialty cafes that have given it a gourmet profile. **Mundo Beat**, run by its owner, Beto, sells curious vintage objects, other kitsch and vinyl records. **Coffee Town** is one of the pioneering specialty coffee shops in a country that is slowly beginning to take an interest in drinking good coffee.

Mercado de San Telmo

Taller Pallarols

Buenos Aires' Most Distinguished Silversmith

Juan Carlos Pallarols is the most famous goldsmith in the country. Since the beginning of democracy in 1983, he has made the presidential baton for each Argentine president. His works are recognized all over the world. Figures such as Lady Di, Melanie Griffith, Madonna and Tom Hanks have bought some of his pieces. The famous artist's workshop is located on Defensa St. Visiting it and seeing some of his antique and current pieces is possible. Most of them are silverware. It is a pleasure to dwell on the texture of each chiselled rose or silver medal. His paintings are also on display. It is open 9am to 5pm Monday to Saturday.

Museo Histórico Nacional
The Renowned Saber of José de San Martín

This museum is situated within the splendid mansion of Parque Lezama. It houses a remarkable collection of objects and images from the revolutionary processes that paved the way for Argentina's independence. This heritage is unparalleled in other museums across the country. Notably, it showcases items like the inkwell used to sign the Declaration of Independence in the province of Tucumán. Personal effects belonging to key figures in Argentine history, such as Manuel Belgrano and Martín Miguel de Güemes, are also on display. Undoubtedly, the centerpiece is José de San Martín's renowned saber – a symbol of liberation that once belonged to the foremost hero in Argentine history. It was the weapon that accompanied the Liberator of America in all the battles for independence. It is a beautiful and straightforward object, without gold pieces, arabesques or other expensive materials, which were popular then. Beyond its permanent Tiempo de Revolución exhibition, the museum hosts rotating exhibitions exploring themes linked to Argentine identity, such as music and soccer. The museum offers free admission and guided tours Wednesday to Sunday.

A PICTURE WITH MAFALDA

The Museo Histórico Nacional frequently organizes exhibitions related to elements of the Argentine idiosyncrasy. A few blocks away, an open-air sculpture speaks of an icon of the country's graphic humour. If you walk down Defensa St to Chile St, you'll likely see people queuing up to have their pictures taken. The monument is small in size. It's a simple square bench featuring a sculpture of Mafalda and some of her friends. This installation pays homage to the internationally renowned comic book character created by the cartoonist Joaquín Lavado (Quino), who was born in Mendoza but chose to reside in San Telmo. The tribute celebrates this endearing character, a curious and ironic girl who brought to light the customs and personality of Argentines.

TRAVELBUENOSAIRES ©

Museo Histórico Nacional

BEST COCKTAIL & WINE BARS

Doppelgänger Bar
Located in San Telmo for over 15 years, Doppelgänger Bar is a haven for mixology enthusiasts. Its specialty lies in the various iterations of Negroni and Martini, although it also offers an extensive range of drinks and snack dishes.

Vina San Telmo
Over 100 different wine labels are on offer for tasting. Additionally, the bar organizes blind wine tastings.

Bierlife
Nestled in an old mansion, Bierlife boasts 70 beer varieties and dishes crafted with this beverage. The spacious garden is perfect for enjoying summer nights.

La Puerta Roja
This bar offers beers, drinks and a good atmosphere. People usually gather here to watch soccer games.

Margal
Craft beer is the protagonist of the place. It has a large terrace.

TRAVELBUENOSAIRES ©

Iglesia Ortodoxa Rusa de la Santísima Trinidad

MORE IN SAN TELMO

A Piece of Russia in San Telmo

A Fabulous Church in Front of Parque Lezama

If you visit Parque Lezama on Brasil St, you will be amazed by the blue domes of a Moscow-style church amid the Buenos Aires landscape. The Iglesia Ortodoxa Rusa de la Santísima Trinidad was inaugurated in 1904. Russian architect Mikhail Preobrazhensky designed the project, although it later underwent modifications by Alejandro Christophersen, known for creating the San Martín Palace in Retiro. Inside, the stained-glass windows and, especially, the paintings displayed in frames are astonishing. Some were created by renowned artists such as Mikhail Nesterov and Viktor Vasnetsov, who worked on Kyiv and St Petersburg cathedrals.

Argentina was a pioneer in freedom of religion issues in Latin America. The church is also a demonstration of that openness. For example, it was the first country in South America to have a non-Catholic Christian temple. Visits are available only one Sunday per month, and you need to reserve a spot at info@iglesiarusa.org.ar. Another way to experience it is by attending a mass, which takes place on Sunday mornings.

 WHERE TO EAT IN SAN TELMO

Café San Juan
This award-winning restaurant features Spanish-inspired tapas and recipes made with quality local ingredients. **$$$**

The Pizza Only True Love
A variety of pizzas, pasta made with organic flour and sourdough, and a cocktail bar. **$$**

El Federal
Has been operating since 1864 as a grocery store, and specializes in cold cuts and cheeses. **$$**

Those Famous Umbrellas

A Gallery with a Rich History

Galería Solar de French is famous for two reasons. The shopping promenade, adorned with dozens of colorful umbrellas, has become one of the most photogenic spots in San Telmo. The other aspect is historical. Domingo French, one of the key figures of the May Revolution that paved the path for Argentina's independence, lived here. The stores are small but feature original designs. As a traveler, you will enjoy the offerings at **Indochina**, a store that specializes in clothing and tourist-themed items. The neighborhood inspires the San Telmo Collection, which includes caps, sweaters and T-shirts.

Satisfy Your Sweet Tooth

Passion for Dulce de Leche

If there are two things Argentines are proud of, it is soccer and *dulce de leche*. La Casa del Dulce de Leche celebrates one of Argentina's passions by offering large pots of classic *dulce de leche* and varieties with chocolate, rum, banana and coffee additions. It also sells liqueurs, *alfajores* and *dulce de leche* chocolates – all ideal for those with a sweet tooth. Other similar establishments in the neighborhood include **La Vaca Lechera** and **Doña Magdalena**. All the ice cream parlours in the city also have *dulce de leche* in different versions.

La Casa del Dulce de Leche

JEFFREY GREENBERG/UNIVERSAL IMAGES GROUP VIA GETTY IMAGES ©

BEST COFFEE IN SAN TELMO

Punto Café
Specialty coffee and pastries in an ideal working environment. Try the Flat Mahal, with chocolate, ginger and sesame.

Café Rivas
A beautiful bar and restaurant with good coffee in an emblematic corner of San Telmo.

La Poesía
This bar has a great history dedicated to literature, and organizes readings and book presentations.

Bar Sur
In addition to coffee, this bar offers tango shows every night.

El Hipopótamo
Cider is the specialty of this old bar of Spanish origin.

WHERE TO EAT IN SAN TELMO

La Brigada
A classic grill where the meat is so tender that you can cut it with a spoon. **$$$**

Pirilo
A classic pizza place frequented by locals. Eating is standing-room only. **$**

Hierbabuena
The concept is defined as 'conscious cuisine'. It offers dishes made with organic and seasonal ingredients. **$$**

FAVORITE PLACES IN SAN TELMO

María Belén Martínez, a tour guide, offers bike tours in San Telmo with La Bicicleta Naranja. *@belu.tour.travel*

Shabu Shabu
This restaurant serves dishes like ramen and sushi in the Mercado de San Telmo. But the curious thing is that when you go up the stairs, you find a 2D Comic Bar. You can order something and feel like you are inside a comic book.

Atis Bar
From the outside, the place doesn't say much. But when you enter, you find an old convent from 1890, with balconies and large halls.

Galería del Viejo Hotel
This old neighborhood hotel has become a space full of studios for artists, designers, and antique dealers.

Souvenirs, San Telmo

Art in an Old Tobacco Factory
A Museum Dedicated to Modern Art

From its beginnings in the mid-1950s, this museum was nomadic. Even journalists called it a 'ghost museum' because it changed venues several times throughout history. Finally, in 2018, Museo de Arte Moderno de Buenos Aires expanded and reopened in the old 1918 building that belonged to an English tobacco company. If you look up at the upper façade of the building, you will see the number 43, which was the name of an emblematic Argentine cigarette brand. It has more than 1500 sq meters of exhibition rooms, a library, educational workshops and a peaceful cafeteria with large tables. The large windows allow natural light to enter the rooms and offer views of San Telmo. The exhibitions are itinerant and focus on works by contemporary artists. The museum covers Argentine art from the 1920s to the present. Its collection includes the Argentine production of contemporary art from the

 WHERE TO STAY IN SAN TELMO

Circus Hostel & Hotel
Offers simple and comfortable rooms, both private and shared. It has a small outdoor jacuzzi. **$**

L'Adresse Hôtel Boutique
An old recycled house with a romantic atmosphere, with only 15 rooms. **$$**

Patios de San Telmo
A former tenement converted into a delicate boutique hotel. It also organizes cultural activities. **$$$**

1940s, 50s and 60s and others that reach the present. There are guided tours every day at 4pm, except on Tuesdays when the museum is closed.

Just Like Old Times

A Bar and Restaurant With a Country Spirit

The *pulperías* of the pampas of Argentina functioned as taverns, way stations and general stores. Throughout its history, Pulpería Quilapán had several uses: a colonial house, a tenement, a dry cleaner, and the headquarters of a foundation. A French couple converted it into a *pulpería*, intending to preserve the house's original forms. Located in the historic center of San Telmo, it bridges the countryside and the city. It features a large patio, a garden, a cistern, and objects that harken back to other times, such as paintings, wine jugs in the shape of penguins, and old refrigerators with wooden doors. In addition to enjoying tango and folklore shows, you can savor succulent dishes based on slow-cooked meat and drinks from bygone eras in a neighborhood social club atmosphere. Don't leave without trying your luck at the **Juego del Sapo**. And take advantage of their curious discounts—for example, 20% off the bill when it rains.

Umbrellas, Galería Solar de French (p101)

WHERE TO LISTEN TO LIVE MUSIC

Centro Cultural Torquato Tasso
Offers shows from Wednesday to Sunday. It is focused on tango, although there are also folklore concerts.

Pista Urbana
Has a busy schedule of shows, mainly tango and folklore. The atmosphere is intimate, and it is easy to feel at home.

Teatro Margarita Xirgu
Offers indie music for young audiences, but sometimes there is theater and art. In the same building, there is Casal de Cataluña, an excellent Spanish restaurant.

Todo Mundo
Located in front of Plaza Dorrego; has daily shows of rock, tango, salsa, jazz, reggae, folklore and ska.

La Scala de San Telmo
This cultural center is located in an old mansion. It has a full schedule of shows.

 WHERE TO STAY IN SAN TELMO

Viajero Hostel Buenos Aires
Offers private and shared rooms. Has a swimming pool and usually organizes barbecues on the terrace. $

Carlos Gardel Hostel
A simple hotel with a tango theme. Only offers private rooms. $

Anselmo Buenos Aires
A small boutique hotel, managed by the Hilton company. Strategically located in front of Plaza Dorrego. $$$

La Boca

FAMED FOR ITS COLORFUL HOUSES, TANGO AND CAMINITO

La Boca was one of the neighborhoods that boosted the city's economic progress with its shipyards, factories and port. It was also where great artists, such as the painters Benito Quinquela Martín and Fortunato Lacámera, lived and worked, and was a refuge for anarchists and the social rebellion of the late 19th century. The tenement houses, full of immigrants who recently arrived in the country, are another of the signs of identity of the place. Some of them are still standing and can be visited on the tour of Caminito, one of the most photographed spots in Argentina. The country's passion for soccer is reflected here in the love for Boca Juniors, one of the most famous clubs on the continent.

☑ TOP TIP

Caminito is one of the busiest spots in the city. To take pictures without crowds, arrive before 11am because most tourist buses arrive from noon. The tourist area around Caminito is safe during the day. You can walk around the site and visit the restaurants, museums and souvenir stores. Be careful around the Boca Juniors stadium.

MILOSK50/SHUTTERSTOCK ©

La Boca

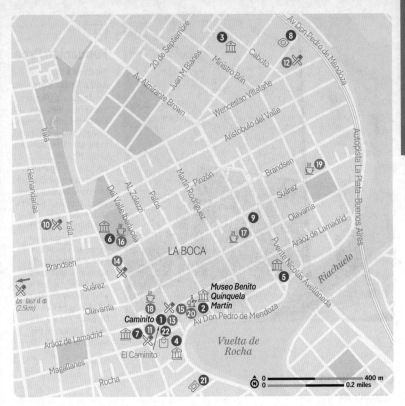

TOP SIGHTS
1 Caminito
2 Museo Benito Quinquela Martín

SIGHTS
3 Barro
4 Fundación Proa
5 Munar
6 Munar

7 Museo de la Pasión Boquense
8 Museo del Conventillo Marjan Grum
9 Usina del Arte

EATING
10 Banchero
11 El Estaño 1880
12 El Gran Paraíso

13 El Obrero
14 El Samovar de Rasputín
15 La Glorieta de Quique
16 Las Gemelas

DRINKING & NIGHTLIFE
17 1905 Bar
18 Bar Roma

19 Café Bar de los Artistas
20 La Buena Medida
21 Lo del Diego

ENTERTAINMENT
22 Colón Fábrica

SHOPPING
23 Almacén Porteño
see 4 Jofre Art Gallery
see 4 Solo Boca

Fundación Proa

**Modern Art
and a Great View**

An old Italianate-style house from 1895 was converted into a modern cultural center dedicated to the artistic movements of the 20th and 21st centuries. It organizes temporary exhibitions of photography, design and video, courses, concerts and conferences. The building comprises three floors, four exhibition rooms with excellent natural lighting, and a bookstore. On the top floor is a restaurant with a terrace, which offers a 360-degree view of Caminito and the most exciting points of the neighborhood.

Fundación Proa

Lo del Diego

Legend's Bar

Diego Armando Maradona is one of La Boca's favorite sons. He was a star and champion with Boca Juniors in the early '80s, returned to play in the mid-'90s, and, as a former player, always went to the stadium to support his favorite team. The soccer legend has a theme bar dedicated exclusively to his figure. There are gigantic photographs; you can buy jerseys of the clubs where he played, with the numbers he used to wear; and see the two statues of Diego, who in Argentina is a sort of god. There are also glasses, mugs and other souvenirs in a place decorated like an old tenement house.

**Museo Benito
Quinquela Martín**

Museo Benito Quinquela Martín

The Great Artist of the Port

Benito Quinquela Martín was not only an exceptional artist who made La Boca the central theme of his work. He was also the creator of the Caminito promenade. His home and studio is an excellent opportunity to learn about his life and work, as well as a way to understand the idiosyncrasy of the neighborhood. There is a collection of more than 300 works, including engravings, drawings and large paintings. It is worthwhile to dwell on those exceptional scenes of his paintings, with the workers and the ships he portrayed. Don't miss the terrace, which offers an excellent neighborhood view. The museum is open from 11:15am to 6pm Tuesday to Sunday.

Museo de la Pasión Boquense
A Tale of Passion

Boca Juniors is, together with River Plate, the most famous club in the country. This museum, located in its stadium, allows visitors to learn about its history, with rooms about its historical protagonists, the different models of jerseys, the great idols, the championships won and the founders of the institution. Of course, a special section is dedicated to Diego Armando Maradona, one of the greatest idols in the club's history. There are 360-degree videos that show the passion that is experienced there on match days. The tour is short – about half an hour – and unfortunately no longer includes access to the field or the locker rooms.

Museo de la Pasión Boquense

Museo del Conventillo Marjan Grum
The Story of Argentina's Immigrants

Marjan Grum's story encapsulates a portion of La Boca's migratory spirit. He was a Slovenian who came to Argentina as a refugee from WWII. He chose to remain and established his art studio in an old tenement. Today, the space shares the history of the immigrants who arrived in the neighborhood – he did an exceptional job restoring the building – and showcases pieces he created, often using iron and other discarded materials. Marjan and his wife Beatriz represent living history, and conversing with them is worthwhile as they are always open to welcoming travelers. It is open daily from 11am to 2:30pm.

El Obrero

El Obrero
Resturant Where Clinton Didn't Get a Table

El Obrero opened in 1954 as a restaurant for the port workers. Today, it is a witness to the history of the neighborhood. Bill Clinton was once attracted by its dishes but had to leave because he couldn't get a table; the owner said they couldn't eject the seated customers. The house specialties are *bife de chorizo*, Spanish omelette and fried calamari. Its walls are full of soccer jerseys and photos of celebrities who once ate there. Open from Monday to Saturday from 8pm.

Caminito

Buenos Aires' Most Famous Colorful Street

The artist Quinquela Martín had the initiative to transform a forgotten alley in La Boca into a colorful and joyful place that would narrate the neighborhood's history. It has become one of the city's most fantastic attractions. It is only 150m long, yet it features the distinctive tenements of various colors where immigrants lived, embodying a part of the vibrant spirit of those homes that encompassed patios, bathrooms and communal kitchens. By immersing yourself in the details of those houses and their histories, you can easily spend hours exploring a converted tenement now functioning as a restaurant, an art gallery or a souvenir shop, entertained by a couple dancing tango. La Feria de Caminito also brings together tango singers, dancers and visual artists who work with leather, wood, metal, fabric, ceramics and *fileteado* – a decorative art style that originated in Buenos Aires in the late 19th century. At 1800 Pedro de Mendoza St, a sculpture stands as a tribute to Quinquela Martín. The statue depicts him in his work attire, holding his tools.

A PICTURE WITH MESSI

The mythical Caminito corner at 837 Magallanes St recently changed its appearance. At the initiative of a group of entrepreneurs, a sculpture of Lionel Messi was installed on the balcony of an *alfajores* shop there. The player is lifting the World Cup, which Argentina won in Qatar in 2022. They manufactured the work using 48 pieces produced by 15 3D printers. To take a photo, go to the store's 2nd floor, where Messi stands happily with his trophy. There is no need to buy anything to take the picture.

TRAVELBUENOSAIRES ©

Caminito

Colón Fábrica

Behind the Scenes of the City's Most Famous Theater

Visiting the Teatro Colón or attending a performance is an exceptional experience in Buenos Aires. But how are its stage designs created? What work is behind those magnificent costumes? A visit to Colón Fábrica offers some answers. Housed in a former French metallurgy building just a couple of blocks from Caminito, visitors can uncover the grand productions that emerge from the workshops of one of the world's few theater factories. The visit can be self-guided or guided. Verónica, one of the guides, can guide you through the visit, explaining the history of the costumes, how they craft every detail of the scenery, and the various techniques used. Walking through these corridors feels like stepping into the fantasy worlds of *Hamlet*, *Turandot* and *Aida*, among other great productions. A screen displays a short video of the theatrical performance alongside each piece. Colón Fábrica is open from Friday to Sunday and on holidays, from noon to 6pm. Guided tours must be booked in advance.

Usina del Arte

Usina del Arte

Cultural Center in Old Power Plant

This former power plant has been converted into a cultural center. The building is a design of Italian Giovanni Chiogna. The grand palaces and castles of the Florentine Renaissance inspired the architect. On the guided tour you can see a variety of semicircular arches, the clock tower, the wrought-iron balconies and a bridge crane that still survives from that era. The 15,000-sq-m site offers various visual arts, music, children's activities and events, and is one of the venues of the **Tango BA Festival y Mundial**. Guided tours take place at 5pm Tuesday to Friday and at 12:30pm and 5pm on weekends.

MY FAVORITE BRIDGE

Bárbara Duarte is a freelance tour guide of Buenos Aires. She frequently tours La Boca.

One of my favorite places in La Boca is the **Puente Transbordador Nicolás Avellaneda**. Inaugurated in 1914, it stands as an icon of the city. During its prime, it facilitated the daily transportation of 17,000 workers. These individuals commuted to the factories and stores in both La Boca and Avellaneda. In the 1990s, during the government of President Carlos Menem, there was an attempt to sell it for scrap. Thankfully, the residents and institutions rallied to prevent this. You can use the bridge to cross from La Boca to Avellaneda. The bridge makes the short transfer only on weekends, free of charge, and provides insight into the neighborhood's history.

SERGIO SCHNITZLER/SHUTTERSTOCK ©. OPPOSITE PAGE: DAVID WALL/ALAMY STOCK PHOTO ©

Puente Transbordador Nicolás Avellaneda

MORE IN LA BOCA

Tango Like the Old Days

Discover the Old Singers of Los Laureles

At the entrance, there is a chalk-written sign that reads: 'Los Laureles. Bar and restaurant. Since 1893.' But this place is much more than that. It's located not in La Boca but in Barracas, but it's worth venturing a bit further south of the city, where time stands still. This restaurant, frequented by locals and tourists, has become increasingly popular over the years, allowing you to immerse yourself in the tango of another era. You won't find extravagant shows with acrobatic dances or sensual staging here. On Thursdays, there's a *Peña de cantores,* where elderly tango singers gather to evoke times gone by, accompanied by live musicians. Tango lessons take place every Wednesday at 8pm, while Fridays feature live bands and *milongas*. The restaurant boasts an unpretentious ambience, yet its dishes maintain a high quality. It offers some of the quintessential classics of Buenos Aires cuisine, including *bife de chorizo*, pasta and *milanesa* (beef schnitzel), among other options. At Los Laureles it is common for people at the

 WHERE TO TRY A CHORIPÁN IN LA BOCA

La Glorieta de Quique
Choripanes and *lomito* sandwiches are the specialties; the *parrillero* serves in the colors of Boca Juniors. $

El Samovar de Rasputín
Some of Argentina's greatest rock stars have passed through here. The *choripanes* come in generous portions. $

Las Gemelas
The barbecue and the table are directly on the street. The *choripán* is delicious. $

A Bar that Resembles a Museum

Bar Roma, an Emblem of La Boca

Buenos Aires has a deep fondness for its historic bars. City residents relish the opportunity to savor a coffee in places brimming with character and history. To enter Bar Roma at 409 Olavarría St, you must push open the swinging door, which instantly transports you to the past. Inside, this momentary journey is experienced with a mixture of joy and nostalgia. Bar Roma is one of the icons of La Boca. Initially, it operated as a grocery and beverage store, an annex to a delicatessen. Later, it transformed into the cafe that both locals and visitors to the neighborhood can enjoy daily. Black and white tiles compose the floor, while exposed bricks adorn the walls. It resembles an antique shop, with vintage posters advertising products such as tires, ointments, soft drinks and Boca Juniors' pennants. Throughout its history, the neighborhood's great personalities, including the painter Benito Quinquela Martín and the musician Juan de Dios Filiberto, frequented the establishment. Bar Roma was inaugurated in 1905. It's challenging to picture La Boca without this place, much like other neighborhoods have bars integral to their identity. Sit at one of the tables facing the large windows on Avs Brown and Olavarría and watch the world go by. The bar opens at 7am.

SOUVENIR SHOPS

Almacén Porteño
Offer *alfajores*, Argentine wines, and a wide variety of *dulce de leche,* all available for tasting.

Jofre Art Gallery
This shop belongs to artist Roberto Jofré. He sells his vibrant paintings, cushions, mugs and bags adorned with themes related to the neighborhood.

Solo Boca
Looking for a T-shirt representing the neighborhood's club? You're in the right place. This store also boasts an extensive range of products associated with the club and some leather goods. You'll find replicas of the cups won by Boca Juniors and items related to Diego Armando Maradona.

Bar Roma

 WHERE TO GET A COFFEE IN LA BOCA

La Buena Medida
It was opened in 1905, the same year Boca Juniors was inaugurated, and still maintains the spirit of that time. $

1905 Bar
Located inside the stadium. Ideal for a drink after a visit to the Museo de la Pasión Boquense. $$

Café Bar de los Artistas
Located in Caminito, the bar evokes a past of painters and musicians. Some live artists often play there. $

The journey to discover the best street art in La Boca begins with ❶ **Bienvenidos a La Boca**, created in 1999 by local artists coordinated by Omar Néstor Gasparini. This work, depicting an everyday scene of immigrants in the area, was mounted on a structure of balconies, metal sheets and doors of an old tenement house.

Continue south to ❷ **Martín Ron murals** on Martín Rodríguez St. Then, because we are in Argentina, the following mandatory stop is at ❸ **San Diego del barrio de La Boca**, a tribute to the soccer legend Diego Armando Maradona, by Alfredo Segatori. Further south, very close to the river, are ❹ **the sand silos**, which Segatori also created in honor of Benito Quinquela Martin, the most famous artist of the neighborhood. The next stop is at ❺ **Caminito**,

perhaps the most photographed spot in the city. It is ideal for discovering not only the colorful houses but also the work of artists and artisans who sell their work and create murals on the area's walls. You can also take a picture with a statue of Messi, celebrating his World Cup achievements. Even further south, almost on the border with Avellaneda, in the province of Buenos Aires, is ❻ **El regreso de Quinquela**, another work that pays tribute to the great artist of the neighborhood in a monumental extension of 2000 sq m.

The tour ends at ❼ **Pasaje Lanín**, one of the city's most attractive urban art exhibits. At the initiative of the artist Marino Santa María, the facades of 35 houses were decorated with different techniques and materials such as *venecitas*.

Buenos Aires Fútbol Tour

The Great Argentine Madness

If you visit Boca Juniors' stadium, appreciate its history, and are a soccer enthusiast, you will undoubtedly be inclined to watch a live match. The Buenos Aires Fútbol Tour, organized by Tangol Tours, offers the opportunity to attend games of top-tier division clubs, including the largest ones. The service encompasses transportation and continuous coordination throughout the match, strongly emphasizing safety. Additionally, it provides guided tours of the Boca Juniors and River Plate museums. Once inside the stadium, the experience can be unforgettable in the term's broadest sense. There are some things that Argentines take for granted, but that will surely catch your attention if you were not born in this country. For example, only the home team's fans go to the stadium. Why? Violence would be widespread if the rivals were in the same space. The fans' screaming is truly deafening and is the fundamental energy transforming it into a unique spectacle. There is another surprising element of Argentine football: the insults. They can be hilarious and full of originality. They are directed at players, opponents, coaches and referees. To complete the experience, you can eat a *choripán* at some street stalls outside all the stadiums. Book tours and check for match dates and availability online. The price of the tours varies according to the games. It also offers the option of watching international tournaments, such as the Copa Libertadores de América and the Copa Sudamericana, which are usually played by Argentine teams.

Boca Juniors' stadium

BEST ART GALLERIES

Barro
Contemporary art gallery located within a renovated industrial building. It curates annual exhibitions while actively engaging in and supporting the creative journey of the artists. It has a store with bags, prints and other items.

Munar
Situated along the riverbanks, Munar occupies a space formerly a rubber factory. The venue hosts exhibitions and provides a workshop environment for resident artists.

Marco
This museum is situated within a historic art nouveau building. It showcases works by contemporary artists and features a laboratory dedicated to experimentation.

WHERE TO EAT IN LA BOCA

El Gran Paraíso
The restaurant, specializing in meats, was set up in an old tenement house in Caminito. **$$**

El Estaño 1880
The place has an old tin bar and a characteristic mural. The specialty is straccinatti pasta with seafood. **$$**

Banchero
The pizzeria, which has several branches in the city, was born in La Boca. The specialty is the pizza *fugazza*. **$**

Puerto Madero

THE PERFECT WALK BY THE RIVER

At the end of the 19th century, driven by the city's expansion, Puerto Madero rose to become the second port of the city, only behind the one located in La Boca. But some time later, the area was abandoned due to its obsolescence, for the new cargo ships. At the end of the 1980s, the place changed its profile and was recovered as an urban space. As a result, it became the city's newest and most expensive neighborhood. Today, it is a vibrant gastronomic center and an ideal place to enjoy a stroll and sunsets by the river. The area has a particularity: each street pays homage to essential women in Argentine history. It is also home to the remarkable museum Colección de Arte Amalia Lacroze de Fortabat and the Reserva Ecológica Costanera Sur, the largest in the city, boasting incredible biodiversity and spanning 350 hectares and providing a temporary escape from the city's noise.

☑ **TOP TIP**

Puerto Madero offers an excellent viewpoint to watch the sunset over the Río de la Plata. The Puente de la Mujer is ideal for taking pictures and enjoying the evening. Another option is the Crystal Sky Bar, a cocktail bar on the 32nd floor that offers a panoramic view of the entire area as well as the Reserva Ecológica Costanera Sur.

WALLPAPER/O/GETTY IMAGES ©

Puerto Madero

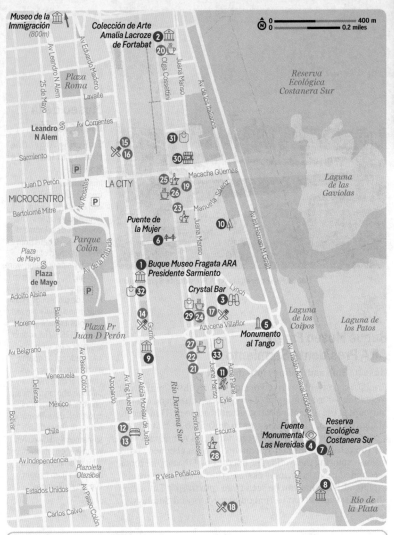

TOP SIGHTS

1. Buque Museo Fragata ARA Presidente Sarmiento
2. Colección de Arte Amalia Lacroze de Fortabat
3. Crystal Bar
4. Fuente Monumental Las Nereidas
5. Monumento al Tango
6. Puente de la Mujer
7. Reserva Ecológica Costanera Sur

SIGHTS

8. Museo de Calcos Ernesto de La Cárcova
9. Pabellón de las Bellas Artes UCA
10. Parque Mujeres Argentinas

ACTIVITIES, COURSES & TOURS

11. Rojo Tango

SLEEPING

see 3 Alvear Icon Hotel
12. Believe Madero Hotel

13. Madero Urbano Studios

EATING

14. Amarra
15. Cabaña Las Lilas
16. La Cabaña
17. Osaka
18. Raíz Plant Mood

DRINKING & NIGHTLIFE

19. Alberto's Lobby Bar
20. Croque Madame
21. La Panera Rosa
see 12 Library Lounge

22. Lobo Café
23. Negroni
24. Ol'Days Coffee & Deli
25. Peñón del Águila
26. Tiendas Naturales
27. Vince
28. White Bar

SHOPPING

29. Havanna
30. I Central Market
31. I Love Gifts
32. Marignan
33. Walmer

Buque Museo Fragata ARA Presidente Sarmiento

Museo de la Inmigración

Exploring Argentine History at Immigrant Hotel

Immigration, primarily from Europe, Asia and Africa, played a fundamental role in the country's development. According to data from 1914, one-third of the country's population were foreigners. The museum is situated where the Hotel de los Inmigrantes welcomed newly arrived immigrants between 1911 and 1953. The rooms are spacious, with knowledgeable guides explaining the various stages of migration through photographs and objects. Many visitors approach the information points to share their surnames and discover when and on which ship their relatives arrived. It is open 11am to 6pm Tuesday to Sunday.

Buque Museo Fragata ARA Presidente Sarmiento

Museum Ship and Journey into the Past

Fragata Sarmiento's first voyage was in 1899, making it Argentina's most iconic ship. Later, it was transformed into a museum of the Argentine Navy, situated at Dock III in Puerto Madero. The tour allows visitors to delve into its history and a part of Argentine history. For instance, its name pays tribute to President Domingo Sarmiento, who envisioned young sailors exploring the world. The operation of the engine room, accommodations, interior decks, and the ports visited are also explained. The ship can be seen from 1pm to 7pm Thursdays and Fridays and 10am to 7pm on Saturdays and Sundays.

Puente de la Mujer

Elegant and Iconic Bridge

Since its inauguration in 2001, this bridge has become one of the most emblematic postcards of Puerto Madero and Buenos Aires, although the Obelisco still holds the first place. Though rarely in operation, the rotating pedestrian bridge opens to give way to the sailboats sailing along the docks. When visiting Puerto Madero, the grand plan is to walk along the four docks connected by bridges. The questions arise when you see it: what does its design mean? What does the shape that Santiago Calatrava gave it refer to? The Spanish architect stated that it is the synthesis of a couple dancing tango, although it takes some imagination to see it. Recently, the wooden floor was replaced by a recycled plastic one. During weekends, there are street performers along the bridge.

Colección de Arte
Amalia Lacroze de Fortabat
Argentine and World Art with a River View

This museum can go unnoticed if you walk along the docks of Puerto Madero. It hides an extraordinary art collection of Amalia Lacroze de Fortabat, the businesswoman and art collector who passed away in 2012. Works by famous artists such as Andy Warhol, Gustav Klimt, Auguste Rodin and Salvador Dalí are exhibited in its spacious halls, with natural light and a river view. However, the most exciting pavilion is dedicated to Argentine art throughout the 19th and 20th centuries. The works end up reflecting the worldview and concerns of its artists over time. The museum is open from noon to 8pm Thursday through Sunday.

Colección de Arte
Amalia Lacroze de Fortabat

Fuente Monumental Las Nereidas

Fuente Monumental Las Nereidas
A Controversial Statue

Lola Mora was one of the greatest Argentine sculptors. This work, which narrates the birth of the goddess Venus, was initially commissioned to beautify the Plaza de Mayo, the most important square in the city. However, the nude figures offended believers when exhibited in front of the Cathedral. This prompted relocation to different parts of the town until it found its place in the Costanera Sur. During those years, at the end of the 1910s, it was on the city's outskirts. It is an exceptional piece, made of Carrara marble and with baroque-style textures. It may need some maintenance, but it is worth spending a few minutes to see the artist's work.

Crystal Bar
Most Impressive Views of the Area

On the 32nd floor, the Alvear Icon Hotel has a bar offering a unique view of Puerto Madero and the city. It is not necessary to stay at the hotel to visit it, but a minimum drink order per person is required. The view from the bar is impressive, especially at night, as it offers a 360-degree panoramic view. All the walls are lined with glass, allowing you to see the lights of the docks, the Puente de la Mujer, the city's urban landscape, the Río de la Plata and the Costanera Sur Ecological Reserve. The menu includes classic and signature cocktails, appetizers, sushi and ceviche. Other dishes have a local flavor, such as chorizo with peppers and the traditional knife-cut meat empanadas.

Reserva Ecológica Costanera Sur
A Walk in the River Breeze

Walking along the riverbank, having a bite to eat at a food truck and visiting the Reserva Ecológica Costanera Sur are some of the favorite activities of the *porteños*. The reserve has the greatest biodiversity in the city and offers more than 350 hectares with about 575 plant species to enjoy. The reserve has two entrances: one on Brasil St and the other on Viamonte St, both separated by about 2km. Once inside, the plan is simple: take a deep breath and follow the trails on foot or by bicycle to escape for a few minutes from the city's noise. The six-trail route is straightforward and leads down to the river, offering a postcard view of the Río de la Plata, a rarity in many parts of the city. In the distance, you can often see large cargo ships and sailboats leaving from the yacht clubs in the northern part of the city. Inside the reserve is space for picnics, and there are food stands at the entrances. There are guided tours at 11am from Tuesday to Friday. In addition, there is a monthly night walk during full moon nights. The reserve is closed on rainy days.

BIRDWATCHING

If you love birdwatching, the Reserva Ecológica Costanera Sur is your place. The reserve has been declared an Important Area for the Conservation of Birds because of the more than 350 species that can be seen, mainly swans, ducks, and a great variety of birds, in the grasslands of the lagoons. Walking along the trails or on Giralt Ave, which borders the Laguna de los Coipos, is ideal to see them. **Buenos Días Birding** organizes specialized visits to the reserve as well as to other places in the country.

YASEMIN OLGUNOZ BERBER/SHUTTERSTOCK ©

Reserva Ecológica Costanera Sur

Yacht Club Argentino

Postales de Buenos Aires

Enjoy the City from the Port

If Puerto Madero connects you to the river and you want to see the city from a boat, there is a tour called Postales de Buenos Aires, which is short but pleasant. It departs from the neighborhood's Dársena Norte every hour, taking about 40 minutes. The tour does not have a guide. A recorded voice narrates the emblematic buildings in the north and south of the city that can be seen from the river. For example, the Museo de la Inmigración, the elegant construction of the Yacht Club Argentino, the Reserva Ecológica Costanera Sur and the skyscrapers of the newer part of the neighborhood are seen. Sturla Viajes organizes the tour starting at 11am, but perhaps the best time is the last one, at 5:40pm, which allows you to see the sunset from the boat. It also organizes other excursions to the islands of Tigre and other alternatives to spend the day on the river. The tour departs from Cecilia Grierson 400, at the corner of Juana Manso St.

Monumento al Tango
Tribute to Buenos Aires Music

Tango is the music of Buenos Aires and deserves this monument inaugurated in 2007. Located at the intersection of Azucena Villaflor and Av de los Italianos, the Monumento al Tango stands proud. This monumental stainless steel sculpture reaches a height of 3.5m, weighs 2 tons and was installed on a 1.7m pedestal. It was created by sculptor Estela Trebiño and engineer Alejandro Coria, with an abstract figure reminiscent of a bandoneon, the most iconic instrument in tango music. The work is intended to encapsulate the essence of tango music and dance in a singular object. During its inauguration, the Monumento al Tango was transported in a grand procession, accompanied by passionate tango enthusiasts and residents.

BEST RESTAURANTS IN PUERTO MADERO

Osaka
Fusion dishes of Japanese and Peruvian cuisine. **$$$**

Amarra
Gathers the best chefs in the country, who rotate in the kitchen. The menu is served for three weeks, and then the chef changes, bringing a new proposal. **$$$**

La Cabaña
A traditional Argentine grill. Its specialty is the 'gran baby beef'. **$$$**

Cabaña Las Lilas
Excellent meats in an Argentine-Brazilian restaurant of great tradition. The chef was awarded several times. **$$$**

Raíz Plant Mood
A cozy place, with world cuisine based on plants. **$$**

Cabaña Las Lilas

MORE IN PUERTO MADERO

The Luxury & Passion of Tango

Show in a Five-Star Hotel

In 2005, this tango show commenced its performances at the Faena Hotel, one of the most exclusive venues in the city. The production re-creates an early-20th-century cabaret atmosphere, showcasing an impressive array of costumes, choreography and live music by the Rojo Tango quintet. The show covers a significant portion of tango's history, from the 1920s to the avant-garde era of Ástor Piazzolla, a key figure in modern tango. The show's standout star is the dancer Carlos Copello, a legend from the iconic Tango Argentino ensemble. Distinguished from other shows in the city, this one offers an intimate proximity to the dancers. At the front, you are seated close to the artists and dancers who perform near your table.

Additionally, the orchestra produces clear and crisp sounds to the left, playing great tango classics from various eras. Of course, the climax comes at the end with 'Adiós Nonino', the beautiful piece composed by Ástor Piazzolla after his father's death, who was affectionately nicknamed Nonino. You can

WHERE TO GET A COFFEE IN PUERTO MADERO

Vince
Offers a brunch called 'Nonno Mico' for four people, with sweet recipes from Argentina and Italy.

Croque Madame
Its menu offers artisan pastries, brownies and croissants, and a variety of teas and coffees.

La Panera Rosa
Nonstop food and coffee with a view of the river. Offers a wide variety of toasts and pastries.

enjoy the show, which commences at 10pm, or opt for dinner at 8pm, followed by the performance. If you prefer the front along with dinner, the menu includes a starter, main course, dessert, champagne, and wines from Argentine wineries. The show takes place every day. Reservations are required.

Art in an Old Port Building
Exhibitions at the River's Edge

The Universidad Católica Argentina (UCA) has been present in the country since 1958. The institution's headquarters in Puerto Madero boasts a cultural space devoted to literature, music and artistic experimentation. This venue is situated in one of the former cargo docks of the old port, retaining its exposed bricks and cast iron beams. Visitors can enjoy exhibitions encompassing painting, sculpture, photography and audiovisual projections. These exhibitions feature private collections, museum pieces, and artworks by various artists. Although its activity is linked to art, the place goes much further. **Pabellón de las Bellas Artes UCA** is also a center for creation and research in history, science, literature, music, film, communication, advertising and journalism. The space is open from 11am to 7pm Tuesday to Sunday, and has free admission.

Tango,
Faena Hotel

BEST BARS IN PUERTO MADERO

Alberto's Lobby Bar
Located in a five-star hotel, this bar offers a menu of signature drinks based on local products.

Negroni
The menu offers burgers, sushi and classic drinks. On some occasions, DJs are featured.

White Bar
An elegant hotel bar, with a terrace to enjoy the views of Puerto Madero.

Library Lounge
Cocktails and live shows in an intimate setting, with plenty of leather sofas and books.

Peñón del Águila
Floating bar overlooking the Puente de la Mujer, with a youthful atmosphere and a menu based on craft beers.

WHERE TO GET A COFFEE IN PUERTO MADERO

Ol'Days Coffee & Deli
A reduced menu but with delicious options and its coffee and tea threads.

Lobo Café
Specialty coffee and a wide variety of cakes. Try the *rogel* cake, with *dulce de leche* and Italian meringue.

Tiendas Naturales
Offers natural products and a wide variety of teas and coffees.

PLACES TO SHOP IN PUERTO MADERO

Marignan
This is a well-known Argentine brand of shoes and sandals made mainly of leather.

Walmer
This place offers many objects to incorporate into your home decoration. Many of them have a minimalist design.

I Central Market
This self-service deli will be a treat for the foodie on the go. It also has a restaurant.

I Love Gifts
This souvenir store has soccer jerseys and objects of the famous Argentine character Mafalda, the creation of the cartoonist Joaquín Lavado (Quino).

Havanna
A classic brand of *alfajores* and other sweet delicacies.

Women Who Made History
A Walk in the Parque Mujeres Argentinas

When you look closer at the streets of Puerto Madero, a fascinating pattern emerges – each one is named after a remarkable woman. It was a decision of the city as a way of remembering vital female personalities in the country. This park pays tribute to those women who marked a path. Its modern layout has a large central square and several levels of height as if it were a theater, providing a panoramic view of the city – the design aims to seamlessly weave together the urban landscape and the natural beauty of the river surroundings.

More than 4000 Years of Art History
A Museum With an Impressive Heritage

Ernesto de la Cárcova was outstanding for his work both as an artist and as a cultural manager. For example, he founded the Escuela Superior de Bellas Artes. The rooms of Museo de Calcos Ernesto de La Cárcova, which are very close to the Reserva Ecológica Costanera Sur, exhibit a collection of casts (original plaster reproductions) of masterpieces of Egyptian, Greek, Roman and Mesoamerican art, among others, which were exhibited in the Louvre in Paris, the British Museum in London and the National Museum of Anthropology in Mexico. It is a journey through more than 4000 years of art history. There is also a room dedicated to Ernesto de la Cárcova's own work. Strolling through the garden and looking at some of the sculptures is a great pleasure offered by the museum. It is open from Tuesday to Sunday.

 WHERE TO STAY IN PUERTO MADERO

Believe Madero Hotel
A casual hotel with a modern design on the border between San Telmo and Puerto Madero. **$$**

Madero Urbano Studios
Offers a good location, close to many of the area's attractions, and spacious rooms. **$$**

Alvear Icon Hotel
This five-star hotel has panoramic views of the city and the river. Its roof bar is one of the neighborhood's highlights. **$$$**

Puerto Madero

Above: Iguazú Falls (p132); Right: Deer, Parque Nacional Iberá (p140)

THE MAIN AREAS

IGUAZÚ
Unmissable
waterfall.
p130

PARQUE NACIONAL IBERÁ
Incredible
wildlife spotting.
p140

CORRIENTES
Beautiful
river city.
p148

Iguazú Falls & the Northeast

WATERFALLS, WILDLIFE AND WONDER

Iguazú Falls is only one of many incredible reasons to make this region part of your itinerary.

LEANDRO HERRANZ/GETTY IMAGES ©

Majestic, ineffable Iguazú Falls often eclipses the surrounding area with its stunning waterfalls that make Niagara seem pale in comparison. Many travelers hop on an overnight bus in Buenos Aires and arrive at Iguazú Falls in the morning, rubbing the sleep out of their eyes, see 'the Falls', and then head back to the city. A shame, because they miss some of the area's other gems that are well worth making time for. The vast expanse of Parque Nacional Iberá, for instance, is one of the best places in the whole country to get up close to incredible wildlife, including the charming, should-have-its-own-crypto-coin-by-now capybara (known in Argentina as a *carpincho*). Add to that the chance, no, the surety of seeing caimans and a host of birds, and this park simply begs to fit in. Nearby, you can visit fascinating ruins of ancient Jesuit missions, whose crumbling walls and arches speak to the grandeur and power of the church that's hard to imagine today. Rivers make for amazing fishing, boating and hiking in the east and south. And the rivers support not only wildlife but some great, vibrant cities as well, with fantastic food, excellent nightlife, and a more relaxed vibe than the Argentine capital. If you only do one thing here, it's Iguazú. But if you can do more, you won't be disappointed.

CONCORDIA	SANTA FE
Relaxed fishing town.	Youthful and vibrant.
p156	p162

Find Your Way

Rivers mark the boundaries of this region and shape what's contained within. In fact, one of the provinces is named exactly that: Entre Ríos. Between Rivers. We've highlighted some of the most memorable places to explore.

0   100 miles

0   200 km

Iguazú Falls, p132

The unmissable highlight of this section, with breathtaking views of one of nature's grandest and most awe-inspiring attractions. Expect brilliant rainbows, thundering water, and hordes of people on both sides of the falls.

Corrientes, p148

One of the many gems of the river Paraná, this laid-back, pretty city has a beautiful golden-sand costanera (beach access), elegant buildings and great restaurants.

Parque Nacional Iberá, p140

A massive wetland preserve that harbors incredible fauna, including reintroduced jaguars, other big cats, rare deer, countless caiman, and the ever-charming capybaras.

Parque Nacional do Iguaçu

Bernardo de Irigoyen

Ciudad del Este

Foz do Iguaçu

Puerto Iguazú

Eldorado

MISIONES

Santa Rosa

Hohenau

Encarnación

Posadas

ASUNCIÓN

Formosa

Pilar

Parque Nacional Iberá

FORMOSA

Comandante Fontana

Corrientes

Resistencia

Las Lomitas

Bermejo

Juan José Castelli

Presidencia Roque Sáenz Peña

Pampa del Infierno

Charata

Villa Ángela

CHACO

Monte Quemado

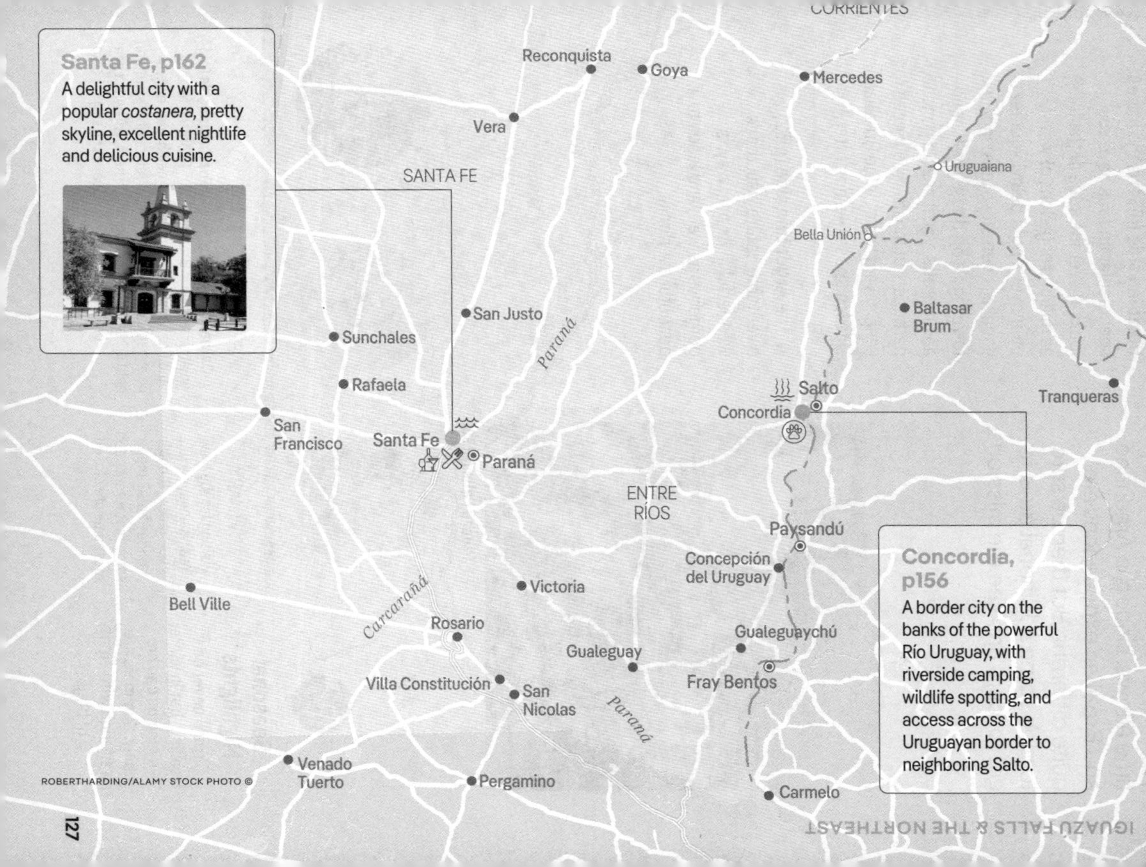

CAR

Driving is very doable, with mostly flat roads that are in better shape than many Latin American roads, and gas stations that are easy to find. Keep in mind many rental agencies don't let you cross international borders.

PLANE

You'll miss out on all the magic in between Buenos Aires and Iguazú Falls, but it's undeniably the fastest way to get there and back. Domestic flights are fairly reasonable, too, with frequent departures.

BUS

Slower than a plane, but easier than a car, with the option to stop and take selfies with the capybaras (er, *carpinchos*) along the way. Some travelers opt to fly out and bus back, stopping at Ibera and elsewhere along the way.

Concordia, p156

A border city on the banks of the powerful Río Uruguay, with riverside camping, wildlife spotting, and access across the Uruguayan border to neighboring Salto.

Santa Fe, p162

A delightful city with a popular *costanera*, pretty skyline, excellent nightlife and delicious cuisine.

ROBERTHARDING/ALAMY STOCK PHOTO ©

127

Plan Your Time

See the falls, from both sides if time allows, since the Argentine and Brazilian experiences are quite different. But then be sure to plan some additional days to get to Iberá and see the missions.

Iguazú Falls (p132)

ANGELA MEIER/SHUTTERSTOCK ©

If You Only Do One Thing

● It's all about the Foz. As much as you can enjoy both sides of the incredible waterfalls (*foz*, in Portuguese) here in Iguazú, the **Brazilian side** (p134) is the more spectacular and will have you looking over the edge of the falls as millions of gallons of water pour over it right below your feet. It makes even those least inclined to vertigo a bit dizzy. You'll need an umbrella, you'll need a poncho, perhaps, but mostly, you'll need to keep saying 'wow'. If the Brazilian side isn't possible, don't fret.

● The **Argentine side** (p132), a veritable nature walk that's wonderful in its own way, is gorgeous as well, and leads to a beautiful overlook.

BOTTOM: SERGIO SCHNITZLER/SHUTTERSTOCK ©, OSABEE/SHUTTERSTOCK ©, LUIS WAR/SHUTTERSTOCK ©

Seasonal Highlights

You'll never be freezing, but in winter evenings can be chilly. Summers are sweltering with plenty of bugs.

JANUARY

Visiting for the New Year is always a fun experience, though holiday hours mean some restaurants and museums are closed.

FEBRUARY

Carnaval (p134) is a great time to be in Brazil, and Foz's festivities are no exception. Sometimes held in March, depending on Easter.

MAY

Foz do Iguaçu's (p134) Fenartec festival celebrates diversity. Although it's autumn here, you won't see leaves changing colors.

Three Days to Travel Around

● Arrive in **Iguazú** (p130) and spend your first day there, then cross to the other side (the Brazilian or Argentine, the side you haven't seen yet). Be sure to hit some of the fun clubs and bars in **Foz do Iguaçu** (p134) when you do.

● If you like shopping, head across to **Paraguay** (p134) for deals and steals on everything from clothing to musical instruments. Or skip the shopping and go instead to the **Güirá Oga** (p135) on the Argentine side or the **Parque das Aves** (p136) on the Brazilian side, where you can see rescued animals such as tapirs and big cats, or birds like toucans.

More Than a Week

● Spend a day at both the Brazilian side and Argentine side of the Falls, then depart for **Posadas** (p146), where you'll check out the beautiful ruins of the Jesuit missions the province is named for.

● End your week with as many days as you can at **Parque Nacional Iberá** (p140), which is best accessed by **Colonia Carlos Pellegrini** (p140). There, you'll see all the capybaras you can imagine, dozens if not hundreds of caiman, and if you're lucky, monkeys, endangered deer, giant anteaters, or even the very elusive jaguar.

JUNE

Winter is beginning, bringing with it colder, crisper nights and migrating bird action.

JULY

Grab a mug and get ready to chug at Santa Fe's **Festival de la Cerveza** (Beer Festival).

OCTOBER

Days are getting warmer, the humidity is rising, and the sun is bright. Summer's on its way.

DECEMBER

It's hot and sweltery. If it's Christmas in your bikini you're looking for, you're in the right place.

BUENOS AIRES

Iguazú

GETTING AROUND

Both Foz and Puerto are easy to walk around in, with plenty of taxis available for longer rides. Hiring a driver for a trip across the border is often the most convenient, even for those with a private vehicle. Access to the falls is restricted so you'll park at the entry gates and then use public transport (bus or train) to reach the falls. For those who like getting wet and wild, boats go upriver to the falls as well.

☑ TOP TIP

If you want to avoid being drenched by the mist, bring an umbrella, or better, a waterproof poncho to put on as you walk out over the falls. Photographers will want to take extra precautions to make sure the mist doesn't blur or mar their lenses.

Nothing compares to Iguazú for its majesty, its beauty, its awe-inspiring wonder. If you're going to pop 'the question', it's the place you'll choose. If you do one thing in this area, it will be to see the falls. On a clear day, with the sun shining, you'll get incredible rainbows arching out over the pristine white falls. Even with the thousands of other tourists, there's a sense that this place is grand enough for those mere humans to be insignificant. Whichever side you choose (but better if you plan for both) you'll just be awestruck by the power of nature and the beauty of it all. But even after seeing the falls, there's lots of fun things to do on either the Brazilian or the Argentine side.

UNDIVIDED/SHUTTERSTOCK © OPPOSITE PAGE: FABIO FERREIRA/GETTY IMAGES ©

Tourist boat, Iguazú Falls (p132)

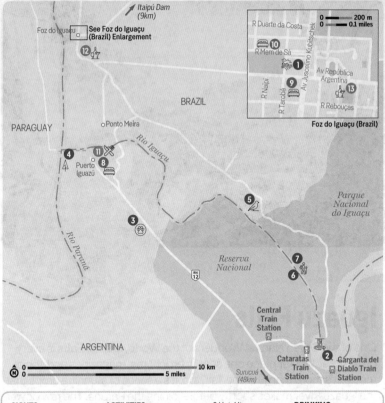

Itaipú Dam (9km)

Foz do Iguaçu **See Foz do Iguaçu (Brazil) Enlargement**

12

BRAZIL

PARAGUAY o Ponto Meira

Rio Iguaçu

4 **11**
Puerto **8**
Iguazú

Rio Paraná

3

Reserva Nacional

RN 12

ARGENTINA

0 ————————— 10 km
0 ————————— 5 miles

Surucué (48km)

Central Train Station

Cataratas Train Station

2 Garganta del Diablo Train Station

5

Parque Nacional do Iguaçu

7
6

Foz do Iguaçu (Brazil)

0 ——— 200 m
0 ——— 0.1 miles

R Duarte da Costa

10 R Mem de Sá

1

R Naipi **9** R Tarobá

Av Juscelino Kubitschek

Av República Argentina

13

R Rebouças

SIGHTS
1 Foz do Iguaçu
2 Garganta del Diablo
3 Güirá Oga
4 Hito Tres Fronteras
5 Parque das Aves

ACTIVITIES, COURSES & TOURS
6 Salto Arrechea
7 Salto Macuco

SLEEPING
8 Casa 24 Puerto Iguazu

see 8 Hotel Itavera
9 Hotel Mirante
10 Pousada Sonho Meu Foz

EATING
11 City Bar – Iguazú
see 9 Gaúcho

DRINKING & NIGHTLIFE
12 Authentic Bar
see 12 Deux Coffee
13 Sudakas

Taking in Puerto Iguazú

A Dusty, Fun Border Town

There's only one reason why Puerto Iguazú exists: to cater to people visiting the falls. As such, it's small, touristy, but fun in its own way. Most of the action is in a small downtown area, close to the river, and there are lots of restaurants, cafes, and bars to enjoy. A small rotary marks the intersection of four different roads: Misiones, San Martín, Perito Moreno, and Av Brasil, and following Brasil uphill will lead you to a warren of spots to choose from. Not surprisingly, you'll find most of the tourists enjoying tasty *caipirinha*, a specialty of Brazil made with *cachaça*. You can grab lunch, a pastry or a drink here, then keep walking on San

Caipirinha

PRACTICALITIES

Scan this QR code for prices and opening hours.

TOP SIGHT

Iguazú Falls

One of the Seven Natural Wonders of the World, **Iguazú Falls** is every bit the spectacular place one sees in brochures, magazines and social media. It's more than just one 'fall', too: it's a series of stunning drops that the Iguazú River makes shortly before joining the Paraná. The raw power of the falls is unparalleled. Plan on being wowed and getting wet.

DON'T MISS

Garganta del Diablo – Argentine side

Garganta del Diablo – Brazilian side

Observatorio de aves Daniel 'Pupi' Somay

Tren Turístico Parque Nacional Iguazú

Parque das Aves

Mirante da Garganta do Diabo

Salto Santa Maria

Garganta del Diablo

Few sights the world has to offer are more spectacular than peering over the Garganta del Diablo (The Devil's Throat). The reactions range from shrieks and squeals to solemn pondering of how small and fragile human existence is. There's just something immeasurably overwhelming here; the force is so powerful you can only gawk and be amazed. Approximately half the river is channeled into the massive falls, which are about 90m wide and almost as tall. At their highest, the flow rate over the falls tops more than a million cubic feet per second, about four times the rate of Niagara. The numbers vary somewhat due to fluctuations in river level, but even at its driest, it's an incredible sight to behold. Whether you see it from above on the Argentine side or view it before you on the Brazilian side, it's simply breathtaking. Be sure to catch a ride on the glass elevator on the Brazil side for a drone's-eye view.

The Nature

These national parks (the twin sides of the Iguazú River) are most famous for their eponymous waterfalls, but they are impressive in other ways, too. The protected jungles harbor a wide variety of fascinating animals and some incredible birds, and some species are found nowhere else in the world. You can have encounters in the wild, with animals such as the coatis, which are anything but wild at this point (be careful, they should not be teased or fed, as a bite may mean a trip-ending visit to a hospital for rabies shots!), and birds (toucans have been known to alight atop the cages of the **Parque das Aves**, whether to tease the caged birds or try to get handouts of food is hard to tell). If you want to maximize your chances of wildlife spotting, try to arrive as early as possible in the morning.

The Exhibits

On both sides of the river there are excellent rescue centers helping to educate about wildlife trafficking and providing shelters for animals and birds that have – for whatever reasons – been unable to be released into the wild. You can learn about the effects of wildlife trade and see some incredible species at the Parque das Aves, where some of the area's most beautiful birds can be seen, as well as many other species (such as flamingos) which don't frequent the Iguazú region but are found elsewhere in Argentina, such as in Miramar (p229).

Trails

While the falls tend to eclipse any other reason to be here, there are a number of beautiful walking and hiking trails through the park's dense forests, some of which lead out to vistas of the falls, others to points along the river, and some that stay entirely in the jungle itself. The surprising thing is that you may find yourself with the trail all to yourself, since so many people opt only to visit the falls before getting back on their tour bus or heading to the airport for home. If time allows, explore the trails to the **Salto Macuco** on the Brazilian side (which has a boardwalk), or **Salto Arrechea** on the Argentine side.

**Ring-tailed coati,
Iguazú Falls**

DO IT IN A DAY

It's not impossible to visit both sides of the falls in a single day, but you'll need to start as early as possible, so be first in line when ticket counters open at 8am. Do the Argentine side first, which will take much of the morning, then have a driver take you across the border and drop you on the Brazilian side. Get there by 1pm and be done by 5pm.

TOP TIPS

- Visit early in the day to minimize crowds and maximize wildlife spotting.
- Don't feed or molest wildlife.
- Bring mosquito repellent for the hikes.
- Bring a rain poncho or umbrella.
- Photographers, take special care to avoid water on your lens, as the airborne mist carries sideways, unlike rain.
- On both sides of the falls, plan on walking for an hour or more.
- Arrange for a ride in advance, as cell service at the falls is spotty.
- Sunrise tours can be dramatic, but rainbows are less likely.

CROSSING THE BORDER

Crossing the border can be quick and painless or it can be a grueling slog through seemingly endless traffic. The quickest way is to take a car to the border and get dropped off, walk though, and have a car waiting on the other side to pick you up. Taking a taxi is faster than going in a private car, as taxis have a special lane they can use that lets them skip much of the (usually) long line for passenger vehicles. You'll need your passport and if traveling with a child, documentation from both parents. Going from Argentina into Paraguay, currently, you are technically required to have a Yellow Fever vaccination, though this is rarely checked.

Hito Tres Fronteras

Martín towards the Paraguay boat ramp. At the river you'll see a different side of the border, looking across at Brazil directly, but if you were to lean out over the water and look to the left, you'd see Paraguay.

If taking in all three countries from one vista sounds fun, go to the **Hito Tres Fronteras**, a small park with a monument intended to signify the point where three countries meet. But guess what? The real spot at which they meet is in the middle of the river, so you can't quite put a foot (and hand?) into three different countries. But you can look at all three and there's a frame to take selfies in. And yes, in case you were wondering, there's a **Hito Tres Fronteras** in Paraguay and a **Marco das Três Fronteiras** in Brazil. A light show here in the evenings often draws crowds.

Fun in the Foz

Brazil's Foz do Iguaçu

The Brazil side of Iguazú Falls is a bigger, more robust city, with more to see and do than at its Argentine sister. This is partly due to economics these days: the Argentine peso doesn't buy what it used to, while the Brazilian real is healthy. So there's more in the way of upscale coffee shops, tasty restaurants and

 PLACES TO STAY AND EAT IN PUERTO IGUAZÚ

Casa 24 Puerto Iguazu
A convenient spot for bus travelers, with a pool, *parrilla*, and attentive staff. $$

Hotel Itavera
A simple, clean hotel close to the tourist center, with free breakfast and hot water for *mate*. $

City Bar – Iguazú
A fusion restaurant with lots of choices ranging from meats to seafood, shrimp, and two-for-one *caipirinha* specials. $$

partying on this side. (It's Brazil, after all – one can expect some good parties!) You can start a fun evening by bellying up to the buffet at **Gaúcho**, a *parrilla* – no, it's Brazil, a *churrascaria* – filled with tasty delights and all the grilled meats you can handle. There's often live music and sometimes dancing. From there, you can head into town along Av Argentina, one of the city's main streets. If it's early in the evening, kill time at **Deux Coffee**, getting your caffeine levels up so that you'll be awake and jittery to have a lot of fun later on. The bar scene here is young and vibrant, there's a mix of music, and the only thing that might be tough is having a conversation. **Sudakas** is popular and fills up after midnight, with patrons spilling out into the street. A more upscale cocktail scene awaits you a few blocks away at **Authentic Bar**, with a mostly under-30 crowd and an adjacent tattoo parlor. If you wake up with a skull and crossbones emblazoned on parts unmentionable, you'll at least know it's...*authentic*.

Learn About Wildlife at Güirá Oga

A Rescue Center with Heart

The **Güirá Oga** (which means 'The House of the Birds' in Guaraní) is located on the way to the falls on the Argentine side, and offers you – and any little ones you may have – a lot of up-close views of wildlife that you likely won't otherwise see on your trip, even though much of it lives right there in the park. It's a rescue, rehab and reintroduction facility that's privately run and is dedicated mainly to rescuing animals and birds that have become part of the illegal wildlife trade or that have been injured (for example, hit by vehicles).

Toucan (p136)

GETTING A DRIVER

Some hotels will try to set you up with a 'group rate' and then claim the others in the group have canceled suddenly, leaving you footing the bill for the entire cab. If you hire someone, ask to see the rate card, as rates are fixed. If they can't show it to you, look elsewhere. Two recommended drivers:

Diego Daniel Aguirre *(WhatsApp: +54 9 3757 43-0235)* is based in Puerto Iguazú and can be hired for visits to either side of the falls, as well as for trips to Paraguay, airport runs, and so on.

Willian Colman *(WhatsApp: +55 45 8807-9367)* is based in Foz do Iguaçu, offering similar services.

 PLACES TO STAY AND EAT IN FOZ DO IGUAÇU

Pousada Sonho Meu Foz
A delightful *pousada* with a large pool, communal kitchen and grill, and sundeck. **$$**

Hotel Mirante
Excellent deal if you're looking for a business hotel ambiance, with breakfast and a pool. **$**

Deux Coffee
Not just great coffees, but tasty sandwiches, snacks and sweets at this spotless cafe. **$**

Blue macaw, Güirá Oga

PARQUE DAS AVES

On the Brazil side of the falls is **Parque das Aves**, an aviary where – similarly to **Güirá Oga** – trafficked, injured and surrendered birds are cared for, specifically those native to the Atlantic rainforest. The park's facilities include large, open-air, walk-in aviaries for species like macaws, where you can interact directly with the uncaged birds. You can learn about bird trafficking, see the history of the park, which was inaugurated in 1994, and of course, see lots of birds. Flamingos, toucans, cassowaries and a variety of colorful parrots make up only some of the many different exhibits. And as mentioned elsewhere, look up and you may even see wild toucans and other species atop the mesh of the cages.

The aim is to release animals back into the wild, but also to provide shelter for those that can't be, as well as release any captive-bred species back into the wild. It's a challenging mission, and many tourists have little or no idea how often species are affected by illegal hunting or trade.

A visit will involve a tractor-pulled wagon ride to the Macuco Center, where you'll see information about the project, the history and future goals. From there, a series of jungle walks extend through the exhibits, which serve both the purpose of rescue and protection, and display for visitors. These vary based on what animals are currently being rescued, but you can expect a variety of mammals that could include anteaters, tapirs, ocelots, pumas, monkeys and even jaguars. Bird species include many types of parrots, but also rare guans, burrowing owls, hawks, falcons and others. There's even a section for insects such as spiders and butterflies.

Beyond
Iguazú

Ciudad del Este
Iguazú Falls
Abai
Nacunday • Puerto Iguazú
• Eldorado
Bernardo
de Irigoyen
PARAGUAY
São Miguel
D'Oeste
Hohenau
ARGENTINA
Encarnación
Missions
of the Guaraní
BRAZIL

Great shopping deals and crumbling Jesuit missions await explorers who want to dip into Paraguay, since it's right there after all.

As much as the falls are the reason you've come all this way, if you've seen it and bought the T-shirt, and enjoyed the towns on both the Brazilian and Argentine sides, the next step is to head into Paraguay. Ciudad del Este is a gritty mix of cultures, most of whom come here to shop – this is the place to get musical instruments, clothes, shoes, knock-off designer bags (at those prices they're certainly not authentic!), and so on. The big malls are conveniently named 'China' and 'Paris', so you know whether to look for inexpensive Asian or faux European items. Beyond lie Jesuit missions that are worth a visit if you're so inclined.

San Ignacio Miní, Missions of the Guaraní (p139)

GETTING AROUND

Buses can zip you to the major cities. To get to the Paraguayan Jesuit ruins you'll want to arrange for a tour or hire a private driver, if you don't have your own vehicle.

☑ TOP TIP

Be cautious especially at night in Ciudad del Este. Of the three border towns, it's the most dicey.

ARTERRA PICTURE LIBRARY/ALAMY STOCK PHOTO ©

Ciudad del Este

BORDER SECURITY

You'll find that crossing the borders is relatively easy and in some cases, a cinch. If you're going from Brazil to Paraguay, for instance, you can just go right on in. It's an open border. Crossing from Argentina to Brazil you'll be asked for papers, and likewise, when returning, but at this time none of the three countries bother to stamp passports. That said, keep in mind that border crossing details often change on a dime due to circumstances or current events. It never hurts to check carefully before embarking, and make sure all papers, shots and documentation are at hand.

Ciudad del Este

TIME FROM IGUAZÚ: **1HR** 🚌

A Burgeoning Border City

Ciudad del Este won't be everyone's cup of *mate*, but it's famous for shopping, and as such, if you're so inclined, you'll want to check out some of the deals. There are two giant indoor malls, known as Shopping Paris and Shopping China, and they have what you might expect: one is more themed towards Asian electronics and other things coming out of Korea and Japan; the other is more European, with clothes and fashions and perfumes and so on that are imported (or at least purported to be) from Europe. It's good to be here with a bit of skepticism since knock-off goods are common and almost expected. You're not here for authenticity but for a good deal. A steal, even, as the case may be.

 WHERE TO STAY AND EAT IN CIUDAD DEL ESTE

Hotel Casino Acaray
One of the swankiest options in Este, this spot has pools, quality rooms and, yes, an on-premise casino. **$$$**

Hotel Sur Brasil
An inexpensive option, yet has on-site parking and free breakfast in addition to friendly, accommodating service. **$**

Ravello Ristorante
Some of the tastiest Italian food Este has to offer, in a low-light, romantic setting that's sure to please. **$$**

Tri-Border Area

The Missions of the Guaraní

The Missions of the Guaraní is a collective term for the many Jesuit missions built in the 1700s along what's now known as the 'triple border' that connects Paraguay, Brazil and Argentina. Undoubtedly, these missionaries brought diseases that caused irreparable harm to indigenous communities, and the harm done has lasted to the present day. These structures stand as a testament to a long-lost history when the power of the church was insurmountable. Interestingly, these missions had the task of protecting the indigenous tribes from human traffickers. Converting to Christianity under the hands of the Jesuits was often the lesser of two evils, as slave ships and marauders often plied these jungles for new people to enslave.

I AM NOT A PIG!

You may see road signs warning of collared peccaries crossing, or if you're lucky, you may see one – or a *squadron* (yes, that's the name for a bunch of them!) – crossing the road. These animals are often confused for wild pigs, but they're actually genetically different, and to find a common ancestor, you need to go back about 40 million years. You may smell a squadron of peccaries before you see it: they have pungent scent glands and use them to mark territory, earning them the nickname 'musk hog' or 'skunk pig'. Just remember, they're not a pig!

ALFREDO CERRA/SHUTTERSTOCK ©

San Ignacio Miní, Missions of the Guaraní

BUENOS AIRES

Parque Nacional Iberá

GETTING AROUND

It's mostly dirt roads around here and while they're generally doable in a normal car, a 4WD may be needed if there's been heavy rain. At times they are impassable, especially going north/south between Colonia Carlos Pellegrini and Posadas. Check with the hotel about conditions before planning to use that road. Coming from the south, via Mercedes, plan on a 90- to 120-minute drive into Colonia Carlos Pellegrini. It's also dirt but is hard and graded. Once you're in town, you can walk anywhere you need to go. If you're driving, go slowly and be aware of crossing wildlife.

☑ TOP TIP

You might be tempted to skip the lagoon tour, especially if you've already spotted capybaras and some cool birds on the way in. You'd be making a big mistake, as a tour can allow you to spot river otters, dozens if not hundreds of caiman, and rare marsh deer.

If you've come to Argentina looking to say 'hi' to the world's largest rodent, the capybara (called *carpincho* here in Argentina), then you've come to the right place. You'll see them everywhere: crossing the road, lying in the road, next to farms and fields, happily wallowing in mud, doing what capybaras love most...munching grass. But Parque Nacional Iberá is much more than just a great time with a great rodent. It's the sixth-largest national park in Argentina and supports a vast range of species, thanks to its diverse habitats ranging from swamp and wetland to thick forests to dry plains. Some of the world's most prized wildlife can be found here: the giant anteater, the flightless rhea, and (recently reintroduced) the jaguar. In many ways, the wilderness of Iberá – though not as spectacular as the Iguazú Falls – is more rewarding.

BUTEO/SHUTTERSTOCK ©

Capybara

140

Cerrudo Cue

Ituzaingo

Loreto

Lomas De Vallejos

General Paz

Manantiales

Mburucuya

Parque Nacional Iberá

Laguna de Luna

Galarza

Río Aguapey

Concepcion

Carayá Trail

Laguna Fernández

Colonia Carlos Pellegrini

Laguna Trin

0   50 km
0   25 miles

Cavorting with Capybaras
The World's Largest Rodent

There's just something about capybaras that makes even the most avid rodent hater's heart melt a bit. Perhaps it's that zen-like expression they always seem to carry. Perhaps it's the fact that – as viral media has shown – they're friends with everybody, from turtles to ducks, cats, dogs, even caimans (a natural predator). Whatever the reason, the human species could learn a lot from this peace-loving oversized rat. For many visitors to Argentina, the chance to see a capybara in the wild is the highlight of any visit. Docile and numerous, you'll likely see them lounging about on the roadside or having a mud bath in one of the drainage channels. If you take an Iberá lagoon tour (p143), you'll see dozens in the swamps and marshes, doing their thing: lazing about or munching vegetation.

While getting too close to a wild animal is never recommended, capybaras may be the one exception, as they're pretty accommodating as long as you're moving slowly and quietly. They're remarkably mellow about being approached, and if they do get perturbed, they're most likely going to take a few steps away from you and then go back to happily munching grass. Yes, there are stories of people even *patting* these lovable critters, but that's usually done by accustoming them to

VISITING PARQUE NACIONAL IBERÁ

Local guide **Luciana Belén Cariaga** *(Instagram: @lucianabelen74)* shares her tips for visiting the park.

Take a lagoon excursion, walk the forest trails, and appreciate the dark night sky. Bring binoculars and cameras to take the best memories of the flora and fauna of Iberá. The emblematic animals to see would be the swamp deer, the Yacaré caiman, the adorable capybaras, the Carayá monkeys, foxes, and many species of endemic birds. If you're really lucky, you might see a giant anteater or even a jaguar.

Things you shouldn't forget to bring are: insect repellent, sun protection, comfortable clothing and rain boots, because we have a variable climate and the weather changes frequently.

 WHERE TO STAY IN COLONIA CARLOS PELLEGRINI

Hospedaje San Cayetano
A lush escape with a pool; rooms have shaded verandas, and it's centrally located. **$$**

Casa Santa Ana del Iberá
Great lagoon access and a large pool, plus welcoming staff and tasty meals. **$$$**

Casa de Esteros
This lovely spot, on the far side of CCP, looks out directly on the marsh and is near a lookout tower. **$$$**

CAIMANS, CAIMANS, EVERYWHERE

If you've ever chuckled at the phrase 'croc-infested waters' and thought it the stuff of Hollywood, you won't think that after a visit to Iberá. These shallow lagoons are teeming with caimans, a relative of the American crocodile. There are two species here, the common *Caiman yacare* and the rarer *Caiman latirostris*. You can tell them apart by looking at their foreheads. The latter have a much more scooped nose, rather than a flat one. While only the largest of these animals pose a threat to humans, they're not to be trifled with, and small pets (or small children!) shouldn't be allowed too close to the water.

Parque Nacional Iberá

you over a series of weeks or months. Don't plan on just walking up to any random rodent and giving it a scratch behind the ears. But a selfie with a capybara a few steps behind you shouldn't be too challenging. That said, capybaras' teeth are as sharp as chisels and their jaws are as strong as a jaguar's, so you don't want to get bitten. Never try to touch or handle a baby, as the mother may defend it and you don't want to be at the receiving end of a bite.

Mind-Blowing Birdwatching

Diversity Means Wealth

This park is a special treat for birdwatchers, who can expect thrilling looks at a whole host of birds, many of which are found nowhere else in the world. Two reasons make it spectacular: the diversity of habitats, and the ease with which you can get close to many birds.

For some reason, in **Parque Nacional Iberá**, the birdlife seems to have much the same blasé attitude as the capyba-

WHERE TO EAT IN COLONIA CARLOS PELLEGRINI

Los Amigos
A simple place, with mostly Italian and Argentine options, that's open late and is inexpensive. $

Don Marcos
Hearty, filling food at this rustic restaurant right at the entrance to town. $$

Despensa y Carnicería La Familia
Good for backpackers, this convenience store has chips, meats and other staples. $

ras. Even herons, typically very flighty, let the lagoon boats approach well within DSLR range. Some species, such as the cheery yellow-billed cardinals, practically beg you to take their picture, hopping around at your feet like sparrows. Out on the plains that border the park, you can often drive right up to everything from rails to rheas. Even the odd, strange-tailed tyrant doesn't seem too concerned about a passing vehicle with a long lens poking out of it.

You'll want to plan to visit as many of these different park habitats as possible: the riparian lagoon areas. Best viewed on a lagoon tour, this will bring you close to all sorts of rails, herons, egrets, storks, ducks, lapwings and other wading/water birds. Not to mention the other wildlife, such as capybaras, caimans and deer. The grasslands are vast and spectacular, with a variety of larks, bobolinks, warblers, sparrows, hawks, burrowing owls, and as mentioned, rheas. The forest trails have trogons, warblers, cardinals, owls and many more. Plan on visiting each for at least four hours, better a full day, and keep in mind you may see different species at dawn and dusk than during the peak daylight hours. At night, watch for potoos, nightjars, owls and whip-poor-wills.

Cruising the Carayá Trail

A Wildlife-Filled Wonderland

People often assume that Iberá is too swampy to be walkable, but there are a host of exciting trails to take that will lead you through great habitats for wildlife and birds. One of the best if you're short on time is the **Sendero Carayá** (Carayá Trail), which is across the street from the information center. It's an easy-to-walk 30-minute trail but will take you through pastureland, forest and swamp, giving you the chance to see a host of fun wildlife and birds. Of course, top of the list are the capybaras, which can often be seen meandering around munching whatever tasty edibles they can find. Caimans are plentiful when you get to the swamp, but if you're lucky, you'll also see monkeys scrambling about above you in the trees. The varied vegetation offers habitat for a diverse number of bird and insect species as well. It's a great trail for little ones, because it's not overly long and offers a lot to see along the way.

Red-crested
cardinal

BEAUTIFUL BUTTERFLIES

Parque Nacional Iberá isn't just a great place for seeing birds and animals. There are lovely butterflies to look for as well. Some even migrate for thousands of miles, either staying here for the season or else stopping before heading onward. Here are three species to keep an eye out for as you hike the trails:

Orange Tiger (Dryadula phaetusa)
Often confused for a Monarch butterfly; the orange and black pattern is tiger-like.

Clearwing Butterfly (Episcada hymenaea hymenaea)
Its transparent wings are unique and beautiful.

Guava Skipper (Phocides Polybius phanias)
A dark butterfly with two distinctive red spots, one on each shoulder.

Beyond Parque Nacional Iberá

Impressively vast, this region has fascinating pockets of history for you to discover, and unparalleled natural beauty.

GETTING AROUND

Paved roads are in good condition here, and there are buses to the bigger destinations. You'll have to have private transport or take an organized tour to get to the more remote areas, and there are no public options for getting to the park.

☑ TOP TIP

The roads here are shoddy, so watch out. Pavement is lumpy, and dirt roads can be drivable one day, then mush after a soaking rain.

There's an almost African sense of grandness in the landscapes here, with fields so big that you can drive through them for an hour and not see the scenery change. Or forests of eucalyptus and pine big enough to build whole cities from. You'll stumble onto lagoons lush with wetland wildlife and birds found nowhere else in the world. It's beautiful monotony, punctuated here and there by small towns and cities that seem perfectly content to be who and what they are. Misiones Province isn't named that for nothing: Jesuit ruins here are some of the grandest the continent has ever seen, even in decay. And places like Parque Nacional Mburucuyá, Iberá's little sister, beg to be explored.

Parque Nacional Mburucuyá

"EDITH POLVERINI"/SHUTTERSTOCK ©

Hornero

Parque Nacional Mburucuyá

TIME FROM PARQUE NACIONAL IBERÁ: **1HR**

Little Sister to Iberá

Don't try to pronounce it, just go: Mburucuyá is a lovely little gem that sits between Iberá to the east and Corrientes to the west, a preserve on either side of a wetland swamp made by the Río Fragosa. Like its larger neighbor, it's possible to see many of the same animals and birds, and yes, if capybaras are on your list you'll see them here. The terrain, however, is drier than much of Iberá, and you'll find saprophytic plants, tall palm trees and other delights – all within a two-hour drive of Corrientes. As such, this is a doable day trip assuming you're willing to get up early and arrive back at the hotel late. Yatay Path is the most popular hike, a 7km trek out to a lookout tower above Santa Lucía estuary. A shorter path, the Che Rhoga, is 4km. Along with the 'usual suspects', you may see gray brocket, a type of deer. Getting here is tricky if you don't have your own private vehicle, as there is no public transportation. This means you'll likely have the park mostly to yourself if you do manage to come.

THE HUMBLE HORNERO

As you travel this area you'll surely notice what look a bit like beehives: soccer-ball-sized round balls made of mud, seemingly everywhere, on fenceposts, on road signs, atop power lines, on tree branches. They're the nest of Argentina's national bird, the hornero (*Furnarius rufusa*), a type of ovenbird about the size of a robin. They're quite common and somewhat unadorned: with a rusty brown color, they don't stand out in a crowd. But their nests sure do, and these chipper chirpers will often be seen peeking out of the small opening or bringing a hapless grasshopper in to feed the young.

WHERE TO STAY AND EAT IN POSADAS

Julio Cesar Hotel
A stately hotel in the town center with a great breakfast, parking and a rooftop pool. **$$**

La Querencia Restaurante
A tasty *parrilla*-cum-Italian spot with starched tablecloths and attentive, vest-clad waiters. **$$**

Bolivar Café
A clean spot on the square with excellent coffee, *medialunas*, pastries, snacks and sandwiches. **$**

POSADAS, YACYRETÁ & PARAGUAY

The grand Río Paraná separates Argentina from Paraguay, a vast border that runs over 300 miles, from Resistencia all the way up to Puerto Iguazú. The only big city in the middle is Posadas, which sits on the upriver side of the giant hydroelectric project of the **Yacyretá Dam**. Posadas is a charming, quiet city with a nice central square, tasty restaurants and a range of hotels. You can cross over to Paraguay via a bridge that connects the two countries. Downstream, the Yacyretá Dam dominates. Its construction changed the landscape, altered the ecology, displaced as many as 40,000 people, and was marred by scandals, such as claims that the census was adjusted downward to lessen the payment to displaced people.

ALFREDO CERRA/SHUTTERSTOCK ©

Parque Nacional Iberá

The Missions of Misiones

TIME FROM PARQUE NACIONAL IBERÁ: **3HRS-8HRS** 🚗

Explore the Impact of the Jesuits

You could say the Jesuits were on a mission to build these missions in Misiones, but that might be missin' the point. All joking aside, this region, Guaraní, spanned what is now parts of Brazil, Argentina and Paraguay. The Jesuits came in the 1700s with dreams of saving 'lost souls' and building numerous missions. Though there was some conversion to Christianity, it was often only adopted as a way for indigenous peoples to avoid human trafficking and enslavement, rather than due to willing adoption of the new religion. Even so, the Jesuits were often attacked. And the places they colonized brought death by disease along with 'salvation'. As was the case all over the Americas, indigenous populations collapsed, and many of the missions were abandoned.

TAKE A LAGOON TOUR

A lagoon tour is one of Iberá's unmissable activities, so you owe it to yourself to take one while you're here. Start at the ❶ **docks**, ideally after lining up a guide the day before. You may find yourself waiting for others if you don't hire the whole boat for yourself. Remember you'll need to purchase the proper park entry bracelet before hopping on the boat. From the dock, you'll head out parallel to the causeway, past the ❷ **Bailey Bridge**, and await confirmation of your visit by the park officials. Just hold up your wrist so they can see you've got your bracelet. From there, you'll go under the bridge and head to see some caimans, at a ❸ **small peninsula** where they congregate due to shallower (and thus warmer) water. Mostly, they're small here, less than a meter long, but you may get lucky and see a large one too. Birders will want to look for herons, grebes, cormorants and bitterns in the reedy shallows, as you head further into the lagoon. At the eastern edge there's a ❹ **channel**, with large caimans and numerous capybaras, which coexist happily. You may even see capybaras climbing over caimans to get to the water's edge. If you're lucky you'll spot a marsh deer, snakes, iguanas and birds. Depending on the guide and the length of tour you've decided on, this may be the end of the trip, but keep your eyes open the whole way, as in the middle of the ❺ **water** you may see river otters, cormorants and turtles.

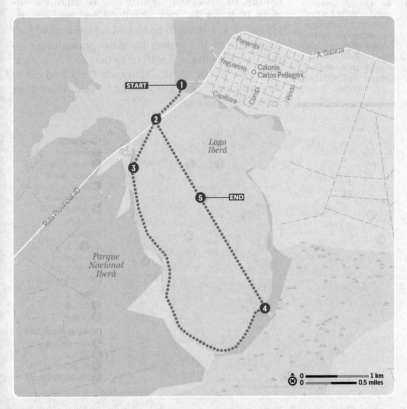

GETTING AROUND

Corrientes is easily reached by bus or plane. Taxis can get you the rest of the way there if you don't have your own vehicle, and it's small enough to walk. Drivers should know that the streets are narrow and traffic snarls are plentiful.

☑ TOP TIP

If you can come for Corrientes' Carnaval, do – it's a full-blown party not to be missed, with all the color, costumes and craziness you'd expect. Get your hotel reservations early, months in advance, or consider commuting from Resistencia if hotels here are full.

Corrientes

This charming river city sits on the eastern bank of the great Río Paraná, and as such, much of its economy revolved (and still does) around river trade. But it's more than just an industrial behemoth. There are quiet avenues, a beautiful beachfront, excellent restaurants, posh hotels, and the vibe of a small town even though it's, in fact, the capital of Corrientes Province. The city hosts one of Argentina's largest Carnaval celebrations and is a hot spot for fishing, drawing both leisure and tournament anglers. It shares the river with its 'sister', Resistencia, across on the western bank and makes a good hub for exploring the region. Its many parks have murals, monuments and statues in honor of historical figures, and the iconic Jacaranda trees and other flowering trees and shrubs make for beautiful spring and summer scenes.

TOP SIGHTS
1 Costanera
2 Museo Arqueológico y Antropológico
3 Museo de Ciencias Naturales
4 Museo Provincial de Bellas Artes

SLEEPING
see 2 DonSuites
5 La Alondra Casa de Huéspedes
6 Turismo Hotel Casino

EATING
7 Cristóbal Café
8 Ginger

DRINKING & NIGHTLIFE
9 Jaiteva Flotante
10 Le Vieux
11 Martha de Bianchetti
12 Monk's Speakeasy Bar

NELSON GONZALEZ/ALAMY STOCK PHOTO ®

Río Paraná

Chill Out at the Costanera

River-Watching at its Best

The Río Paraná is one of the world's greatest rivers, sitting comfortably along with the Amazon, the Mississippi, the Danube, the Yellow and the Nile. It served as the main corridor for trade throughout the country's history and still offers incredible views of cargo freighters chugging by, along with pleasure boats, sailing and fishing vessels, and even kayaks, SUPs and canoes. Bring your *mate*, your beach towel and your friends, and plan on enjoying some sunshine and watching life unfold on the water. With its views, the boats, and the golden hue of the sand, it's little wonder this is called the prettiest *costanera* in all of Argentina. It's not just a great spot for sunbathing either, as the 5km of walkway extends around the shoreline, making it perfect for jogging, running, biking or walking the *perrito* (dog).

Because the water is west of the shore, it's also a perfect spot for sunset chasing, with beautiful skies as a background to the lights of the suspension bridge that connect the two sides of the river. You'll also see a number of people fishing, rods and reels out, hoping to catch some of the prized fish the river holds, such as dorado, surubí, and pacú, which will

SOMETHING FISHY

The Río Paraná, yes, does have piranhas, as well as a host of other fish. Piranhas are even caught by fishermen and taken back to the table. Unlike the myth, you're unlikely to be stripped to the bone in seconds by a frenzied school, but now and then, piranha attacks happen, and in some cases, people have died. You can best avoid being bitten by not swimming in water with lots of reeds, lilypads and other vegetation, as this is where piranhas often hide. They're also more likely to attack in areas where they're nesting. Before taking a dip, always ask locals if there's anything to be aware of. Snakes, caiman or piranhas...better safe than sorry.

 PLACES TO STAY IN CORRIENTES

Turismo Hotel Casino
A snazzy, posh spot that's nicely located next to the *costanera*, with (duh!) a casino attached. $$$

La Alondra Casa de Huéspedes
A spiffy spot with a great outdoor pool, a restaurant and affable service. $$$

DonSuites
A nice spot close to the *costanera*, Don offers modern rooms, fridges, microwaves and a pool. $$

TEATRO JUAN DE VERA

This stunning belle-époque building is a must-see even if you aren't able to take in a performance, and is lovingly referred to as the 'Temple of Culture of Corrientes'. The red velvet seats, elegant chandeliers, triple balconies, and the beautiful mural on the ceiling dome all make it well worth stopping for. If anyone's at the ticket office, ask if they'll let you take a quick peek. Otherwise, you may want to just get a ticket, because no matter what the show is, you'll surely enjoy taking it in style.

Carnaval, Corrientes City

be brought back home and grilled with cassava and lime. Anglers, you may want to get out the rod yourself and take a cast or two. And take note, there are plans underway to put in a second bridge connecting the two sides. It's possible that the landscape will look a little different in the near – or not so near – future.

Museocultural

Enjoy Corrientes' Many Museums

Corrientes is not just a nice place to look at the river; you can actually learn about the city, its history, its art, and that of Argentina as well, at its many museums, most of which are housed in beautiful antique buildings and are in themselves worthy of appreciation. One of the common stops is the

 PLACES TO EAT IN CORRIENTES

Martha de Bianchetti
A delicious, nay, revelational pastry, ice cream and coffee shop in the center of town. **$**

Ginger
Offering Real. Good. Food. Ginger has everything from sushi to specialty pizzas, steps away from the *costanera*. **$$**

Cristóbal Café
A nice lunch, dinner and live-music spot near the *costanera*, with burgers, pizzas, tacos and more. **$$**

Museo Arqueológico y Antropológico, in what is known as Casa Martinez, a beautiful building that dates from the mid-1700s. The collection here is small, but with a guide (Spanish speaking) you can get a more robust picture of the leaders the house served, as well as understand Guaraní culture and funerary rites. If history and anthropology aren't your thing, check out the collection of stuffed animals at the **Museo de Ciencias Naturales**, where you can view a wide range of species, and even see re-creations of some extinct animals that once roamed the Argentine plateaus.

Rheas, foxes, capybaras, maras, guanacos, and even butterflies and spiders are all on display behind glass protective cases. It's a great way to learn about some of the animals you may see as you journey through Argentina. Housed in the residence of the governor of Corrientes, Dr Juan Ramón Vidal, the **Museo Provincial de Bellas Artes** has a lovely collection of local and national painters, sculptors and folk art, as well as rotating galleries.

Go Carnaval Crazy

A Rowdy, Gaudy Good Time

Corrientes may not be Río, but it sure does put on a good show for its yearly Carnaval, arguably the biggest in Argentina. It shuts down the *costanera* for four separate weekends leading up to the Easter holiday, with everything you'd expect: scantily clothed dancers, costumes with feathered headdresses large enough to make a Maya king jealous, festive floats of all shapes and sizes, brash bands marching and belting out tunes, and plenty of vivacious onlooking, glitter, glitz, beverage consumption and dancing.

Juried shows are held in the city amphitheatre and the Corsódromo Nolo Alías, where performers compete to win the year's big awards. Of course, they crown a King and Queen, but there's also crowns for the King and Queen of several different categories, such as the children's group, the individuals, best musical, and so on. Big bucks are spent to make this a spectacle that people all over the country – and all over the world – will come to see, and if you like dazzle and dancers, this won't disappoint.

**Carnaval,
Corrientes City**

BEST CORRIENTES BARS

There's a surprisingly varied, fun cocktail scene here in riverside Corrientes, whether you pick a spot overlooking the water or something more intimate in the city center. Expect mostly to be at tables; you won't find many traditional sit-at-the-bar bars here.

**Monk's
Speakeasy Bar**
A dimly lit, often packed spot with a nice range of classic and creative cocktails. Come for the drinks; the food is sub-par.

Le Vieux
A nice open-air spot with lots of tables, often with live music, and a patio for dancing.

Jaiteva Flotante
You can't get closer to the water without being wet at this floating platform that has food, beers and cocktails.

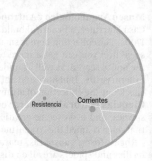

Resistencia   Corrientes

Beyond
Corrientes

GETTING AROUND

Resistencia is easy to walk around, but is spread out, so for longer trips you may want to use a taxi. Collectivos and buses also can take you to most of the larger destinations.

Corrientes is only part of the magic of this area, which has other cities, natural wonders, river adventures and beautiful wildlife.

Beyond Corrientes, the top place to go is the dusty, yet surprisingly artsy, Resistencia, the capital of neighboring Chaco Province. While it doesn't quite have the architectural beauty of its haughty sister, Corrientes, it's got its own charm, making up for the rather plain buildings with a number of interesting sculptures; it even has a biannual sculpture event that draws artists and onlookers from all around the country. The town center is small, safe, and there's a nice nightlife scene once the bars open. If you only pick one city, it's hard not to choose the other side of the river, but if time allows, you'll be glad you checked out both.

PAULO HOEPER/GETTY IMAGES ©

Resistencia

☑ TOP TIP

Garages here often close at night; if you need to depart early in the morning, be sure they'll be open.

BEST BARS IN RESISTENCIA

It's no surprise that a city that values its street art has some artsy, creative places where those sculptors can unwind. You'll find a bevy of great bars and coffee shops in and around the city, many just steps from Plaza 25 de Mayo.

Eleven Rooftop
Can't beat this fun, hip, happening rooftop spot a few blocks away from 25 de Mayo Plaza.

Nanas Suena Bien!
A young 20- to 30-something vibe here, with craft cocktails, decent food items, and a clean, raw brick and black table decor.

Olegario Café
Has the feel of an Italian village spot, with men outside sipping coffee or wine at all times of day.

Resistencia

TIME FROM CORRIENTES: **30MINS** 🚌

Plazas, Prayers & People

Resistencia's main plaza, the 25 de Mayo, elevates this somewhat dusty city to the ranks of the worth-stopping-for. It's as if the city, knowing that it lacked the waterfront *costanera* beauty of its sister, Corrientes, decided it would beautify its side in many other ways. Argentine towns often lack a main center, but here you feel grounded in a place around which, surely, the city grew. Plaza 25 de Mayo has beautiful shade trees and a cathedral overlooking it, and when the jacaranda trees are blooming, the cathedral is postcard-pretty. Sculptures (p154) are scattered throughout the city, making for interesting, thought-provoking discovery as you walk along.

Outside the cathedral, you'll find examples of these works of art, such as the Picassoesque statue of San Fernando to the left of the doors. Look for other sculptures around and in

 WHERE TO STAY AND EAT IN RESISTENCIA

Niyat Urban Hotel
A chic, modern hotel with free breakfast, right on the plaza. **$$**

Hotel Diamante
A modest, clean business hotel with free parking and free breakfast. **$$**

Coco's Resto
This relatively swanky spot has excellent mostly Italian food, friendly service and reasonable prices. **$$**

THE MUSEO DEL HOMBRE CHAQUEÑO

If you're looking for an activity that won't take you traipsing all over a city, check out the **Museum of the Chaco Man**, a small but interesting place dedicated to the anthropological history of Chaco up to the modern day. It focuses on three main areas of humans here, the indigenous Chaco people, the Criollos, who were a mix of locals and European colonists, and then the 'gringos', who came as a wave mostly in the 19th century onward. There are ceramics exhibits, musical instruments, dioramas, displays, and a 4th floor devoted to mythology. And while most of the exhibits are in Spanish, some of the very accommodating staff may be able to translate or explain in English.

the park itself, as well as on the street, such as in front of the wave-shaped Casa de las Culturas, which has a radio station, art gallery and auditorium, where you can often catch an exhibition or a show. Other key buildings, such as the Banco de la Nación Argentina, make the square stately and picturesque.

The City of Sculpture

Immerse Yourself in 650 Works of Art

Not many cities of Resistencia's size can boast of having over 650 sculptures dotting its streets, paths, parks and venues. You can't toss a stone without nicking a work of art, thanks to the city's biannual sculpture festival, called Bienal.

Every July, the city welcomes sculptors to build, and then display, their non-perishable creations in the city's Parque Intercultural, where events, festivities and judging take place. The works are then installed throughout the city, meaning that the number of incredible works of art grows each year. It's an exciting event, but even if you're not here for the festival itself, you can enjoy wandering the streets, first looking for the art, then admiring it.

Though some statues, such as the one in the center of Resistencia's Plaza 25 de Mayo, commemorate famous historical figures, you'll find that many, if not most, are avant-garde, quirky, interesting and fun. Replicas of Michelangelo's David, strange spherical forms, and human forms abstracted to the near unrecognizable are all things you may find as you wander around.

You can find out more about this festival and see many of the previous year's entries by stopping in at the museum, where you can get more info and pick up a brochure mapping where the sculptures can be found throughout the city. There's even an app, apparently, that can do that for you as well (though it was not available at the time of research).

Roadside fish stand near Resistencia

Concordia

A beautiful border town just downstream of the vast reservoir made by the Salto Grande Dam across the Río Uruguay, Concordia is a fun spot to stop for a day or two, with day trips across the border, thermal springs to relax, play, or swim around in, a decent food and restaurant scene, and some nice parks and scenery. You can camp by the river if you like; there's great fishing, and yes, if you hang around long enough, you'll see those ever-cute, ever-cuddly capybaras. You can explore cool, somewhat creepy castle ruins if you've got some time on your hands. The city makes a great hub for other day trips, such as to Parque Nacional El Palmar, or for forays into historic Salto, in Uruaguay.

☑ **TOP TIP**

If you plan to go to Salto, time it so you're not stuck in traffic rush hour, as waits can be long otherwise. It used to be that shoppers went from Argentina to Uruguay for cheap deals; now it's reversed; Uruguayans come to Concordia for everything from electronics goods to gasoline.

GETTING AROUND

Downtown Concordia is pretty small, and you can easily walk across the entire city in an hour. Getting to the thermal springs or the farther camping grounds will require wheels – Bus 2 goes out that way, as do taxis.

SIGHTS
1 Castillo San Carlos
ACTIVITIES, COURSES & TOURS
2 Termas Concordia
3 Termas y Parque Acuático del Ayuí
SLEEPING
4 Camping la Tortuga Alegre
5 Camping Las Palmeras
6 Florentina 'El Origen'
7 Hotel Salto Grande
8 Posada Bamby's

Parque Nacional El Palmar

Get Yourself into Hot Water

Try the Relaxing Thermal Springs

There's nothing like a hot bath, but it's even better when it's a naturally heated swimming-pool-sized experience, such as the one you'll find at the delightful thermal springs here in Concordia. There are several; the closest to the city is the aptly named **Termas Concordia**, a hot spring and amusement park with a lot more to do than just dip in the heated water. There's a variety of pools, ranging in heat from about 40°C to a toasty 44°C, as well as suspended tree bridges, walkways and picnic areas. There's something for the whole family to enjoy, and lifeguards ensure safety.

Similarly, at nearby **Termas y Parque Acuático del Ayuí**, you can splish and splash in soothing heated waters. Here, the focus is more on the water, and a variety of different spas, pools and submerged seats let you sit, soak or even massage yourself with the hot water. Kids will find there are plenty of pools shallow enough for them to bathe safely. (None of them are deep.) The non-bath attractions here are the animals: a number of resident peacocks make this spot their home, and it's not uncommon to see a herd of capybaras munch their way across the river side of the property.

WORLD-CLASS FISHING

If you're an angler, you may just want to plan to stay here for a couple of days; some stay for weeks. The waters of the Río Uruguay and the smaller tributaries around it offer some fantastic fishing. Depending on water levels, the river may be rock-strewn or very flat, but a good guide will know the right places to cast your lure. Known as 'La Zona', the area downstream from the dam is heavily restricted, so you can only come with a guide and only on certain days. But the regulations have allowed the golden dorado to grow to world-record-setting sizes. Who knows, you may be the next person to catch that famous fish!

 WHERE TO STAY AND EAT IN CONCORDIA

Posada Bamby's
Delicious meals (breakfast free, dinner extra) and a you're-at-your-home kind of attitude at this inexpensive hotel. $

Hotel Salto Grande
A stately option in the center of town, with alfresco tables on the street, clean rooms, writing desks and friendly service. $$

Florentina 'El Origen'
A spic-and-span coffee shop with excellent lattes, espressos and iced coffee, plus pastries and sandwiches. $$

157

Both places have restaurant facilities, and though you may find service and quality is better elsewhere, you can't beat the convenience of barely drying yourself off before dining, and then returning to another blissful soaking sesh.

Creepy Abandoned Ruins

See Castillo San Carlos

The Jesuits weren't the only ones to build and then abandon structures. Rich people did it too. The **Castillo San Carlos** is a strange place, built in 1888 by Éduard Demanchy, a French industrialist. The materials to make it were imported from Europe, so no expense was spared, and at the time, it had amenities found nowhere else in the region, such as heated floors, running water and centralized gas lamp light. Despite its opulence and expense, it was only lived in for three years before the Demanchys left, so suddenly that all they took with them was their clothes. Rumors about why they disappeared have remained unfounded and the disappearance remains a mystery. Left abandoned, the building has seen its share of action, including a visit – an emergency landing – by none other than famed French postal mailman turned novelist Antoin de Saint-Exupéry, who actually stayed here for a time, presumably until his airplane was patched up enough to take to the air again. A **large statue of the Little Prince** is in the castle gardens. The building was also, at various times, a fruit stand, a salting factory and even a candle shop.

Today, it sits, beautiful and forlorn, overlooking the water. You can walk through the structure in a number of guided walkways, read plaques with information about the history, and admire the splendid grandeur of the decay. A small museum room has papers, documents, photos and a replica of Sant-Exupéry's plane. To get there from Concordia, take Bus 2 and get off at the entrance, where it's only a short walk through the lawns and gardens to get to the house itself.

CAMP WITH THE CAPYBARAS

If getting up and greeting the sunrise amid a herd of friendly capybaras sounds like your 'cupybara' of tea, then you may want to find a site at the water's edge. Note that as with any riverside, you may find there's more need to wear bug repellent, especially in the evenings when the bloodsuckers come out in force. You can't beat the morning sunlight though, scintillating over the placid river's surface as you coax water to boil for that morning pick-me-up.

Camping Las Palmeras
A nice family campsite with a sandy beach and facilities, grills for cooking, and outdoor showers.

Camping la Tortuga Alegre
A casual spot popular with fishers, with beach access and boat launches.

Castillo
San Carlos

You'll start this tour where everyone does: the entry gate. But take time to check out the ❶ **visitor center**, as the kind staff can offer tips about the daily conditions, give you maps, and explain park rules and regulations. An important one is to keep the vehicle going under 40km/h, to minimize the chance of hitting and injuring wildlife (turtles, snakes, lizards, rodents...even capybaras!).

From there, drive about 6.5km to a rotary, and turn right. Follow the road to your first stop, the ❷ **Yatay Trail**. It's a short 500m loop that brings you through some pretty scrub and of course, plenty of palms. Further on, you'll get to ❸ **Glorieta Trail**, where a 900m walk brings you through forest, along a small river, and back up to the parking area, where there's a beautiful overlook of the palms.

After that, backtrack to the rotary and continue (on the entrance road) to the right, towards the water. Then, about 9.2km from the entrance, you'll make another right. If you're a hiker, start looking on the left for the beautiful, 4.2km-long ❹ **Pastizal Trail** parking area. This is a spectacular in-out hike that takes you to the Río Palmar. If you're *not* a hiker, keep going and you'll soon come to a shorter trail, the 350m long ❺ **Arroyo del Palmar trail**, for a similar peek at the river. Once you're done, head back, again turn right at the main road, and follow it to the camping area, where there are ❻ **facilities and a gift shop**. If you want to plunge into the ❼ **Río Uruguay**, now's your chance.

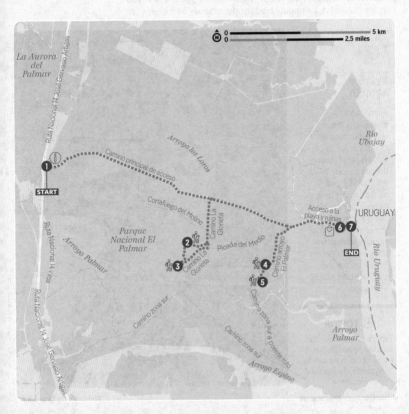

Beyond
Concordia

The dam, the border, and some great parks to explore make the area worth taking time for.

One of the area's biggest hydroelectric projects divides the Uruguayan and Argentine borders, with the beautiful, stately city of Salto across the way. You can easily make a day trip there, or a fun overnight, but traffic across the border can be heavy at times. To the south, you'll want to check out Parque Nacional El Palmar, the 'Palm Park'. Yatay palms like these once dominated the landscape for thousands of square miles, but as the land was converted into cattle farming and eucalyptus trees, the palm ecosystems shrank to almost nothing. This is one of the rare places where you can see this habitat – and its birds and animals – as it once was.

GETTING AROUND

Salto is an easy city to walk around in, and buses and *colectivos* run to various parts around the city as well. Taxis are plentiful, and if you're coming from Concordia, consider hiring a driver to take you across, as it's not violently expensive and gives you the flexibility of going exactly where you want to go.

☑ TOP TIP

Especially in summer, this area can be beastly hot. If you're hiking, make sure to bring plenty of water...and sunscreen.

LARRY LARSEN/ALAMY STOCK PHOTO ©

Fishing, Río Uruguay

Hydro electric power plant, Salto

Salto TIME FROM CONCORDIA: 1HR (+BORDER CROSSING TIME) 🚌

Crossing the Border

Salto is a lovely day trip, with Colonial-era architecture, snazzy malls and quiet fishing spots hidden away from the bustle. From Concordia, you'll head past the Termas and cross the Salto Grande hydroelectric project (itself a worthy sightseeing destination; it's massive, and the contrast between the up and down river sides is stark!). Then you'll likely want to check out the Plaza de los 33 Orientales, the city's most picturesque square. It's clean, green, and with its newly renovated fountains and its modern public bathrooms, it's really a cut above the rest of the squares you'll likely see. You can bring *mate* and sip it with amigos, find a coffee shop on the square, or visit the beautiful twin-steepled Parroquia Nuestra Señora del Carmen, which overlooks the plaza. From there, it's an easy walk to the river to enjoy views of this massive waterway any time of year.

Depending on when you come, the levels will be higher or lower. At times (such as after heavy rains in Brazil), it can even flood several of the nearby streets. But most of the time it's more docile. As with anywhere along the Río Uruguay, there's a chance you'll come across some peacefully grazing capybaras. North of the city you'll find the Parque Indigena, a spot for events, fiestas and competitions. If you have your fishing rod, keep going north and find the Cuevas de San Antonio, a collection of naturally eroded caves and rock formations that marks the spot of one of the best fishing sites in Salto. It's interesting even if you don't plan to fish (and if you do, be sure you have the proper permits, as this is heavily restricted).

PLACES TO STAY & EAT IN SALTO

Salto has its share of decent hotels and some tasty restaurants, as well as inexpensive street food around the main plaza.

Salto Hotel & Casino
A snazzy upscale spot right on the square, with beautiful views of the cathedral from the upper floors and rooftop pool area. **$$$**

Hotel Español Salto
A casual hotel with nice common areas, clean rooms and a free breakfast, with easy walking access to the plaza or the river. **$$**

La Trattoria
With a name that Italian you'd expect the pastas to be spectacular, and they are. **$$**

Cavern
A tasty, classy spot a few blocks from the main plaza, with burgers, fries, *tostadas* and plenty to drink. **$$**

161

Santa Fe

GETTING AROUND

Santa Fe's maze of narrow, often one-way streets can be daunting for drivers, and parking is a bit of a hassle. Non-drivers will find it's easy to taxi or bus about, and ride-share service is available as well. There's nothing to keep you from using your two feet, either: it's a pretty city to walk around in.

☑ TOP TIP

Despite its size, and the fact that the city had four railway stations in the past, the city is not served by any trains at this time. The closest you can do is arrive in Rosario by train from Buenos Aires, then take a bus the rest of the way.

Of all the big Río Paraná cities, Santa Fe (officially Santa Fe de la Vera Cruz) has the nicest combination of size, culture, beauty and *je ne sais quoi*, making it a delight to visit any time of year. Its beautiful bridges, the tranquil *costanera*, the architecture, the pedestrian avenue, and the dining mean that it has something for anyone, and even though it's a big city (the country's fourth largest), it has a sweet, small-town feel to it. A tunnel runs underneath the Paraná (the river), connecting it to Paraná (the city), making it easy to hop across the river and visit that side as well. Come here to drink, dine and walk its busy avenues while enjoy building facades. Or just to sip *mate* with a special friend on the *costanera* as you watch a sunset together. It's a choose-your-own-adventure kind of town.

Plaza of the Three Cultures, Santa Fe

ROBERTHARDING/ALAMY STOCK PHOTO ©

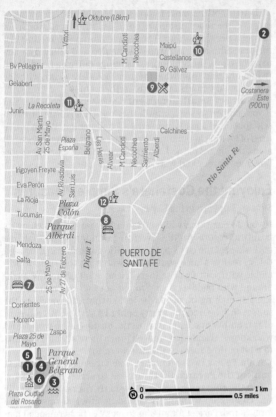

SIGHTS
1 Casa de la Gobierno
2 Costanera
3 Lago Sur
4 Monumento a la Biblia
5 Plaza 25 de Mayo
6 Templo y Museo de San Francisco

SLEEPING
7 House Park Boutique Hotel
8 Los Silos

EATING
9 Paladar Negro

DRINKING & NIGHTLIFE
10 Barrio Latino Cocktail Club
11 Insert Coin
12 One Six Roof Bar

Plazas, Cathedrals & Architecture

Visiting Plaza 25 de Mayo

Like so many other Argentine cities, Santa Fe too has a **Plaza 25 de Mayo**, and it's a great spot to start exploring the city. You can easily spend an afternoon here – or a whole day – looking at the impressive, imposing buildings, then crossing the busy street (be careful!) and checking out the views along the waterfront. The **Casa del Gobierno** vies for top spot visually, with its impressive facade, beautiful Greco-Roman architecture, and austere presence overlooking the square. Other buildings around the square are almost equally impressive. From there, walk southeast to the pretty Plaza of the Three Cultures, where the **Templo y Museo de San Francisco** is.

 WHERE TO STAY AND EAT IN SANTA FE

Los Silos
This fancy, casino-adjacent hotel has beautiful waterfront views. The name comes from its converted grain silos. $$$

House Park Boutique Hotel
A clean, friendly spot near the plazas, with excellent breakfast and helpful staff. $$

Paladar Negro
Varied mains, with tasty craft cocktails and a nice view of the park. $$

163

Ray Bartlett, writer

I connected with Santa Fe on so many different levels. I love cities with a river, and the Paraná is quite a river. Being able to sit and watch sunsets on Santa Fe's *costanera* with *mate* in hand felt so wonderfully Argentine. It has beautiful architecture and is a big city, but really feels more like a friendly small town compared to its other large neighbors. I also love that it's large enough for me to get a decent cocktail and have more to eat than just Italian food. And the fact that the university is there means there's a youthful, vibrant aspect to the place as well.

Though not the most impressive of buildings in terms of exterior, the relics inside are quite beautiful, well worthy of taking a peek...or a tour. The temple has an interesting history, including a priest who was mauled and killed by a jaguar who chose the building as its refuge during a flood. Hard to imagine that from what the area looks like today, with the nearest wild jaguars far north, in Iberá (p140).

Nearby is a **small monument** dedicated to the Bible, and if you happen to see a crowd, they're perhaps listening to a self-appointed apostle, using the spot as a pulpit. When you're tired of looking at buildings, cross the street and enjoy a stroll along the shores of the **Lago Sur**, a cove with a pretty shoreline, reeds, trees and waterfowl.

Enjoying the Costanera's Simple Pleasures

Sunset, Sipping and the Skyline

If you do one thing while in Santa Fe, you need to enjoy its beautiful *costanera*, the riverfront walking areas that line both sides of the city's part of the Río Paraná. It can be anything, really: a nice walk while watching the river, a preamble with your favorite furry friend, a bit of kicking a ball around with buddies, a spot to put out the yoga mat and get some stretching in, or maybe just sitting and watching the sunset sink behind the pretty Santa Fe skyline. It's a breath of tranquility and calm in a hectic, hustle-bustle world, and who knows, science may indeed prove there's health benefits to a bit of time spent at the *costanera* too.

Santa Fe has two *costaneras*. One faces east, on the **west bank of the Paraná**. It's the easiest to access if you're staying in the city, and great for those early risers. You'll get the sun coming up with the river and its ethereal mists in the foreground. Perfect for an 'I'm so lucky to be here' social media post. But the other side, **Costanera Este** (East Costanera), accessed by a beautiful suspension bridge and thus a bit harder to get to, faces west, and is the go-to spot for sunset chasers. You'll want to cross the bridge and then make a left, going north of the bridge. You'll find a broad bank with lots of parking and green grass, some picnic areas, and bathrooms. There are casual beach bars if you're in the mood to add a beer or cocktail into the equation. The spot can be just as pretty after dark, too, with the city's lights reflecting off the majestic Paraná's slow-moving waters.

 BEST BARS IN SANTA FE

One Six Roof Bar
Come here for creative craft cocktails and an eagle's-eye view of the city, spectacular any time of day.

Barrio Latino Cocktail Club
A great spot to chill and take in some of the city's best jazz, drink in hand.

Oktubre
One of the bars with a pool table, that also hosts live music events.

Beyond
Santa Fe

Vibrant cities, important historical monuments, interesting ruins, and a big beautiful river running through it all.

Several important cities, and, interestingly, the ruins of Cayastá line the Río Paraná. Cayastá was the initial location of what's become Santa Fe de la Vera Cruz. Though there's a similarity between most of these places, in that a river runs through them (or near them), if you take the time to explore, you'll find each one has its own distinct character. The big brother of them all, Rosario, is rich with history and architectural beauty, while peaceful Paraná has quiet streets and a tasty food scene. In between are cattle grazing lands, beautiful birdlife, and the river, never too far away.

GETTING AROUND

Buses and *colectivos* can bring you to all the spots mentioned here. You'll need to take an early bus to do a day trip to Cayastá. To and from Paraná you'll find frequent buses.

☑ **TOP TIP**

Car window 'smash and grabs' are on the rise in Rosario, so drivers should use off-street parking when possible.

ANIBAL TREJO/SHUTTERSTOCK ©

Monumento Histórico Nacional a la Bandera (p167)

165

THE RUINS OF CAYASTÁ

Also known as Santa Fe La Vieja, Cayastá sits about 75km north of Santa Fe on the banks of the Río Javier. It was Santa Fe's original location, and while much of the original site has sadly vanished into the river, a few key ruins remain that make it an interesting trip. At the top of the list is Iglesia de San Francisco, where almost 100 burials have been discovered. They are covered with a protective enclosure, and the original bones replaced with well-done replicas, but they remain a solemn testament to those early settlers who died in a distant land. Many of the graves are of named individuals. There's a museum, a few other ruins, and a gift shop, as well as a small town that's sprung up nearby.

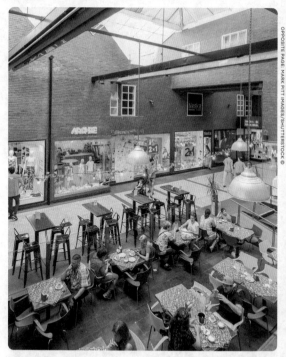

OPPOSITE PAGE MARK PITT IMAGES/SHUTTERSTOCK ©

Restaurants, Rosario

Paraná

Santa Fe's Sister City

TIME FROM SANTA FE: **40MINS** 🚌

Trek through the tunnel beneath the Río Paraná and enter the city of the same name. It's a sweet spot but smaller than its neighbor across the river. It's the capital of Entre Ríos (Between Rivers) Province, and as such, has its own pretty *costanera* and some quiet plazas. Paraná makes a good day trip if you've been based in Santa Fe and want to do something different for a bit. The Museo y Mercado Provincial de Artesanías is a top spot to stop and learn about – or buy – souvenirs. Objets d'arte, shoes, hats, fabrics and wooden toys are all on display, and the staff can explain the intricate processes involved in crafting them, which certainly adds to the value of a regional souvenir. There's also the Museo Histórico de Entre Ríos, which details the short-lived Republic of Entre Ríos, giving you a sense of the turbulence and time it took to

 WHERE TO STAY AND EAT BEYOND SANTA FE

Roberta Rosa de Fontana Suites
Easy walks to the *costanera*, restaurants and bars. **$$**

Hotel Coé Verá
Welcoming motel that's clean and has a free breakfast, as well as Fernet for sale if you need an evening tipple. **$$**

Ristorante Giovani
Possibly the best restaurant in Paraná, the Giovani is as friendly as it is fancy, with a lovely dessert selection. **$$$**

craft the Republic of Argentina that we know today. The city was the capital of the Argentine Confederation (which didn't include Buenos Aires) from 1853 to 1861.

Feeling the urge to sunbathe? Check out the city's two beaches, Playa Municipal, just west of the Paraná Rowing Club, or the nicer Playas de Thompson, which are about 1km east, beyond the port. Both offer the chance to dip or laze at the water's edge, though there's not much in the way of shade. The latter has a nearby kids' jungle gym and a decent swimming pool, if bathing in the river isn't your cup of tea.

Rosario

TIME FROM SANTA FE: **2HRS**

Rough & Ready Rosario

As of late, Rosario has had some tough times, mostly due to increased crime that's made it often at the top of the headlines for drug-related and other crimes. It's become less popular with tourists, and you need to be a bit more careful here than in some other cities, but that doesn't mean you should stay away. It's a fine spot to stop for a night or for a day trip. Rosario is a big enough city to offer lovely things to see and do. It's hugely famous for being the birthplace of two Argentine greats: Ernesto 'Che' Guevara and famed soccer star Lionel Messi. (Chances are you'll see more people wearing Argentine colors here than anywhere else in the country!) There's been a revitalization happening along the *costanera*, too, with hip brewhouses and restaurants replacing derelict warehouses. The *rosarinos* (people from Rosario) are as warm and welcoming here as anywhere in Argentina.

HONOR THE FLAG

Nothing symbolizes Argentina more than its flag. There's a lovely solidarity here;, you'll find people all over the country wearing white and blue, and they'll stop and lovingly admire an Argentine flag atop a mountain peak or flying proudly in the midst of a town square. The person responsible for creating the flag is honored here in Rosario. Manuel Belgrano rests in a crypt beneath the massive **Monumento Histórico Nacional a la Bandera**, topped with an obelisk, adorned with plaques, and thronged with adoring photo-takers. You can ride an elevator up to the viewing area and take in the pretty vistas of the Paraná. Whether or not you're a fan of patriotism, it's a key sightseeing stop in any Rosario visit.

Rio Paraná, Rosaria

Salta & the Andean Northwest

MOUNTAINS, INDIGENOUS CULTURE AND FOLKLORE

Adventure awaits amid the cactus-strewn, sun-drenched landscapes of the Andean northwest.

The Andean northwest is a region of awesome natural wonders, with ecosystems that change with the altitude. From the cloud-forest-covered hills of the Yungas emerge the colorful rockscapes and cacti of the *precordillera* (Andean foothills), beyond which lie the high-altitude plains and shimmering lakes of the puna (Andean highlands). Each layer is home to different wildlife, from pumas, guanacos and vicuñas to flamingos and condors.

The region's people venerate the power of nature and the land itself. The mountains are dotted with *apachetas* (stone altars), placed to give thanks to and ask for the protection of the Pachamama (Mother Earth). Throughout the northwest, you'll see the Wiphala,

the square emblem comprising squares of seven colors, which represents the indigenous peoples of the South American Andes.

For visitors to the region, Andean culture can be experienced in the form of flavorsome food and a vibrant folk music scene. From the site of Argentina's Declaration of Independence in Tucumán to the museum housing Inca mummies in Salta, the northwest's cities are steeped in history and culture; they are also excellent places to sample Argentina's best empanadas and dance to folk music at *peñas* (folk music venues).

The northwest is also known for its handicrafts, including handwoven ponchos; this item of clothing even has its own dedicated festival in Catamarca.

MARCEL BAKKER/SHUTTERSTOCK ©

THE MAIN AREAS

SALTA
Folk music
and wine.
p174

TILCARA
Quebrada de
Humahuaca village.
p186

TUCUMÁN
Historic city
surrounded by hills.
p197

CATAMARCA
Gateway to
the Andes.
p205

Left: Parque Nacional Los Cardones (p181); Above: Parque Nacional Talampaya (p213)

Find Your Way

Northwest Argentina encompasses a large area of scenic mountainous landscapes traversed by roads that make for epic trips by car, bike or bus. Distances are immense, so be strategic. Keep your camera handy.

PARAGUAY

Doctor Pedro P. Pena

Yacuiba

Tartagal

General Ballivian

Los Blancos

Bermejo

Bermejo

Pichanal

San Ramon de la Nueva Oran

Libertador General San Martin

San Pedro

General Guemes

Monte Quemado

Salado

Joaquin V Gonzalez

Rosario De La Frontera

Humahuaca

Tilcara

Jujuy

Salta

Cerrillos

Trancas

San Antonio de los Cobres

Cachi

Cafayate

Susques

Molinos

Salar De Pocitos

Antofagasta De La Sierra

Salta, p174

The historic city of Salta is home to a museum housing Inca mummies, as well as *peñas* where Argentina's best folk singers perform.

Tilcara, p186

This lively village makes the ideal base for visiting the colorful rock landscapes and indigenous communities of the Quebrada de Humahuaca.

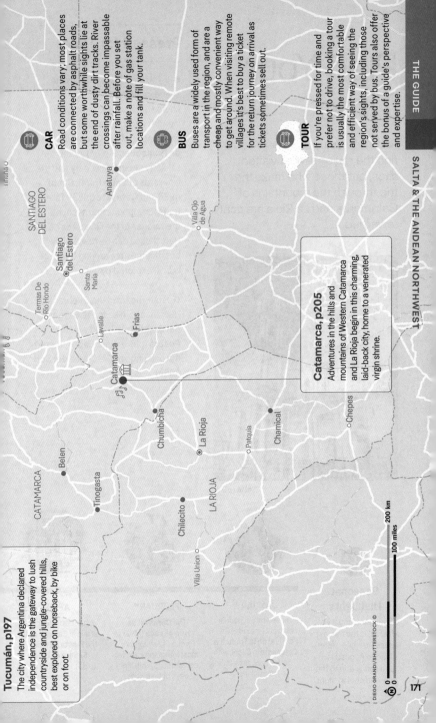

CAR

Road conditions vary; most places are connected by asphalt roads, but some worthwhile sights lie at the end of dusty dirt tracks. River crossings can become impassable after rainfall. Before you set out, make a note of gas station locations and fill your tank.

BUS

Buses are a widely used form of transport in the region, and are a cheap and mostly convenient way to get around. When visiting remote villages it's best to buy a ticket for the return journey on arrival as tickets sometimes sell out.

TOUR

If you're pressed for time and prefer not to drive, booking a tour is usually the most comfortable and efficient way of seeing the region's sights, including those not served by bus. Tours also offer the bonus of a guide's perspective and expertise.

Tucumán, p197

The city where Argentina declared independence is the gateway to lush countryside and jungle-covered hills, best explored on horseback, by bike or on foot.

Catamarca, p205

Adventures in the hills and mountains of Western Catamarca and La Rioja begin in this charming, laid-back city, home to a venerated virgin shrine.

SANTIAGO
DEL ESTERO

Tinuña

Anatuya

Santiago
del Estero

Termas De
Río Hondo

Santa
María

Villa Ojo
de Agua

Lavalle

Frías

Catamarca

CATAMARCA

Belén

Tinogasta

Chumbicha

La Rioja

Patquía

Chamical

Chepes

LA RIOJA

Chilecito

Villa Unión

0 — 200 km
0 — 100 miles

DIEGO GRANDI/SHUTTERSTOCK ©

Plan Your Time

Salta and Jujuy are where you'll find the region's most visited sites, but those who make the trip through the mountains of Catamarca and La Rioja are richly rewarded.

Salta (p174)

Pressed for Time

● If you have just a few days to spend in the northwest, make a choice between the indigenous villages and spectacular landscapes of the **Quebrada de Humahuaca** (p186), or the similarly stunning scenery and the vineyards of **Salta** (p174), **Cachi** (p181) and **Cafayate** (p183). Take transport options into account: the villages of the Quebrada de Humahuaca can be reached by bus, but the area around Cafayate is best explored by car.

● From Tilcara in the Quebrada de Humahuaca, hike to the **Garganta del Diablo** (p187) and visit the **Pucará** (p188). Near Cafayate, see the paintings at the **Cueva del Suri** (p183).

Seasonal Highlights

Summer (January to March) is the rainiest season, while winter (June to August) is dry and sunny during the day and cool at night.

JANUARY

The region's schedule of events includes the **Festival de la Tradición Calchaquí** in Cachi, with performances by folk musicians.

FEBRUARY

The **Carnaval de Humahuaca** (p192) is one of Argentina's most intriguing carnival celebrations, with eight days of festivities.

APRIL

After Easter, pilgrims arrive in Catamarca for the **Fiesta de Nuestra Señora del Valle** (p213), including a city procession.

ANJELOU/SHUTTERSTOCK ©

BOTTOM: SIMON MAYER/SHUTTERSTOCK ©, MARCELO AGUILAR LOPEZ/SHUTTERSTOCK ©, ALE GRUTA FOTO/SHUTTERSTOCK ©

A Week in the Northwest

● After a day in **Tucumán** city (p197), head into the hills of **Tafí del Valle** (p202) for hiking and horseback rides.

● Then continue north to **Cafayate** (p183), stopping at **Amaiche del Valle** (p201) and **Quilmes** (p204) on the way. Spend a day visiting the area's vineyards, then travel through the **Quebrada de Cafayate** (p185) to Salta.

● After a day or two in the city, head north to **Tilcara** (p186). From there, take your pick of day trips: to **Purmamarca** (p191) and the **Salinas Grandes** (p191), or to **Humahuaca** (p186) and the **Serranía de Hornocal** (p193).

Ten Days to Explore

● Start in **Tilcara** (p186), then head north to the **Iruya** (p194) for epic hikes. Stop in **Humahuaca** (p186), before heading south to **Salta** (p174).

● From here, drive through the **Parque Nacional Los Cardones** to **Cachi** (p181), then take the bumpy road to **Cafayate** (p183), stopping at bodegas along the way.

● Next, head south on the Ruta 40, via **Quilmes** (p204), to the village of **Belén** (p211) and the nearby ruins of **El Shincal** (p210).

● Take the **Ruta del Adobe** (p211) to **Fiambalá** (p211), then drive the **Ruta Los Seismiles** (p209) to the Chilean border.

JUNE

Gauchos gather in Salta for the **Guardia bajo las Estrellas** (p179) in honor of independence hero General Güemes.

JULY

Winter events include the **Fiesta Nacional del Poncho** (p213) in Catamarca and independence day celebrations in Tucumán.

AUGUST

On August 1, Andean communities hold ceremonies to celebrate and thank Mother Earth on the **Día de la Pachamama** (p202).

OCTOBER

Iruya's festival in honor of **Nuestra Señora del Rosario** involves folk music, dancing and processions on horseback.

BUENOS
AIRES

Salta

GETTING AROUND

Salta city centre is relatively small, easy to navigate and safe to walk around. To use local buses, you'll need a Tarjeta SAETA, which is sold at the airport and in some kiosks. The bus terminal, near Parque San Martín, has regular services to Jujuy and Tucumán, among other locations. There are daily buses to Cafayate and Cachi, but no buses between the two. There are plenty of car rental companies; Alto Valle (altovallerentacar. com.ar) is a reliable option.

☑ TOP TIP

Salta Free Tour offers walking tours of the city center Monday through Friday at 10am in Spanish and 6pm in English. The meeting point is in front of the Cathedral in Plaza 9 de Julio. There's no need to book, but tours are sometimes cancelled if it rains. Pay by tipping the guide.

Nicknamed *la Linda* (the Pretty), Salta is a sophisticated city packed with historic buildings, including a large number of churches. There are also some interesting museums, including the city's star attraction, the Museo de Arqueología de Alta Montaña (Museum of High Altitude Archaeology). Here you'll find the mummies of three children whose deaths formed part of an Inca religious ceremony.

In Salta, you can while away hours strolling the city's cobbled streets and the nearby forested hills, browsing local produce and sipping coffee or beer at the sidewalk tables of bars and cafes. The city has a vibrant cultural scene that centers around art and music. You can hear *música folclórica* in the city's *peñas*, folk music venues that also serve regional food. Add in a few bottles of Malbec or Torrontés from local vineyards, and it's no wonder this is a city where people tend to linger.

Catedral Basilica de Salta (p179)

0 — 500 m
0 — 0.25 miles

SIGHTS
1 Catedral
Basílica de Salta
2 Güemes Monument
3 Iglesia de la Merced
4 Museo de Arqueología de Alta Montaña
5 Museo Güemes

ACTIVITIES, COURSES & TOURS
6 La Vieja Estación
7 Paseo de los Poetas
8 Punto de Diseño

SLEEPING
9 All Norte Hostel
10 Kkala Hotel Boutique
11 La Candela

EATING
12 Aires Caseros
13 Alfajores Hidálgo
14 Doña Salta
15 El Charrúa
16 El Charrúa
17 In Bocca al Lupo

DRINKING & NIGHTLIFE
18 Antares Salta

19 Café del Tiempo
20 Café Tucán
see 8 Pacha Wine

SHOPPING
see 21 Björk
21 El Camino
22 Mercado San Miguel
23 Una Tienda Con Propósito

The Children of Llullaillaco
Visit the Site of Ceremonial Rituals

By the late 15th century, the Inca empire included the western areas of modern-day Jujuy and Salta. The high peaks of the Andes were considered sacred ground and were the chosen sites for ceremonial rituals, including the sacrifice of children as an offering to the gods. The chosen children first attended the *capacocha,* a huge celebration packed with pilgrims in the Inca capital of Cusco, before making the journey to the mountaintop. In 1999, the

175

mummified bodies of three such children were found near the summit of Volcán Llullaillaco (6739m), at the border with Chile. They are preserved using a sophisticated technological system at the MAAM.

MORE MOUNTAIN MUMMIES

The small **Museo del Hombre** (p154) in Fiambalá contains the naturally preserved remains of an Inca-era man and woman discovered in Loro Huasi. However, unlike the children in Salta, these two people did not die as part of a ritualistic sacrifice.

View Inca-Era Mummies
The Children of the Mountain

It was a controversial decision to display the mummified bodies of the children whose deaths formed part of an Inca sacrifice ritual. Nonetheless, the **Museo de Arqueología de Alta Montaña (MAAM,** pictured p175), where the mummies can be seen, is one of the region's most important museums. It contains a number of galleries with informative displays on Inca culture in both English and Spanish. Buy tickets online in advance to avoid waiting in line.

The mummified bodies of three children – a 15-year-old girl, a girl aged around six, and a boy aged around seven – are displayed one at a time on rotation; at the museum entrance, an information board lets visitors know which of the three children can currently be seen in the museum gallery.

After watching the introductory video, head to the top floor to view the objects found with the children. Display boards explain the historical context and the rituals and beliefs surrounding the sacrificial offering of the children, which was part of an important religious ceremony. Pieces include items for the children's journey to the afterlife, such as blankets, a drinking vessel and a textile bag, as well as figurines of animals and humans, and miniatures of objects related to common activities for the Incas. Look out for the mountain shoes, which were worn when hiking through snow at the mountain peaks.

Coming face-to-face with the mummy is a powerful experience; how you feel about it depends on your personal views. Their plaited hair and clothes are perfectly preserved.

Downstairs, the *Reina del Cerro* (Queen of the Hill) exhibition displays the mummified body of a girl found at the top of Chuscha in Cafayate in the 1920s, and tells the story of how the body was recovered from a private collection in Buenos Aires and brought to Salta.

ANIBAL TREJO/SHUTTERSTOCK ©

WHERE TO STAY IN SALTA

All Norte Hostel
Well-run hostel in an old house with high ceilings, a kitchen and a gorgeous garden. **$**

La Candela
This villa-like hotel has a courtyard garden with a pool and rooms with hardwood floors. **$$**

Kkala Hotel Boutique
Located in an upmarket neighborhood, this stylish hotel has private jacuzzi decks with city views. **$$$**

Convento San Bernardo

Begin your stroll at Plaza 9 de Julio in the heart of the city centre. First, pop into the **❶ Museo de Arte Contemporáneo (MAC)** to see the current exhibition, then head to the pink **❷ Catedral Basílica de Salta**, entering via the pretty courtyard with pots of lavender, to the east of the main entrance. Allow around two hours to explore the exhibits at the **❸ Museo de Arqueología de Alta Montaña** (p176). Nearby is the elaborate beaux-arts **❹ Centro Cultural América**, built in 1912 for an elite social club. Head inside to see the tiled floors and decorative doorways of the 1st-floor rooms, which now display the work of local artists. Walk up the grand central staircase to view the stained-glass windows, and be sure to take a peak at the ballroom on the 2nd floor. Continue around the square to the **❺ Cabildo**, the restored 18th-century town hall that now houses the Museo Histórico del Norte. Inside, take a look at the pre-Columbian ceramics, before heading to the 1st-floor balcony for views across the square. Continue east along Calle Caseros (p178). Make a stop at the **❻ Museo Casa de Uriburu**, the former home of the Uriburu family, including José Evaristo Uriburu, president of Argentina from 1895 to 1898. The 18th-century adobe construction around a central courtyard is typical of the buildings of the period. On the next corner is the striking **❼ Iglesia San Francsico**. Buy a ticket for a tour of the 54m-tall bell tower for views over the city. Head east to view the exterior of **❽ Convento San Bernardo**, a 16th-century convent that is home to Carmelite nuns. Don't miss the carved 18th-century algarrobo door.

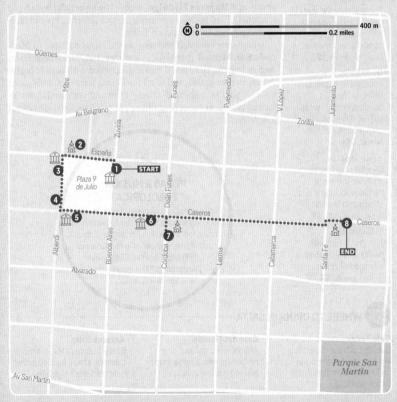

Boutique-Hopping on Caseros
Browsing Salta's Independent Stores

Lined with cafes and boutiques located in some of Salta's oldest buildings, Calle Caseros is a pleasant place to shop for local specialties. One block east of Plaza 9 de Julio, pop into **Pacha Wine** to browse the local produce, including Salta wines, spices, craft beer and artisan gin made with local botanicals. If you aren't able to visit the vineyards of the Valles Calchaquí (p182), you can book a wine tasting here instead. In the same gallery is **Punto de Diseño**, which sells the work of six local designer-makers who take turns to work in the shop.

The ceramic cactus lamps are particularly beautiful. One block east is **Una Tienda Con Propósito** (a store with a purpose), stocked with high-end fair-trade artisan blankets, rugs, bags and clothes made by local indigenous communities. On the next block, stop at **El Camino** to see the Uruguayan-style *mates* (gourds), made in Salta using squash husks, leather and alpaca.

Pop into the next-door store **Björk**, for fun cactus print bags and other souvenirs. Continue one block east to sample the goods at **Alfajores Hidálgo**, where the sweet *dulce de leche* (caramel) filled cookies are made using a generations-old family recipe that includes corn flour.

To bag some bargains and shop as the locals do, head to **Mercado San Miguel**, three blocks southwest of Plaza 9 de Julio on Av San Martín. Here you'll find stalls packed with bags of herbs, spices, maize, grains and local medicinal remedies, nuts, coca leaves, llama salami, goat's cheese, fruit and veg stands, and informal restaurants serving filling plates of regional dishes for low prices.

BEST PLACES TO EAT IN SALTA

In Bocca al Lupo
Hole-in-the-wall pizza joint selling Neapolitan-style pizzas. **$**

Viracocha
This place has a beer garden and a youthful vibe, and serves good-value, creative regional dishes. **$$**

Doña Salta
Traditional restaurant in an old brick building serving local specialties such as empanadas and *locro* (stew). **$$**

Aires Caseros
Overlooking Plaza 9 de Julio; the menu includes various salads and *humitas* (a local corn dish). **$$**

El Charrúa
This restaurant with two branches in the city specializes in grilled meats. **$$**

PEÑAS & MÚSICA FOLCLÓRICA
Salta is just one of many places to hear folk music in northwestern Argentina. In Jujuy, folk musicians perform nightly in restaurants and *peñas* in **Humahuaca** (p193) and **Tilcara** (p186), while **Tucumán** (p197) is also known for its folk music.

 WHERE TO DRINK IN SALTA

Café Tucán
Quality coffee and pastries in a bright airy cafe; open for breakfast and *merienda* (afternoon tea).

Café del Tiempo
Atmospheric bar and restaurant with a large terrace and regular live music.

Antares Salta
Buzzy branch of the Argentine brewpub chain, located in the heart of Salta's nightlife.

La Vieja Estación

AA WORLD TRAVEL LIBRARY/ALAMY STOCK PHOTO ©

Learn about Local Independence Hero General Güemes

Leader of the Gaucho Army

If you're interested in Argentine history, Salta's museum honoring Martín Miguel de Güemes is worth a visit. Housed in what was once Güemes's family home, **Museo Güemes** uses talking holograms and creative audiovisual displays to tell the life story of the Salta native who led an army of northwestern *gauchos* to battle against royalist forces loyal to Spain during the War of Independence (1810–1818). The entertaining audiovisual tour offers a patriotic narration of events; English subtitles are available.

The highlight is the central courtyard display of clay figures celebrating the ordinary people who used improvised weapons to defend their territory.

In the east of the city is the **Güemes Monument**, where in June thousands of gauchos on horseback gather to pay homage during the Guardia Bajo las Estrellas. General Güemes's remains are housed in the **Catedral Basílica de Salta**.

A Night Out in Salta

Folk Music and Dancing

Salta is known for its *música folclórica* (folk music). The best place to hear local musicians is in a *peña*, a bar or social space where people gather to play folk songs, eat regional dishes, and dance (there are traditional dances to accompany each particular style of folk music).

If you want to dance, head to **La Casona del Molino**, housed in a former mansion and patio where musicians work around the tables (closed Mondays). It's aimed at tourists, but is nonetheless a classic Salta experience. Arrive early to be sure to get a table. Another well-established *peña* is **La Vieja Estación**, with nightly music and dance shows in an atmospheric dining room. It's best to book a table online in advance.

ART & MUSIC IN SALTA

Salta native **Alejandro Calatayud** shares his tips.

Paseo de los Poetas
This street is full of small bars where you can hear different types of music. My friend runs open mic nights in a bar in a garage there. Musicians often play jazz, blues and soul but in a style that's influenced by traditional northern folk music and using local instruments.

Iglesia de la Merced
Thanks to its high Gothic roof, this church has excellent acoustics. Look out for concerts by the Orquesta Sinfónica de Salta.

Vineyard museum
If you book a tour at **Bodega Colomé** near Molinos you can visit the **James Turrell Museum**. For me the art is in the shadows produced by the structures.

Beyond
Salta

Salta's surroundings offer the opportunity for epic road trips through spectacular landscapes of cactus forests and striking rock formations.

South of the city of Salta, the Valles Calchaquíes offers rugged landscapes, adobe villages and top vineyards. The RN 68 winds through the glowing red rocks of the Quebrada de Cafayate as it approaches Cafayate village, which, with its wineries and paved highway, presents quite a contrast to more remote settlements such as Angastaco or Molinos. The village of Cachi, accessible from Salta via a spectacular road that crosses the Parque Nacional Los Cardones, makes a charming destination for an overnight stop.

The remote puna settlement of San Antonio de los Cobres can be visited on a day trip from Salta, which includes a ride on the high-altitude train to the clouds.

GETTING AROUND

One of the most popular ways to explore the Valles Calchaquíes is to hire a car and drive the loop from Salta with overnight stops in Cachi and Cafayate. If you aren't planning to drive, you can take the bus from Salta to Cachi or Cafayate, but not between the two. Several places in Cafayate offer bicycle rental. It's an easy drive via a paved section of the Ruta 40 from Cafayate to Quilmes (p204) and nearby Amaiche del Valle (p201).

☑ TOP TIP

If you aren't hiring a car, consider staying in Cafayate, where there are bodegas within walking or cycling distance of the town centre.

ELKENEIZE/SHUTTERSTOCK ©

Parque Nacional Los Cardones

Cachi

Cachi

TIME FROM SALTA: 4½HRS

Drive through Cactus-Strewn Landscapes

Located around four to five hours by car from Salta, the village of Cachi can be reached via a spectacular drive through **Parque Nacional Los Cardones**, a park named for its dominant plant species, the cardon cactus.

From El Carril, the RP 33 winds along the riverbank, ascending through verdant forest, which gradually gives way to dusty open plains with views of distant mountain peaks. Parts of the road are unpaved, with tight bends. The road climbs the **Cuesta del Obispo** to 3457m, where the **Piedra del Molino** viewpoint marks the beginning of the Parque Nacional Los Cardones. Stop here to see the tiny San Rafael chapel and take in the mountainous panorama. The next section of road goes through the **Valle Encantado**. Here there are several viewpoints and short walking trails, including the **Mirador Ojo del Condor** viewpoint and the **Secretos del Cardonal** path, a 200m interpretative trail through the cacti.

Soon you'll reach the enchanting adobe village of **Cachi**, a charming place for an overnight stop. At the tree-filled Plaza 9 de Julio, take a look inside **Iglesia San José**, where the barrel-vaulted ceiling and confessional booth are constructed

CLOSE ENCOUNTERS IN CACHI

Located 3km north of Cachi's Plaza 9 de Julio is a strange UFO landing pad, known locally as the **Ovnipuerto** (UFO port). Occupying an area the size of four city blocks, the Ovnipuerto is a remarkable installation comprising the outlines of 12 stars of different sizes, marked out with stones. The largest of the stars has a 48m diameter and 36 points.

Officially called *Estrella de la Esperanza* (Star of Hope), the work was created by Swiss artist Werner Jaisli. In 2008 Jaisli claimed he saw two UFOs measuring 12m to 15m in diameter at the site. The extraterrestrials asked Jaisli to create a large star, so he got to work.

 ## WHERE TO STAY IN CACHI

Viracocha Art Hostel
A cheery place in the centre of town, with colorful dorms with bunks and private rooms. **$**

Hostería Villa Cardón
This guesthouse has bright, minimalist-style decor, helpful owners and an excellent breakfasts. **$$**

El Cortijo
Sophisticated boutique hotel with off-white furnishings, ceiling beams, landscaped gardens and a pool. **$$$**

FOOTAGEMEDIA/SHUTTERSTOCK ©

SALTA'S WINES

In the Valles Calchaquíes, the stony, sandy ground, dry climate, consistent bright sunshine and wide temperature span between hot days and cool nights are ideal conditions for producing wine. There have been vineyards in the region since Jesuit priests planted the first vines in the 18th century; varieties of French Malbec and Tannat grapes were brought to the area a century later. But Salta's signature wine is Torrontés, produced with a grape variety that some believe to be native to Northwest Argentina (its origins are disputed; the grapes may have been brought from Spain). In March, the **Vendimia** (grape harvest) is celebrated with traditional folk dancing.

JEROEN MIKKERS/SHUTTERSTOCK ©

Ruta 40

from cardon cactus wood. Nearby is the **Museo Arqueológico**, displaying local ceramics and archaeological finds; booklets with English translations of the signage are available. Don't miss the intriguing rock with petroglyphs on both sides, one human and the other feline. Next, take a walk over the river to the hilltop **cemetery**, with views of the snow-capped mountain peaks.

Longer walks from Cachi include the 10km stroll through the valley to the tiny village of **Cachi Adentro**. To return a different way, bear left at the church and follow the road to Las Trancas. From here the road winds back to Cachi via the village of La Aguada.

Valles Calchaquíes

TIME FROM SALTA: **4½HRS** 🚌

Visit the Bodegas on the Cachi to Cafayate Wine Route

Located amid the spectacular landscapes of the Andean foothills, some 200km south of the city of Salta, the vineyards of the Valles Calchaquíes are some of the highest in the world. The bodegas (wineries) in and around Cachi and Cafayate form part of the so-called Ruta del Vino. Here the dry, temperate climate is perfect for producing Torrontés, as well as other varieties including Malbec, Tannat and Syrah.

 WHERE TO EAT IN CACHI

Viracocha Restaurant
Bar and restaurant serving good-value plates of typical Andean dishes. $

El Zapallo
Serves regional dishes and grilled meats, including goat and lamb, cooked on the roadside parrilla. $$

Oliver
At Plaza 9 de Julio, this restaurant and wine bar serves pizzas and typical local fare. $$

The section of road between Cachi and San Carlos is unpaved and can be challenging to drive; ask locals about current conditions before setting out. Allow at least five hours for the drive from Cachi to Cafayate, with stops.

Bodega Puna, 8km east of Cachi at an altitude of 2600m, produces award-winning Malbec Reserve and Torrontés. Book ahead for lunch, tastings, or a free guided tour. Next, head south from Cachi along the sandy Ruta 40 for 77km to reach Bodega el Cese, a boutique winery in a picturesque setting; tastings and quick tours are free. It is worth stopping in the nearby village of Angastaco; there are several places to eat lunch around the pretty square. From here, the Ruta 40 south to Cafayate passes the striking jagged rock formations of the Quebrada de las Flechas. Pull over at the Mirador Monumento Natural Angastaco and climb up to the viewing platform to take in the panorama.

Shortly before the town of San Carlos, 130km south of Cachi, the Ruta 40 becomes paved. Just north of Cafayate, look for the turnoff for Piattelli, an upscale vineyard. Book ahead for tours of the state-of-the-art winemaking equipment, a range of tastings, or lunch; if you only do one vineyard tour, this is a good one to choose. Finca las Nubes is located in a particularly beautiful spot near the Río Colorado (p184), 5km southwest of Cafayate, and offers scheduled tastings and tours. From Cafayate, it's an easy bike ride to both Piattelli and Finca las Nubes; a number of places in town offer bicycle rental.

Near Cafayate's Plaza San Martín are the bodegas (the bottle stores and tasting rooms, but not the vineyards) of several wineries, including Bodega Nanni, a traditional, family-owned vineyard producing organic wines, and El Porvenir, where the enologist Paco Puga is one of the region's most highly regarded. Both offer tastings.

Finally, don't miss Cafayate's Museo de la Vid y el Vino, where thorough displays in English and Spanish describe the history of winemaking in the region. The highlight is the evocative display covering the life of the vines in Valles Calchaquíes through a series of poems.

Cafayate

TIME FROM SALTA: 3HRS

View Cave Art & Waterfalls

Located 5km west of Cafayate (15 minutes by car or 25 minutes by bike) are two worthwhile sites that can be visited with guides from the indigenous Diaguita community. First, look for the roadside sign to the Cueva del Suri. From here, a guide will take you up to the hillside to see a number of sites: a cave with a palpable energy, used as a place of shelter

BEST PLACES TO EAT IN CAFAYATE

Finca las Nubes
The shady gardens at Finca las Nubes are an idyllic place for lunch or snacks (empanadas, salads and cheese plates) made with fresh local ingredients. **$$**

Piattelli
Book ahead for the lunchtime tasting menu with paired wines and weekend grills at this vineyard. **$$$**

Bad Brothers Wine Experience
Located in Cafayate town (and not at the vineyard), Bad Brothers offers a menu of small plates paired with their own wines; reserve in advance. **$$$**

La Despensa
Excellent regional dishes and *picadas* (sharing plates), with performances by local and visiting musicians. **$$**

Pacha
High-end contemporary restaurant serving creative plates made with local ingredients and impeccable deserts. **$$$**

WHERE TO STAY IN CAFAYATE

Rusty-K Hostal
Well-run hostel with cozy rooms, terracotta tiles and a vine-filled patio garden with mountain views. **$**

Portal del Santo
This cool white hotel has spacious, well-equipped rooms set around a pretty pool. **$$**

Killa
Centrally located and tastefully decorated boutique hotel; rooms overlook the garden and pool. **$$**

CHEWING COCA LEAVES

Chewing coca leaves has been part of Andean culture for thousands of years. In fact, the coca shrub is one of the oldest cultivated plants in South America.

Possessing small quantities of unprocessed coca leaves is legal in northwest Argentina, and bags of coca leaves and coca candies are sold in shops and at market stalls across Salta and Jujuy. Putting a few leaves inside your cheek (don't swallow them) or sucking on coca candies produces a mild stimulant effect that helps combat altitude sickness. The leaves can also be used to make tea.

Coca leaves are also used in certain spiritual practices, including ceremonies honoring the Pachamama (Mother Earth).

EDITH POLVERINI/GETTY IMAGES ©

Polvorilla Viaduct

and storage; ancient cave paintings; and milled rocks used to track the position of the stars.

Less than 1km south, past the entrance to the Finca las Nubes winery, is the starting point for walks along the Río Colorado. Here the local community offers guided walks (going without a guide is not permitted). There are seven waterfalls to see here; the 5km trip to the third waterfall and back takes around 1½ hours; allow three hours for the full 9km hike to all seven waterfalls. The hike is easiest in winter when water levels are low.

Puna de los Andes
TIME FROM SALTA: **3HRS**

Ride into the Clouds on the Tren a las Nubes

One of Salta's most popular excursions is the Tren a las Nubes (Train to the Clouds), though these days, most of the journey is by bus. The day trip from Salta begins with a bus ride to the town of El Alfarcito for breakfast and continues through the multi-colored landscapes of the Quebrada de las Cuevas to the puna town of San Antonio de los Cobres (3775m), a typical highland settlement with a stone church. From here, passengers board the train for the 22km journey to the impressive Polvorilla Viaduct, which spans a desert canyon at 4220m. Nurses are on hand to administer oxygen to those struggling to adjust to the change in altitude. Spaces sell out so book in advance.

VINEYARDS IN NORTHWEST ARGENTINA

Though Salta's vineyards are the region's most well known, there are also highly rated wine producers in **Catamarca** (p205), **La Rioja** (p213), and even in the Quebrada de Humahuaca in **Jujuy** (p195).

One of Argentina's most memorable drives is the road from Salta to Cafayate. This driving tour follows the RN 68 as it winds through the Quebrada de Cafayate, a spectacular landscape of multicolored sandstone and unusual rock formations carved out by the Río de las Conchas.

Traveling south from Salta, the scenery begins to change after you pass the town of ❶ **Talapampa**. After 12km, look for the turnoff to ❷ **Alemania**, named in honor of the German construction workers who built the railway here between 1916 and 1920. The railway ran between Alemania and Salta city until 1971; now most of the town's buildings lie empty. Stop to see the former railway station and bridge.

Return to the RN 68 and continue for 35km to reach the ❸ **Garganta del Diablo**, where you can walk through the huge circular opening in the red rock. Next, drive 1km south to ❹ **El Anfiteatro**, a vast chasm with excellent acoustics. Continue for 10km to reach ❺ **El Sapo**, a rock shaped like a toad. Then follow the winding road for 7km until you see a roadside shop signed Tienda la Yesera. Nearby is the starting point for the ❻ **Sendero los Estratos**, a 30-minute walk to remarkable rock stacks where the twisted sedimentary strata exhibit an array of tones, from rich ocher to ethereal green. Drive for 11km to reach ❼ **Los Colorados**; stop here to take a closer look at the colors of the surrounding hills. The rock formations are particularly beautiful at dusk, when they glow in the light of the setting sun. Continue for 12km to see the sand dunes of ❽ **Los Médanos**, before driving on to ❾ **Cafayate**.

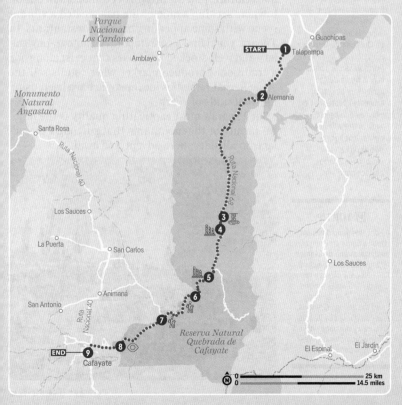

Tilcara

BUENOS AIRES

GETTING AROUND

Tilcara is small enough to explore on foot. You can also get around on horseback; ask at the tourist office. From the bus terminal, there are frequent services to San Salvador de Jujuy, Humahuaca, La Quiaca (the border with Bolivia) and Purmarmarca. There is one bus a day to Iruya (buy tickets in advance). Note that you need to pay to park in the village center; look for the people wearing yellow vests who collect payment.

☑ TOP TIP

For something different, book a llama-trekking trip with **Caravana de Llamas** (caravanadellamas.com). The company offers a range of guided walks around Tilcara, Purmamarca and the Salinas Grandes, accompanied by llamas who carry the bags packed with a picnic lunch. Wear sunscreen and a hat.

Home to some 6000 people, Tilcara is a lively village that makes an ideal base for exploring the outstanding landscapes of the surrounding Quebrada de Humahuaca. The village is named for the Tilcaras, an indigenous group that formed part of the Omaguacas communities of the Quebrada; today, you can visit the reconstructed remains of their hilltop settlement at the Pucará, just south of modern-day Tilcara.

The combination of traditional village life, indigenous culture, and the arrival of cosmopolitan out-of-towners seeking a quieter life has created a vibrant scene with some appealing bars and restaurants. In Tilcara, you'll find a contemporary photography gallery and well-stocked wine bars that exist alongside a traditional produce market where stalls sell the same herbal remedies local people have been using for thousands of years.

But Tilcara's most captivating quality is the natural beauty of the mountains that surround the village on all sides; here adventures await.

OPPOSITE PAGE: LUCA QUINTINI/SHUTTERSTOCK ©

Pucará de Tilcara (p188)

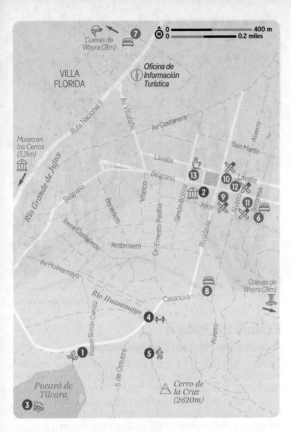

SIGHTS
1. Botanical Garden
2. Museo Arqueológico
3. Pucará de Tilcara
4. Railway Bridge

ACTIVITIES, COURSES & TOURS
5. Cerro de la Cruz

SLEEPING
6. Antigua Tilcara
7. La Calabaza
8. Patio Alto

EATING
9. Bien Me Sabe
10. El Nuevo Progreso
11. La Chacana
12. La Picadita

DRINKING & NIGHTLIFE
13. La Ekeka

Hike to the Garganta del Diablo

Waterfall Walk

One of Tilcara's most popular hikes is to the **Garganta del Diablo** (the Devil's Throat), a waterfall located a 4km walk east of Tilcara along a signed trail (it is a 6km drive by road). From the entrance hut, a steep, narrow path leads down to the river to reach the waterfall, which gushes down between jagged rocks. Note that bathing is not allowed. You will find locals offering horseback riding excursions near the entrance to the falls.

The site is managed by the Ayllu Mama Qolla indigenous community, who also offer guided hikes to the **Cuevas de Wayra** (Wayra Caves) in the nearby mountains. The walk takes two to three hours and passes a number of archaeological sites on the way to the caves, which were created in the volcanic rocks by a process of erosion. Tilcara's tourist office can provide contacts for local guides.

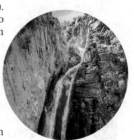

Garganta del Diablo

BEST PLACES TO EAT IN TILCARA

La Ekeka
Cafe within a bookshop, selling a range of local texts as well as coffee, sandwiches and cakes. **$**

Bien Me Sabe
Homemade pastas are the house specialty at this cozy restaurant; good pizza and desserts, too. **$$**

La Picadita
A bar stocked with local wines serving flavorful dishes such as *pastel de llama* (minced llama with mashed potato). **$$**

La Chacana
Excellent salads as well as typical regional dishes, served at indoor and outdoor tables. **$$**

El Nuevo Progreso
An artsy ambiance and imaginatively prepared plates including llama dishes and gourmet salads. **$$$**

MARTI BUG CATCHER/SHUTTERSTOCK ©

Railway bridge, Pucará de Tilcara

Explore the Pucará
Reconstructed Pre-Columbian Fortification

Located 2km south of Tilcara are the reconstructed remains of the Pucará de Tilcara, a hilltop village that was home to the Tilcara indigenous group. The Tilcaras lived here from around the 10th century, and the village was a regional capital during the Inca period. The site was abandoned after the Spanish gained control of the area in the late 16th century.

Athough *pucará* is a Quechua word for fortress, there are no defensive constructions at the site. From Tilcara's main square, it's a pleasant 25-minute walk to the Pucará via the photogenic former **railway bridge**. Just past the bridge is the **Cerro de la Cruz** trail; the views from the top are best in the late evening light.

At the Pucará, take a stroll around the complex's **botanical garden**. Stop to strike the **piedra campana**, a volcanic stone that makes a sound like a bell. From here, follow the signed route through the reconstructed buildings, which include houses, a cemetery and an Inca ceremonial space. The techniques used to reconstruct the buildings in the 1950s do not reflect the original methods or materials, but they do give an idea of what the village was like.

 WHERE TO STAY IN TILCARA

La Calabaza
This property has a two-room cabin that's perfect for families, plus a private double. **$**

Antigua Tilcara
A red adobe building with well-decorated rooms, a spacious cafe area and a guest kitchen. **$$**

Patio Alto
This stylish hotel has rooms with colorful floor tiles and serves great breakfasts. **$$**

Where the main square would have been, there is now an objectionable monument to the archaeologists who uncovered the site, which includes an erroneous and offensive reference to the *'pueblo muerto'* (dead/disappeared people) of the Quebrada's indigenous communities.

At Plaza Prado in Tilcara, don't miss the **Museo Arqueológico**, which houses ceramics and jewelry found at the Pucará and elsewhere in the Quebrada.

See the Photography of the Museo en los Cerros

Hike to a Hillside Museum

The **Museo en los Cerros** (MEC) is a photography gallery in a beautifully designed adobe building, located in a scenic mountain setting. It's 4.5km southwest of Tilcara, and can be reached on foot, by car or on horseback. Alternatively, take a taxi here and walk the mostly downhill route back.

The museum's gallery spaces display the work of a number of Argentine photographers. One room is dedicated to the late local musician Ricardo Vilca and has with headphones to listen to his music. There is also a cozy library full of photography books to browse.

Museo en los Cerros

THE QUEBRADA DE HUMAHUACA

Isabel Albiston,
writer

Sometimes, it feels as though the Andes mountains of northwestern Argentina, northern Chile and southern Bolivia have a magnetic force field that pulls me in time and again. I will never tire of this region's landscapes and culture. Nowhere is more special to me than the Quebrada de Humahuaca, a place that seems imbued with magic. It can be sensed in the glow of the mountains in the evening sunlight, the glimpse of hummingbirds drinking from a stream, and the spread of stars across the night sky. Add in some of Argentina's most flavorsome food, accompanied by local wine and informal performances by talented folk musicians, and the Quebrada de Humahuaca edges close to perfection.

Beyond
Tilcara

Tilcara sits amid the mountains of Quebrada de Humahuaca. East of Jujuy Province lie the cloud forests of the Yungas.

Tilcara enjoys a strategic location in the Quebrada de Humahuaca, near the center of Jujuy Province. From the provincial capital of San Salvador de Jujuy, the RN 9 climbs through Yungas forest before emerging into the colorful Quebrada, a Unesco World Heritage Site. Here, the sedimentary strata have been eroded into spectacular scalloped formations, revealing a spectrum of colors in undulating waves. Throughout the Quebrada, there are indigenous villages with artisan markets, interesting adobe churches, and opportunities for breathtaking hikes to nearby multihued rocks and caves.

In 2023, the indigenous communities of Jujuy staged a series of protests to draw attention to violations of their rights, the targeting of community activists, and institutional racism in the province.

GETTING AROUND

San Salvador de Jujuy's bus terminal is 7km east of the city center; it has excellent facilities, including a tourist office. To use local city buses, you'll need a SUBE card, available from the terminal (Buenos Aires SUBE cards work too). There are flights to Buenos Aires, Mendoza and Córdoba from Jujuy airport, 30km southeast of Jujuy. From Jujuy, buses run north along the Ruta 9 through the Quebrada de Humahuaca, to Tilcara, Humahuaca and La Quiaca at the border with Bolivia. Buses connect Tilcara with Purmamarca and Iruya. For the Salinas Grandes, drive or take a tour from Purmamarca or Tilcara. In summer, ask about road conditions before driving on unpaved roads, including the road from Humahuaca to Iruya, which can become impassable after heavy rain.

Cerro de los Siete Colores

MATYAS REHAK/SHUTTERSTOCK ©

Purmamarca

TOP TIP

Come prepared for blazing sunshine during the day (bring sunscreen and a hat); temperatures drop dramatically at night.

LITHIUM EXTRACTION AT THE SALINAS GRANDES

In 2023, members of the indigenous communities of the Quebrada de Humahuaca set up road blocks in protest at plans to extract lithium from the **Salinas Grandes** and **Laguna de Guayatayoc**. The communities believe that extraction poses a threat to the water supply, and goes against the communities' spiritual practice of honoring the Pachamama (Mother Earth). The protest was also connected to state reforms, which the communities say undermined land rights. The Jujuy state government has already tendered the rights to several mining projects to a number of international companies.

Purmamarca

TIME FROM TILCARA: **30MINS**

Count the Tones of the Cerro de los Siete Colores

The village of Purmamarca, 3km west of the Ruta 9, sits beneath the celebrated Cerro de los Siete Colores (Hill of Seven Colors), a dramatic hillside with neat, multihued layers of sediment. It is 30 minutes by bus and an easy day trip from Tilcara. Taxis and tours leave from Purmamarca for the Salinas Grandes.

Purmamarca's charms attract a steady stream of visitors, who come to photograph the famous hill and shop. There is a flourishing artisan market in the village plaza; it's hard to pass by without being pulled in by the vibrant fabrics. At the plaza, stop to take a look at the Iglesia Santa Rosa de Lima, a 17th-century church fronted by an ancient algarrobo tree.

For views of the hillside, look for signs to the Paseo los Colorados, an easy but rewarding 3km walk around the hill.

WHERE TO EAT & STAY IN PURMAMARCA

La Casa del Sol
Colorful bar serving pizzas, empanadas, salads and warming bowls of stew, with live music. $

Los Colorados
At an unbeatable location, tucked into Purmamarca's famous hill, are these boutique adobe cabins. $$

Huaira Huasi
On the edge of town, this lodge has majestic valley views and rooms decorated with local textiles. $$

CARNAVAL DE HUMAHUACA

In February or March, the towns of the Quebrada celebrate the Carnaval de Humahuaca, one of Argentina's most intriguing carnival celebrations. Here indigenous traditions have melded with Catholic customs to produce a vibrant celebration, with dancing and parades. The carnival begins with the resurrection of the devil figure, who is dug up from the place where he was left the previous year. The devil then walks the streets, knocking on doors to ask for food and to bring people out to join the festivities. Rather than representing evil, the devil is a character who tempts people to have fun. Finally, the devil is buried again, signalling the end of the raucous partying.

MAJORITY WORLD/UNIVERSAL IMAGES GROUP VIA GETTY IMAGES ©

Revelers, Humahuaca

Salinas Grandes

Explore the Salt Flats

TIME FROM TILCARA: 1½HRS 🚗

These dazzling salt flats, which span the boundary of Salta and Jujuy Provinces, are best reached from the Quebrada de Humahuaca in Jujuy via the RN 52, which passes through Purmamarca. The site can be visited on a day trip from Tilcara (around 1½ hours' drive) or Purmamarca by car, tour or taxi. West of Purmamarca, the paved RN 52 climbs to 4170m as it winds through the mountains (take care on the hairpin bends), before descending to 3350m at the **Salinas Grandes**.

To enter the salt flats, you need to go with a guide from the cooperative of local indigenous people who manage the site. Register in the parking area, and the guide will accompany you in your vehicle as you drive out onto the crusty white plains. Surrounded by mountain peaks, the 525-sq-km salt flats is the site of a former lake. Bring sunglasses to protect your eyes from the reflected sunlight.

The guided trip out to the flats includes stops for fun photographs (you can play with perspective and make it look like you are balancing on a bottle, for example). You'll also see **piletones**, constructed rectangular pools where salt is extracted, and the **Ojo de Salar**, a natural pool in the cracked salt surface.

 WHERE TO STAY IN HUMAHUACA

La Humahuacasa
Excellent hostel with shared dorms and private rooms set around a bright patio; there's a kitchen, too. $

Inti Sayana
Offers well-priced rooms with private bathrooms and shared dorms; breakfast is included. $

Tikay Humahuaca Refugio de Tierras
These self-catering apartments on the edge of town have mountain views. $$

Humahuaca

TIME FROM TILCARA: **45 MINS** 🚌

History & Folk Music in the Quebrada

The Quebrada's largest settlement is Humahuaca, a town known for its folk music and carnival celebrations (p42). Its cobbled streets, sleepy plaza and produce market are a great place to experience local life. The town can be visited on a day trip from Tilcara (45 minutes by bus), and combined with a visit to the Serranía de Hornocal. If you are planning to visit Iruya (p194), you might stop in Humahuaca overnight.

Overlooking Plaza Sargento Gómez is the impressive Monumento a los Héroes de la Independencia, which pays tribute to the people of Humahuaca who fought in Argentina's War of Independence (1810–1818). It was designed by Ernesto Soto Avendaño in 1926, but was not completed until 1950. Take a walk up the steps for a closer look at the figures represented in the piece. Soto Avendaño captured the facial features of the local people in his depiction of the *gauchos norteños* (northern cowboys) who defended northwestern Argentina; he also featured women in the scene, including one with a baby on her back. Nearby is the Torre Santa Bárbara, all that remains of a 1695 Jesuit chapel. The tower was originally located at the site of the monument, but was moved on wheels at a pace of 50cm per day to make way for Soto Avendaño's new work.

At the Plaza, take a look at the 1940s Cabildo; at noon, a figure of San Francisco Solano emerges from its clock tower. Nearby, browse the fair-trade blankets and scarves at Manos Andinas.

For views over town, cross the bridge at the eastern end of Calle Salta and follow the road for 2km to the rocks of Peñas Blancas.

Serranía de Hornocal

TIME FROM TILCARA: **1½HRS** 🚗

See the Magical Mountains

The colorful, jagged 'teeth' of the **Serranía de Hornocal** are one of the Quebrada de Humahuaca's most awesome sights. The mountains can be seen from a viewpoint located 25km (50 minutes' drive) east of Humahuaca via an unpaved road. Drivers at Humahuaca's bus terminal offer shared trips to the site in 4WD vehicles; check current road conditions before setting out in your own car.

Look out for vicuña on the epic road trip up the Hornocal viewpoint, located at 4350m. The Hornocal is most beautiful in the late afternoon, when the western sun brings out vivid hues.

SOLAR-POWERED TOURIST TRAIN

At research time, work was underway to repair the railway that once ran through the Quebrada de Humahuaca and operate a new tourist service using the world's first solar-powered trains. The reopening will begin with the 46km stretch of track from Volcán to Humahuaca, with stops in Tumbaya, Purmamarca, Maimará and Tilcara, scheduled to begin operation in late 2023. The plan is that in the future trains will run all the way north to La Quiaca, at the border with Bolivia. The original train line from San Salvador de Jujuy to La Quiaca was inaugurated in 1908, but ceased operating in 1993.

 WHERE TO EAT & DRINK IN HUMAHUACA

Aisito
Cozy restaurant serving local specialties including llama, quinoa and empanadas, plus pizza. $

Pachamanka
Creative variations of traditional regional dishes, wines from nearby bodegas, and live music. $$

Humahuagica
This lively bar on Calle Buenos Aires hosts regular performances by local folk musicians. $

Uquía

TIME FROM TILCARA: **30MINS**

See Armed Angels & Colorful Hills

Located just off the Ruta 9, the village of Uquía is easy to visit by bus or car from Tilcara (30 minutes) or Humahuaca (15 minutes). Here the 17th-century church includes paintings of *ángeles arcabuceros,* weapon-wielding angels.

From Uquía, you can hike to the Quebrada de las Señoritas, a striking mountain landscape of red, white and black rock, with canyons and caves. You'll need to go with a local guide; allow around three hours.

Afterwards, stop for a meal at Cerro Las Señoritas, where dishes are prepared from scratch using produce fresh from the garden.

Iruya

TIME FROM TILCARA: **4HRS**

Hike through Breathtaking Landscapes

Perched on a rock ledge overlooking the river, surrounded by epic mountain scenery and soaring condors, is the beguiling village of Iruya. This traditional indigenous village is four hours from Tilcara by bus; there are more frequent services from Humahuaca (three hours). From the Ruta 9 turnoff, 25km north of Humahuaca, an unpaved road ascends to a 4000m mountain pass at the border of Jujuy and Salta Provinces. From here, the road winds through a spectacular valley, until the pretty yellow and blue church of Iruya comes into view.

From Iruya, a wonderful 8km hike (two hours each way) leads to the neighboring village of San Isidro. From Iruya's plaza, follow the road past the car park and down into the valley. From here, the path bears left to follow the river, cross-

MORE YUNGAS FORESTS

The hills near Tucumán city have similar vegetation to those of the same height in Jujuy. Learn about Yungas flora and fauna at the **Reserva Experimental Horco Molle** (p200), then hike the nearby forest trails.

BEST TUNES FOR A NORTHWEST ROAD TRIP

Luna Tucumana
Atahualpa Yupanqui's beautiful ode to the Tucumán moon shining over the Tafí hills.

El Carnavalito (El Humahuaqueño)
Classic carnival song that's emblematic of the Quebrada de Humahuaca.

Viva Jujuy
Folklore group Los Tekis' celebration of their home province of Jujuy.

El Diablo de Humahuaca
Salta band Los Huayra's song about the Carnaval de Humahuaca's main protagonist.

Zamba Para Olvidarte
Salta native Daniel Toro's sad *zamba* about lost love; also covered by Mercedes Sosa.

WHERE TO EAT AND STAY IN IRUYA

Las Cachis
Restaurant on Iruya's main square selling simple but tasty plates of typical local dishes. $

Hostal Milmahuasi
Welcoming guesthouse with a cozy rooms and a fabulous terrace overlooking the hills. $

Hotel Iruya
Located at the top of town, this boutique hotel has tastefully decorated rooms with TVs and heating. $$

Iruya

INCA TRAILS IN THE QUEBRADA

Recognized as a Unesco World Heritage Site, Qhapaq Ñan (the Camino del Inca or the Inca Trail) is the name of the 30,000km Inca road network through the Andean mountains. In some places the Inca made use of existing trails to build a system across extreme terrains, traversing an area extending from Colombia to northwest Argentina, where it passes through Jujuy, Salta, Tucumán, Catamarca, La Rioja, San Juan and Mendoza.

Sections of the Camino del Inca pass through the Quebrada de Humahuaca. You can pick up the trail in the remote village of **Santa Ana**, south of the Serranía de Hornocal (p193), and hike into the Yungas forest of Valle Grande.

ing it in several places (look for strategically placed stepping stones). It's a peaceful trail beneath the open sky (wear a hat), surrounded by red, green and gold-hued mountain scenery and grazing donkeys. The path begins to climb on the approach to San Isidro, a lively little village that sits at the top of a flight of steps. There are several shops here selling water and snacks. Head to the terrace at Teresa's for empanadas; you might be serenaded by local folk singers.

Shorter walks in Iruya include the 15-minute stroll up to the Mirador de la Cruz, and the steep climb up to the Mirador del Cóndor on the eastern bank of the river. The best time for spotting condors is the afternoon.

Jujuy

TIME FROM TILCARA: 1½HRS 🚌

Market Grazing & Urban Walks

San Salvador de Jujuy is a vibrant city with a youthful feel and a culture rich with indigenous traditions but few visitor attractions. It is 1½ hours by car or bus south of Tilcara and two hours' drive north of Salta. Jujuy's airport is the closest for visiting the Quebrada de Humahuaca, making the city a convenient place to stop.

Start at the spotless Mercado Central 6 de Agosto, where the

🍽 WHERE TO EAT, DRINK AND STAY IN SAN SALVADOR DE JUJUY

Madre Tierra
Vegetarian cafe and bakery that uses its own homemade wholegrain flour; has a leafy patio. $

Casa Tomada
Bohemian events space, bar and vegetarian cafe; hosts regular live music and various workshops. $

El Arribo
Elegant family-run hotel with a patio garden and pool, large rooms and a central location. $$

YUYOENELESPACIO/SHUTTERSTOCK ©

Parque Nacional Calilegua

BEST JUJUY SPECIALTIES

Tortillas rellenas
Filled tortilla wraps cooked on a street-side charcoal grill; try the *caprese* (cheese, tomato and basil). Look for them in Tilcara and Purmamarca.

Quinoa
This grain is used to fill empanadas and is added to soups and salads.

Papas andinas
Small, multicolored potatoes with a nutty, earthy taste.

Llama
Look out for dishes prepared with llama meat.

Humita en chala
Grated corn mixed with onion and spices, wrapped in a *chala* (corn leaf) and steamed.

central food court sells specialty coffee, fresh fruit smoothies and savory tarts and pastries. Next, head to Plaza Belgrano to see the city's 18th-century cathedral, which has a gold-laminated baroque pulpit. Stop at one of the nearby pubs to drink a craft beer on the terrace, overlooking the square.

A lovely place for a walk, run or cycle is Parque Xibi Xibi, a lineal park extending for 2km along both banks of the river.

Discover Vibrant Cloud Forest

Explore the Parque Nacional Calilegua

Eastern Jujuy is a humid subtropical zone, with areas of cloud forest. At its center is Parque Nacional Calilegua, a biodiverse park extending to the Serranía de Calilegua range. If you have a car, the park can be visited on a day trip from San Salvador de Jujuy (1¾ hours); it is three hours' drive from Tilcara. Alternatively, you can book a tour.

Tucumán

The city of San Miguel de Tucumán is known across the country as the place where Argentina declared independence from Spain on July 9, 1816. The Casa de Independencia, where Congress met, is now a museum visited by streams of school children and Argentine families.

Tucumán has a down-to-earth vibe; the city center is clogged with traffic, noisy and alive. Temperatures are baking hot in summer and pleasantly warm on winter afternoons when the streets are brightened by the fruit of the orange trees. The afternoon siesta is observed year-round.

To the west of the city, the leafy neighborhood of Yerba Buena has high-end restaurants and country clubs. Beyond it lie the forest-covered hills of the Yungas.

Tucumán also has a strong folk music tradition, with musicians performing at the city's *peñas*. It was the birthplace of singer Mercedes Sosa, whose childhood home is now a museum.

Visit the Building where Argentina Declared Independence

The Room Where It Happened

For Argentines, the city of Tucumán's star attraction is the **Casa de la Independencia** (closed Mondays), a museum dedicated to the Declaration of Independence of July 9, 1816. The original room in which the Tucumán Congress met has been preserved; the rest of the museum is a reconstruction.

In the first room, where displays set the scene of colonial-era Tucumán, look for two of the building's original wooden doors, which were salvaged by a construction worker during demolition works in 1903. Decorated with portraits of the men who formed the Congress of 1816, **La Sala de la Jura** is the room where the Declaration of Independence was made. It was originally two rooms in a family home; an adobe wall was knocked down to accommodate the Congress attendees.

In the outdoor courtyard, two bronze reliefs by Tucumán artist Lola Mora celebrate the Revolution of May 25, 1810 in

GETTING AROUND

To use most city buses, you'll need a transport card (Tarjeta Ciudadana), available from a kiosk at the bus terminal. For bus routes and times, download the Tucubondi app or pick up a list from the tourist office. Buses 118, 102 and 100 link Tucumán city centre with Yerba Buena; bus 100 continues to Horco Molle, and bus 118 goes to the top of Cerro San Javier. Buses connect Tucumán with Tafí del Valle, Salta, Cafayate, Jujuy, Catamarca and La Rioja. There are several flights a day from Tucumán airport to Buenos Aires.

☑ TOP TIP

Tucumán is considered by many to produce Argentina's best empanadas, though some insist Salta's are superior. Empanadas from Salta are usually made with olives and potatoes as well as meat, while *empanadas tucumanas* are juicier, and made with fattier cuts of beef, onion and egg.

TUCUMÁN SALTA & THE ANDEAN NORTHWEST

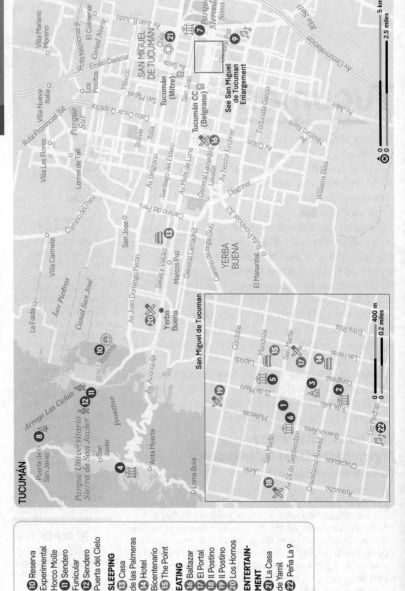

SIGHTS
1 Casa de Gobierno
2 Casa de la Independencia
  see 1 Casa Padilla
3 Catedral Metropolitana
4 Cristo Benedicto Statue
5 Federación Económica
  see 10 Jardín Botánico
6 Museo Folclórico
7 Museo Mercedes Sosa
8 Parque Sierra San Javier
9 El Cardon
10 Reserva Experimental Horco Molle
11 Sendero Funicular
12 Sendero Puerta del Cielo

SLEEPING
13 Casa de las Palmeras
14 Hotel Bicentenario
15 The Point

EATING
16 Baltazar
17 El Portal
18 Il Postino
19 Il Postino
20 Los Hornos

ENTERTAIN-MENT
21 La Casa de Yamil
22 Peña La 9

ACTIVITIES, COURSES & TOURS
9 El Cardon

San Miguel de Tucuman

Parque Universitario &
Sierra de San Javier

See San Miguel de Tucuman Enlargement

5 km
2.5 miles

400 m
0.2 miles

Buenos Aires and the signing of Declaration of Independence of 1816. María Remedios del Valle was a Black woman who fought on the battlefields of Salta and Tucumán during the War of Independence (1810–1818), and was awarded the title of captain by General Manuel Belgrano. She was later injured in battle, captured by Spanish royalists and subjected to a public flogging. Though she faced execution on several occasions, she survived the war and returned to live in Buenos Aires. However, she struggled to receive recognition as a captain and the corresponding salary.

In 2021, artists were invited to create portraits of Remedios del Valle. A digital copy of one of the winning entries can be seen in the Casa de la Independencia.

At night, the museum hosts a **sound and light show** that tells the story of Argentina's independence; buy tickets for the night's performance earlier the same day.

Explore Plaza Independencia
Tucumán's Central Square

Plaza Independencia has a number of interesting buildings. Begin in the southwestern corner at the **Catedral Metropolitana**; the neoclassical cathedral has a pediment depicting the Exodus. Take a short detour one block west along Av 24 de Septiembre to visit the **Museo Folclórico**, which displays gaucho paraphernalia and musical instruments including an armadillo *charango* (a small Andean guitar). Next, pop into the museum in **Casa Padilla**, a restored mid-19th-century house with a collection of Chinese pottery. Next door is the **Casa de Gobierno**, with an impressive facade that combines French baroque, Italian and art nouveau architectural styles. On the northern side of the square, a French-style building houses Tucumán's **Jockey Club**. Nearby, take a peek at the decorative tiles in the **Federación Económica**.

A Beloved Singer's Childhood Home
Visit the Museo Mercedes Sosa

Mercedes Sosa (1935–2009) was one of Argentina's most beloved singers, with a distinctive, powerful voice. The small house that was home to the Sosa family from 1880, and where Mercedes lived as a child, now houses a museum dedicated to the singer.

Displays include family photos and postcards, and details (in Spanish) of the key events in Sosa's life. In the 1960s, she was part of the Nuevo Cancionero music and literary movement. Then, during the Military Dictatorship of 1976–1983,

BEST PLACES TO EAT IN TUCUMÁN

El Portal
Rustic, city-center restaurant with indoor and outdoor tables; serves regional dishes and grilled meats. **$**

Il Postino
Pizza and pasta restaurant with branches on Junín and Córdoba in the city center. **$$**

Baltazar
This contemporary cafe, bar and restaurant in Yerba Buena has a large sunny terrace; it is open all day. **$$**

Los Hornos
Empanadas are baked the traditional way in the clay oven at this Yerba Buena restaurant. **$$**

WHERE TO HEAR FOLK MUSIC IN TUCUMÁN

La Casa de Yamil
This *peña* hosts regular performances by folk musicians, including a Sunday afternoon show.

Peña La 9
Lively *peña* with a young crowd and performances by a range of folk singers.

El Cardon
Come here for regional dishes – including excellent empanadas – accompanied by traditional folk music and dancing.

Sosa and her musicians were detained by police while performing on stage in La Plata; she spent the following years living in exile in Europe, before returning to Argentina in 1983. You can watch video recordings of Sosa performing in what was once the bedroom she shared with her parents.

In front of the museum, look for street art depicting Sosa playing a *bombo legüero* (an Argentine drum), and with her friend and collaborator Charly García.

Discover the Flora & Fauna of Cerro San Javier
Jungle Wildlife and Walks

The hills to the northwest of Tucumán are known as **Las Yungas**, which is also the name of the type of forest found here and in other areas of the eastern Andean foothills. Yungas forests are humid and biodiverse areas that are home to an array of wildlife.

You can learn about the Yungas ecosystem at the **Reserva Experimental Horco Molle**, at the western edge of Yerba Buena. Here you can visit the reserve's rehabilitation centre for native wildlife, where rescued animals and birds are nursed to health and released into the wild when possible. Join a guided tour to see tapirs, anteaters, macaws, toucans, pumas, and several species of native wildcats, among other wildlife. Nearby, take a walk around the reserve's expansive **Jardín Botánico**.

From Horco Molle, it's a 1.5km walk west to the starting point for several trails through the forests of **Parque Sierra San Javier**. The **Sendero Funicular** is a 2.5km linear trail along the tracks of a former funicular railway. The highlight is crossing three bridges, from which you can look down on the treetops below. After the third bridge, retrace your tracks; just before the first bridge look for the signed turnoff for the **Sendero Puerta del Cielo**. This steep 2km trail leads up Cerro San Javier; emerging through the trees are grassy areas with views across Tucumán city.

From here, you can follow the road south (uphill) for 2km to reach the 28m-high **Cristo Benedicto statue** at the top of Cerro San Javier. At dusk, the statue is lit up during a sound and light show. From here, you can take the 118 bus back to Tucumán.

YERBA BUENA

The leafy residential neighborhood of Yerba Buena extends east from Tucumán city to the hills of Las Yungas. Several hotels and guesthouses are located here, and there are a number of excellent cafes, bars and restaurants on Av Aconquija, the neighborhood's main thoroughfare. It makes a good base for exploring Cerro San Javier, and it's an easy journey by bus or taxi between Yerba Buena and the city centre. However, you'll need a Tarjeta Ciudadana transport card to pay for the city centre bus. You can get a transport card from the kiosk at the bus terminal.

WHERE TO STAY IN TUCUMÁN

Casa de las Palmeras
Upstairs bedrooms in a lovely family home in Yerba Buena, with attentive hosts and excellent breakfasts. $

The Point
Good-value, well-equipped and spacious self-catering apartments located in the city centre. $$

Hotel Bicentenario
City-center hotel with a rooftop pool and sundeck and a secure car park. $$$

Beyond
Tucumán

Ciudad Sagrada
de Quilmes

Amaicha del Valle

Tucumán

Tafí del Valle

El Mollar

From hiking through verdant mountains to visiting the ruins of Quilmes, there's plenty to explore in Tucumán's surrounds.

Though the province of Tucumán is relatively small (by Argentine standards), there is plenty to see. Opportunities for adventure abound, from horseback riding through the Tafí Valley to cycling through the hills. The area also has no shortage of cultural attractions, from a network of artisan home studios to an outdoor museum of carved standing stones.

Beyond Tafí are the extensive ruins of the Ciudad Sagrada de Quilmes, the remains of a city that was once home to a group of Diaguita Calchaquíes people. The site looks out over the valley towards the nearby village of Amaiche del Valle, where the Museo Pachamama houses remarkable sculptures honoring local deities.

GETTING AROUND

There are several buses a day from Tucumán city to Tafí del Valle; if you're driving, be aware that the road is steep and winding in parts. From Tafí, buses loop around the valley, but check times in advance to make sure you don't get stranded. You can also get around the valley by car, bike or on horseback.
Buses from Tafi del Valle to Cafayate stop in Amaiche del Valle, and can drop you at the turnoff for the Ciudad Sagrada de Quilmes, from where it's a 5km walk (there's no shade; bring water and a hat).

☑ **TOP TIP**

Don't rush through Tafí del Valle. With crisp mountain air and scenic walks, you'll want to stay a night or two.

JULIO RICCO/GETTY IMAGES ©

Ciudad Sagrada de Quilmes

HONORING THE PACHAMAMA

On August 1, communities in Jujuy, Salta and Tucumán hold ceremonies for the **Día de la Pachamama**, during which offerings are made to Mother Earth by placing items including coca leaves, maize, tobacco and chicha (a traditional fermented drink) in a hole in the ground.

Throughout the region, you'll see *apachetas*, altars composed of stones placed to give thanks to the Pachamama and ask for her protection; they are traditionally found on dangerous routes and mountaintops.

In February, the town of Amaiche del Valle in Tucumán hosts the **Fiesta Nacional de la Pachamama** to celebrate and give thanks for the harvest, with folk music, parades and parties.

IMAGEBROKER.COM GMBH & CO. KG/ALAMY STOCK PHOTO ©

El Mollar

Tafí del Valle

TIME FROM TUCUMÁN: 2½HRS

Follow the River to El Mollar

Surrounded by rolling hills, the valley town of Tafí del Valle, 110km by road from Tucumán city, offers plenty of opportunities for hiking, biking and horseback riding. One short, easy hiking trail climbs to the Mirador Cerro de la Cruz, from where there are views over town.

For a longer hike, follow the western bank of the Río Tafí south for 12km from Tafí del Valle to El Mollar, passing grazing horses and the Angostura Reservoir. Near El Mollar, look for a signed 1km trail past archaeological remains at Casas Viejas; these include old animal pens and two large rocks used for ceremonies and astrological observation.

In El Mollar, don't miss the Reserva Arqueológica de los Menhires, an outdoor museum housing 125 menhirs (carved granite standing stones) transported here from around the valley. The stones are around 2000 years old, and include representations of humans, cats, llamas and serpents. They were used for Andean rituals relating to ancestors and the land. Look for El Blanquito, a stone carved with two faces, and a nearby stone depicting a serpent with a human face. From El Mollar, you can catch the bus back to Tafí.

 WHERE TO EAT & STAY IN & AROUND TAFÍ DEL VALLE

Rancho de Félix
This large restaurant is a reliable spot for regional dishes, grilled meats and local wine. **$$**

Estancia Los Cuartos
Historic building with plenty of character, mountain views and grazing llamas out front. **$$**

Estancia Las Carreras
Surrounded by hills, 14km south of Tafí, this relaxing *estancia* offers horseback excursions and makes cheese. **$$$**

Shop for Crafts on the Ruta del Artesano

The Home Studios Include Ceramics, Textiles and Jewelry

The Ruta del Artesano driving or cycling route from Tafí del Valle features the home studios of some 20 artisans, whose work includes ceramics, textiles, jewelry and musical instruments. The Tucumán Turismo website (tucumanturismo.gob.ar) has a downloadable map of stops on the 45km loop around the valley, which includes home studios in Tafí del Valle, El Rincón and El Mollar. Stop at Estancia Las Carreras (built in 1718) to visit the cheese factory and take in the views.

Following the route is a lovely way to see the countryside, meet local people, and support their work.

Amaicha del Valle   TIME FROM TUCUMÁN: 4HRS

Visit the Museo Pachamama

The town of Amaicha del Valle, 50km north of Tafí del Valle, is the location of a remarkable collection of stone sculptures created by the artist Héctor Cruz in 1996 in celebration of the Pachamama (Mother Earth). A visit to the Museo Pachamama can be combined with a trip to the nearby archaeological site of Quilmes (p204).

Part museum, part outdoor art gallery, the Museo Pachamama houses remarkable large-scale stone sculptures honoring traditional local spiritual beliefs' key figures and deities. Pick up a booklet from the museum reception explaining the significance of the pieces, which are surrounded by the scenic backdrop of the hills of the Valles Calchaquíes.

First, look for a representation in the paving stones of the goddess who provides water for crops. Nearby is an impressive sculpture of a shaman. The Pachamama Mask sculpture is Cruz's of-

WEAVERS IN WESTERN CATAMARCA

In **Belén** (p211) and **Londres** (p210), visit weaving workshops and to see artisans producing ponchos, blankets and rugs using traditional techniques.

WALKS NEAR TAFÍ DEL VALLE

Tucumán local **Carla Acosta** shares her favorite local walks.

Molle Solo
A lovely rural area by the river, at the foot of Cerro Muños, 8km south of Tafí. It can be accessed from Ovejaria.

Cascada de los Alisos
This waterfall is quite popular, but most people access it from Las Carreras. An alternative route is to walk from Santa Cruz, passing archaeological sites and some beautiful natural pools where you can take a dip. It's best to go with a local guide.

Cascada el Rincón
This is a smaller waterfall that not many people know about, located in the greenest, most picturesque part of the valley, 20km southwest of Tafí.

 ## WHERE TO EAT & STAY IN & AROUND TAFÍ DEL VALLE

Casa Alpiste Comiste
Lovely B&B on the edge of Tafí with an onsite vegan and gluten-free cafe. $

Descanso de las Piedras
Riverside cabins in a bucolic setting, with hammocks and a heated pool; great for families. $

Restaurante el Museo
A historic Jesuit chapel is the atmospheric location of this lunchtime restaurant serving local dishes. $

fering to Mother Earth; it has two sides, one representing the sun god (Inti) and the other representing the moon goddess (Quilla). Both have feline crowns representing the guardians of the gods.

There are also galleries with displays on the region's geology and culture, with re-creations of early dwellings. The museum gift shop sells locally produced rugs and handicrafts.

Ciudad Sagrada de Quilmes

TIME FROM TUCUMÁN: 4½HRS

Discover the Remains of the Sacred City

Located 5km west of the Ruta 40, 75km northwest of Tafí del Valle, are the remains of the Ciudad Sagrada de Quilmes. Here, you can visit the ruins of what was once a thriving city, home to a group of Diaguita Calchaquíes people known as the Quilmes.

Start at the site's modern museum, where you can learn about the history and culture of the Quilmes before visiting the ruins. Detailed displays offer explanations (in English and Spanish) of the Quilmes people's spiritual and religious practices, farming techniques and everyday life activities. The city was invaded by the Inca in 1480, after which time the Diaguita language of Kakán was replaced with Quechua, and then by the Spanish in 1535; the Quilmes people resisted the Spanish for 130 years until they were finally defeated in 1665. In the museum, an evocative film depicts the 1300km march across Argentina to Buenos Aires that the Spanish forced the defeated Quilmes to take.

Next, a local guide will introduce you to the site (most of the guides are from the same ethnic group – the Diaguita Calchaquíes – as the people who once lived here, and might even be their descendants). You can place a stone on the *apacheta* as an offering to the Pachamama, then follow the arrows around the remains. The settlement includes defensive outposts and houses; high on the hillside were the buildings where soldiers and shamans lived. Look out for the ceremonial millstones. Follow the trail up to the northern *pucará* (defensive fort) for views over the remains and across the valley to the distant hills; it's a great spot for photos.

BEST ACTIVITIES IN TUCUMÁN

Horseback Riding
Explore Tafí del Valle on horseback on a guided ride (p202).

Paragliding
Take a tandem flight over the Yungas from Loma Bola on Cerro San Javier.

Hiking
Explore the Yungas (p200) and the hills surrounding Tafí del Valle.

Mountain Biking
Hit the hills on two wheels on some of the northwest's best trails.

High Ropes Course
Balance on narrow planks and zipline between trees at Parque Aéreo Raki.

Kayaking
Celestino Gelsi reservoir in El Cadillal is a scenic spot to go for a paddle.

OTHER ARCHAEOLOGICAL SITES

Don't miss the extensive remains of an Inca city at **El Shincal** (p210) near Belén in Catamarca Province. On the outskirts of Catamarca city, visit the remains of an Aguada Culture settlement at **Pueblo Perdido de la Quebrada** (p207).

Catamarca

BUENOS
AIRES

San Fernando del Valle de Catamarca, or SFVC for short, is a youthful, affluent city that makes a pleasant place to spend a couple of days before or after adventures further west.

The city's notably pink cathedral houses the Virgen del Valle; twice a year, she's dressed in a new hand-embroidered robe and paraded through town. Catamarca's most interesting sight is the Pueblo Perdido de la Quebrada, where you can visit the remains of an Aguada culture settlement in a beautiful spot by the river. Ceramics found at the site can be seen in the city's excellent archaeological museum.

Catamarca's hotels book up fast during the Fiesta Nacional del Poncho in July, which is celebrated with huge outdoor artisan markets, folk concerts and plenty of regional food. Local specialties to try include wine, olives, cheese and walnuts.

GETTING AROUND

To use local buses you'll need a SUBE card, available at kiosks (SUBE cards issued in Jujuy and Buenos Aires work here). To reach Pueblo Perdido, take bus 101 from Calle Salta, between Republica and Esquiú. You can also get around by e-bike. Buses for La Rioja, Tucumán and Belén leave from the city center terminal.

☑ TOP TIP

Bici Catamarca offers electronic bike rental and guided city cycling tours from its office in Plaza 25 de Mayo. It's necessary to book in advance by calling or sending a Whatsapp message to +54 9 3834 50-2844. Locations to visit include the dam at **Lago Lumeal** in the west of the city.

Virgen del Valle (p206)

Catamarca's city center sights are clustered within a few blocks of Plaza 25 de Mayo. Start at the ❶ **Museo Arqueológico Adán Quiroga**, an archaeological museum with a large collection of ceramics from different cultures and eras. Don't miss the black Aguada ceramics decorated with animal motifs.

South of the museum, on Calle Sarmiento, stop to browse sidewalk stalls selling local produce including olive oil, honey, walnuts, spices, and a huge range of medicinal herbs. On Calle Esquiú, look for ❷ **Burrata Vinoteca y Delicatessen**, stocked full of Catamarca wines, cheeses and salamis, as well as cigars made with local tobacco.

Walk one block south along Sarmiento to reach ❸ **Plaza 25 de Mayo**, with a statue of independence hero José de San Martín astride his horse in its center. On the west-

ern side of the square, look for the bright pink exterior of ❹ **Catedral Basílica de Nuestra Señora del Valle**, the 19th-century cathedral housing the Virgen del Valle. When you enter the main cathedral you'll see her back. Take the side entrance from the pedestrian lane next to the cathedral to reach the Camarín de la Virgen chapel, with beautiful floor tiles, ornate moldings and stained glass, where you can come face to face with the Virgin.

Continue along the alley around the back of the cathedral to reach the ❺ **Museo de la Virgen del Valle**. Here you can see artistic representations of the Virgin; don't miss the room devoted to her hand-embroidered capes. Twice a year (two weeks after Easter and on September 8) hordes of pilgrims arrive in Catamarca to join the procession as the venerated Virgin is led through town.

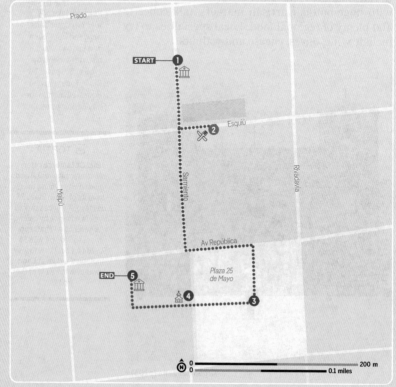

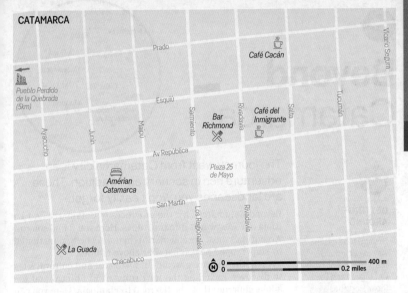

CATAMARCA

Prado

Café Cacán

Pueblo Perdido de la Quebrada (5km)

Esquiú

Bar Richmond

Café del Inmigrante

Av República

Plaza 25 de Mayo

Amérian Catamarca

San Martín

La Guada

Chacabuco

0   400 m
0   0.2 miles

Vicario Segura

Tucumán

Salta

Rivadavia

Sarmiento

Maipú

Junín

Ayacucho

Los Regionales

Rivadavia

Discover the Hilltop Ruins of the Pueblo Perdido de la Quebrada

Riverside Remains

On a beautiful hillside beneath higher mountain peaks, 6km west of Plaza 25 de Mayo, are the remains of an Aguada culture settlement known as the **Pueblo Perdido de la Quebrada**. The ruins are just off the main road, opposite a pretty stretch of the **Río el Tala**, where there are walking trails along the riverbank. It is a lovely spot for a picnic, under the shade of the trees. The road here is popular with local cyclists.

The remains can be visited on guided tours, during which you'll see residential dwellings with curved doorways to prevent llamas from getting in, workshops where ceramics and arrowheads were found, and a shared kitchen. The site was inhabited between 200 and 450 CE by people from the Aguada culture, and was not occupied by the Inca. One of the culture's gods was the jaguar, who is represented on ceramics founds at the site and housed in the Museo Arqueológico Adán Quiroga. At the top of the hill is a ceremonial space; here stones mark the position of the summer and winter solstice, used to mark time for sowing crops and harvesting.

Don't miss the small museum, housed in a building that replicates the style of the village's original stone and adobe constructions, but constructed using modern materials. Images show how the village would once have looked.

BEST PLACES TO EAT, DRINK & STAY IN CATAMARCA

Bar Richmond
Overlooking Plaza 25 de Mayo, it serves excellent pizzas. **$$**

Café del Inmigrante
A beautifully restored building makes an elegant setting for a latte, brunch, or afternoon cocktail. **$$**

Café Cacán
Specialty coffee, pastries and *merienda* (afternoon tea). **$**

La Guada
A blackboard menu lists the day's dishes, including meat grilled on the *parrilla*. **$$$**

Amérian Catamarca
The Catamarca branch of the Amérian chain offers well-equipped rooms. **$$**

Beyond
Catamarca

El Shincal
de Quimivíl
Fiambalá •
• Belén
Lavalle
Tinogasta • La Gruta
Catamarca Frías
Chumbicha
Chilecito
Villa Unión •
• La Rioja
Parque Nacional
Talampaya
Patquia
Chamical

GETTING AROUND

Driving is the easiest way to get around the provinces of Catamarca and La Rioja. Hertz has a car rental office in Catamarca; book ahead. Buses connect Catamarca and La Rioja, La Rioja and Chilecito, Catamarca and Belén, and Catamarca and Fiambalá, but there are no buses between Belén and Chilecito. You can reach Parque Nacional Talampaya by bus from Chilecito (via Villa Unión) or La Rioja. To explore Western Catamarca beyond Fiambalá, you'll need to drive or to take a tour.

☑ TOP TIP

During the afternoon siesta (between 1pm and 5pm) expect to find businesses closed and streets empty throughout Catamarca and La Rioja.

The journey west from Catamarca city is an adventure rich in scenery and tradition. These are landscapes you won't easily forget.

Beyond Catamarca city, the provinces of Catamarca and La Rioja rise westwards into the Andes. Here you'll find some of Argentina's most spectacular highland scenery, punctuated by snowcapped peaks that soar above 6000m.

Along the way are a wealth of historical and cultural sites to discover, including the Inca ruins at El Shincal and the adobe churches that line the road to Fiambalá. Here you can spend the morning sandboarding down desert dunes and the afternoon soaking in hot springs.

In Catamarca and La Rioja, the journey is really the best part: the drive south from Tinogasta to Chilecito is breathtaking, as is the route from Chilecito to Parque Nacional Talampaya, via the Cuesta de Miranda.

WIRESTOCK CREATORS/SHUTTERSTOCK ©

Ruta Los Seismiles

From Fiambalá, the paved Ruta 60 climbs through desert, red rock and high mountain plains to Paso de San Francisco at the Chilean border. It makes a stunning drive. Los Seismiles, for which the route is named, are the area's six peaks above 6000m, including Ojos del Salado (6893m), the world's highest volcano. It's 200km each way from Fiambalá; allow five hours for the round trip and fill up with fuel before setting out.

After 23km, look for the turnoff for **❶ Cañón del Indio**, where you can hike to see rocks that resemble the faces of local indigenous people. Drive along the sand road to reach a parking area, then hike 2km through the peaceful canyon to see the formation. The route involves some scrambling over rocks.

Back on the Ruta 60, the road follows the river and soon begins to wind through the dramatic red rock escarpments of the **❷ Quebrada de las Angosturas** (be sure to slow down for the bends) before emerging into the high mountain plains.

The only place to stop for supplies along the way is **❸ Hostería Cortaderas** (p211), a hotel 95km from Fiambalá, where the restaurant offers hot meals with incredible views. At night the clear, dark skies are perfect for stargazing.

From here, you'll pass through icy wetlands teeming with flamingos, yellow tundra home to grazing vicuñas, and see the spectacular Seismiles behind other snowcapped peaks.

For most of the year, the road ends at **❹ La Gruta**, the Argentine border post 21km from Chile. The **❺ San Francisco** border crossing opens once a week on Wednesdays; if you plan to cross into Chile, check the border is open before setting out (argentina.gob.ar).

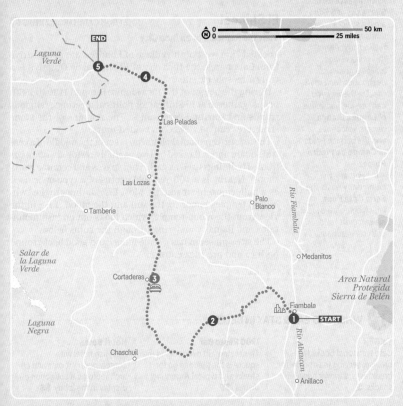

RODRIGO.FOTOSI/SHUTTERSTOCK ©

Iglesia de San Pedro, Ruta del Adobe

ADVENTURES IN THE WILD NORTHWEST

High in the mountains of northwest Catamarca, 300km (five hours by car) beyond Belén, the village of **Antofagasta de la Sierra** sits at 3320m amid a spectacular landscape. If you are feeling adventurous, this puna village makes a great destination for a road trip. On the way you can see the flamingos of **Laguna Blanca**, remote volcanoes, and the pumice fields of **Campo de Piedra Pomez**.

In February, the community hosts the **Feria de la Puna**, which celebrates local artisan crafts and cultural traditions.

El Shincal

TIME FROM CATAMARCA: **3½HRS**

Visit the Remains of an Inca City

Located 7km west of the village of Londres, 3½ hours' drive from Catamarca, the Inca city of El Shincal de Quimivil is a truly atmospheric site.

During the height of the Inca empire (around 1430 to 1580) people gathered at El Shincal for political meetings, religious rituals and spiritual ceremonies. The remains of the stone structures can be viewed on guided tours.

The *ushnu* (ceremonial platform) is set in the middle of a central square and is flanked by two partially restored *kallankas* (roofed buildings used as gathering spaces and ceramic workshops). Nearby is a 400-year-old cactus of a type once used as a hallucinogenic medicine. Most fascinating are the twin hilltop temples honoring the sun and the moon. Take in the view from the moon temple, which looks out on lush mountains and llamas wandering through the ruins below.

The site's museum has a scale model and good background on Inca and pre-Inca culture.

WHERE TO EAT & STAY IN BELÉN

Ya'Güir
Cafe with local books to browse, serving tea and coffee, breakfasts, sandwiches and snacks. $

1900 Resto Bar
This restaurant overlooking the square is the place to go for steaks and typical Argentine dishes. $$

Hotel Belén
A stylish hotel with contemporary rooms and an archaeological collection on display in the lobby. $$

Belén
TIME FROM CATAMARCA: **4HRS**

Watch Artisans at Work

In Belén, four hours' drive from Catamarca city, you can visit the cooperative workshop Arañitas Hilanderas. Here artisans will show you the different stages of the weaving process, from cleaning and spinning the wool, coloring it with natural dyes (different shades are produced using *yerba mate* and nut shells, among other items), and weaving the pieces on traditional looms. Items are sold at the site's shop.

Elsewhere in town, stop by to see the artisan ponchos of Rua Chaky. Nearby, Familia Avar Saracho has a range of high-quality pieces, including shoes.

Tinogasta to Fiambalá

TIME FROM CATAMARCA: **3½HRS**

Visit the Churches of the Ruta del Adobe

Beginning just south of the dusty town of Tinogasta, 3½ hours' drive from Catamarca, the RN 60 to Fiambalá is known as the Ruta del Adobe on account of the historic adobe buildings located near the main road. These are built with thick walls of mud and straw and have cane roofs supported by algarrobo beams.

The first stop is the ruins of the Capellanía Pituil Viejo in the hamlet of Copacabana. Nearby, the historic Finca la Sala is a lovely place to stop for lunch.

Continue north through Tinogasta, then take a detour through the village of El Puesto to see the Oratorio de los Orquera, a small adobe chapel next to an ancient olive tree. The most impressive building along the route is the Iglesia de Andacolla; look for the turnoff on the left just before crossing the river, 2km north of El Puesto. At the southern entrance to Fiambalá is the whitewashed Iglesia de San Pedro, which dates from 1770.

See the Mummies of Fiambalá
TIME FROM CATAMARCA: **4½HRS**

The Museum of the Mummified Inca

In Fiambalá, the Museo del Hombre is a small regional museum that houses the mummified bodies of an Inca man and woman that were found near Loro Huasi. Displayed nearby are woven textiles and a miniature female statue that were found with the bodies. You can also see some quality ceramics dating from 650 to 850 AD, including anthropomorphic figures.

BEST PUNA WILDLIFE

Flamingo
See them at the lake at Cortaderas on the Ruta Los Seismiles (p209).

Red Fox
Look out for them in the mountains near Fiambalá.

Vicuña
See them near the Paso de San Francisco on the Ruta Los Seismiles.

Puma
Catamarca is home to Andean Pumas, though you probably won't spot them.

Rhea (South American Ostrich)
You might see rheas near Fiambalá.

Vizcacha
These creatures look like a cross between a rodent and a rabbit.

 WHERE TO EAT & STAY IN WESTERN CATAMARCA

Casona del Pino
Lovely boutique hotel in an old *casona* in Fiambalá. Breakfast is eaten around a shared antique table. **$**

Finca la Sala
Historic Finca near Tinogasta with elegant rooms, lush gardens and an excellent restaurant. **$$**

Hostería Cortaderas
Located at 3000m on the Ruta los Seismiles, this hotel and restaurant has an unbeatable mountain setting. **$$**

MINING IN FAMATINA

Chilecito's cable car was constructed in 1904 by a German engineering company and used to transport gold, silver and copper from Famatina mountain down to the railway terminus at Chilecito.

The minerals were loaded into trolleys at **La Mejicana**, at an altitude of 4600m, more than 3500m higher than Chilecito and nearly 40km away. The cable car ceased operating in 1927.

Since then, several multinational companies have sought to resume mining at Famatina, but protests by the local population have prevented any new mining projects from going ahead. The mountain is the source of the area's water supply, and the slogan *El Famatina no se toca* (Don't touch Famatina) can be seen across the region.

Parque Nacional Talampaya

GUILLERMO CAFFARINI/SHUTTERSTOCK ©

Sandboarding and Hot Springs

TIME FROM CATAMARCA: **1HR** 🚗

From Thrill to Chill in the Same Day

The stunning golden sand dunes located 15km north of Fiambalá are a beautiful place to go sandboarding. Similar to snowboarding, the sport involves standing on a board and riding down the slopes of tall sand dunes; you can also sit on the board, or lie on your belly. The Duna Mágica is east of the village of Saujil (the route is signed); a number of places in the Saujil rent boards, as do most accommodations in Fiambalá. It is best to come in the morning, before the winds pick up, when you can spend hours trudging up and riding down the dunes. You'll need your own vehicle to get here.

Afterwards, you can soak your tired muscles in the nearby Termas de Fiambalá. These hot springs are located in a truly magical setting, in a verdant creek between the mountain rock face, looking out over desert plains. Tickets are sold at the tourist office at Fiambala's Plaza Principal (bring ID), from where it's a 15km (20 minute) drive through desert dunes to the termas. At the complex, hot water cascades down through a series of pools, ranging in temperature from 24°C to 48°C.

WHERE TO EAT & STAY IN CHILECITO

El Rancho de Ferrito
A neighborhood favorite that hasn't changed in years, serving grilled meat and local wines. **$$**

Borussia
This bar on the main square has great decor and good vibes; it serves the usual pizzas and burgers. **$$**

El Viejo Molino
This guesthouse has warm, helpful owners and bright modern rooms with mountain views. **$**

Chilecito

TIME FROM CATAMARCA: **4HRS** 🚐

Cable Cars & Colorful Rivers

Set amid cactus-covered rocks, against a backdrop of snow-capped Sierra de Famatina mountain peaks, the former mining town of Chilecito has wineries and a number of worthwhile sights to visit. It is four hours by car from Catamarca city.

The town's top attraction is the Museo de Cablecarril, which includes museums at the first two stations of the town's former cable car. Start at Estación 1, where a museum documents the extraordinary engineering project. The cable-car system was built in the early 20th century to transport gold, silver and copper down from the mines; exhibits include old photographs and mine workers' boots. Outside the museum are the rusted structures of the cable-car terminus. Next, head 11km northeast to Estación 2, where you can see the motors and machinery of the steam-powered system. The hilltop industrial structures and mountain backdrop make for great photos.

From Estación 2, you can take a 5km detour along a dirt road to see the incredible Unión de los Ríos. Here the bright yellow waters of the Río Amarillo meet the sky-blue Río de la Quebrada del Agua Negra (the name is deceptive). Follow signs to a parking area, from where you can walk 200m to the exact spot where the colored rivers meet.

Parque Nacional Talampaya

TIME FROM CATAMARCA: **4HRS** 🚐

View the Impressive Rock Formations

Parque Nacional Talampaya encompasses a vast expanse of remarkable red rock formations and sandstone cliffs, four hours' drive from Catamarca.

Access to the park is only permitted by guided tour. From the Cañón de Talampaya entrance, tours set off by bus or jeep, with stops at the green oasis of the Jardín Botánico and at various dramatic rock formations. You'll also see fascinating petroglyphs, some of which could be as much as 2500 years old. The engravings include depictions of llamas and an image thought to have been drawn by a shaman while under the influence of hallucinogenics.

Tours by 4WD to the rock formations at Ciudad Perdida and Cañón Arco Iris start from an entrance 14km south. Nighttime tours are offered when there is a full moon.

BEST FESTIVALS IN CATAMARCA AND LA RIOJA

Feria de la Puna
Llamas take center stage at this celebration of traditional Andean culture, held in Antofagasta de la Sierra in February.

Fiesta de Nuestra Señora del Valle
Two weeks after Easter and on December 8, the Virgen de la Valle is led on a procession through Catamarca city.

Fiesta Nacional del Poncho
This celebration of local handicrafts and folk music takes place in Catamarca city in July.

La Chaya
In February, La Rioja residents get soaked in a huge water fight.

El Tinkunaco
On December 31, this ceremony in La Rioja reenacts friar Francisco Solano's 1593 mediation between the Diaguitas and Spanish colonialists.

Above: Catedral Nuestra Señora de la Asunción (p222); Right: Capilla del Monte (p254)

Córdoba & the Central Sierras

VIBRANT, AUSTERE, DESOLATE AND CHARMING

While the vibrant city of Córdoba oft eclipses its surroundings, the region holds a diverse spread of beauty, activities, history and charm.

The second-largest city in Argentina, and arguably the second most important after the capital of Buenos Aires, Córdoba has all the joys of a big city – wonderful museums, great restaurants, beautiful architecture, a vibrant nightlife – yet still feels in many ways like a small, easygoing town. Step out of the city, though, and you'll quickly find it as varied and different a place as anywhere in Argentina. Drive less than an hour and find a range of odd, rock-strewn mountains home to the iconic Andean condor. Pop into tiny mining towns that somehow still hold on to Argentine traditions of a century ago. Seek out lagoons, reservoirs and salt flats for otherworldly, almost lunar landscapes and amazing birdlife, or head to the spectacular Parque Nacional Sierra de las Quijadas, which, despite its beauty, manages to feel as isolated and pristine as can be. If you haven't spotted condors in the Sierras, look for them in the eroded, iron-red canyons. Ruins of Jesuit missions and supposedly haunted hotels await the adventurous. Then, hop back by nightfall for a delightful evening at a fancy restaurant, followed by Argentine tango at one of Córdoba's beautiful, welcoming *milongas*. The region can be explored in a series of day trips or by moving from place to place – either way, you'll find more than enough to enjoy.

MICHAL KNITL /SHUTTERSTOCK ©

THE MAIN AREAS

CÓRDOBA	SAN LUIS	THE SIERRAS
Argentina's second-largest city. **p220**	Capital of San Luis Province. **p230**	Hiking and natural beauty. **p239**

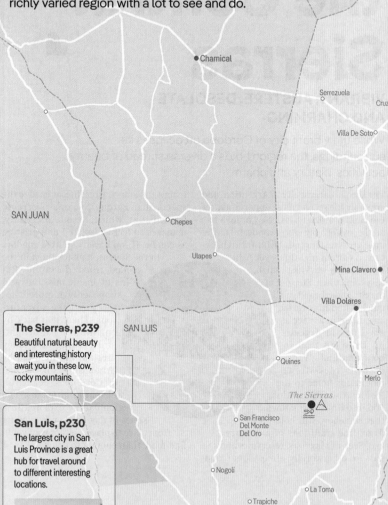

Find Your Way

Córdoba and the surrounding region are oft overlooked as people zip to Tierra del Fuego or north to Iguazú Falls, but it's a richly varied region with a lot to see and do.

Totoralejos

Chamical

Serrezuela

Cruz D

Villa De Soto

SAN JUAN

Chepes

Ulapes

Mina Clavero

Villa Dolares

The Sierras, p239

Beautiful natural beauty and interesting history await you in these low, rocky mountains.

SAN LUIS

Quines

Merlo

The Sierras

San Francisco
Del Monte
Del Oro

San Luis, p230

The largest city in San Luis Province is a great hub for travel around to different interesting locations.

Nogolí

La Toma

Trapiche

San Luis

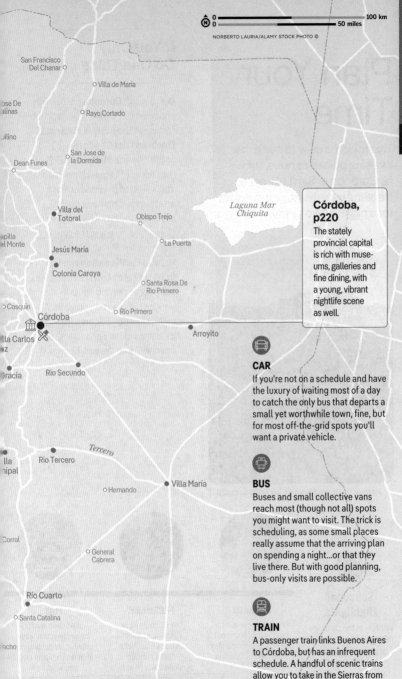

NORBERTO LAURIA/ALAMY STOCK PHOTO ©

San Francisco
Del Chanar

Villa de María

ose De
alinas

Rayo Cortado

uilino

San Jose de
la Dormida

Dean Funes

*Laguna Mar
Chiquita*

Córdoba, p220

The stately provincial capital is rich with museums, galleries and fine dining, with a young, vibrant nightlife scene as well.

Villa del
Totoral

Obispo Trejo

apilla
el Monte

La Puerta

Jesús María

Colonia Caroya

Santa Rosa De
Rio Primero

Cosquin

Córdoba

Río Primero

lla Carlos
az

Arroyito

Gracia

Rio Secundo

Tercero

lla
nipal

Rio Tercero

Villa María

Hernando

Corral

General
Cabrera

Río Cuarto

Santa Catalina

acho

CAR

If you're not on a schedule and have the luxury of waiting most of a day to catch the only bus that departs a small yet worthwhile town, fine, but for most off-the-grid spots you'll want a private vehicle.

BUS

Buses and small collective vans reach most (though not all) spots you might want to visit. The trick is scheduling, as some small places really assume that the arriving plan on spending a night...or that they live there. But with good planning, bus-only visits are possible.

TRAIN

A passenger train links Buenos Aires to Córdoba, but has an infrequent schedule. A handful of scenic trains allow you to take in the Sierras from the comfort of a railcar.

217

Plan Your Time

This region is easy to see either by using places as hubs, such as Córdoba or San Luis, or by traveling linearly, staying in a spot for a night or two before moving on.

Parque Nacional Sierra de las Quijadas (p236)

If You Only Do One Thing

● In a word: **Córdoba** (p220). This charming city makes a perfect hub for seeing the **Parque Nacional Quebrada del Condorito** (p242) or the mystical **Miramar** (p229) on the shores of Laguna Mar Chiquita. You will want to spend at least an afternoon, perhaps several, exploring the city itself, enjoying the architecture and the canal.

Head to the **Plaza San Martín** (p372) to catch quiet Córdoba life, see people playing cards in the park, or kids chasing pigeons. At night, seek out **Güemes** (p255) for its warren of bars and cafes, all open well into the wee hours.

Seasonal Highlights

Winters in the cities are mild overall but can dip at night. The Sierras can be quite cold. Summers are hot and, at times, quite humid.

JANUARY

Keep your eye out for the Festival Nacional del Folklore, a nine-day affair held in Cosquín.

FEBRUARY

The Cosquín Rock Festival, a kind of Córdoba Coachella, draws famous musicians and their fans from around the world.

MAY

Antipodean winter is beginning. You'll see the locals putting on their down puffer coats and wool hats.

Three Days to Travel Around

● You'll want to spend at least a night in **Córdoba** (p220), exploring what the city has to offer. Then head west to the Sierras, where you can explore tiny towns and villages with beautiful riverside *balenarios* (swimming spots), such as **Mina Clavero** (p240) or **La Cumbrecita** (p250).

● From there, explore **San Luis** (p230) and its salt flat, check out some birdlife at **La Florida** (p238) reservoir, and then head north, to mystical **Miramar** (p229), where haunted hotels and flocks of flamingos await.

More Than a Week

● More than a week gives you the luxury of really delving into everything that makes **Córdoba** (p220) tick, then meandering through the mountains, stopping and appreciating every small town. They're all different; each has something special to offer the traveler.

● From **Mina Clavero** (p240) and **La Cumbrecita** (p250) to the lesser visited spots of **El Volcán** (p247) and **La Florida** (p238).

● Do an overnight (or at least a whole day) exploring the incredible **Parque Nacional Sierra de las Quijadas** (p236), where you may see Andean condors.

JULY
Festival Nacional del Tango draws dancers from around the country to Córdoba's **La Falda** (p227) town.

SEPTEMBER
Bookworms will want to look for the Feria del Libro, held in mid-September in **Córdoba** (p220).

OCTOBER
Beer-guzzlers will be sure to enjoy the region's many Oktoberfests, celebrating the area's German heritage.

NOVEMBER
Team Summer, rejoice: it's warm and summery and even hot. Grab a *mate* and some mates and welcome the sunshine.

BUENOS
AIRES

Córdoba

GETTING AROUND

Córdoba is served by an international airport, trains, and an excellent bus system for transport in and around the city. Taxis are easy to flag, and metered service means you shouldn't be charged more than what's expected. Electric bicycles are fast becoming an alternative way to get around.

☑ **TOP TIP**

Don't withdraw money from ATMs here (or anywhere in Argentina). The usurious conversion rates and paltry max withdrawals make it feel like robbery. Use Western Union or another money sending service and send to yourself, at the vastly better 'blue' rates.

Landlocked and far away from Buenos Aires, Córdoba might be easily overlooked by travelers, but those who do are missing out. Argentina's second-largest city is rich with hip, hot, up-and-coming spots to explore, and a vibrant, youthful nightlife scene. Its many universities mean there's lots of artsy, avant-garde projects going on.

That's not to say the city doesn't also have an austere, stately, elegant side. Its wide avenues, colonial-era buildings, Jesuit missions and many parks balance the rainbow-colored hair, tattoos and piercings. In one day you can see some of the world's finest art, dine on anything from cheap street eats to white tablecloth and candle-lit luxury, and then party until sunup in clubs every bit as trendy as those in Buenos Aires. When the city tires, escape to beautiful mountains, dusty plains or mystical lagoons.

SAIKOSP/SHUTTERSTOCK ©

Plaza San Martín

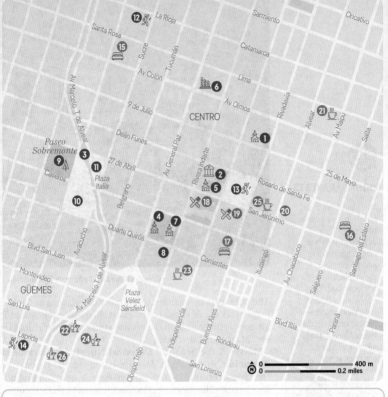

A Park, Pigeons & Parakeets...Oh, My!

Beautiful Plaza San Martín

Córdoba has a delightful wealth of parks and outdoor spaces, but one of the most impressive – and arguably the most important – is the beautiful **Plaza San Martín**. Named (as are all the Plazas San Martín in Argentina) after the historical figure José de San Martín, it's a charming part of the city.

Catedral Nuestra Señora de la Asunción

MONK PARAKEETS

You can't miss them, not even if you close your eyes. They're as loud as they are bright; squawking and squabbling, they'll circle in a flock overhead, then alight and – despite their vivid colors – almost vanish in the trees. These flashy, neon-green birds are so common they'd be a nuisance if they weren't so darn pretty. Monk Parakeets (also called the Quaker Parrot) are a 'true parrot'. For the ornithologists, they're an official member of the family Psittacidae. They're widespread here in Argentina but are a hardy bird infamous for establishing colonies (due to escapees) as far north as Massachusetts, USA.

The parakeets here almost outnumber the pigeons and make huge nests out of sticks in the giant shade trees or squabble among themselves atop the bronze statue of General José de San Martín on horseback.

Marvel at the beautiful **Catedral Nuestra Señora de la Asunción**, one of many Jesuit missions in the region and the oldest continually functioning church in all of Argentina. Construction began in 1582, but it wasn't officially consecrated until the early 1700s. The building's exterior is austere and grand, but if you've got time, duck inside to see the spectacular ceilings and decorations: ornate, gilded woodwork, lofty arches with frescoes and murals. It's a beautiful, calming place even for the non-religious. Next door is the stately **Cabildo de Córdoba**, a combined museum and performance space, where, if you're lucky, there'll be an orchestra performing or an art show. In a sprawling city like Córdoba, it's often tricky to decide what feels like the 'center', but here, it's not hard to sit on a park bench, close your eyes, and imagine yourself transported back a few centuries to a bustling 1700s-era town, parakeets and all.

PLACES TO EAT IN CÓRDOBA

El Solar de Tejeda
Alfresco dining in the shadow of Nuestra Señora de la Asunción. $$

Oriental Plaza
This clean, non-greasy spoon diner is open 24 hours. $

Bursátil
This stylish coffeeshop and more has great service, good food and reasonable prices. $$

Architecture Everywhere
Córdoba's Streets Are a Museum

Even those with only a scant interest in architecture will find it hard not to stop at every street corner and marvel at the buildings here, and not just the Jesuit missions. There's plazas, artsy galleries and public administration buildings, which lend a stately, regal air to even the most casual of walks here. Add the fact that you're likely to see parakeets instead of pigeons jostling for position atop statues in the parks, and you've got a city that's truly like no other. Elaborate moldings and cornices, columns adorned in Corinthian, Doric or Ionic styles, the beautiful arches that make even the most humble doorway seem as if it has a frame around it.

Certainly, you'll want to visit Plaza San Martín, but other places well worth meandering about are the **Paseo Marqués de Sobremonte**, where the Córdoba capital building sits, with its regal Greco-Roman style majesty and playful fountains. It's a lovely park that's perfect for jogging or walking, or pushing a stroller around (if you're traveling with little ones). Nearby is the **Cañada**, the 'emblem' of Córdoba, a canal that runs through the city and offers beautiful (and in places, not so beautiful) riparian and water views. Efforts to keep the channel clean are ongoing. Crossing over the Cañada, you'll come to the **Plaza Italia**, a nice spot for a rest or to perhaps listen to some busking. Back again on the other side of the Cañada, you'll hit the near-obligatory **Plaza de la Intendencia**, **Héroes de Malvinas** park, with its monument to the fallen in what the world knows as the Falklands War, but which in Argentina is called the Malvinas War. It's worth noting that this spot is lovely during the day and gets a bit dicey after dark.

Cañada

JESUIT SIGHTS IN CÓRDOBA

There are so many Jesuit missions in Argentina that there's even a whole province named after them: Misiones. In Córdoba city, top among the dozens of spots are:

Manzana Jesuítica (the Jesuit Block)
This block of museums and religious structures is a Unesco-listed site.

UNC Historical Museum – Manzana Jesuítica
A museum in the Jesuit block with excellent information on the area's history.

Capilla Doméstica Jesuita
Known for its ornate chapel.

Iglesia Compañía de Jesús
A still functioning church with gorgeous decorations.

Cripta Jesuítica
This once-forgotten Jesuit crypt has been restored and is now a creepy must-see.

PLACES TO SLEEP IN CÓRDOBA

Hotel Everest
This friendly, inexpensive hotel is within walking distance of Plaza San Martin. $$

Aldea Hostel
Welcoming if basic hostel, no breakfast, but great location, *terraza* and price. $

Windsor Hotel
Stately, elegant and refined, with fine dining, a bar and a rooftop pool. $$$

BEST TANGO IN CÓRDOBA

Taking lessons beforehand is vital to being able to enjoy the event known as the *milonga*. You'll find that most venues offer free or inexpensive beginner lessons beforehand as a one-shot deal, or if you're in the area for a week or longer, consider a group class or private lessons.

Tsunami Tango
Hosts a popular *milonga*, plus has other dances like bachata as well.

Milonga Plaza San Martín
A lovely outdoor *milonga* held at the Plaza San Martín.

Caminito Tango
A center-of-town spot with lessons, *practicas* and *milongas* in a friendly environment.

Tango, Cordoba

Learning to Tango
Don't Ask 'Shall We Dance?'

If you thought tango was that cliché of two people charging across a room with a rose in their teeth, think again. Tango, or we should say correctly, *Argentine* tango, is vastly more than that. It's a community, and Córdoba is a great place to dip into learning this amazing form of dance. Aficionados will claim it's actually more than a dance; it's a language, but whatever you call it, if you're in the mood to check it out, seek out the kind, welcoming environment at **Tsunami Tango**. Classes are held at all skill levels, and beginners may want to get to a few of the lessons before trying their skills in a *milonga* (dance party). That's where tango dancers from all walks of life – and all parts of the world – come to socialize amid incredible tango music, often with wine and snacks (empanadas, anyone?). Close your eyes, and you might even think you've been whisked back to the Golden Age of tango,

 FIND MATE IN CÓRDOBA

Casa Nostra – La Casa del Mate
A boutique solely devoted to the hallowed *yerba*.

Punto y Banca
A smoke-shop and game store with a number of *mates*, *bombillas* and more.

Gava
Hand-painted, unique, cutesy *mates* that will make great souvenirs.

the 1930s and '40s, with the black-and-white tile floors, the elegant dresses and the dim light.

Sit a while at the edge and you'll notice the *ronda*, the circular motion the dancers make as they move around the floor. It's been said that a tango dancer dances not only to the music, not only to their partner, but to the room as well. At the end of a triplet or quartet of songs (known as the *tanda*) the dancers freeze. For an instant, the entire room, swirling and moving, is as still as if you're looking at a photograph. Couples then move to the edges of the dance floor, find their seats, while some other music (the 'curtain', or *cortina*) plays. When it finishes and a new *tanda* begins, you'll see eager dancers staring intensely at prospective partners, a form of invitation known as the *mirada*. When two dancers' eyes meet, the leader will nod their head (the *cabeceo*), the follower will nod back, and they will move out to the dance floor.

Whatever you do, don't just walk up to someone, stand in front of them, and say, 'Would you like to dance?' Doing so is a big no-no, as experienced dancers know that if someone hasn't been looking in your direction, she or he isn't interested. To force it by asking a question marks someone as a rank beginner (which may be why the dancer wasn't looking at you in the first place!). If your chosen dancer isn't looking your way, keep looking; chances are someone else will meet your gaze, smile and nod.

Dive into Córdoba's Dive Bars

Visiting the Güemes District

One of the things that makes Córdoba so vibrant is its youth. University students hit the books during the day and enjoy themselves at night. Güemes is a great district known for hip bars, cafes and coffeehouses, most – if not all – of which are open long into the night. Dozens of bars span the gamut from British-style pub to funky electronica vibe, and the district is split in the middle by the atmospheric Cañada, the walled river channel. In winter you'll see groups bustling, red-cheeked, from bar to bar. In summer, there'll be buskers playing guitar or singing for spare pesos on the street corners.

Fernet and cola

BEST GÜEMES BARS

There are dozens of great places to have a pint (or Fernet and cola!) with friends new or old, but if you're looking for places to begin an evening on the town, here are some suggestions. Be aware that most drinking spots here have table seating; the stand-up bar is a rarity in these parts.

Los Infernales
A big, boisterous place with lots of tables, excellent food and decent prices.

The Journey
Its bottle ceiling makes this bar unique, and the actual bar (not just tables) lets you sidle up and make new friends.

Club Paraguay
Hosts performers and rock bands who perform to packed, standing-room-only crowds.

Villa del Totoral

Miramar

Jesús María
Colonia Caroya
La Falda
Arroyito
Córdoba
Rio Secundo

Beyond
Córdoba

The vast and varied region around Córdoba includes beautiful mountain ranges, flat farming plains, and eerie salt-laden lagoons.

GETTING AROUND

You'll be able to get to the bigger towns and to places like Miramar with public transport, but getting further off the grid will require a private vehicle. Birders especially will value the ability to screech to a stop and pull off the roadside when a new Life List bird appears.

☑ TOP TIP

Without a private vehicle you'll want to plan your trips conservatively, as schedules can leave you stranded if you're not careful.

Córdoba makes a great hub for some fantastic day trips. Birders will love the range of habitats that are all within a few hours of each other, enabling you to go from mountain peaks to marshland in mere hours. History buffs will love exploring the small towns and villages, and nature lovers will find a wealth of trails and trekking options, bird and animal life, and great swimming spots perfect for a cool-off plunge. Jesuit missions are another reason people love to explore this part of Argentina, and let's not forget that even the small towns often have a tango scene where you can put on those dance shoes and make new friends.

La Falda

PABLO RODRIGUEZ MERKEL/SHUTTERSTOCK ©

Flamingos, Cordoba

La Falda

TIME FROM CÓRDOBA: **90MINS**

Fabled Tangoland

Nestled in a valley northwest of Córdoba, you'll find the beautiful sleepy town of La Falda – sleepy, that is, any other time than its tango festival, held each year in July. Then there's no sleep at all, as the town swells with visitors from all over the country and beyond to dance, see and listen to the music Argentina is famous for – tango.

Enjoy the various tango-themed statues around town, and if you plan to visit during the festival, reserve your hotel stays months in advance unless you fancy a 90-minute ride in the wee hours all the way back to Córdoba. The first festival was held in 1965 and included Aníbal Troilo; subsequent festivals included Osvaldo Pugliese (among many famous others), and the list of tango stars now reads much like a who's who of Argentine tango. Though faced with every possible setback, from tornado strikes to economic problems to Covid-19, the festival continues and is one of the best reasons to venture away from Córdoba if you're here in July.

For the rare few looking for something other than tango, head to the reservoir and its beautiful 7 Cascades swimming hole, a beautiful spot for a dip, where waterfalls – *cascadas* – plunge down a rock face in sheets that look like fine lace curtains. At the main town square (eponymously known as La Falda) is a cute labyrinth that kids or the young-at-heart will enjoy. It's overlooked by the charming Parroquia Santisimo Sacramento, visible from the hillsides around town. Inside, ornate stained-glass windows and a beautiful altar make it well worth stopping for.

FAMOUS TANGO COMPOSERS

Osvaldo Pugliese
Arguably the greatest of the Golden Age greats, he is known for challenging tunes with drama and lyricism.

Aníbal Troilo
His birthday, July 11, is commemorated nationwide as National Bandoneon Day.

Francisco Canaro
Born in Uruguay, Canaro grew from abject poverty to international acclaim as a tango composer and violinist.

Juan d'Arienzo
Known as the 'King of the Bea', d'Arienzo is a beloved paragon in the tango world, even today.

Miguel Caló
Considered by many to be one of the tango world's greats, his compositions are a standby in *milongas* around the world.

Grab those binoculars or that fancy zoom lens you've been dying to try out, and head out to Miramar, renowned for its amazing birding along the shores of the odd, inland sea known as Laguna Mar Chiquita –the 'Little Sea Lagoon'. Evaporation makes a thick haze even on the brightest, clearest of days, and locals will tell you about the white salty residue that gets left on windshields and tabletops. It's a bizarre place, but birders are in for a treat. The shallow saltwater shorelines hold a host of birds. Park your car (or get dropped off) at the ❶ **Torre Copacabana**, which, despite the name, is nothing more than a dilapidated brick tower that's as good as any landmark to start a birding walk. If you haven't spotted some flamingos yet, you will soon. Oddly, here, they're often seen chest-, shoulder- or even neck-deep in the water – an odd behavior for birds often

seen in shallows. From there, walk along the *costanera* (street closest to the water) towards the ❷ **Muelle Playa Central**. Keep an eye out for flamingos, of course, but you stand a good chance of spotting roseate spoonbills, and a variety of ibis, herons, grebes, and other shorebirds. On the inland side of the road, look for giant wood-rails and warblers. Keep walking until you reach the ❸ **Gran Hotel Viena**, then turn inland on Rivadavia. You'll now be in farmland. Look for burrowing owls and scimitar-billed woodcreepers, among other field and farmland birds. Follow until you reach a five-way intersection and turn sharp right. Turn right again onto ❹ **Sarmiento** street and follow it over the ❺ **marshy area** (another spot for great birding), and back to the shores of the Mar Chiquita.

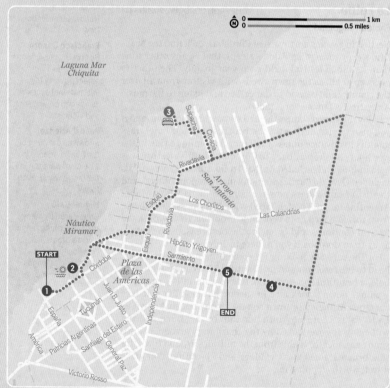

Miramar

TIME FROM CÓRDOBA: **3HRS** 🚌

A Creepy, Haunted Hotel

There's perhaps no better setting in all of Córdoba for a zombie apocalypse movie than the Gran Hotel Viena. It sits, crumbling away, on the receding, eerie shores of the Laguna Mar Chiquita, amid desolate dead tree trunks and crusty salt formations. You can only visit the inside of the hotel with a pre-arranged tour, which are only held a few times during the day and sometimes not at all – almost as if there's something evil lurking there, waiting... Well, OK, maybe not quite that bad, but it's a cool, desolate, creepy spot to check out. The hotel construction began in 1940 and was completed in 1945, aimed as a good place for those afflicted with psoriasis, but the hotel operated for less than a year before closing due to conflicts with labor and complications with the world's political scene. The lone security guard who remained looked after the place for years, living alone in the solitary building until – rumor has it – he was poisoned (or killed himself). People claim to have seen him wandering the halls, and heard his clumping footsteps and the rattling of his key ring.

MORE ABOUT TANGO

To really dance tango takes years of practice, but it's accessible to anyone who cares to invest the time. If you're looking for more info about this fascinating Argentine pastime, you can read about it in our **tango** essay, p519.

FLAMINGOS

For many visitors, the chance to see flamingos is a vacation highlight, and if you visit Miramar you'll find they're here (along with many other beautiful birds) in abundance. For many casual observers, if you've seen one flamingo you've seen them all, but birders will delight in knowing that, depending on the time of year, up to three different species of this uniquely adapted bird can be seen. The most common is the Chilean flamingo, which lives on the lake year round, with beautiful courtship and nesting rituals in September. But you can also see the Andean flamingo and the James flamingo if you're lucky, as they stop by during the months of June, July and August.

WHERE TO EAT AND STAY IN MIRAMAR

Hotel Comedor Marchetti
An on-the-water hotel with a pretty pool, great shoreline access and tasty meals.

Parrilla Marchetti
Restaurant with a large buffet and grilled meat selection.

Renacer
A *costanera* spot that's casual and inexpensive, with fries, burgers and other diner-type fare.

BUENOS
AIRES

San Luis

Dusty, working-class San Luis makes a good hub for some area attractions that are well worth checking out if you're out here, and has a quiet charm that grows on you the longer you stay. It was founded in 1594, only to be abandoned and then founded again in 1632. It remained obscure until the arrival of the railway, which was built to reach the wine-making regions of Mendoza – San Luis was a great middle stop along the way. Today, the city is the capital of San Luis Province, a vibrant hub with industry, tourism and farming. Salt production at the nearby *salinas* is another revenue source.

Tourists will find the city has a reasonable number of sights, some good museums, and a restaurant and bar scene that makes it easy to stay here a night or two.

GETTING AROUND

San Luis has a small airport, and buses and microbuses can get you around the city itself. Private taxis may be the best option for reaching spots that are farther away (such as the *salinas*) if you don't have a rental car.

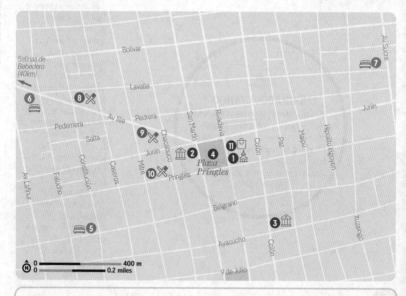

SIGHTS
- **1** Catedral de San Luis
- **2** Colegio Nacional Juan Crisóstomo Lafinur
- **3** Museo Dora Ochoa de Masramón
- **4** Plaza Pringles
  see **4** Statue of Colonel Pringles

SLEEPING & EATING
- **5** Casa Blanca Hostel
- **6** Hotel Premium Tower Suites
- **7** Hotel Punta Lavalle

EATING
- **8** 4 Reinas
- **9** La Rosa
- **10** Maria Bonita

SHOPPING
- **11** Regionales Mercedes
  see **11** Santería Catedral

Plaza Pringles

☑ TOP TIP

If you visit the Salinas de Bebedero at sunrise (as many tourists do, catching the rays of morning light glinting off the salt formations), be sure to check the sunrise schedule carefully, lest you wait in pitch dark for hours. Argentines have three classifications of twilight, and only the last has enough light for photography.

TEAM THIS, TEAM THAT

Anyone visiting Argentina will find it cute, comical or even disturbing how team-oriented the Argentines are. You can't go anywhere without seeing the white and blue. And of course, it manifests itself with team sports, notably football (aka soccer), where spectators often get rowdy. Wear the wrong colored T-shirt or have luggage that's in the colors of a different team, and you'll hear about it. But you'll also hear people talk about how they're 'Team Summer' or 'Team Winter'. There's also 'Team Mate' and 'Team Coffee'. 'Team Fernet', 'Team Vermouth' and 'Team Vino'. Even among the 'Team Mate' there's 'Team Bitter', 'Team Sweet' and 'Team Cold'.

Discover the Museo Dora Ochoa de Masramón

Natural History and More

The Museo Dora Ochoa de Masramón is undergoing (at the time of research) a lengthy restoration and is a wonderful place to spend a rainy day. The house once belonged to Dr Alberto Arancibia Rodríguez, a governor of San Luis Province. Its current name was christened in honor of the famous writer, Dora Ochoa de Masramón. Inside, there's a diverse quantity of historical and scientific relics, ranging from furniture of specific periods and other antiques to stuffed animals and fossils, indigenous artifacts and tools. Artwork, statues, fabrics, and even 1900s-era photography equipment are all on display. It's an interesting building to meander around with grand rooms, decorative moldings, and beautiful wooden floorboards. One of the most popular exhibits for kids is a giant armadillo, with front claws the size of a saber-toothed tiger's incisors. The collection includes over 700 pieces, many of which are unique to the San Luis area.

Take in Plaza Pringles

Not a Munchie

Plaza Pringles (no, not related to the famous snack) is the main plaza around which San Luis grew. It's surprisingly stately and lush compared to the surrounding working-class city. Inside the main square are a number of tall shade trees (of course, with plenty of the ubiquitous monk parakeets squawking in the branches) and even some beautiful palms. In the center, surrounded by flowers and flowering trees, is a

WHO WAS COLONEL PRINGLES?

Juan Pascual Pringles was a revered military man who was born in San Luis in 1795 and eventually rose through the ranks to become a Colonel, before his death at the hands of one of Facundo Quiroga's men. He distinguished himself in a number of famous battles and also helped to liberate Peru before returning to Argentina, where he fought against Quiroga in Buenos Aires, in a brutal civil war. A number of squares and public spaces throughout Argentina bear Pringles' name in his honor, and San Luis is proud to call him their own. There's no apparent connection between this military hero and the beloved potato snack.

Salinas de Bebedero

statue of Colonel Pringles himself, seated atop a horse and wearing his full uniform. A fence protects the monument from vandalism, but you can easily fit a camera through the bars to get a good photograph. On the park's southeastern corner, you'll find the **Catedral de San Luis**, a twin-steepled building with an exterior that's been damaged by the elements. Between the steeples, the entrance almost looks like the Parthenon, with a flat, triangular roof and Corinthian columns below. Inside, there's a stunning altar surrounding a statue of the Virgin Mary and gorgeous paintings on the ceiling. It's also refreshingly cool inside on those hot Argentine summer days. If the visit has enthralled or inspired you, check out the **Santería Catedral**, a religious bookstore with all the statues, crucifixes, effigies, rosaries and books you could want. If religious souvenirs aren't your cup of...*mate,* then try the shop next door, **Regionales Mercedes**, where you'll find a host of novelties and unique gifts, including *mate* gourds and unique *bombillas*. On the other side of the plaza, there are low buildings of the campus of **Colegio Nacional Juan Crisóstomo Lafinur**, which is gorgeous when the jacaranda trees are in bloom.

 WHERE TO EAT IN SAN LUIS

4 Reinas
A chic, stylish gastropub with a good wine selection and nice Italian fare. $$

La Rosa
With live music, alfresco dining, a decent menu and excellent service, this is a hit. $$

Maria Bonita
If you're missing Mexican food, this is a tasty reminder, with tacos, salsas, quesadillas and *cervezas*. $$

A Not-So-Wasted Wasteland

The Salinas de Bebedero

About a 45-minute drive southwest of San Luis is a vast flat plain that once, eons ago, was an inland sea much the same as Córdoba Province's Laguna Mar Chiquita. Now it's all but dried up, and like all inland seas, the salts have concentrated due to evaporation. This wasteland stretches as far as the eye can see, and if you visit during the day, bring sunglasses. It's a blindingly white, snow-like plain made of dry, crystallized salt. While not as vast as some of the world's other famous salt works, such as Guerrero Negro in Mexico's Baja, and not as picturesque as the mountainside salt evaporating pools of Bolivia and Peru, it's nonetheless impressive, with mountains of salt that are piled as high as a three-story building, longer than football fields. The area is also used by the Argentine military to conduct training exercises, so you may see military vehicles there at certain times.

One of the most popular times to visit is sunrise when there is less glare and the angled morning sunlight lends itself to wonderful photography. Sunset is also a great time to come for similar reasons. If you come in a private vehicle, make sure to obey any signs, particularly warnings about where you can and can't safely drive, as there may be trenches hidden by only a thin crust of salt; much like a skater can break through thin ice, so too can a car tire get swallowed if it's in the wrong place at the wrong time. Keep in mind that large sections of this area are a working salt factory, so heavy machinery such as front-end loaders or giant dump trucks may be passing by. Be especially aware of traffic if you have little ones.

STERILIZING SALT

Salt may seem, today, to be a humble, even boring mineral, and when you look out at a vast plain of the stuff, the magic wears off relatively quickly. But it's important to remember that before refrigeration, salt – along with sugar – was one of the only ways to preserve foods out here, making it indispensable in households here in the Argentine frontier. If you killed a deer, you might have a week or two to eat it before it went bad. Yet when properly salted, it could last the whole winter, or even years. Salt was also vital as an antiseptic, helping to clean wounds long before the days of antibiotics and vaccines.

Catedral
de San Luis

 WHERE TO STAY IN SAN LUIS

Casa Blanca Hostel
A cheap, friendly hostel option with private rooms and helpful, welcoming staff. $

Hotel Premium Tower Suites
A higher-end spot in a good central location with a swanky rooftop pool. $$$

Hotel Punta Lavalle
A midrange option with a pool, dining area and comfortable rooms. $$

Parque Nacional
Sierra de las Quijadas

San Francisco
Del Monte Del Oro

Nogolí

Trapiche

La Punta

San Luis

Beyond
San Luis

A wide and wonderfully diverse region awaits
you beyond the borders of San Luis proper.

GETTING AROUND

No question about it, you'll be best off exploring these regions with your own car. It's not impossible to reach places by bus, but schedules are often hard to pin down and travelers have complained that a whole day or two gets wasted trying to plan around a limited window of when buses will arrive. If a rental isn't an option, inquire in your hotel about finding a driver who can bring you where you want to go, wait, and return again for a fixed fee.

☑ **TOP TIP**

You'll likely want your own transportation to get to many of these spots, especially the more out-of-the-way ones.

San Luis sits in the center of several distinct regions and, as such, makes a great hub for exciting day trips or overnights as you explore the region. The star attraction is the incredible Parque Nacional Sierra de las Quijadas, with its iron-red cliffs, unique wildlife and sweeping canyons. It's the kind of place that only grows on you as you spend more time here. But the park isn't the only attraction. The nearby Sierras Puntanas have a lot of offer, from tiny vacation hamlets to birdlife-filled reservoirs, to craggy peaks with Andean condors. You'll also find cute historic mining towns and lots of beautiful nature as you delve in.

CLWPHOTO/SHUTTERSTOCK ©

Parque Nacional Sierra de las Quijadas

HERNAN4429/GETTY IMAGES ©

La Florida (p238)

LOOKOUT POINTS

If you're stopping to take a photo somewhere on these winding roads, be extremely careful to do so in a safe place. Make sure your car isn't blocking the roadway or crushing roadside flowers and plants, which leads to road-destroying erosion. As tempting as it may be to stop anywhere and everywhere, it's often safest, and the most conscientious, to stop where there's a dedicated pullout. This is as much for your own safety as others, as Argentine drivers are known for passing in places they might not expect to find an oncoming or parked car.

La Punta

TIME FROM SAN LUIS: **40MINS** 🚗

Gasp at the View

Not far north of San Luis is a relatively new, urban-planned town known as La Punta. Head east from there into the mountains on a wending and winding road that, if you're prone to motion sickness, will make you a bit queasy. Those who like roller coasters, on the other hand, will enjoy the ride. And it's all worth it to reach the Mirador de la Punta, a vista point on a hairpin turn that offers a commanding view of 270 degrees, including the town of La Punta and San Luis. On a clear day, you can see all the way to the Salinas de Bebedero (p233). Those without a car may find it a bit challenging to get to, but if you have your own set of wheels it's a worthy stop. You can even use a big frame for those social media selfies. Vistas like this allow you to really appreciate the geography, geology and natural history: turn the clock back, add a bit of heat, and imagine this entire flatland below you filled with a shallow inland sea. Today, all that remains of that vast, tropical swamp are the salt flats, which look about the size of a postage stamp from this vantage point.

When you're done taking photographs and gawking at the view, you can keep going (for more hairpins) and get to the town of El Volcán, or turn around and return to San Luis.

 ## WHERE TO STAY AND EAT AROUND SAN LUIS

Cabaña El Balcón de Trapiche
Lovely spot with sweeping mountain views, pool, and friendly hosts. **$$$**

Cabañas La Cascada
Rustic cabins with individual grills, a pool, and vistas of the Trapiche river. **$$**

Parrilla y Restaurante 'Los Armenio'
Grilled meats, colossal burgers, tasty fries and pastas at this brick-red spot in Trapiche. **$$**

SUZANNE LONG/ALAMY STOCK PHOTO ©

PRACTICALITIES

Scan this QR code for prices and opening hours.

TOP SIGHT

Parque Nacional Sierra de las Quijadas

The grandest of the area's national parks, this spectacular park features over 70,000 hectares of desert, including canyons, valleys, highland scrub, cliffs and mesas. Some of Argentina's most unique and revered fauna can be found here, such as the Andean condor, the quirky Chacoan mara, and the odd, almost unreal fairy armadillo. Cougars, hooved mammals, foxes and coyotes can be seen as well.

DON'T MISS

Dinosaur footprints and fossils

Hornillos de Hualtarán

Potrero de la Aguada

Trail Las Huellas del Pasado

Interesting wildlife

Trail Guanacos

Trail Farallones

Dinosaur Footprints & Fossils

It's hard to imagine now, but this barren landscape used to look like *Jurassic Park* in the, sorry, not Jurassic, the Cretaceous Albian era, when Andean condors paled in size to their giant *Pterodaustro* cousins, with a wingspan of almost 4m. The first fossils of this incredible species were found here in the 1950s and further paleontology has uncovered not dozens, but hundreds of important fossils. There are also footprints of gigantic sauropods you can hike out and view. As you trek over these crumbling sandstone cliffs and look out from the vistas, keep your eye on the ground. Who knows, the next big fossil discovery might be your own!

Hornillos de Hualtarán

They're easy to miss but even at the entrance of the park you'll find fascinating remnants of ancient human settlements in the form of circular clay rings, which, while eroded, are the vestiges of ovens that were once used by indigenous people to cook with. The fact that the Potrero de la Aguada was a reliable water source may have made human habitation possible despite the severe dryness during most of the year.

Potrero de la Aguada

This beautiful and unique area is filled with eroded canyons, arroyos, washes, and rocks shaped into fascinating structures by weather, wind and time. You can use your imagination and see shapes in the rocks (some look like the Sphinx of Egypt, for example); they are beautiful structures that will evoke mystery and beauty in anyone who sees them. This area, interestingly, is landlocked for the most part, with only one outflow, so in times of heavy rain, water can actually collect here and stay for weeks or months – the only place in the park where this occurs. As such, it offers much-needed water for birds and wildlife. Walking here will increase your chances of spotting foxes, pumas and the beautiful wild guanacos, relatives of the llama.

Las Huellas del Pasado

This trail, accessible only with a guide, takes you out through the beautiful landscapes to the location of some dinosaur footprints. It's about a two-hour round-trip walk, requiring moderate ups and downs. The prints, visible clearly in the deep red sandstone rock, are incredible, and impress on anyone the sheer size of these long extinct creatures.

Interesting Wildlife

But extinct creatures aren't the only prime attraction here. There are lots of very alive critters to look for too. Along with the graceful guanacos, you may see collared peccaries (a piglike mammal), maras (a largish rodent with a square nose and almost rabbit-like features), the curious, black-masked vizcacha (another rodent, vaguely resembling a chinchilla), and beautiful endangered brown brocket deer.

Trail Guanacos

One of the best self-guided trail options of the park, this three- to four-hour round-trip hike will take you through stunning landscapes where guanacos are known to frequent. You'll also have great birdwatching opportunities. Pay keen attention to the skies, as Andean condors can be seen wheeling and circling above you. Bring plenty of water lest the condors get their wish and you keel over, letting them make you their next meal.

Trail Farallones

The longest of the standard guided tour options, this four-hour round trip will take you through the valley and across stunning peaks. It ends near the cliffs called 'Fallarones', a broad shelf of beautifully eroded sandstone, dotted here and there with stunted desert vegetation. It can be tricky to find a guide, so try to arrange at least a day in advance if you don't want to be disappointed.

GETTING GUIDES

Most of the site's signage is in Spanish and some trails require a guide. Most only speak Spanish, though with an offline-capable translator you can get a lot done these days (there's wi-fi at the park building, but nothing once you're on the trails). The park has a list of guides, so contact the visitor center and take things from there.

TOP TIPS

- Check bus schedules carefully to avoid long waits or being stranded.
- Bring plenty of water, even in winter.
- Bring food and snacks, as there's nothing available within the park.
- The parking area and nearby lookouts are accessible to some degree for those with wheelchairs or strollers; none of the trails are.
- Drive slowly, as wildlife – especially the critically endangered pink fairy armadillo – may be crossing the road at exactly the wrong time.
- Photographers, be aware that this is a highly dusty area and there may be strong winds. Bring appropriate lens-cleaning items.

A DAM GOOD FISHING SPOT

Fishermen may want to check out the nearby reservoir known as **Represa Saladillo**, a popular getaway spot for anglers from San Luis. It's a pretty spot nestled up in the mountains, a bit like a mini version of La Florida. The dam itself has places for casting, though you'll want to bring sun protection, as there's little to no shade and very few trees. Early mornings are a great time to come, and you'll find *pejerrey* (silversides) are a common catch. Sunsets are popular here too. Birders may want to look for shorebirds, wading birds such as herons and egrets, and a variety of ducks. Be sure to bring those binoculars!

FOTO 4440/SHUTTERSTOCK ©

Parakeet

Trapiche

TIME FROM SAN LUIS: **40MINS** 🚌

A Florida Without a Panhandle

La Florida reservoir, high above San Luis in the Sierras Punta-nas and near the tiny town of Trapiche, is a delightful escape from the dry plains and deserts. Here, even with low water levels due to climate change, you'll find a tranquil blue expanse dotted with inlets, coves and even an island or two. Tall conifer groves line some of the coastline, and birders will delight in the ease with which they can spot not only waterfowl on the surface, but wading birds along the shorelines. Other riparian birds can be seen in the nearby trees. Monk parakeets chatter constantly, but you'll also spot woodpeckers, warblers, doves, herons, ducks and birds of prey. Those with a car can drive the circumference of the lake in under an hour (longer if you stop for birds). If you don't have a car, see if a taxi near the Trapiche bus drop-off will take you around or take you part of the way.

Interestingly, the dam that created the reservoir had been envisioned as early as 1891 as a way to ensure the then-small but growing town of San Luis would have a reliable water supply. But the dam wasn't completed until half a century later, in 1953. It now serves both San Luis and Villa Mercedes.

The Sierras

Though not the stereotypical mountains one imagines when thinking of Argentina, the Sierras here are nonetheless lovely experiences for the traveler, and are well worth exploring if you're in the area. Tiny historic mining towns, delightful national parks, signs of ancient civilizations long gone, and beautiful winding roads where you stand a chance of spotting some of Argentina's uniquest wildlife and birds. It's also – thanks to the elevation – cooler here even in the summer, a welcome respite for those seeking to escape the heat. Some of the area's best and most beautiful swimming happens here too, with riverside swimming holes, waterfalls and sunbathing spots. Get out the bikini, Team Summer, you're going to like it here.

GETTING AROUND

No surprise, getting around the Sierras requires a vehicle, unless you're willing to hop overnight to overnight from town to town. It's just not feasible to do multiple day trips and still have time to do any of the activities you're planning to do while you're there. So hire a vehicle or rent one, and you'll be able to make it to many of these and still be back in San Luis or Córdoba by Argentine dinnertime (read: 10pm).

☑ TOP TIP

Don't be deceived by the lack of snow-capped peaks: these mountains can be markedly different in temperature than the big flatland cities below. Bring a few different layers to wear, especially something warm to put on after a dip in the swimming holes.

JAVIER GHERSI/GETTY IMAGES ©

La Cumbrecita (p250)

BEST BALNEARIOS IN MINA CLAVERO

Note that in these river-based swimming holes, the swimmability depends greatly on seasonal water levels, which can fluctuate wildly, as can water temps, varying anywhere from feels-like-bathwater to geeez-that's-icy, depending on the season. As with any water-related sport, be aware of the surroundings and the currents, and keep an eye on kids.

Nido del Aguila
Arguably the most scenic of all the spots, with giant rocky cliffs and overlooks.

Balneario de Mina Clavero
A central spot with a bridge and cement retaining walls to ensure deeper swimming spots.

Balneario Las Conanas
Wide beaches and shallow water make this popular for families.

Balneario Los Elefantes
Known for its elephantine rocks that line the shores.

OPPOSITE PAGE: NESTOR. J. BEREMBLUM/ALAMY STOCK PHOTO ©

Mina Clavero

Rest & Recharge in Mina Clavero
A Mountain Hideaway

Mina Clavero is one of many pretty, picturesque, quaint towns that dot these beautiful sierras. Originally the home of indigenous Comechingones, who left rock art and other pictographs, the area was thoroughly colonized by the Spanish after mining explorations brought them here in the mid-1500s. By the 1700s, it was a retreat town, as mining hopes never quite materialized. Today, the Mina Clavero river offers lovely swimming spots, and that's the primary reason to day-trip here – get away from the heat with a refreshing splash. The swimming spots, and there are several, each with its own character, have a beach area with picturesque rocks, eddies and shallows. At certain times of year, you might even see a waterfall. The Mina Clavero riverway was recently named one of Argentina's top seven most beautiful rivers.

Be aware that these riverside swimming spots (known as *balnearios*) can sometimes be very crowded, especially in summer when city-dwellers are escaping the heat. If you're expecting an idyllic dip in serene waters that feel like you're the first person to find this spot, you're in for disappointment. If you want to sunbathe in a fun, party-type environment amid *mate* and beer drinkers, see families with beach umbrellas and kids kicking balls around, then this will be exactly the swimming you're looking for. If you're planning to make a day out of it, pack a lunch, some beverages and some tunes and get ready to relax Argentine style.

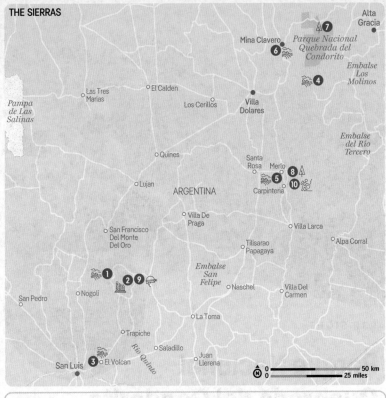

THE SIERRAS

Alta Gracia

Mina Clavero 6

Parque Nacional
Quebrada del
Condorito

△ 7

Embalse
Los
Molinos

Las Tres
Marias

El Calden

Los Cerillos

Villa
Dolares

4

Pampa
de Las
Salinas

Embalse
del Río
Tercero

Quines

Santa
Rosa

Merlo

8

Lujan

ARGENTINA

5
Carpinteria

10

San Francisco
Del Monte
Del Oro

Villa De
Praga

Villa Larca

Alpa Corral

Tilisarao
Papagaya

Embalse
San
Felipe

Naschel

Villa Del
Carmen

San Pedro

Nogolí

1

2 9

La Toma

Trapiche

Río Quinto

Saladillo

Juan
Llerena

San Luis

3 El Volcan

N

0   50 km
0   25 miles

SIGHTS
1 La Carolina
2 Casa de Piedra Pintada
3 El Volcán
4 La Cumbrecita
5 Merlo
6 Mina Clavero

7 Parque Nacional Quebrada del Condorito
8 Reserva Natural de Merlo

ACTIVITIES, COURSES & TOURS
see 6 Balneario De Mina Clavero

see 3 Balneario La Hoya
see 6 Balneario Las Conanas
see 6 Balneario Los Elefantes
see 1 La Carolina Mines

9 Inti Huasi Cave
see 4 La Olla
10 Mirador de los Condores
see 6 Nido del Aguila

**Ziplining,
San Luis (p230)**

PEDRO SUÁREZ/ALAMY STOCK PHOTO ©

PRACTICALITIES

Scan this QR code for prices and opening hours.

TOP SIGHT

Parque Nacional Quebrada del Condorito

DON'T MISS

The condors (of course!)

Sendero Secretos Bajo Nuestros Pies

Sendero a la Quebrada

La Cascada Escondida

Centro de Visitantes

Sendero Río de los Condoritos (with guide only)

The Giant Condor statue

The Andean Condors

Non-birders may look up in the sky and think anything soaring above them is an Andean condor, but there's all sorts of raptors, buteos, falcons and vultures that could be in the skies. Not all are Andean condors. If they're far away, you'll need binoculars to pick out the distinctive shape of their head. They also have a characteristic wing shape and pattern, which the rangers here will be happy to describe. If you're a birder, the difference between an Andean condor and, say, a turkey vulture is as obvious as the colors of two basketball team jerseys. They're here, and if you're lucky, you'll see them.

Sendero Secretos Bajo Nuestros Pies

This trail translates to 'The Secret Beneath our Feet' and for good reason: this short trail brings you to an overlook, where you'll see that there's a surprising amount of water pooled below in an often-dry brook. In periods of heavy rain, the brook will run, but at other times of year, the stagnant pools provide water for the park's wildlife. This is a short walk from the vis-

Andean Condor

NOT JUST CONDORS

You'd be surprised at how many other animals call this incredible spot home. Pumas, several species of fox, deer, smaller rodents (no, no capybaras) and, of course, dozens of bird species are all quite comfortable here in these grassy, open hills. Hikers can plan on spotting a few of these cool critters on the longer trails.

itor center, so it's a good option for those with little time or those who aren't able to walk far, such as parents with toddlers. (Note that due to the cliff drops, you'll want to keep a close eye on little ones!)

Sendero a la Quebrada del Condorito

This four- to five-hour trail takes you out through rock-strewn copses and little valleys, eventually ending at the spectacular overlook where (if you're lucky) you'll see the Andean condors. They're majestic, beautiful birds, and from the vantage point at the Quebrada, you may even get to see them up close if they're circling nearby. It's a good half-day hike, so be sure to bring plenty of water.

La Cascada Escondida

This isn't named 'the Hidden Waterfall' for nothing. Tucked away in the rocks, and almost circled by a sharp hairpin curve of the highway, lies a beautiful hidden waterfall that, depending on the season, is deep enough to swim in. Most people, their eyes on the road, don't even notice it. Those that do, however, will often be seen pulling over, stripping to their skivvies, and plunging in for an icy dip. It's also a nice spot to see tinamou, grouse-like birds that scuttle off into the grasses when they realize they've been spotted.

The Condor Statue

This unmissable landmark sits at the entry to the park, a giant, rather sorry-looking condor made of metal and wire. It's an iconic selfie spot, so plan on a quick pull-over and to snap a shot or two.

TOP TIPS

- Wildlife spotting is best in the early morning or late in the day.
- Bring plenty of water, as the standing water in the park is not safe to drink.
- Even on cloudy days, the sun is very strong. Wear hats, bring sunblock, and remember to reapply it frequently.
- The condors will likely be soaring high above you, but if you come across ones that are on the ground, do not approach them or try to scare them into taking flight.
- The best, most sweeping views are at the end of the longer, multi-hour hikes. Plan accordingly.

La Carolina

WHY I LOVE THE SIERRAS

Ray Bartlett, writer

I expected 'mountains' in Argentina to be the Andes, snow-capped peaks so tall they scratch the sky. But despite their relatively low, humble altitude, the Sierras amazed me. They're an otherworldly mix of rocks, crevasses, ridges and grassy fields, and are full of surprises. Come around a hairpin corner and see a gurgling brook so hidden you might have never known it was there. Turn another corner and surprise a pair of Andean condors, who hop awkwardly out of the road, looking at you accusingly for interrupting their roadkill lunch. And then there are the little towns and villages, each one so different from the next. I was glad to have had my own car, too, as it allowed me to stop wherever I wanted to explore.

MORE IN THE SIERRAS

An Ancient Art Museum
Cave Paintings in Three Places

If marveling at ancient rock art is your thing, visit the **Casa de Piedra Pintada**, a series of three large cliff walls decorated with strange figures, geometric shapes and animals, which look out on a beautiful grassy hillside that vanishes into farms and fields and forests far below. It's a nice spot to bring a picnic lunch, see the paintings, then contemplate their vast history as you enjoy the pretty landscape.

Unfortunately, the site has also been 'decorated' by some less-than-ancient art, so expect to see lovers' names scratched into the walls as well. There's a sturdy metal walkway you can use to reach some of the art. It's open 8am to 8pm in summer (December–March), and 10am to 5pm during the rest of the year. You don't have to have a guide but you may find you get more out of the site if you do, and usually someone's willing to give you a tour for a small fee.

 WHERE TO STAY IN MINA CLAVERO

Balcon del Río
A lovely spot overlooking the river, with a pool and gracious hosts. **$$**

Hostel El Viaje Casa Alternativa
A colorful and funky hostel, with its own beach access and parking. **$**

Apart Hotel Costa Serrana
If a swanky pool and clean, tile-floor rooms by the river suit you, this is the place. **$$**

The House of the Sun

Explore Inti Huasi Cave

With a backdrop of meadow, boulders and some dramatic dromedary-shaped rock formations, **Inti Huasi Cave** is believed – if the radiocarbon dating is correct – to have been inhabited as long as 8000 years ago. The name means 'House of the Sun' in Quechua, and its discovery caused a lot of hullabaloo in the archaeological circles, as previously, it was thought humans populated the region much later on in prehistoric time. So though unassuming at first glance, the cave has vital archaeological value and ranks among the top sites in the Americas thanks to its being so pivotal in forming our understanding of prehistoric humanity. While there are plenty of mysteries still to be solved about the cave and the people who lived here, we do know a fair bit about these early inhabitants of the region. Inti Huasi was home to the Ayampitín people, and they left behind hundreds of items like arrowheads, mortars and bone tools. Some replicas are displayed at the cave, while others are in museum collections worldwide. It's a wide, shallow cave with metal walkways that allow those in wheelchairs or strollers to get around inside. Though there's no rock art or cave paintings, visitors love the delicate, vivid green ferns covering the far wall's lower part. They provide shelter for some interesting modern inhabitants. Look down and you may find some interesting 'creepy crawlies', like spiders and centipedes. Look up (or listen) and you may see bats. Though signs are mostly in Spanish, the small museum has lots of photographs and other items worth a peek even if you're unable to read the Spanish. Several buses a day bring visitors here from nearby La Carolina; ask at the visitor center for the current schedule.

Mining for History

La Carolina: Inca Mining Town

High up in the foothills of the Cerro Tomalasta (2020m) is the small town of **La Carolina**, once a spot where the Inca found gold. It was exploited heavily in the late 1700s, when the Spanish cashed in (literally) on the hills' wealth. But the mines petered out, leaving the town with the quaint boom-bust feel so common to other mining areas. Today, it's a pleasant spot with historical discoveries, a few nice restaurants, beautiful scenery, and a relaxed, everyone-knows-you feel. Most of the buildings are made of stone, making them incredibly photogenic. Many visitors opt to wander about with their cameras or phones at the ready, making memories.

THE AYAMPITÍN

Inti Huasi was the site of some key archaeological discoveries that vastly reshaped the views of early human settlement in the Americas. The Ayampitín were cave dwellers who left unique signs of their culture, though it's what they didn't leave behind that's sparked an interest. While researchers found stone tools, grinding stones, and intricately shaped spear blades and arrowheads, they did not find any pottery, an enigma and defining characteristic. The discovery in this cave helped disprove earlier theories about the pre-colonial indigenous inhabitants of the Americas. The lack of ceramic crafts pointed to a culture significantly older than what was previously thought.

WHERE TO EAT IN MINA CLAVERO

Rincón Suizo
Often packed, this teahouse has a nice overview of the river and good Swiss food. $

Coronado Restaurant
A friendly option with alfresco seating for those with pets. Food is average: Italian pastas, pizzas and sandwiches. $$

Restaurant El Viejo Nogal
A nice garden and daily specials make this a good option, with popular raviolis taking the spotlight. $

As you enter the town, be sure to stop at the **overlook**, just before the entry gate with the metal miner statues. It's a short walk up steps to a photo-worthy viewing area above the valley, and still retains a decidedly Wild West feel. Then keep going in and stop at the **visitor center** for maps and answers to any questions you may have. (They also have public restrooms, if you've been getting desperate after the long drive!)

The **labyrinth**, atop a hill near the museum, is a fun challenge for those who enjoy that sort of thing. There's a beautiful **stone church** to peek into. It's been built and rebuilt several times, but always in the same location; thus, it's been standing and operating since 1732.

The star (or golden) attraction is a visit to the **mines** themselves. You need to go with a guide, but he or she will take you down through the tunnels into the shafts, which can actually be dangerous. The classic hit-your-head-on-the-beam is common, and the dank rocks can be slippery at times, especially after rains. So there's a bit of a 'You're Indiana Jones for an hour' feel here. The tours are mostly given in Spanish, but you can ask if an English-speaking guide is available. Journeying into the shafts will give you a sense of not only the labor required to mine, but the dangers and injuries the enslaved workers endured at the hands of European mine owners. You'll also learn about the different types of minerals, not just gold, that were formed and the geology of the cave. You'll see early formations of stalactites and stalagmites in the shafts thanks to the mineral-laden water that seeps down through the rocks, collecting and then depositing, drop by drop. A tiny amount of calcified sediment grows over

MUSEO DE POESIA

If you've been dying to read about 1700 manuscripts by acclaimed Carolina poet Juan Crisóstomo Lafinur, and other Spanish-speaking greats, then you've come to the right place. High up in these gentle hills is a museum dedicated to Spanish poetry. The location was the birthplace of Lafinur, who was born in Carolina in January 1797 but died in exile in Chile. His remains were returned to San Luis. Interestingly, the internationally acclaimed poet Jorge Luis Borges is related to Lafinur, a distant nephew. This is not going to be every visitor's cup of tea, but for those with an appreciation of the beauty of Spanish and its writers, this will be a spot you'll not want to miss.

Mina Clavero (p240)

WHERE TO STAY IN LA CAROLINA

Rincón del Oro Hostel
A hidden-away gem (currently undergoing renovation), with inexpensive rooms and a nice communal dining area. $

El Refugio Carolina
Cabins with nice comfortable beds, private baths, and better privacy than the nearby hostels. $$

Hostal El Tomolasta
Nice views, clean, spartan rooms, and excellent value for those looking for inexpensive accommodations. $

Parque Nacional Quebrada del Condorito (p242)

hundreds or thousands of years into the dripped-candle-like formations we appreciate today. Here in the shafts, there's only small ones, but give it a few million years, and they may be as spectacular as any. Tours may be canceled for safety issues at certain times, such as after heavy rainfall.

Come in January for the town's **Gold Festival**, a few days of fun and merriment that kicks off on the first weekend of the year. Among the events are age-appropriate treasure hunts that let you pretend you're a prospector and cry, 'Eureka!'

Cool off in El Volcán

A Recent Summer Resort

Unlike so many of the towns in this area, **El Volcán** was founded relatively recently, in 1949. It was created specifically as a summer resort, a place where San Luis residents could go to escape the summer's heat and drudgery. In some ways, not much has changed since then: it's still a great spot to head up into the mountains, cool off in pristine rivers, and get away from it all. Interestingly, despite its name and persistent rumors to the contrary, there's no geologic evidence of this spot ever being a volcano. Yet people still claim that from

LABERINTO DE LAS PIEDRAS

Not far from the **Museo de Poesia**, if you cross the small creekbed and head up the other side, is a small rock **labyrinth**, with walls about a meter high, dedicated to the poet Jorge Luis Borges. It has about five concentric layers before you get to the center, where a small monument stands. While it may be a bit underwhelming for adults, especially since it's only waist high, anyone with toddlers may find themselves having to pick the kiddos up, kicking and screaming, and drag them away. Be warned! Also, as these walls are not cemented, please be sure not to remove rocks or alter the structure in any way.

WHERE TO EAT IN LA CAROLINA

Huellas Cafe-Bar
A nice lunch and dinner spot next door to the eponymous Huellas Turismo. **$$**

El Bodegón de Oro
Possibly the best food in town, this spot serves crêpes worth saving space for, as well as excellent mains. **$$**

Lo de Chacón
Tasty soups, pastas, and hearty mains at this friendly, family-run restaurant. **$**

TO DRINK OR NOT TO DRINK

That is indeed the question. If you're traveling, it's tempting to toss caution to the wind and drink from the seemingly pristine waters you see as you hike. Keep in mind that some of the world's most dangerous microbes might be contained in that careless sip you take. Argentina is blessed with potable water. Most of the hotels offer tap water you can drink safely. But in any kind of stream, you risk fecal contamination from foxes, deer and other mammals, which can lead to serious – even untreatable – illnesses. Most, like giardia, will just make you sick and may cut your trip short if you need hospital care. But some can have lasting effects for years. So you're best to avoid drinking water that's not coming from a tap.

La Cumbrecita (p250)

above, it looks as if it's in the center of a volcano, and the color of the rocks, and the depth of the river waters...this is used as evidence of a volcano. It's not to be believed, yet you'd be surprised how easily people cling to fake news these days. Or perhaps it's always been a part of human need to invent fictional stories to replace the less-than-exciting reality? Whether you choose to believe the volcano hype or roll your eyes about it, the tale certainly adds some mystique and mystery to a place that otherwise is pretty dull. But that's not meant as a slight to this lovely spot. Dull is in fact the whole point: it's a sleepy, quiet spot to escape and spend your time lounging in La Hoya swimming hole, refreshing yourself with the chilly water and (perhaps) an equally chilly beer.

Interestingly, the Volcán River is one of the few that people claim is potable, thanks to its being spring-fed, though take that with a grain of salt, as it doesn't take much happening upstream to spread giardia. The river also flows – uncharacteristically – from east to west. Thanks again to its being spring-fed, it flows year-round, unlike many other rivers, which dry up during the hot summer months, from November to March.

WHERE TO STAY IN LA CUMBRECITA

Hostel Cumbrecita Planeta
A lovely spot with incredible views, decent breakfasts, and helpful staff. Also has both dorms and private rooms. **$$**

Hotel La Cumbrecita
If you like balconies, come here – most rooms have big ones. It's in a building that was La Cumbrecita's first house. **$$$**

Hospedaje El Ceibo
Rooms are simple but the views make up for it, and there's decent food here as well. **$$**

Splish & Splash at Balneario La Hoya

A Spectacular Swimming Hole

Anyone who spends time at El Volcán will, at some point, be coaxed to don their swimming trunks and wade, walk, crawl or plunge into the crisp waters of **La Hoya**, a swimming hole that's one of the town's prime attractions. And those who went grudgingly will wonder why they didn't give in sooner. It's a wonderful, special little spot. Given you'll be swimming with a couple of waterfalls, there are concrete entry steps for slip-free swimming, and the water is refreshing yet not too icy, so many visitors will want to plunge in. Depending on water levels and how tall you are, the 'hole' may be waist deep or it might be neck deep (or deeper), but it's always a great way to cool off, especially for those 'Team Summer' moments when the outside air seems hot enough to scald. The rocks make for perfect sunbathing; you'll almost certainly need to share the spot with others. Families, couples, solo travelers, the random heron or squirrel – just about everyone wants to swim here at some point. Another benefit to this simple life joy is that it's actually easy to take good selfies (for those ubiquitous social media moments!), because it's usually shallow enough that you can safely wade out with your phone (or have a friend follow you) and do the poses and voguing, without needing the hassle of a waterproof case. Just make sure you don't – oops! – let it drop!

Rainbow trout

FISH FINDING

Don't be the angler who comes to Argentina without your rod and reel. You'll regret it. If you're using live bait, be aware that you may have to contend with a hungry turtle or two. You'll find there are a number of fish species in the reservoir, but the game fish you'll want to catch are listed below:

Pejerrey
One of the prime fish to catch here, the pejerrey can be found in both shallow and deep waters.

Trout
Rainbow trout are a prize catch for any angler, as pretty to look at as they are tasty.

Carp
Though less sought after than the above, carp are often strong fighters and fun to catch.

 WHERE TO EAT IN LA CUMBRECITA

Bar Suizo
Famous for its delicious *spaetzle* (a kind of pasta), this rustic eatery is one of La Cumbrecita's mainstays. **$**

La Colina
Grab some hearty pork chops and applesauce or just sip a great imported beer. **$$**

Edelweiss
German-style food such as sausages and schnitzels, and other tasty treats, as well as a delicious tea service. **$$**

A Slice of Switzerland

Quirky La Cumbrecita

Mention that you're going to Córdoba, and inevitably someone will ask you if you plan to visit La Cumbrecita – if you don't have it on your radar, you will after they entreat you to go. It's a gorgeous gem, enclosed on all sides by mountains, with the feel of a Swiss ski resort...only without the skis. In fact, many of the hotels and houses even have that distinctive white wall and brown trim that you'd expect to see somewhere in Europe, and some establishments even market themselves that way. Yet, La Cumbrecita has its own unique qualities too. One of the many prime attractions is the swimming: the river here is crystal-clear, and there are several swimming holes, and fairly high waterfalls, making it very picturesque. There's also several delightful shallow bends in the river with nice beaches, for those who don't fancy a plunge as much.

It's also notable for another reason: there are no cars! Yes, that's right, it's a 'pueblo peatonal', a 'walker's town'. If you come by private vehicle, you'll need to park it outside the town limits and walk the rest of the way. Which feels wonderful, making you wonder why more places don't do the same thing.

The town has a cute little church to pop your head into, plus several longer hikes that take you to fun riverside spots such as **La Olla**, 'The Pot', which offer nice swimming as well. Around town, you'll find whimsical wooden statues carved into shapes like gnomes or fishermen. It may not be everyone's cup of tea, but nobody will claim it's not as unique and quirky a town as this area has to offer, and beautiful too.

MIRADOR DE LOS CONDORES

If you can't fly like a condor, here at least maybe you can *feel* like one: by partaking in one of the many altitude-defying activities here.

Ziplining
Probably as close to soaring as you'll get while still being safely attached to the ground.

Suspension bridges
You can inch along wire bridges hooked into safety harnesses; just don't look down.

Rock climbing
Try your skill at this sport as you clamber up to take in the stunning views.

Hiking
There's lots of exploring to do in them thar hills.

Photography
You don't have to even own a drone to feel like you're in one, with some stunning vistas.

La Cumbrecita

WHERE TO STAY IN MERLO

Merlo Hostel
A centrally located hostel that's got a pool, hammocks and a nice beer garden, good for meeting other travelers. **$**

Parque y Sol Hotel
A motel-style spot close to the casino that's spic-and-span, has a large pool, and is kiddo-friendly. **$$**

Epic Hotel
If you're looking to splurge, the Epic is a reasonable one, with nice rooms, great breakfast and heated pools. **$$$**

Mirador de los Condores

Be Eagle-Eyed at Reserva Natural de Merlo
Fantastic Wildlife in the Sky and on the Ground

You couldn't ask for a nicer spot to go with some friends and share *mate,* surrounded by nature, looking out over the dry hills at a beautiful plain below you. A rushing stream guides you much of the way. Along the way, you can meet the now-famous aguila mora (mora eagle) and happen on a friendly fox or two. Please remember the maxim: a fed fox is a dead fox. Don't be tempted by those cute furry faces. They shouldn't be fed and often become dependent on humans. Take photos, but keep your distance, please.

As the hike progresses, you'll notice trees getting taller and changing into conifers, then petering out completely if you go high enough. Above, high above, you may even see Andean condors, and somewhere up there is the **Mirador de los Condores**, so you may want to plan to do both things at some point, assuming you don't have a fear of heights. If you do, this quiet, beautiful nature walk will be just the kind of 'high' you're looking for.

Expect to spend at least two hours, maybe twice that, depending on how quickly you hike and whether you view it as a meander or as exercise. Much of the way there's little shade, so make sure you have good sun protection, and bring lots of drinking water, ideally in a reusable bottle.

BEST EATS IN MERLO

In this small town, your best bets for food are around the main square, the Plaza Sobremonte, where there are a number of small, mom-and-pop spots with alfresco seating. In the evening a few vendors sell snacks and sweets from pushcarts. While it's not exactly a town of culinary fame, there's something sweet and special about dining here, people-watching as you enjoy a quiet meal.

Pulpería Lo de Urquiza
In a building here since 1880, serving stick-to-your-gullet options like bean soups, pastas and tasty empanadas.

Franchesca Resto
A solid, alfresco option on the plaza, with burgers, pastas, pizzas and more.

El Nazareno
Chocolate and pastries at this on-the-square confectionary. *Medialunas* anyone?

Capilla
del Monte
La Cumbre
The Sierras
Córdoba
Mina Clavero
Alta Gracia
Río Secundo
Villa Dolares
Río Tercero
Villa Rumipal
Papagayos

Beyond
the Sierras

The Sierras are a loose collection of mountain ranges, but there's more to see near and beyond them.

GETTING AROUND

You'll need a car to make the most of time here, but buses will bring you to the bigger towns, and often hotels or hostels will know how to set you up with a tour or driver. Smaller towns like Capilla del Monte are easy to walk around in.

☑ TOP TIP

Be sure to download your maps directly onto your phone for offline use, as many areas have bad connectivity.

The Sierras break up a vast area that runs north to south and is shared by both Córdoba and San Luis Provinces. There are foothill towns as well as sections worth a visit that may be a day trip or so from your Sierra-based hotel. The landscapes range from forested to barren, from farmland to field, from rock-strewn river to water inching along the bottom of a mostly dry arroyo. It's a very diverse area, with quirky tourist spots and beautiful nature, and everything in between.

Capilla del Monte (p254)

Paragliding

La Cumbre

TIME FROM CÓRDOBA: 1½HRS

Paragliding in La Cumbre

There are some folks who won't be caught dead without both feet firmly on solid ground, but if you look at birds green with envy, paragliding in La Cumbre might be your kind of thing. This tiny town rose to international paragliding fame when it hosted the 1994 World Paragliding Cup. It has a great launch site, almost 400m above the valley made by the Río Pinto, and the options for gliding include tandem rides, where you'll be strapped on (essentially as baggage) while someone with experience does the flying. But if this sport is your thing, there are ample opportunities to take classes here, get individual instruction, and rent equipment. Once you've decided to go, you'll head up to the launch site, strap into the equipment, wait (not unlike a condor) at the edge of the cliff for a benevolent updraft...and whoosh! Into the sky you go.

For those who don't know the terminology, there's often confusion about what paragliding is, and is it the same as parasailing, and then, if so, how does it differ from hang-gliding? The answers are relatively easy: parasailing and paragliding both use a soft, collapsible, parachute-like wing to provide the lift, but with parasailing, you're being pulled from be-

PARAGLIDER COMPANIES

Paragliding (*parapente*, in Spanish) is best done with an experienced tour operator.

Voler Paragliding School
A respected standard in the area with years of experience and several locations.

Parapente Capilla del Monte
A tandem operation that's based north of La Cumbre.

Vuelos Tandem de Parapente
As the name suggests, this operator does popular tandem flights around the area.

Parapente Marcos
A one-man operation based in La Cumbre.

WHERE TO STAY IN CAPILLA DEL MONTE

Monte Adentro
Beautiful private cabins, one of which has a pool. Rooms look out at the mountains, perfect for sunsets or UFO-watching. $$$

Dos Aguas
Get into the UFO spirit with a stay in one of these freaky (yet chic!) geodesic dome rooms. $$$

Posada del Árbol
You may be greeted by little green men at the door of this nice, upscale spot in town. $$

THE CRESTED CARACARA

You may be tempted to call any bird you see an eagle, a hawk or a condor, but it just might be that the bird you're looking at is a crested caracara. These large, hawk-like birds have unique characteristics that make them easy to tell from the other similarly sized birds. First, they have a crest, usually easy to see even when they're flying. They also tend to perch atop cacti or in treetops rather than lower in the vegetation like many hawks do. They have a thick, sharp, eagle-like bill, but a patch of red skin around the base of the beak and to the eyes, similar to a turkey vulture's. Bright, long, yellow legs, black wings, and a white, mottled breast are other distinguishing marks.

Hiking, Capilla del Monte

low, usually on a speedboat, and there's a long cord keeping you attached to the vehicle. With paragliding, you're free as a bird. Hang-gliding is also free, but with a very different kind of equipment, a fixed, wedge-shaped wing that is kept aloft by the skill of the pilot. With a paraglider, you don't have to really do much until you reach the ground; it practically flies itself, except for a bit of direction you give it by pulling the cords.

Capilla del Monte
TIME FROM CÓRDOBA: 1¾HRS

Keep Your Eyes on the Skies

If you've seen every *X-Files* episode, you may want to schedule some time in Capilla del Monte, where you just might spot the next UFO. The first sightings began in the 1930s and the otherwise unknown town certainly didn't mind a little international attention. Since then, it's become a fabled spot among UFO hunters, who claim the crafts are drawn here by energy vortexes that crisscross the spot. Theories don't stop just at energy vortexes. They range wildly, from connections between the Holy Grail and Voltán of the Comechingones to the UFOs trying to enter a vast subterranean city where, of course, the human race will be able to retreat before spreading out across the galaxies.

Uritorco is the nearby peak, atop which UFO-hopefuls will wait, but the sightings don't seem to be only reserved for wear-

 WHERE TO EAT IN CAPILLA DEL MONTE

Buddhi
Lots of vegan options in this Buddha-themed spot, serving a variety of excellent Asian fusion dishes. $

Sabia que venias y prepare un pastel
A delightful cafe with whimsical names for the great mains, cakes, pastries and coffee. $$

Alfonsina Parrilla Gourmet
If you're looking for meat, this won't disappoint, but there's more here than just what's on the grill. $$$

ers of tinfoil hats. In 1986, a pair of locals claimed to have seen a spaceship land that was big enough to leave a 122m by 64m burn mark on the ground. Huella del Pajarillo it was called, and while it's been debunked, the mystique lives on. As do the sightings. As many as 300 people saw, or claimed they saw, a craft that left a mark 41m in diameter some years later. A burn mark was found in 1991 that, according to geologists, had heated the rocks beneath it to approximately 3000°C, well beyond what a normal lightning strike might have left.

Not surprisingly, these events have given rise to huge numbers of alien-seeking tourists, and there's even a festival, held each February, that brings the usual suspects (folks with Geiger counters, radios that pick up certain frequencies, and costumed characters from Star Wars, ET, and Dr Who). More importantly for the town, these aliens bring cold, hard, and very earthly cash to a small town that certainly doesn't mind the boost to its economy.

Papagayos

TIME FROM CÓRDOBA: **4HRS** 🚗

An Unexpected Oasis

As odd as it may sound, there are palm oases here in the region and visiting one is a fun experience. In Papagayos they are caranday palms, which have a beautiful sage color and which – despite being classified as 'coconut palms' – do not produce any coconuts. They're mostly decorative, and when they bloom, they produce bright yellow racemes of tiny flowers. In Papagayos you'll see plenty of them, as it's located in an arroyo, and floods help spread the seeds far and wide. If you've been looking for unique souvenirs to bring home, consider one of the wooden handicrafts made from these interesting palms, which only grow in this particular part of San Luis and a few other places nearby in Argentina and Paraguay.

Crested caracara

A PLANT PRIMER

These dry areas support a surprisingly varied number of desert and semi-desert plants.

Nopal
These 'beaver tail' pad cacti are unique, easy to spot, and edible.

Agave
Thick, sharp leaves that are hard and woody. Flower stalks can be up to 10m high.

Chin Cacti
Low-growing *Gymnocalyciums* have beautiful pink and yellow flowers and are a popular house plant.

Siphocampylus
These beautiful plants have long, often brightly colored flowers that are a popular food for hummingbirds.

Mesquite
A low, thorny shrub that can grow to tree size, with incredible taproots that can find water far below the surface.

Mendoza and the Central Andes

BLENDING WINE COUNTRY WITH THE ANDES

Immerse yourself in wine culture, dine at bodegas and brace yourself for adrenaline-fueled Andean adventures in Mendoza.

The central west region comprising the provinces of Mendoza – Argentina's leading winemaking hub – and San Juan is a fantastic playground for wine aficionados and *bons vivants*, while extreme sports lovers will relish conquering the Andes.

Founded in 1561, Mendoza capital is the central Andes' buzziest city, its leafy squares and irrigation canals dating back to pre-Hispanic times. Andean snowmelt is the city's, and region's, lifeblood, watering vineyards and people who otherwise couldn't easily exist in this semi-arid desert.

Once you leave Mendoza capital, vineyards will soon start springing up on both sides of the RN40, the winemaking past and present shown in century-old red-brick edifices sharing terroir with contemporary bodegas (wineries). Your vino adventure really starts in the stunning valleys of Luján de Cuyo and Valle de Uco, where wine is free-flowing and the Andes are seemingly within reach.

While scaling Aconcagua, the southern hemisphere's highest summit, isn't for everyone, you can still get a taste of the mountains by hiking, rafting or horseback riding. Whether you're kayaking near San Rafael or tasting Malbec in Barreal, the jagged backbone of South America always looms large.

WESTEND61/GETTY IMAGES ©

DON'T MISS

MENDOZA CAPITAL
Historic provincial city. **p262**

LUJÁN DE CUYO
Biking and bodegas. **p270**

VALLE DE UCO
World-class wineries. **p280**

SAN JUAN PROVINCE
Gateway to lunar landscapes. **p292**

Left: Malbec grapes, Mendoza; Above: Vineyard, Mendoza   257

Find Your Way

To an Andean backdrop in central western Argentina, Mendoza and San Juan account for 90 percent of all vineyards. While the two provinces are large, it's relatively easy to get around if you have a car, although there is more off-roading to be had in San Juan. We've picked the places that reveal this unique elevated wine culture so you can savor their flavors.

San Juan Province, p292

Low-key wine country and lunar landscapes reveal themselves in diverse corners of this largely undiscovered Central Andean province.

Mendoza Capital, p262

The historic capital of the eponymous province is home to picturesque plazas and museums, and is a great base

Luján de Cuyo, p270

In the Malbec heartland, book tastings and lunches at world-class wineries with stunning Andean vistas, then work it off cycling or

La Rioja

San Agustín Del Valle Fértil

Marayes

Punta Del Agua

Tucunuco

Mogna

San José de Jáchal

Las Flores   *Rodeo*

Iglesia

SAN JUAN

Talacasto

Matagusanos

Vallecito

Las Casuarinas

San Juan

Cañada Honda   *Media Agua*

Calingasta

Villa Pituil

Barreal

San Juan

Nueva California

Jocolí

Mendoza 🏛

Uspallata

Punta De Vacas

Cerro Aconcagua (6960m) ⛰

Mendoza

COQUIMBO

PACIFIC OCEAN

VALPARAÍSO

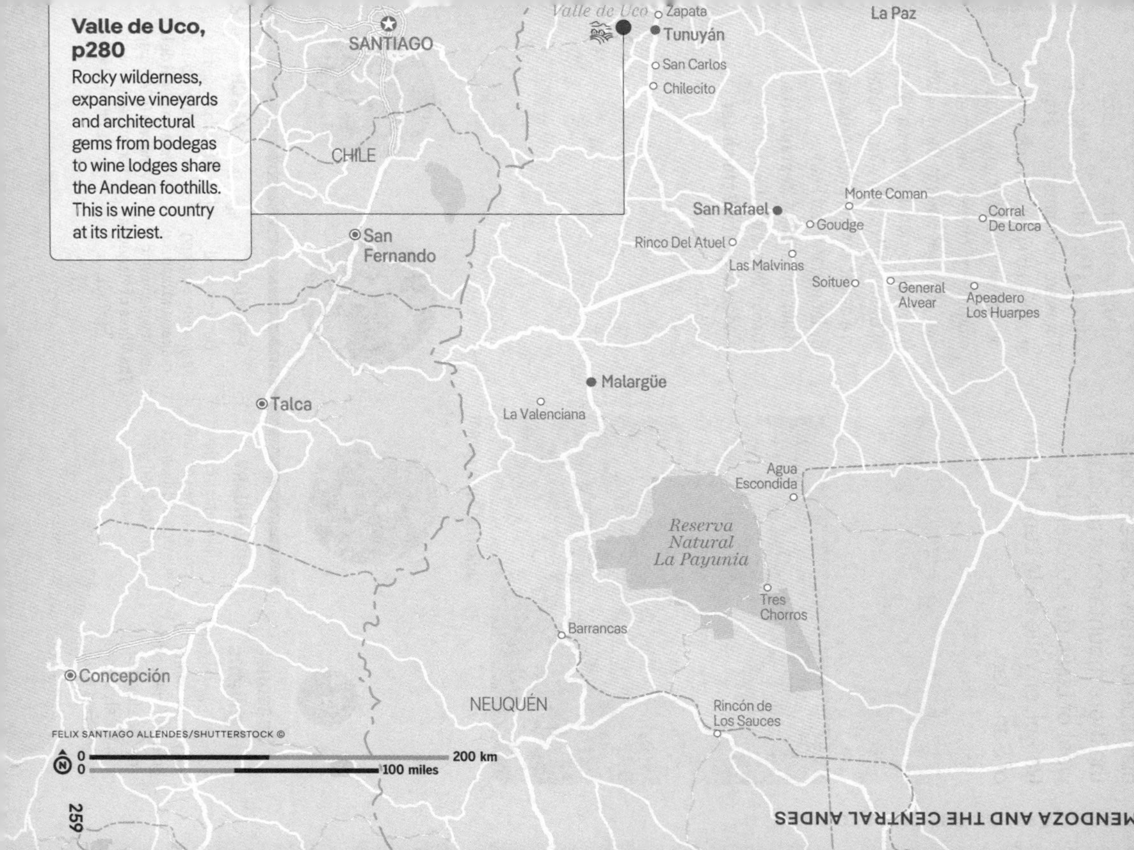

CAR

Hiring a rental car is the best way to get to know Mendoza and San Juan wine country. Exploring higher up into the Andes along rutas provinciales requires a 4x4 drive, so plan ahead. If you're drinking, hiring a private driver is an option.

TRAM

An efficient way to travel between Mendoza capital and Maipú is on the metrotranvía (tram). The single 17km-long line has 26 stations along its route, which means you're never far from your destination.

BUS

If you use Mendoza capital as your base, you can take buses to Maipú and Luján de Cuyo, provided you have a topped-up SUBE smart card (p483). For Valle de Uco, San Rafael or San Juan capital, take a micro (comfortable double-decker bus) from Terminal de Mendoza.

Valle de Uco, p280

Rocky wilderness, expansive vineyards and architectural gems from bodegas to wine lodges share the Andean foothills. This is wine country at its ritziest.

La Paz

Corral De Lorca

Apeadero Los Huarpes

Monte Coman

General Alvear

Goudge

Soitue

Valle de Uco

Zapata

Tunuyán

San Carlos

Chilecito

San Rafael

Las Malvinas

Rinco Del Atuel

Agua Escondida

Tres Chorros

Reserva Natural La Payunia

Rincón de Los Sauces

Malargüe

La Valenciana

Barrancas

NEUQUÉN

SANTIAGO

CHILE

San Fernando

Talca

Concepción

FELIX SANTIAGO ALLENDES/SHUTTERSTOCK ©

200 km

100 miles

Plan Your Time

Hitting the wineries is a must, but also spend a few days exploring the more mountainous regions west of Luján de Cuyo and San Rafael, or Valle de la Luna, north of San Juan.

Cañón del Atuel (p289)

If You Only Do One Thing

● Gourmands should make Mendoza capital their base for one night. It's close enough to a handful of bodegas in **Godoy Cruz** (p265) and **Maipú** (p267) for visitors to sample Mendoza's delicious food and wine offerings. There are accommodations to match all budgets, so splash out on wining and dining. In the morning, go olive-oil tasting at Pan y Oliva at **Bodega Santa Julia** (p267), enjoy lunch in the gardens of **Casa Vigil** (p268) winery, revel in a paired tasting menu prepared by legendary chef Francis Mallmann at **1884 Restaurante** (p265), then wind down with a cocktail at **The Garnish Bar** (p264).

Seasonal Highlights

Summers are hot and dry, while winter is cold and, depending on the elevation, it will likely snow in Mendoza Province.

JANUARY

Take refuge in the cooler climes of Valle de Uco and luxuriate in the food and wine scene.

FEBRUARY

Get first-hand experience picking grapes and learning about winemaking at **The Vines of Mendoza** (p283).

MARCH

Mendoza capital comes alive with the **Fiesta Nacional de la Vendimia** (p265) grape harvest festival, with parades in the streets.

Three Days to Travel Around

● Stay in **Luján de Cuyo** (p270) and get to know the winemaking history of this valley, visiting an array of contemporary and historical bodegas. Rent a bike and cycle between cellar doors such as **Carmelo Patti** (p274) and **Bodega Lagarde** (p270), savor tasty lunches with Andean panoramas at **Riccitelli Bistró** (p275) or **5 Suelos – Cocina de Finca** (p271) and, if your budget allows, lap up the luxury at **Cavas** (p272) or **SB Winemaker's House** (p272).

● For mountain vistas in the great outdoors, add some adventure to your day and go **white-water rafting** (p277) out of Potrerillos on the Río Mendoza rapids.

More Than a Week

● After a few days tasting your way around Luján de Cuyo, head south for Andean vistas and open wine country in Valle de Uco. Appreciate Uco's glitzy side thanks to wonderful architecture at **Zuccardi** (p283) and **Clos de los Siete** (p287), dine in harmony with full or new moon lunar phases at **Sitio La Estocada** (p282), or enjoy a remote lunch at **Ruda** (p282).

● Given the Andes' proximity, saddle up for a horseback expedition with the gauchos at **La Quebrada del Cóndor** (p284).

● For a laidback winery route, head further south and spend a night in **San Rafael** (p289) to go condor spotting and kayaking at **Cañón del Atuel** (p289).

APRIL
The clear night skies are perfect for stargazing at **Complejo Astronómico El Leoncito** (p297) near Barreal, San Juan.

JUNE
Pay respects to South American liberator San Martín in the **Manzano Histórico** (p286) on the anniversary of his death.

JULY
Bring your snow gear and take to the uncrowded slopes of **Las Leñas** (p290) for skiing and snowboarding.

OCTOBER
As spring begins, enjoy the blossoms across **Rancho 'e Cuero** (p285) mountain estate on a horseback ride.

BUENOS
AIRES

Mendoza Capital

GETTING AROUND

The center of Mendoza capital is walkable, as it's fairly flat with gentle inclines, but you should be prepared for a tiring uphill hike if you decide to go by foot to the San Martín monument in the eponymous park. Public transport includes buses to move you around the city, and there's also a tram out to Maipú, Godoy Cruz and Las Heras. If you're driving, you should park in an *estacionamiento,* denoted by a large E; fees are hourly or daily. Having your own wheels will make it easier to visit the wine estates beyond the city.

☑ **TOP TIP**

Mendoza's El Plumerillo airport is a 20-minute drive from downtown Mendoza. While the 680 bus runs from the terminal to Plaza Independencia in the city center, a SUBE travel card is required, so it's more efficient to take a taxi or rent a car at the airport.

Mendoza is the liveliest and largest city in the Central Andes and, despite its size, is easy to navigate. Founded in 1561, the eponymous province's capital was originally formed as part of Spain's Chile colony and was liberated by military hero José de San Martín. Three centuries later, future president Domingo Sarmiento recruited a French agronomist to create a wine industry here. Among the Bordeaux vines shipped to this fertile land was Malbec, today the country's star red grape.

The area is prone to earthquakes, with the most devastating in 1861, ensuring no pre-Hispanic and little colonial architecture remains. Much of Mendoza was rebuilt after the quake, and today it's a relatively low-rise city whose straight streets are lined with *acequias*, pre-Hispanic irrigation canals, and London plane and sycamore trees providing shade and keeping *mendocinos* cool during the hot summer months. Though the city itself is relatively flat, the nearby Andes mountain range promises adventures ahead.

Mendoza's Plazas and Parks
Exploring Green Spaces by Foot

The city's numerous green spaces along with its relatively flat terrain make exploring the center on foot highly enjoyable. The central square, **Plaza Independencia**, is the city's social focal point. Its four blocks of green space invite you to wander the artisans' fair at the weekend or just watch the world go by from a bench under the shade of the acacia and magnolia trees that smell magnificent in summer. As its name denotes, the plaza celebrates Argentina's history with fountains and a mural of high-relief sculptures that recounts its independence story. There's also a lofty 17m-high national coat of arms that is illuminated at night. Fanning out from this plaza are four more squares, mapped out rather like the number five on a dice by landscape designer Julio Gerónimo Balloffet.

SIGHTS
1 Espacio de Fotografía Máximo Arias
2 La Enoteca – Centro Temático del Vino
3 Memorial a la Bandera del Ejército de los Andes
4 Museo Carlos Alonso
5 Museo de Arte Moderno de Mendoza
6 Parque General San Martín
7 Plaza España
8 Plaza Independencia
9 Plaza Italia
10 Plaza San Martín

EATING
11 Azafrán
see 11 Centauro
12 Fuente y Fonda

DRINKING & NIGHTLIFE
13 Chachingo
14 La Central Vermutería
15 The Garnish Bar

WINE LINGO

If you're unsure of wine lingo, this glossary will help decipher some common terms.

A *degustación* means a tasting. You will likely try *vino tinto* and *vino blanco*, red and white wine. If you're driving, ask for an *espiter* (spittoon).

When visiting a bodega or winery, seeing the *viñedos* (vineyards) and *cava* (cellar or barrel room) is part of the package.

To order a young fresh wine, ask for *un vino joven y fresco*. For something aged in oak barrels, ask for *vino con un paso por barrica*.

Argentina has its share of *cien puntos* (100 points) wines, an industry benchmark awarded by critics.

Three pay tribute to – and are named after – the key migrant communities of Spain, Italy and neighboring Chile in Mendoza, while the fourth again honors South America's liberator José de San Martín, the general depicted atop his steed in a bronze statue. With Andalusian ceramic tiles complemented by fountains and monuments, **Plaza España** is the prettiest, the frieze that wraps around **Plaza Italia** depicts agricultural scenes that helped boost the region in the 19th century, while benches in **Plaza Chile** pay a colorful tribute to that country's flag.

From Plaza Independencia it's a straightforward 30-minute walk west uphill to **Parque General San Martín**, then a much steeper trek up to **Cerro de la Gloria**, the park's peak at 1700m, where sweeping views of the city and the Andes await. Renowned landscape artist Charles Thays applied a rational design to the park, whose lovely green corners include a rose garden as well as plane- and palm tree–lined avenues. A vital lung thanks to the 50,000 trees, it's also home to a lake, riding and tennis clubs, restaurants and an amphitheater, while at the summit lies **El Monumento al Ejército de Los Andes** (Monument to the Army of the Andes).

MAKE IT MALBEC

The success of Argentina's most famous wine is down to two French migrants: Michel Pouget and the Malbec grape. Tasked by future president Domingo Sarmiento, who had *grape* expectations of seeding a viticultural industry, agronomist Pouget looked to his Bordeaux roots to explore noble varieties, returning to Mendoza in 1853 with a Malbec vine. A star was born.

One of many French grape varieties that Pouget imported, today Malbec rules the roost. Winemakers began experimenting with novel approaches to growing the grapes 30 years ago, planting them at ever-higher elevations or aging the wine in smaller barrels rather than huge vats. It's proved its versatility time and again: depending on your taste, you can sample young fresh wines, 15-year-old barrel-aged vintages, rosé and sparkling Malbec – and even white versions.

Cerro de la Gloria (p263)

Museum Hopping

Wine, Patriotism and Art Come Together

Mendoza is quite the cultural city, and there are plenty of sights and museums to dip into that blend together wine, art and patriotism. Among the wine-related options, the highlight is **La Enoteca – Centro Temático del Vino**, south of the city center. A former viticulture school and winery, it has been repurposed to recount the history of Argentina's wine. You can even take a tasting on the rooftop, best appreciated in the evening while the sun is setting behind the Andes.

In terms of national history, *mendocinos* are hugely proud of General José de San Martín, one of South America's heroes, who, while born in Corrientes, formed his army in Mendoza and played a key role in Argentina's independence. The purpose-built **Memorial a la Bandera del Ejército de los Andes** just south of the city center houses the flag of the Andean army dating back to 1816.

On the arts side, it's well worth visiting the **Espacio de Fotografía Máximo Arias**, west of the center, which celebrates the late photographer whose lens captured the daily travails and social injustices in Mendoza; the permanent collection is housed in a former hospital. Also warranting a look is the **Museo de Arte Moderno de Mendoza**, tucked away under

WHERE TO DRINK IN MENDOZA CAPITAL

The Garnish Bar
Refresh yourself with a gin and tonic or a signature drink such as the refreshing Basil Oil Smash at this cocktail bar. $

La Central Vermutería
Stop by to sample the solid collection of vermouth on tap; stay for tasty small plates. $

Chachingo
Sip a pint of something crafty at this artisanal brewer that goes beyond IPAs to play around with grapes and barrel aging. $

the Plaza Independencia, which houses works by contemporary Argentine artists such as Antonio Berni. Elsewhere, the **Museo Carlos Alonso** displays hundreds of illustrations by the eponymous visual artist in a beautifully restored old house, Mansión Stoppel. And a 15-minute drive east, in Guaymallén, is **La Casa del Escultor Roberto Rosas**, where the namesake sculptor's workshop pays tribute to his life's works.

Celebrating the Sacred Grape
Where Harvest Festival Meets Carnival

There's definitely a carnival vibe with a Mendoza twist at the annual **Fiesta Nacional de la Vendimia** (grape harvest festival) as parades take to the provincial capital's streets in late summer and early fall. The province's 17 departments show off their agricultural prowess that goes beyond cultivating grapes to include tomatoes, squash, zucchini and orchard fruits.

Mendocinos have celebrated their bountiful harvests this way for over 80 years, and while the festival's beauty pageant – culminating in the crowning of the grape harvest queen – feels dated, the party spirit overall makes it a great time to visit the city. Revelers follow a procession of floats, mules and gauchos wearing their finest garb out of Parque San Martín and along the city's main avenues to a folk music soundtrack. To get into the grapey groove, take a bag to catch some of the seasonal fruits and vegetables thrown down by the 'princesses' from the floats. Catching cantaloupe melons is all part of the occasionally messy fun. The finale takes place in the Teatro Griego amphitheater – entry tickets are required – where an extravaganza of music, dance and opera finishes with the *vendimia* queen's coronation and an epic fireworks display that lights up the sky.

DRINKING ARGENTINA
Mendoza's wine varieties such as Malbec and Cabernet Sauvignon might be Argentina's best known, but there are lots more options from across the country for enthusiasts to discover.
See **Argentine Wine** on p506 for further information.

BODEGAS 15 MINUTES FROM MENDOZA CAPITAL

If you want to visit bodegas but are short on time, you can still wine and dine at one less than 15 minutes' drive from Plaza Independencia.

The 1922-founded **Los Toneles** in Guaymallén has been spruced up to tempt wine lovers in for more than a guided winery visit: book a table at Abrasado restaurant and order the dry-aged beef.

Operating out of a former auto body and paint shop in nearby Godoy Cruz, the vibe is relaxed at **Casa Tano**.

Sip their orange wine over a three-course tasting menu at in-house Capannina Bistró. Meanwhile, 1884 Restaurante at **Escorihuela Gascón** is one of legendary chef Francis Mallmann's outposts. Enjoy a romantic candle-lit dinner within its 140-year-old adobe walls.

WHERE TO DINE IN MENDOZA CAPITAL

Azafrán
Restaurant serving a delectable wine-paired tasting menu that works for both date night or a business meeting. $$$

Centauro
Ingredients sourced from Mendoza's ecoregions form the dining concept at this 2023 opening. $$$

Fuente y Fonda
A colorful local favorite located opposite Plaza Italia that serves vast platters to share, such as tasty *milanesa* and lasagna. $$

265

Beyond
Mendoza Capital

Move outside of Mendoza capital and discover
the traditional roots of wine country in rural
bodegas that keep their culture alive.

GETTING AROUND

While the
metrotranvía (tram)
service runs between
the center of Mendoza
capital and Maipú, it's
more convenient to
reach wineries by car.
Uber and Cabify both
operate in Mendoza,
but as cars can take
more than 30 minutes
to arrive in rural areas,
it's best to plan ahead
and book a car in
advance, paying a
little extra.

☑ TOP TIP

While the center of
Maipú can be reached by
metrotranvía (tram), it's
more convenient to visit the
wineries by car.

Head southeast of Mendoza capital towards Zona Este and you
don't have to go far before the urban landscape gives way to open
farmland. This wine region – known, together with Luján de Cuyo
(p270), as the Primera Zona or First Zone – has long been one of
Mendoza Province's most bountiful breadbaskets, home to wineries, many of which are found in the Maipú district. One-hun-
dred-year-old vineyards share the terrain with apple and peach
orchards, olive groves and bodegas, whose distinctive architectural styles rise above the vines. Driving along the winding country
roads gives a colorful picture of rural life: you'll come across trac-
tors, trucks transporting winery materials, dogs snoozing in the
midday sun and even a few goats – a lovely place to spend a day.

KAROL KOZLOWSKI PREMIUM RM COLLECTION/ALAMY STOCK PHOTO ©

Bodegas López

Maipú

Wineries Steeped in History

While it's usually considered that Mendoza Province produces mountain wines, **Maipú**, one of Zona Este's key grape-growing districts and the province's lowest-elevated at a rather lowly 650m above sea level, is an exception. The climate here is arid and the soil is loaded with clay, rather than Andean rocks. The area's star grapes are Cabernet Sauvignon, Bonarda and Malbec, slow-ripening reds that use the hot and dry climate to their advantage. A handful of 100-year-old vineyards in this district cultivate these varieties and take immense pride in retaining and highlighting their traditional winemaking methods.

At **Bodegas López**, three blocks from Gutiérrez tram station, you can take a guided visit of the 1898-founded winery; upgrade to pay for a wine tasting. The fourth-generation López family, led by winemaking director Carlos López and his brother Eduardo, continue using immense French oak casks of up to 40,000 liters for aging classic vintages such as their Montchenot red blend. The winery is living history, with hand presses and agricultural tools of the trade forming part of this museum experience as you walk among the enormous oak vats.

Another fourth-generation-run winery in Maipú is **Luigi Bosca**, founded by the Arizú family in 1901. Book ahead for the three-hour guided visit and tasting at its **Finca El Paraíso** vineyard near Barrancas, which includes a scenic walk through some of the 500 hectares of vineyards and olive groves. The gentle stroll, accompanied by birdsong, tasty snacks and an extra virgin olive oil tasting, ends at a beautiful mansion with a four-course lunch, paired with the bodega's star vintages.

Bodega Santa Julia

Drizzle Olive Oil Over Everything

A 20-minute drive northeast of Maipú lies the Zuccardi family's **Bodega Santa Julia** winery in the district of Santa Rosa. Running a 300-hectare organic vineyard, third-generation Miguel Zuccardi also cultivates olive groves to make Zuelo, the family's award-winning line of extra virgin olive oils. A mixture of Italian and Spanish varieties, including Genovesa, Coratina, Frantoio and Picual, is grown on this terrain, as well as the oldest variety to be cultivated in Argentina, the fresh and spicy Arauco. Olive harvest takes place in the fall: book your spot to get involved in the picking process, shaking and stirring the trees to release the green and black olives, and then see exactly how the oil is produced. There's nothing quite like the grassy aromas of the first press, extra virgin olive oil freshly squeezed in less than 40 minutes.

Another way to get closer to the land is to hire bicycles and roam the olive groves on two wheels. Pedal a little bit hard-

A WINEMAKING HISTORY LESSON

From century-old agricultural tools to extremely vintage vintages sporting peeling labels, Maipú's most relevant museum, the **Museo Nacional del Vino y la Vendimia**, exhibits a wealth of winemaking artifacts such as manual presses, many dating back more than 100 years. But perhaps the buildings that house these collections are even more special than the wine museum itself. Having previously belonged to notable winemaking families, the Gargantinis and the Giols, the two mansions were designed in the Italian Art Nouveau *stile floreale* architectural style. Stained glass windows depicting life in the vineyard have been beautifully restored, as have the Carrara marble staircases, summoning you to step back in time both agriculturally and architecturally.

WINE ON THE LINE

As you drive along Mendoza's country roads, every now and then you have to slow down to cross over a bumpy railroad track. A hundred years ago, trains transported wine in bulk between Mendoza and Buenos Aires, with bodegas and warehouses strategically constructed next to railway lines in both cities (Bodegas López's Palermo Soho warehouse still operates today). Once it arrived, the wine was divided up, often into concrete tanks, bottled into demijohns (three-gallon bottles enclosed in wickerwork), then sold to clients. One of the best examples of the old railway lines is at Trapiche, where old wagons are parked in perpetuity and the original platform remains perfectly preserved. By 1963, bulk wine transportation had been outlawed.

Bodega Trapiche

er and you can work up an appetite for lunch at **Pan y Oliva**, the on-site Mediterranean-style restaurant. Chefs use the estate-grown extra virgin olive oil in every dish, from drizzling it on top of the beef carpaccio to mixing it into the homemade ice cream.

Casa Vigil, Chachingo

TIME FROM MENDOZA CAPITAL: **30 MINS** 🚗

Great Vineyard in the Middle of Nowhere

The name 'Chachingo' literally means 'middle of nowhere' to *mendocinos*, but despite an unpromising name, this sleepy village has become a prime destination after **El Enemigo** winery at **Casa Vigil** ranked 10th in the World's 50 Best Vineyards list in 2023.

WHERE TO EAT IN ZONA ESTE

Casa del Visitante
Skip breakfast so you're ready for the *asado* (roast meat) experience at Bodega Santa Julia's other restaurant. **$$**

Casa Agostino
Many ingredients that go into the Italian-Mediterranean menu here are picked from the organic garden each morning. **$$**

Mil Suelos
Rib-eye, short ribs and flank steak are some of the cuts ready to be paired with some top vintages. **$$**

Chachingo is surrounded by orchards, vineyards and olive groves, a rural setting that winemaker Alejandro Vigil and his wife Maria Sance chose to move to in order to raise their family. After creating El Enemigo and basing this winemaking project in his Chachingo backyard, he then followed it up with the **Casa Vigil** restaurant, making a new wining and dining destination out of this part of Zona Este. A restaurant for 30 guests cocooned by vineyards with the Andes in the distance, serving trout empanadas, slow-grilled rib-eye and refills of El Enemigo, quickly turned into a restaurant accommodating 200 diners after word got out that this was a fun spot to while away an afternoon. Those with a penchant to learn more about enology are able to browse the concrete-egg fermentation tanks, covered in chalk illustrations.

This is one of the few Mendoza Province winery restaurants to accept reservations for both lunch and dinner, but before eating, guests go down into the candle-lit tunnels and cellar, which is decorated with works painted by Mendoza artists Osvaldo Chiavazza and Sergio Roggerone. Whether you choose a la carte or the tasting menu, delightful staff are receptive to your needs, and can help you choose the pairings or a top-scoring vintage such as Gran Enemigo Cabernet Franc Gualtallary to accompany your meal.

Museo Nacional del Vino y la Vendimia (p267)

JON G. FULLER/VWPICS/ALAMY STOCK PHOTO ©

MATERIAL WORLD: CLAY, OAK AND CONCRETE

Visiting bodegas and becoming familiar with the materials used to make wine over the years helps visitors understand the history of winemaking in Argentina.

It all began in the 16th century when Jesuit monks fermented 'mission' grapes in hide bags or clay jugs. In the late 19th century, the grape juice was aged in enormous oak casks that could hold 50,000 liters or more – barrel makers were much in demand.

Smaller vessels holding 225 liters made from new or used French or American oak became the norm in the mid-20th century.

Today's bids for fresher styles aim for less wood intervention; concrete-shaped eggs and stainless steel vats are popular – and the clay jugs have come full circle as the new generation experiments with these pots.

BEST BODEGAS IN ZONA ESTE

Trapiche
Book a tour of the iconic Renaissance-style red-brick winery, then sample the produce on a tasting.

Trivento
Sampling single vineyard vintages at this bodega takes place among picturesque Malbec vines.

Tempus Alba
Here, you can undertake a self-guided tour or live the harvest experience pruning bunches of grapes during *vendimia*.

Luján de Cuyo

BUENOS
AIRES

GETTING AROUND

While Luján de Cuyo and its 15 districts are accessible by bus, it's more convenient to visit wineries, cellar doors and restaurants by car. Order Uber or Cabify cars in advance to avoid waiting times in Luján's more rural areas.

☑ TOP TIP

Almost all bodegas require reservations ahead of time and it is unlikely you will get a table or into a tasting without one. Remember that many only open for lunch, so it might be more difficult to lock down dinner reservations.

Approximately 19km south of Mendoza capital, Luján de Cuyo town and namesake region bring you ever closer to the Andes and the great outdoors. Grapevines gently creep up the foothills here and the panoramas become ever more expansive – this is where you start to live Mendoza wine country.

As you drive the straight roads, old industrial bodegas rub shoulders with contemporary wineries, many of which have well-run visitor centers where you can taste wine or olive oil, book in for lunch, try a wine-blending class, tour the facilities or cycle through the fields.

While the region is large, many of the best-known wineries are within a 20- to 30-minute drive from each other. It makes sense to plan a day wining and dining in Luján's sub-districts such as Vistalba, Mayor Drummond, Agrelo, Chacras de Coria or Las Compuertas.

Malbec Heartland
What Lies Behind a DOC

While Malbec has proved its mettle all over the country, it's the town of Luján de Cuyo that is famous as Argentina's cradle of this renowned wine – meaning this is the place to come to visit bodegas and wineries which focus on this celebrated red grape and to learn just why it received its own Denominación de Origen Controlada (DOC – a sign of quality) back in 1989, the first given to wine in South America.

You can try Malbec DOC at some of the country's most respected wineries, and you can pick no place better than those that were also instrumental in obtaining that classification. At **Nieto Senetiner** in Vistalba, sample your juicy red with a fabulous Andean view, as recommended by Mendoza-based photographer Martín Orozco. At **Bodega Lagarde** in Mayor Drummond, enjoy a glass right next to the centenary Malbec vineyards from where its DOC is sourced. And at 1895-built

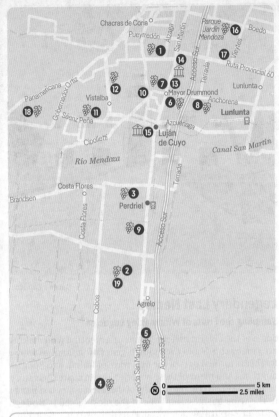

SAVORING THE VISTA

From some Luján de Cuyo wineries, you can enjoy spectacular views of the Cordón del Plata section of the Andes, which is always covered in a snowy white blanket but is particularly magical following heavy winter snowfall.

Enjoyed with a lazy lunch and some wine, the peaks are what memorable Mendoza Province experiences are made of. At **Quimera Bistró** at Achaval Ferrer winery in Luján sub-district Agrelo, order eclectic small plates such as endive salad and sweetbreads to complement a terrace-side table and bold reds.

5 Suelos – Cocina de Finca at Familia Durigutti winery in Las Compuertas sub-district, offers an epic 14-course paired menu set amid vineyards, while empanadas and ribeye under the vine trellis await at **Ramos Generales by Francis Mallmann** at Bodega Kaiken in the Vistalba sub-district.

SIGHTS

1. Bodega Alta Vista
2. Bodega Bressia
3. Bodega Casarena
4. Bodega Catena Zapata
5. Bodega Chandon
   see 12 Bodega Gieco
6. Bodega Lagarde
7. Bodega Luigi Bosca
8. Bodega Mendel
9. Bodega Norton
10. Bodega Viamonte
11. Bodega Vistalba
12. Bodegas San Huberto
13. Bodega Trivento
14. Museo Provincial de Bellas Artes
15. Museo Regional y Americanista
16. Nieto Senetiner Bodega
17. Otero Ramos
18. Riccitelli Wines
19. Susana Balbo Wines

EATING

see 18 Riccitelli Bistró

Bodega Norton, take your Malbec DOC with a piece of architectural history in the red-brick cellar room at the Perdriel-based winery. Other places that helped start Luján de Cuyo's classification story include **Luigi Bosca**, **Otero Ramos** and **Chandon**; you can take guided visits and tastings at them all.

During the past three decades, other wineries including **Casarena**, **Vistalba**, **Mendel**, **Bressia** and **Trivento** have joined Luján's exclusive DOC club. You can reserve a table for lunch at the restaurants at both Casarena and Vistalba, or book tastings at the others.

BEST LUXURY WINE LODGES

Cavas Wine Lodge
Standalone suites in a secluded Agrelo vineyard with private plunge pools, rooftop terraces for lapping up Andean sunsets, and a well-stocked cellar. **$$$**

Entre Cielos
The room to book at this Vistalba hotel is the adorable pod on stilts overlooking the Malbec vines – though the vineyard cabins are just as cozy. Revitalize your drinking arm with a spell in the spa. **$$$**

SB Winemaker's House & Spa Suites
Legendary winemaker Susana Balbo turns her hand to hospitality at this seven-suite luxury hotel in the heart of Chacras de Coria, which has wellbeing as its central tenet. **$$$**

Catena Zapata

Legendary Last Names
Sampling the Fruits of Winemaking Legacies

Some of the biggest bodega names in Argentine winemaking are run by third- and even fourth-generation families whose forebears formed part of the first wave of Italian and Spanish migrants, and many of these wineries love to share their story.

Luján de Cuyo is home to many of these legendary last names in the wine business, and one of the most fabled is **Bodega Catena Zapata**, which was declared the World's Best Vineyard in 2023 by the World's 50 Best rankings. While visitors have long been able to get involved wine tasting sessions at Catena Zapata's pyramid-shaped winery, the latest addition to the Agrelo-based bodega is **Angélica Cocina Maestra** restaurant, where fourth-generation vintner Laura Catena puts family vintages first, challenging chef Iván Azar to pair them with first-rate food.

Roberto de la Mota, meanwhile, follows in father Raúl's footsteps at **Mendel Wines** in Lunlunta. One of Argentina's most revered winemakers, Raúl pioneered single-varietal wines, and the father and son then worked together at Chandon (p271). Today, Roberto makes world-class Semillón and Cabernet Sauvignon.

BEST BIODYNAMIC WINERIES TO VISIT

Alpamanta
Try some of the 18-strong portfolio of wines over a picnic lunch and a yoga class near Ugarteche.

Krontiras
Drive past the llamas and taste Argentina's first natural Malbec before undertaking a horseback ride through the vines.

L'Orange
Sample Ernest Catena's line of organic and biodynamic wines, one of the longest-standing such projects in Argentina.

Trailblazing Susana Balbo was the first Argentine woman to qualify as an enologist. At **Susana Balbo Wines**, she tries all the produce prior to bottling with son José Lovaglio, director of enology. She opened a luxury hotel in 2022 with her daughter Ana Lovaglio.

Sofía Pescarmona's wine-loving grandfather bought **Bodega Lagarde**, founded in 1897. She's the third generation to run this Mayor Drummond winery. Self-appointed guardian of the few remaining bottles of Lagarde's legendary 1942 Semillón, she's also added two restaurants, Fogón and Zonda, olive oil production and an organic garden. Lagarde's iconic red blend is named Henry, for her father, while Sofia also makes Chardonnay and Pinot Noir with sister Lucila.

In Las Compuertas, Matías Riccitelli leads the new generation of winemakers creating skin-contact wines at **Riccitelli Wines**, following in his old man Jorge's footsteps in the winemaking game. They make a powerful Malbec-Cabernet Franc blend, and sister Verónica manages the bistro.

You can book ahead to visit all these wineries.

On Your Bike
Cycling Between Bodegas and Vineyards

Taking to two wheels to cycle between Luján de Cuyo's dozens of bodegas is an enjoyable way to get to know the area's countryside – and your reward for scaling the Andes' gradual gradients by bike is sampling a glass of Malbec (don't forget to spit). There are 110km of *ciclovía* bike lanes in Mendoza Province, which ensure you cycle past vineyards and adobe farmhouses, roads lined with poplars and snowy peaks popping up now and then.

Hire a bicycle from **Vistalba Bikes** in Vistalba or **Baccus Biking** in Chacras de Coria: they are available for full-day experiences, and you can pedal as much or as little as you like. The teams will happily put together an itinerary for you and provide maps and helmets as required. Pedaling up the hills and then freewheeling back down is a fun way to visit some of the lesser-known wineries such as **Bodega Gieco**, **Bodega Viamonte**, **Bodega Alta Vista** and century-old **Bodegas San Huberto**, stopping off along the way to try their wares. With some careful planning, you can squeeze in five wineries, pausing for lunch and tea, as most of the bodegas on the circuit also have a restaurant or food trucks. Why not savor a charcuterie platter at one winery and a cheese selection at the next? Should a certain vintage tempt you, the bike shop you rented from can pick up any cases you purchase and hand them over when you drop off your ride.

WHERE TO TAKE THE BEST PHOTOS

Martín Orozco, photographer of Estudio 365, shares his recommendations for where to snap vineyards with an Andean backdrop in Luján de Cuyo.

Anaia Wines
The views from this new Agrelo winery's tasting room are spectacular – a trick of the light makes it seem like there's an infinite vineyard, with vines running to the foot of the mountains.

Nieto Senetiner
Whether you point your lens from the arched entrance built in 1888, the restaurant's grill or the vineyards, the view of the Andes is always fantastic here so you're guaranteed a great shot.

Catena Zapata
This Agrelo-based winery has some of the finest mountain vistas given that its vineyards face the Andes; very few bodegas have this advantage.

BEST ASADO EXPERIENCES

Nieto Senetiner
A traditional barbecue awaits at this winery, where a dazzling selection of beef cuts is slowly cooked on an enormous grill. **$$**

Ramos Generales by Francis Mallmann
Catch Mallmann's show at Kaiken restaurant, where his team cooks over fire pits. **$$**

Fogón
An array of cooking techniques make for an exciting and fiery dining experience. **$$**

A REFRESHING TASTING WITH CARMELO PATTI

Many wineries run slick hospitality operations geared towards foreign visitors, so arriving at Carmelo Patti's unglamorous winery – basically a warehouse – is highly refreshing. Plus you get to taste with the hands-on winemaker himself. Located on main drag San Martín in Mayor Drummond, there's barely a sign to guide you into the parking lot, but that's all part of the magic. And no need to speak Spanish; wine is Carmelo's language. Known for his barrel-aged Cabernet Sauvignon and Malbec, his philosophy is old school, which means only releasing his vintages after several years, when he considers them ready. Try three wines in a free tasting.

HEMIS/ALAMY STOCK PHOTO ©

Bodegas Norton (p271)

Stars in Their Eyes
Explore Argentina's Michelin Dining Guide Area

Paired tasting menus and lunchtime *asado* experiences are the backbone to wining and dining in Luján de Cuyo, but some winery chefs have gone beyond the traditional steak and barbecue remit. It makes sense, given the province's outstanding quality of fruits and vegetables, and the new wave of menus that buck the area's barbecue obsession caught the Michelin dining guide's eye, which launched its first Argentina guide in November 2023.

BEST PAIRED TASTING MENUS

Angélica Cocina Maestra
The dishes here are chosen to match vintages at Bodega Catena Zapata's establishment. $$$

Brindillas
The well-stocked cellar at this Chacras de Coria restaurant means the sommelier has plenty of options. Dinner only. $$

Osadía de Crear
The sommelier team at the Susana Balbo Wines' restaurant draws from the extensive cellar. $$

Creating a multiple-course tasting menu that's paired with house vintages is an easy way to attract an audience, but at **Zonda** at Bodega Lagarde in Mayor Drummond, visitors get more involved than merely eating and drinking. First, you're invited to wander through the hundred-year-old Semillón and Malbec vineyards, past the shady olive grove to the organic garden to pick herbs and vegetables. Then, at the stylish restaurant, Zonda's friendly cooks teach you to make beef empanadas using your freshly picked ingredients, crimping the edges like a pro. The sommelier has the pick of Lagarde's cellar, mixing vintages that date back to the 1970s and 1980s with the contemporary line for the eight-course menu. Book a table for lunch or dinner. At **Riccitelli Bistró** in Las Compuertas, chef Juan Ventureyra loves to put plants first on his micro-seasonal five-course tasting menu. He cultivates the province's star garden product, heirloom tomatoes, as well as eggplant, carrots and herbs next to the Malbec vineyards. Dishes include pasta stuffed with potatoes and celery with a butter emulsion, and onion tempura with a parsley, spring onion and almond gremolata, matched with winemaker Matías Riccitelli's vintages such as Old Vines From Patagonia Semillón and Kung Fu Criolla. Enjoy a wine tasting at the bodega before, or after, lunch.

Culture Vultures
Art and Archaeology in Wine Country

Besides being steeped in winemaking history, Luján de Cuyo also houses two museums that make for a pleasant cultural break from wine tastings. At the **Museo Provincial de Bellas Artes** in Mayor Drummond, enjoy the permanent collection by artist and sculptor Fernando Fader, which includes murals, as well as a collection from Mendoza-born artists Roberto Azzoni, Antonio Bravo and Fidel De Lucía.

The **Museo Regional y Americanista** brings together local and American continental history, housing an interesting archaeological collection that reflects on the region's indigenous communities as well as exhibitions featuring original-size reproductions of friezes, steles and sculptures from the Olmec, Maya and Aztec cultures in the Mesoamerican region. The villa that houses the museum is also of historical interest, retaining original architectural features that date back to its 1908 construction.

HAMMING IT UP

Fuel up when you're on the road with a quick pit stop to try Mendoza's specialty cured ham sandwiches.

Food truck on RN7
Edgardo Campos only makes and sells one single product: his enormous home-cured ham sandwich to share. Enjoy it as the lorries burn past his food truck on RN7 and Cobos street en route to Chile. **$**

La Jamonería
A lunchtime-only spot at Bodega Vistalba. The charcuterie such as *bondiola* (pork shoulder) and *jamón crudo* (Serrano-style ham) prepared by expert Miguel Martín is the standout. **$**

Puesto jamonero on RN40
Look for a battered green truck as you head south towards Valle de Uco and pull over for Marcelo Gianuzzo's home-cured ham, drizzled with olive oil and dried oregano. It's a 20-minute drive south of the center of Chacras de Coria. **$**

 BEST PLACES TO STAY

Casa de Coria
Just off Chacras de Coria's main square lies this comfy property with spacious rooms and a large garden to relax in. **$$**

Casa Naoki
A private chef attends to your every whim while the infinity swimming pool overlooks vineyards and farms. **$$$**

Finca Adalgisa
This farmhouse turned boutique hotel is tucked so tightly into the vineyards you can pick grapes while floating in the pool. **$$$**

Beyond
Luján de Cuyo

GETTING AROUND

Some tour operators can arrange pickups from your lodging when you book a white-water rafting expedition. To explore the mountains, it's best to rent a car.

The landscape changes radically as you swap Malbec tastings for mountains high and rivers and valleys low.

Leaving behind the beautiful bodegas of Luján de Cuyo, within 45 minutes' drive on the RN7 – also known as the Ruta Alta Montaña – towards Chile, you are a lot nearer to the rocky Andean foothills and a more austere landscape. This corner of Luján is home to the southern hemisphere's highest mountain, Aconcagua.

While scaling its 6962m is for experienced climbers only, there are plenty of easier outdoor options here. The Río Mendoza rapids make for an exhilarating watery ride, while calmer Potrerillos Reservoir welcomes kayakers and stand-up paddleboarders. In summer, drive higher into the mountains along the Uspallata Pass for closer glimpses of Aconcagua.

HERNÁN E. SCHMIDT/SHUTTERSTOCK ©

Uspallata (p278)

White-water rafting, Cañón del Atuel (p289)

Potrerillos

TIME FROM LUJÁN DE CUYO: **45 MINS** 🚗

White-Water Rafting on Río Mendoza

Snowmelt from the Andes feeds rivers such as the Río Mendoza and Río Diamante and provides water for both the region's vineyards and its inhabitants, filling the irrigation channels throughout the province.

One of the most thrilling ways to get out on the water is riding the Andean white-water rapids on an inflatable raft, bouncing along a rocky mountain river, and the best-organized expeditions start near **Potrerillos**, Mendoza Province's adventure tourism hub. Aquatic adventures start with **Potrerillos Explorer** or **Argentina Rafting**, both a 45-minute drive from central Luján de Cuyo and close to the Potrerillos Reservoir.

The Río Mendoza exhibits its greatest flowing power during the summer months, which makes for a more dynamic expedition, but choose a trip that best suits your experience and time. There are options for all abilities, from a 5km one-hour Class II float to a full-day or even two-day descent with an overnight camping stay. A full-day is a four-hour expedition of moderate difficulty that covers around 30km of rapids, with plenty of river to bounce along. Don't forget to look up for uninterrupted views of the Andes; you are rafting through and over the Cordón del Plata. Tour operators provide all necessary equipment, such as life vests and safety helmets.

If rafting over rapids seems a bit much, Potrerillos Reservoir is equally good for more gentle water sports. Hire a stand-up paddleboard or a kayak from the same operators and glide over the calm surface; the Andean panoramas are just as outstanding.

☑️ **TOP TIP**

Go prepared for the rugged landscape with comfy clothes, sun hat and sunscreen for your close-up with the majestic Andes.

ADRENALINE KICKSTARTERS

Rappelling
With so many Andean rock faces to choose from, it's time you tried rappelling. Expeditions last a couple of hours and combine trekking with rappelling; one fantastic circuit with **Kahuak** tour operator takes you to waterfalls including the Quebrada del Salto.

Ziplining
Called canopy surfing in Argentina, this is as close as you'll get to feeling like an Andean condor as you fly through mountain passes. A two-hour circuit takes you above the Río Mendoza for around 1.4km; shorter circuits last roughly one hour.

Fly-fishing
Passionate anglers' excitement will peak when they catch sight of the trout in Potrerillos Reservoir and clear mountain streams. The season runs September through May; Potrerillos Explorer can hook you up.

277

AUTUMN SKY PHOTOGRAPHY/SHUTTERSTOCK ®

Parque Provincial Aconcagua

DANCING IN THE MOONLIGHT

Sunday afternoons haven't been the same since **Las Palapas** installed sound systems and dance tents next to a vineyard on Potrerillos Reservoir; entry is close to Hotel Potrerillos. DJs spin electronic dance music from 3pm until 10pm and the mountains reflecting in the water to a party soundtrack make for a unique experience. Wine, of course, is the tipple of choice; dress up, but take warm clothes.

Closer to downtown Luján de Cuyo, **Bodega Maal Wines** hosts electronic music parties at its Las Compuertas vineyard. The vibe is festival-oriented, with attendees donning extravagant costumes. And just across the way, **Family Durigutti** winery has been known to throw the odd EDM bash with Buenos Aires–based DJ Oliverio curating the magic.

Uspallata
TIME FROM LUJÁN DE CUYO: **90 MINS** 🚌

While the views along the RN7 to Parque Provincial Aconcagua are breathtaking, the altitude can be too, so pause in Uspallata, 90 minutes' drive from central Luján. Hikers use this small town as a starting base for park treks, and you can also undertake horseback rides in the mountains and discover abandoned mines that are dotted along the Uspallata Pass, which connects Argentina and Chile. Also close by is a curious monument – the cupolas of Las Bóvedas in San Alberto, domed chimneys of smelters used for refining iron that date back to the early 1800s; inside is a tiny museum.

Continue west past the Cementerio de los Andinistas to Puente del Inca, a naturally formed bridge of red rocks and yellow sulfur. Legend says that an Inca chieftain traveled here to be cured by the thermal waters.

Parque Provincial Aconcagua
TIME FROM LUJÁN DE CUYO: **2 HRS 45 MINS** 🚌
Climb the Southern Hemisphere's Highest Summit

Drive west from Mendoza capital via Uspallata and in a few hours you'll reach Parque Provincial Aconcagua, the snow-capped heart of the Andes. In summer, the park attracts mountaineers from all over the world, eager to undertake the three-week expedition to conquer the namesake summit, which, thanks to its 6962m peak, takes the title of highest mountain in both the southern and western hemispheres.

RN7 – the highway between Argentina and Chile – takes you through Cacheuta, known for its therapeutic thermal waters and spa, past the Potrerillos Reservoir and the fertile valley of Uspallata, you'll then hit the notable natural bridge and sulfurous hot springs at Puente del Inca, close to Aconcagua's base camp. In winter, check forecasts before setting out for the provincial park; if there's been heavy snowfall, it makes driving difficult.

Permits to scale Aconcagua are mandatory and most easily acquired through a specialist tour operator. The season is mid-November through mid-March. Given that Argentine summer holidays take place in January, this is the busiest and most expensive month to visit. Of the three approaches, the western Plaza de Mulas (Mule Square) route is the most accessible, though very experienced climbers will want to follow more demanding trails, such as Glaciar de los Polacos (Polish Glacier) or via Plaza Francia (France Sqaure) base camp and Los Horcones. Climbers looking to cut their teeth on slightly lower mountains in the park should consider scaling Cerro Catedral at 5335m and Cerro Tolosa at 5432m.

Every year, a handful of mountaineers do not return from their attempt to conquer Aconcagua, one of the world's toughest summits to scale, so go on a poignant pilgrimage to pay respects at the **Cementerio de los Andinistas**.

A 10-minute drive west of Los Penitentes village and 1km from the Puente del Inca, the cemetery was created in the late 19th century for railway laborers who didn't survive the harsh conditions while working on the Ferrocarril Trasandino (Transandean Railway) linking Mendoza with Chile. At the turn of the 20th century, other civilians and, later, mountaineers came to rest here; a pioneering QR code project shares some of their stories in a bid to keep their memories alive.

SAFETY FIRST

Clothing
Driving through the Andes means you are susceptible to fast-changing weather. Wear layers that you can peel off or throw back on, and carry a hat and sun protection.

Check ahead
Always be aware of road conditions, especially in winter, and check in with ACA automobile club or tourism offices before setting off.

Fill up
Gas stations and other services are few on your way to Parque Provincial Aconcagua, so fill your tank before departing.

Light and water
Carry extra bottles of water, a rug or blanket and a flashlight just in case you break down and have to spend longer in the mountains than expected.

Scan this QR code for more information on Cementerio de los Andinistas.

Climbing, Parque Provincial Aconcagua

ALMAZOFF/SHUTTERSTOCK ©

Valle de Uco

GETTING AROUND

Valle de Uco is a 90-minute drive from Mendoza capital. It makes sense to hire a car to reach the spread-out wineries, hotels and restaurants. If you're going to drink, remember to spit or, alternatively, book a private driver to shuttle you between wineries. Uber and Cabify offer sporadic service in Valle de Uco. If your accommodation is in Mendoza capital, consider taking the hop-on-hop-off Bus Vitivinicola, which has several pick-up points in the city and heads into Valle de Uco once a week.

☑ TOP TIP

Visit Valle de Uco's Bodega Salentein on April 17, Malbec World Day, when it lends its basement barrel room to classical music concerts.

Winemaking dates to the late 19th century in Valle de Uco. At the turn of the 20th century, European growers and investors saw the valley's potential, and these days some of the world's high-altitude vines are cultivated here. Along with fabulous vintages, handsome winery architecture also vies for your attention – Valle de Uco is Mendoza Province's wine culture at its finest.

From Luján de Cuyo, it's thirty minutes south to Tupungato in northern Valle de Uco; further south are Tunuyán (60 minutes) and San Carlos (90 minutes). These are the valley's three principal departments. As you drive, the topography opens up and snow-capped mountains are ever closer. Once near 6570m-high Tupungato Volcano, Uco is within your sights, as is the opportunity for hiking or horseback riding.

NICK PHOTOWORLD/SHUTTERSTOCK ©

Vineyards, Valle de Uco

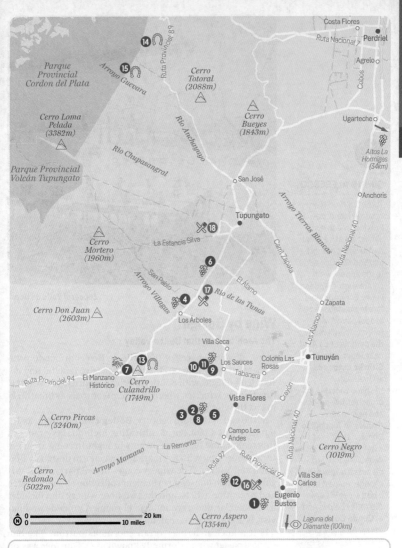

SIGHTS
1 Bodega Alfa Crux
2 Bodega DiaMandes
3 Bodega Rolland
4 Bodega Salentein
5 Clos de los Siete
6 Domaine Bousquet
7 Manzano Histórico
8 Monteviejo
9 Piedra Negra
10 SuperUco
11 The Vines
of Mendoza
12 Valle de Uco

ACTIVITIES,
COURSES & TOURS
13 El Viejo Manzano
14 La Quebrada del
Cóndor
15 Rancho `e Cuero

EATING
16 Cundo Cocina
17 La Azul
18 Ruda
see 6 Sitio La
Estocada

PABLO DUCROS/SHUTTERSTOCK ©

Zuccardi Valle de Uco

DINING ALFRESCO

Three hundred days of sun in Mendoza Province mean it's almost always a great day to dine outdoors – and Valle de Uco adds to the appeal with uninterrupted Andean views. For traditional fare (empanadas and *asado*) paired with folk music, sit under the pergola at **La Azul** near Tupungato. At **Sitio La Estocada** in Gualtallary, the bijou winery organizes full-moon and new-moon dinners. In Tupungato Winelands vineyard estate is **Ruda**, whose vegetable-forward menu is a refreshing change – plus it has a bird's-eye view of the valley below. And at **Cundo Cocina** in Paraje Altamira, chef Seba Juez only uses ingredients sourced from the Valle de Uco for his delicious tasting menu.

Wine by Design
The Architecture that Built a Valley

The wide open spaces of the Valle de Uco continue to present a blank canvas for architects to conceive fanciful and design-led bodegas with South American identity. The result is functioning wineries where the architecture is as breathtaking as the vintages.

At the end of the 20th century, **Bodega Salentein** near Tupungato was a pioneer in cultivating high-quality grapes in this region, and its Dutch owners brought in some architectural pioneering with a remarkable cruciform design by Bórmida and Yanzón. The winery comes in two parts: Killka art gallery, which houses a permanent collection showing Dutch and Argentine artists; and the two-floor winery that includes a spectacular underground barrel room. A guided two-hour visit is ample time to soak up art and wine.

Is it a nuclear bunker or an enormous button? The San Carlos–based winery formerly known as O. Fournier was renamed **Alfa Crux** in 2018 when it changed ownership, but its curious design remains intact. Built in 2007, in Eugenio Bustos, and also designed by Bórmida and Yanzón, iron and glass fuse to create a striking profile topped with a steel can-

WHERE TO STAY IN VALLE DE UCO

Casa de Uco
Book a suite or spacious two-room villa at this stylish hotel, which boasts Andean views and spa treatments. **$$$**

La Morada Lodge
A peaceful haven surrounded by vineyards. Check into a pocket-size cabin, then luxuriate in the wide open spaces. **$$**

Alpasión
Pitch up in one of six king-size glamping tents among organic vineyards in Los Chacayes; three include a hot tub. **$$$**

tilever umbrella roof. While the exterior is a talking point, the interior reflects a more passive attitude: the barrel room, reached by walking along a catwalk, is a haven of tranquility.

Not all bodegas have million-dollar budgets, however. At **SuperUco**, located at The Vines of Mendoza near Tunuyán, biodynamic agricultural practices are the inspiration for this family-run project led by the four winemaking Michelini brothers. Not only are the vines cultivated in a radiating circular fashion, but the austere and innovative concrete winery itself is shaped like an octagon in homage to the circle of life. Designed by their father Rufino Julio Michelini, SuperUco has picked up numerous accolades for sustainability.

The Art of Hospitality
The Zuccardi Family Does it Best

Hospitality comes easy to *mendocinos* – all they have to do is light a fire, uncork a great vintage and cook an *asado* before an incredible mountain backdrop. Taking hospitality to a new level, however, is **Zuccardi Valle de Uco**. The three-time winner of the World's Best Vineyard between 2019 and 2021 awarded by World's 50 Best, the legendary Zuccardi winemaking family upped its game when it unveiled its Uco Valley bodega in Paraje Altamira in 2016, known as Piedra Infinita. It was designed by architects Eugenia Mora, Fernando Raganato and Tom Hughes, who took inspiration from the Andes' jagged peaks and wanted the roof to replicate the horizon. Thousands of tons of rock removed from the terroir to make way for vineyards received a new lease of life when they were used to construct the buildings. Both the landscape design and the innovative architecture have picked up a slew of awards.

Third-generation Julia Zuccardi – after whom sibling winery Bodega Santa Julia (p267) is named – takes care of every last detail at Zuccardi Valle de Uco, whether it's a sun hat to keep the rays at bay while you sip Concreto Malbec or a lamb's wool blanket for when the sun drops behind the mountains. Whet your appetite with a guided visit, where concrete egg-shaped fermentation tanks allow the grape juices to sing, then try the wines in a tasting or over lunch.

The latter is a hearty four-course lunch paired with greatest hits such as Emma Bonarda and Finca Piedra Infinita Gravascal. The uninterrupted Andean views work delightfully with squash hummus and an enormous T-bone steak. Belly filled, top up your glass and soak up the views or wander the estate planted with Malbec, Cabernet Franc, Bonarda and Tempranillo to a backdrop of clouds hugging the peaks.

REMOTE STAYS IN VALLE DE UCO

In La Carrera in Tupungato department, unwind at one of these out-of-the-way stays.

Bella Viña
At these two charming cabins, there are unobstructed views of the Cordón del Plata mountain range. When Jeff and Veronica Mausbach aren't tending their vines, they rent out these peaceful properties.

Estancia El Totoral
It's an adventure getting to one of six en-suite rooms at this Colonial Jesuit-style guest lodge, as it's only possible to cross the mountains in a four-wheel drive. Highlights include the gaucho-cooked *asado* and roaming the estate on horseback.

Rancho 'e Cuero
Breathe deeply before driving up 2500m to this huge working ranch, owned by the Palma family for 250 years. Cozy rooms ensure an intimate stay.

 WHERE TO STAY IN VALLE DE UCO

Posada Salentein
This winery's secluded lodge harbors 16 spacious rooms sporting rural design set among the vines and gardens. **$$**

Huentala
Boutique Gualtallary hotel boasting art installations and spectacular views of Tupungato Volcano. **$$**

The Vines of Mendoza
Treat yourself to a villa at the Los Chacayes hotel that put Uco hospitality on the map. **$$$**

Make Your Own Wine

A Vineyard Dream Come True

The Vines of Mendoza is one of the winemaking province's hospitality success stories, thanks to its outstanding 28-villa lodge, Siete Fuegos restaurant, directed by chef Francis Mallmann, and spa. Its beginnings pioneered winemaking for those who long dreamed of having their own vineyard. Today there are around 180 private vineyard owners who collectively produce more than 300 vintages a year.

While you might not have the budget to snap up a few hectares of terroir, you can still turn your tastebuds to the task. Visitors – and lodge guests – can live a little of the winemaking dream by booking in for an array of activities, but be prepared, it can be rather gruelling under the hot summer sun.

The most hands-on activities take place during harvest season (Feb–Mar), so grab a pair of pruners and getting to work picking. Bunch selection is key, as is tasting and cutting the grapes from the vine in the right place, filling your metal basket with bunches as you go. Once it's full, carry it to the drop-off point, earn your token, then repeat the process, like a real grape picker.

A morning in the vineyard also includes the soul-lifting experience of some old-fashioned grape stomping with your bare feet. You can also hand-bottle your own personal Uco Valley vintage as part of the visit.

Should this sound like too much hard work, book into Siete Fuegos restaurant for lunch or dinner, and simply order a vintage produced by one of the 180 private vineyard owners.

The Andes by Horseback

Riding From Sunrise to Sunset

From a dawn trek, eating *medialuna* pastries and drinking *yerba mate* with gauchos in the foothills as the sun rises, to a full-on five-day Andean expedition, all levels of riders can saddle up and take to the mountains in Valle de Uco.

The gauchos at **La Quebrada del Cóndor** in La Carrera lead small groups through cattle pasture on a two-hour excursion into the Andes on relaxed steeds, though the 2000m elevation might lead them to huff and puff on steeper slopes. The view from the top is incredible, offering a true feel of the valley's breadth – you might even spy curious wild horses or condors. Ride it or hike it with your own two feet (sneakers are fine for this walk) – either way, you'll work up an appetite and your prize is a tasty *asado* (and a glass of wine) awaiting at the log cabin.

 BEST ORGANIC WINERIES

Domaine Bousquet
Sustainability comes first at this French-run winery whose range includes crisp Chardonnay and Malbec Nouveau.

SuperUco
This family-run winery, part of the Vines of Mendoza estate, has picked up awards for its sustainability efforts.

Sitio La Estocada
Personal project of Matías Michelini and his children, this biodynamic and organic winery produces all their lines.

Horse-riding, Mendoza

Gaucho Nino Masi at **El Viejo Manzano** starts his horseback expeditions in the Manzano Histórico, a short 20-minute drive if you're staying at Casa de Uco or the Vines of Mendoza. On an early-morning trek to the Pampa del Durazno valley, your trust is invested in your four-legged friend as, little by little, darkness gives way to dawn and the vertical drops become a lot more real.

The gauchos at **Rancho 'e Cuero** estate in La Carrera know the mountains like the back of their hand. Book a day out in the Andes and traverse cliffs, river valleys and meadows on a trip that takes you over the highest point at 2500m.

Advanced riders can book an epic five-day adventure, crossing the Andes with Buenos Aires–based equine adventure specialist **MacDermott's Argentina**.

CELLAR DOORS WITH A DIFFERENCE

Canopus Vinos
For zero-kilometer drinking, sample cold-climate Pinot Noir and Malbec made by Canopus' Gabriel Dvoskin during a romantic vineyard tasting in the great outdoors of El Cepillo in San Carlos.

Corazón de Sol
This winery, which outgrew its space at The Vines of Mendoza, uses Mother Nature for refrigeration, plucking bottles of single-vineyard Semillón and Grenache from a nearby stream's snowmelt waters.

Cundo Tasting Room
Only hand-selected small vintages sourced from around Valle de Uco can be tried by the glass at this cellar door in Paraje Altamira, run by the Suárez Lastra siblings.

DEDE VARGAS/GETTY IMAGES ©

Laguna del Diamante

WHAT'S IN AN IG?

Before a wine region can become a DOC (see p506), it first needs to receive Indicación Geográfica (IG) approval, and there are several Valle de Uco IGs hoping one day to become DOCs.

Four of the most recent to be approved by the INV (National Wine Institute) are San Pablo and Pampa El Cepillo in 2019, Los Chacayes (2017) and Paraje Altamira (2016).

While IGs don't define winemaking standards, they are extremely helpful in defining which grape varieties are cultivated in certain regions, as per European denominations.

San Pablo and Pampa El Cepillo, for example, stand out for Sauvignon Blanc, Chardonnay, Malbec, Cabernet Franc and Pinot Noir, helpful information for consumers.

San Martín's Siesta
A Historic Resting Place

Even though he was born in Corrientes Province, *mendocinos* are most proud of one man, José de San Martín, the general who freed Argentina from its Spanish rulers. They've named plazas and streets after him, but it's in a quiet corner of Valle de Uco, where the RP94 from Los Chacayes veers right and heads north, that a more singular reminder of the soldier, a famed apple tree, stood and gave its name to the **Manzano Histórico** village. It was under said *manzano* (apple tree) that the victorious general is said to have rested with his troops after liberating Chile and Peru in 1823. While the original tree has since died, a younger example was planted in its place, and close by is the stone *Retorno a la Patria* monument created by artist Luis Periotti. While you can't buy apples here, you can browse the outdoor craft fair next to the monument. A protected natural reserve, this area is the gateway to the Andes: many horseback expeditions start here, or you can also undertake short treks past rocky streams and waterfalls such as the Puente del Salto cascade under your own steam.

Foreign Affairs
A New Wave of Winemakers

While Valle de Uco's winemaking tradition dates back more than 150 years, the region attracted renewed interest from European winemakers at the end of the 20th century, starting with the French and the Dutch. Back in 1992, Dutch businessman Mijndert Pon saw potential in elevated Tunuyán and began cultivating Malbec, Chardonnay and Pinot Noir vineyards. While Bodega

Salentein's wines are regular top scorers, his greatest legacy is perhaps the stunning winery itself, modern yet unobtrusive architecture that has blended into the terroir.

Around the same time as Pon was eyeing Uco, the world's most renowned flying winemaker, Michel Rolland, joined forces with French counterparts to build the four-winery complex **Clos de los Siete** in Los Chacayes. An ambitious project for the time, **DiamAndes**, **Monteviejo**, **Cuvelier Los Andes** and Michel's own winery **Bodega Rolland** today make world-class Bordeaux-influenced wines using Argentine grapes that are barrel-aged; all four bodegas host tastings, and the former two open for lunch.

Other French influences include François Lurton, whose **Piedra Negra** winery in Los Chacayes notched its 30th *vendimia* grape harvest in 2023, while Anne Bousquet and husband Labid Al Ameri lead organic winery **Domaine Bousquet**. Italian flying maker Alberto Antonini has been involved with **Altos Las Hormigas** from day one. There's also North American interest: US wine lover Michael Evans co-founded the neighboring **The Vines of Mendoza** in 2004. You can visit all these wineries and appreciate how these imports have turned their hands to Uco terroir.

Laguna del Diamante Adventure
Dive into the Gorgeous Lagoon

Involving a three-hour drive from Tunuyán to Pareditas, then onwards along 60km of dirt track in the southern part of San Carlos department, visiting Laguna del Diamante is an invigorating outdoor adventure.

Named for the diamond-shaped reflection that the towering Maipo volcano projects onto the lagoon's cobalt waters, the lagoon is located in the reserva provincial of the same name. Given Laguna del Diamante's high altitude at 3325m, intense weather conditions are likely, with a blustery wind whipping about your person, so bring suitable clothing.

For an easy activity, spend an hour or two hiking around the freshwater lake observing a herd of guanaco – look out for the dominant male keeping watch on higher ground – in this starkly beautiful habitat, before hunkering down from the wind for a picnic. Bring binoculars because you might also spot foxes and flamingoes that live in the reserve.

More experienced hikers can undertake the challenging 17km route up to the first elevation of the volcano, whose peak tops out at 5323m. It takes a little more than four hours and you will be rewarded by marvellous vistas of the lagoon. Whichever trail you decide to take, it's unlikely you will bump into many other people along the way. The reserve is only open during summer between January and April.

BEST CULTURAL EVENTS

Wine Rock
Annual rock festival at Monteviejo with winemaker and guitarist Marcelo Pelleriti and Argentina's finest rock musicians in late fall.

Rally de las Bodegas
Now in its third decade, this rally sees vintage car lovers take to their automobiles in a 700-km competition in March.

Música Clásica por los Caminos del Vino
One of the main draws to March's *vendimia* (harvest) celebrations are the classical music concerts held in bodegas.

Beyond
Valle de Uco

GETTING AROUND

It makes sense to rent a car to easily reach wineries and accommodations and to undertake expeditions under your own steam in this region. Buses run between San Rafael and Malargüe; there are also buses from San Rafael's bus terminal to Valle Grande and El Nihuil.

☑ **TOP TIP**

Many of San Rafael's traditional bodegas have fixed schedules for visits and can easily accommodate large groups, so reservations aren't usually necessary. This is the region to buy easy-drinking wines rather than investment vintages.

Slow down the pace and get close to a different Andean landscape, using the towns of San Rafael and Malargüe as your base.

From Valle de Uco's Tunuyán, it's a 2hr drive to southern Mendoza Province's main hubs of San Rafael and Malargüe. The RN40 divides at Pareditas: continue on it for Malargüe and Las Leñas ski resort, or take the RN143 to San Rafael.

The pace of life is slower in this southern stretch of the province, and the landscapes are more wide open as the Andes begin to shrink in the distance. There are dozens of historical wineries to visit in San Rafael, and it's also a convenient jumping-off point for exploring the great outdoors, such as whitewater rafting in Cañon del Atuel and volcanoes near Malargüe.

San Rafael
TIME FROM VALLE DE UCO: **2 HRS** 🚗
Slow the Pace Down in San Rafael

Once out of Valle de Uco, the scenery accompanying your drive along the RN40 on the way to San Rafael quickly turns into steppe, with slopes rather than mountains forming the landscape. Look in your rearview mirror – the Andes have disappeared behind you.

Best described as a large town, San Rafael is a microcosm of the provincial capital, with its irrigation canals and shady avenues. The pace is laid-back – here people still actually sleep during siesta. The area is also known for wine – drive 15 mins out of the center to find open farmland and vineyards where the winemaking remains firmly in traditional territory. There are few bells and whistles to speak of here, and it's refreshing to see wine in a less marketing-focused environment. Whitewashed walls and century-old farm tools are on show at the cluster of bodegas on RP173, also known as calle Cubillos. Most offer guided visits at set times for free or a small fee, such as

© OLIVIA...

Cañón del Atuel

Finca El Nevado, **Bodega 1920** and **Bodega Labiano** (the latter is notable for its 'Malbec' hued fountain). Given the warm climate, try bold reds such as Cabernet Sauvignon, Bonarda and Malbec.

Big-name wineries such as **Bianchi** and **Suter** have also made their mark on San Rafael's wine industry; both are open for visits. A contemporary and more luxurious addition is **Algodón Wine Estates**; those on a big budget can stay the night.

Cañón del Atuel TIME FROM VALLE DE UCO: **2 HRS 30 MINS** 🚗

Water and Mountains Meet at Cañón del Atuel

A 40-minute drive from San Rafael is **Cañón del Atuel**, a gem of a natural canyon that encompasses two aquamarine-colored reservoirs, rugged terrain and lots of outdoor activities. The drive on RP173 through Valle Grande past Villa El Nihuil becomes more interesting when the road starts to twist and turn, rocks begin to jut out of the earth and pink pepper trees and weeping willows line the way to the Río Atuel. While the Embalse Valle Grande and Embalse El Nihuil reservoirs are manmade, the rock formations that cocoon them offer beautiful reflections of the low-lying mountains that line them.

You can park at **La Barra** restaurant, located just after the Embalse Valle Grande reservoir's bridge, and strike out on an easy trek around the shores to soak up the magnificent mountain and water views. Another leisurely experience is taking a catamaran from the Embalse Valle Grande's jetty to while away an afternoon on the sandy beach at Playa Portal del Atuel. For this and other outdoor adventures – whitewater rafting, canyoning, rappelling and exciting nighttime rafting and trekking expeditions – book with tour operator **Portal del Atuel**. As condors make the Cañón del Atuel their home, keen bird spotters should continue to the Mirador de

ARGENTINA'S FIRST BIODYNAMIC WINERY

While many San Rafael bodegas focus on quantity rather than quality, the region is home to the first winery that was certified for biodynamic agriculture in Argentina. After years working in the family business, third-generation winemaker Alejandro Bianchi set up his own project. Today, **Finca La Encantada**, a charming four-room lodge that he built by hand, shares a century-old farm surrounded by **Finca Dinamia**, with its loquat trees and vines, his organic and biodynamic winemaking project a 15-minute drive south-west of San Rafael.

Specializing in Malbec, he produces two wines in concrete-egg fermentation tanks and French oak barrels at La Encantada; you can browse the tiny facility with Alejandro. Besides producing wine, there's also a small organic chocolate factory on site.

los Cóndores, an eight-minute drive from La Barra. The enigmatic Andean avian surfs on the air currents, barely beating its wings before dramatically dropping or soaring up into the sky. Given that they breed in the canyon, your chances of observing one are good.

Follow the mountain road alongside the Embalse Valle Grande southwest for an hour to see the second reservoir, Embalse El Nihuil. This is the place to go kitesurfing; book with operator **Nihuil Kite & Aventura**.

Malargüe   TIME FROM VALLE DE UCO: 2 HRS 40 MINS 🚗

What small Malargüe lacks in big-town energy, it makes up for in impressive geology and volcanic landscapes. It also makes a decent if distant base for Las Leñas ski resort, 70km away, if you're on a tight budget. A fascinating mix of parks, lagoons and even a witches' cave make up the town's surrounding geography; you'll need your own transport to reach these places.

Bird spotters will enjoy the wetlands at Reserva Provincial Laguna de Llancanelo – a photogenic high mountain lake 60km southeast of Malargüe that is home to ducks, black-necked swans, gulls and teals among 100 other species; you can also spot Andean flamingoes. Volcano fans should head to the spectacular Parque Provincial La Payunia, 200km south of Malargüe. The 4500-sq-km park has the highest concentration of volcanic cones in the world, more than 800, which make for breathtaking scenery like something from another planet. A little closer to Malargüe, 65km away, lies Caverna de las Brujas, a 5km-long witches' cave made out of limestone and full of stalactites and stalagmites that's recognized as a national natural monument. Allow for two or three hours to explore it with a tour operator such as Karen Travel.

Las Leñas   TIME FROM VALLE DE UCO: **3 HRS** 🚗
Snow Season in Las Leñas

One of Argentina's most upmarket ski resorts, **Las Leñas** is where, between June and September, snow-loving *mendocinos* head to spend the weekend. *Porteños (*people from Buenos Aires) make a beeline here too, flying directly into San Rafael airport from Aeroparque Jorge Newbery, then driving the 200km to the resort. This is also the choice for northern hemisphere pros, who make the most of the south's winter to continue training – bask in the fact that you're in excellent company. Wherever they arrive from, though, the draw is the same: there's nothing more exhilarating for powder fans than skiing down the Andes.

AROUND
SAN RAFAEL

Bodega Tornaghi
The oldest winery in San Rafael has been operating continuously since 1883; pick up some easy-drinking Malbec to enjoy.

Laberinto de Borges
An a-*maze*-ing labyrinth tribute to the Nobel-prize winning Argentine author Jorge Luis Borges that's bursting with literary symbolism.

Salinas del Diamante
Parts of these ancient salt flats are still being harvested after a century of commercial use; book ahead to drive through a snow-white natural landscape.

🛏️ WHERE TO STAY BEYOND VALLE DE UCO

Finca La Encantada
Charming four-room lodge; winemaker Alejandro Bianchi used mostly recycled materials to build it himself. **$**

Algodon Wine Resort
Delightful lodge surrounded by vineyards and the eponymous winery. Golfers will love doing the rounds. **$$$**

El Nevado
On the outskirts of Malargüe, this budget yet comfy hotel is run by very helpful owners. **$**

Snowboarding, Las Leñas

Las Leñas resort nestles at 2240m, while its mountain reaches 3430m and has 30 runs to ski or snowboard on, meaning there's room for everyone. Ski school gets beginners up and running on the nursery slopes, while old hands can simply clamber onto El Marte lift, which takes you to the more difficult terrain for off-piste and black runs. In recent years, with climate change, the season has increasingly become shorter, so Las Leñas often relies on snow machines to ensure visitors can ski away to their heart's content.

There are five hotels to book into and several 'apart hotel' facilities, whose self-catering rooms accommodate groups of up to six and also have room service. The hotels offer package deals that include ski passes, though if you're on a budget but still want to hit the slopes, it can be cheaper to rent a room or chalet an hour's drive from Las Leñas in **Los Molles**.

BEST NATURAL WONDERS

La Payunia
Spot guanacos and ñandús roaming the terrain at Parque Provincial La Payunia.

Flight of the Condors
Take binoculars to ensure a fascinating close-up of condors flying around Cañón del Atuel.

Pozo de las Ánimas
Two almost identical lakes filled with turquoise water make for an off-the-beaten-path photo opportunity en route to Las Leñas.

BUENOS
AIRES

San Juan Province

GETTING AROUND

The best way to get around San Juan Province to visit its spreadout attractions is by car; rent a vehicle – and consider a 4WD to take on rocky mountain roads and dirt tracks – at the airport if you're planning to explore further afield.

☑ TOP TIP

San Juan capital is a charming and small city that is easily walkable. Spend a night here to enjoy its relaxed pace. If you're going to explore the province, be sure to hire a vehicle, preferably a four-wheel drive.

A leisurely pace awaits in low-key San Juan Province, its eponymous capital and the surrounding valleys – although it is full of natural surprises if you're up for exploring. The tradition and siesta-as-standard are welcome after Mendoza's visually arresting wineries and restaurants; relaxed San Juan hasn't really caught up with its neighboring province in many respects.

Wandering the long shaded boulevards of the provincial capital at a sedate pace is welcoming and a pleasant opportunity to recharge if you have just visited Mendoza. Home to a few decent restaurants and a few museums, including a wine-focused one, the city also makes a useful launchpad for exploring the wider region's rugged landscapes, as there are several hotels here. There is also a Ruta del Vino wine trail, albeit not as extensive as Mendoza's – but that's a positive, as it means fewer crowds and the likelihood of one-on-one time with the winemakers themselves.

You can reach the city via a 1hr 45min flight from Buenos Aires or a 2hr 45min drive north from Mendoza city on RN40.

Plaza 25 de Mayo

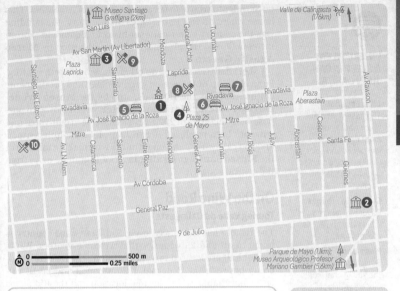

SIGHTS
1 Catedral de San Juan Bautista
2 Museo Agustín Gnecco
3 Museo y Biblioteca Casa Natal de Sarmiento
4 Plaza 25 de Mayo

SLEEPING
5 Del Bono Central Hotel
6 Hotel Provincial
7 Hotel Selby

EATING
8 Club Español
9 Club Sirio Libanés
10 Mesa Uno

Exploring Central San Juan Capital
Strolling the Home of the Sun

It's easy to explore the downtown of San Juan capital on foot. Founded in 1562 by Spanish colonialists, the city's low-rise buildings, vintage signage and storefronts take you back to a bygone era. Its spacious **Parque de Mayo** and plazas offer respite during the hot summer months – the capital's nickname is Residencia del Sol (home of the sun) thanks to the 300 sunny days a year it enjoys.

Start a self-guided walking tour at the verdant central square **Plaza 25 de Mayo**, home to **Catedral de San Juan Bautista**, whose architecture is surprisingly modern in such an old city – but with good reason. San Juan's geographical location near tectonic plates means earthquakes in this small urban landscape are regular occurrences. As a consequence, few buildings are more than 80 years old and, following the damaging 1944 earthquake, this cathedral was rebuilt three decades later in 1979, resulting in its contemporary architecture. It's worth climbing the red-brick bell tower for a panorama of the Río San Juan valley to appreciate the city's relevance in the region.

Then walk to **Museo y Biblioteca Casa Natal de Sarmiento**, named after the educator and journalist Domingo Fausti-

SAN JUAN BODEGAS

San Juan Province is home to several grape-growing valleys of which Pedernal, Calingasta, Zonda, Ullum-Zonda, Iglesia and Jáchal are the best known; each has a Geographical Indication, known as IG, that confirms the wine's origin. **Valle de Tulum** is home to the largest cluster of bodegas in the area, and you can visit traditional and well-known regional winery names such as **Augusto Pulenta**, **Argus**, **Callia** and **Champañería Miguel Más** to learn how they have contributed to the local wine industry through short guided visits and tastings.

WHERE TO EAT & SLEEP IN SAN JUAN CAPITAL

Club Español
The basement of this place packs out every night thanks to its low prices and solid Spanish-style staples, such as tortilla and paella.

Club Sirio Libanés
Savor platters of meze amid Alhambra-style architecture.

Mesa Uno
Book here to see how the young chef works closely with local farmers to create dishes such as roast lettuce with stewed tongue.

Hotel Provincial
Just off Plaza 25 de Mayo, this hotel makes for a comfy one-night stay and includes parking.

Hotel Selby
Simple and well-sized rooms are great value for the downtown location.

Del Bono Central Hotel
Contemporary design, a rooftop swimming pool and a spa are some of the details at this located hotel.

no Sarmiento who also became president of Argentina. This house where he was born shares his life story; the building was the country's first national historic monument. For an introduction to the province's history, also stop by **Museo Agustín Gnecco**.

A short drive away are two other museums worth visiting. For a close-up of the region's archaeology and pre-Hispanic cultures such as the Huarpe's, stop by the **Museo Arqueológico Profesor Mariano Gambier**, which moved to purpose-built facilities in 2023. Grapes have been cultivated and wine has been produced in San Juan since the 16th century, and you can learn about one family's winemaking mission at the **Museo Santiago Graffigna**; it's a 10-minute drive from the central square.

On the Wine Road

Touring Valle de Calingasta

The remote but extremely lovely San Juan wine country is home to around 25 wineries that welcome visitors. While almost half are located in Valle de Tulum, the rest are divided up between the Pedernal, Ullum-Zonda and Fértil valleys – but thanks to its elevated location and the Río de los Patos that runs through it, **Valle de Calingasta** offers the best range of outdoor activities, such as rafting or kayaking, paired with spectacular Andean scenery as well as wine tastings and guided visits to bodegas.

This attractive valley is a four-hour drive, at times along dirt tracks, from San Juan capital. Enjoy the meandering drive, which takes in views of Cordillera de Ansilta's seven breathtaking peaks; you might also catch a glimpse of Aconcagua. Valle de Calingasta is home to seven bodegas that welcome visitors, in the villages of Sorocayense, Villa Pituil and Barreal. In the latter, you can go tasting at **Cara Sur**, **Los Dragones**, **Entre Tapias** (the village's first boutique bodega) and **Finca Basin**; the former two both make terroir-driven organic and natural wines. Barreal is also 20km from **Parque Nacional El Leoncito** (p294), which is a great half-day excursion for a change in scenery. In Sorocayense you can taste at **Alta Bonanza de los Andes**, or enjoy local charcuterie with a three-wine tasting at **35.cinco** in Villa Pituil. Most bodegas produce reds such as Malbec and Bonarda, although Cara Sur has rescued old Criolla Blanca and Criolla Negra vines.

 WHERE TO STAY IN CALINGASTA

Posada de los Patos
Stay in one of the 10 adobe-constructed suites at this stylish and peaceful retreat south of Barreal. **$$$**

Acrux Barreal
After bedding down in a spacious room, enjoy breakfast with Andean views at this option south of Villa Pituil. **$$**

Posta Celestino
A cozy hotel with simple design; amenities include an outdoor swimming pool. **$$**

Valle de Calingasta

Beyond
San Juan

Lunar landscapes and dinosaur remains are some of the treats in store in this largely undiscovered Central Andean province.

GETTING AROUND

To explore San Juan's wonderful parks and outdoor spaces, rent a car, preferably a 4WD. Or to let someone else do the driving, look into a guided tour to Parque Provincial Ischigualasto leaving from San Juan capital; ask at the tourism office for more info.

☑ TOP TIP

Given the long distances and rough roads, remember to fill up your fuel tank and check for gas stations and places to eat en route before setting out. Take warm clothes, water and sun block too.

With astonishing lunar landscapes and low-key wine country offering a whole new perspective on mountain vino, traveling into the depths of San Juan Province can be extremely rewarding. While neighboring Mendoza produces the majority of Argentine wine, San Juan holds its own, making 16 percent.

You're closer to the Andes, less snowcapped and more rock face here, and given the sparse population, it can often feel like you are the only person on this bit of the planet. Traversing the *rutas provinciales* can be challenging, given the rough terrain, dirt roads and distances, but the breath-taking **Parque Provincial Ischigualasto** and **Parque Nacional El Leoncito** are well worth the effort to get to.

Parque Provincial Ischigualasto

SUNSINGER/SHUTTERSTOCK ©

Valle de la Luna

Parque Provincial Ischigualasto

TIME FROM SAN JUAN CAPITAL: **3 HRS 30 MINS**

A Geologist and Paleontologist's Dream Destination

If you've dreamed of walking on the moon, seize the opportunity to come close with a visit to **Parque Provincial Ischigualasto**. The name translates as 'lifeless land' in the Diaguita indigenous language, but this place is more commonly known as Valle de la Luna or Moon Valley. A three-and-a-half-hour drive north of San Juan capital on RN40, it makes sense to bunk down in the small town of San Agustín del Valle Fértil, which is 70km from the park via RP150.

A desert valley that's home to incredible 180-million-year-old fossils, this park is the only place in the world where you can witness every stage of the Triassic period – hence its Unesco cultural heritage badge. Herrerasaurus and Eoraptor lunensis dinosaurs ran riot between the park's two sedimentary mountain ranges; some of their fossils are on display at the museum. There is an entrance fee, payable at the visitor center, where you can also sign on with a ranger to guide you through the park.

The three-hour accompanied tour in your own vehicle takes you through the most curious of rock formations made from red sandstone, volcanic ash and clay with nicknames such as **El Gusano** (the worm), **El Submarino** (the submarine) and **El Hongo** (the mushroom). The latter two are some of the park's most photographed natural wonders. Of the five predetermined routes, the Diurno Tradicional is the most lunar-like, while the Quebrada de la Peña is the most physically demanding; for full-moon hikes through the park or a mountain biking expedition, book ahead on www.ischigualasto.gob.ar. Despite the 'lifeless land' moniker, herds of guanaco have made this region home. Keep an eye out for them bouncing over the shrubs and rocks.

PARQUE NACIONAL EL LEONCITO

The space theme continues at **Parque Nacional El Leoncito**, which, thanks to low light pollution and some of the clearest skies in the world, is a leading astrotourism destination; entry to the park is free. A four-hour drive west of San Juan capital on RN40 and RP149, and 35km from Barreal, the **Complejo Astronómico El Leoncito** located within the park is home to two world-class observatories and Argentina's most powerful telescope, the Jorge Sahade, named after the respected Argentine astronomer. Serious stargazers should plan visits around the new moon cycle as the full moon blocks out many constellations; for night visits to the observatories, you need to book well in advance at https://reservascasleo.com. There are a few dorms at the observatories, so do ask about staying overnight (dinner and breakfast included) when you make your reservation.

Above: Asado, San Antonio de Areco (p304); Right: Mar del Plata (p334)

The Pampas & the Atlantic Coast

GAUCHO COUNTRY, ESTANCIAS AND BEACH FORESTS

Grasslands of *estancias*, polo clubs and ruins lead to the tamed dunes of the coast where paranormal activities, summer parties and craft beer await.

This area encompasses all of the province of Buenos Aires, the country's most populated region. Its fertile grasslands, home to nearly 40 percent of the nation's cattle, give rise to the Sierras de Tandil in the west, coastal forests in the south, a salt sea in the north, and the architectural cornucopia of the provincial capital of La Plata in the east.

The Criollo horse and the Argentine polo pony come from here, but colonies of flamingos and sea lions, and solitary swamp deer, are also present. The Spanish brought the horses when they began colonizing Argentina in the 16th century, but it was indigenous groups (the Querandíes, Pampas and Tehuelches originally inhabited these plains) who developed the pampas'

famed horse-whispering technique. A large concentration of polo clubs and *estancias* (ranches) offer tourists the chance to experience country life here, complete with an *asado* (barbecue) and horseback rides with gauchos (cowboys of the pampas).

On the coast, an emerging wine region has sprouted up near Mar del Plata, but the city's far better known as the birthplace of craft beer in Argentina, and the national party destination come summer.

The province is also the religious heartland of the country. Pilgrimages occur semi-frequently, and stories of paranormal activities, be they alien abductions or woodland apparitions, allude to many ilks of faith.

THE MAIN AREAS

Find Your Way

The province of Buenos Aires is the country's largest at 307,571 sq km. It can take over 10 hours to cross by bus, and far more time to drive over 1200km of its coastline.

CAR

Renting a car will give you the most freedom to explore, and allow you to easily reach destinations in the north where buses are sparse. You'll also be able to check out many of the province's towns that most foreign tourists never see.

BUS

Long-distance buses run throughout the region between towns and cities, and from the city of Buenos Aires to the major cities of the province. All of the major cities have a public bus system, as do some of the larger towns.

TRAIN

For traveling to Mar del Plata, La Plata and some of towns around these cities, trains are cheap and are one of the easiest ways to get to these destinations from the city of Buenos Aires.

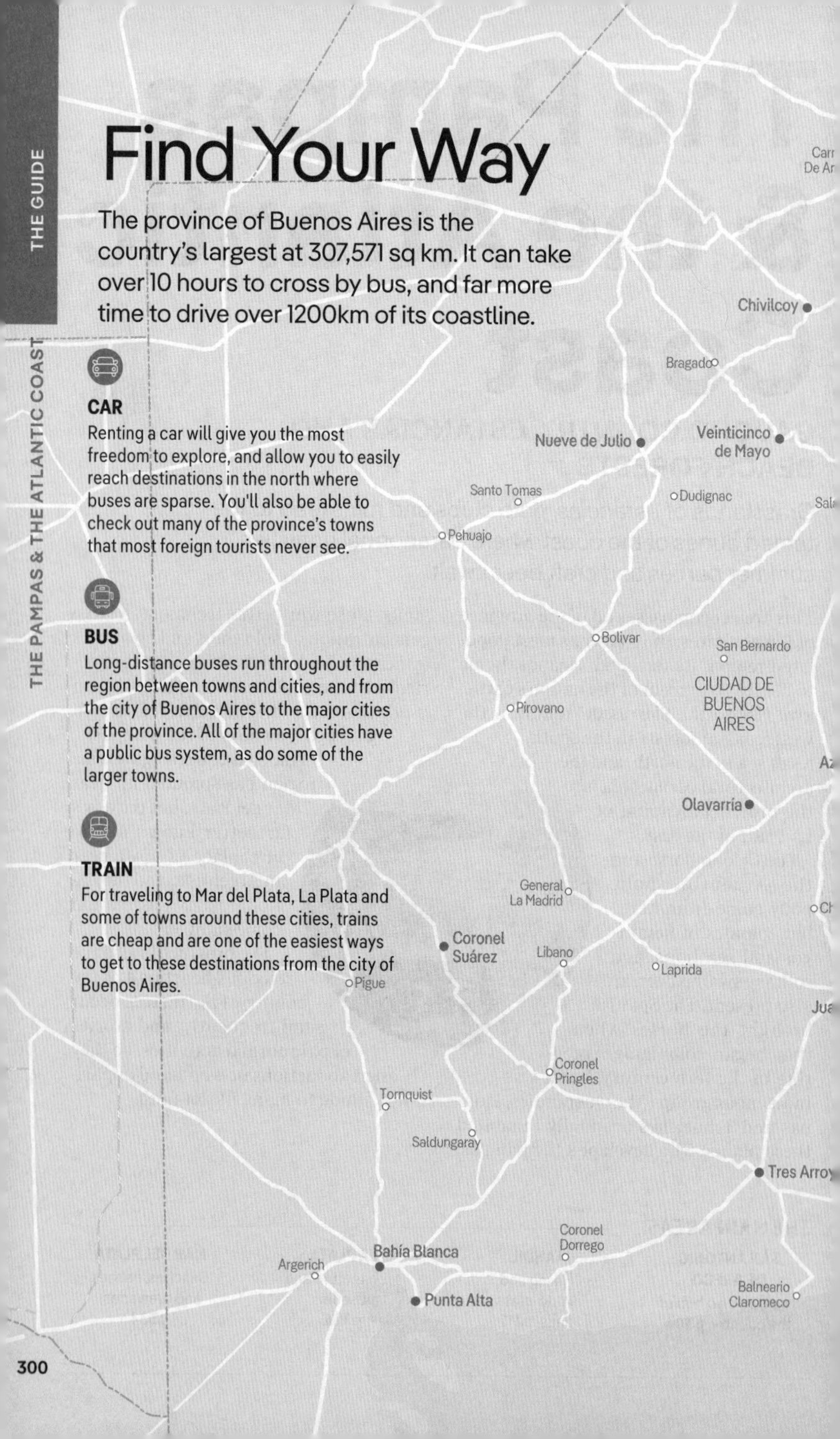
Chivilcoy
Bragado
Nueve de Julio
Veinticinco de Mayo
Santo Tomas
Dudignac
Pehuajo
Bolivar
San Bernardo
CIUDAD DE BUENOS AIRES
Pirovano
Olavarría
General La Madrid
Coronel Suárez
Libano
Laprida
Pigue
Coronel Pringles
Tornquist
Saldungaray
Tres Arro
Coronel Dorrego
Bahía Blanca
Argerich
Punta Alta
Balneario Claromeco

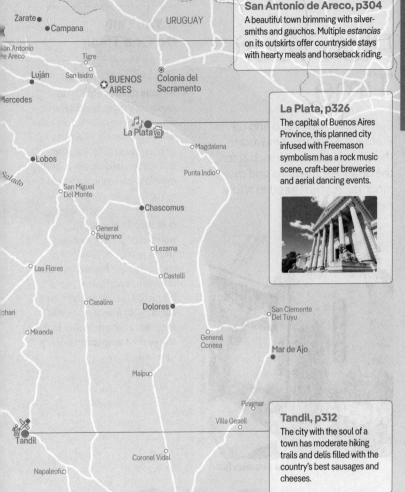

San Antonio de Areco, p304

A beautiful town brimming with silver-smiths and gauchos. Multiple *estancias* on its outskirts offer countryside stays with hearty meals and horseback riding.

La Plata, p326

The capital of Buenos Aires Province, this planned city infused with Freemason symbolism has a rock music scene, craft-beer breweries and aerial dancing events.

Tandil, p312

The city with the soul of a town has moderate hiking trails and delis filled with the country's best sausages and cheeses.

Mar del Plata, p343

The main summer beach destination of the country sees masses of sunbathers during the day and clubgoers at night, with concerts and plays throughout the season.

URUGUAY

Zarate
Campana
San Antonio de Areco
Tigre
Luján
San Isidro
BUENOS AIRES
Colonia del Sacramento
Mercedes
La Plata
Magdalena
Lobos
Punta Indio
Salado
San Miguel Del Monte
Chascomus
General Belgrano
Lezama
Las Flores
Castelli
Casalins
Dolores
chari
Miranda
General Conesa
San Clemente Del Tuyu
Maipu
Mar de Ajo
Pinamar
Villa Gesell
Tandil
Coronel Vidal
Napaleofu
Balcarce
Mar del Plata
Yraizoz
General Alvarado
nergia
Necochea

N

0 ————————— 100 km
0 ————————— 50 miles

Plan Your Time

San Antonio de Areco and La Plata are a day trip away from the city of Buenos Aires, but for the beaches, the ruins and the mountains, you'll need to allow more time.

Epoca de Quesos (p316)

If You Only Do One Thing

BOTTOM: MAGAIZA/SHUTTERSTOCK ©, LAUTARO SOTO/SHUTTERSTOCK ©, MAXYM/SHUTTERSTOCK ©

● Head to the town of **San Antonio de Areco** (p304) to experience Argentine countryside life and gaucho culture. Take a day tour of an *estancia*, where you can go horseback riding, eat *asado*, and watch a folkloric show, or stay overnight to see the town itself the next day.

● Browse its silversmith workshops and buy your own knives, jewelry or silver-inlaid *mate* gourds, then head for a meal of generous portions at one of the rustic bars. It's a short trip to **Luján** (p310) from there to visit Argentina's patron saint, or to the vineyard in **Campana** (p311) for a wine tasting.

ALEXANDR VOROBEV/SHUTTERSTOCK ©

Seasonal Highlights

Summers bring crowds to Mar del Plata's beaches. Fall and spring draw hikers to Tandil.

JANUARY

The summer season begins in Mar del Plata and the surrounding beach towns, with concerts, theater shows and parties.

MARCH

At Easter, thousands of pilgrims walk through the forest visiting the stations of the cross in Tandil's **Vía Crucis** (p317).

JULY

Try 100 brews from local craft brewing associations at La Plata's **Festival de la Cultura Cervecera Platense** (p327).

Five Days to Travel Around

● Begin with a day in **La Plata** (p326) where you can walk around and see the city's architecture, including the Le Corbusier-designed Casa Curutchet, then visit the Museo de La Plata's extensive bone collection of prehistoric animals.

● Spend a few days in **Tandil** (p312) eating *picada* in its many delis and hiking its gentle mountain trails. Take the chairlift to cruise through the pine forest, and if you're there during warm weather, look for capybaras on its lake.

● Finish the trip at the ruins of **Epecuén** (p318) and stay in nearby **Carhué** (p322) to float in its thermal baths.

More Than a Week

● Surf, tan or party in **Mar del Plata** (p334) when you're not eating seafood or drinking craft beer. Visit the forests of **Villa Gesell** (p340) and **Miramar** (p229), as well as the coastal winery in hipster village **Chapadmalal** (p341).

● Continue onto **Bahia Blanca** (p319) for museums and possible alien sightings, then go inland to hike at **Parque Provincial Ernesto Tornquist** (p323) and **Cerro Tres Picos** (p324).

● If the weather's cool, skip the coast, and go *estancia*-hopping in **San Antonio de Areco** (p304) and around **La Plata** (p326) or stay in a castle in **Lobos** (p333) and learn how to play polo in **Cañuelas** p(332).

AUGUST
See flamingos at the ruins of **Epecuén** (p318), then get out of the cold at the nearby thermal baths.

SEPTEMBER
Hike in **Parque Provincial Ernesto Tornquist** (p323) to see the rare iguana de cobre.

OCTOBER
In the **Peregrinación a Pie de la Juventud** (p310), over a million people walk to Luján to see Argentina's patron saint.

NOVEMBER
Gauchos go to the **Fiesta de la Tradición** (p307), and film buffs to the Mar del Plata International Film Festival.

San Antonio de Areco

BUENOS AIRES

GETTING AROUND

Public buses run through town, but most places (other than *estancias*) that you'll want to go are all within walking distance of each other. Having a car is great for getting to the estancias or exploring nearby towns. Alternatively, you can book transport directly with the *estancia* or through one of the several *remise* companies in town to reach the countryside. There are multiple bike rental companies, and many locals travel via bicycles or mopeds around town.

☑ TOP TIP

Most everything shuts down from noon to 3pm for the afternoon siesta. Not all restaurants open every day. Fridays, Saturdays and Sundays have the most options of activities and restaurants. If there is a holiday, businesses will alter their schedules to stay open, then take the following day off to rest.

Walk San Antonio de Areco's cobblestone streets and you'll find a *pulpería* (gaucho saloon) before long, numerous silversmith workshops crafting *facones* (gaucho knives) or *rastras* (gaucho belts), and the local artisanal chocolate shop. Tradition, quality and slow living meet in its pretty tree-lined streets, and out-of-towners find themselves feeling more patient and calmer than they were before arriving.

The line between real and imaginary blurs here. The writer of the gaucho novel *Don Segundo Sombra*, Ricardo Güiraldes, based the main character of Don Segundo on local gaucho Segundo Ramírez, who was also a strong influence in the drawings of Osvaldo Gasparini. San Antonio de Areco is the gateway to the majesty of the pampas, both rough and inspiring, and staying at an *estancia* on its outskirts is one of the best ways to enter that world of folkloric singing, horse whispering and daily *asados*.

SUNSINGER/SHUTTERSTOCK ©

Gauchos, Fiesta de la Tradicion (p307)

SIGHTS

1 Centro Cultural y Museo Usina Vieja
2 Mariano Draghi Orfebre
3 Museo de Arte La Recova
4 Museo Evocativo Osvaldo Gasparini
5 Parque Criollo y Museo Gauchesco Ricardo Güiraldes
6 Puente Viejo

ACTIVITIES, COURSES & TOURS

7 Alquimia
8 El Fogón

SLEEPING

9 Estancia La Cinacina
10 Hostel Casa Suri
11 Hotel Draghi

EATING

see 3 Almacén de Ramos Generales
12 La Olla de Cobre
13 Pulpería lo de Tito

DRINKING & NIGHTLIFE

14 Boliche de Bessonart
15 La Vieja Sodería
16 Tucano

THE ORIGIN OF DOMA INDIA

Horses are not native to Argentina. When the Spanish began importing them as they colonized the pampas, several escaped and began to breed in the wild, eventually becoming the Criollo breed. When indigenous people began working with the horses, they developed a form of horse whispering that was non-violent, taming them through different kinds of whistles, shouts and nudges – now known as 'Doma India'. Eventually, the gauchos learned it from the indigenous people, and began using it to tame their horses. The gauchos would not train all their horses this way, only the ones they intended to keep.

Horseback Riding & Horse Whispering

Stay at El Ombú de Areco

A day or night at an *estancia* will allow you to experience the pampas as they were hundreds of years ago: many of the traditional customs like singing, grilling and horseback riding, are daily occurrences. While *estancias* started as a form of land gifting to Spanish colonizers, they went through multiple iterations, eventually downsizing but still being run by wealthy families who would hire gauchos to tend them. This signaled the end of the nomadic era of the gaucho, but also provided them more stability than their former freewheeling lifestyle in the pampas.

Estancia El Ombú de Areco is the most expensive *estancia* in San Antonio de Areco, but it's worth the money (full board per person from US$375), and they can arrange transport if you don't have a car. While the *día*

GAUCHO GUIDE

To read more about **gaucho** history and its impact on Argentine culture, turn to p510.

CHOCOLATE STOP

On Matheu St stands a small brick and wood building that any Argentine will tell you is an obligatory stop when visiting San Antonio de Areco: **La Olla de Cobre** (The Copper Pot). A family-run artisanal chocolate and *alfajores* factory, La Olla is most famous for its chocolate-covered *alfajores* (*dulce de leche* sandwich cookies). The front of the store displays the chocolate bar, full of *marroc* (chocolate and peanut butter), white chocolate with almonds, chocolate-covered rum raisins, and many more varieties. Sample a few, enjoy the aroma of chocolate in the air, and peer through the window to the kitchen to see the artisans preparing the chocolate. The *alfajores* in particular make great gifts for Argentine friends.

SUNSINGER/SHUTTERSTOCK ©

Fiesta de la Tradición

del campo (country day tour) option is the more economical choice, spending a night here ensures access to the very same activities, plus more meals, more horseback rides, and a country chic room with a wood burning stove in the Italian-style farmhouse built in 1880.

Upon arrival, a short tour and talk about the history of the property leads to a lunch of multiple cuts of grilled beef, pork and chicken, while a troupe of folkloric performers play music and sing songs of gaucho tales. They'll also invite you to dance. Afterwards, you can see a Doma India (horse whispering) demonstration, then go horseback riding with the gauchos on the 300-hectare cattle-filled property. Dinner, breakfast and a morning horseback ride round out the stay.

Shop the Silversmith Workshops

Handmade Knives, Jewelry and Mates

Silversmithing in Buenos Aires Province dates back to the 16th century and was popularized primarily by Spanish and Portuguese immigrants. San Antonio de Areco, home to about 100 silversmiths, is the place in Argentina to buy beautiful gaucho pieces (daggers and horse adornments), as well as jewelry and *mate* kits (silver-adorned drinking gourds and *bombillas*, the filtered straws used to drink *mate*).

WHERE TO STAY IN SAN ANTONIO DE ARECO

Hostel Casa Suri
A centrally located, clean hostel with friendly owners, good vibes and good cats. $

Hotel Draghi
Stay at the back of a silver workshop in luxurious refurbished stables. $$

Estancia La Cinacina
A 180-year-old *estancia* that's only a 10-minute walk from the center of town. $$$

Chief among the silversmiths is the Draghi family, who have both a workshop and museum, **Mariano Draghi Orfebre**, on the main square. The museum (tickets US$2) has displays in both English and Spanish about the history and art of silversmithing in Argentina, and opens to the workshop where you can see the silversmiths in action. They forge traditional gaucho knives as well as rings and necklaces. Several pre-made pieces for sale are displayed in the front, and you can commission custom pieces.

Two other silversmiths worth stopping by are the more alternative **Alquimia** on Arellano, specializing in delicate, creative jewelry of silver, copper and bronze, with many gingko-leaf-inspired pieces; and **El Fogón** on Alsina, specializing in all things *mate*. (It also has a giant *mate* that makes for a fun photo.) You can talk to the artisans directly in many of the shops. Prices vary greatly depending on what you're looking for and what details you desire, as well as if you're buying something pre-made or ordering a special commission. If you just want a quality but cheap souvenir, a *bombilla* (about US$2) is a good option.

Attend the Fiesta de la Tradición

A Gaucho Gathering

One of the largest gaucho events in Argentina takes place in San Antonio de Areco: the **Fiesta de la Tradición**. The three-day festival pays homage to the history of the gaucho, the Criollo horse, and the traditions of the pampas. Since 1939 the festival has taken place annually on the birthday of José Hernández, author of the epic poem 'Martín Fierro', which immortalized gaucho culture.

Two thousand gauchos ride through San Antonio de Areco's streets in *boinas* (floppy berets) and *bombachas* (gaucho pants); you can see their parade from Plaza Ruiz de Arellano, the main square. However, most of the activities take place in **Parque Criollo** at the **Ricardo Güiraldes Gaucho Museum**, like races and the *carrera de sortija*, a competition where gauchos try to thread a metal ring held between their teeth while riding their horses. There's also a massive grilling station where you'll have your pick of meat cuts and steak sandwiches. Other activities include folkloric singing by elementary groups dressed in gaucho garb, an artisan fair, and gaucho bards.

Entry per day ranges in price but is generally no more than US$2. Book accommodation well in advance for this as it's the year's largest event in San Antonio de Areco. Take sunscreen and bring lots of water, as most of the events are outside. A

RICARDO GÜIRALDES, GAUCHO AUTHOR

Ricardo Güiraldes wrote his most celebrated work, *Don Segundo Sombra*, in San Antonio de Areco at his family's *estancia*, La Porteña. The coming-of-age tale revolves around a seasoned gaucho, Don Segundo, and a boy he begins to mentor, imparting wisdom and work ethic to him. Don Segundo was based on Segundo Ramírez, a real-life gaucho who worked at La Porteña. Güiraldes won the Literary National First Prize in 1925, and San Antonio de Areco became a tourist hub as the popularity of the book grew. The writer's friend, author Jorge Luis Borges, said that the work was clearly influenced by Rudyard Kipling's *Kim* and Mark Twain's *Huckleberry Finn,* but that it was no less Argentine for it.

WHERE TO EAT & DRINK LIKE A GAUCHO

Boliche de Bessonart
A 200-year-old general store–turned-tavern, where the real-life Don Segundo Sombra used to eat. $

Almacén de Ramos Generales
Open daily, this restaurant has expertly grilled meats, lots of wine and antique country decor. $$

Pulpería lo de Tito
Enjoy empanadas, *picada* and beer at this restaurant near the river. Open Friday through Sunday. $$

THE PAMPAS & THE ATLANTIC COAST

Christine Gilbert,
writer

I love the Pampas and the Atlantic coast because they are rich with stories. From tales of pop-up dwarfs in Miramar's forest to the people who generously shared memories of the flood in Epecuén with me, it was as if this region said: 'Tell me what you think you know of Argentina, and I will show you something completely different.' It's a region of dreamers, madmen who tried to tame dunes, and pilgrims who believe in divine help and cardio. People care about art and quality. Sometimes they see aliens. Gauchos even cuddle their horses here. Everyone eats well, especially in Tandil, and when you have a conversation with someone, they really listen.

full schedule of events is posted on sanantoniodeareco.com, though if figuring it out seems overwhelming, the tour company **BA Cultural Concierge** (baculturalconcierge.com) can organize a custom tour around the event.

San Antonio de Areco's Museums

Gaucho Art and a Plane

San Antonio de Areco is officially the National Capital of Tradition in Argentina, and visiting its museums will help you understand why.

The **Parque Criollo y Museo Gauchesco Ricardo Güiraldes** is a museum dedicated to the writer of *Don Segundo Sombra*, Ricardo Güiraldes, and is housed within a re-created *casco* (ranch house) and restored *pulpería* (general store–cum-bar), **La Blanqueada**. See Güiraldes' desk and exhibits of gaucho adornments and tools, and snap a picture of the bar – though it's only an exhibit and not functioning as a watering hole any longer. The **Puente Viejo**, the pink bridge you must cross to enter the property, is also a national historic landmark. Built in 1857, it served as Argentina's first toll bridge.

To buy affordable gaucho paintings, stop by the **Museo Evocativo Osvaldo Gasparini**. There, you can speak with Gasparini's son and grandson, artists in their own right, who can tell you wonderful stories about their family history as you tour the small museum. If you like what you see, there's even more of Gasparini's art a short walk away at **Museo de Arte La Recova**.

Just off the main square, housed in the old power plant, the **Centro Cultural y Museo Usina Vieja** focuses on the history of the town of San Antonio de Areco itself. Outside, there's a garden with metal sculptures and wooden carvings of gauchos and horses, while inside, you can see various artifacts, like the Arequero G1, an experimental plane that Aroldo Gómez, a local inventor and founder of the town flight club, built himself in the 1980s.

 WHERE TO DRINK COFFEE IN SAN ANTONIO DE ARECO

Tucano
Specialty coffee bar with some of the best cakes in Argentina. Great for reading. $

La Tolderia Deli & Café
Excellent lattes, *alfajores* from La Olla de Cobre, a wooden playground, and strong wi-fi. $

La Vieja Soderia
Argentine-style bar and cafe in an old soda factory. Get the churros with your coffee. $$

Beyond San Antonio de Areco

Wine country mixes with religious tourism and biodiverse wetlands in the northern reaches of the province.

The area to the northeast and southeast of San Antonio de Areco has farmland, industrial towns and, eventually, the Paraná River with its hulking swamp deer and electric blue spiders. It's a part of the country characterized by religious tourism, thanks to the many pilgrimages people make throughout the year to the statue of the Virgin of Luján. Even some of the forefathers of Argentina's independence, Generals Manuel Belgrano and José de San Martín, passed through here to ask for divine help in the war against Spain. Under the surface of the elaborate religious festivals and quirky celebrations, there's a subtle mysticism and deep faith here that continue to inspire hope throughout the entire country.

Basílica de Luján (p310)

GETTING AROUND

Self-driving or hiring a *remise* (like Remis Sol 02326 45-5444) are the easiest ways to get from San Antonio de Areco to Luján and Campana. You can also book a tour directly to the winery from Buenos Aires, if you want to start from there instead (where there are also several public transportation options from which to choose). If you do the pilgrimage walk from Buenos Aires to Luján, there are multiple bus and train options to take you back to the Buenos Aires Metropolitan Area, like the Sarmiento trainline that runs to Liniers.

☑ TOP TIP

Bus Line 228d connects Luján and Campana., but renting a car and driving is more enjoyable.

THE RARE SWAMP DEER

Just outside of Campana is one of only two national parks in Buenos Aires Province: **Parque Nacional Ciervo de los Pantanos** (Swamp Deer National Park). The park is named for its population of endangered swamp deer, the largest deer in South America at 1.27m (just over 4ft tall). The deer have hooves especially suited to swimming in the park's river, preventing them from sinking when walking through the swamplands. Several nature trails in the park allow visitors to see this rare species and other wildlife like otters, capybaras and blue-tipped tarantulas. Birders also frequent the park, where 200 types of birds, including guans and kingfishers, can be observed.

Basílica de Luján

Luján
Visit the Virgin

TIME FROM SAN ANTONIO DE ARECO: **1HR**

Buenos Aires Province is the site of several pilgrimages, the most famous being the Peregrinación a Pie de la Juventud (Youth Pilgrimage on Foot) from the city of Buenos Aires to Luján. Between one and two million make the trek, making it the largest pilgrimage in the country. It happens on the first Sunday in October, with the 60km route starting from the Santuario de San Cayetano in the Buenos Aires neighborhood of Liniers to the Basílica de Luján, a neo-Gothic minor basilica with 106m-high pink towers where the Virgen de Luján, the patron saint of Argentina, is housed.

Many pilgrims start at dawn. The journey takes about 15 hours, and though tiring, the walk is not boring. Just some of the sights you'll see along the way include hawkers with clotheslines of socks on makeshift stands, priests hearing confessions by the side of the road in moveable confessionals, a blessing station, and carts with hundreds of rosaries for sale. Many people open their homes to be used as public bathrooms for a small fee. Parts mirror long-distance road race hydration checkpoints, as various volunteer groups offer pilgrims water, tea and other beverages.

 MORE FESTIVALS IN LUJÁN

Luján Flota
Ride in hot-air balloons at the hot-air balloon fest on August 26.

Easter
Festivities include mass foot washings, orchestra performances, fireworks, and burning an effigy of Judas.

Peregrinación Boliviana
Part Bolivian dance party, part pilgrimage; happens in front of the basilica in early August.

If you can't make it to Luján during the pilgrimage, there are events throughout the year that the basilica acts as a nucleus for (like Immaculate Conception Day), and you can always find the Virgin behind the main altar. Also, consider a tour of the basilica's crypt to see its collection of Virgin statues from around the world.

Campana

TIME FROM SAN ANTONIO DE ARECO: **1HR** 🚗

Countryside Libations

Just under an hour's drive from San Antonio de Areco, **Bodega Gamboa** in Campana also happens to be the closest winery to the city of Buenos Aires, making it an easy option for those visiting the country who don't have time to visit the wine regions in Mendoza or Salta.

A family-run affair, Gamboa produces about 1000 bottles of wine a year. It makes Malbec, Pinot Noir, Cabernet Franc, and a blend, all from grapes exclusively grown in its vineyard. The small-batch production means that one of the only ways to taste these wines is to physically come to the vineyard, as they are not typically sold outside of Gamboa. The best way to experience Gamboa is by booking a full-day tour (US$40 per person) through the website bodegagamboa.com. ar, or through external guides like Viator (US$149 per person with transportation).

Tours start at midday with a sparkling glass of wine and a walk around the vineyard, where a guide will tell you about the 10 varietals grown here, before taking you to the warehouse where the wine is aged in oak barrels. After, guests can taste three wines (at least one being a Malbec), paired with cheeses. The day finishes with a late three-course gourmet lunch of seasonal ingredients, with steak, fish or portobello mushroom as the main course.

Open Wednesday through Sunday, Gamboa can only be visited with prior reservations. Consider making the trip in the spring, when the grapes are in full bloom, best for vineyard photo ops.

Virgen de Luján

THE STORY OF OUR LADY OF LUJÁN

You'll see images of the Virgen de Luján everywhere in Argentina, even in the subway, where people stop and pray to her while switching lines. The statue – depicting the Immaculate Conception with Mary clothed in a hooded blue and white dress standing on a half-moon – has been credited with healing and moving of its own volition. In 1630, a Portuguese landowner in Santiago del Estero sent for a statue of the Virgin from Brazil. En route to Santiago del Estero, the ox-driven cart carrying the statue got stuck by the river in Luján and moved only when the statue was taken off. The Virgin was enshrined in the area and moved to the Basílica de Luján years later.

BUENOS
AIRES

Tandil

GETTING AROUND

Tandil's bus system will take you to most of the important sights in town, and its streets are walkable, though slightly hilly. Most lines run from 6:30am to 11pm. Expect to wait 10 to 30 minutes for a bus. Call one of the *remise* companies, like Remis Tandil (0249 442-3333), or drive to get to hikes on the edge of town, as taxis are not plentiful. If driving, be aware that some streets require paid parking with a SUMO tourist card that can be purchased at kiosks with yellow SUMO signs on them.

☑ TOP TIP

Plaza Independencia is the main square of the city. Just across from it on the street General Rodriguez, you'll find the tourist information office. It's open from 9am to 5pm everyday but Sunday, when it's only open until 1pm.

In Tandil, you're never far from good food or green spaces. This city in the humid pampas has a population of 124,631, but feels like a town, where world-famous delis give you heaping portions of *picada* (charcuterie) and one of the main pastimes is hiking the hills of the Sierras de Tandil, a 2.5-million-year-old mountain range that surrounds the city.

Evidence of both its indigenous and European immigrant history is everywhere. The name 'Tandil' is a combination of two Mapuche words meaning 'beating' and 'rock', in reference to the city's famous once-teetering stone, Piedra Movediza. The Europeans can be credited with making Tandil the *picada* capital of Argentina, as Italian and Basque immigrants started producing artisanal salamis and cheeses here, said to be the best in Argentina. A large number of European stonecutters also came to work the quarries, the ruins of which you can see on some hikes.

Chairlift at Cerro El Centinela

Legend and a Celtic Horoscope

A short walk uphill from the car park, see the boulder balanced on end for which **Cerro El Centinela** (Sentinel Hill) is named. Legend has it that Yanquetruz, a young indigenous man, waited for his love, Amaiké, on the hill, not knowing that she had been captured by the Argentine army. Moved by his love and dedication, the gods turned his spirit into the rock.

Take the **chairlift** (US$5 per person) to get to the top of Cerro El Centinela. Lasting about nine minutes, the ride offers panoramic views and cuts through swaths of pine forest until it reaches the top (298m above sea level) where skilled chairlift operators scoop you off your seat. Walk left to the

SIGHTS
1 Cerro El Centinela
2 Monumento a Don Quijote de La Mancha
3 Mulita Footgolf de Tandil
4 Parque Independencia

ACTIVITIES, COURSES & TOURS
5 Monte Calvario
6 Valle del Picapedrero

SLEEPING
see 8 Hostel B&B Tandil

7 Hotel Roma
see 7 Mulen Hotel Tandil

EATING
8 Almacén Serrano
9 Bello Abril
10 Bistro Verde
11 El Banqueano Tandil

12 Época de Quesos
13 Huellas del Tandil
14 La Quesería
15 Ladran
16 Sydquet

Celtic Horoscope, a garden with over 20 different kinds of trees. The trees correspond to different phases of the moon, Celtic deities, and their virtues. While there's a map, it's fun to walk through the paths to try to find your birth tree, as trees are well marked. On the other side of the chairlift, a short trail (450m) leads down a rocky slope, then through a pine forest to a spring with potable water where you can fill your water bottle.

In high season, the chairlift is open every day from 11am to 5pm. In low season, it's only open on Saturdays, Sundays and holidays. You can also rent mountain bikes, go down water slides, and horseback ride near the car park. There are two restaurants: one at the base and one at the top of the chairlift.

Cerro
El Centinela

This walk takes you around Lago del Fuerte (Fort Lake) in a little over an hour but can easily be stretched to an hour and a half or more, depending on how long you spend at each stop.

Start with the **❶ Jardín Vertical Tandil**, a vertical garden spelling the word 'Tandil'. While it's a popular picture stop, the reason to pause here is behind the sign. On warm, sunny days, capybaras come here to snooze by the water. Walk over the lake along the concrete dike, the **❷ Dique del Fuerte**, for the best view of the lake. After you cross, you'll see the **❸ Monumento al Fundidor**, a statue made with foundry material, depicting one of the workers who built Tandil. Follow the paved path downhill to an island on your right. Here you can fish or rent a kay-

ak from **❹ Centro Náutico del Fuerte**. The path stays flat until you go left at the fork and walk uphill for the next 20 minutes to the **❺ Monumento al Quijote**, white metal statues of Don Quijote and Sancho Panza next to a large windmill. Return the way you came, then go left at the lake until you come to the **❻ Puñon Mapuche**. Here you can read some history of the native Mapuche people, next to the Mapuche face carved into the rock. Follow the path down and around the playground to reach the red metal bridge of the **❼ Paseo de los Españoles**, where you can also go through the hedge labyrinth. Once you make your way out, continue uphill to reach **❽ El Mirador Drinks & Food** for a hearty lunch and coffee.

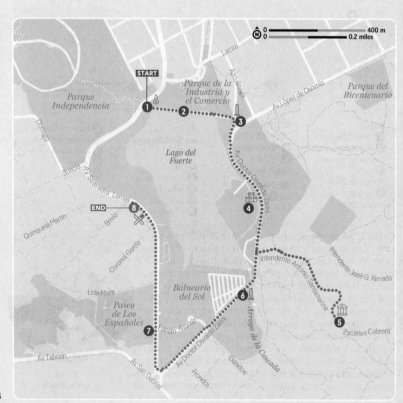

Castle, Tandil

Follow the Footsteps of the Stonecutters

Hiking the Sierras de Tandil

Tandil's rolling hills and abandoned quarries make it a trail runner's or moderate hiker's dream. You'll generally find some sort of surprising monument or structure at the top of its most popular hikes, and nearly all of Tandil's trails are free.

Head up the rocky steps of **Cerro Movediza** where you'll find a 300-tonne metal rock, a replica of the teetering rock Tandil was named for (the rubble of the original can be seen below), then follow the path down, all easily done in 30 minutes. Another popular hike or drive is to the Moorish castle through **Parque Independencia**, which offers a panoramic view of Tandil.

If you want to hike a bit outside of the city, go to **La Cascada**, a 1km roundtrip hike, the trailhead of which is just up the road from the Amaike Hotel Gold & Spa. Just past the metal gate by the parking area, you'll see signs pointing to the trail towards the Virgen de Fatima. Go the opposite way through the other gate, then past the trees on the right and up the hill to see the waterfall. To lengthen the hike, go to the virgin shrine as well; all of this can be done in under an hour.

Both trail runners and hikers will enjoy the well-marked 6km roundtrip dirt trail of the **Sendero de las Animas**, which also has signs for various panoramic viewpoints. The **Paseo de los Pineros** offers a hiking-friendly road to the top of Cerro del Mate, from which you can see the old quarry.

BEST DELIS IN TANDIL

Sydquet
Known for high quality and prices, Sydquet sells artisanal cheeses, massive ham hocks, and sandwiches. **$$**

El Banqueano Tandil
Near Cerro El Centinela, this cozy shop offers craft beer, salmis, cheeses, marmalades and liquors. **$**

Huellas del Tandil
Buy ready-to-go *picada*, savory spreads and wine, for edible souvenirs or a convenient lunch. **$$**

Almacén Serrano
Spice-encrusted salamis pair wonderfully with the artisanal liquor also on offer, like the local brand Picapedrero Vermouth. **$$**

La Quesería
At this cheese store, buy a vat of *dulce de leche,* salamis, marmalades and *alfajores,* and all the necessary *picada* tools like knives and cutting boards. **$**

 WHERE TO SLEEP IN TANDIL

Mulen Hotel Tandil
Centrally located, the stylish Mulen offers big beds, a quality buffet breakfast, climatized pool, and sauna. **$$**

Hostel B&B Tandil
A clean, cheery hostel with optional gluten-free breakfast, located just a few blocks from Independence Park. **$**

Hotel Roma
Only two blocks from Tandil's main square, this family-owned hotel has excellent customer service. **$**

A QUIXOTIC PRESENCE

Spend some time in Tandil and you'll notice a surprising amount of Don Quixote fan art: the Monumento a Don Quijote de La Mancha up the hill from Lado del Fuerte, the wall-length mural of Quixote near the intersection of the streets Maipú and General Paz, the Sancho Panza statue in Ladran, and even more homages. The reason for all this fan art is probably due to Tandi's proximity to the city of Azul, a Unesco-declared 'City of Cervantes', a 90-minute drive away. In addition to the city hosting the Miguel de Cervantes Festival every year, its Casa Ronco library holds the most editions of *Don Quixote* of any collection in the country.

KM/SHUTTERSTOCK ©

Época de Quesos

Eat Picada at Época de Quesos

Sweet Dreams Are Made of Cheese

Eating *picada* is the quintessential experience in Tandil, and the best place to order a heaping board of the city's finest meats and cheeses is **Época de Quesos** (open 9am to 11pm). Built in 1860, the building was originally a post for wagon drivers coming from Buenos Aires. Later, it was a general store, then declared a historical landmark before becoming a restaurant turned store in the '90s. Stepping into it feels like you've entered a delicious time machine that has carried you back to Argentina's past. Salamis, hams and over 100 varieties of cheese in wheels big and small act as both product and decoration, lining shelves and topping tables. The front of the building is the deli and also sells flavored salts, *mate* blends with lavender, and vacuum-sealed boxes of pre-cut *picada* to-go. Start here and sample some of the items to make a better-informed decision about what to order for lunch at the back of the building, which functions as a restaurant.

Sit at one of the tables with mismatched tablecloths in one of the cool, dark rooms inside, or head to the vine-filled courtyard for some sun. There you'll find chickens pecking by a rusty automobile, an old well, and motorcycle tourists ordering sandwiches or splitting *picada*. Wine, beer and fondue are also on offer, in addition to desserts.

FAMILY OUTDOOR ACTIVITIES IN TANDIL

Valle del Picapedrero
Zip-line, rock climb and cross the suspension bridge amid the stonecutter ruins in this 24-hectare adventure park.

Mulita Footgolf de Tandil
Play footgolf, a game combining the holes of golf with the ball of soccer.

Cabalgatas El Penacho Familia Heredia
Horseback ride through the sierras with a family of gauchos. Call 0249 463-1975 to reserve.

Take your time here, and be patient if the bill is a bit slow; it's all part of the experience. After lunch, revisit the deli for some items to take home.

Find Peace at Estancia Ave María

Relax and Ride Horses

For a well-rounded trip to Tandil, a short stay in the country is just as essential as experiencing the city. To be nourished, cared for, and immersed in nature, book a stay at one of the many *casas del campo* (country homes) or *estancias* (country mansions–turned-inns) located in the countryside just outside the city. In particular, **Estancia Ave María** (rooms from US$80), located about a 20-minute drive from Tandil, has exceptional hospitality.

Run by owner Asunción, who can easily be found onsite (just look for the small pack of Jack Russell terriers that follow her around), the French-style house has 11 sunlit, comfortable rooms (some with their own fireplace and canopy bed) named after members of her family. The *estancia* was built in the 1960s by an influential immigrant family, the Santamarinas, and purchased in the 1990s by Asunción, who restored it with her own hands.

Guests can ride horseback through the property's fields and meadows of magnolia and oak trees, with the option of visiting a nearby massif. Rides are accompanied by a gaucho guide and can be tailored to beginners. While the scenery is picturesque, the winds are strong, making the sitting room's fireplace with its always-stoked flames an antidote to the cold after a ride, especially if you have a good book to read by it.

Breakfast and dinner are included with the stay and feature high-quality meat, as well as produce from the onsite organic garden of pumpkins, rhubarb and peppers. Guests also have access to the outdoor pool and can book in-room massages.

Pilgrimage to Monte Calvario

Join Thousands on Vía Crucis

Monte Calvario, a forested hill of eucalyptus and pine trees, hosts thousands of pilgrims every Easter who come to walk its Vía Crucis (Way of the Cross). The trail's 14 different stations of statues of the Passion of the Christ are complemented by the Capilla de Santa Gemma, a chapel that holds choir concerts, bathing the forest in a cappella harmonies. Down the stone steps from the chapel, a grotto is set into the hill with an amphitheater in front of it, used for Holy Week productions. Outside of Easter, the area is peaceful, with lampposts and a stone table that puts one in mind of scenes from *The Lion, the Witch and the Wardrobe*.

SALAMI PAR EXCELLENCE

Tandil's world-renowned salamis are one of eight Argentine national products that bear the Denomination of Origin (DOT) seal, ensuring a high-level standard of quality in both the food and the conditions in which it was produced. Salami's origin is linked to Italian and Basque immigrants in the 1800s. The quality and taste of the sausage can be attributed not just to the skill of those curing the meats, but also to the robust livestock and cool climate of Tandil. Buying a DOT salami means it has exact proportions (two parts beef, one part pork and one part bacon), it has been aged and cured in Tandil, and the beef was grass-fed.

WHERE TO EAT IN TANDIL

Bistro Verde
A restaurant, hotel and artist house in one, serving mostly plant-based food alongside cocktails and mocktails. $$

Ladran
Enjoy the gorgeous back patio while dining on steaks, pastas and *picada*. Excellent chocolate mousse. $$$

Bello Abril
Creative cuisine here spans seafood, pastas, ramen, and red wine ice cream. $$$

Azul

Olavarría

Carhué   Tandil

Coronel Suárez

          Juarez

Parque Provincial
Ernesto Tornquist

       Tres Arroyos

Bahía Blanca

Punta Alta

Beyond Tandil

The coastal city of Bahía Blanca, thermal baths,
ruins, and Parque Provincial Ernesto Tornquist's
mountains make up this eclectic region.

GETTING AROUND

Having a car is the
most efficient way
to get around this
region. For public
transport, there's a
daily bus from Tandil
to Bahía Blanca, and
several daily from
Bahía Blanca to Sierra
de la Ventana and
Tornquist, the towns
where most hikers
base themselves
for trekking Cerro
Tres Picos and the
trails in Parque
Provincial Ernesto
Tornquist. Tornquist
Municipality's buses
run throughout the
day between the base
of Cerro de la Ventana
and Tornquist.
These routes can be
found by searching
plataforma10.com.ar.
Carhué is the
hardest to reach via
public transport, but
Grupo Plaza runs
several buses a day
between Carhué and
Bahía Blanca. Check
termasdecarhue.gov.
ar for up-to-date info
on routes.

The area west of Tandil has some of the most diverse sights
in all of Buenos Aires Province. Here, you might see guanacos while hiking to Tres Picos in the mountainous part of the
Pampas, or sight a UFO in Bahía Blanca at a former factory turned museum. Astral photographers take advantage of
the low light pollution and striking ruins of Epecuén, while
spa tourists come to float in the nearby thermal baths of Carhué. Several horror films and a Red Bull biking short have
been filmed around Epecuén. And the box office flop *There
Be Dragons* was filmed outside of Sierra de la Ventana. You'll
also find art deco slaughterhouses and cemeteries as well as
geodesic dome glampgrounds.

Epecuén

Museo Taller Ferrowhite

☑ **TOP TIP**

Long-distance buses are infrequent and not well connected. Book accommodation in mountain towns in advance, especially during holidays.

Bahía Blanca

TIME FROM TANDIL: **4½HRS** 🚗

History & Mystery at the Port

A mere 4½ hours from Tandil by car, Bahía Blanca has some of the most interesting museums on the coast. Head to the port where the Museo Taller Ferrowhite and the Museo del Puerto are only a short walk from each other. The former is a museum workshop with exhibits on Argentina's shipping and railroad history, while the latter tells the stories of immigrants who came to build their lives around the port through models of the settlement, clothing, letters, and re-created living scenes, like a school house and barbershop. Both have free entry, and are open every day, save Monday for the Museo del Puerto.

The Museo Taller Ferrowhite is housed in three structures, the most striking of which is the former power plant built by Italian immigrants in the 1930s. Resembling a castle more than a modern-day power plant, only a small part of it is used for artistic workshops, with plans to open more of it soon to the public. Visitors can freely roam the grounds and peer through broken windows to try to spot UFOs, or head inside the former regional maintenance workshop directly opposite it, which contains the actual exhibits, including a zorb-like lifeboat.

The best day to visit Museo del Puerto is on Sunday when they serve a themed menu each week based on different countries' cuisines.

Plan for about three hours between the museums. It's worth the money to take a taxi or rideshare out to the port, as it's a long way from the center.

ALIEN HAPPENINGS IN BAHÍA BLANCA

Nicolás Testoni, Director of the Museo Taller Ferrowhite, who was born and raised in Bahía Blanca, shares some of the stories of paranormal activity associated with the museum's old power plant.

In 1975, railwayman Carlos Diaz was allegedly abducted by a flying saucer just meters from the place the museum occupies today, between the railway tracks of the port of Ingeniero White. Diaz said the aliens flew him to Buenos Aires, where they dropped him off. Recently, the groundskeeper of the museum and her daughter, who live onsite, saw colored balls of light hovering around the factory one night. They called the police to come investigate, but the police were unable to determine what they were.

Message on
WhatsApp for
prices and
opening times:
+54 29 2342-7092

TOP SIGHT

Villa Epecuén

Once a spa town, Villa Epecuén sat on the Epecuén Lake, with water as salty as the Dead Sea. In 1985, the lake flooded Epecuén, and residents spent the following days evacuating without any casualties ensuing. Later, a second flood submerged Epecuén completely. After two decades, the waters receded, revealing the salt-bleached ruins of buildings and petrified trees that tourists now come to photograph.

DON'T MISS

Complejo
Balneario
Municipal

Matadero

Cementerio
Abandonado de
Carhué

Centro de
Interpretación
y Museo de las
Ruinas

Avenida de Mayo

Casa de Pablo
Novak

El Cristo

Planning & Arrival

The closest town to Epecuén is Carhué, from which you can easily walk, bike or drive to reach the ruins. While most of the ruins are concentrated in a paid area, the cemetery, Christ, Matadero, petrified forest and the swing *(hamaca)* are all free. Driving down the Camino Epecuen/Carhué (the road that hugs the lake) will take you to most of the free sites, while the cemetery is located closer to Carhué at end of the road Laprida, just over the levee. To visit all of the sights, plan for five hours.

Matadero

One of the best-preserved buildings, the Matadero (slaughterhouse) was designed by Italian architect Francisco Salome, whose art deco works can be seen throughout Buenos Aires Province in graveyards, city buildings and cemeteries. Its grand arched edifices are now skeletons, and the only sounds you can hear are the cawing of birds, giving it an eerie feeling compounded by the petrified forest of eucalyptus trees next to it.

Cementerio Abandonado de Carhué

The cemetery was the site of a massive exhumation to relocate the dead once the flooding ensued. Some of the broken crypts and graves have fresh flowers on them from loved ones who still come to visit. Impressive headstone statues bleached white from the salt are scattered throughout.

Centro de Interpretación y Museo de las Ruinas

Stop here before you go into the paid area to learn more about the factors that contributed to the flood, as well the history of Epecuén, from its indigenous heritage to its heyday as a spa town (all of which is only written in Spanish). There are also salvaged items, the pizzeria's animal sculptures, a vintage bathing costume, and windowpanes from the castle.

Flamingos & Salty Beaches

Epecuén is home to a nature reserve where 22,000 flamingos live during part of the year, making it one of the largest colonies of flamingos in Argentina. The only animal that lives in the lake's waters, artemia salina (brine shrimp), is a favored food of the flamingos. You can see the birds throughout Epecuén, but just southwest of the swing is one of the best spots to watch them feeding.

Avenida de Mayo

This was the main drag that leads to what was the pinnacle of the town: the Municipal Spa Complex (Complejo Balneario Municipal), now with the salt-bleached remains of waterslides and the old cistern, marked with a line to show the level the floodwaters reached. Some of the best-labeled and most-intact structures can be found along this street, including the old school, the Monte Real hotel and the staircases of the Confitería Corradini.

Casa de Pablo Novak

Located a few blocks away from the paid area is Pablo Novak's house. The nonagenarian has garnered fame as being the sole resident of Epecuén. It's possible to visit him at his home or run into him strolling around the ruins on his daily walk with his dog. He's very open to sharing stories from his youth in Epecuén and memories of the flood.

LIVING THROUGH THE FLOOD

Alicia Pazos, resident of Carhué and owner of Departamentos Jacarandá, shares her experience: After the cemetery flooded, some of the coffins floated to the surface. People contracted divers to break into crypts to get their loved ones' coffins out and move them to other cemeteries. My brother had to get permission from the municipality to break my dad out.

TOP TIPS

- Epecuén has little light pollution, making it a hot spot for astrophotography, especially by the Matadero.
- The best light for daytime photos at the ruins is in the late afternoon.
- To walk the cemetery by yourself, go just after a rainstorm.
- The paid section is totally exposed. It can get very cold in winter and hot in summer. Dress accordingly, and bring water.
- Norma Berg (normabergturismo @hotmail.com) is a guide for hire who speaks English.
- If driving, look out for big potholes on the road to Pablo Novak's house and near the museum.

THE HEALTH PROPERTIES OF LAGO EPECUÉN

Indigenous groups, like the Tehuelches and Araucanians, bathed in the waters of Epecuén long before the Spanish arrived, but it wasn't until the 1880s that an Italian chemist started investigating the water's mineral properties. The lake contains calcium, magnesium, sodium, potassium, copper, zinc and silica, among other minerals. Soaking in the lake is said to help with skin regeneration, insomnia, muscular contractions, osteoarthritis, rheumatoid arthritis, psoriasis and eczema. Locals recommend letting the water dry on your skin until a salt residue forms, then exfoliating whatever part of the body you are trying to heal with the salt, before returning to the water.

LADANIFER/SHUTTERSTOCK ©

Cerro Bahía Blanca

Carhué

TIME FROM TANDIL: **4½HRS** 🚌

Lago Epecuén, A Post-Apocalyptic Spa

Epecuén Lake has salinity levels on par with the Dead Sea. Its waters get pumped into the pools of the spas and campground complexes of the neighboring town of Carhué, just above the levee from the ruins of Epecuén. Wellness tourists come to soak in its waters for its healing properties. With a range of price points, there's options in town for budget travelers, like the Spa Cabañas y Camping Levalle (open 10am to 8pm), as well as those seeking more luxury, like the Complejo Termal & Lúdico Mar de Epecuén (open 11am to 7pm), with multiple pools and water park features.

You don't have to stay at a complex to access its pools; purchase a day pass (starting from around US$4) with multiple entry options. You can also book add-ons, like fango treatments (full body masks with mud from Lake Epecuén), massages and chocolate body masks.

The water is from the lake, meaning it's not pristine and can have a green hue. Be careful not to get it in your eyes – the salt burns and you'll have to exit the pool to wash your eyes immediately if you do. However, it's easy to avoid, as the complexes put floating devices and handrails in the pools.

 WHERE TO EAT & DRINK IN BAHÍA BLANCA

Casamonte
Welcoming staff serve sandwiches, soups and large pieces of cake in this colorful cafe. **$$**

Coffee Tiger Co
A specialty coffee shop that also sells bags of beans from roasters around the country. **$**

El Dorado
A speakeasy and restaurant known for its curries, cocktails and gnocchi; come here for dinner. **$$$**

While many complexes offer climatized pools, there's also the option to bathe in the lake directly by heading to the Eco Sustainable Beach located in Epecuén itself. Anywhere you can soak, you'll find jars of fango for sale as well, making for an interesting, if heavy, souvenir.

Parque Provincial Ernesto Tornquist

TIME FROM TANDIL: 3½HRS 🚗

Hiking in Parque Provincial Ernesto Tornquist

Less than a four-hour drive from Tandil, the 67-sq-km Parque Provincial Ernesto Tornquist is an easily accessible hiking destination, with plenty of lodging in the nearby towns of Sierra de la Ventana, Tornquist and Villa de la Ventana.

Most trails are easy to moderate in difficulty and begin from one of the park's two entrances: Base de Cerro de la Ventana and Base de Cerro Bahía Blanca. Gates open at 9am, and trails close at 4:30pm. A day pass (US$0.60) gets you into both entrances. The park's Facebook page lists up-to-date trail info: facebook.com/ParqueProvincialTornquistCerroVentana.

Cerro de La Ventana offers the most popular hike in the park: a trail of moderate difficulty to the window-shaped rock of the 1150m-high Cerro de la Ventana. The six-hour hike can only be accessed with a paid guide (show up on Saturday at 9am at the ranger station by the parking lot to use the park guide or hire an external one). Another paid guided hike, to the Garganta del Diablo, is a six-hour trek through foothills and a ravine to a 15m-high waterfall. The self-guided hikes are shorter, like the Garganta Olvidada, about an hour-long roundtrip along a rocky stream to a small waterfall.

The Cerro Bahía Blanca entrance has the Centro de Visitantes with info on the flora and fauna of the park, such as the endemic cobra lizard. Self-guided hikes are the way to go here, including the two-hour roundtrip trail to the top of 1400m-high Cerro Bahía Blanca, and Claro Obscuro, which winds through a forest of pine and eucalyptus.

THE BEST PLACES TO EAT & DRINK NEAR PROVINCIAL ERNESTO TORNQUIST

Modesto Café
This cafe in Torquist serves a decent coffee and carrot cake, even during afternoon siesta. **$**

El Molino de La Casa Azul
This restaurant in Sierra de la Ventana experiments (in a good way) with Argentine classics. **$$**

Puente Blanco Restaurant
Located inside the Puente Blanco glampground, this restaurant offers grilled meats, fish, and vegetarian dishes. **$$**

Kupinski Restobar Unsina del Arte
Coffee, pastries, and engaging conversations with the owner can be found at this artsy restobar. **$**

Obrador
This bakery serves delicious croissants and espresso-based beverages, as well as lunch options for celiacs. **$$**

WHERE TO EAT IN CARHUÉ

Pizza Epecuén
The most popular pizza joint in town has won awards for its pizza and empanadas. **$$**

Hado
Open all day, this ice-cream and pastry shop makes the best coffee in town. **$**

La Cambacita
Buy *alfajores* at this cookie factory that relocated from Epecuén to Carhué during the flood. **$**

The Highest Hill: Cerro Tres Picos

Cerro Tres Picos, the highest point in Buenos Aires Province at 1239m above sea level (4065ft), is a short drive from Parque Provincial Ernesto Tornquist. Managed by Fundación Funke (with whom trekkers are required to register beforehand via its online form), the trail takes seven to nine hours as a day hike. Hikers can also camp along the trail to split the 21km (13 miles) roundtrip into two days with or without a guide.

❶ Camino a Glorieta (Glorieta Path)

Drive or take a *remise* to Estancia Funke. After check-in and orientation (7.30am to 8.30am for day hikers), drive or walk to the car park at Camino a Glorieta. As you go through the gate, you'll see Cerro Tres Picos on your right.

The Hike: Follow the dirt path through the gate, across the stream and past the bulls. You'll see the entrance to the pine forest about 3.5km from the trailhead.

❷ Bosque de Pinos (Pine Forest)

Take a break at the start of the forest to rehydrate, as this part of the trail has the steepest incline. You'll start to feel the increase towards the 996m elevation gain to reach the top.

The Hike: About an hour from the trailhead, the trail turns to gravel when you reach the forest. Once you reach the wire fence, head east, then take a left at the fork.

Cerro Tres Picos

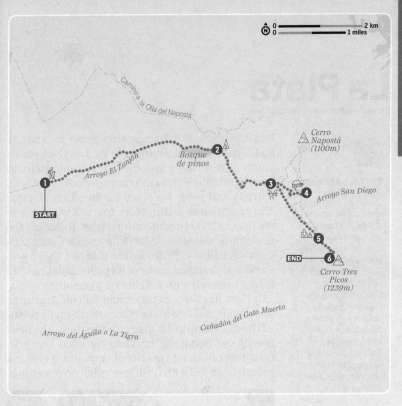

❸ Paso Dinamitado (Dynamited Pass)

After Paso Dinamitado, you'll see the window-shaped rock formation of the Cerro de la Ventana in the distance on a clear day. The pass is also a camping area for overnight hikers.

The Hike: From the wire fence, it's about 45 minutes to Paso Dinamitado. Continue along the path and go left again at the fork by the corral.

❹ Cueva Guanacos (Guanacos Cave)

See guanacos here, and fill your water bottle at the stream downhill from the cave. You can camp inside the cave, the wide mouth of which acts as a frame for stunning sunsets and sunrises over the valley.

The Hike: After the rock ridges past the corral, go right at the first fork, then left at the second. If not camping, you can skip this section, and instead head right at the second fork towards the summit.

❺ Piedra Bote (Boat Rock)

Stop here for a photo on top of the boat-shaped rock, then get ready to use your hands to scramble to the top.

The Hike: From the cave to Boat Rock, it's about 45 minutes. Return to the main trail via the shortcut indicated on the map from the orientation.

❻ Cumbre (Summit)

You'll have uninterrupted views of the Sierra and strong winds in this section. Once you reach the summit, you can snap the obligatory picture sitting on top of the metal stool.

La Plata

GETTING AROUND

There's no need to rent a car for getting around La Plata: the city's streets are on a grid, and they are flat and walkable. They aren't always labeled, though, so having Google Maps open on your phone will help you get your bearings. Buses run regularly and are plentiful. Taxis are cheap and easy to find. Multiple rideshare apps, like Cabify and Uber, function here. You can use the same public transportation card, SUBE, that you use in Buenos Aires to pay for buses as well as the train, the Tren Universitario, which runs in a half-circle around part of the city.

☑ TOP TIP

From the city's center, Plaza Moreno, you can walk to any part of the city within its original grid in 40 minutes or less. Two major roads that run diagonally, Diagonal 73 going east to west, and Diagonal 75 going north to south, meet at Plaza Moreno.

La Plata, capital of Buenos Aires Province and the first planned city in South America, has always been highly advanced – it was the first Argentine city to have lightbulbs – though often overlooked by both tourists and *porteños* since its founding in 1882. The exception is architecture tourists who visit to see the city's vast architectural styles, including the neo-Gothic Catedral de La Plata and Le Corbusier's Curutchet House. Pedro Benoit planned the city on a grid and designed many of its public buildings, infusing his work with Freemason symbolism.

La Plata has been an important hub for Argentine rock bands and one of the places that heavily resisted the dictatorship. Its many universities – the most prestigious being the La Plata National University, which produced two Nobel laureates – give it a college-town feel with fresh energy but no pretension.

Museo de La Plata

SIGHTS
1. Casa Curutchet
2. Centro Cultural Estación Provincial
3. Museo de La Plata

EATING
4. Carne
5. Lebrel

DRINKING & NIGHTLIFE
6. Amsterdam Cervecería
7. Fisher
see 7. Laurus
8. Llama Coffee Roasters
9. Walden

BEST BARS FOR CRAFT BEER

Astor Birra
Award-winning beers and pop-ups by guest chefs. $$

Walden
Taps from brewers in La Plata, including Desobediencia Civil, the owner's sours line. $

Laurus
This local brewery has superb sours, stouts and IPAs. $

Amsterdam Cervecería
With more than 20 taps and including gluten-free, you'll find a beer for you. $$

Fisher
Of the 20 beers on tap, the one to try is Bullying Beer, brewed by the owner. $$

A History of the World

Tour Museo de La Plata

Of La Plata's many museums, the must-see is **Museo de La Plata**, a world-class natural history museum where you can touch a meteorite and see the fossilized skin of a giant sloth. Bruce Chatwin wrote about visiting the museum specifically to see the skin in his travel-writing classic *In Patagonia*, to solve the mystery of the origin of a prehistoric pelt his grandmother owned. Today, it has a catalog of 3.5 million pieces ranging from the bones of dinosaurs and other giant prehistoric animals, such as a pack of glyptodons (like massive armadillos) and the skeleton of a towering giant sloth, a favorite of visitors to photograph.

✷ FUN FESTIVALS IN LA PLATA

Festival de la Cultura Cervecera Platense
For three days in July, sample over 100 beers brewed by local craft-brewing associations.

Aniversario de La Plata
Celebrate the founding of the city with concerts, dancing and visual art in November.

Museos a la Luz de la Luna
The city's museums stay open until midnight, hosting concerts, workshops and talks in November.

Most of the specimens come from South America, though there's also an Egyptian section with mummies that was donated by the Sudanese government. The permanent exhibitions take up 20 rooms on two floors, charting earth's and humanity's evolution. Exhibit themes include invertebrate and vertebrate zoology, biological anthropology, ethnography, archeology, and the Jesuit Missions.

Argentine explorer Francisco 'Perito' Moreno founded the museum in 1884, served as its first director, and donated its initial collections from his personal library. The building's design incorporates elements of both neoclassical and baroque styles, including six Corinthian columns at the front. Several pre-Colombian reliefs are on the facade, and two statues of sabertoothed tigers (a species that once roamed the pampas) guard its entrance.

Plan for at least an hour and a half to visit. The museum is not open on Mondays and Tuesdays.

Casa Curutchet, a Modernist Masterpiece

See a Le Corbusier-Designed House

One of the main reasons architecture buffs come to La Plata is to tour **Casa Curutchet**, one of only two works in the Americas by French-Swiss architect Le Corbusier (the other being Harvard's Carpenter Center for the Visual Arts). A pioneer of the modernist architectural movement, Le Corbusier made minimalist designs with industrial materials, like reinforced concrete. He hoped that this would make housing more affordable, something he was highly aware of as a city planner.

Argentine surgeon Pedro Curutchet commissioned the house in 1948, and after Le Corbusier sent the plans, it was project managed by Amancio Williams, designer of Mar del Plata's famed Casa Puente. Later, the house was named a Unesco World Heritage Site in 2016, along with 17 other of Le Corbusier's works.

Casa Curutchet is an example of Le Corbusier's five points of architecture: an open floor plan, long windows, open facades, pillars, and a roof garden. Sleek and functional with clean lines, it has a ramped walkway and four levels connected by a spiral staircase, with a poplar tree in the middle of the space. When you walk it, you might have a weightless feeling – something else for which his designs were known.

The house is now managed by the Colegio de Arquitectos

ARGENTINE DANCE PIONEERS

Argentine performance art company De La Guarda helped to boost awareness and acclaim for combining aerial dance and theater when it began touring the world in the 1990s. The show required audiences to stand in place while performers scaled the walls above and around them, oftentimes splashing them with water. After performing in Seoul, Berlin and London, the company did a six-year off-Broadway stint of 2475 performances at New York City's Daryl Roth Theatre. Though the company disbanded, you can still find its influence in productions like the popular dance-theater show Fuerza Bruta in Buenos Aires, and Cuerda Producciones, which was started by former members of De La Guarda.

WHERE TO EAT & DRINK IN LA PLATA

Lebrel
Order a vermouth with your loaded sandwich made with fresh-baked bread at Argentina's first *focacceria*. $$

Carne
An upscale burger joint by Michelin-starred chef and La Plata native Mauro Colagreco. $$

Llama Coffee Roasters
A local specialty coffeeshop chain with several locations throughout the city. $

(Buenos Aires Professional Association of Architects), with whom you can pre-arrange a brief guided tour that can sometimes be done in English (email info@capba.org.ar). After, you can stay as long as you like to explore. No prebooking is necessary to see the house, but tours require prior arrangement. The house is only open Thursday to Sunday.

Bouncing Off the Walls

Aerial Dance at Estación Provincial

It's very Argentine to take an old building, repurpose it, and add in some artistic, surprising element. That's exactly what the Caro Aérea aerial dance seminars do: allow participants to attach themselves via dance harness and rope to several rigging points on the top of **Centro Cultural Estación Provincial**, then rappel down to the building's mid-section to run Spiderman-style along the walls of the old provincial train station.

The founder of the company, Carolina Castillo, leads participants in a light warm-up on the ground (incorporating many of the moves used in the air) before doing a safety talk and equipment checks with the rigger. Appropriate for novices and advanced aerial dancers alike, the seminar (US$30) lasts from 10am to 3pm, allowing everyone two to three dancing sessions, with time to recover between each. If participants get comfortable with horizontal running, turning and flipping, they can try simple duo and trio choreography, looking like a flock of majestic iguanas to those watching from the ground. The building no longer functions as a train station but acts as a cultural center. You can see various art exhibits inside and read about its history while waiting for your turn; it's a good way to stay cool in the heat, should you be there in summer.

The seminars run about once a month. Check Caro Aérea's website for upcoming dates (caroaerea.store/index.html) and be prepared to communicate mostly in Spanish. It's a 35-minute walk from the center to the train station or a bus ride on one of the 237 lines to reach it.

ANOTHER WORTHWHILE CEMETERY

For those interested in seeing another fascinating cemetery, consider going to Buenos Aires' **Cementerio de la Recoleta** (p88), known for its own lore and famous gravesites, including Evita Peron's.

A MINI CITY & MASONIC SYMBOLISM

El Cementerio de La Plata (the La Plata Cemetery) was designed by Pedro Benoit, the Argentine architect who designed La Plata. Built to be a mini version of the city, the cemetery emulates its placement of diagonal streets and small squares, using the same architectural styles of its buildings in its crypts: neo-classical, art deco, neo-Gothic, and Egyptian modernist, among others. Benoit was a Freemason, and local guides will point you to masonic symbolism throughout, including mentioning the cemetery's location at the end of Diagonal 74, a street that starts at La Plata River. The water represents birth and life, and the street's ending after heading east to the cemetery represents death.

On this two-hour tour, you'll see the city's most famous buildings spanning a wide range of architecture. If you're coming from Buenos Aires via train, it's a great introduction to La Plata, as it starts from where you'll disembark.

Begin at **❶ Estación del Ferrocarril Roca**. Its massive green dome with circular windows makes the station look like a large train itself and art nouveau petal-shaped roofs frame the entrances. Head down Av 1 and turn right on Av 53 to arrive at **❷ Casa Curutchet** (p328), the only Le Corbusier house in Latin America. You'll be able to admire its clean white lines and poplar tree, even if you don't venture inside. Continue along Av 53 to Plaza San Martín to reach the **❸ Residencia de Gobierno**. Designed by Belgian architect Jules Dormal in a neo-Renaissance style, its white

Corinthian columns and large balcony are accented by exposed red bricks. Just off the plaza you'll also find **❹ Paseo Dardo Rocha**, a former train station built in the Italian neo-renaissance style, and the **❺ Palacio de la Legislatura**, a German renaissance-style palace. From the plaza, continue down Av 51 to reach **❻ Teatro Argentino**. If this Brutalist building doesn't quite fit with La Plata's aesthetic, it's because it was a replacement after the original one partially burned down. Walk down Av 51 to finish your tour at Plaza Moreno. There you'll be able to see the **❼ Palacio Municipal**, a Renaissance-style town hall, and the neo-Gothic **❽ Catedral de La Plata**, the tallest church in the country. Relax in the grassy plaza and take in the many parts of its facade: gargoyles, stained-glass windows, and reliefs of saints' stories.

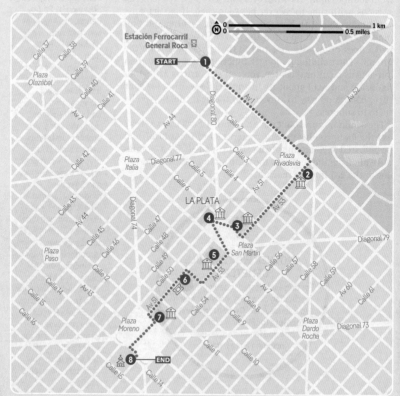

Beyond
La Plata

Go west from La Plata to enter a land of *estancias*, polo and extreme sports.

This region, within a two-hour radius of La Plata, is where *dulce de leche* was invented, and Argentina's most influential president, Juan Domingo Perón, was born. Cañuelas has the highest concentration of the country's polo clubs, including La Dolfina, the project of Adolfo Cambiaso, one of the best players in the world. It's also where you can learn how to play polo at the *estancia* and polo club Puesto Viejo. Further west in Lobos, the skydiving capital of Argentina, you'll find other extreme sports, like windsurfing and kitesurfing, and you can stay in a castle, the Estancia La Candelaria, which is, of course, also a polo club.

GETTING AROUND

Renting a car will be your fastest choice of transport, and allow you to explore some of the smaller towns in the area between Cañuelas and Lobos. Direct long-distance buses run from La Plata to Lobos and Cañuelas and between Cañuelas and Lobos. If you're patient, public transportation (a series of buses and trains) will get you from La Plata to these areas too, but this will be much longer than the other options and require several transfers.

☑ TOP TIP

Book individual tours to either *estancia*, or opt to do both in one trip with your own car.

Estancia La Candelaria (p333)

MEET THE ARGENTINE POLO PONY

If you're playing polo in Argentina, you might notice that your horse is smaller than other horses you've ridden on previous horseback rides. Smaller horses are common in polo, where players need to be able to reach the ground with their mallets, and the Argentine polo horse is particularly sought after, making the country one of the largest exporters of polo horses in the world. The Argentine polo horse is a variant of the Argentine Criollo horse that was bred with English thoroughbreds. This gave it the adaptability and endurance of the Criollo horses and the speed of the thoroughbreds, resulting in a horse both fiercely competitive and surprisingly calm under pressure.

MARIA ELISA ROL/SHUTTERSTOCK ©

Polo, Argentina

Cañuelas

TIME FROM LA PLATA: **1HR** 🚆

Polo Day at Puesto Viejo

When British settlers came to the Pampas, they began playing polo on the flat grasslands. The River Plate Polo Association was founded in 1892, and later the Argentine Polo Association in 1922. Now, 80 percent of the highest-rated polo players in the world are Argentine, and the Pampas has become a destination for polo players to train in the offseason of the northern hemisphere (as polo can be played year-round in the Pampas) and for leisure tourists looking for an affordable option to try polo.

About an hour's drive away from La Plata is Puesto Viejo, a polo club and *estancia* in Cañuelas, that will teach you how to play polo. You don't have to have prior horseriding experience to participate, and classes can be taught in English or Spanish. You'll get outfitted with all the necessary equipment – helmet, mallet and horse – and be walked through proper swinging technique, trying to hit balls on the ground while standing on a stool, before you get on a horse. The instructor will show you how to ride the horse and get it to stop, spending adequate time going over the basics before you go on the field to put it all together. After class, they provide lunch and

ADVENTURE TOURISM IN LOBOS & CAÑUELAS

Argentina Extrema
A rural biking tour takes you down backroads from the Cañuelas train station to Uribelarrea.

Laguna de Lobos
Multiple campgrounds rent kayaks as well as windsurfing and kitesurfing gear to use at Lobos Lagoon.

Skydive Lobos
Jump out of a plane at one of Argentina's oldest skydiving schools.

you can watch a polo match of four on four, as well as use the *estancia's* infinity pool and bicycles to explore the property more. Polo days are US$195 per person, with transport provided from Buenos Aires capital, or you can book just the polo class for US$80.

Lobos

TIME FROM LA PLATA: **2HR** 🚌

Stay in a Castle

Provencia de Buenos Aires has several castles, but only one you can stay a night in: La Candelaria, an *estancia* and polo club near Lobos. A two-hour drive from La Plata, the 123-year-old structure was built after Manuel Fraga Calveyra and Rebeca del Mármol, a newly wedded Argentine aristocratic couple in the 1890s, decided they needed their own castle after returning from their European honeymoon. Five years later, the massive neo-renaissance French-style château was complete; many years later, it was the first *estancia* in Argentina to open its doors to tourists that would later include the Rolling Stones and Prince Harry.

Room prices at La Candelaria (book at estanciacandelaria. com) include access to all activities at the *estancia:* horseback riding, biking, and swimming in the pool. There are also day-dependent activities, such as empanada-making classes, a history talk about the castle, and a folkloric show. Also included in the room price are three meals and tea-time snacks, as well as access to the trails in the forests of araucaria, cedar and pine trees.

Wellness services (yoga, sound baths, massages and facials) can also be booked for an additional cost. A night in the castle starts at just over US$80, but budget for more if you want some of the additional services. Another option is day access to the castle and its activities (the Día de Campo option), which also comes with lunch and plenty of time to take photos of the castle. La Candelaria is especially welcoming to families, providing lots of children's activities, plus a nanny service for an additional cost.

Iglesia de Nuestra Señora de Luján, Uribelarrea

AN EVITA FILMING LOCATION

Alan Parker's 1996 movie *Evita*, starring Madonna and Antonio Banderas, was shot partially in the town of Uribelarrea, less than a 30-minute drive from Cañuelas. If you've seen the movie, you'll recognize the church, the Iglesia de Nuestra Señora de Luján, from the scene of the wake, when Evita escapes into it to kiss her deceased father. Parker paid to have stained glass installed in the church, which you can still see today, and you might recognize some of the funeral goers from the movie as well: several of the extras were Uribelarrea townspeople.

Mar del Plata

GETTING AROUND

Mar del Plata has buses, but walking can often be faster, due to long wait times. Taxis and rideshares, like Uber and Cabify, are available and usually the quickest way to get to a place if you don't have a car. Rideshares are still in a legal gray area, meaning your driver might ask you to sit in front, making it less obvious the journey is a rideshare. Driving is easy, though stressful, as aggression at unmarked four-way stops is common. Parking, especially in the center and around Paseo Güemes, can be difficult to find.

☑ **TOP TIP**

The tourist office, located next to the Casino Central on the main street, Av Patricio Peralta Ramos, is worth a visit to discover current offerings of festivals, talks and concerts. Follow the sun in the summer, meaning you should head to the southern beaches for the most daylight and the most parties.

Mar del Plata is the biggest little city on the Argentine Atlantic coast. Made popular by Argentine president Juan Perón in the mid-1900s, it's still the main beach resort Argentines vacation at during the summer holiday season of January and February – so much so that it can be hard to find a spot to lay your towel on the sand. While there's more to do here than anywhere else on the coast in the off-season, it feels less like a city than a town, as some businesses close for an afternoon siesta. A literary hub and gambling destination at various points in history, Mardel (as the locals call it) has gone through many iterations, the most recent being in the 1990s, when it established itself as Argentina's preeminent craft-beer hub. Other draws include seafood, surfing and pastries. After all, it's where Havanna, a global brand of Argentine *alfajores*, began.

Searching for Sea Lions

Hang Out at the Docks

The sea lion is the most emblematic animal of Mar del Plata, as evidenced in both the city's wildlife – packs of sea lions sun themselves at the port and the nature reserve – as well as in the city's art – stone sea lion sentries guard Playa Bristol's beach, and Museo Mar's massive gold sea lion statue was once famously covered in wrappers of Havanna *alfajores*. To see the real thing, head to the **Banquina de Pescadores**, at **Puerto Mar del Plata**. The sea lions like to sleep, fight and bark at the edge of the wharf where you can buy fried seafood, beer and hot dogs for lunch from the different stalls. You can also pick up fresh-caught fish to cook later or cans of fish for souvenirs.

If you tire of crowds of tourists and high schoolers on field trips at the wharf, it's a short drive or long walk out to the **Sea Lion Reserve**. The reserve runs along the jetty and starts just past the ship repair section of the port. You'll be able to smell the sea lions before you can see them. Even more can be found here than by the fish stalls, and their snoring sounds almost harmonized.

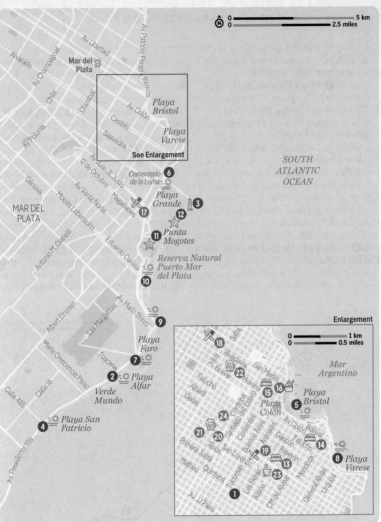

SIGHTS
1 Centro Cultural Villa Victoria Ocampo
2 La Caseta
3 Monument to San Salvador
4 Acantilados
5 Playa Bristol
6 Playa Grande
7 Playa Helena
8 Playa Varese
9 Playa Waikiki
10 Punta Mogotes

ACTIVITIES, COURSES & TOURS
11 Banquina de Pescadores
12 Sea Lion Reserve

SLEEPING
13 Hotel Sainte Jeanne
14 Hotel Sirenuse
15 Los Arcos

EATING
16 Havanna
17 Lo de Fran
18 Sarasanegro
19 Yin & Toni

DRINKING & NIGHTLIFE
20 Antares
21 Bohr Bar
22 Hops
23 Kiva Café
24 Proyecto Bar

THE GUIDE

MAR DEL PLATA THE PAMPAS & THE ATLANTIC COAST

See many of Mar del Plata's icons on this hour-and-half-long walk around part of the coast and ending in the center.

Start at ① **Playa Varese**. In the offseason, you can have a peaceful morning *mate* by the ocean here, but in the summer, you'll see huge crowds and nary an open space. Walk down the beach until you reach the Balneario Bahía Varese, then head uphill to take Almirante Brown to Mendoza to reach ② **Torre Tanque**, an 88m-high water storage tower that looks like it was broken off of a castle. Climb the 194 steps to the top for panoramic views of the city and port. Go back down Mendoza until you hit Av Colon, then left two blocks to arrive at the ③ **Museo Municipal de Arte Juan Carlos Castagnino**, whose crests and pinnacles are a cross between French manor and Anglo-Norman architecture. Head towards the coast along Carlos Alvear until the road ends at ④ **Torreón del Monje**, a tower commissioned by Ernesto Tornquist. Today it houses a restaurant, gift shop and exhibition space. Make your way along the shore down ⑤ **Playa Las Toscas** or on the paved promenade above, running along Primero Jesús de Galindez, to get to ⑥ **Playa Bristol**, the city's central beach. Take a picture with the sea lion statue, the ⑦ **Monumento Lobos Marinos**, then pass the casino and cross the avenue to buy *alfajores* at ⑧ **Havanna**. This was the site of the original Havanna factory that was started in 1948 and would lead to the worldwide chain. Save room for the next stop: churros at ⑨ **Manolo**. Afterwards, cut over to the pedestrian street of San Martín to finish at the neo-Gothic ⑩ **Basílica de los Santos Pedro y Cecilia**.

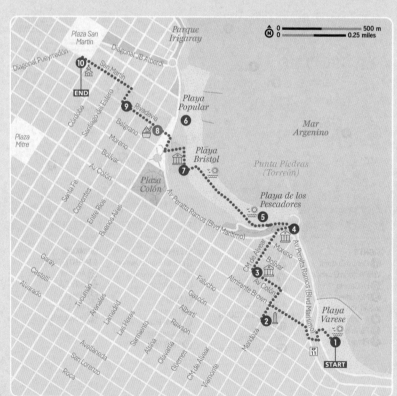

Continue down the jetty, and you'll reach the massive **monument to San Salvador**, the patron saint of fishers. Here, you'll have an amazing view of Mar del Plata's coastline and waves crashing behind you on the rocks, perfect for some *Little Mermaid*–inspired pictures. Both the port and reserve are free to enter and open 24 hours.

The Gastronomy of Mar del Plata
There's Something in the Water

Mar del Plata's gastronomy has always been tied to its water: its ocean – the largest fishing port in the country – and the aquifers from where the city sources its water. Being naturally potable, the national consensus is that the city's water quality has contributed to the deliciousness of its cuisine, especially its pastries (even if some are only made with milk).

Churros come filled with *dulce de leche* here, and you'll see *marplatenses* lining the streets, waiting to eat at their favorite churro spots on Saturday mornings. Mar del Plata is also synonymous with *medialunas*, croissant-like pastries made with lard or butter. Even the journey to Mardel from Buenos Aires has, for any Argentine, meant an obligatory stop between the two cities at Parador Atalaya to buy *medialunas*. Within Mardel, though, the best place is highly debatable, but **Confitería Boston** and **La Fonte D'Oro** are two of the most popular bakery chains in the city. Do your own research by picking a new shop to try each day. However, the pastry that put Mar del Plata on the global gastronomy map was *alfajores*: **Havanna**, the *alfajores* and chocolate shop that's now a globally franchised cafe chain, started here.

For seafood, you'll find calamari, mussels, prawns, paella and much more in restaurants all along the coastline, with some of the most famous and touristic restaurants at the port.

Antares, now a national craft-beer brand, started in Mar del Plata. Visit the original location in Los Troncos, then check out the slews of breweries and craft-beer bars on Constitución Ave and Olavarría St.

Mar del Plata's Beaches
Sunbathing, Surfing and Paragliding

In Mardel, going to the beach is the number one activity in summer. Locals begin planning for the next summer immediately after the season ends by booking spots at *balnearios* (bathing resorts with umbrellas, chairs and tents for rent) for the following summer, thus getting the best price. You can

THE BEER SCENE IN MAR DEL PLATA

Alayh Rivera, owner of Celebra Tequeños, which sources food for over 25 bars in Mar del Plata, shares how to experience the city's beer culture: **Bohr Bar** and **Hops** have a rotating lineup of taps showcasing beer from different breweries. Get the Escondido IPA, Cachalote's session IPA, and, the one I think is the best beer not just in Mar del Plata, but in Argentina: Jamming's IPA. Locals also like La Paloma's cream ale. **Antares** was the first brewery here. You can try it, but I'd also recommend **Proyecto Bar**. It feels like you're in a friend's home with cool events, great food and good beer.

NIGHTLIFE IN MAR DEL PLATA

The Center
Find bars and clubs within the triangle of Plaza Mitre, Plaza Colón and Plaza San Martín.

Playa Grande
Restaurants by day turn into some of the city's most sought-after *boliches* by night.

Güemes Centro
Great for bar-hopping or a chill date spot in one of the many restaurants.

book per day when you show up, but if you plan on staying in Mardel for a while, ask for a cheaper rate.

The most central beach is **Playa Popular**, also known as **Playa Bristol**, directly behind the casino and sea lion statues. It's a public beach and the most crowded in Mar del Plata. Though easy to access, it's far from the cleanest or prettiest beach; there's an excellent skatepark there. **Playa Varese** is a short walk away, where you can take surfing classes or rent equipment (including SUP boards) from **Mar del Plata Surf Club** (contact them on Instagram @mdp.surf.club). Continuing south, there's the fashionable **Playa Grande**, full of restaurants and clubs, and good for surfing and kitesurfing. Another popular surf spot is **Playa Waikiki**, next to **Punta Mogotes**, one of the preferred beaches for families with its many beach services and a wide coastline. Further down the coast, **Playa Helena** hosts lots of concerts in the summer, and **La Caseta** is a favored beach by Argentine celebrities where it's easy to get a massage and find yoga classes. Further south, going towards Chapadmala, you'll find the less crowded **Playa Acantilados**, a free beach overlooked by a large cliff that's a paragliding hot spot.

Read Up on the Ocampo Sisters

And Their Prominent Literary Family

The Ocampo family was a prominent literary force in Argentina in the mid-1900s. Victoria Ocampo founded the literary magazine *Sur,* which acted as a conduit between Argentine literature and the global literary scene. Her sister, Silvina Ocampo, was an award-winning writer. The sisters' circle included Virginia Woolf, Graham Greene and Jorge Luis Borges, among many other writers and intellectuals. Victoria liked a good hat, and apparently a good bath, judging by the number of tubs in **Villa Victoria**, the family's summer home, now a cultural center in Mar del Plata's Los Troncos neighborhood. There you can see artifacts from the family, attend literary and musical events, and stroll the large garden full of lavender bushes.

 WHERE TO SLEEP IN MAR DEL PLATA

Los Arcos
Complimentary breakfast, small but clean rooms, and only a few blocks from the beach. **$**

Hotel Sirenuse
This family-run, centrally located hotel feels like a mountain abode; it has strong wi-fi. **$$**

Hotel Sainte Jeanne
A boutique luxury hotel with a spa by Playa Grande. Come here to pamper yourself. **$$$**

Villa Gesell
Coronel Vidal
Balcarce
Mar del Plata
Yraizoz
Chapadmalal
Miramar

Beyond
Mar del Plata

Diverse forested beach towns, from the hippie to the hip, dot this part of the Atlantic coast.

Outside of Mar del Plata, beach towns sprung up around areas where enterprising businessmen planted forests to stabilize shifting dunes. It makes for a distinctive landscape where the pampas run up against the forest and then, suddenly there's the coast. Stretching from Miramar, 46km south of Mardel, to Pinamar 126km to the north, this region was visited by both Albert Einstein and Che Guevara for very different reasons. The summer high season (January and February) has the most events, while winter offers calm, solitary stretches of beaches. Each town has its own distinctive flavor: the hipster surf scene of Chapadmalal, the enigmatic forest of Miramar, and the festival party scene of Villa Gesell.

Villa Gesell

MEL-ART94/SHUTTERSTOCK ©

GETTING AROUND

Having a car makes a trip to the coast much more enjoyable, especially if you want to travel in winter when not all bus lines run as frequently. Driving your own car is also the only way to go to smaller beach towns in a short period of time, like Mar de las Pampas, Mar Azul and Cariló, which are also in this area. Bus company Costa Azul runs buses from Mar del Plata to Miramar (212) every 30 minutes and other routes from Mar del Plata to Villa Gesell and Pinamar. Message it on WhatsApp at 2233 02-4560 for schedules. Mar del Plata's public bus 511 will take you to Chapadmalal in about 50 minutes.

☑ **TOP TIP**

If you come during the summer, book accommodation well in advance. Many places will only rent rooms by the week.

ARGENTINA'S CLOTHING-OPTIONAL BEACHES

There are two nude beaches in all of Argentina. **Playa Escondida** and **Playa Querandí** are hidden away on this part of the Atlantic coast. Playa Escondida, the easier to access and more built up of the two, is 25km from Mar del Plata, off RP11 between Chapadmalal and Miramar. It has beach bars, spa services, and wooden stairs down to the sand. The other, Playa Querandí, has no infrastructure and is part of the reserve located near the lighthouse of Villa Gesell, a 5km walk from Mar Azul. Though there's an understood code of ethics, it's best to avoid the forested area at Escondida, as some people go there for romantic trysts.

ANDRES CONEMA/SHUTTERSTOCK ©

Forest, Villa Gesell

Villa Gesell

TIME FROM MAR DEL PLATA: 1½HR

Forest Delights: Reserva Pinar del Norte

Reserva Pinar del Norte, the place where Villa Gesell started, began as a forestation project to stabilize the beach's shifting dunes by inventor and entrepreneur Carlos Gesell. The dunes were so wild that he had to build a door on each side of his house to be able to enter it without being pummeled by sand. After his associate Héctor Manuel Guerrero created Cariló up the coast via forestation, Gesell moved onto the land where the reserve is now located, and worked for nearly 10 years to plant a mix of pine, acacia, poplar and ash trees, as well as sunflowers, vegetables and clover, in specially made tubes to tame the land. Today, the forest contains several trails, a bee-keeping association and a plant nursery – all sans flying dunes.

WHERE TO EAT ALONG THE COAST

El Viejo Hobbit
Meat lovers, beer drinkers and vegetarians alike appreciate the portions in Villa Gesell's hobbit-themed restaurant. **$$**

Tante
A German-inspired menu from strudel to stroganoff, with a wide selection of teas, in Pinamar. **$$$**

Casa Oxalis
A casually luxurious brunch spot with buddha bowls, fresh juice and more in Pinamar. **$**

Free to enter and open 10am to 3pm Tuesdays through Sundays, the reserve holds Gessell's former homes, which have been repurposed: the Museo y Archivo Histórico Municipal de Villa Gesell, telling the history of the Gesell family, and the Chalet de Don Carlos, a cultural center that hosts art talks and classes. Nestled into the reserve is also El Tinglado, a bohemian cafe, and the Municipal Ceramics and Pottery Workshop that holds public classes (signup information at facebook.com/TMCVillaGesell). While this area is popular in summer, check hours for the cafe and workshop in winter, as they can be irregular. In addition to many picnic-appropriate areas, you'll also find a museum dedicated to the Falklands War, some kitschy wooden structures that look like they were erected by cartoon elves, and public toilets.

Go to the Night Circus

Roll Up, Roll Up for Some Big Top Fun

When the summer season starts in Villa Gesell, performances sweep the city. Buskers juggle on street corners while plays, folkloric shows and even operas run at the Municipal Theater (see what's playing at gesell.tur.ar). One of the mainstays of summer is Circo del Aire, a circus that has been playing the season in Villa Gesell since 2009. Put on by Maria del Aire, a pillar of the circus community in Buenos Aires, the circus is similar to the feats you'd see in Cirque du Solei but more rustic, romantic, and with a sea breeze from the ocean just a few blocks away. No animals are used in the show.

Chapadmalal
TIME FROM MAR DEL PLATA: **1HR**

Drink Wine on the Coast

Less than an hour's drive south of Mar del Plata in Chapadmalal is the emerging wine region of the Atlantic coast. Costa & Pampa, the closest Argentine winery to the ocean and part of the highly awarded Bodega Trapiche family, can be found 6km from Chapadmalal's beaches down a bumpy dirt road. The vineyard produces light, fresh wines of strong aromatic complexity, which patrons can sample in one of two tasting options. The Mar y Montaña Tasting (10am or 3.30pm, US$12 per person) includes four wines, two of which are Costa & Pampa, plus a tour of the property, including the wine cellar. The other, Mundo Costa & Pampa Tasting (11.30am or 1.30pm, US$15 per person), is the better option for true wine lovers, as it only offers varietals produced on the estate (three non-sparkling white or rosé wines and one sparkling),

ARGENTINA'S CIRCUS HISTORY

There's a long history of circus in Argentina, and circus subcultures can be found in its major cities. Argentina developed its own style of circus, Circo Criollo, a combination of theater and circus in which the gaucho was a central figure. While the circus was introduced into the country in the 19th century by nomadic circus troupes, it was not until after its resurgence in the post-dictatorship years of the 1980s that it started being studied in academic spaces, like the University of Buenos Aires. Circus is taught at universities in Buenos Aires and Rosario, where students receive degrees in circus performance art. Some rising circus stars have even competed on the *Got Talent Argentina* TV show.

WHERE TO STAY IN VILLA GESELL

Hotel del Cine
A centrally located movie-themed hotel with a micro theater, pool and complimentary breakfast. **$$**

Hostería Santa Barbara
Big, sunlit rooms come with balconies surrounded by plants in this spotless boutique hotel. **$$**

La Deseada Hostel
This colorful hostel has dorm or private rooms, a kitchen, grill and outdoor dining area. **$**

BIRDING PARADISE

Between Mar del Plata and Villa Gesell lies the sleepy beach town of Mar Chiquita, where you can find the Albúfera Mar Chiquita, a Unesco Biosphere Reserve. The 35km-long lagoon is the only one of its kind in the country; it receives salty ocean water from the Atlantic and freshwater from the mountain streams of the Sierras de Tandil. The two sources mix, giving it a sweet salinity and creating a habitat where over 200 species of birds can be found, making it the best bird-watching spot on the coast. Another popular activity here is sportfishing, as the lagoon holds over 55 species of fish.

including a juicy Pinot Noir. Afterward, you can shop for bottles of Costa & Pampa or Trapiche varietals from Mendoza. Sometimes there's a food truck on the grounds where you can buy lunch and have a picnic in the vineyard after the tour.

Miramar
TIME FROM MAR DEL PLATA: 1HR

Magnetic Waves in Bosque Energetico

Just an hour away from Mar del Plata off Ruta 11, Miramar's Bosque Energetico (Energetic Forest) radiates a strange magnetism that draws scientists, psychics and tourists to traipse through its trails, perform experiments and hug trees. The most common activity here is to pick up two sticks, one arched and one stripped down to a point at one end, then balance the arched stick on the other in a 'T' shape – then observe how the sticks stay balanced without support. Other activities here include hiking, biking, meditating and practicing yoga along the trail winding through three of the hectares of the 500-hectare forested area.

Sneaky Creatures in the Dark Forest

If You Go Into the Woods Today ...

The trees of Bosque Energetico's branches grow together, forming a canopy impenetrable by light. This phenomenon, called 'the dark forest', makes the air of the forest floor fresh and cool. The name has a bit of a double meaning, though, as mythological creatures are said to inhabit this part of the forest. Once under the dark canopy, snap some photos, then check your camera for shadowy figures that you didn't see when taking the pictures. Many photos have surfaced (from both film and digital cameras) of short human-like figures leaning against or climbing trees. The reason locals say these beings are dwarfs? Because they're usually wearing little hats in the images.

 HIPSTER BEACH HANGS IN CHAPADMALAL

Bai Bai
A chic cafe and surf hostel where even the dogs are cool. Good for lunch.

Santori Yoga
Yoga, sound healings and massages keep everyone looking and feeling good at this holistic center.

Luva Café
Specialty coffee and avocado toast get served to stylish beach bums on crate furniture.

Egrets, Mar Chiquita

343

Bariloche & the Lake District

BREATHTAKING LANDSCAPES AND EPIC DRIVES

Adventure awaits in one of Argentina's most spectacular playgrounds. Towering peaks, sprawling hiking networks and lakes of every shade of green, blue and gray.

The region we call Bariloche & Lake District is a little deceiving. We have to focus on Bariloche because, well, it truly is a magical place and there is no need to ask why it tops the tourist lists in Argentina. But more specifically, the area covered by this chapter is what we could say is Northern Patagonia – from the region's tallest peak in the north, Volcán Domuyo (commonly known as the roof of Patagonia), to the region's capital in the east, Neuquén, the frontier with Chubut in the south at El Bolsón and El Hoyo and the Andes, which line the west. There are lakes (everywhere), but there are also volcanoes, remote rock wall carvings, mighty rivers, ancient trees and landscapes peppered with peaks in every corner of the map.

The province of Neuquén roughly covers most of this area, a region with strong Mapuche and Pehuenche communities coupled with a more recent past wrapped up in Argentina's 19th-century Campaign of Desert. When the indigenous people were removed from their lands, Swiss and German immigrants crossed the border from Chile to Argentina and established themselves in towns like Bariloche and San Martín de los Andes. The intricate network of hiking *refugios*, the chocolates and alpine architecture are just some of the remnants of this history.

THE MAIN AREAS

BARILOCHE
Soaring mountains and great eats. p350

EL BOLSÓN
Hippy markets and endless summers. p361

SAN MARTÍN DE LOS ANDES
Slow travel, trekking and volcanoes. p370

NEUQUÉN
Desert landscapes, wineries and dinosaurs. p381

Left: Hikers, Volcán Domuyo (p389); Above: Cerro Campanario (p356)   345

Find Your Way

Traversing three provinces – Neuquén, Río Negro and Chubut – Northern Patagonia covers some ground. The region's two primary road transport hubs are Neuquén and Bariloche.

Neuquén, p381

Dinosaur discoveries and Pinot Noir combine in this desert capital, the largest city in Patagonia and the meeting place of the rivers Limay and Neuquén.

San Martín de los Andes, p370

Adventurer's paradise on Lago Lacár with all the mountains, volcanoes, hikes, lakeside beaches and river rapids of Bariloche without the crowds.

Bariloche, p350

One of Argentina's most scenic cities, with picture-postcard views of soaring peaks and glistening lakes everywhere you look, coupled with a top-notch food scene.

El Bolsón, p361

Mellow town in a fertile valley with locally grown organic produce, an infamous hippy craft market and a huge network of hikes at Cajón del Azul.

MENDOZA

Chos Malal

Rincón de
Los Sauces

25 c

Auca Mahuida

Cat

Mariana
Moreno

Paso De
Los Indios

Añelo

Neuquén

Barda Del Medio

Las Lajas

Zapala

Cutral Co

Neuquén

Puesto
El Sauce

Senillosa

Alumine

Picun Leufu

Trica C

Junín de
los Andes

Limay

El C

Piedra Del
Aguila

La Esperan

San Martín
de los Andes

Corral De
Piedra

Mencue

Villa La
Angostura

Paso Flores

Laguna
Blanca

Los Menuc

Bariloche

Comallo

Ingeniero
Jacobacci

Maquincha

San Carlos
de Bariloche

Villa Mascardi

Las Bayas

Quetrequile

Diaz

El Bolsón

El Maiten

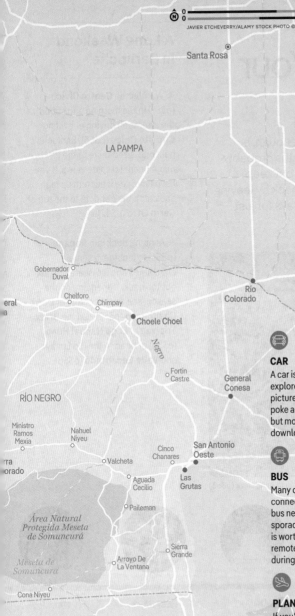

0 | 200 km
0 | 100 miles

JAVIER ETCHEVERRY/ALAMY STOCK PHOTO ©

Santa Rosa

LA PAMPA

CIUDAD
DE BUENOS
AIRES

Gobernador
Duval

Chelforo

Chimpay

Río
Colorado

Choele Choel

Negro

Fortín
Castre

General
Conesa

RÍO NEGRO

Ministro
Ramos
Mexia

Nahuel
Niyeu

Valcheta

Cinco
Chanares

San Antonio
Oeste

Aguada
Cecilio

Las
Grutas

Paileman

*Área Natural
Protegida Meseta
de Somuncurá*

Sierra
Grande

*Meseta de
Somuncura*

Arroyo De
La Ventana

Cona Niyeu

CAR

A car is the best option to explore the region, with more picturesque drives than you can poke a stick at. Fuel is cheap but mobile reception is sparse: download maps before you go.

BUS

Many cities and towns are connected by an extensive bus network. Service can be sporadic to smaller villages so it is worth planning ahead. Some remote roads have limited hours during snowy winters.

PLANE

If you're arriving in Buenos Aires, flights are available to Bariloche, Neuquén, San Martín de los Andes, El Bolsón and Chos Malal. There are no direct flights between any of the airports.

Plan Your Time

A few days is not enough, a few weeks or months probably won't cut it either, but keep expectations in check by leaving some downtime days for just soaking it up.

Villa la Angostura (p353)

A Long Weekend in Bariloche

● Wander the **Centro Civico** (p352) in the morning and spend the afternoon driving or cycling **Circuito Chico** (p356), Bariloche's best bite-sized taste of the magnificent lakeside views. If you have time, see it all from up high and catch the gondola to the top of **Cerro Otto** (p352).

● At night, duck into **Rapanui** (p353) to indulge in some chocolates and ice-skate the rink out the back. Depending on the season, see the fall colors at **Cerro Challhuaco** (p352), sail the **Brazo Tristeza** of **Lago Nahuel Huapi** (p353) or head to the Río Limay and **Valle Encantado** (p358).

Seasonal Highlights

Each season is a unique experience. Take in a 10pm sunset in summer, while in fall, see the red and yellows of the *lengas* and *ñires*.

JANUARY

Peak summer, the lakes are warm(er)! Pick **Villa Llanquín** (p358) lavender on the Río Limay and soak up the atmosphere in El Bolsón.

FEBRUARY

Party time with the **Fiesta Nacional de la Confluencia** (p388) in Neuquén and the huge hops harvest festival in El Bolsón.

MARCH

The weather cools and the crowds start to fade. Pick grapes at the wineries in **Neuquén** (p386).

One Week in Bariloche

● After you've done the classics (see left), head out to **Pampa Linda** (p359) or go whitewater rafting on the mighty **Río Manso** (p359).

● Next, head north for a few days and do the loop to **Villa la Angostura** (p353) and back via **San Martín de los Andes** (p370) and **Villa Traful** (p379). Don't miss gawking at the ancient, cinnamon-colored trees at **Parque Nacional de los Arrayanes** (p353) and the stunning scenery of the **Ruta de los Siete Lagos** (p378).

● If you have a day to spare, don't miss the **La Feria Regional Artesanal** at El Bolsón (p363).

Two Weeks or More to Travel Around

● Spend some time in **Neuquén** (p381) visiting the dinosaur sites and wineries before getting off the beaten track and exploring **Chos Malal** (p389) and the *techo* (roof) of Patagonia, **Volcán Domuyo** (p389).

● For more volcano visits head to the top of **Volcán Batea Mahuida** (p380) to see eight volcanoes on the border. Or in summer, visit the twin towns of **Copahue** and **Caviahue** (p388), where Volcán Copahue smolders and the earth bubbles with mineral-rich hot springs.

APRIL
Search for easter eggs and see the world's biggest chocolate bar at the chocolate festival in **Bariloche** (p352).

JULY
Snow starts to fall and the powder hounds descend on snow zones at Cerros Catedral, Chapelco, Perito Moreno and **Caviahue** (p388).

OCTOBER
It's time to feast upon Patagonia's gastronomic delights at the week-long food festival, Bariloche a la Carta.

DECEMBER
In **San Martín de los Andes** (p370) hop between the Christmas festival and the Mapuche music and dance gathering, Trabún.

BUENOS
AIRES

Bariloche

GETTING AROUND

Bariloche's center is compact but very steep, with stairs in places. Cycling is a good option for longer distances but be prepared to share the road with vehicles. A car can be great for exploring further but traffic can be heavy on the two main roads (Av Exequiel Bustillo and Av de los Pioneros) that lead west to many of Bariloche's main attractions. Don't leave valuables in sight and make sure to lock your car.

Buses run to Colonia Suiza (10), Puerto Pañuelo (20) and Cerro Catedral (55) but can be very full and slow in peak season. Bring a SUBE card with you as Bariloche often runs out and the office at Centro Civico is closed on weekends. The tourist office (open seven days) has bus schedules. Also, ask for up-to-date information on where to recharge SUBE cards: the recharge machine in Centro Civico only accepts Mercado Pago.

San Carlos de Bariloche (Bari to locals) hugs the southern shoreline of the region's largest and deepest lake, Lago Nahuel Huapi, and induces slack-jawed gaping with its spectacular string of 2000m+ mountains. It hardly entertains a tourist lull, with an activity for every season – snow for winter, mild temperatures and clear days for hiking in summer, fall foliage to feast upon in March and wildflowers aplenty in spring. And if getting active isn't part of your holiday plan, the town is brimming with culinary delights and local craft beers. Just sit back and relax.

It is the heart of the Lake District and both domestic and international tourists count it as one of Argentina's top destinations. The classics are well-trodden but if you take the time to explore, you can still find some peace and solitude in Argentina's oldest national park, Parque Nacional Nahuel Huapi.

☑ TOP TIP

The last two weeks of July (Argentine school holidays) and January are absolute peak times and best avoided. Travel in September for late ski season or March for warm days and smaller crowds. May is a quieter month but many tourist companies carry out maintenance and can be closed.

Cathedral, San Carlos de Bariloche

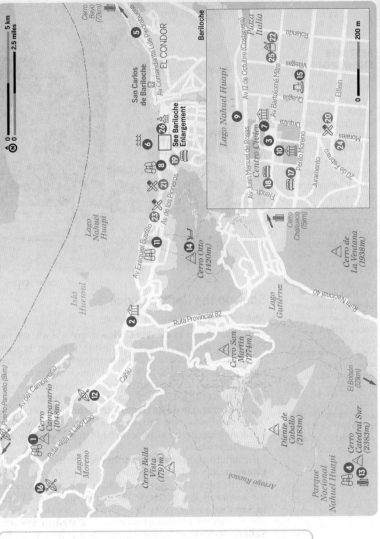

SIGHTS
1 Aerosilla Cerro Campanario
2 Balseiro Institute
3 Centro Cívico
4 Cerro Catedral see 26
Chemamull
5 INVAP
6 Lago Nahuel Huapi
7 Museo de la Patagonia
8 Parque Ecoturístico Cerro Viejo
9 Puerto San Carlos
10 Secretaría de Turismo Bariloche
11 Teleférico Cerro Otto

ACTIVITIES, COURSES & TOURS
12 Brazo Tristeza
13 Cerro Catedral
14 Cerro Otto
15 Feria Artesanal Bariloche
16 Playa Sin Viento

SLEEPING
17 Hospedaje Penthouse 1004
18 Hotel Tirol
19 Selina

EATING
20 Chimi Deli Cocina
21 La Cabrona
22 Mamushka
23 Manush
24 Manush
25 Rapanui

INFORMATION
26 Catedral Nuestra Señora del Nahuel Huapi

351

BEST SKI & SNOW SPOTS

Cerro Catedral
The place to ski, board and trek in Argentina, with plenty of lifts and runs, and excellent infrastructure.

Cerro Otto
Five kilometers from town, if you are short on time, catch the gondola to the top for a fun kids' snow zone. Be sure to take your own gloves for *culipatin*.

Cerro Challhuaco & Refugio Neumeyer
Great spot for beginner backcountry skiing. In winter, access is via 4WD only, or book an excursion. In warmer months, dome accommodation is available.

Cerro Bayo
On the opposite side of the lake, ski the slopes at this more exclusive, boutique resort.

SAIKO3P/SHUTTERSTOCK ©

Centro Civico

Soak up the Centro Civico

Architecture, Museums & Chocolates

Start in the heart at **Centro Civico** where you will see the emblematic stone buildings designed by architect Ernesto de Estrada in 1940. The plaza is an important cultural and social meeting point for both tourists and locals alike, with many gathering in the late afternoons for chats and *mate* sessions against the backdrop of **Lago Nahuel Huapi**. The excellent **Secretaria de Turismo Bariloche** sits on one edge of the plaza, while the **Museo de la Patagonia** (closed on weekends) has an excellent natural history collection and Mapuche artifacts.

For nature and culture, head through the park, past the **Chemamull** wooden totems looking east by Mapuche Chilean artist Bernardo Oyarzún, to find the lake shore. Wander the boardwalk and check out the exhibitions within **Puerto San Carlos**. Follow Av 12 de Octubre a couple of blocks east to visit the unfinished white stone **Catedral Nuestra Señora del Nahuel Huapi**, designed by architect Alejandro Bustillo, who also designed Hotel Llao Llao.

For shopping and eating, pass beneath the stone arches and run the gauntlet of souvenir shops on **Calle Mitre**. It's hectic but worth it to step into dreamy chocolate shops like

 WHERE TO EAT IN BARILOCHE

La Cabrona
Locals flock to this lakeside food truck with a seasonal gourmet menu. Don't miss it. $

Chimi Deli Cocina & Chimi Bar de Choris
Deli for superb salads and veg options, or cross the street for beers and *choripan*. $$

Manush (Centro & Km 4)
Local *cervecería* with excellent burgers and pub grub; both locations are top notch. $$

Rapanui (with its own ice-skating rink) and **Mamushka** (many claim it to be the best) – just be prepared to line up with the hordes. For local crafts, head up the hill to **Feria Artesanal Bariloche**, where you will also find the **Zuem Mapuche Cooperative** selling quality textiles. If lunch or dinner are on your mind, many excellent eating options are huddled together on **Calle Ada Maria Elflein**.

The Deep Blue Lake

Ancient Forests, Mythical Creatures

With Lago Nahuel Huapi everywhere you turn, it would be re-miss not to get out onto or into it. At 767m above sea level and with a measured depth of 425m, it's said to play host to Bari-loche's answer to Loch Ness, **Nahuelito** (the subject of a re-cent documentary by Bariloche filmmaker Miguel Ángel Rossi).

Boating tours leave from **Puerto Pañuelo** at Llao Llao, a 30-minute drive from Bariloche. Choose from excursions that visit stunning **Puerto Blest** and the waterfall **Cascada de los Cantaros** or **Isla Victoria** (Victoria Island) and the un-missable **Parque Nacional de los Arrayanes** (p379). The boat trip only allows for a limited time on land, so if you wish to see both the awe-inspiring stands of ancient trees and the rock paintings, it is best to drive to **Villa la Angostura** and wander through the park at your own speed. Catch the 10am boat for fewer crowds.

For a more intimate sailing experience, explore **Brazo Tris-teza** on the 32-person boat *Kaikén Patagonia*. Book ahead and hop on at Bahía Lopez, a stunning bay on Circuito Chi-co. The trip includes a visit to the waterfall **Cascada del Ar-royo Frey** and a one-hour hike where you might just catch a glimpse of a condor.

For kayaking, SUP or diving, head to **Playa Sin Viento** on **Lago Moreno** (also on Circuito Chico), where the sheltered spot is ideal. Elsewhere, ask locals for advice and preferably stick close to shore – in the center of Lago Nahuel Huapi, the weather can be unpredictable.

BEST VIEWS (NO HIKING REQUIRED)

Teleférico
Cerro Otto
Pick a clear day for this charming cable car and be rewarded with spectacular views over the lake.

Aerosilla Cerro Campanario
A classic Circuito Chico open-air chairlift that takes you over wildflowers to the summit.

Cerro Catedral Telecabina
Amancay & Telesilla Diente de Caballo
Head to the slopes of Catedral year round for the highest, easily accessible summit. Hop in the cable car and then connect with the chairlift to the top.

Parque Ecoturístico Cerro Viejo
Great for all ages and right in town; take the chairlift to the top and slide back down the giant slippery dip.

WHERE TO STAY IN BARILOCHE

Hospedaje Penthouse 1004
One of Bariloche's first hostels and still going strong. Roomy, light, and killer views. $

Selina
Social vibe with helpful staff, nestled in forest on the edge of the city center. $$

Hotel Tirol
Charming, central hotel. Request a lakeside room for views and less street noise. $$$

CONTROVERSIAL STATUE

The horseman at the center of Centro Cívico is former Argentine President General Julio Argentino Roca. Known as the father of modern Argentina, some claim he also committed genocide as the leading figure behind the 19th-century Conquest of the Desert, a military campaign which removed the indigenous population from the region and unintentionally paved the way for European migration from Chile. In 2023, Bariloche local council decided to remove the statue of Roca, but the decision was then overturned by the courts. It's a complex and controversial subject in Argentina where locals are reckoning with their past, but one to consider in Bariloche when looking at all that alpine architecture (and the St Bernard dogs).

Kayaking, Lago Nahuel Huapi

Frauds & Newton's Apple

Science by the Lake

Bariloche is a scientist hotbed thanks, in part, to an embarrassing failure by former president Juan Perón. Austrian scientist Ronald Richter convinced Perón to invest in a nuclear fusion project which turned out to be a big old fraud. Richter's abandoned bunkers are on Isla Huemul in Lago Nahuel Huapi, and although the island is technically closed, some local companies do half-day kayak tours to the island, leaving from **Playa Bonita** at Km 8, Av Bustillo.

It's not all bad news: Richter's costly prank led to an eventual significant investment in Argentina's scientific future. Now, Bariloche is home to some of Argentina's premier science institutions – the globally prestigious **Balseiro Institute** (for students of experimental physics and nuclear engineering and where a reputed descendant of Newton's apple tree can be seen in the library garden), the **Bariloche Atomic Centre** and **INVAP**, a private company that designs and manufactures aerospace technology like satellites and flight radars. Post-pandemic, Bariloche Atomic Centre no longer receives visitors, but **Historias de Bariloche Walking Tours** (check online for English tours) runs a fascinating science-themed tour (Perón in Bariloche) in the surrounding area for those wanting to dive deeper. It is possible to take a guided tour at INVAP but plan ahead and email visitas@invap.com.ar long before you arrive. Be prepared to wait for a response.

Beyond Bariloche

Río Limay

CHILE

ARGENTINA

Comallo

Bariloche

Pampa Linda

Cerro Las Buitreras

Get up close with Andean condors in an otherworldly landscape and explore the turquoise waters of the Río Limay.

Bariloche isn't all chocolates, lakes and alpine architecture and you don't have to stray far for it. Put it this way, Parque Nacional Nahuel Huapi consists of almost 2 million acres of land – there's so much to explore, a lifetime hardly seems enough time to touch the surface. Head to the heart of the park to check out Pampa Linda and get up close to Cerro Tronodor, that thundering beast of a mountain. For the thrill-seekers, don't miss the mighty river Manso where Class III and IV rapids lead to the Chilean border on waters fed from one of Tronodor's seven glaciers. For some solitude, head to the south to watch the giant condors play.

Bahia Lopez (p357)

GETTING AROUND

Once you leave Bariloche, there are very few local buses. Buses run to major towns but to explore Río Limay, Valle Encantado, Villa Llanquín, Las Buitreras or Pampa Linda, you will need your own transport or to join an excursion. In summer, both Transitando lo Natural and Travel Light Turismo do transfers to and from Pampa Linda. RN237 is a well-maintained highway, but there is no mobile reception. Fill up with petrol in Bariloche, pack snacks and water, and download maps. Gravel road RN82 to Pampa Linda is in very poor condition. It is closed to general traffic in winter. The dirt road to Las Buitreras is also in poor condition.

☑ TOP TIP

Out of town, cell reception and gas stations can be hard to come by. Take cash, maps, snacks and water.

Circuito Chico

This Lake District loop is, as the Argentines say, *un clásico!* Drive, walk or cycle – it's 60km that can be done in a couple of hours or slowly over a day. Short on time? It's still the best snapshot of Bariloche's lakes and landscapes. For cyclists, head in a clockwise direction for fewer hills. Local buses 10 and 20 will get you part of the way.

❶ Bariloche

Starting in town at Km 0, grab some gourmet *alfajores* for the road from the Brucherie food truck (Km 4.5) or stop for a swim at Playa Bonita (Km 8).
The Drive: Drive west along Av. Bustillo, hugging the lake shoreline.

❷ Cerro Campanario

Catch the chairlift or walk the 30-minute trail to the summit for one of the best 360-degree views of Bariloche.

The Drive: Stop at Km 17.5 for the entrance. Early mornings are best to avoid crowds.

❸ Punto Panoramico

The first of the *miradores* (viewpoints) for an awe-inspiring panoramic view of the lake and surrounds. On windy days, you'll hear the trees whistling.
The Drive: At the roundabout after Cerro Campanario, turn left onto RP77 where the Circuito Chico officially begins. The viewpoint is on the right-hand side of the road after the bridge.

View from Cerro Campanario

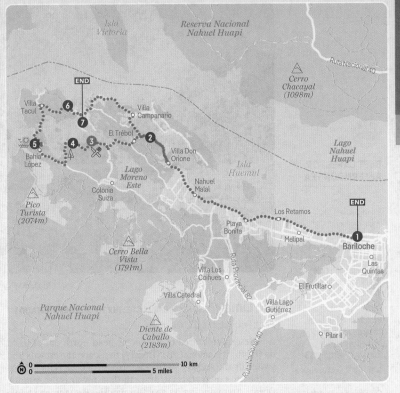

④ Patagonia Cervecería & Parque Nahuelito

Stop in at one of Bariloche's most famous breweries. Walk the trails or just sit back and relax. A truly magical setting, but be warned: it can be swamped with people. Across the road, Parque Nahuelito offers one-hour walks through the dinosaur forest, a great outing for kids.

The Drive: Parque Nahuelito is located on the left-hand side of RP77 at Km 24.5. Patagonia is on the right-hand side.

⑤ Bahía Lopez

In summer, stop off for a dip in this dreamy bay. For hikers, the 1.5km trail to the Mirador Brazo Tristeza leaves from here. Classified as easy, the walk does have some steep parts – wear decent shoes.

The Drive: Stop at Km 32 and park to the left of Hotel Alun Nehuen. Walk across the beach and find the start of the trail within the little forest.

⑥ Cerro Llao Llao

For longer trails, the section between Bahía Lopez and Llao Llao has various options for walking in Parque Municipal Llao Llao (free entry and many are family-friendly).

The Drive: Pull into one of the parking grounds along this stretch and start walking. For information on available hikes, stop at the sign 800m before the entrance to Puerto Pañuelo.

⑦ Llao Llao Resort & Puerto Pañuelo

Stop here to visit Argentina's most famous five-star hotel (book ahead to splurge on a decadent high tea) and for boat tours that leave for Puerto Blest and Isla Victoria.

The Drive: For Llao Llao Resort, detour to the right, up the hill.

JACINTO ESCARAY/SHUTTERSTOCK ©

Río Limay

BEST CAFES FOR AFTERNOON TEA

Bruncherie Patagonia Truck & Bruncherie Café & Deli
Choose between the lake-side food truck or the garden cafe; the *alfajores* are a must. **$$**

Bellevue Salón de Té
Pioneering but busy *casa de té* nestled in the forest in a fairy-tale setting. **$$**

Chiado Restaurante & Casa de Te
Quirky, cozy feel; be sure to nab a spot on the best deck on Circuito Chico. **$$**

Blanco es Negro
Original menu and excellent coffee; the sweet treats are close to perfection. **$$**

Winter Garden at Llao Llao Resort
Book ahead and splurge on a high tea at this five-star hotel with stunning views. **$$$**

Río Limay   TIME FROM BARILOCHE: **1HR TO VALLE ENCANTADO** 🚗

Rock Formations & Lavender

A little-explored area of Bariloche, head north out of town on the Ruta Nacional 237 (RN237) to escape the crowds and switch up the scenery. At the eastern end of Lago Nahuel Huapi, the Río Limay starts to drain the lake towards the Atlantic Ocean, first winding its way through the Patagonian steppe towards Neuquén. It's a stunning blue-green river that pops against the earthy colors of the hills and the blush-colored sauces in winter. In summer, the banks are dotted with yellow and violet wildflowers.

This stretch of road is technically part of the Circuito Grande (as opposed to the Circuito Chico on the western side of Bariloche), but it's a less-traveled route for tourists. Be sure to stop at the amphitheatre viewpoint to take in the incredible landscape. The road rims the river until the confluence of the Río Traful, an easy one-hour drive from Bariloche. Stop by the only small village on the road in summer, Villa Llanquín. Here you can step back in time and pop your car on the free vehicle raft (or just watch the process) to cross the river into the province of Río Negro and visit Lavandas del Limay (closed in winter), a local lavender farm. There is also a pe-

LUXURY STAYS BEYOND BARILOCHE

El Casco Art Hotel
Boutique five-star hotel with curated contemporary Argentine art rooms and sculpture garden. **$$$**

Charming Luxury Lodge & Private Spa
Lakeside Playa Bonita location with unique views of Cerro Catedral. **$$$**

Estancia Peuma Hue
Escape the hustle and bustle and connect with nature at this sumptuous eco retreat. **$$$**

destrian bridge. Contact Cultura Rural Patagónica for other rural tourism activities if you are interested in visiting other local families and producers.

Just five minutes further down the road, the landscape reveals the spectacular Valle Encantado – towering, craggy volcanic rock formations well known for climbing. Book an excursion with Kairos Patagonia for a guided, short, steep hike into the hills and caves with views over the river and the confluence.

Río Limay is a great option for rainy Bariloche days (there might be a few!) as it tends to have a drier climate, despite being only 60km from town. And you might just spot a guanaco or two.

Cerro Tronador & Pampa Linda

TIME FROM BARILOCHE: **2HR** 🚌

Black Glaciers & Roaring Rivers

Cerro Tronador is the soaring hero of Parque Nacional Nahuel Huapi. This extinct volcano sits 3554m high and straddles Argentina and Chile. In Spanish, *tronador* means 'thunderer', a reference to the sound of the cracking glaciers, of which it has seven. Climbing Tronador requires technical expertise, but you don't need to train to see it up close. It's a two-hour drive into Pampa Linda and the heart of Parque Nacional Nahuel Huapi – head south on the famed RN40 and, after Villa Mascardi, turn right onto RP82, a notoriously narrow, rough road. If you're planning to drive in and see the sights in a day (summers only), avoid arriving at 10am to visit the Cascada de los Alerces with the rest of the tourist companies.

Drive towards Pampa Linda first and view the Río Manso (an excellent glacial river for whitewater rafting), Ventisquero Negro (a black glacier located a 6km drive from Pampa Linda, or one-hour walk) and the base of Cerro Tronador; just be sure to enter before 2pm when the road closes to incoming traffic.

In summer, Bariloche enjoys long days with the sun setting at 10pm. In winter, the trip is best done with an excursion, as the road is only open to 4WD vehicles with chains. To base yourself in the park, book ahead to stay at Refugio Otto Meiling or Agostino Rocca, camp at Pampa Linda, or splurge at the seriously stunning Hotel Tronador (open November to April).

HIKING IN PARQUE NACIONAL NAHUEL HUAPI

Argentina's oldest national park, Parque Nacional Nahuel Huapi was established in 1922 from initial land donations made by Perito Francisco Moreno, who was gifted land for his work securing Argentina's sovereignty over the area.

The Parque Nacional Nahuel Huapi office in Bariloche (closed weekends) is an excellent source of maps, advice and information alongside barilochetrekking. com, which is where you must register your details if you plan on hiking within the park. Club Andino Bariloche no longer provides information to the public.

From low difficulty, short hikes to strenuous multiday treks, Nahuel Huapi has a huge range of walks, all with spectacular sights. Bring pesos to pay the park entrance fee or prepay online via Bariloche Trekking.

WHERE TO EAT BEYOND BARILOCHE

La Luna Bar & Inefable Libros & Cafe
Lakeside bookshop and vegetarian cafe by day; cocktail bar and live music by night. $

Lupino
Top-notch pizza and organic wines from Argentina and Chile, from Buenos Aires transplants. $$

Casa Cassis
Intimate dining experience including kitchen garden wander and conversation with chef China Müller. $$$

THE GREAT OUTDOORS

Gabriella Chavez, photographer and co-founder of *@Kairos.Patagonia*, shares her top treks.

Every day I feel like a tourist in my own city because Bariloche has this thing that you can't put your finger on – you arrive, and you don't want to leave!

Three or four or five days is never enough to see the best of Bari. Do the classics but try to hike the mountain trails and stay in the *refugios*. Your perception of the city changes when you connect to the nature it has on offer. One of my favorite places is the Mirada del Doctor near Cerro Tronador. At the top, there are 24km of incredible panoramic views in every direction!

EMA REYNARES/SHUTTERSTOCK ©

Cerro Las Buitreras

Cerro Las Buitreras

TIME FROM BARILOCHE: **45MINS** 🚗

Up in the Sky

Drive 45 minutes south of Bariloche and you'll find yourself on another planet. A wind- and rain-eroded landscape (like giant sandy ant hills) rises from the earth, and if you look up you'll see that Cerro Las Buitreras is the playground for hundreds of Andean condors.

To get there, be prepared to drive slowly on a dirt road before reaching the entrance to La Lucha, a private *estancia* owned by the Crespo family. At the gate, kind Quela will welcome you and ask you to register and pay a small entrance fee. Las Buitreras is a very fragile environment and can be closed to visitors at short notice. The walk has a few options within the 8km loop of low difficulty, but a standard level of fitness is required. In summer, enter towards the end of the day, when the sun transforms the hills, but respect the birds by keeping your drones at home. Bring snacks and water and note that there is no mobile reception.

In winter, hikers must visit with a guide, but be warned that the site is often closed due to poor road conditions. In summer, enter between 9am and 4pm (closed Tuesdays and Wednesdays). If you wish to visit without a guide, contact the owner Quela Crespo via WhatsApp +54 294 4597230 to ask permission to visit.

For stargazing in this magical part of the world, contact Daniel Chiesa at Astropatagonia to visit his nearby custom-made observatory at Ñirihuau Arriba.

El Bolsón

El Bolsón is a common day trip from Bariloche as tourists race Ruta 40 to check out the sprawling Feria Artesanal, take a peek at Lago Puelo and head back to Bari. Alternatively, hikers drive straight through on the long-haul bus to El Chaltén and miss out completely. But El Bolsón certainly deserves a longer stay. Spend a couple of summer days in this fairy-tale, fertile valley and you'll soon see why. With a strong hippy past (and present), El Bolsón is the easygoing sister city to alpine Bariloche. And with hundreds of *chacras* (small farms) dotting the valley, you'll find fresh raspberries, strawberries, mushrooms, truffles and hops (feeding the excellent local craft-beer scene) on your doorstep. Summer brings harvest parties, week-long hikes staying in the incredible system of *refugios* in the Cajón del Azul, or just plain old chilling under the embrace of Cerro Piltriquitrón.

El Bolsón

ATIKINKA/SHUTTERSTOCK ©

GETTING AROUND

You can fly into El Bolsón or arrive by bus from Bariloche, Neuquén or Esquel in the south. Locally, the bus system is extensive in summer but sporadic in the off season. Contact Grado 42 for excursions to Bosque Tallado and Cerro Piltriquitrón. Buses for Wharton for Cajón del Azul leave from Plaza Pagano. Timetables are available on the tourist office window. Otherwise, share a taxi to get dropped off at the trailhead. El Bolsón is an easy town to walk around in; hire a mountain bike to explore further.

☑ TOP TIP

El Bolsón really turns it on in summer – it's busy and beautiful and you'll need to book accommodations ahead of time, especially in the camping grounds. In winter, it is a sleepy (and rainy) town with many hostels, campgrounds and activities closed for the season.

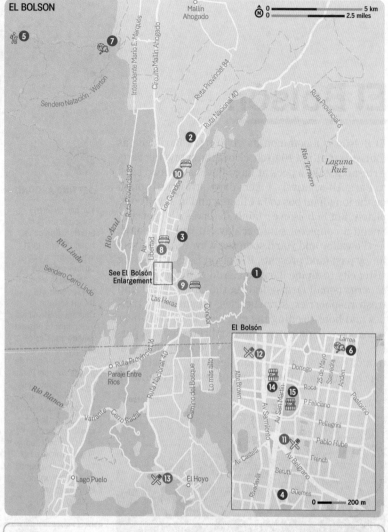

EL BOLSON

SIGHTS
1 El Bosque Tallado
2 Granja Larix
3 Humus
de la Montaña
4 Lumina

ACTIVITIES,
COURSES & TOURS
5 Cajón del Azul

6 Earthship
Patagonia Eco Hostel
7 La Confluence
Lodge & Farm

SLEEPING
8 Hostel
La Casita Naranja
9 La Aguada
Bed & Breakfast

10 La Casona
de Odile Hostel

EATING
11 El Tablón
Pizza a la Piedra
12 Iori
13 Restaurante Pirque

DRINKING
& NIGHTLIFE
see **3** Heladería
Humus

SHOPPING
14 Feria Franca
15 La Feria
Regional Artesanal

Mate cups, El Bolsón

BEST NEW AGE EXPERIENCES

Lumina
An El Bolsón icon; Lumina is a spiritual workshop space housed in a mystical pink building with eyes for windows.

La Confluence Lodge & Farm
This sustainable lodge close to Cajón Del Azul offers yoga, Wim Hof intensives, and tai chi and meditation retreats.

Earthship Patagonia Eco Hostel
Handcrafted with love and the spirit of hippy El Bolsón; this long-established hostel offers holistic yoga retreats and communal dinners.

El Bosque Tallado
Take a meditative forest bath surrounded by 60 figurative sculptures carved by local and international artists from tree stumps left after devastating fires on the slopes of Piltriquitrón.

Scratching the Surface of El Bolsón

Explore the Market

Arrive on market day (Tuesday, Thursday, public holidays or the weekend) and you'll want to stay in El Bolsón forever. Under the watchful gaze of Cerro Piltriquitrón and to the ever-present soundtrack of the *tambores* (drums), hundreds of artists and craftspeople set up stalls at **La Feria Regional Artesanal** along the eastern edge of Plaza Pagano in the very heart of town. A remnant from El Bolsón's hippy past (it was the first place in Latin America to declare itself a nuclear-free zone), the market has been running since the 1970s when young artists started selling their wares in the park. Today, it is bigger than ever, and although it's a little different these days, the spirit of the hippy movement still exists, with all products needing to be handmade to be offered for sale. From handcrafted *mate* gourds and *bombillas* to children's toys, art, textiles, ponchos, knits and knives, there is an incredible range of products, many not found elsewhere.

WHERE TO EAT IN EL BOLSÓN

El Tablón Pizza a la Piedra
Locals' favourite with classic Argentine wood-fired pizzas in a cosy corner sports bar. $

Iori
Creative Asian gem with outstanding sushi, vegan options, delicious ramen and great gin and tonics. $$

Restaurante Pirque
Pirque feels like home; you'll want to return. Don't miss the *lomo con morillas*. $$

MUSHROOMS

Each year, from the beginning of September until October, the hunt begins for a very special mushroom – the *hongo del ciprés* (Cypress tree mushroom or morel), also known as the *morilla* in Argentina. Unable to be commercially harvested, the wild organic *morilla* is one of the world's most rare and expensive mushrooms and it grows sporadically in the forests surrounding El Bolsón. With its distinctive shape and taste, it is handpicked by locals each season, with prices for the delicacy upwards of hundreds of dollars per kilo fresh, and thousands of dollars per kilo dried. Often seen on menus in the *comarca andina*, the *morillas* at Restaurante Pirque in El Hoyo are particularly good.

Cajón del Azul

During harvest, you'll also find fresh berries on offer alongside locally produced jams, pastries, cheeses and craft beers.

Even if you keep your hands in your pockets, the atmosphere is delightful, especially on sunny days when over 400 stalls pack the plaza. Saturdays are the pick of the week and Sundays operate at half-tilt.

Taste the Town

Berries, Beer and *Chacras*

The fresh, local ingredients on offer in El Bolsón should come as no surprise. It's an incredibly fertile valley with a particular microclimate, so raspberries, strawberries, hops and mushrooms grow in abundance. El Bolsón is the *lúpulo* (hops) capital of Argentina, while nearby El Hoyo boasts berries of all varieties. You'll find jams and in-season sweet and juicy strawberries and raspberries at both the Feria Regional Artesanal and the open-air farmer's market, **Feria Franca**. To get up close to some *chacras* in town, take a tour of organic berry and dairy farm **Humus de la Montaña** (Mondays, Wednesdays and Fridays at 5pm; bookings essential). Just a five-minute drive from the center of town, this little oasis produces delicious cheeses and *dulce de leche* – you can visit its on-site store any day or stop by in the afternoons for one

 WHERE TO STAY IN EL BOLSÓN

Hostel La Casita Naranja
Cheap and run by volunteers, in a quiet street a few blocks from town. **$**

La Casona de Odile Hostel
This paradise by a river is one of Argentina's best hostels (open September–April). **$**

La Aguada Bed & Breakfast
Boutique offering with contemporary rooms, peaceful grounds and views of Cerro Piltriquitrón. **$$$**

of Argentina's best ice creams at its café **Heladería Humus** (open Thursday–Saturday).

In February, El Bolsón parties hard to celebrate the hops harvest with the huge **Fiesta Nacional del Lúpulo**, a free music and food festival held at the aerodrome. The event runs for four days and it's a great opportunity to taste-test the wide variety of craft beers that use the locally grown hops – the rest is used for export.

El Bolsón is also known for its trout farms, some of which you can also visit. One of the oldest, **Granja Larix** offers free tours of its rainbow trout facilities with the opportunity to purchase smoked trout in its small shop.

Cajón del Azul

Sprawling Network of Cabins

Post-pandemic, El Bolsón has perhaps become best known for **Cajón del Azul**, a hike and site that particularly lends itself to Instagram-worthy selfies on the *pasarelas* (the rickety wooden bridges) that swing above the breathtaking blues of the **Río Azul** below. The six-hour trail has become so popular that there's now a daily limit of 1000 people and you must register online with ANPRALE. In peak season, pack your patience, as only one person can cross the *pasarela* at a time. But there is much more to this region than meets the eye – for one, it has the largest network of *refugios* in all of South America, with 13 places to stay in total. Cajón del Azul is just one of these walks and *refugios* – to explore the others, you could potentially walk for some weeks, staying a night or two in each one.

The whole system is very accessible, well maintained and well organized, and some of the better *refugios* are higher up, like the social **Casa del Campo** near an incredible stand of alerce trees. Another spectacular spot is the basic *refugio* **Hielo Azul**, which is best reached leaving from **Camping Hue Nain**. From the *refugio* it is a two-hour uphill hike to reach the glacier Hielo Azul and the stunning green lake. If conditions are right (ask at the *refugio*) you can also visit the ice caves that lie an easy 30 minutes from the hut. Take your time to map out your route; Cajón del Azul is certainly well worth the hike, but you will be rewarded if you explore further.

Fresh strawberries

CERRO PILTRIQUITRÓN

Soraya Parra, born and bred in El Bolsón, shares a little of what it is to live beneath the mountain.

Piltriquitrón means hanging from the clouds in the Mapuche language. He's imposing but very protective of those who need him. His presence is so strong that people can become very attached to his company. When I can't see Piltriquitrón I become a little anxious! I don't like being at the sea or on the plains for too long. El Bolsón, with its guardian Cerro Piltriquitrón, together they are a tribute to life! They always provide a warm welcome to their visitors, whether they are here to holiday or to live.

Beyond
El Bolsón

GETTING AROUND

Having a car offers greater freedom beyond El Bolsón but the bus system is also generally extensive, with less frequent buses in the off season. Buses run between El Bolsón and El Hoyo, or catch a taxi. Local companies offer excursions and transfers to Lago Puelo, Cerro Perito Moreno and Mallín Ahogado.

☑ **TOP TIP**

Take it slow. Ruta 40 has spectacular scenery but it is full of potholes and trucks.

Get lost in a labyrinth in El Hoyo, camp out at Lago Puelo or ski the slopes at Perito Moreno.

Head south out of El Bolsón and you will find yourself crossing state lines into Chubut. But all of these little villages belong to La Comarca Andina del Paralelo 42 (it technically runs from Bariloche in the north to Esquel in the south) and locals tend to feel connected to the *comarca* rather than the respective province. El Hoyo is just 15 minutes from El Bolsón. Use your intuition to find your way out of South America's largest labyrinth, and then sit back and sip cider or eat treats from the garden. Ski at Cerro Perito Moreno in winter, a very chilled out resort with none of the pretension of nearby snow zones.

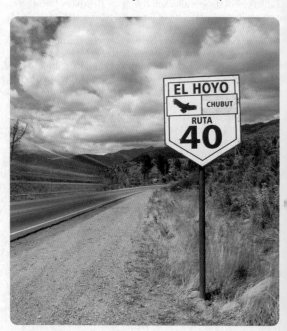

Ruta 40

Parque Nacional Lago Puelo

Parque Nacional Lago Puelo

TIME FROM EL BOLSÓN: 30MINS 🚗

Long Summer Days

Just a 20-minute drive from El Bolsón (but crossing over state lines into Chubut) you'll arrive in the town of Lago Puelo. Take a detour via RP16 and stop at the Pasarela Río Azul, a serene spot with a wooden suspension bridge that crosses the Blue River. You can enter the Motoco Cadenas community and follow the 20-minute trail to the waterfall, Cascada Motoco Cadenas, best seen in winter when plenty of water flows. Alternatively, walk the easy 2km trail to the Mirador del Río Blanco. Next, drive a further 10 minutes to the turquoise lake, the namesake of the Parque Nacional Lago Puelo.

A long stretch of pebbly beach, this is a stunning spot to kayak or swim (the water does warm up in summer) or to simply while away the hours or days. The water is shallow near to the shore before it drops off and, in a natural amphitheater surrounded by mountains, the view is nothing short of incredible. Like El Bolsón, there are plentiful campgrounds, and January and February are the months to visit. Hire a mountain bike to explore the area with ease. For bird watching,

THE WATER DIVISION

All along the Argentine side of the Andes there are huge lakes – some that flow to the Pacific Ocean via Chile and others that drain to the Atlantic Ocean in Argentina. Lago Puelo is one that runs to the Pacific (the invisible water division lies between Lago Gutiérrez and Lago Mascardi) as does Lago Lacár (p373) at San Martín de los Andes. Interestingly, it was explorer and academic Perito Francisco Moreno who surveyed much of the border area and later disproved Chilean claims to the continental divide in the Southern Cone by proving that many Patagonian lakes draining to the Pacific Ocean were actually part of the Atlantic Ocean basin.

 WHERE TO STAY BEYOND EL BOLSÓN

Villa Escondida
Fourteen self-contained cabins nestle into nature on this stunning private property at El Hoyo. $$

Linaje Boutique Hotel
Adults-only Lago Puelo hotel on a 20-hectare farm; beautiful grounds, pool and breakfast. $$$

La Confluencia Lodge & Farm
Top spot for large groups with organic food, wellness programs and doorstep access to hikes. $$$

BEST COMARCA ANDINA FESTIVALS

Fiesta Nacional de la Fruta Fina (January)
This long-running El Hoyo harvest festival celebrates all the berries.

Fiesta Nacional del Lúpulo (February)
Huge four-day festival of music and food celebrates the hops harvest in El Bolsón.

Fiesta Nacional del Bosque (February)
Summer arts and music festival in Lago Puelo.

Fiesta Provincial de la Chicha (April)
Head to Mallín Ahogado for this traditional celebration of *chicha*, a drink with Incan origins.

Fiesta de la Tradición (November)
Celebrate *criollo*-style with a 500-gaucho-strong parade in El Bolsón.

Laberinto Patagonia

explore the sandbanks and dreamy waters of Brazo Desemboque where the Río Neuquén runs into the lake. You have to pay a fee to enter the private campgrounds at the mouth of the river or simply stay overnight. To get out on the lake, Nautica Puelo offers a variety of excursions including sailing trips to the Chilean border. They also offer campground transfers and fishing trips. Horseback-riding trails are also possible.

El Hoyo
TIME FROM EL BOLSÓN: **15MINS**

El Hoyo & the Labyrinth

El Hoyo suffered a disastrous bushfire in 2021 and, as you enter the town, just 15 minutes from El Bolsón, you will see the still scorched hills lined with temporary housing. Right on Ruta 40, just past the viewpoint, take the driveway to Restaurante Pirque. The best little restaurant in the area, chef Gabriela Smit's family home is a delight, with excellent views of Cerro Pirque and the valley below. And the food? Well, Gabri-

WHERE TO GRAB A LOCALLY MADE DRINK IN EL BOLSÓN AND SURROUNDS

AWKA
Tiny but mighty drinking hole with takeaway taps of AWKA's craft beers.

Valkyria Gin
Try Rodrigo Carbajal's export-quality, organic, handcrafted gin at his distillery just out of town.

Sidrería Laberinto
Try a cider degustation (if you can escape the maze) made with the labyrinth's apples.

ela and her son, Manuel, offer up excellent home-grown plates from their *huerta* (vegetable garden) with all the warmth and affection of truly gracious hosts. You could do worse than to eat here every day. Book ahead in summer when long lunches bleed into the afternoons.

Just 3.5km from El Hoyo, South America's largest garden labyrinth can be found at Laberinto Patagonia (open December–April). Created by Doris Romera (she also studied gastronomy with Francis Mallmann) and Claudio Levi in 1996, the design mixes knowledge of kabbalah, sacred geometry and ancient mythology. A lot of love has gone into the maze (it is surprisingly difficult to find the exit!), and the owners have developed the entire site, including an on-site cafe offering macaroons and kitchen garden cakes and plates, excellent home-grown cider and fresh juices, and GAL, an immersive digital art space – it is easy to while away an entire day here.

In summer, drive a further 30 minutes to Puerto Patriado at Lago Epuyen. Locals say this serene lake is the warmest spot in which to swim or explore with a kayak or SUP to explore.

Cerro Perito Moreno   TIME FROM EL BOLSÓN: **40MINS** 🚗

Hippy Skiing at Cerro Perito Moreno

In the last few years, the road to Cerro Perito Moreno (not to be confused with the mega glacier in Santa Cruz of the same name!) has been improved and new chairlifts have been added, the result being that winter tourism is starting to open up in El Bolsón. Laderas, the ski resort at Perito Moreno, is a little hidden gem with the most economical pass and rental prices in the region, and a warm and welcoming attitude (think hippies on the slopes). Perito Moreno has no pretensions, so it is a great place to learn to ski, especially for kids. On weekends there is generally family-friendly entertainment and the vibe is decidedly chill.

When conditions are good for advanced skiers, the upper levels offer decent off-piste and backcountry fun. For non-skiers, it is worth visiting the base plateau, which has a great view of the valley. Currently, there are no accommodations on the mountain – apart from the basic Refugio Cerro Perito Moreno – so most people stay in El Bolsón and drive 40 minutes up the hill each day. Plans are in development for ski village accommodations, but this will take some years. The company is associated with British magnate Joe Lewis who has his controversial private luxury estate in the area.

Since 2021, Laderas has also operated in summer, the chairlifts taking visitors to 1650m for access to viewpoints. Trails are open for walking, horseback-riding on Pampa de Ludden, and mountain biking. On the plateau there is also an aerial park with challenging obstacles for those eight years of age and older.

MALLÍN AHOGADO

Just 10 minutes from El Bolsón, Mallín Ahogado is a fertile, rural valley where much of El Bolsón's produce is grown, including the town's large plots of *lúpulos* (hops), which are grown for export. You can drive the signposted Circuito de Mallín Ahogado and visit various agritourism businesses including Trufas del Mallín Ahogado, who provide guided tours of their truffle grounds if you call ahead.

The town is also home to an 80-person-strong community of Sufi Muslims and Argentina's most southern mosque. To visit the peaceful grounds of the Mezquita Sufi (inside the Sheik Raúf Abdul Felpete's *chacra*) turn up around lunchtime when there is generally someone to welcome you in.

San Martín de los Andes

BUENOS AIRES

GETTING AROUND

Chapelco Airport has frequent flights from Buenos Aires, Córdoba and Rosario. The Terminal de Omnibus has prime real estate one block from the shore of Lago Lácar, where there are frequent daily buses to Bariloche, Buenos Aires, Neuquén, Villa la Angostura, Zapala and Paso Mamuil Malal for entry into Chile (sit on the left for views of Volcán Lanín en route). To get to Aluminé, change buses in Zapala or Junín de los Andes. In town, SMA is compact, flat and easy to walk or cycle. Local buses depart frequently (less during winter) for Hua Hum, Playa Catrite and Lago Lolog. If travelling outside of summer, think about renting a 4WD. It is a requirement to carry chains during winter. Mobile reception is often nonexistent in Parque Nacional Lanín, and be prepared with fuel, water and snacks. If taking a rental car off road doesn't tempt you, excursions are available to most sites.

If you're looking for all the action and adventure of Bariloche but packaged in a smaller and more mellow town, San Martín de los Andes is your pick. A compact *centro cívico* nestled on the southern shore of Lago Lacár, San Martín is a great base for exploring the ancient trees, little-known trails, crystalline lakes and smoldering volcanoes of Parque Nacional Lanín. In winter, Cerro Chapelco is a well-developed ski zone just 20km from town. In summer, tourists flock to the azure waterholes of Lago Lacár, or go rafting and fly-fishing in nearby Río Chimehuín.

Just 45km from the Chilean border, San Martín de los Andes has a motley crew of inhabitants. With *pueblos originarios* from both sides of the border, descendants from European immigrants and 19th-century logging families, soldiers, *paisanos*, polo players, new-wave adventurers and post-pandemic *porteño* transplants, it is a surprising melting pot.

YASEMIN OLGUNOZ BERBER/SHUTTERSTOCK ©

San Martín de los Andes

☑ **TOP TIP**

San Martín de los Andes has two peak periods – summer in January and skiing in July and August. Otherwise it is a quiet little town, especially compared with Bariloche. Best to visit in early December or end of February for warm days and few visitors around.

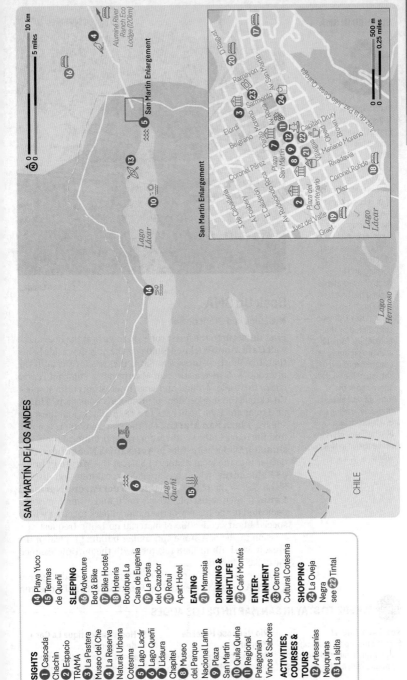

SAN MARTÍN DE LOS ANDES

San Martín Enlargement

CHILE

Lago Lácar

Lago Queñi

Lago Hermoso

Alumine River
Ranch Eco
Lodge (120km)

10 km
5 miles

500 m
0.25 miles

SIGHTS
1 Cascada Chachin
2 Espacio TRAMA
3 La Pastera Museo del Che
4 La Reserva Natural Urbana Cotesma
5 Lago Lacár
6 Lago Queñi
7 Lidaura Chapitel
8 Museo del Parque Nacional Lanín
9 Plaza San Martín
10 Quila Quina
11 Regional Patagonian Vinos & Sabores

ACTIVITIES, COURSES & TOURS
12 Artesanías Neuquinas
13 La Islita
14 Playa Yuco
15 Termas de Queñi

SLEEPING
16 Adventure Bed & Bike
17 Bike Hostel
18 Hotería Boutique La Casa de Eugenia
19 La Posta del Cazador
20 Rotui Apart Hotel

EATING
21 Mamusia

DRINKING & NIGHTLIFE
22 Café Montés

ENTER-TAINMENT
23 Centro Cultural Cotesma

SHOPPING
24 La Oveja Negra
see 22 Tintal

SUMMER IN SMA

Mauri Spisso, a transplant from La Plata, Buenos Aires, shares his love for SMA.

I will live the rest of my life here. My favorite spot is Lago Lacár and the infinite beaches – the campgrounds, the summer nights filled with stars, the smell of smoke and wood burning and long, deep conservations around the fire.
I love my drive to work in town, driving surrounded by the tallest pine forests with the picture-post-card background setting of the white, snow-capped mountains. I always think I am driving in a hand-drawn illustration. This is my place to live in this world.

Lago Lacár

Soak Up SMA

Museums and Great Coffee

First things first: the finest coffee in town is at the hole in the wall **Café Montés** (closed Sundays), the only downside being that, like most businesses in SMA, it closes for siesta in the afternoons. Coffee aside, San Martín has a compact *centro cívico* to wander around and some interesting cultural spots. Check out the independent printmaker's bookshop, **Tintal**, next door and then head back to Av San Martín and the main square, **Plaza San Martín**. On the eastern corner, you will find the tourist office with useful transport information, and stunning Mapuche textiles in **Artesanías Neuquinas**. Dive deeper into the local history of SMA at the **Museo Primeros Pobladores**, which has archaeological items on display. Stroll across the plaza to the **Museo del Parque Nacional Lanín** (closed weekends) where you'll find a small museum dedicated to the history of the national park together with a special library collection of material on Lanín (request permission to view). A stone and timber building typical of the area, it was built in 1948 together with the Bottini-designed Plaza San Martín.

For art and culture, check out the newly opened **Espacio TRAMA** or the long-standing **Centro Cultural Cotesma**

 WHERE TO STAY IN SAN MARTÍN DE LOS ANDES

Rotui Apart Hotel
Sumptuous rooms in a timber lodge with manicured grounds, complete with a little creek. **$$**

Río Hermoso Hotel de Montaña
Boutique hotel on a property 30 mins from SMA, beside the aptly named beautiful river. **$$$**

Hostería Boutique La Casa de Eugenia
Historic home with comfy beds, a pool and peaceful gardens. **$$$**

(includes the SMA cinema) – both host a varied program of music and theater performances. Excellent local and regional contemporary art can be seen at **Lidaura Chapitel**, a council-run exhibition space. After all that sightseeing head back to Av San Martín, grab an ice cream at **Mamusia** and wander southwest towards Lago Lacár's leafy shore and pier.

Summer Around Lago Lacár

Dreamy Lakeside Beaches

Lago Lacár is home to some delightful swimming spots which are at their warmest (read: still chilly) in the summer months. Heading out on Ruta 40, just a five-minute drive (or one-hour walk) from town, you'll see the turnoff to **Playa Catritre**. Take the dirt track to the right and you'll find a small pebbly beach with a campground and a fast-flowing creek. A further 30 minutes down the road (take RN108), you could easily spend the day at **Quila Quina**, a Mapuche Curruhuinca community-owned stretch of beach with a restaurant and grassy grounds. From the pier in San Martín de los Andes, Naviera boats do frequent daily transfers to the beach. Or hire a kayak to explore the lake's gigantic granite cliffs and visit **La Islita**, a rocky outcrop just a 5km paddle from town.

For crystal-clear blue swimming holes in a calm, sandy bay surrounded by boulders, try **Playa Yuco** on the western side of Lacár. Take the dirt road RP48 or hop on a bus heading to Hua Hum; it is a short walk to the lake from the bus stop. It's worth driving all the way to Hua Hum where the **Río Hua Hum** drains Lago Lacár into Chile and the Pacific Ocean. Jump into the river rapids to whitewater-raft to the Chilean border or hike the 3kms to **Cascada Chachin**, a stunning waterfall reached via ancient Valdivian temperate rainforest.

Most of the popular swimming spots have lifeguards during summer. Take cash to pay the indigenous community entrance fees.

San Martín
de los Andes

BEST LOCAL SHOPS

Mamusia
Sweet treats to take home from San Martín's homegrown chocolate and ice-cream store.

Tintal
Curated printmaker's bookshop with children's titles, local art and workshops.

Artesanías Neuquinas
Mapuche cooperative with high-quality textiles and carvings, next door to the tourist office.

Regional Patagonian Vinos & Sabores
Top-shelf Argentine wines, Patagonian beers and gins.

La Oveja Negra
In SMA since 1982, stock up on unique winter woollies and local handcrafted gifts.

 WHERE TO STAY IN SAN MARTÍN DE LOS ANDES

Bike Hostel
Not just for cyclists; there are light and airy dorms and private rooms in this fun hostel. **$**

Adventure Bed & Bike
Spacious with great chill-out areas, ideal for large groups. A shuttle takes guests into SMA. **$**

La Posta del Cazador
Rustic and charming, alpine-style inn with warm service; located one block from Lago Lacár. **$$**

La Pastera Museo del Che

BIRD WATCHING IN SMA

Just 7km from the center of SMA on Ruta 40, the 38-hectare wildlife sanctuary **La Reserva Natural Urbana Cotesma** provides visitors with guided bird-watching tours and a small viewing hut for spotting a wide variety of Patagonian birdlife on the wetlands. Book via the website rnu. cotesma.com.ar.

Driving further afield, stop by **Observatorio De Cóndores**, a purpose-built viewing platform on Ruta 40 (20 minutes from Junín de los Andes towards La Rinconada) where it is possible to spot the elusive Andean condor. Arrive early morning or around dusk for more chance of locking eyes with these majestic creatures. Have patience and soak up the impressive landscape; it is a truly magical place to appreciate the flight of these birds.

Exiles & Revolutionaries Passing Through

Pablo Neruda and Che

During their formative first trip through Latin America (which inspired Guevara's memoir, *The Motorcycle Diaries*), Ernesto 'Che' Guevara and Alberto Granado arrived in San Martín de los Andes on their motorbike, *La Poderosa II*. The director of the Parque Nacional Lanín gave the hungry and tired pair food and offered them an old barn to sleep in. Today, this old barn, **La Pastera Museo del Che**, is the site of a small museum that details Che's life and includes a bookshop with titles about the revolutionary.

A couple of years earlier, in 1948, Chilean poet Pablo Neruda sought refuge in Argentina and crossed the Andes on horseback, ending up in **Lago Queñi**, an isolated but stunning lake to the south of Lago Lácar. To retrace his steps and take a dip in the natural hot springs, **Termas de Queñi** (December to April only), hop on the road to Hua Hum near the Chilean border (Neruda crossed at clandestine Paso Lilpela) and continue towards Lago Queñi. The narrow, rough dirt road is suitable for 4WDs only. The creek crossing prevents vehicle access from May to December when the gate is locked. The 4km (1½ hours of moderate walking) trail to the springs starts near the campground and the welcoming park ranger. After all that adventure, the reward is a relaxing soak in the small waterholes – beware, one is much hotter than the other! It's bite-sized compared to the journeys of Che, Alberto and Neruda, but half the fun is getting there.

Beyond
San Martín de los Andes

Ancient *pehuén* stands, religious sites, fly-fishing and more volcanoes than you can poke stick at.

Remote, storybook landscapes await those who venture north from San Martín de los Andes. For religious pilgrims and fly-fishers alike, Junín de los Andes beckons. It is also a great base for adventurers wanting to tackle the ascent of Volcán Lanín, the star attraction of Parque Nacional Lanín, or whitewater-raft the Class III rapids of Río Chimehuín. Further north, base yourself at Villa Pehuenia to drive the quiet Circuito Pehuenia (a day-long loop around the lakes and towering stands of ancient araucaria trees) or see how many volcanoes you can spot from the top of Volcán Batea Mahuida.

Volcán Lanín

GETTING AROUND

Transfers are available to Cerro Chapelco and Lago Hermoso Ski. Local buses run regularly to Villa Pehuenia and Junín de los Andes for Río Chimehuín and in summer to Lago Huechulafquen. A car is best for exploring further north. Check road conditions ahead of time and always carry chains in winter. Many roads are *ripio* (gravel), including the road between Zapala and Villa Pehuenia, RP61 to Puerto Canoa, and the national park entrance for the ascent of Volcán Lanín.

☑ TOP TIP

The further north you head from San Martín de los Andes, the less well-trodden the road becomes.

RELIGIOUS TOURISM

A 40-minute drive from San Martín de los Andes, Junín de los Andes is a much more humble affair, with religious tourism at the forefront. Many Christian pilgrims travel to Junín to walk the Vía Christi, a hillside climb past 23 stations of the cross sculptures, and to visit the austere Iglesia Nuestra Señora de las Nieves, which also honours Blessed Laura Vicuña.

Approximately 60km from Junín, the remains of the young Mapuche Ceferino Namuncurá lie at the architecturally striking Santuario de Ceferino. Beatified in 2007 by the Catholic Church, it's said that Blessed Ceferino sang with Carlos Gardel in the Colegio Pío IX choir in Buenos Aires in 1901.

Skiing, Cerro Chapelco

Cerro Chapelco & Lago Hermoso
TIME FROM SAN MARTÍN DE LOS ANDES: **20MINS**

Huskies, Horseback Riding & Tetrathlons

The development of Cerro Chapelco, San Martín de los Andes' ski resort just 20 minutes from town, opened up this mountain village to winter tourism back in the 1970s. Less crowded than other mountains in the region, Chapelco enjoys excellent views to Volcán Lanín and Lago Lacár and has a wide variety of runs. Non-skiers can reach 1600m by gondola and hike in the snow or enjoy the trails on snowmobiles. It's also possible to race through El Bosque de los Huskies with a professional guide and a huskie-led sled – a dreamy snow experience for kids and adults alike. For athletes, each September, Chapelco plays host to Tetra Chapelco, a tetrathlon that has been running for almost 40 years. Competitors ski 17km, mountain-bike 44km, kayak 10km in the icy waters of Lacár and finish with a 17km run. Phew! A 25-minute drive from SMA, on the Ruta de los Siete Lagos, is the smaller and more exclusive option, Lago Hermoso Ski, where activities include horseback riding trails in the snow. Tip: take cash, as foreign cards are often not accepted. Some restaurants only accept Mercado Pago for Argentine bank account holders.

 WHERE TO EAT IN SAN MARTÍN DE LOS ANDES

Vieja Deli
Busy, lakeside location with all the usual suspects, but good-value *milas* hit the spot. **$$**

Pizza Cala
Hands down the best wood-fired pizza and empanadas at this cosy and warm restaurant. **$$**

Morphen
Book ahead at this intimate restaurant, SMA's finest, with excellent service and an ever-changing menu. **$$**

Volcán Lanín

TIME FROM SAN MARTÍN DE LOS ANDES: **1.5HRS** TO THE NORTHERN FACE OF VOLCÁN LANÍN

Lanín from All Sides

The prize peak of Parque Nacional Lanín is its namesake, the 3776m Volcán Lanín. Visible from various points given its towering size and distinctive cone (and from as far away as RN237 on the way to Neuquén), the best views, without tackling the ascent, are from the park's largest and most accessible lake, Lago Huechulafquen. Buses run from San Martín and Junín to the lake during summer, but otherwise take an excursion or drive the unpaved and winding RP61 from Junín, which offers outstanding vistas of the volcano (2½ hours from San Martín de los Andes).

There are plenty of Mapuche-owned campgrounds along the lake; you can also take a boat trip from Puerto Canoa or kayak the calm, sheltered waters. Andestrack also offers a five-day kayak and camping trip across three lakes in the southern shadow of Lanín, including the remote Lagos Epulafquen and Paimún. For the big business end of town, the ascent of Lanín's north face is one for the bucket list. It is a tough physical challenge over two days, but is an accessible climb for most fit hikers with an experienced guide (the park offices in San Martín have lists of authorized guides).

Register with pnlanin.org.ar before you leave. If you are short on time, it is worth doing the two-hour (but steep) hike to the mirador at the base of Lanín's north face. Park at the ranger's station off RP60 (1½ hours from San Martín de los Andes) to start the trail to stunning panoramic views of the volcano and Lago Tromen. Best to visit from November to April.

Volcán Lanín

EXTREME SPORTS

If religious tourism is big in Junín de los Andes, San Martín de los Andes is known for its extreme sports tourism. Each April, runners take over the city to race in the Patagonia Run, competing in ultramarathons of 110km and 100 miles (and it's not flat!). And for the last 40 years, athletes have been competing in the Tetra Chapelco on Cerro Chapelco, which includes ski, run, cycle and swim legs. For water adventurers, the Class III rapids of Río Chimehuín north of San Martín de los Andes are a significant drawcard, while the rocks at Villa Meliquina pull the climbers. Experienced bikepackers also tackle the Patagonia Beer Trail, cycling the 220-mile route from SMA to El Bolsón.

FESTIVALS IN SAN MARTÍN DE LOS ANDES

Fiesta de Fundación
February parade to celebrate the anniversary of the town and its varied inhabitants.

Fiesta Nacional del Montañés
A woodchopping spectacle held in August in conjunction with the ski season.

Trabún
Chilean and Argentine *pueblos originarios* perform folk music and dancing at this December festival.

THE GUIDE

BEYOND SAN MARTÍN DE LOS ANDES BARILOCHE & THE LAKE DISTRICT

PRACTICALITIES

Scan this QR code for route information in English.

TOP SIGHT

Ruta de los Siete Lagos

The most iconic section of Ruta 40, La Ruta de los Siete Lagos (The Seven Lakes Drive) is a 110km scenic stretch from San Martín de los Andes to Villa la Angostura, where the road rims seven lakes in the region. Every Argentine has done it and every tourist wants to.

DON'T MISS
Playa Quina Quela
Mirador Pil Pil
Lago Machónico
Río Pichi Traful
Cascada Ñivinco
Lago Espejo
Río Correntoso

Take the Day...or More

Take your time and give yourself the freedom to stop, hike a trail, sit on a beach or have a chat. Tourists tend to rush this route, but aim to savour it. There is a lot to explore if you stay along the way or spend a night or two at either end.

Cycling

It is a very popular road to cycle, with plenty of camping available, and the distance is about the right size for an easy multiday trip. The roads are good, including the gravel – the only thing is the 1500m elevation gain. It's trial by fire, with the first section from San Martín being an immediate climb. You can hire bikes in San Martín and return them in Villa la Angostura.

Cascada Ñivinco

You'll see the parking area for the 30-minute hike to this stunning waterfall, which in summer is suitably packed. Some of the walks here have been closed in recent times because there is a population of torrent ducks that call the area home. Very sensitive to environmental changes, the ducks live in the Andes near very fast running water. They don't like to be disturbed by humans, let alone drones and trash, so do the right thing.

Seven Lakes & Counting

Not surprisingly, there are more than seven lakes in the region and some are easily accessible from the road. Lago Hermoso is a stunning lake – some say the most beautiful – and it is just a short detour from the main road. Lago Traful is a longer detour but worth a stopover, with sights like the Bosque Sumergido, a group of 60 cypress trees that are submerged in the crystal-blue water. Lago Espejo Chico is a very short 2km detour; do it.

Winter on the Road

Between July and September, vehicles must carry chains and can only drive between 9am and 6pm due to snowy conditions. Check road conditions before you leave. The beach and banks of Lago Faulkner covered in snow are a sight to behold. The landscape between Faulkner and Lago Machónico is also particularly pretty in winter – with the green lichen-covered trees, gray boulders, red branches and white snow all combining in a rainbow of alpine colors. Watch out for wildlife and farm animals.

Parque Nacional de los Arrayanes

Not technically part of La Ruta de los Siete Lagos, it is just geographically easy to access at either the beginning or end of the trip in Villa la Angostura. Tourists tend to take the boat trip to Isla Victoria from Bariloche to experience the incredible stand of 650-year-old trees, but the boat only allows for a limited time in the forest. To spend a day with these rare ancient trees (and check out the indigenous rock wall paintings) enter the park from the land entrance. The trees are at the southern end of the peninsula, so if you are pressed for time, you can also catch the ferry over from Puerto Quetrihué in Villa la Angostura.

**Parque Nacional
de los Arrayanes**

TAKE THE DETOUR

If you are driving the loop (Bariloche to San Martín de los Andes and back), detour via Villa Traful on the return journey. The tiny town is worth a stop, and when the road meets up with RN237 at the confluence of the rivers Traful and Limay, you'll be greeted with the impressive sight of Valle Encantado (p358).

TOP TIPS

● Slow down and take your time. You could drive the route in two hours, but where would be the fun in that?

● There's no harm in driving the road in either or both directions; the views are completely different. The same goes for different seasons. Don't be put off driving the road in winter; the lakes are a spectacular sight to see surrounded by snow.

● If you're camping, plan to see sunrise at Lago Espejo – you'll find out why it is called the mirror lake.

● Did you know? Río Correntoso claims to be the shortest river in the world.

Volcán Batea Mahuida

THE MONKEY PUZZLE TREE

The pehuén (araucaria or monkey puzzle) tree is a survivor from the Jurassic era, more than 45 million years ago. Slow growing and reaching heights of 48m, the trees are considered living fossils and are of huge cultural importance for the *pueblos originarios* who collect the *piñones* (seeds) to either make flour (the seeds are naturally gluten-free) or eat toasted, as they are very rich in nutrients like magnesium and calcium. Large-scale commercial harvest is prohibited in the interest of protecting the increasingly rare species. This sacred tree is celebrated at the Fiesta Nacional del Pehuén at Aluminé (April) and at the Fiesta del Piñonero y del Artesano Mapuche in Villa Pehuenia (January).

Circuito Pehuenia & Volcán Batea Mahuida   TIME FROM SAN MARTÍN DE LOS ANDES: 3½HRS

Eight Volcanoes & Ancient Trees

Head north from San Martín de los Andes and you'll quickly notice that the number of tourists starts to fade dramatically. The idyllic lakeside village of Villa Pehuenia, a 3½-hour drive from San Martín de los Andes, is the starting point for Circuito Pehuenia, a scenic 120km gravel road loop encompassing Lago Moquehue, Lago Ñorquinco (the northern limit of Parque Nacional Lanín), Lago Pulmarí, Lago Aluminé and the ancient pehuén (araucaria) trees that give this region its name. There are incredible rock formations, seemingly prehistoric landscapes and a variety of walks, including the 14km trail to the viewpoint for Cascada Coloco, which leaves from the ranger's hut at the southern end of Lago Ñorquinco.

From December to March, drive a further 30 minutes north to the easily accessible Volcán Batea Mahuida, where you can park near to the top of the volcano and then walk an easy two hours to the summit at 1948m. From here, you can view the string of eight volcanoes that straddle the border of Argentina and Chile – from Lanín in the south to Copahue in the north. There is a stunning blue lake in the crater of Batea Mahuida. In winter, it is possible to ski at the family-friendly Batea Mahuida Parque de Nieve, which is owned and run by Puel Mapuche. It has a small number of runs, very reasonably priced passes and a long season from June to October. Be sure to take chains, as the access road can be heavy with snow; otherwise, taxis do transfers from Villa Pehuenia.

Neuquén

Neuquén is Patagonia's largest city, and although not a top tourist spot, it's starting to garner more attention for its year-round dry climate, spectacular landscapes and dinosaur discoveries. Located at the confluence of the Ríos Limay and Neuquén, which join to form the Río Negro, it is an important fruit-growing area with large swathes of apple and pear orchards. Neuquén also lies on the Vaca Muerta, a geological formation from the late Jurassic period and host rock for major shale oil and gas deposits, with drilling operations visible throughout the surrounding desert landscape. And there's a lot more underground, with various dinosaur fossils having been unearthed in the 20th century. These include some of the world's largest known beasts, from the 40m-long *Argentinosaurus huinculensis* found near Plaza Huincal to the carnivorous *Gigantosaurus carolini* at Villa El Chocón.

Confluence of the Rivers

Mighty Waters and Wildlife

The **Río Limay** drains Lago Nahuel Huapi in Bariloche and runs all the way to Neuquén, where it joins with the **Río Neuquén** to create the **Río Negro**, which then flows all the way to the Atlantic Ocean near Viedma. The mighty confluence is a sight to see and best enjoyed from the **Paseo a la Costa**, a great park to walk or cycle, with smooth paths along the river shore. Near the entrance to **Parque Sur** from Av Río Negro, you will also find a good selection of craft beer and food trucks, a superb spot to while away summer nights. On the shore side of the large office building, you will find **Tecim Eco Navegación**, one of the only companies who offer small boat excursions on the river with an informative guide.

Wander all the way to the end of the walking paths and you will find a welcome center for the newly created protected

GETTING AROUND

Neuquén is a hub for domestic and international flights and bus services. The city is mostly flat with walking paths and is well-lit at night. There is an extensive bus network and trains run on the Tren del Valle route between Plottier and Neuquén, stopping at both the Terminal de Omnibus Neuquén and the airport. Plaza Huincal, El Chocón and Rincón de los Sauces can all be reached via buses from the Terminal de Omnibus Neuquén. To reach Centro Paleontológico Lago Barreales or the wineries past San Patricio del Chañar, you need a car or to organize an excursion.

☑ TOP TIP

Best to go from March to May when days are mild. Temperatures soar in summer and shade is hard to come by. Accommodation are competitive, with lots of business-style hotels and self-contained apartments to host the petrochemical industry, and standards are generally high.

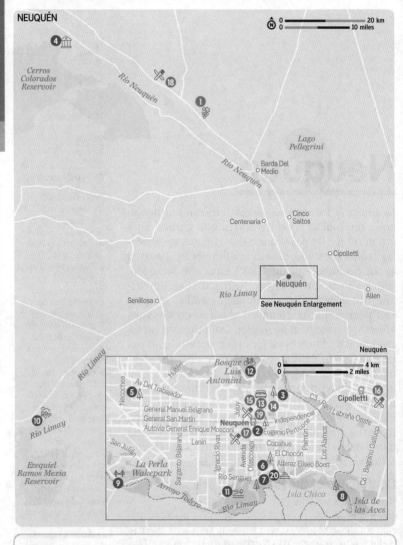

NEUQUÉN

Cerros Colorados Reservoir

Río Neuquén

Río Neuquén

Lago Pellegrini

Barda Del Medio

Centenaria

Cinco Saltos

Cipolletti

Río Limay

Neuquén

See Neuquén Enlargement

Senillosa

Allen

Neuquén

Río Limay

Bosque Luis Antonini

Cipolletti

C3 - Raúl Labraña Oeste

Necochea

Av Del Trabajador

Huiliín

Jujuy

Independencia

C6 - Bagimo Galíluga

Río Limay

Exequiel Ramos Mexia Reservoir

General Manuel Belgrano

General San Martín

Autovia General Enrique Mosconi

Neuquén

Eugenio Perticone

Paimún

Los Álamos

San Julián

Lanín

Ignacio Rivas

Sargento Belgrano

Avenida Olascoaga

Copahue

El Chocón

Alferez Eliseo Boerr

La Perla Wakepark

Río Senguer

Isla Chica

Arroyo Todero

Río Limay

Isla de las Aves

SIGHTS
1 Bodega Familia Schroeder
see 18 Bodega Malma
2 Parque Central
3 Parque Este
4 Parque Geopaleontológico Proyecto Dino
5 Parque Oeste
6 Parque Sur
7 Paseo a la Costa
8 Península Hiroki
9 Puente Las Perlas
10 Villa El Chocón

ACTIVITIES, COURSES & TOURS
11 Balneario Sandra Canale
12 Dirt World Fly Park
see 12 Parque Norte

SLEEPING
13 Cyan Soho Neuquén Hotel
14 La Morada Petit Hotel
15 Punto Patagonico Hostel

EATING
16 Casa Tinta
see 10 La Posada del Dinosaurio
17 La Toscana
18 Malma Restaurant
19 Restaurante Estación Q

TRANSPORT
20 Tecim Eco Navegación

Start in the afternoon at the **❶ Museum Nacional de Bellas Artes** to check out the latest exhibition at this singular outpost of the national fine arts gallery in Buenos Aires. Then wander through **❷ Parque Central** to the contemporary art space **❸ Sala de Arte Emilio Saraco**, which hosts excellent local works in a 1911 railway shed constructed by the British-owned Buenos Aires Great Southern Railway. Stop by the **❹ Tranquera de los ingleses**, a replica of the gate once used by the British railway company to divide the city of Neuquén in two. In 1936, in a fit of despair, then Neuquén Mayor Amaranto Suarez ordered the gate be pulled down in order to bring the people together once again. Head along the tracks to **❺ Museo Gregorio Álvarez** (closed Sundays and Mondays), another restored historic railway building with an excellent local

ethnographic collection. For an afternoon drink, go upstairs at **❻ Antares** to enjoy the sun setting over the park in a unique historic residential home built by Ukranian immigrants. It was one of the only houses to have stained-glass windows and a street-facing garden. Take the diagonal and head back to Av Argentina find the humble **❼ Catedral de Neuquén María Auxiliadora**, whose first Bishop Jaime de Nevares was a leading figure during the military dictatorship for those needing refuge. Wander Av Argentina to the **❽ Feria de los Artesanos**, a market that harks back to 1979 when hippies stopped by Neuquén on their way south to El Bolsón. Continue up the hill to the **❾ Plaza de las Banderas** and finish the evening at the intimate **❿ Observatorio Astronómico de Neuquén** to see the desert sky stars.

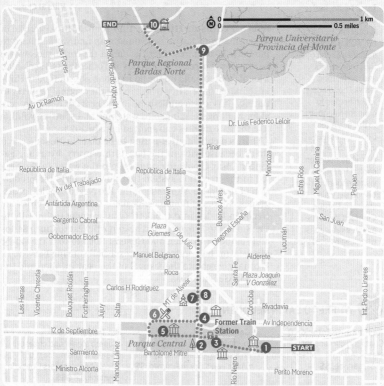

FREE CITY TOURS

The local Neuquén council offers free minibus and walking tours covering many of the city's highlights. Guides are typically very passionate about their city's history, making the whole experience well worthwhile. Minibus tours cover the Río Limay shoreline, stopping at its various viewpoints and visiting some of Neuquén's historic landmarks, such as the ghostly ruins of the 19th-century Torre Talero, and the grounds of the former jail, Ex Carcel U9. Walking tours include a circuit of the city's murals and the historic railway buildings which helped to connect Neuquén to Buenos Aires. Bookings essential via Eventbrite; visit @turismo.neuquen. capital for links or visit the tourist office beside the train station in Parque Central. One of the minibus vehicles is wheelchair-accessible.

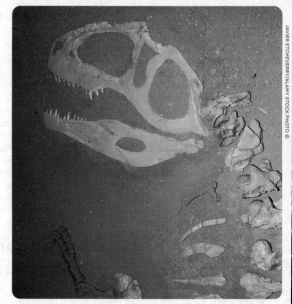

JAVIER ETCHEVERRY/ALAMY STOCK PHOTO ©

Villa El Chocón

reserve **Península Hiroki**. In 1927 Tomizu Hiroki arrived in Argentina from Japan as a young man and worked hard to purchase 50 hectares of fertile land at the confluence, where he grew strawberries, raspberries and other fruits. He planted a lot of trees to build up the flood-prone site, and today Hiroki's children have gifted 8 hectares of the original property to the city. It is a peaceful escape in the heart of Neuquén, ideal for walking, relaxing, bird watching and spotting wildlife like the gato montés cub spotted here in 2023.

There's plenty of great eating to be done in Neuquén, and that's because back in the late 19th century, hydraulic engineer César Cipolletti's studies into the water in the area led to the irrigation system that now supports the production of the entire Alto Valle of the Río Negro. Apples, pears, grapes, almonds, tomatoes, peaches and plums – cross the Neuquén bridge into Cipoletti (you are now technically in the Río Negro Province) and head northwest to Cinco Saltos and southeast to Allen and General Roca to tour the valley. Many farms have guided tours, especially during harvest. In February, celebrate the festival of the pear in Allen and the apple in General Roca.

WHERE TO EAT IN NEUQUÉN

Restaurante Estación Q
Charming corner spot with classic Argentine offerings and great service. **$$**

Casa Tinta
Intimate Cipoletti space with an inspiring local menu by chef Emma Leiva. Try the *chivito*. **$$**

La Toscana
Superb steaks and cheese platers at this outpost of local cheesemakers Quesería Ventimiglia. **$$$**

Get Outdoors in the City

Parks and Trails for Days

You don't need to wander far to feel like you are out in nature in this very liveable compact city. With parks at each point of the compass, there are kilometers of trails and vistas to enjoy on your doorstep, and *neuquinos* are out enjoying them year-round. The entrance to **Parque Norte** (North Park) is at the top of the hill that climbs Avenida Argentina and is filled with a system of trails with a long 4.5km circuit, the Observatorio Astronómico de Neuquén (entrance fee AR$1000, bring cash), and **Balcon del Valle**, which is a great viewpoint to see the neighboring towns and orchards of Cipoletti, Centenario and Cinco Saltos. Below the observatory, you will also find **Dirt World Fly Park**, a BMX bike park with dirt jumps. **Parque Sur** (South Park) offers the coastline of the Río Limay and the **Paseo a la Costa** along with **Balneario Gustavo A Fahler**, a popular summer swimming spot with lifeguards. If you are cycling, another peaceful park to have a dip in is **Balneario Sandra Canale**, or ride the 15km stretch of smooth paths that run beside the Río Limay heading south to the **Puente Las Perlas**. In the west of the city, **Parque Oeste** (West Park) has a skatepark and a small lagoon with birdlife (and mosquitos!). **Parque Central** (Central Park) runs along the railway tracks in the heart of town, while **Parque Este** (East Park) has lovely views of the Río Neuquén, a sundial, and is the perfect spot to see the moon rise.

Follow the Footsteps of the Dinosaurs

Twenty-Four Hours in El Chocón

An hour's drive from Neuquén, **Villa El Chocón** is a popular day trip with a couple of great dinosaur sites. Follow the painted dinosaur footprints on the road to the small but mighty **Museo Municipal Ernesto Bachmann**, which boasts the remains of the giant *Gigantosaurus carolini* found by fossil hunter Rubén D Carolini in 1993. At the time, it was the world's largest-known carnivorous dinosaur, even bigger than the popular *Tyrannosaurus rex*. The museum has excellent staff and information in both English and Spanish. For a wilder experience, head back to the main road and then follow the signs to the **Parque Náutico** and aerodrome until you see a purple sign for **Las Huellas** (footprints). There are two viewing platforms on the reservoir shore where the rocks below reveal the heavy and huge footprints of prehistoric dinosaurs. Keep driving and you will see a small rocky beach with a lifeguard shelter. Take care when you are parking as there

TOP DINO SPOTS

Beyond El Chocón check out these dino hotspots:

Museo Municipal Carmen Funes, Plaza Huincul
Gawk at the replica of the *Argentinosaurus huinculensis*, an incredible 40m-high dinosaur (the world's largest at the time) found by a local in 1989.

Parque Geopaleontológico Proyecto Dino, Lago Barreales
Must-visit working palaeontology site in a remote paradise. Book ahead for tours (twice daily). Worth visiting if you head out to the wineries for the day.

Museo Municipal Argentino Urquiza, Rincón de los Sauces
Further afield, this museum is for hard-core fans and holds the only known fossils of a *Titanosaurus* and its eggs.

 WHERE TO SLEEP IN NEUQUÉN

Punto Patagonico Hostel
Central location near lots of nightlife with a pool, patio and friendly staff. $

La Morada Petit Hotel
Light, spacious rooms with terraces, garden views, pool and included parking. Children over six welcome. $$

Cyan Soho Neuquén Hotel
Standard contemporary rooms with an in-house restaurant and a gym down the road. $$

are numerous exposed dino footprints to walk among; locals have outlined the sites with small pebbles. It is a very quiet spot in winter but busy with swimmers in summer. To the left of the town, it is worth driving down to the water to see the impressive dam wall of the **Embalse Ezequiel Ramos Mexía**, used to generate the largest hydroelectric power station in Patagonia. Drive across the bridge and take the dirt track to the right for 30 minutes to see **Los Gigantes**, impressive rust-colored rock formations jutting out of the blue water.

On the Neuquén Winery Trail

Grapes Above, Dinosaurs Below

An hour's drive north of Neuquén capital, near San Patricio del Chañar, there are a string of spectacular wineries that have been pioneering this special grape-growing area over the last couple of decades. Two of the Bodegas del Neuquén – **Bodega Familia Schroeder** and **Bodega Malma** – offer guided tours of their wine production, and have a cellar door and excellent on-site restaurants for lunch. Pick between the two or visit both. Bodega Familia Schroeder is slightly more family-friendly in that there is a dinosaur in the mix. During the early days of the winery, the fossil of the dinosaur *Panamericansaurus schroederi* was unearthed. You can also reserve a Saurus Picnic to eat among the vineyards. Both wineries are closed Mondays and require reservations for tours and lunch. If you wish to have an English tour, book at least a couple of days ahead. **La Vendimia Neuquina** celebrates the harvest in March each year with events at both wineries. Patagonia's largest winery, Bodega del Fin del Mundo, also has its vineyard in this region, but it is no longer open to the public. If you have time before or after a winery tour, it is well worth checking out the working palaeontology site and museum, **Parque Geopaleontológico Proyecto Dino**, 45 minutes further north on **Lago Barreales**. Book ahead for three-hour tours (closed Mondays) at either 10am or 3pm. The staff are extremely knowledgeable and it's in a stunning location. In warmer months, drive RP51 and stop off for a dip in the reservoir, **Mari Menuco**, where you'll also spot drilling operations for the petrochemical industry.

PINOT NOIR

Dry conditions, the wide temperature range (very hot in summer with freezing nights in winter) together with the ever-present Patagonian winds make the wine-growing area of Neuquén perfect for producing a unique Pinot Noir. The color is extremely light and could be mistaken for a rosé. One of the best-known organic and biodynamic Pinot Noirs comes from Italian winemaking royalty Piero Incisa della Rocchetta and his Bodega Chacra in the Alto Valle del Río Negro. They produce award-winning pinots, Chacra 55 and Chacra 32; dip into your savings for a singular taste of the terroir of Patagonia.

Los Gigantes

Beyond
Neuquén

Relax and restore in bubbling, hot-mud pools or tackle the *techo* of Patagonia, the towering Volcán Domuyo.

There is so much to pack into a trip to the remote, northern parts of Neuquén. You could easily focus on this area alone for a couple of weeks. Head to Caviahue in winter for a guaranteed ski season and check out the smoking volcano, Volcán Copahue. Or go hiking in summer after the snow melts and visit the Copahue hot springs complete with mineral-rich mud pools. Further north, the former capital Chos Malal is a pretty little oasis town that acts as the gateway to Patagonia's highest peak, the 4702m-tall Volcán Domuyo, where you can tackle the ascent or traverse the area on mountain bikes.

Waterfall, Copahue

GETTING AROUND

Having your own wheels is the best option to explore this area, but there are frequent buses to Caviahue and Chos Malal from Neuquén. In summer there are regular buses running between Caviahue and Copahue. Cautivar Patagonia in Neuquén also organises excursions to the north. For many roads in Neuquén it is compulsory to carry chains in your vehicle during winter. Check road conditions for daily updates. After visiting Caviahue and Copahue, you could choose to head south to San Martín de los Andes and Bariloche or north to Chos Malal. If you are heading north, you'll have to drive the unsealed but scenic RP21, then take RN6 rather than RN4.

☑ TOP TIP

Distances are long in northern Neuquén. Check road conditions, fill up when you can, and carry snacks, water and maps.

Caviahue & Copahue

TIME FROM NEUQUÉN: **4½HRS** 🚗

Powder Mountains & Hot Springs

In the northwest of the province, the twin towns of Copahue and Caviahue are about a 4½-hour drive from Neuquén. It's a less explored part of Argentina and you'll be treated with spectacular vistas. Twenty minutes before arriving in Caviahue you will see Los Riscos Bayos, a fascinating rock formation in the hills to the left of RP26. Said to be 'volcano tears', they are a very rare phenomenon formed from a unique set of volcanic ash cloud conditions.

In winter, Caviahue turns it on with a guaranteed five-month season of powder snow due to the particularly cold and dry climate. The ski resort is just 1km from town and has a variety of runs and excursions, including snowmobile trips to the frozen waterfall Cascada Congelada del Valle de Jara. In summer, the snow melts and there are plenty of incredible hikes and sights to enjoy in this little village dotted with araucarias. The Salto del Agrio, all rust red and green water, is a waterfall from another planet with striking colors from the mineral-rich area and with smoking Volcán Copahue looming in the background. Located about 30 minutes from town (take RP26 and then RP27 before turning off), it is easily accessible and for that reason can be busy in summer. Arrive at midday to take full advantage of the high sun to bring out the outstanding hues. For the more adventurous, hike to Puente de Piedra, a natural rock bridge formation on the banks of Lago Caviahue. It's a medium difficult hike due to the initial steep section; be sure to wear decent shoes, plus sun protection in summer. Drive towards Loncopue on RP26 where the entrance to the start of the trail is 3.5km from Caviahue. Be prepared for strong winds.

Copahue is only open from December until the end of April as snow prevents access, but in summer the town is filled with Argentines bathing in the curative thermal springs at Termas de Copahue. Steaming pools and a bubbling hot-mud pool (Laguna del Chancho – the pig's lagoon!) are set in a natural amphitheater with the mountain range behind. You can also see wild thermal waters bubbling at Las Maquinas just outside of Copahue, where there is a military base in ruins. Just be careful where you step!

Stone bridge, Caviahue

WEEKENDS IN NATURE

Paola Carazo, photographer and teacher, shares her love for Neuquén's nature.

I love the weather; you can enjoy all the seasons, and nature is very close. In summer or winter, there are incredible places to visit and sports to do surrounded by nature – by rivers and lakes, on the mountain range or by the sea. It is all very accessible to go for the weekend. I love the birds, the flowers in spring and winter, the trees – our pehuenes (araucarias) are beautiful, a blessing to behold. We also eat well and in season with local fruits and vegetables. It is a great place to live where the people are affectionate and kind.

✦ FESTIVALS IN AND AROUND NEUQUÉN

Fiesta de San Sebastián
Religious procession and celebrations in Las Ovejas in January.

Fiesta Nacional de la Confluencia
Huge, free music festival in Neuquén capital in February each year.

Fiesta Nacional del Chivito, la Danza y la Canción
Thousands gather in Chos Malal each November to sing, dance and feast on goat.

Chos Malal & Northern Neuquén

TIME FROM NEUQUÉN: 4½HRS

The Road Less Traveled

Take the little-driven northern Ruta 40 and you'll reach Chos Malal, a 4½-hour drive from Neuquén. The largest town in the region, with a historic center and located at the picturesque convergence of the rivers Neuquén and Curi Leivú, Chos Malal is the best option as a base to explore further north. It is also one of the few towns in the area with a reliable gas station, so be sure to fill up (take cash to buy gas in Andacollo, Varvarco or Las Ovejas to be on the safe side and be aware that they can have limited hours and/or fuel). Explore further north and you'll find a couple of wonderful, rarely visited attractions like hot springs and geysers, Volcán Domuyo (Patagonia's tallest peak), and an archaeological site featuring *pueblo originario* rock art.

The drive north rewards the adventurous with spectacular scenery at every turn. Not only does Cerro Domuyo loom in the distance, but it is also possible to view Volcán Tromen (4114m) and Cerro Wayle, which has a small ski resort in winter. Two hours north of Chos Malal, or 17km south of Varvarco, the impressive Parque Arqueológico Colomichicó has over 600 examples of Pehuenche rock art, one of the most important collections in Patagonia. The mysterious carvings can be seen during a three-hour trek with a local guide between January and April each year. Tours leave at both 6am and 8am.

The small settlement of Varvarco is another option as a base for exploring further north. One hour north of Varvarco, visit the Termas Aguas Calientes to soak in the natural hot springs at the base of Volcán Domuyo. They are hailed as some of the most mineral-rich waters in Argentina. The rocks can be very hot, so take care to wear proper footwear. On the way, take the detour to Los Bolillos, where the eroded rock formations create a lunar-like landscape nothing short of otherworldly. West of the hot springs you'll also find Los Tachos, geysers which spurt up to 2m. It is just a 20-minute walk each way into the canyon and you might just spot one of the world's largest and strongest birds, the Andean condor.

Situated in the heart of the park, Sistema Domuyo, the *techo* of Patagonia is said to be Volcán Domuyo, which towers over the landscape at 4702m. The adventurous can tackle the ascent, or Andestrack Patagonia has a six-day mountain-bike traverse which starts in Varvarco and includes the hot springs, Los Bolillos and pink flamingo–filled Lake Varvarco Tapia.

LAGUNA BLANCA & THE SWAN

A little-visited national park, Parque Nacional Laguna Blanca is just 30km from Zapala and a handy detour driving Ruta 40 north or heading west from Neuquén. The relative isolation of this harsh, desolate landscape has helped to protect these important wetlands, which are home to a large variety of birds. Laguna Blanca itself is a shallow lake that was formed when lava flows dammed two small streams. The name comes from the vision of the vast lagoon filled with its large flock of black-necked white swans. It is best to visit between November and March when birdlife is most abundant and the winds have subsided a little. Basic camping is available.

WHERE TO TAKE A SOAK IN HOT SPRINGS

Termas de Copahue
A large modern establishment with pools and mud pits. Only open December to April.

Termas Aguas Calientes
Mineral-rich and wild. Hop into these hot springs near Volcán Domuyo.

Termas Caviahue
During winter, the warm waters are pumped to Caviahue so skiers can soak après-ski.

DEYAN DENCHEV/SHUTTERSTOCK ©

Above: Perito Moreno Glacier (p421); Right: Seal cub, Patagonia

Patagonia

JAGGED PEAKS, GLACIERS AND MARINE WILDLIFE

Spot southern right whales along the coast, hike snowcapped mountaintops in the Andes and gallop on the Patagonian Steppe.

Patagonia presents visitors with two distinct geographical regions: the snowy, serrated mountaintops of the Andes and temperate forest in the west, and the bright blue coastline with rugged high cliffs in the east. Wildlife is a key feature too. Whales swim in the ocean, joined by penguins, sea lions and elephant seals. Guanacos, sheep and cattle graze the semi-arid steppe covered in grass and desert shrubs. There's history here as well. In the late 1800s, the Welsh colonized the area, leaving behind indulgent afternoon teas and churches. In Trelew, there's an excellent dinosaur museum. And scattered around the provinces of Chubut and Santa Cruz are swaths of million-year-old petrified forests. Making up more than a third of the country, but home to less than two million people, Patagonia is a sparsely populated part of Argentina, making it the perfect place to get away from it all. Some parts do get busy though – in January and February the majority of Argentines enjoy their summer vacations, and places like Perito Moreno glacier and hiking hub El Chaltén see lots of visitors. To escape the crowds, head to Bahía Bustamante and Cabo Raso along the mostly unpaved RP1 in eastern Chubut. Wherever you set foot, silence, adventure and a deep connection to a land that Bruce Chatwin dedicated a whole book to, and where the Tehuelche people hunted rheas and guanacos, awaits.

OLGA KOT PHOTO/SHUTTERSTOCK ©

THE MAIN AREAS

PUERTO MADRYN	ESQUEL	EL CALAFATE	EL CHALTÉN
Sea lions, penguins and whale watching.	Rivers, lakes, hiking and skiing.	The country's most famous glacier.	Mountains and Argentina's hiking capital. p429
p396	p408	p419	

Find Your Way

Patagonia covers a third of the eighth largest country in the world so traveling by land takes time. Flying can be expensive but is the most efficient way to see the region's highlights.

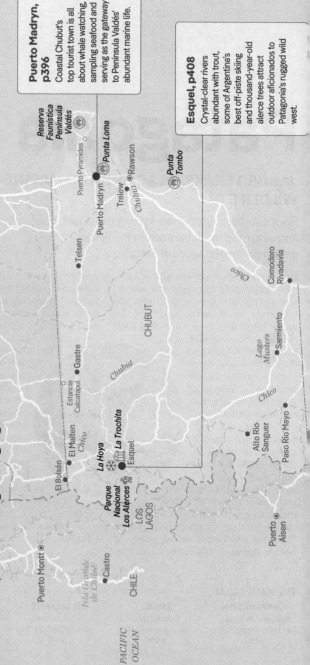

Puerto Madryn, p396

Coastal Chubut's top tourist town is all about whale watching, sampling seafood and serving as the gateway to Peninsula Valdés' abundant marine life.

Esquel, p408

Crystal-clear rivers abundant with trout, some of Argentina's best off-piste skiing and thousand-year-old alerce trees attract outdoor aficionados to Patagonia's rugged wild west.

Reserva Faunística Península Valdés

Punta Loma

Puerto Pirámides

Puerto Madryn

Trelew

Rawson

Chubut

Punta Tombo

Telsen

CHUBUT

Chico

Comodoro Rivadavia

Gastre

Chubut

Lago Musters

Sarmiento

Estancia Calcatapul

Chico

El Maitén

La Trochita

El Bolsón

La Hoya

Esquel

Alto Río Sanguer

Paso Río Mayo

Parque Nacional Los Alerces

LOS LAGOS

Puerto Aisén

Puerto Montt

Castro

Isla Grande de Chiloé

CHILE

PACIFIC OCEAN

CAR

Renting a car is a convenient way to get around and comes highly recommended if you want to access Patagonia's isolated natural beauty. Gravel roads are common in the area and easily affected by rain and snow – always check road conditions before heading out.

BUS

Long-distance buses are comfortable and usually cheaper than flying. A handful of companies operate to and from Buenos Aires to various destinations in Patagonia, including Andesmar and Don Otto. Marga Taqsa buses connect Esquel and El Calafate during peak season (January and February).

AIR

Very useful if you are short on time. The region is well served by routes from Buenos Aires (carriers include Aerolíneas Argentinas and Flybondi). Flights between destinations within Patagonia are much scarcer and in general more expensive.

Puerto Deseado

Puerto San Julián

Comandante Luis Piedrabuena

Los Antiguos

Cochrane

CHILE

Gobernador Gregores

Chico

Villa O'Higgins

Lago Cardiel

Tres Lagos

Río Santa Cruz

El Chaltén

Lago Viedma

El Calafate

Lago O'Higgins

Cerro Fitz Roy

Parque Nacional Los Glaciares

Glaciar Perito Moreno

Río Gallegos

28 de Noviembre

Gallegos

Puerto Natales

CHILE

El Calafate, p419

This town's main focus is one of the world's most famous glaciers, although there are excellent and truly remote *estancia* stays in the area too.

El Chaltén, p429

Situated at the foot of the Andes, mountain town El Chaltén is surrounded by trails taking you to beautiful glacial lakes and snowy peaks with sublime views.

R.M. NUNES/SHUTTERSTOCK ©

0   200 km
0   100 miles

Plan Your Time

Make sure to give yourself enough time for Patagonia. It's vast and travel between places can be slow, especially if your destination is served only by bus or car.

Perito Moreno Glacier (p421)

If You Only Do One Thing

● From El Calafate visit Patagonia's top attraction, the irresistible **Perito Moreno Glacier** (p421) in Parque Nacional Los Glaciares. Take a tour or drive yourself; either way you'll be astonished by this massive block of ice advancing at 2m a day, with chunks of it dropping off and crashing into the milky gray-blue Lago Argentino.

● Continue to **El Chaltén** (p429) and spend a couple of days exploring the numerous trails, using the town as your base. There's everything from easy day walks to longer multiday climbing expeditions.

Seasonal Highlights

Patagonia has something for every season – hiking and horseback riding in spring and summer, whale watching in fall and skiing in winter.

JANUARY

The peak of summer and vacationers flock to **El Calafate** (p419) and **Puerto Madryn** (p396). Expect crowds.

FEBRUARY

The tiny village of **Cholila** (p417) hosts Fiesta Nacional del Asado, a huge barbecue party with roasted lamb.

MARCH

Fiesta Nacional del Trekking takes place in **El Chaltén** (p429) with rock-climbing and wood-cutting competitions.

Six Days To Travel Around

● Fly to **Puerto Madryn** (p396) to access one of Argentina's best wildlife hotspots. Here, along Chubut Province's east coast, there are plenty of animals including whales, penguins and elephant seals.

● If here between June and December, visit **Playa El Doradillo** (p398) to watch southern right whales and their young swim just a few meters away from you.

● Then head south to **Punta Loma** (p399) and get a taste of the region's desolate but impressive coastline. Stand at the viewpoint and watch the strong Patagonian sun shine on the cobalt-blue Atlantic Ocean as a colony of sea lions go about their everyday business on the beach below.

More Than A Week

● With time and your own transportation, you can explore Patagonia's remotest locations. In **Puerto Madryn** (p396), rent a car and drive south to **Cabo Raso** (p406), a refuge from the modern world: no wi-fi or phone reception, just kilometers of coast, an elephant seal colony and the Atlantic Ocean.

● Stay in an old city bus or set up a tent and stargaze. Continue south to **Camarones** (p407), once a busy port for the wool industry, today a laid-back town and a perfect base for **Cabo Dos Bahías** (p407) – a lonely spot that's home to thousands of nesting penguins. Don't be surprised if it's just you and these cute seabirds.

JULY

Whale season really kicks off in **Puerto Madryn** (p396). Watch southern right whales and their calves from the shore.

OCTOBER

Eisteddfod del Chubut is a Welsh music and literary festival dating back to 1875, held in **Trelew** (p405).

NOVEMBER

Weather is getting warmer so from now until March is the best time to drive along Ruta Nacional 40.

DECEMBER

A good time to head to **El Calafate** (p419). Summer has started but it's cheaper and less crowded than January.

★ BUENOS
AIRES

GETTING AROUND

Puerto Madryn is very walkable and the city center is easy to navigate, with the action centered around two parallel avenues, Roca and 25 de Mayo, together with the *costanera* (the road that runs along the shoreline). Many hotels and some tour agencies rent out bikes if you want to explore further afield, including surrounding beaches. There are plenty of taxis and *remises* (taxi service with fixed rates which you have to book by phone) available for trips to Playa El Doradillo north of town to watch southern right whales, and to Punta Loma with its sea lion colony south of the city. There are a few bus lines serving Puerto Madryn but they're not very helpful for the visitor sites in town.

☑ TOP TIP

If you're going on a whale safari, plan a stay of at least 3–4 days. Boats only depart weather permitting (and that Patagonian weather can stop activities for a number of consecutive days). If a tour is cancelled companies will usually honor your booking the following day.

Puerto Madryn

Located along the Golfo Nuevo in northeast Chubut Province, Puerto Madryn is Argentina's second-largest fishing port (after Mar del Plata) and gateway to Reserva Faunística Península Valdés. The reserve is home to whales, guanacos, rheas, penguins, sea lions and elephant seals. The sprawling city, established by Welsh settlers in 1886, is Patagonia's star destination for marine wildlife watching. This is where southern right whales come to breed – spot them from the beach at Playa El Doradillo and view sea lions on the shores at Punta Loma. What will most likely be a highlight of your trip is also on offer: swimming with inquisitive sea lions.

ALEXIS FIORAMONTI/GETTY IMAGES ©

Southern right whale, Península Valdés (p399)

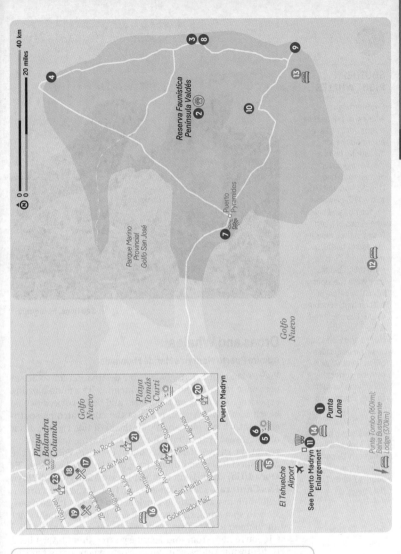

TOP SIGHTS
1. Punta Loma
2. Reserva Faunística Península Valdés

SIGHTS
3. Caleta Valdés
4. Estancia La Ernestina
5. Playa El Doradillo
6. Playa Las Canteras
7. Puerto Pirámides
8. Punta Cantor
9. Punta Delgada
10. Salina Chica

ACTIVITIES, COURSES & TOURS
11. Madryn Buceo

SLEEPING
12. Estancia El Pedral
13. Estancia Rincón Chico
14. Hotel Territorio
15. La Calandria B&B
16. La Tosca Hostel

EATING
17. Chona
18. Hotel Península Valdés
19. Hotel Tolosa
see 17 Matilde

DRINKING & NIGHTLIFE
20. Barrika Bar de Tapas
21. Cervecería Artesanal Kaiser
22. Cervecería Cerro Parva
23. James Bar

SOUTHERN RIGHT WHALES

Southern right whales, or the *ballena franca austral*, have enormous heads measuring up to a third or a quarter of their total body. Hunted from the 17th to the 19th centuries for their oil and baleen (the series of filters found in their mouths instead of teeth), their name derives from the belief that they were the 'right whale' to catch, due to their high economic value. The sheltered waters of Golfo Nuevo and Golfo San José, on both sides of Península Valdés, provide perfect conditions for them to give birth to and raise their calves, meaning around 500 whales arrive here in early June and stay until early December before continuing south towards Tierra del Fuego.

FOTO 4440/SHUTTERSTOCK ©
OPPOSITE PAGE: POL CALCA/SHUTTERSTOCK ©

Sea lions, Patagonia

Orcas and Whales
Admire Puerto Madryn's Marine Mammals

Puerto Madryn is Patagonia's star destination for some superb once-in-a-lifetime wildlife watching. It's a mind-blowing experience standing on the brown and beige-colored pebble beaches of Golfo Nuevo, north of the city, watching southern right whales play around in the high tide right in front of you. Every year in mid-June, these marine mammals arrive at the shores of eastern Chubut to breed. For one of the most spectacular sightings, drive or take a taxi to **Playa El Doradillo,** about 11km north of Puerto Madryn, and **Playa Las Canteras**, a few kilometers further. If you hire a driver, a 90-minute wait is always included in the fee. It's also possible to spot whales in the city itself; during season it's not uncommon to see calves playing in the harbor at high tide.

If you're here from mid-February through mid-April head to Península Valdés and Punta Norte where orcas hunt by sliding on to the beach to catch unsuspecting sea lion pups. Even if you're not lucky enough to see them on the land, just spotting the orcas' fins in the water is a thrilling experience. Always check when high tide is before you head off – many

 WHERE TO STAY

Hotel Tolosa
Modern and bright hotel with welcoming staff. Great breakfast buffet with eggs and small desserts. **$$**

Hotel Territorio
Located south of the city center and close to the beach; all rooms have ocean views. **$$$**

La Tosca Hostel
Clean and spacious hostel with a lovely garden and a well-equipped shared kitchen. **$**

hotels have the weekly schedule printed out and posted in the elevator/reception, or ask the very helpful tourist office on Av Roca for one.

Exploring Península Valdés
Whale Watching, Kayaking and Penguins

To get the most out of the **Reserva Faunística Península Valdés**, rent a car. Devote at least a couple of days to soaking up the views of the sandstone cliffs, listening to the brawling seals on the Atlantic shores and, if visiting between March and April, watching for orcas hunting in **Punta Norte**. From mid-June to mid-December people flock to Puerto Pirámides – the only town in the reserve, named after a pointed cliff in the bay – to board boats and catch a glimpse of the southern right whales temporarily inhabiting the waters. There are five licensed tour operators charging the same; one, Southern Spirit, also offers a trip on their semi-submersible Yellow Submarine with underwater views of the huge animals when visibility is good.

In addition to Puerto Pirámides, the reserve can be divided into three parts: Punta Norte in the north; **Punta Cantor** in the east; and **Punta Delgada** in the south. Use Puerto Pirámides as your base or stay at **Estancia Rincón Chico**, just southwest of Punta Delgada. Included in your room rate at Rincón Chico is a guided visit to the *estancia*'s private beach, where 10,000 elephant seals and up to 3500 sea lions gather to breed from December to March each year. Dolphins, orcas, whales and penguins can also be spotted along the property's 16km-long coastline. From Punta Delgada, driving inland on the unpaved RP2, make a stop at **Salina Grande** and **Salina Chica**, two salt flats which, at 42m below sea level, are some of the world's lowest continental depressions.

Penguin,
Chubut

BEST PLACES FOR WILDLIFE SPOTTING

Península Valdés
One of Patagonia's most famous wildlife spots for cetaceans including orcas and southern right whales.

Punta Tombo
With roughly a million Magellanic penguins, this is continental South America's largest nesting ground for these seabirds.

Bahía Bustamante
Private *estancia* with plenty of wildlife including dolphins and the endemic steamer duck.

Punta Loma
South of Puerto Madryn, this small natural reserve is home to a lively sea lion colony.

Cabo Dos Bahías
Punta Tombo's younger cousin has its fair share of Magellanic penguins, but without the human crowds.

WHERE TO EAT

Matilde
The best and most popular *parrilla* in town. Don't miss their delicious Patagonian lamb. $$

Chona
Extensive menu featuring pasta, meat and a few seafood dishes such as shrimp with butter and garlic. $$

Hotel Tolosa Restaurante
Affordable restaurant inside Hotel Tolosa run by a friendly matriarchy. The meat empanadas are a must. $$

399

TICIANA GIEHL/SHUTTERSTOCK ©

TOP SIGHT

Reserva Faunística Península Valdés

PRACTICALITIES

Scan this QR code for more information.

An hour's drive north from Puerto Madryn, Reserva Faunística Península Valdés, a magically blue coastline filled with nesting penguins, southern right whales and elephant seals, takes home the gold for spotting Argentina's wildlife up close. It's one of the most important marine reserves in the world and the only place on Earth where you can watch orcas hunt on land.

DON'T MISS

Puerto Pirámides

Punta Pirámides

La Ernestina

Punta Norte

Punta Delgada

Caleta Valdés

Planning & Arrival

To make the most of the peninsula, stay in Puerto Pirámides and rent a car. This way you can set out early in the morning and beat the crowds. Also, by staying in Puerto Pirámides you only pay the reserve's entrance fee once. To start, decide which animals you want to see and plan accordingly. For orcas hunting on the beach, there are two seasons: March and April, when they head to Punta Norte to try their luck grabbing newborn sea lion pups; and October through December when they hunt for elephant seal pups in Caleta Valdés, 30km from Punta Norte. The reserve might look small on the map but you can easily spend days exploring it: one day for the north section, a second for the eastern parts and one day in Puerto Pirámides if opting for a whale tour. It's also important to remember that weather can be unpredictable and affect your plans; boats don't depart if the winds are too strong and rangers shut roads if the rain has been particularly heavy.

Sea lion colony, Península Valdés

WHERE TO STAY

There are not many options outside of Puerto Pirámides and most people would claim that there's no lodging in Punta Norte at all – but this is not entirely true. There is one: La Ernestina. It's a working sheep ranch with six guest rooms and is home to Punta Norte Orca Research, so it has unique access to many of the beaches where orcas hunt on land.

Puerto Pirámides

Puerto Pirámides is the main town on Península Váldes and from where all the whale safaris depart. Except for when busloads of tourists arrive to head out to try to spot southern right whales between June and December, this is a quiet place. If you're staying overnight – there are a couple of decent options – a truly local experience is standing on the beach in the dark, trying to hear the whales out in the ocean. Starting northwest of town, a 5km walk around the headland takes you to Punta Pirámides, a good spot, especially in January, to catch sea lions. You can also drive there.

Punta Norte

Located on the very northern tip of the peninsula, Punta Norte is less than 80km north of Puerto Pirámides along a gravel road. This is the prime location for watching orcas ambush sea lion pups on the beach from March to April. The rest of the year you can see Magellanic penguins and elephant seals. Drive with caution as both wild animals and sheep roam the area, and stock up with food and petrol if you plan to spend a whole day here; there are no stores or gas stations, just restrooms.

Caleta Valdés

Occupying the central coast of the reserve, Caleta Valdés is around 75km by gravel road from Puerto Pirámides. From roughly the end of September to mid-April you can watch Magellanic penguins who come here to nest. On the southern tip of Caleta Valdés, also called Punta Cantor, is a group of elephant seals who station themselves on the shores to breed and shed their winter coats. Here you find public restrooms, an information board and trails along the coastline.

TOP TIPS

- Always check road conditions with the rangers at the entrance or the Centro de Visitantes Istmo Carlos Ameghino.
- The RP2 from Puerto Madryn to Puerto Pirámides is paved; the rest of the road network is gravel and affected by poor weather.
- Rangers shutting roads due to heavy rain/snow or wildlife accidents is fairly common.
- Tours from Puerto Madryn don't usually include Punta Norte; if they do, they don't take the tides into account (essential to spot orcas from the beach).
- If you're committed to watching orcas it's best to arrange your own transportation.

BEST PLACES TO STAY IN COASTAL CHUBUT

Bahía Bustamante
Private wildlife haven with endemic birds, penguins, whales and sea lions. Stay in a seaside cabin for the best views. **$$$**

Cabo Raso
Isolated *refugio* with kilometers of coastline offering camping, B&B rooms and sleeping in old city buses. **$-$$**

Estancia Rincón Chico
Stylish, secluded ranch on Península Valdés with views of the Patagonian Steppe. **$$$**

Estancia El Pedral
1920s ranch where you can see Magellanic penguins in September. Prices include all meals. **$$$**

La Calandria B&B
A few kilometers from Playa El Doradillo, this cute B&B offers cozy bungalows surrounded by lavender fields. **$$$**

CHRISSTOCKPHOTOGRAPHY/ALAMY STOCK PHOTO ©

Estancia El Pedral

Savoring Seafood and Patagonian Lamb

Try Regional Delicacies

It's not surprising that Puerto Madryn, Patagonia's biggest fishing port, offers some of the freshest seafood in Argentina. *Arroz con mariscos* – the city's take on a Spanish paella with rice, shrimp, squid and mussels – is a local specialty, best enjoyed with a cold glass of Chardonnay. The beachfront has a handful of restaurants serving up other treats from the ocean. Just about every eating option in the city features at least one or two seafood dishes, including the *parrillas* (steakhouses). At **Barrika Bar de Tapas** there's plenty of sushi on the menu, plus small dishes similar to tapas. Pick the tortilla topped with battered shrimp and the squid *escabeche* which uses the traditional Spanish method of marinating cooked or pickled food in an acidic sauce.

For gratinated scallops with a cold glass of Pinot Grigio, grab a window seat at **Hotel Península Valdés'** dim-lit restaurant. Since 1977, the lamb festival (Fiesta Nacional del Cordero) has been held in Puerto Madryn, celebrating the regional meat delicacy. The smell of whole roasted lamb fills the streets of the city for three days in mid-February, and events showcasing the local gauchos' sheep-shearing skills draw the

WHERE TO DRINK

James Bar
Popular *cervecería* near where the cruise ships dock. Flavorful IPAs on tap.

Cervecería Cerro Parva
Beer made with pure spring water from the Parva peak in the center of Chubut Province.

Cervecería Artesanal Kaiser
Small, friendly beer house making their own IPAs, porters and ales. Happy hour 6–8pm.

crowds, as does the annual coronation of La Reina del Cordero (lamb queen). If you're in Puerto Madryn any other time of year, you can savor succulent grilled lamb from the area's *estancias* at **Matilde**, washing it down with a bottle of red blend. Servings are generous – a grilled platter of meat for two should feed three to four people.

Get Close to the Wildlife

Snorkel with Sea Lions

Puerto Madryn's coast is home to an abundance of sea lions meaning this is *the* place to swim with these playful and curious animals. The breed you find in the waters around the city are South American sea lions, distinguished by a coat of short hair, usually brown with an orange and yellow belly. For your own close encounter with them, **Madryn Buceo** arranges trips. The tour includes a brief training in responsible snorkeling, an English-speaking instructor and a return boat trip to Punta Loma, 20km south of Puerto Madryn, where a colony of 500 sea lions live.

The tour company will instruct you to keep quiet so as not to scare the animals and to stay at a respectful distance once you are in the water, letting the sea lions approach you rather than you them. Groups are also kept small (usually never more than 10 people) to disturb the colony as little as possible. There are daily departures (weather permitting), but book 24 hours ahead. The tour lasts roughly 2½ hours, and you get about 45 minutes in the water with the creatures. If you have a PADI certificate, you can dive with them too. It costs a bit extra but is worth it if you want an even closer experience. **Costas de Patagonia** stick to experiences with sea lions on rather than below water level in the Golfo de San José in Península Valdés; you can kayak among them all year round.

Traditional asado roasted lamb

PATAGONIA LANDSCAPES/SHUTTERSTOCK ©

THE PATAGONIAN COAST

Madelaine Triebe, writer

Sitting by the Patagonian coast at night, listening to the Atlantic Ocean under a starry sky, calmed by the waves and the Patagonian wind is one of my dearest travel memories. We got to Cabo Raso by car on the unpaved RP1 not really knowing where we were heading. There was a sense of adventure and freedom, the thrilling feeling of not knowing what to expect that any road trip in Patagonia evokes. Once there, we stepped out of the car and looked around. It felt like we had stepped into a movie scene depicting Earth abandoned by humans. It's exactly those things I love about Patagonia's coast; desolate, vast and seemingly impervious to human domination.

Beyond
Puerto Madryn

Puerto Madryn's surrounding area includes Welsh teahouses, a superb dinosaur museum, a petrified forest and a desolate coastline dotted with wildlife.

You don't have to travel far beyond Puerto Madryn to sample some very different Patagonia experiences. In Trelew, 65km south, there's Welsh culture and the excellent and beautifully organized Museo Paleontológico Egidio Feruglio exhibiting massive dinosaur skeletons and eggs. A few hours further south along RP1, you find what seems like endless views of the arid Patagonian Steppe, some of the country's largest penguin colonies and remote accommodations and *estancias* – one even with its own private 60-million-year-old petrified forest – perfect for spending your days close to the ocean without another person in sight, connecting to nature and being treated to big skies by the dramatic Patagonian coast.

GETTING AROUND

It's essential to have your own wheels. Public transportation is very limited, and although cities and towns are served by regional buses most of the time, tourist and natural sights are usually not.

MAF/ALAMY STOCK PHOTO ©

Museo Paleontológico Egidio Feruglio

Ty Gwyn

Trelew

TIME FROM PUERTO MADRYN: **50 MINS-1HR**

Homemade Cakes and Scones, Welsh-Style

Coastal Chubut Province is synonymous with Welsh heritage to most Argentines. This is where – of all the places in the world – new arrivals from Wales settled at the end of the 1800s. Coming by boat, they were looking to escape oppression at home and to preserve their culture and language, which they felt were being threatened. They made a home in the Chubut Valley, cultivating the land, and later founded both Puerto Madryn and **Trelew**. Today, most visitors can get a taste of Welsh heritage by visiting one of the many *casas de té* that still serve an indulgent, traditional afternoon tea. For the most famous and biggest selection of teahouses, travel to **Gaiman**, a tiny village in a river valley 20km from Trelew.

This is where locals pride themselves on telling the story of when the late Princess Diana came to the town and had tea. Every year, a candle is lit on the day of her death to honor the former Princess of Wales. Two of the best teahouses are local favorite **Ty Gwyn** and the charming **Plas y Coed**, with Welsh-language posters and photos decorating the walls. Expect a bottomless pot of tea served with an assortment of cakes, including the mandatory Torta Negra (dark fruit cake),

☑ **TOP TIP**

Having your own vehicle is the best way to get around. Rent a car to access the area's remote places.

CHUBUT'S WELSH HERITAGE

In 1865 the first Welsh immigrants arrived in Patagonia looking for religious and political freedom, but life on the South American continent proved hard at first. The land that was promised to the 150 settlers who had traveled 8000 miles with the desire to protect their culture and language was originally territory occupied by the indigenous Tehuelche and not fertile. Growing crops was a futile operation due to both droughts and floods, but thanks to irrigation systems and the help of the locals who taught them to hunt, the Welsh managed to survive, establishing themselves on Chubut's east coast where they later founded both Puerto Madryn and Trelew.

 WHERE TO STAY IN TRELEW & GAIMAN

La Casona del Río (Trelew)
Charming posada with helpful English-speaking owners and garden, and rooms with parquet floors. **$$**

Posada Los Mimbres (Gaiman)
Enjoy lush countryside a short walk from town at this inn with spacious, bright rooms. **$$**

Hostería Gwesty Plas y Coed (Gaiman)
Pair your stay with Welsh cakes and scones served in the tearoom next door. **$**

THE TEHUELCHE PEOPLE

Before Europeans arrived, the Tehuelche people inhabited the eastern Patagonian plains.

They were nomadic and divided into northern and southern branches, each with their own distinct culture and dialect.

Believed to hunt solely on foot for over 3000 years, they were introduced to the horse by the Spanish in the early 1700s and the animals became an integral part of their lives.

The Europeans also brought war and disease and a rapid decline in Patagonia's native populations. By the end of the 1800s, only an estimated 1500 Tehuelche survived.

Today there's no evidence that there are any Tehuelche people left – the last ones were believed to have lived on two reserves in Santa Cruz Province. There are, however, a number of communities still claiming Tehuelche heritage.

OPPOSITE PAGE: FOTO 4440/SHUTTERSTOCK ©

La Ernestina

homemade scones with jams and bread. To burn off the culinary delights, a leisurely stroll around the town center past its stone houses and rose gardens is a good option.

Cabo Raso and La Ernestina

TIME FROM PUERTO MADRYN TO CABO RASO: **3HRS 25 MINS** 🚗

TIME FROM PUERTO MADRYN TO LA ERNESTINA: **2HRS 30 MINS** 🚗

Hit Patagonia's (In)famous Gravel Roads.

The area around Puerto Madryn offers some strikingly isolated spots. Which makes sense, given that Patagonia is home to more sheep than people while covering almost all of southern mainland Argentina with its 673,396 sq km. To access this secluded beauty and its clear blue coastline, rent a car – public transportation is scarce. From Trelew, drive south on the unpaved but well-maintained RP1 until you get to the unique refuge that is **Cabo Raso**, a former thriving sheep-ranching settlement abandoned in the 1950s, now a remote retreat created by a lovely Patagonian couple from Trelew.

You can book a room in the wonderfully decorated guesthouse or stay in one of the stone houses. For budget travelers, there are refurbished buses with no electricity or heating – where you sleep in a bunk bed listening to the howling Pa-

WHERE TO EAT IN TRELEW & GAIMAN

Sugar (Trelew)
In front of Trelew's main square, this contemporary restaurant serves elegantly composed meat and seafood dishes. **$$$**

Restaurante de Hotel de Libertador (Trelew)
Classic restaurant serving meat and seafood dishes and with an extensive wine list. **$$$**

Na Petko (Gaiman)
Dine accompanied by the rippling sound of the Chubut River at this charming gastro pub serving homemade pizza. **$$**

tagonian wind outside – and a campsite by a *quincho* (patio and barbecue area) where you can set up your tent. Heading instead north from Puerto Madryn towards Península Valdés, make the remote sheep farm of **Estancia La Ernestina** your home for a few nights. Almost at the end of gravel road RP47 towards Punta Norte, you'll enjoy 20km of private coastline, passing hours hunched on the beach, trying to see the site's claim to fame – orcas hunting on land.

Head South
Off the Beaten Path

TIME FROM PUERTO MADRYN: **3HRS 40 MINS–9HRS** 🚗

Straying south from Puerto Madryn, it's fairly easy to have a more intimate moment with the marine fauna, though you need time and a car to do so. From the city, drive south on RN3 and then take a left onto RP30 to get to **Camarones**. Stay the night in this sleepy fishing village. In the morning, drive 30km southeast to **Cabo Dos Bahías**, a natural reserve where you can see guanacos, rheas and foxes, but barely any humans, together with a healthy colony of Magellanic penguins which nest, in the South American spring and summer, under the wooden boardwalk that takes you down to the beach here.

In winter, look for whales and fur seals. Lining up to get fitted with a life vest and a rain poncho together with 40 other people before being ushered onto a boat in Puerto Pirámides to spot whales, or being one of the numerous visitors heading to Punta Tombo to watch Magellanic penguins, now seems far away. A little further south there's **Bahía Bustamante**; an 80-hectare private *estancia* with penguins and sea lions dotted along its deserted coast. The excursions here are for guests only and are run by English-speaking naturalists. About a 9hr drive south from Puerto Madryn you find another unfrequented gem; the estuary of **Río Deseado**, full of marine wildlife including dolphins, seabirds and rockhopper penguins with their mullet-like hairdo.

Guanacos,
Península Valdés

BEST MUSEUMS BEYOND PUERTO MADRYN

Museo Paleontológico Egidio Feruglio
Trelew museum housing one of the continent's most important paleontological collections spanning 300 million years.

Centro de Visitantes Istmo Ameghino
Reserva Faunística Península Valdés' visitor center with lots of information on the reserve's wild animals.

Museo Pueblo de Luis
Housed in Trelew's old train station, this museum tells the story of the Mapuche and Tehuelche people, and Patagonia's Welsh settlers.

Museo Historico Regional Gales
Gaiman's regional museum focuses on the history and development of the village's Welsh community and heritage.

Museo de la Familia Perón
Multistory museum covering the life of Argentine president Juan Perón who led the country between 1946 and 1955.

BUENOS AIRES

Esquel

GETTING AROUND

Esquel is easy to get around on foot; the town is small and divided into square blocks, making it easy to navigate. If you are pressed for time, take a taxi, or if you don't want to walk and are on a budget there are three town buses, lines 1, 2 and 3, but you need a prepaid bus card from a *kiosko* (small shop) in town.

☑ TOP TIP

Summer (December through February) and winter (July and August) are when accommodations prices in Esquel and around reach their peak. Visit in low season instead to get large discounts, though remember that many establishments shut in Parque Nacional Los Alerces after Easter and usually don't re-open until November.

Esquel, in northwestern Chubut Province, is a straightforward, unpretentious town that lets the surrounding natural beauty speak for itself. Its location close to the Patagonian Andean Forest and just 45km east of Parque Nacional Los Alerces means most visitors use Esquel as a base to explore the wider region – and to ride the endearing *La Trochita,* one of Patagonia's beloved steam trains. Founded in 1906 by Welsh immigrants, the town is a center for livestock and commerce. It's surrounded by the arid *meseta patagónica* (the plateau making up northern Patagonia), a landscape covered with shrubs and grass. In contrast to the lush forest with its relatively wet weather, summers in Esquel are dry. Come winter, the Andean peaks are painted with white powder, drawing skiers and snowboarders to Cerro La Hoya.

La Trochita

TOP SIGHTS
1 La Hoya
2 Parque Nacional Los Alerces

SIGHTS
see 12 Beviamo Wine House
3 Glaciar Torrecillas
4 La Hoya
5 La Trochita
6 Lago Futalaufquen
7 Lago Krüger
8 Lago Menéndez
9 Nahuel Pan
see 2 Parque Nacional Los Alerces
10 Puerto Chucao
11 Villa Futalaufquen

ACTIVITIES, COURSES & TOURS
12 Patagonia Verde
13 Rossi Ski Rental

SLEEPING
14 Carrileufu River Lodge
15 Dormis Acá
see 22 Hostería Canela B&B
16 Hostería Cumbres Blancas
17 Ibai Ko Mendi
18 Laguna Larga Lodge
see 12 Las Bayas

EATING
19 Coolibreat
20 Don Chiquino
21 PilPil Sabores de la Patagonia

DRINKING & NIGHTLIFE
22 La Gintonería de Cinco Cerros
23 Rider Brewing Bar

IN THE FOOTSTEPS OF AN ABANDONED TRAIL

There's Sweden's Kungsleden, the USA's Appalachian Trail and in Patagonia there was supposed to be the Huella Andina, a 600-km-long walking route through five national parks in the region's north. It was initiated in 2008 by wife and husband Estefanía Chereguini and Walter Oszust, and the couple received government funding for the project. But in 2016 when the tourism board in Argentina stopped receiving money from the ruling party, the dreams of a free trail running from Lago Aluminé in Neuquén to Lago Bagillt in Chubut stopped. The official website is long gone, but the trails and a few signposts are still there, including the last stretch to Bagillt Lake, a challenging 15km hike starting at RN259, 55km southwest of Esquel.

OPPOSITE PAGE: ALFREDO CERRA/SHUTTERSTOCK ©

Snowboarding, Esquel

Hit the Slopes

Skiing in the Andes

Of all the ski resorts in Argentina, **La Hoya** – named after the mountain shape that consists of a wide glacier on top of a basin – is considered one of the most affordable and, though it offers some of the country's best powder, is also relatively unknown. Located only 12km north of Esquel, it's one of the country's most accessible resorts, and has a season that runs from June all the way through to October.

Stay in Esquel, where you have plenty of superb accommodations choices and chilled places to down regional artisanal beer with relaxed snowboarders. Check into 4-star hotel **Las Bayas** and get your gear from **Rossi Ski Rental** on Av Fontana (or onsite at **Ski Rental de la Hoya**). Heading to the mountain, you don't really need your own car; there are plenty of inexpensive minivan shuttles taking you from your hotel to the slopes. Alternatively, you can call a *remise* to make the 20-minute drive on an unpaved, albeit broad and usually well-maintained, road.

Once at La Hoya you have 30 runs catering to different abilities to choose from. If you are after some adventure, join the thrill-seekers going off-piste – plenty of short backcountry

 WHERE TO FISH

Río Futaleufú
Chile's turquoise river flows through the Andes into Argentina, where it's also called Río Grande.

Río Pico
About 2½ hrs drive south of Esquel this small river attracts fishers for its big trout.

Arroyo Pescado
A spring creek entirely on private land just over a 40-minute drive southeast of Esquel.

hikes take you to some of the region's best descents. For beginners, there's a small ski school. To miss the crowds, avoid July when Argentine kids go on winter school holidays, and families flock to the slopes.

Connect with Nature

Hiking and Camping

Take advantage of Esquel's gorgeous natural setting and pack your camping gear; the town's surroundings offer tranquil campsites near clear green rivers and accessible trails through temperate forests in **Parque Nacional Los Alerces**. This is uncharted territory for most travelers. Reach the park, which protects some of the largest forests of the endemic alerce (Patagonian cypress) trees in Patagonia, by public transportation – in peak season, two daily buses run here from Esquel's bus terminal; check with the tourism office for the timetable. Alternatively, and more easily as with most places in Patagonia, bring your own wheels.

Regional food delicacies such as cheese and homemade jams are often sold along the road, but pack enough provisions to last your whole stay: there are only a couple of very basic stores in **Villa Futalaufquen**, situated within the national park some 12km beyond one of the park's three entrances, Centro Portada. Set up your tent by the turquoise shores of **Lago Futalaufquen** at the eponymous campsite and choose from the wide range of day hikes that can be done around the lake. There is the very accessible and easy **Pinturas Rupestres route**, which passes 3000-year-old indigenous paintings, and the much more challenging trek (you must

Lago Futalaufquen

WINE IN CHUBUT

Mendoza may be the queen of wine production in Argentina, but there are vineyards as far down south as Chubut in Patagonia. One of the southernmost places in the world to grow grapes like Chardonnay, Sauvignon Blanc, Pinot Noir and Torrontés, the province is home to a small number of producers, including **Viñas del Nant y Fall** in the Trevelin Valley and **Otronia** in Sarmiento, close to Lago Chubut. As expected, winters are cold and temperatures below zero are common. To get around this, all vineyards in the province are situated around large rivers and lakes as the bodies of water help mitigate the frost damage on the harvest.

WHERE TO DRINK

La Gintonería de Cinco Cerros
Gin bar where you'll find bottles of Esquel's very own Gin Bräse, plus occasional live music.

Rider Brewing Bar
Cervecería with a vast choice of regional craft beer on tap. Happy hour 6–9pm.

Beviamo Wine House
Stylish bar with a great selection of boutique wines by the bottle or glass.

BEST PLACES TO STAY

Hostería Canela B&B
A comfortable and friendly bed-and-breakfast a few kilometers from town featuring a fireplace and mountain views. **$$**

Ibai Ko Mendi
Cozy cabins with kitchen and private bathroom. Heated indoor pool and sauna onsite too. **$$**

Hostería Cumbres Blancas
Charming inn with Andes views and a restaurant, just off Esquel's main avenue. **$$**

Las Bayas
Six sleek and bright suites with king-size beds, adjacent to a wine and tapas bar in the center of town. **$$$**

Dormis Acá
Modern and minimalist hostel in the center of town with snug beds, spacious dorms and plenty of common areas to hang out. **$**

LAURA VANHORLEGAN/SHUTTERSTOCK ©

Lago Menéndez

register at the visitor center in Villa Futalaufquen before you start) to the campsite and refuge at the south end of **Lago Krüger**; you can do it in a day, about 12 hours stiff walking, or break up the long hike, camp on Playa Blanca and return the following day the same way you came, or by boat.

Chasing Adventure
Get your Adrenaline Going

With its high mountains, wild and desolate landscape and open spaces, Patagonia attracts adventurers from all corners of the country and the world. And the small corner of it occupied by Esquel is no exception. Here, thrill-seekers swoosh down **Río Corcovado** white-water rafting, kayak on the **Río Grande** or go hiking to high glacier lakes surrounded by Andean peaks. There are plenty of options to push your adrenaline levels. Parque Nacional Los Alerces (p411) is close by: drive 45km southeast on RP259 and continue west on RP71 and you arrive at Centro Portada, the main entry point to the park.

To discover its clear rivers and lakes, woodlands and mountains, take one of the trails that wend through it – ranging from easy to difficult, there's a trek for every ability. To find out more, visit Esquel's tourism office on Av Alvear to start

 WHERE TO EAT

Don Chiquino
One of Esquel's most popular places, with plenty of pasta on the menu, including lamb ravioli. **$$$**

PilPil Sabores de la Patagonia
Regional ingredients are important at this restaurant, with both lamb and trout on the menu. **$$$**

Coolibreat
Young and vibrant pasta bar where hip bartenders mix delicious and good-looking cocktails. **$$$**

with; the staff's English is limited, so if your Spanish is not up to par check out their decent website instead. In winter, nothing beats an off-piste adventure in Cerro La Hoya, while in summer you can take the boat from **Puerto Chucao** on **Lago Menéndez** to **Puerto Nuevo** and from there do the 2hr ascent to **Glaciar Torrecillas**, hiking through forests of alerce trees. Long-running **Patagonia Verde** has more than 30 years' experience and can take you rafting in the region, or bike down unpaved roads and zip-line with **EPA Expediciones**.

Board the Old Patagonian Express

Take a Steam Train

La Trochita, which translates to Little Narrow Gauge, is a popular tourist attraction and one of South America's classic train rides. Originally part of Ferrocarriles Patagónicos – a network of railways in Argentine Patagonia that ran from the south of Río Negro Province to Esquel between 1945 and 1993 – today it serves as a charming tourist train chugging through Chubut's open grassland. Boarding in Esquel takes you through the property of one of Patagonia's largest landowners, Italian fashion family Benetton, looking out over the arid rolling steppe of northern Chubut where you can spot guanacos, maras and even condors if you are lucky.

Internationally, *La Trochita* was made famous by Paul Theroux's novel *The Old Patagonian Express*, in which he describes it as a railway at almost the end of the world. Although this is not true – there are railways way further south in Argentina – a trip on this steam train with its wooden benches and open windows feels like stepping onto the set of a Wild West movie. So much, in fact, that on selected days each year (usually in May and September but check the website beforehand), a spectacular show called Asalto al Tren is added to your trip, when galloping horseback-riding robbers approach, hijacking the 100-year-old train.

Most visitors take a half-day excursion from Esquel to the small village of **Nahuel Pan**, a little more than 20km away, but there are also departures throughout the year from **El Maitén** to the border of Río Negro Province and then back again. Check latrochita.org.ar for the timetable and to buy tickets.

TOP SIGHTS IN ESQUEL AND AROUND

El Abuelo
A gigantic 2600-year-old alerce tree measuring 2.2m in diameter and 57m in height.

La Trochita
Narrow gauge-train running from Esquel to Nahuel Pan and from El Maitén to Ñorquincó and back.

Playa Blanca
Beautiful beach in Parque Nacional Los Alerces where you can camp (park permission needed).

El Dedal Circuit
Rather steep hike to El Dedal peak, with lovely panoramic views; takes 6–7 hours round trip.

Los Vascos
General store from 1926 with wooden shelves and ladders selling everything from hats to groceries.

Lago
Epuyén
Epuyén

Cholila

Esquel

Trevelin

Beyond
Esquel

Crystal-clear lakes, dense temperate forest and Welsh heritage – the region around Esquel is a mix of enticing nature with a splash of settler history.

Lying between the deep forest and lakes of the Andean foothills and the Patagonian Steppe, Esquel's surroundings have their fair share of natural beauty – wide stretches of shrubland, lush pine forests and trout-filled rivers and lakes. Nearby waters offer excellent fly-fishing, and a couple of hours' drive along RN40, small Cholila is where you can follow in the footsteps of Butch Cassidy and the Sundance Kid, who both settled here in the 1900s. A 30min drive southwest of Esquel along RN259 will take you to Trevelin, the only Welsh settlement in inland Patagonia, and further west, the elusive, endemic and endangered huemul (South Andean deer) live high up the Andean mountains.

GETTING AROUND

Public transportation is scarce although smaller towns are served by regional buses. To truly enjoy the highlights and less visited sites of the region, rent a car.

☑ **TOP TIP**

Visit in shoulder season (Sept-Nov & March-April) when accommodations are usually cheaper. Bear in mind that during Semana Santa (Easter week) prices soar.

Sulo/Shutterstock ©

Tulips, Trevelin (416)

SUNSINGER / SHUTTERSTOCK ©

Piedra Parada

Ruta Nacional 40

Experience Indigenous Culture and its Glorious Past

Explore indigenous culture and history as well as underexplored highlights on this celebrated highway. Pick up your rental car in Esquel and get on the RP259 towards Nahuel Pan. After 12km, turn right onto RN40. After 3km – when you see the restaurant Sabor de Mapuche – turn left. Follow the road for 1km and turn left to arrive at Nahuel Pan's Museo de Culturas Originarias Patagónicas, which covers the story, culture and crafts of Chubut's Mapuche people. It's open when La Trochita (p413) makes a stop here, plus during special events. To further immerse yourself in indigenous history, continue north on RN40 and visit the private estate of one of the biggest landowners in the country, Estancia Leleque, owned by the Italian fashion family Benetton. Museo Leleque, situated along RP15 just off the RN40 in a charmingly restored building, is the only part of the ranch open to the public.

Spread over four rooms, this museum tells the history of the Tehuelche people and their relationship with the European arrivals. Don't miss the general store and canteen where you can have a drink and a bite to eat surrounded by old, well-preserved knickknacks. From the museum, continue north

WHERE TO STAY FOR FLY-FISHING AROUND ESQUEL

Fly-fishing is a big deal around Esquel, drawing angling enthusiasts who stay at specialist lodges that are equally accommodating to non-fishers.

Carrileufu Valley Lodge (Cholila)
Impeccably decorated lodge with wooden walls, a high ceiling and a big fireplace in the Carrileufu Valley. $$$

Estancia Tecka Lodge
Working sheep ranch with wi-fi, spacious rooms and 96 miles of private land to catch trout. $$$

Laguna Larga Lodge
Situated by a lake in Parque Nacional Los Alerces, this hotel has a private beach and pier. $$$

 OTHER SIGHTS TO SEE

Viñas de Nant y Fall
The area's first winery produces excellent Pinot Noirs. There's also an inn and a campsite.

Piedra Parada
A 200m-high rock in the middle of the Patagonian Steppe attracts advanced rock climbers.

El Campo de Tulipanes
Tulip fields in various colors in the Nant y Fall valley. Open Oct to beginning of Nov.

THE SOUTH ANDEAN DEER

Standing at a little less than 1m at the shoulder, the huemul, a small Patagonian deer native to Argentina and Chile, is as short as it is endangered. Due to deforestation, poaching, massive habitat loss and competition over land with domestic livestock, fewer than 1500 are left in the wild today. Two-thirds of those are in Chile, while in Argentina your only chance of seeing one is is in Patagonia's Parque Nacional Los Alerces. Here, in winter, if weather conditions are particularly harsh, they descend from the mountains to Playa El Francés on the shores of Lago Futalaufquen in search of food.

Butch Cassidy and Sundance Kid's former home

on RN40 and stop in El Maitén – a lesser-known point of departure for the La Trochita steam train – to visit the Railway Museum as well as the workshop to get an insight into the maintenance work of this narrow gauge steam train. To return to Esquel, follow the RN1S40 for 30 minutes, then turn left onto RN40.

Trevelin
TIME FROM ESQUEL: **30 MINS**
Welsh Cakes and Culture Clash in Patagonia

Most Welsh settlements are near Patagonia's coast – with the exception of **Trevelin**, a small village 24km south of Esquel. The first colonizers to explore this region were colonel Fontana of the Argentine army and Welsh settler John Evans, arriving in 1885 and founding the village soon after. Meaning town (*tre*) mill (*velin*) in Welsh, in reference to flour mills built by pioneers, its inhabitants take pride in their heritage – visit at the end of October for the Eisteddfod (cultural celebration) or visit one of the town's two *casas de té* (teahouses) any time. The best is **Nain Maggie**, dating back to the late 1800s and serving delicious tea and cakes; the other, **La Mutisia**, offers big, homemade servings.

Things were not always so tranquil. There were clashes in the

CAMPSITES AND AROUND TREVELIN

Complejo La Balsa
A well-run campsite with toilets and hot showers in lush surroundings by the Río Futaleufú. $

Puerto Ciprés
Open only in summer, this family-run place has sites for both campervans and tents. $

Aiken Leufú
Pet- and family-friendly option 12km from Trevelin with a laidback atmosphere, wi-fi and kayak rental. $

region between the indigenous people who already inhabited the land and the new arrivals. When Evans and some Argentine troops were caught in a bloody encounter with Mapuche warriors, everyone was killed except the Welshman. For more on this history, pay a visit to **Museo Cartref'Taid**, where the great-grandchild of John Evans – whose story was told by Bruce Chatwin in his travel book *In Patagonia* – Clery Evans lives. She runs a small museum filled with memorabilia from the beginning of the colonizing days and will gladly tell the stories of her ancestors for hours (in Spanish only though).

Cholila

TIME FROM ESQUEL: **1HR 40 MINS**

Visit Butch Cassidy and the Sundance Kid's Homestead

In 1901, after a series of armed bank robberies and with a price on their heads, Butch Cassidy and the Sundance Kid escaped the American Wild West for a new life in Argentina. They arrived – together with Etta Place, one of their gang members – in Patagonia, where from 1902 to 1907 the three ran a ranch in Chubut Province, just outside Cholila, which you can still visit today. Situated just off RP15, the trio's homestead, made up of three partially refurbished cabins, still attracts a small stream of curious visitors, though you're most likely to have the place to yourself. Entry is free of charge, and except for a few information boards there's not much else to do than to soak up the atmosphere and ponder the fact that some of the USA's most famous bank robbers once lived outside a tiny town in Patagonia most people have never heard of.

Tea house,
Trevelin

THE GUIDE

BEYOND ESQUEL PATAGONIA

BEST PLACES TO STAY

Arroyo Escondido (Trevelin)
These beautiful bungalows with private jacuzzi in the midst of Patagonian forest deliver stunning mountain views. **$$**

Challhuaquen Lodge (Trevelin)
A luxurious lodge right by the Río Futaleufú featuring an outdoor pool and sauna. **$$$**

Lemuria Cabañas & Habitaciones (Epuyén)
Affordable, pleasant *hostería* close to Lago Epuyén offering rooms and cabins with a communal kitchen. **$**

Huemules Reserva de Montaña (Esquel)
Observe Patagonia's nature from the comfort of your own dome. 23km northwest of Esquel. **$$$**

Piuke Mapu Patagonia Hostel (Cholila)
Bright, charming hostel providing breathtaking views of the Andes and warm service. **$**

BEST PLACES TO EAT

Nikanor (Trevelin)
Homemade ravioli and meat dishes by a husband and wife team in an airy space with exposed brick walls. **$$$**

Restaurante Ruta 71 (Trevelin)
Restaurant just off RP 71, serving various meat dishes including lamb, homemade bread and pizza. **$$$**

Fonda Sur (Trevelin)
Head chef Paula Chiaradía composes elaborate plates like tagines with dried fruit and lamb paté with passionfruit. **$$$**

La Perla (Trevelin)
Stop by for a great atmosphere, delicious gin and tonics, homemade pasta and meatballs. **$$$**

Laguna Larga (Parque Nacional Los Alerces)
Excellent restaurant with an extensive wine list – there's more than 100 handpicked bottles. **$$$**

Lago Epuyén

Epuyén and Lago Epuyén
Mountain Villages and Blue Water

Situated between El Bolsón and Cholila along RN40, the little village of **Epuyén** is often missed by tourists, except for a few months during summer (January and February) when regional and national tourists arrive to enjoy the mountains and the lake area here. It's the perfect little Patagonian village to base yourself in to relax and explore for a few days. In the summer, kayaking on the clear blue waters of **Lago Epuyén,** where water vehicles are forbidden, is a good way to enjoy the tranquil setting. **Kayak Puerto Bonito** by the lake can rent you one – they also arrange group trips on the water in high season. On a hot summer's day visiting the lake area, small **Playa Las Rocas** makes the perfect stop for a refreshing dip in the clear water.

After your swim, pop by the small wooden cabin selling handmade crafts and homemade jams, affiliated with the much bigger **Centro Cultural Antu Quillen** overlooking the lake. In March, when the autumn colors pop, the trees are colored bright red and yellow, the sun is still shining and temperatures are pleasant, Lago Epuyén invites you to enjoy leisurely hikes along its shore. Starting at **Puerto Bonito**, the 10km **Bahía Las Percas** trek will take you along the lakefront through the pine forest until you arrive at a secluded bay.

El Calafate

Named after the calafate berry that, once eaten, will inevitably bring you back to Patagonian soil (according to the local legend), El Calafate, in Santa Cruz Province, has one thing going for it that will get any visitor hooked – the irresistible allure of Glaciar Perito Moreno. This jaw-dropping, gigantic glacier transformed El Calafate from a quaint little town in the 1960s to Argentina's most-visited tourist destination today, filled with high-end restaurants, steakhouses, cafes, luxurious hotels and busy hostels. There are all sorts of travel services, including numerous tour agents offering everything from boat trips on Lago Argentino to 4WD trips in Parque Nacional Los Glaciares, souvenir shops selling various trinkets and *cervecerías*. As convenient as it is comfortable (and sociable if you are staying in a hostel), it's the perfect launchpad for exploring the glacier and surrounding beautiful area.

GETTING AROUND

El Calafate is small and easily explored on foot. There's no public transportation to get around the town itself, so if you want to get to the outskirts, walk or take a taxi.

☑ TOP TIP

Visit in shoulder season (Sept-Nov & March-April) when accommodations are usually cheaper. Bear in mind that during Semana Santa (Easter week) prices soar.

Perito Moreno Glacier (p421)

419

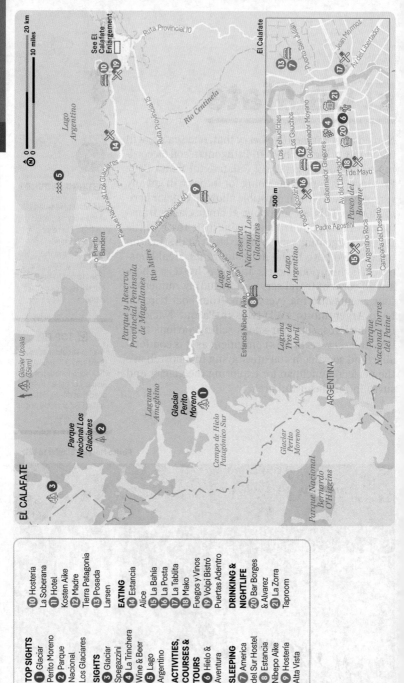

EL CALAFATE PATAGONIA

TOP SIGHTS
1 Glaciar Perito Moreno
2 Parque Nacional Los Glaciares

SIGHTS
3 Glaciar Spegazzini
4 La Trinchera Wine & Beer
5 Lago Argentino

ACTIVITIES, COURSES & TOURS
6 Hielo & Aventura

SLEEPING
7 America del Sur Hostel
8 Estancia Nibepo Aike
9 Hostería Alta Vista
10 Hostería La Soberana
11 Hotel Kosten Aike
12 Madre Tierra Patagonia
13 Posada Larsen

EATING
14 Estancia Alice
15 La Bahía
16 La Posta
17 La Tablita
18 Mako
19 Volpi Bistró
Fuegos y Vinos
Puertas Adentro

DRINKING & NIGHTLIFE
20 Bar Borges & Alvarez
21 La Zorra Taproom

MEUNIERD/SHUTTERSTOCK ©

Tourist boat, Perito Moreno Glacier

One of the World's Most Famous Glaciers

Gawp at Perito Moreno Glacier

Watching big chunks of ice calve down **Perito Moreno Glacier** – one of the world's few advancing ice fields, creeping forward at a speed of up to 2m a day – into the milky blue water below is, simply put, a thrilling experience. Attracting a whopping 450,000 visitors a year, this is one of Argentina's most popular attractions. Situated in the southern sector of **Parque Nacional Los Glaciares**, 80km southwest of **El Calafate**, the glacier viewpoint is a short hike from the national park's main entrance.

There are three different ways to appreciate this awesome spectacle of nature: from the viewpoint, by boat, or ice trekking on it. The latter is one of the most unique and exciting ways to see and feel the force of the glacier and it's important to book ahead as spots are limited and the activity is popular. **Hielo & Aventura**, the only licensed tour operator arranging treks on the glacier, offers a short 2hr hike or a more demanding 4hr option. Further away, there are lesser known, albeit bigger, icy marvels to see. **Glaciar Upsala** is one of South America's biggest glaciers; at roughly 7km wide and 60km long it covers an area three times the size of Buenos

BEST ESTANCIAS

Estancia Nibepo Aike
Working cattle ranch with a beautiful farmhouse run by a Croatian family; 60km outside El Calafate. **$$$**

Estancia Hostería Helsingfors
Stay in comfortable, spacious rooms with old-style furniture three hours from El Calafate. **$$$**

Estancia Cristina
Accessible only by boat from Puerto Punta Bandera, a stay at this amazing *estancia* includes all meals and a guided expedition to Glaciar Upsala. **$$$**

Estancia El Condor
Remote and charming with a strong focus on conservation, this option even has its own nature reserve. **$$$**

Hostería Alta Vista
A huge working sheep ranch from the 1920s, with seven charming guest rooms. **$$$**

 WHERE TO EAT

La Posta
Elegant hotel restaurant with a wide-ranging menu including various meat and pasta dishes. **$$$**

Volpi Bistró Puertas Adentro
The only true fine-dining experience in El Calafate is reservation-only and housed in the home of chef Volpi. **$$$**

La Bahía
Gourmet dining where the highlights on the menu include guanaco sashimi and Patagonian lamb. **$$$**

421

Aires. Admire this gigantic chunk of ice from one of the catamarans navigating **Brazo Upsala**. For the tallest glacier of them all, seek out the impressive **Glaciar Spegazzini** with a wall measuring between 80m and 135m high. Just like Upsala, it's accessible only by boat, weaving through icebergs in the canals of **Lago Argentino**.

Succulent Lamb and Regional Culture
A Principal Part of Patagonia Cuisine

No food says Patagonia more than lamb and El Calafate is a great place to sample it. Visiting the town's *parrillas* you'll see lamb roasted whole on spits above red-orange embers and, once cooked, chopped up and dished out sizzling hot to hungry guests. The meat is crispy, juicy and succulent, all at the same time, dripping with juices from the fat as you eat it from the bone. To try for yourself, there are several options. Make a reservation at immensely popular and traditional **La Tablita**, El Calafate's most famous steakhouse, to get a taste of Patagonia's staple food, and wash it down with a good bottle of Malbec. For fine dining, head to **Mako Fuegos y Vinos**; start with lamb sweetbreads, then enjoy tender ribs served with potatoes and a Caesar salad.

There are also heartwarming lamb stews with portobello mushroom and pancetta and homemade ravioli stuffed with lamb on the menu. Elsewhere around Santa Cruz Province are many working sheep ranches which have turned to tourism. **Estancia Nibepo Aike**, a 1½hr drive southwest from El Calafate along RP15, provides an insight into the daily life of just such a ranch. It offers day-trip experiences (transfers from El Calafate and back at an additional cost) that include a sheep shearing demonstration and a traditional country lunch with barbecued lamb. On the way to Perito Moreno Glacier is **Estancia Alice**, 22km west of El Calafate, where you can spend the day watching kelpie sheepdogs and border collies herd flocks, followed by skilled gauchos shearing the animals' thick wool. End your visit eating lamb back at the ranch.

THE CALAFATE BERRY

The box-leaved barberry, calafate in Spanish, is an evergreen shrub that grows to around 1 to 2m high and whose yellow flowers cover the Patagonian landscape each September. Native to southern Argentina and Chile, it's the symbol of this rugged place, and legend has it that whoever eats the black-blue berry will return swiftly to Patagonia. Locally, they're eaten fresh or used for making jams, and you might even encounter them bottled as a sweet, dark red liqueur. High in antioxidants, they are also known for their medicinal benefits and the indigenous Tehuelche knew the berry for its energy-giving properties.

 OTHER SIGHTS AND EVENTS IN EL CALAFATE

Laguna Nimez
Nature reserve with flamingos among roughly a hundred other species of birds; a 15-minute walk from town.

Cerro Frías
Peak with stunning views of Cerro Fitz Roy and Torres del Paine on a clear day.

Festival del Lago Argentino
This is Patagonia's biggest festival, held in mid-February and with lots of cultural activities and live music.

Start with a visit to ❶ **Museo Regional** on Av Libertador in the center of town. This tiny, free museum exhibits a diverse collection including fossils, photos of the pioneers who founded El Calafate, various archaeological objects and some indigenous crafts. Continue northwest along Av Libertador before turning right onto José Pantin. After 350m the street turns slightly left and becomes Gobernador Moyano. After 55 meters turn right onto José Pantin again and stop for a *café con leche* (coffee with milk) and a *medialuna* (an Argentine pastry resembling a small French croissant) at ❷ **Paseo de Compras**. From there it's a 10-minute walk along José Pantin and Almirante G. Brown to the ❸ **Centro de Interpretación Histórica Calafate** showcasing Patagonia's natural and human history. Learn about the detrimental impact European settlement

had on indigenous communities, the workers' strike in 1920–1921, glaciers and dinosaurs. Head back to the center and stop for a hearty lunch at ❹ **Isabel Cocina al Disco**, where filling stews are cooked over the fire in deep black pans (*al disco* in Argentina), before you get the shuttle bus from the car park on Calle 1 de Mayo to ❺ **Glaciarum**, El Calafate's excellent, modern glacier interpretation center with multimedia exhibitions on everything ice-related. It also has Argentina's first ice bar, ❻ **Glaciobar**, where you can order a cocktail. For something warmer, there's a cafe where you can sip on a glass of red and snack on a lamb empanada enjoying the fine view of Lago Argentino. Grab the shuttle back to town and end your day with a treat from the extensive wine list at intimate and stylish restaurant ❼ **La Zaina**.

Riding in the Andes

Gaucho Culture, Mountains and Horses

From El Calafate, venture out to spend the day in the saddle. There are several travel agents in town offering *cabalgatas* (horseback riding), from a couple of hours to full-day excursions including lunch. Choose wisely – paying a little extra usually means better horses and better tack. Kitted out with boots and a windproof raincoat (riding hats are usually not provided in Argentina) and accompanied by a gaucho leading the way, you'll explore the dramatic landscape on sturdy and reliable *caballos de campo* (country horses that are not a specific breed). Comfortable on soft, warm sheep skins and the reins in one hand, you'll ride through meadows and grassy steppe covered with thorny calafate bushes, passing grazing white and brown guanacos as you slowly ascend Cerro Frías.

Pretty soon you reach the top of the mountain and are rewarded with sweeping views of Parque Nacional Los Glaciares' snowy peaks and Lago Argentino – the park's ice-blue glacial lake and biggest body of water with a total length of 125km. On a clear day you can see all the way to the peaks of Chile's Torres del Paine and El Chaltén's Cerro Fitz Roy. For a ride on private land **Cabalgatas del Trekking** pick you up at your hotel in the morning and take you to **Estancia del Roca** for an hour's ride uphill not meeting a single soul. Once at the top, and most likely with the Patagonian wind in your hair, look out over Perito Moreno Glacier and lakes.

**Horse-riding,
El Calafate**

BEST PLACES TO STAY

Hotel Kosten Aike
Within walking distance of El Calafate's main strip, this Alpine-style hotel features a restaurant and large rooms. **$$**

Hostería La Soberana
Right by the lake, this new place offers warm service and tidy rooms outside of town. **$$**

Posada Larsen
Charming brick building with wooden details and a beautiful view of Lago Argentino. Rooms have big windows and are impeccably decorated. **$$**

Madre Tierra Patagonia
Boutique hotel with a cool interior and friendly staff. All suites have modern bathrooms and wooden floors. **$$$**

America del Sur Hostel
Popular and spacious hostel featuring laundry facilities, hair dryers and an outdoor terrace. **$**

Beyond
El Calafate

Estancia El Condor

Estancia Hostería
Helsingfors

ARGENTINA

CHILE

Estancia Cristina

El Calafate

Parque Nacional
Torres del Paine

Continue inland and along the Andes to admire vistas of turquoise lakes and frozen mountaintops and explore Patagonia's wild beauty.

Mossy beech forests, high snowy peaks, remote *estancias*, glacial lakes and icy blue rivers – the lower reaches of the Andes and inland Patagonia are just waiting for you to venture into their untamed and alluring landscapes. A few hours west of El Calafate you find Chile's stunning Torres del Paine with its glaciers and inviting azure lakes and towering mountains where pumas hunt guanacos on the slopes. In all directions beyond El Calafate, you find numerous *estancias,* which despite their remote locations and harsh weather have managed to raise cattle and sheep for decades. Many are still working ranches and some have also turned to tourism. A few, like Estancia El Condor, offer pack trips into the mountains, camping and staying in rustic shelters along the way.

Torres del Paine

GETTING AROUND

Distances are great once you get out of El Calafate. It's best to have your own car if you want to explore the surrounding area freely, though organized tours to some places do exist.

☑ TOP TIP

Distances are long and the landscapes invite you to slow down and connect to nature, so allow plenty of time to travel.

425

BRUCE CHATWIN'S IN PATAGONIA

Written in the 1970s, *In Patagonia* is, for many, *the* travel book on Argentina. The British author Bruce Chatwin wrote the novel, which broke the barriers for conventional travel writing at the time, after his adventures in Chile and Argentina, which he embarked on after quitting his job as a correspondent at the *Sunday Times*. The book is a series of self-contained anecdotes and tales about everything from Butch Cassidy and the Sundance Kid and their cabin in Cholila to the history of Welsh settlers such as John Evans. The long-lasting power of his writing still draws a steady stream of fans to the far-flung places he visited.

PANTHER MEDIA GMBH/ALAMY STOCK PHOTO ©

Estancia Cristina

Far West Santa Cruz Province

TIME FROM EL CALAFATE: 3HRS

Spend Your Days Horseback Riding

Leave El Calafate behind and book a stay at one of Santa Cruz's remote *estancias* in the far west of the province. It's only in one of these that you can stay in the middle of the dramatic and isolated landscape of the region without having to compromise on comfort. Some of the ranches are situated within the borders of Parque Nacional Los Alerces. **Estancia Hostería Helsingfors** and **Estancia Cristina** are among those breathing country-chic luxury into their properties whilst simultaneously speaking to the adventurer in you. Welcoming visitors since the mid-90s, Helsingfors is a former Finnish pioneering ranch blessed with a stunning location, on the edge of Lago Viedma and with beautiful vistas of Cerro Fitz Roy.

With only nine rooms, it's intimate and relaxed – here you pass your time in the living room in front of the fire after a long day trekking or horseback riding. At secluded Estancia Cristina, accessed from Puerto Punta Bandera by boat heading up the beautiful Bahía Cristina, you can indulge in some of the best trekking in the region before spending the night in one of their bright cabins with glorious views. A stay here also includes boating to Glaciar Upsala.

 OTHER SIGHTS TO SEE

Lago Roca
The southern branch of Lago Argentino, unfrequented by visitors, where you can see 3000-year-old rock art.

Torres del Paine
The continent's finest national park is on the other side of the border in Chile.

Cerro Cristal
A roughly 5hr hike starting at the RP15 takes you up this peak, with stunning views of Torres del Paine.

Hit the Road
Drive along Argentina's Route 66

The Patagonian part of the epic **Ruta Nacional 40** (RN40) is a road trip for the books. It's Argentina's most famous highway, running from Santa Cruz in the south to Salta in the north, and the longest national *ruta* in the country, measuring about 5200km. Some people dedicate a whole trip to the South American country's answer to Route 66, but just to do a stretch of it is a worthwhile experience. You need a car and time on your hands; undertaking a journey in this part of the world has its challenges, but in many ways, this is also what makes it so enticing.

There is nothing quite like driving for hours without a house in sight, surrounded by flat steppe and what seems to just be you, your car and the occasional guanaco. Starting in El Calafate and heading south, once you have come this far south in Argentina you might as well cross the border into **Chile**. It's fairly straightforward to take a rental vehicle into the neighboring country; you just need the right paperwork from the rental company. Drive along the RN40 towards **Puerto Natales**, 3½hr from El Calafate, not including the time it will take to cross the border. Once in Chile, stay the night at **Wild Patagonia** – a joyful hostel with pleasant rooms and a fire pit in the courtyard. In the morning, drive towards **Torres del Paine** – one of South America's finest and most famous national parks.

Estancia El Condor & Around

TIME FROM EL CALAFATE: **5HRS**

Trail Rides in the Mountains

There are plenty of far-flung areas beyond El Calafate where you can have your very own horseback adventure. **Cabalgatas Andora** can take you on a six-day-long pack trip starting at **Estancia El Condor**. After being picked up in El Calafate in the morning you'll arrive at the *estancia* five hours later, traveling 150km on paved road and then the rest on gravel. After getting to know the horses and seeing the 100-year-old tack room, you stay the first night in the comfortable rooms of the *estancia* where you have both running water and electricity. On day two, a more rustic adventure awaits.

Once the saddle bags are packed with the necessary gear for your next few days of riding, you set off towards **Laguna Corazón**, riding through beech forest and under towering mountains. Here you set up camp for the night and have

PLANNING FOR THE RN40

If you want to do a stretch of the legendary Ruta Nacional 40 road, there are a few things to keep in mind. With your own wheels, make sure to leave enough time. This is not a trip to be rushed as the weather can be unpredictable, especially in the south where crosswinds can be extremely strong. Although most of the route is now paved, it's worth investing in a 4WD if you have the budget for it, as many side roads still aren't paved. If you don't want to drive at all, several travel agencies, including El Chaltén Travel, offer minivan transports between El Calafate and Bariloche via El Chaltén. For something more hardcore, Bariloche-based Ruta 40 offers 10-day journeys between October and April along the epic highway.

 WHERE TO STAY

Camping Lago Roca
Top-notch campground with a restaurant bar, games room and bike and fishing-gear rental. $

Eolo
Relais & Châteaux hotel on the Patagonian Steppe with an outdoor jacuzzi, sauna and horseback riding. $$$

Aguas Arriba
Lodge on the eastern shores of Lago del Desierto in an area frequented by the endangered huemul. $$$

427

dinner under the starry sky. The following morning prepare yourself for seven hours in the saddle, making a stop for lunch at **Río Grande**. The next day you'll ride to the western end of the 400 sq km *estancia* and the border of Chile. You're in true Patagonian wilderness and you'll set up your tent for the night looking out over massive **Lago San Martín** and the **O'Higgins volcano** in Chile. On day five, you'll ride through ravines and lagoons, followed by fishing if you want. On the sixth and final day, enjoy a ride along the turquoise water of Lago San Martín.

Chile's Parque Nacional Torres del Paine

TIME FROM EL CALAFATE: **3.5 HRS** 🚗

Hike in the Spectacular National Park

Just across the border west of El Calafate is one of South America's finest national parks, the sublime Parque Nacional Torres del Paine. Here, turquoise rivers and glaciers, azure lakes and emerald-green forests compete for your attention with the three eponymous gigantic granite peaks and icons of the park, the Paine Towers. Rather than visiting on a rushed day trip from El Calafate, get your own vehicle and drive to Puerto Natales in Chile, staying a couple of nights. Check into the excellent Vinnhaus and start the following morning with some of the best coffee you've had in South America before heading to the national park – a 112km drive north will take you to Portería Sarmiento, the main entrance. Torres del Paine can be explored on foot, on horseback, aboard a catamaran or in a car, although it is to Chile what El Chaltén is to Argentina – the country's top trekking destination.

Two of the most popular hikes are the lengthy Circuito Grande trail, taking you through the park's main attractions with stellar views of Glaciar Dickson and the Southern Ice Field, and the Sendero W, a roughly four-day hike along a route that follows the shape of a W and takes you to three of the park's major highlights – the Torres del Paine, Valle del Francés and Glaciar Grey. For superb views of Lago Nordenskjöld on a shorter walk, opt for the one-hour hike (one way) to Mirador Nordenskjöld. Starting at Guardería Pudeto, the trail passes the powerful waterfall of Salto Grande, taking you through beech forest and thorny bushes on the way to the viewpoint.

GUAXININ/SHUTTERSTOCK ©

Parque Nacional Torres del Paine

El Chaltén

El Chaltén is a must-include for hikers and adventurers on any Argentina itinerary. It's an increasingly popular destination, just a three-hour drive from El Calafate along RN40, which, since its establishment in 1985, has grown from a successful attempt to claim territory from neighboring Chile to a booming tourist town with plenty of accommodations and restaurants. Surrounded by the serrated, snowcapped peaks of the Andes, El Chaltén's appeal lies in its proximity to a multitude of treks, trails and climbs in the northern sector of Parque Nacional Los Glaciares. It's also where you find the highest peak in the Patagonian part of the Andean *cordillera,* the pointy Cerro Fitz Roy, reaching 3375m above sea level. Despite what some see as uncontrolled development, the town has managed to retain a laid-back and friendly atmosphere.

GETTING AROUND

El Chaltén is very small – though it has grown substantially over its four-decade existence – and is easily navigated on foot. Las Lengas has minivans to Lago del Desierto but if you want to explore the surroundings at your own pace, you are best off renting a car.

☑ TOP TIP

Contrary to what you might think, the best weather conditions for trekking in El Chaltén are not in the summer and peak season (January and February). Instead, they're during the Patagonian fall when there is less wind (and fewer people around), so, if possible, visit in March and April.

Cerro Fitz Roy

ANTON PETRUS/GETTY IMAGES ©

429

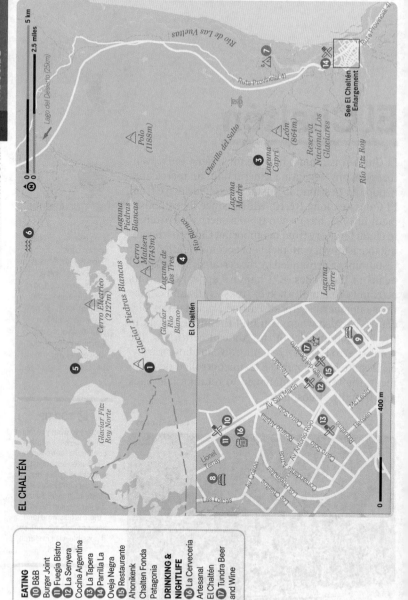

EL CHALTÉN

SIGHTS
1 Cerro Fitz Roy
2 Cerro Torre
3 Laguna Capri
4 Laguna
de los Tres
5 Paso
del Cuadrado
6 Río Electrico

SLEEPING
7 Chalten
Camp
8 Hostería
El Puma
9 Hostería
Senderos

EATING
10 B&B
Burger Joint
11 Fuegia Bistro
12 La Senyera
Cocina Argentina
13 La Tapera
14 Parrilla La
Oveja Negra
15 Restaurante
Ahonikenk
Chalten Fonda
Patagonia

**DRINKING &
NIGHTLIFE**
16 La Cerveceria
Artesanal
El Chaltén
17 Tundra Beer
and Wine

MOCHILAOSABATICO/SHUTTERSTOCK ©

Piedra del Fraile

BEST TREKS

Laguna de los Tres
A 10km walk for hikers in good physical shape through windswept forest to a glacial lake.

Laguna Capri
Walk for about three hours to enjoy a stunning view of Cerro Fitz Roy.

Chorrillo del Salto
Short and easy trail leading to a 20m-high waterfall in the middle of the mountain range.

Laguna Torre
An 18km hike through hilly country to a lake reflecting Cerro Torre, weather permitting.

Mirador Maestri
Add 40 minutes to the Laguna Torre trek for more spectacular vistas of Cerro Torre plus Cerro Grande.

Seeking Adventure
Adrenaline-Filled Mountain Experiences

El Chaltén is the perfect launchpad for mountain-focused adventures – there's rock climbing, ice trekking and mountain biking all within an hour's drive. Start planning at the tourist office just at the entrance to the town where you can get an idea of the activities on offer. For serious mountain expeditions, including ascending Cerro Fitz Roy and Cerro Torre, a guide is mandatory and sensible; conditions with gusts of winds and snow storms can be incredibly unforgiving.

If you're after a rewarding hike you're spoiled for choice – El Chaltén is Argentina's de facto hiking capital. One of the lesser known trails with stellar views is to **Piedra del Fraile**, a good option for a medium-level trek. Start by taking a 15-minute minibus from El Chaltén operated by Las Lengas bound for Lago del Desierto and get off just before the bridge at **Río Electrico** on the RP23. The path starts to the left of the river and is well signposted, slowly peeling away from the river to the gravel of the Río Blanco Valley and through the sub-Antarctic forest of the Río Electrico Valley before reaching a magnificent view of Glaciar Marconi. At Piedra del Fraile there's a *refugio* (mountain hut) and a campsite.

BEST TOUR GUIDES

Chaltén Mountain Guides
Mountain guides for treks and rock climbing in Parque Nacional Los Glaciares. They have climbing courses too.

Casa de Guías
Offers day hikes and longer expeditions.

Patagonia Aventura
Runs boat trips to a couple of scenic lakes (Viedma and del Desierto) and can arrange fishing trips.

HIKING INTO CHILE

There's the option to trek into Chile for those with the stamina and persistence to hike the southern part of the ice field, starting at the south shore of Lago del Desierto, 33km northeast of El Chaltén, and ending in Candelario Mancilla on the Chilean side, where you can take a ferry to Puerto Bahamondes. From there you can catch the bus to Villa O'Higgins, the last stop on Chile's Carretera Austral. The trip takes one to three days – depending on if you choose to take a boat or walk certain stretches – and can be done between November and March when the border is open. You need to bring all provisions, your passport, Chilean currency and rain gear. For more information visit the tourism office in El Chaltén.

OPPOSITE PAGE: MATTHEW WILLIAMS-ELLIS/GETTY IMAGES ©

Cerro Fitz Roy

Very experienced mountaineers can continue to **Paso del Cuadrado** from here. It's a 6–7hr return hike with a 1200m ascent from Piedra del Fraile. Once at the top, beware of the ferocious wind as you're looking out over one of the most dramatic views you'll encounter in the national park, gazing over **Cerro Torre**, **Fitz Roy** and **Polone**. If you want an experienced guide accompanying you, contact **El Chaltén Mountain Guides** or **Fitz Roy Expediciones**.

Strap on Your Walking Boots
Argentina's Number One Hiking Town

The monumental Andes mountains towering above El Chaltén reach their peak with the snow-clad spires of **Cerro Fitz Roy** at 3045m – which the Tehueleche referred to as El Chaltén (the mountain of smoke) – and imposing **Cerro Torre**. As you hike trails taking in forest, ravines, wooded slopes and rivers, each step brings breathtaking views – sometimes snowy mountaintops and glacier lakes, sometimes waterfalls and river valleys. There are routes catering to all abilities and in all directions from town. Before deciding on where to go, check with the national park office, 1km south of town, for advice on which ones suit your experience. **Laguna de los Tres** hike starts at a yellow-roofed pack station and is a chal-

 WHERE TO STAY

Hostería Senderos
Tastefully decorated three-star hotel with mountain views, a wine bar, and rooms with comfortable beds. **$$$**

Hostería El Puma
Bright and sleek rooms with queen-size beds and views of the Andes. **$$$**

Chalten Camp
Luxurious glamping beyond the town border on the other side of Río Las Vueltas. **$$$**

lenging, somewhat strenuous yet stunningly beautiful 10km trail taking you to an alpine lake. After roughly four hours walking one way you are rewarded with one of the most photogenic spots in the national park – a still glacial body of water with a view of Cerro Fitz Roy. If you want to break up the trek there is an excellent free campsite at **Laguna Capri**, about an hour's walk along the route. For something slightly shorter, opt for the 18km round-trip Laguna Torre trail. Start by turning off Av San Martín by Viento Oeste shop, following the marked path at the base of the hill. Once you arrive at the lake at the end, you can see Cerro Torre reflected in the water on a clear day.

A Night Out on the Town

Drinking and Nightlife

Spending a night barhopping and eating your way around El Chaltén is a good way to enjoy the friendly and bustling atmosphere in peak season (January and February) when visitors from around the world flock to this small mountain town. Start early if you're aiming for a long evening, as most restaurants and bars open (6pm and onwards) and close (usually midnight at the latest) earlier than in other parts of Argentina (especially Buenos Aires). Begin with a couple of meat empanadas and *pintas* at **Tundra Beer and Wine** listening to the DJ spinning records; take full advantage of the 6–8pm happy hour. Continue to **B&B Burger Joint** and order one of their juicy grilled burgers with melted cheese and topped off with bacon and caramelized onions. There's a good selection of beers on tap; choose between stouts and red and golden ales from regional microbreweries including Cervecería Esquel. Once you are done, jump next door to **B&B Tacos y Burritos**. This little joint serves tacos and tasty drinks including ice-cold margaritas. At **La Cervecería Artesanal El Chaltén** they brew their own beer (make sure to try the crisp and refreshing pilsner) and the staff speaks English (never a given in Argentina). The atmosphere is friendly and sometimes there's live music too.

Patagonia lamb stew

BEST PLACES TO EAT IN EL CHALTÉN

La Tapera
Excellent restaurant that fills up quickly in high season. Try the salads for something light and fresh. **$$$**

Restaurante Ahonikenk Chalten Fonda Patagonia
Serves lamb empanadas and a hearty lentil stew, just a short walk from El Chaltén main street. **$$$**

La Senyera Cocina Argentina
Friendly, family-run restaurant where the homemade food is comforting and portions are generous. **$$**

Fuegia Bistro
Open for lunch and dinner, this place is good for steak, trout, lamb ragù and wine. **$$$**

Parrilla La Oveja Negra
Set in an attractive wooden cabin, this steakhouse is perfect for long, meaty dinners. **$$$**

Beyond
El Chaltén

Sarmiento
Puerto Aisen
Perito Moreno
CHILE
Bajo Caracoles   Cueva de las Manos Pintadas
Parque Nacional Perito Moreno
Reserva Los Huemels
ARGENTINA
El Chaltén

GETTING AROUND

Like most parts of Patagonia, it's ideal if not mandatory to have your own wheels to explore these far-flung parts of the region. There are buses serving El Calafate from El Chaltén, but for smaller places like Reserva Los Huemules, as well as Bosque Petrificado Sarmiento, you need a car or to arrange a taxi. For Perito Moreno National Park it's essential to have a car. Many *estancias* can pick you up with prior reservation at an extra charge.

Explore a 65-million-year-old petrified forest, visit one of Argentina's most stunning national parks and marvel at ancient rock art.

Patagonia is huge and the highlights 'beyond El Chaltén' can be several hundred kilometers away from the town – but are worth the effort. From awesome national parks and prehistoric art to ancient petrified forests unfrequented by international visitors, peace and offbeat gems await.

Along the Andes mountain range, a 450km drive north from El Chaltén, lies one of Argentina's first national parks, Parque Nacional Perito Moreno. Despite boasting impressive peaks and beautiful lakes, this place attracts an astonishingly low number of annual visitors – around 1000. Further inland, 500km from Argentina's hiking capital, in the middle of the Patagonian outback, Cueva de las Manos Pintadas wins the prize for South America's finest examples of rock art. Traveling further north along RN40 for more than 800km, then east towards the outskirts of small-town Sarmiento, perfectly preserved petrified tree trunks, from when Patagonia was made up of lush forest 65 million years ago, are scattered around the lunar-like landscape.

☑ TOP TIP

When driving through these remote expanses of Patagonia, towns and supplies are very limited. Stock up on everything and fill the tank before heading out, and top up on fuel whenever you can – service stations sometimes run out so don't risk waiting until the next one.

BERND ZILLICH/SHUTTERSTOCK ©

Bosque Petrificado Sarmiento (p438)

Cueva de las Manos Pintadas

Cueva de las Manos Pintadas

Canyons and Cave Paintings

One of South America's finest examples of rock art, **Cueva de las Manos Pintadas** is not to be missed – even if you have to drive around 8hr north from El Chaltén to see it. Located in the sparsely populated area between the small towns of Bajo Caracoles and Perito Moreno (not to be confused with Glaciar Perito Moreno or Parque Nacional Perito Moreno), the cave is the reason most visitors venture to this part of Patagonia. The name, 'cave of the painted hands', comes from the many stenciled human hands on the rock walls, believed to have been made by the hunter-gather communities that used to inhabit the land between 9500 and 13,000 years ago. The site can be accessed by car from a rather rough side road just north of Bajo Caracoles or, better, by hiking up the canyon it looks on to – the beautiful **Cañón del Río Pinturas**,

RESERVA LOS HUEMULES

Reserva Los Huemules is a private nature reserve offering 25 marked trails that are notably quieter than those around El Chaltén. Once here you can opt for something easy or challenging. Loma del Diablo is the latter, a 4hr hike up through lenga forest to a magnificent view of Cerro Fitz Roy. A more moderate trail (3hr one way) is to Laguna Diablo which ends at a lake overlooking Glaciar Cagliero. Stay the night in the modern and stylish mountain refuge (reserve ahead), just by the lake. The reserve's fauna includes pumas, red foxes and, most notably, the endangered huemul deer; there are breeding areas for this small creature in the reserve, but they're off-limits to visitors.

 WHERE TO STAY IN PERITO MORENO AND AROUND

Camping Municipal
No-frills campsite ideal for travelers on a limited budget in the southern part of town. $

Hostería & Cabañas Río Fénix
A short walk from Perito Moreno's bus terminal with comfortable and spacious rooms. $$

Hostería Cueva de las Manos
Former *estancia* with double and triple rooms just off RN40, 60km from Perito Moreno. $$-$$$

Parque Nacional Perito Moreno

Intrepid travelers are in for a treat at Parque Nacional Perito Moreno, a wild, unspoiled-by-tourism spot, 450km from El Chaltén on the border with Chile. Be one of the few who make it here each year and tour the park by car (preferably a 4WD) on an excellent two-day road trip on which you can enjoy its beautiful lakes, high flying condors, grazing guanacos, impressive views and abundance of solitude.

❶ Gobernador Gregores

Before heading to the park, stop at the small town of Gobernador Gregores to stock up on food and fuel – there are no services in the park save for some offered by local *estancias*.

A few basic campsites offer somewhere to pitch a tent, but bring your own gear and remember that fires are prohibited – buy a gas stove if you want warm food.
The Drive: Drive northwest from Gobernador Gregores on RN40 to Las Horquetas, then take unpaved RP37. From the park office, continue a couple of kilometers to Estancia Belgrano. From there, head west towards Lago Belgrano.

❷ Lago Belgrano

Marvel at the intense turquoise color of one of the most remarkable lakes in the park that's accessible to visitors. Unlike many Patagonian bodies of water, this lake has been spared from introduced species and is filled with native fish (although fishing is prohibited).

GALYNA ANDRUSHKO/SHUTTERSTOCK ©

Lago Belgrano

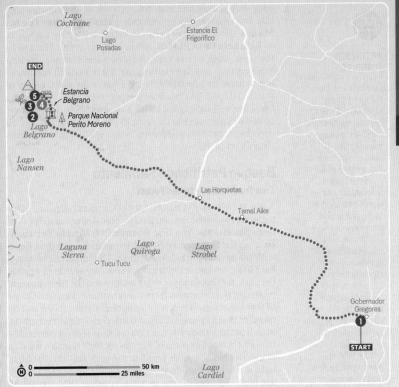

The Drive: From Estancia Belgrano drive 8km west until you reach Península Belgrano, accessed by foot through an isthmus. There's a parking lot just before the narrow strip of land.

③ Península Belgrano

Península Belgrano is covered by shrubs and troops of guanacos attracting a fair share of pumas. Follow the three-to-four-hour-long Circuito Chico trail through *mata negra* bushes passing by the graceful lamoids – and bones the feline predators have left behind. Set up camp for the night at Refugio Caleta Huala with beautiful views of the lake, 900m from the parking lot.

The Drive: Head back east. Once you have passed Estancia El Belgrano again, turn left on RP37 and head north to reach the clearly marked turnoff to Estancia La Oriental.

④ Estancia La Oriental

One of very few accommodations options in the area, the charming working ranch Es-

tancia La Oriental is situated in a peaceful valley with views of Lago Belgrano. There are a few hikes taking you to some seriously dazzling views, including the 3½ hr one to the summit of Cerro León, 1434m above sea level, affording panoramas of the heartland of the park.

The Drive: Roughly 3km further north you have Cerro de Los Cóndores. To enjoy the view of this peak, park the car at Estancia La Oriental and hike 1.5km to La Condorera viewpoint.

⑤ Cerro de Los Cóndores

Marvel at South America's most majestic bird; the Andean condor. With cliffs stained white, this is the *condorera* (nesting area) used by about 30 individuals. You're never guaranteed to spot them but the chances are high as they regularly come here to teach their chicks how to fly. For a great view of the park and *condorera,* hike up Cerro León; it takes 3½ hrs from Estancia La Oriental. Head back to the *estancia* and stay the night before returning to Perito Moreno.

PETRIFIED FORESTS

Petrified wood is the name given to fossilized trees created by minerals invading cavities between and in the cells of natural wood. It is created when a plant is buried in sediment and doesn't decay due to the protection from oxygen and organisms. Simply put, petrified wood is trees turned into stone, usually so accurate to the original shape of the tree that the cell structure of the plant can be noted millions of years later.

More than 60 million years ago the landscape in Patagonia was made up of verdant forest and palm trees and looked very different to the dry steppe that you find here today. In the Tertiary period, though, the Andes rose and stopped humid air and rain coming in from the west over what is today inland Patagonia, and the climate and terrain changed. At the same time, volcanoes erupted, covering the landscape and the ancient forest in ashes, which marked the start of the slow organic process of turning the wooden trunks into stone.

with deep gorges and rust-colored rock walls. The day-long hike has two starting points: either **Hostería Cueva de las Manos**, 60km south of Perito Moreno via RN40 in the north, or **Estancia Casa Piedra**, 82km south of Perito Moreno, in the west. Both routes take you down the canyon, crossing Río Pinturas, and are challenging: leave early in the morning to allow enough time; bring a hat, sunscreen, plenty of water and food. You can hire a guide to go with you, but the trails are well signposted so it's also possible to do it on your own. The caves are too far from El Chaltén to do in a day, so stay the night in Perito Moreno before venturing to the caves the following day.

Bosque Petrificado Sarmiento
Tree Trunks and Petrified Forest

A long drive from El Chaltén, 12hr or so, takes you to one of Patagonia's most striking petrified forests. Approximately 30km from **Sarmiento**, you find **Bosque Petrificado Sarmiento**, a perfectly preserved 65-million-year-old petrified forest with massive fossilized tree trunks. The mineral-rich water here has permeated the trunks, randomly scattered around the park, for thousands of years and turned the trees, brought by strong river currents from the mountain regions millions of years ago, into stone. It's a remarkable sight to see and remember that as you walk around the 2km-long circuit all visitors have to follow, you are putting your feet on Mesozoic – the last (before our own) of Earth's geological eras – wooden chips. The most popular trunk in the park and also the highlight is a hollow fossilized log that almost looks like a drainage pipe. Get here in your own car or ask at the very helpful and enthusiastic tourist office on Calle Pietrobelli in Sarmiento to book you a *remise*. If you're in charge of your own time, try to stay until sunset when **Cerro Abigarrado** and the surrounding rounded hills in the petrified forest are bathed in red and orange light. To prepare for your visit, bring plenty of water, sunscreen, a hat and some food if you are planning to stay for a while – there are toilets but no other services. If you want a guide, the tourist office in Sarmiento can put you in touch with one. They can provide you with maps and information on lodgings too.

Bosque Petrificado Sarmiento

Tierra del Fuego

SOUTHERNMOST ENDS OF THE EARTH

The world's most southerly well-populated land is a storied island where the windswept, subpolar pampa makes way for snowcapped mountains, glacial waters and Antarctic wildlife.

Perilous journeys, treacherous seas and stupendous feats: Tierra del Fuego is one of the world's most storied maritime geographies. A subpolar archipelago of shipwrecks and adventures, explorers and villains, rushes and revivals and subantarctic seas backdropped by snow-capped mountains – few places on the planet combine such epic scenery with world-famous history. The southernmost tip of the Americas, Isla Grande (the 'big island'), separated from the South American mainland some 6000 years ago when the melting glaciers flooded the Magellan Strait. In the latter half of the last millennium, explorers such as Captain Cook, Sir Francis Drake and Charles Darwin began navigating around the mysterious land of fire – so called by the first European to sail its seas,

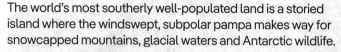

Ferdinand Magellan, who sighted smoke rising from the fires lit by the indigenous population across the archipelago.

December to February is the most accessible time due to the mild climate – perhaps too much so, given the throngs of South American tourists who book out the south during high season; temperatures reach around 15°C, and this is the best time for hiking. In winter frozen Ushuaia transforms into a Nutcracker-style snow globe, though penguins and whales migrate north, so perhaps the ideal times to visit are the shoulder seasons of autumn and spring.

Like those who came before, get ready to discover your own storied adventure on this island at the end of the world and leave with a more profound understanding of our planet.

THE MAIN AREAS

USHUAIA	RIO GRANDE	TOLHUIN
Snow globe at the Earth's end. **p446**	Steppe wildlife and northern culture capital. **p461**	Pristine glacial lakes and low-key tourism. **p471**

Left: Ruta 3 (p468); Above: Alice Island (p448)   441

Find Your Way

With Argentina's half of Tierra del Fuego spanning just over 21,000 sq km, the Ruta 3 highway connects the Chilean border with San Sebastián in the north, sweeping down past the island's towns to Ushuaia.

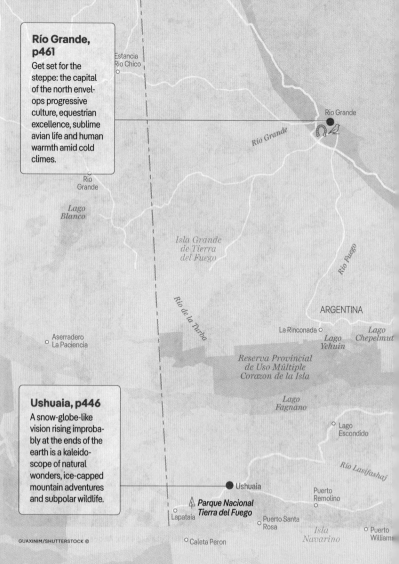

Río Grande, p461

Get set for the steppe: the capital of the north envelops progressive culture, equestrian excellence, sublime avian life and human warmth amid cold climes.

Ushuaia, p446

A snow-globe-like vision rising improbably at the ends of the earth is a kaleidoscope of natural wonders, ice-capped mountain adventures and subpolar wildlife.

GUAXINIM/SHUTTERSTOCK ©

INTER-REGIONAL TRANSPORT

Reliable minibus shuttles by Monciel and Lider run 12 times per day from the early morning to evening, connecting the cities of Río Grande and Ushuaia with a stop at Tolhuin en route. Bus Sur departs daily for Punta Arenas in Chile from Río Grande.

ON WHEELS

Two or four wheels are optimal for exploring the island. Off the Ruta 3 – gritted continually in winter – wind a series of smaller *rutas complementarias* leading to more off-the-beaten-track destinations. You'll need a 4WD to negotiate these during winter.

BIKES & BOATS

The flat terrain of the northern steppe is optimal for cycling. To explore the sites along the Beagle Channel's coastline you can take a boat tour from Ushuaia during summer.

ATLANTIC
OCEAN

ancia
Ewan

o Cabo San
Pablo

huin

Tolhuin, p471

The folk heart of the island ushers formidable Andean glacial lakes, eclectic creativity and a burgeoning epicurean scene amid striking beauty and tranquil tourism.

Río Bueno

io Moat

Río López

Beagle
Channel

Isla
Picton

N
0 — 50 km
0 — 25 miles

Plan Your Time

Ushuaia holds the lion's share of sights and tour agencies on the island. Start here, then head east and north to explore the island.

Train, Parque Nacional Tierra del Fuego (p450)

POLA DAMONTE/SHUTTERSTOCK ©

Whirlwind Tour

● You've just arrived in the southernmost well-populated city in the world. Roll on the **Tren del Fin del Mundo** (p450) into **Parque Nacional Tierra del Fuego** (p450), then revel in a hike, tour or canoe ride amid the preternaturally idyllic mountain-topped cocoon of forests, lakes and lagoons.

● After, feast on centolla (king crab) at **La Cantina Fueguina de Freddy** (p454) or merluza negra (black hake) at **Volver** (p454) to get you in the spirit for following in the wake of Darwin and Captain Cook on a boat tour around the **Beagle Channel archipelago** (p457).

● Cap off the day with *ushuaiense* (from Ushuaia) **artisanal chocolates** (p453) or **beer** (p454) when you alight.

Seasonal Highlights

The seasons pivot from mild summers to snow-blanketed winters. December to February is high season.

JANUARY

The high season – when temperatures reach their mildest – sees South Americans flood tourist destinations and hiking is more accessible.

APRIL

The end of the summer shoulder season, when subantarctic marine wildlife migrates north and some tourist sites close.

JUNE

The beginning of winter, when daylight hours shorten, snow covers the south and winter resorts reopen.

Long Weekend

● Check into a mountain *cabaña*, campsite or hotel. The next morning, wake up, pour a glass of glacier water and breathe in the clean air, feeling fresh before the shuttle collects you to join a hike to climb the Fuegian Andes and explore the **Vinciguerra Glacier** (p457).

● That night, warm up with an artisanal gin under striking constellations on **Cerro Martial** (p448) at **La Cabaña Beerpoint** (p449). The next day, head for **Estancia Harberton** (p460). Explore the marine skeletons at the visitor center and walk among the penguins of **Isla Martillo** (p448).

● Reflect on your experiences at the end of the world over freshly caught subantarctic seafood at **Puerto Almanza** (p457).

A Week on Isla Grande

● Set off to explore the north and east of the island along the iconic **Ruta 3** (p468). Stop by Paso Garibaldi for captivating views of **Lago Escondido** (p477) beneath the snowcapped Andes en route to **Lago Fagnano** (p469).

● Take lunch in one of **Tolhuin's cabin restaurants** (p475), then drive east to spend a couple of nights on an *estancia* lining the Ruta Complementaria A and visit the **Desdemona shipwreck** (p478) at San Pablo.

● Afterwards, head north and walk among subpolar birds on the beaches of the **Reserva Costa Atlantica** (p461) while exploring Río Grande before catching your flight or driving on to mainland Argentina via the border with San Sebastián.

JULY
The **National Winter Festival** takes place over the second weekend with celebrations, gourmet food and live music.

AUGUST
Join or watch the magical nighttime torchlit descent down the slope of Cerro Martial during the **Bajada de Antorchas**.

OCTOBER
The start of the tourist season. As snow thaws, days become longer, marine wildlife returns and seasonal sites reopen.

NOVEMBER
Museums and cultural centers stay open until midnight for **La Noche de los Museos'** island-wide program of events and exhibitions.

Ushuaia

GETTING AROUND

Those planning to base themselves in the center and embark on organized tours don't need anything beyond two feet. All the museums and most restaurants are based in proximity to Av San Martín and tour operators make shuttle and bus runs to collect visitors from accommodations for day trips; boat tours depart from Puerto Turístico. Shuttles depart for destinations such as Glaciar Martial, Tren del Fin del Mundo, the winter centers and the trailheads of Laguna Esmeralda and other walks from the station at the junction of Av Maipú and Juana Genoveva Fadul. The main taxi station is located at the junction of Av Maipú and Comodoro Augusto Lasserre Sur.

The descent into Ushuaia is among the most dramatic in the world, flying above shifting clouds, mountain peaks and stormy seas. The small but growing city – pronounced Oos-uw-why-a, meaning deep bay in the indigenous Yaghan (pronounced Shargan) language – is a mix of multicolored Tyrollean, mock-Tudor and Scandinavian architecture creeping up the slopes of the snowcapped crenelations of the Martial mountain range. It was first settled as a point of proximity between temperate (relatively: this is, after all, one of the closest lands to Antarctica) mountain-shouldered arable land and the Beagle Channel, where the Yamana – renamed by the missionaries who formalized the territory – sea nomads dwelt.

Today, it's a portal to pristine natural adventures: hiking, mountaineering, Antarctica and the Beagle Channel, and home to a sophisticated epicurean scene. If at any point the melange of souvenir shops, hyped-up tour groups and the occasional penguin onesie overwhelm, just gaze at the astonishing panorama of mountainscape and subantarctic sea to remember that you're standing at the edge of the world.

☑ TOP TIP

Most restaurants close during the afternoon, opening between noon and 3pm for lunch and 7pm to 11pm for dinner. Reserve a table if you don't wish to queue. Outside of these sittings cafes remain open throughout the day. Book accommodations well in advance, especially during the high season or national holidays.

SAIKO3P/SHUTTERSTOCK ©

Ushuaia

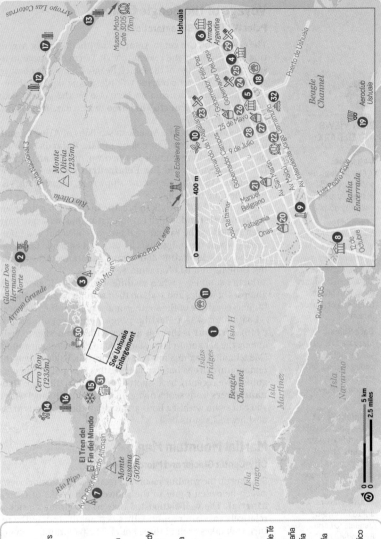

SIGHTS
1 Bridges Island
see 16 Canopy Ushuaia
2 Cascada de los Amigos
3 Cerro Alarkén Nature Reserve
4 Galería Temática Historia Fueguina
5 La Antigua Casa de Gobierno
see 4 Museo del Fin del Mundo
6 Museo Marítimo de Ushuaia
7 Parque Nacional Tierra del Fuego
8 Paseo de los Antiguos Pobladores
9 Plaza Islas Malvinas
10 Reserva Natural Urbana Bosque Yatana

ACTIVITIES, COURSES & TOURS
11 Alice Island
12 Centro Invernal
13 Cerro Castor
14 Cerro Martial
15 Club Andino Ushuaia
16 Escuela de Esquí
17 Llanos del Castor
18 Piratour
19 Ushuaia Divers

EATING
20 Ana é Juana
21 Chocolates Edelweiss
22 Jeremy Button Gintonería
23 Kaupé
24 La Cantina Fueguina de Freddy
25 La Casa de los Mariscos
26 Laguna Negra
27 Ramos Generales el Almacén
28 Tante Sara
29 Volver

DRINKING & NIGHTLIFE
30 Chloe Casa de Té
31 Garibaldi Cerveza de Montaña
see 16 La Cabaña Beerpoint
see 16 La Cabaña Casa de Té

TRANSPORT
32 Puerto Turístico

447

Voyage of the Beagle Channel
Polar Wildlife on Subantarctic Isles

The closest you can get to Antarctica without leaving Argentina, and arguably the reason to visit Tierra del Fuego in itself, the archipelago of the fabled Beagle Channel is home to captivating Antarctic marine wildlife, iconic sights and subpolar fauna unmatched anywhere else on the planet. Boat tours depart from **Puerto Turístico** twice a day, in the mornings and afternoons.

Say hello to the South American sea lions of **Alice Island**, delight in the cormorant colony of **Isla Pajaros** (also replete with barking pinnipeds when we visited) and survey the iconic, century-old **Les Eclaireurs** lighthouse. It's the site of the MS *Monte Cervantes* shipwreck, occasionally visible when the tide is low.

Book a tour with a walk to breathe in the crisp marine air on **Bridges Island**, which carbon dating has shown to have been settled by the Yaghans – there's a replica hut and information about the indigenous history and endemic fauna set against the scintillating 360-degree panorama of surrounding Ushuaia and Isla Navarino.

During summer – when wildlife watchers will also catch glimpses of whales and seals on their sailings along the mountainous coastline of the southernmost point of the Americas – boats tour to Isla Martillo *pinguinera* (penguin colony; p448). **Piratour** is the only agency with permission to walk among the penguins of the island and to tour here year-round. (Magellanic Penguins migrate to Peninsula Valdés when the temperature drops but Papua penguins stay put). King penguins have recently been spotted on Isla Martillo too. **Ushuaia Divers** leads scuba diving in the Beagle Channel where you can swim with sea lions and explore the notorious array of shipwrecks at its base.

Martial Mountain Magic
City-Center Glacier and Micro-Resort

Snaking up the winding mountain road, Beagle Channel views sweep below en route to the snowcapped peaks of **Cerro Martial**. The well-signposted hike to the cirque glacier is relatively easy after an initially steep uphill stretch; the return trek takes around three hours. The panoramic views of the surrounding mountains and Beagle Channel are slightly more impressive than of the glacier itself.

At the resort base stand hiking and snow outfitters. Longstanding log cabin **Escuela de Esquí** also runs ski and snow-

BEST VIEWS AFTER DARK

Dog Gone
Whizz through the snow-covered forests of the Tierra Mayor valley by dogsled.

Fire and Ice
Revel in the contrast of cold air and thermal waters over panoramic views via alfresco hydrotherapy during a night visit to the spa of Arakur Resort.

Dark Skies
Stargaze at dazzling subantarctic constellations on the beach and nature reserve of Playa Larga.

Midnight Feast
Take a guided night hike and ski lesson on Cerro Martial then dine in a forest dome with Patagon Mountain Agency.

Starlit Waters
Join a tour from Ushuaia to Lago Escondido for a sunset kayak beneath the stars and cordillera.

 WHERE TO DRINK IN USHUAIA

La Cabaña Beerpoint
Set at the base of Cerro Martial, grab an artisanal beer around the garden fire of this log cabin bar.

Dublin Pub
Irish bar faithful to its name set off the main drag and open into the early hours.

Club 1210
Open until dawn with electronic music nightly, this club near the seafront is perfect for going out.

boarding classes in season. In 2023 the **Centro de Montana Glaciar Martial** opened in the revamped former chairlift station with guided treks encompassing night hikes.

Continue the adventure by coursing the nine zip lines of **Canopy Ushuaia** or ski cross-country with **Francisco Jerman**, which is part of veteran **Club Andino Ushuaia**, with whom you can book a snowboarding, mountain-climbing or ice-skating class.

Afterwards, join the queues for a table at **La Cabaña Casa de Té**: this vivacious, pastel-hued tea parlor might be the closest South America gets to Hygge. For something stronger, grab a fireside artisanal beer in the garden or log cabin of **La Cabaña Beerpoint**. Taxis back down the mountain are on standby outside for tired legs and buses leave on the hour during afternoons. If you can't make it up the mountain then the mountain can come to you: Glaciar Martial provides most of the tap water to Ushuaia.

Urban Nature

City Hikes with Mountain Views

Warmups for daylong hikes and with iconic mountain views, pockets of nature cross the city center. Well-signed trails lead around the **Cerro Alarkén Nature Reserve**, accessed behind the Arakur Ushuaia Resort, snaking between the trees marked with yellow and blue paints, as well as a more demanding red hike. It's set on a spur with views of Cinco Hermanos, Monte Olivia and, on a clear day, the Vinciguerra Glacier.

Approximately halfway down the same unnamed road, a sign and car park marks the beginning of the 8km, four-hour round trip to the effervescent, deep-drop **Cascada de los Amigos** in the Río Chico valley. Walk the path until it splits and then follow the left fork. Cross the river and walk through the woods until you reach the foot of the waterfall.

Just a few blocks north of Av San Martín sprouts **Reserva Natural Urbana Bosque Yatana**, an enchanting urban forest. Dotted with art installations, re-creations of indigenous lodgings and facts surrounding the endemic fauna, the craft center to the front is the meeting point for the various classes and events held here. A precious introduction to the surrounding nature and feast for the soul.

GREAT GLACIERS

To experience the real deal and climb the mountains that you see all around, head to p457 to learn more about the best glacier trekking on **Isla Grande**.

STANDING ROOM ONLY

Jostling with fellow passengers for a view of subantarctic marine wildlife is unforgettable on a number of levels... Terramar Turismo and Rumbo Sur are travel agencies accommodating larger groups for those who thrive in the throng. Ché Turismo, Tierra Turismo and Tierra del Fuego Aventura specialize in smaller vehicles and vessels. With group sizes of between 10 and 20 people, they've the ability to adjust tour itineraries to optimal timings and closer, quieter views. For last-minute tickets or to get an overview of the range of tours by different providers, visit the booths next to the Puerto Turístico.

WHERE TO DRINK IN USHUAIA

Moat
Sophisticated speakeasy-style cocktail bar tucked underneath a tapas restaurant serving great gin. Closed Tuesdays.

The Birra
Bottle shop below, beer stop up top. This sleek beer bar has superlative craft draughts.

Cervecería Grut '84
Log cabin in the Dos Banderas district with locally crafted pints poured from wooden beer pumps.

MATYAS REHAK/SHUTTERSTOCK ©

TOP SIGHT

Parque Nacional Tierra del Fuego

PRACTICALITIES

Scan this QR code for more information.

The most visited site of the archipelago has a different terrain and mode of exploration for every age, weather, ability and inclination. Set across nearly 700 sq km and extending to the border with Chile, whether explored via a whirlwind tour or the stirring isolation of a multiday hike, straddling subpolar sea, snowcapped mountains, glacial lakes, emerald lagoons and pony-grazing valleys, this Unesco World Heritage Site is a microcosm of the highlights of Argentina.

DON'T MISS

Lapataia Bay

Tren del Fin del Mundo

Lago Acigami

Lago Roca Canoeing

Bahía Ensenada Zaratiegui

Beagle Channel

Laguna Verde

Tren del Fin del Mundo

In general, anywhere in Ushuaia branded 'end of the world' should come with a buyer-beware warning. However, this evocative steam locomotive winding between lenga forests and snowcapped mountains lives up to the hype. This re-creation of the 7km journey made by the city's first immigrant wave – prisoners exiled to the turn-of-the-20th-century penal colony of Ushuaia to mine the land to build the city – meanders from the faux-period station towards Parque Nacional Tierra del Fuego. Insightful commentary about the prison history of Ushuaia in four languages is inevitably upstaged by the rolling views of wild horses grazing tundra snaked by glacial streams, La Macarena waterfall stop, comedy prisoner photo ops and panoramic mountain-topped surroundings.

Take a Hike

Through lenga forests fringing glacial waters beneath towering snowcapped mountains, trails span from coastal walks weaving from sea to lake to arduous mountain hikes and short waterfall detours. The Senda Costera trail (closed May to November) leads from Bahía Ensenada Zaratiegui to Lago Acigami along the iconic western coastline of the Beagle Channel through forests, hidden coves and beaches. The Cerro Guanaco is a challenging uphill mountain hike to binary views of the sea and Fuegian Andes (to embark on this you must register with the Alakush Visitors Center prior), while the stroll to Río Pipo waterfall is an easy 15-minute ascent. The trail up the mountains to Laguna del Caminante and Lago Superior spans several days, starting in the national park.

Water Wonders

Opening like a lunar crater is the perfect sphere of Lago Acigami – a pristine expanse of glacial water sentinelled by imposing ice-capped mountain escarpments and Chile beyond. Various trails lead around the crescent-shaped pebble beach – follow it to fruition on the Hito XXVI trail to reach the border with Chile; there are log benches for lakeside contemplation en route. With summertime canoeing (the only official activity allowed in the national park) and camping, Lago Acigami unveils novel ways to explore the heart of Parque Nacional Tierra del Fuego. Short trails of 10 minutes or so lead around the wooden walkways lining Lapataia Bay, the culmination of the Pan-American Highway. Thirty minutes beyond shimmer the emerald waters of Laguna Verde.

Refuge at the End of the World

The handsome surrounds of the capacious Alakush Visitors Center welcome with a small exhibition explaining the glacial, anthropological and constructed evolution of the national park and a roomy cafeteria with panoramic views and a fire. Seek out the space to the back right with views of the ice-capped mountains fringing the Lapataia River.

To send a postcard from the end of the world, Bahía Ensenada Zaratiegui is the last place to do so! Closed when we visited, others reported that septuagenarian postmaster Carlos de Lorenzo, self-declared prime minister of the Republic of Rhodonda (the island where the post office was formerly based) opposite, is increasingly absent of late. Still, the highly decorated pier-top hut makes for a requisite scenic photo stop. Those who've brought their passports to be stamped might bear in mind that novelty markers can render documents invalid.

SIGNS OF LIFE

Hikers will likely encounter silver foxes, beavers and a myriad of birds. Look out for raised mounds of earth along the coastline – these could be middens, left by the Yaghans who dwelt here. Try spotting the Alakush flightless steamer duck, which lends its name to the visitors center, and guanacos and condors along the Cerro Guanaco trail.

TOP TIPS

- Try to reach sights such as Lapataia Bay in the morning or late afternoon.
- Take the Tren del Fin del Mundo one way, then hike or join a tour to explore the park before or after.
- Camping grounds are located at Bahía Ensenada, Lago Roca, Laguna Verde, Río Pipo and Bahía Ensenada Zaratiegui.
- Some hiking routes close during winter.
- When we visited it was essential to have a tour booked after alighting from the End of the World Train in winter.
- Buses leave Ushuaia for the park on the hour each morning. There are six stops, including at Bahía Ensenada Zaratiegui, the Alakush Visitors Center and Lapataia Bay.

Galería Temática Historia Fuegina

PEAK PRICING

Tierra del Fuego has the second highest income and is among the wealthiest regions of Argentina. Pair that with a unique end of the world tourism proposition and prices climb high in Ushuaia. For our costings $$ covers a room in budget accommodations in the city, while for price indicators of $$$ expect to bag yourself somewhere midrange. Luxury hotel prices scale the same levels of their equivalents in the cities and resorts of western Europe and the US – hospitality costing more in line with the rest of the country can be found in and around Tolhuin and Río Grande.

MORE IN USHUAIA

Museums: East

Ushuaia's Defining Museum Triptych

Tours by a Yaghan lecturer, a national-level museum set in a panopticon and an audiovisual tour of Ushuaia through the millennia: step inside the city's major museums situated around the east of Av San Martín.

Each of **Museo Marítimo de Ushuaia's** five wings is devoted to a different local fascination – from the maritime history running from the Magellan Strait, to Antarctica and the Yaghan provenance. The most atmospheric of all is the backstory of Ushuaia and the 19th-century panopticon in which the museum stands, a former penal colony dubbed the 'Siberia of the South', set across cells once occupied by Argentina's most notorious prisoners.

Spend an hour and a half exploring tableaux depicting the history of Tierra del Fuego, from the indigenous communities who lived here c 4000 BCE through to the adventures of Shackleton and Darwin, on an audiovisual tour set across four stories at **Galería Temática Historia Fuegina**.

 ## WHERE TO STAY IN USHUAIA

Los Acebos
Sister hotel and neighbor to Las Hayas has stupendous views, great restaurants and fantastic service. $$$

Arakur Mountain Resort
Luxury mountaintop retreat with outdoor hydrotherapy, horse riding, onsite trails and views for days. $$$

Los Cauquenes
Luxury resort hotel set on the seafront just outside the center with an extensive program of activities. $$$

Every day, lecturer Victor Vargas Filgueira, member of Ushuaia's small Paliakoala indigenous community and son of Cristina Calderón, the last Yaghan speaker in the world (d 2022), gives talks in Spanish about the region's indigenous history and culture at 11am. Ask to see his ancestral basketry and handicrafts before exploring the absorbing exhibits on Antarctic wildlife and human history of Tierra del Fuego at the **Museo del Fin del Mundo**. It's spread over two veteran buildings on Av Maipú. The second, **La Antigua Casa de Gobierno**, built in 1890, covers the sinking of MS *Monte Cervantes* through original footage and first-person accounts. Tickets to this and Museo Marítimo de Ushuaia allow reentry over a couple of days: you may wish to come back for more.

Sweet Love in a Cold Climate
Extraordinary Cold-Beating Confectioneries

From the ubiquitous chocolatiers lining Av San Martín to destination mountain teahouses, Ushuaia's dizzying array of cake and chocolate shops dot and decorate the city.

On Av San Martín, pick from eight Patagonian chocolate *providores*. **Laguna Negra** has superlative sweets and – like most of its contemporaries – doubles as a hot chocolate stop – while **Chocolates Edelweiss** is a traditional independent gem. *Fuegian* (from Tierra del Fuego) patisserie **Tante Sara's** *chocotortas* and other cakes are so loved that there are now two smart but traditional cafes on Av San Martín and another in Río Grande. **Ana é Juana** is a contemporary Patagonian baker purveying artful South American desserts.

Stepping into **Ramos Generales el Almacén** on Av Maipú feels like entering Ushuaia circa the Victorian era; it doubles as a museum with vintage toys, cash registers and treasure chests lining the century-old interiors alongside glass counters displaying decadent desserts. For brews with a view, **La Cabaña Casa de Té** with its polygonal gift shop is a picture of pastel-hued Patagonian perfection, while reservation-only **Chloe Casa de Té** pours homemade infusions at this mountainside tearoom and dome with views extending over the Beagle Channel.

Neptune's Lure
Sensational Subantarctic Seafood

With a gastronomy scene mature beyond its age, Ushuaia's seafood menus are unparalleled anywhere else on the planet. Centollas (king crabs, pronounced centosha) can grow to 19cm and live for up to 30 years – many meet their fate on a plate

TAKE TO THE SKIES

For more extensive mountain adventures get a bird's-eye view over the region's most beautiful – and inaccessible – sights. Soar over Laguna Esmeralda, get closer to the peak of Ushuaia's highest mountain, Monte Olivia, glean sights of Chilean Tierra del Fuego and alight at the top of Alvear, where you can heli-ski, too. Take a shortcut to lunch at Puerto Almanza and penetrate the Península Mitre. HeliUshuaia flies passengers in choppers over Ushuaia and the Fuegian Andes mountaintops, while Aeroclub Ushuaia can take passengers in light aircrafts over Isla de los Estados (and the lighthouse that inspired Jules Verne's *The Lighthouse at the End of the World*), Cordillera Darwin and Cape Horn.

WHERE TO EAT IN USHUAIA

Mercado del Jardín	Isla Vegana	Xpresso
Tyrollean food court on Av Martin with everything from a sushi truck to pizzas. $	Meat-free bakery located off eastern Av Maipu serving excellent burgers, sandwiches, cakes and salads. $	Humming all-day upstairs cafe in Av Martin with smoothies, bakery and Beagle Channel views. $

Cerro Castor

TANGO AT THE END OF THE WORLD

Trot the tango at the southernmost point in the world. Masdanza is a dance studio with a program of various classes tucked just above and off Av San Martín. For fanatics of Argentina's national dance, Tango B'n'B is a themed accommodation helmed by a family of musicians showcasing live concerts and accordion courses to guests. Equal parts immersive experience, supper club and museum, at Cavas del Fin del Mundo the dining experience travels the rooms of this vintage museum building where tango and music are instrumental to the experience. For the all-encompassing introduction, dedicated nights with shows, supper and dancing are held every Wednesday and Friday evening at Onírico Sur's theater space.

after a sojourn in the myriad of window-front tanks lining the city. They are best undressed or *gratinated* – a regional specialty where the crustacean's plump, meaty legs are covered and baked in a ramekin with oozing parmesan cheese.

Pescatarians appreciate that plump, oily salmon from the Beagle Channel is among the most flavorsome in the world, and merluza negra (black hake or toothfish) is a delicacy caught by divers deep in the Beagle Channel – you can almost taste Antarctica in the delicate, crisp flakes.

On Av San Martín **La Casa de los Mariscos** and **La Cantina Fueguina de Freddy** are accessible seafood restaurants. For occasional dining, intimate **Volver** on Av Maipú is evocatively styled like a fishing hut, fronted by a celebrated chef and famed for its ceviche, while **Kaupé** has won multiple awards for its immaculate and imaginative seafood dishes.

Good Libations
Where the Craft Is

It'll be love at first sip when you try Ushuaia's sublime heavenly water. Where else in the world can you not only drink subantarctic glacial water on tap but bathe in it too? Over the past decade it's also spurred on the island's thriving artisanal distillery and brewery scene.

 GET YOUR SKATES ON

Laguna del Diablo
This city-center lagoon becomes a vast ice hockey pitch when the water freezes over.

Cerro Castor
Upscale ice-skating in the winter resorts' only ice skating rink. Free entry with a ski pass.

Carlos Tachuela Oyarzún
Set on the western waterfront, this outdoor municipal rink is the hub for locals hitting the ice.

In Tierra del Fuego beer isn't so much an après-hike thought as an obsession. A burgeoning collection of micro-breweries craft beer from glacial water, Patagonian hops and mountain herbs. The most famous, Cerveza Beagle, can be found in every bottle shop and bar in town, while **Garibaldi Cerveza de Montaña** brews its beers onsite.

For something stiffer, Gin 3005 can be visited at Haruwen's **Museo Moto Cafe 3005** (free shots to anyone who enters). **Jeremy Button Gintonería** is a buzzing seafront bar and gin distillery, and is less unfortunate than its namesake – a Yaghan apparently sold for a button, then kidnapped by Robert FitzRoy to be paraded around England, before returning on the HMS *Beagle* with Darwin some years later. Whatever your poison, would-be returners should sample a pint or spirit infused with calafate – local lore decrees that those who try the Patagonian berry are destined to return.

Powder & Hounds

Frozen Adventures at the Winter Centers

The Tierra Mayor valley, like much of the lowlands lining the southern tip of Tierra del Fuego, was formed from a giant glacier that broke off from the Darwin range 25,000 years ago, molding the flat, baking dish shape that so dramatically accents – and affords access to – the surrounding peaks.

Those visiting between June and September can enter a Narnian winter wonderland without climbing a mountain. Go husky-sledding through lenga forests from the **Centro Invernal** or ice-climb a frozen waterfall. Snowmobile through the 12 acres of snow-swept valley at **Llanos del Castor**, then hit the 19 slopes of the only full-scale ski resort in the extreme south of the Americas, **Cerro Castor**. This is a sophisticated enterprise of a former Olympian, with chairlifts, restaurants, après-piste deejays and lodgings; some slopes have engineered snow guaranteeing skiing from when the season starts on the day after the winter solstice. They're particularly appealing after dark, when twinkling lights and hot chocolate heighten the contrast of night sky and snow. All have homey onsite restaurants serving excellent *parrilla*.

Next Stop: Antarctica

Cruise Control Trips South

From October to March each year, cruise ships bound for Antarctica stop at Ushuaia to collect passengers before heading to the seventh continent. The cost is around US$10,000 – last-minute spaces can be found in agencies such as 4x4 Ushuaia and Rumbo Sur, with prices reduced to around US$4000. The minimum time needed to reach Antarctica is a five-day round trip to the South Georgia islands, but most sailings take two weeks or more. There are two-hour flights from Punta Arenas in Chile from December to February to King George Island, with itineraries ranging from one-day round trips to fly and sail packages. Those curious to explore cruise options can visit a number of travel agencies on Av San Martín specializing in these.

SURF THE TURF

Of course, Tierra del Fuego is renowned not only for its surf – but also its turf, as the birthplace of Argentine sheep farming. You can navigate through a range of *parrillas* serving fresh lamb from the island's *estancias*. Fuegian *cazuelas* (casseroles) are a hearty, slow-cooked specialty. Isabel Cocina al Disco on Av Maipú serves generous sharing dishes overlooking the Beagle Channel, while Kaur's *cazuela* is an explosion of warming flavors. Accessible Estancia la Parrilla and Moustachio serve reliable lamb fired on the spit, although to truly sample farm-to-table freshness the *parrillas* of Tolhuin and Río Grande lead, situated on the doorstep of Tierra del Fuego's *estancias*.

Beyond
Ushuaia

GETTING AROUND

The shuttle station in Ushuaia has regular minibuses running to the base of Laguna Esmeralda and the Centros Invernales. Taxis from the town publish a list of set fares to Harberton, Almanza and all destinations outside the city. Snow poles, equipment and crampons are available from the Centros Invernales and outfitters in town. During summer, tours taking in the Beagle Channel archipelago travel by boat and land to Estancia Harberton, and to Puerto Almanza year-round. The Ruta Complementaria J requires confident driving and a 4WD in winter.

☑ TOP TIP

Travel times deviate dramatically in the winter months when conditions can be precarious. Factor in a possible time increase of 20% to 50% for off-the-beaten-track hikes or drives.

Head north for ambitious hikes on impossibly beautiful mountains to breathtaking glaciers. Dining and historic settlements delight deep along the southern coast.

If Ushuaia is the embarkation, then its surroundings are the revelation. With snow- and icescapes covering its upper climes year-round, you can get closer to the iconic peaks of Cinco Hermanos and Monte Olivia on day hikes or longer exploring the Fuegian Andes escarpment. It's an ice kingdom of marine-hued lagoons, altitudinous snowcapped summits, grottos, hidden glaciers and waterfalls. Heading east along the southern coast, you'll discover a surprise sea-to-table gourmet hamlet, majestic marine wildlife with views of Puerto Williams so close that phones reset to Chilean carriers, and Tierra del Fuego's first *estancia*, whose founders played a pivotal role in the formation of Ushuaia.

Carbajal Valley

Carbajal Valley TIME FROM USHUAIA: 20 MINS 🚗

Glacier Trekking in the Mountains

Among Ushuaia's greatest lures, the surrounding glaciers have been formed over tens of thousands of years, presenting a taster to its neighbor 1000km south, Antarctica. Set in the cradle of the Fuegian Andes, hours- or days-long mountain adventures begin in valleys within the city or a 20-minute drive beyond Ushuaia.

The most challenging of Ushuaia's entry-level day hikes are to the surrounding glaciers. To reach Vinciguerra Glacier leave from the gate in Camino del Valle to enter the Andorra Valley and trek the steep ascent through forest paths to the Laguna de los Tempanos. Follow the right-hand curve around the turquoise lagoon to reach the glacier; you'll need a guide and equipment to negotiate this in winter. Vinciguerra's ice caves can be visited, but it's strongly discouraged to enter these or any others without a guide or official notification that it's safe to do so. In late 2022, a person died from falling ice at the region's Jimbo cave.

The ascent to the Alvear Glacier is among the area's most ambitious – and magnificent – to undertake, necessitating overnight camping on the vicinity's third-tallest mountain. Compañia de Guías de Patagonia are experienced mountain guides steering this adventure and others nearby – they can adjust itineraries to individual abilities and interests. The Ojo del Albino is among the island's most spectacular glaciers – only readily accessible in winter, when Laguna Esmeralda freezes over. Adventurers will still need crampons and ice picks to reach it. The same is true for Monte Olivia – the tallest peak at 1326m – which can only be scaled in the coldest climes.

Puerto Almanza to Harberton/The Beagle Channel Coast TIME FROM USHUAIA: 1½ HOURS 🚗

Catch of the Day

About 1½-hour's drive beyond Ushuaia, past winding forest tracks, Lago Victoria, gaucho *refugios* and roaming cows, lies the fishing hamlet of Puerto Almanza. The Ruta Complementaria K, known locally as La Ruta de la Centolla, curls right off the Ruta J and is lined by traditional wooden cottage dining rooms idyllically facing and fishing from the Beagle Channel. Gaze 5km across the strait to Isla Navarino's Puerto Williams (so close that phones reset to Chilean carriers along this stretch). La Mesita de Almanza and La Sirena y el Capitán are two highly rated, intimate dining rooms welcoming just a dozen or so diners each. The latter is highly decorated and

TIERRA DEL FUEGO'S TALLEST PEAKS

Monte Olivia is the highest mountain in the range visible from Ushuaia – you'll notice it towering like Mt Zermatt, 1326m high and crowning the peaks above the city. Its glacier is named after Salesian father Alberto de Maria Agostini, the first person recorded to have climbed Monte Olivia, in 1913.

Iconic Cinco Hermanos is just dwarfed by Monte Olivia at 1280m – it's named after Thomas Bridges' five sons for its jagged five-peaked summit. The trail, 867m up its face, is a challenging 4½-half-hour round trip.

The highest mountain in Tierra del Fuego is Monte Darwin across the border in the Chilean icescape of the Cordillera Darwin range, standing at 2488m tall.

MOUNTAIN GUIDES & TOURS

Arpon Turismo
Excellent family-run agency leading small-group tours to the Vinciguerra and Ojo del Albino glaciers.

Canal Fun
Long-established tour operator with a comprehensive array of small-group day hikes and tours.

Patagon Mountain Agency
Agency steering intrepid – and varied – day hikes around the glaciers, ice climbing and more.

Begin the adventure by driving or taking the 10am shuttle from Ushuaia to the **❶ Valle de Lobos**, 19km east of the city off the Ruta 3. Make sure to bring waterproof clothing: hiking or Wellington boots are essential, plus water and food to enjoy at the lagoon. Heading north, begin at the sign marked 1 and course the wooden walkway to head through towering lenga forests for around 1km on this four- to five-hour out-and-back hike.

Alight into a clearing with dazzling views of the mountain-backed Carbajal Valley. Head right to follow the river and, after 700m, re-enter the **❷ forest**, following the blue signs on the trees (or an organized group) uphill. Watch out for silver foxes and beavers along the way. Exiting the forest after 1.3km, you enter the **❸ peat bog area**. This is the most challenging terrain – but also one that's endemic of Tierra del Fuego – on the ascent, fully fledged falls are common. In general, following the left-hand side can be least dense, but look for a group to see where the pros are navigating.

After you pass this, follow the Río Esmeralda again (perhaps washing footwear and hands off in its waters), and be sure to turn around and admire the panorama of the mountains before you and river valley below. As you veer steeper up the ascent for a further kilometer, observe how the stream becomes a deeper green in color, flowing by the rocks at its summit. Surmount these to reach the perfect sphere of **❹ Laguna Esmeralda** – enjoy the peace of the emerald green waters nestled in the ring of mountains, admiring the **❺ Ojo del Albino glacier** beyond, before retracing your steps back to base.

overlooks fishing folk pulling in the day's catch. Sometimes, customers lend a hand in helping to reel it in, too.

Five kilometers past the small port, Alma Yagan is a cookery concept helmed by Tierra del Fuego's only female captain, who guides visitors in preparing seafood dishes at her cosy Beagle Channel–side forest *cabaña* before they sit down to devour the fruits (de mer) of their labors. Winding along the waterfront, past the tiny settlement of Punta Parana, beckons Puerto Pirata. The restaurant of the same name is nearly as decorative as the gourmet dishes here: Cascada del Duende flows behind it for those seeking to walk off fish suppers. Watch out for roaming whales and playful sea lions basking in the Beagle Channel, who no doubt come here for the great seafood, too.

Tierra del Fuego's First Estancia

Lucas Bridges' seminal autobiography *Uttermost Part of the Earth* reads like a thriller, depicting the 1870s founding of Ushuaia that might have been forgotten if not for his diary. His father, Thomas, was the first European colonizer in Tierra del Fuego, assigned as an English missionary to convert the Yamanas to Christianity, and wrote the only dictionary of their now archaic language. When he rescinded his church role in 1886, he was awarded the land now lying some 75km from Ushuaia along the Ruta J. His descendants still own and run the collection of dreamily pastoral red-roofed white buildings, surrounding islands and the pastures flanking the Beagle Channel as a museum, restaurants and a homestay.

Accommodations are set in the simple original cottages of Estancia Harberton, with packages ranging from bed-and-breakfast to full-board, complete with private tours of the

SEA TO PLATE

To sample the island's finest and freshest centolla head to **Puerto Almanza** (p457), where king crabs are caught before your eyes and served in the up-and-coming gourmet fishing hamlet's seafront restaurants.

NOT THE END OF THE WORLD

Even the last city in the world faces competition: in 2019 Chile declared Isla Navarino (whose capital, Puerto Williams, vividly faces Puerto Almanza at just 5km away) a city, technically making that the southernmost in the world. The channel crossing between Argentina and Chile closed during the pandemic, with boat trips from Ushuaia (mornings daily, November to March) only recommencing in autumn 2023. Reaching Isla Navarino year-round is possible via Punta Arenas in Chile. DAP Airlines runs flights, while the Yaghan ferry voyages via Cordillera Darwin's Glacier Alley. It's well worth the journey, with the world's largest living Yaghan community, Dientes de Navarino hike – part of which is named after a Lonely Planet writer – and Cape Horn beyond.

WHERE TO STAY ON RUTA K

Oveja Verde B&B y Cabañas
Rustic posada set in Puerto Parano with helpful hosts and restaurant onsite. **$$**

Refugio Punta Parana
Isolated log cabin set in nature with basic furnishings and glorious sea views. **$**

Biblioteca Rural José Larralde
Just past Puerto Pirata, this small farm and library sometimes welcomes visitors wishing to stay. **$**

THE END OF THE ROAD

Along the track around 20km east of Estancia Harberton, at the end of the Ruta J, stands the huge domain of Estancia Moat. Established by one of Thomas Bridges' fellow missionaries, it's home to vast swathes of Beagle Channel coastline, fields and rivers. The wild horses and guanaco herds are synonymous with the island's east. It's also the entry point for exploring the Peninsular Punta Mitre's south coast – the most historical shoreline of the protected wilderness – by foot. Alma Calma Expediciones has a three-day hike from here to Cabo San Pío, and Terre de Feu Authentique leads week-long rambles along this coast.

Acatushun Visitors Center

MORE EXCELLENT ESTANCIAS...

The Ruta A to **Cabo San Pablo** (p479) is an hour's drive from Río Grande and lined with excellent *estancias* such as Las Hijas, San Pablo and Rolito, where you can stay the night or take a day tour to experience life on a working farm.

islands. Daytrippers can tour the Acatushun Visitors Center, which has an impressive array of marine skeletons and fossils salvaged from the islands' shores; you can also tour replica Yaghan huts in nature walks, reserve a visit to Isla Martillo and delight in afternoon tea overlooking the Beagle Channel every day from 2pm to 7pm except Tuesdays. The reservation-only restaurant offers Fuegian fine-dining for lunch.

Estancia Harberton is only open from October to May, when many tour operators visit here from Ushuaia by boat, incorporating activities such as hiking on Gable Island, sea kayaking, lunch in nearby Puerto Almanza, and perhaps the highlight of the entire Beagle Channel: the Isla Martillo penguin colony. Piratours is the only agency allowed to walk in the *pinguinera* (penguin colony) and takes groups of 20 passengers, with 10 people alighting on the islet at a time.

Río Grande

Combining a big city feel with a small town's warmth, Río Grande is the capital of northern Tierra del Fuego and a sprawling industrial hub. The antithesis of its rival Ushuaia, both in landscape – set at the heart of the Steppe – and its utilitarian architecture and 1950s grid layout, Río Grande is a textbook study in urban planning. While its surrounding *estancias* and Misión date back to the late 1800s, the city itself grew to accommodate the influx created by the successive gold, livestock, hydrocarbon and tax-free rushes of Tierra del Fuego's north. Numbering some thousand residents in 1945, the population roughly doubled during each successive decade until the '80s when it grew to 38,000. Today 120,000 people live here. What Río Grande lacks in prettiness, it makes up for with a serious and progressive cultural scene, island-leading equestrianism, subpolar bird watching and windswept walks on its steppe coastline.

Walk on the Wild Side
Coastal Bird Watching and Walking

Swooping the flightpath of a soaring array of interpolar migratory and Patagonian seabirds, the Reserva Costa Atlantica avian sanctuary sweeps Isla Grande's northeast coast.

Cross the Punta Mosconi over the Río Grande to reach **Punta Popper**, an important protected nature reserve home to birdlife distinct in the world. Wander among hundreds of falcons, albatrosses, oystercatchers and loicas pecking at supersized peach-colored conches and arctic shells along the dark sand seashore to the flocks gathered on the estuarine spit flanked by the big river.

Returning to the center, continue north along the seafront to search out the giant bird sculpture crowing **Centro de Interpretación Ambiental**. Spend two hours tracking the extraordinary life of the subpolar ebb and flow along the beach trail surveying the skeleton of a beached whale en route, or join the ecological center's free guided nature walks.

Resident flamingos fly from **Laguna de los Patos** when it

GETTING AROUND

Río Grande is best explored with wheels, and is flat and largely constructed to an immaculate grid layout. The central bus station is located on Av Belgrano, with connections around the city as well as further-flung locations such as Punta Delgada and Punta Arenas in Chile. Destinations outside the city center can be reached via car, bicycle or taxi too. For the latter, most establishments will call an operator to arrive within 15 minutes.

☑ TOP TIP

Río Grande's museums and cultural attractions are closed or only partially open during weekends. Misión Salesiana and Centro de Interpretación Ambiental open Monday to Friday, Museo Virginia Choquintel opens 3pm to 6pm on weekends, while the Museo Fueguino de Arte Niní Bernardello is closed on Sundays. Check online or visit the excellent Tourist Information Center on Plaza Almirante Brown for more information.

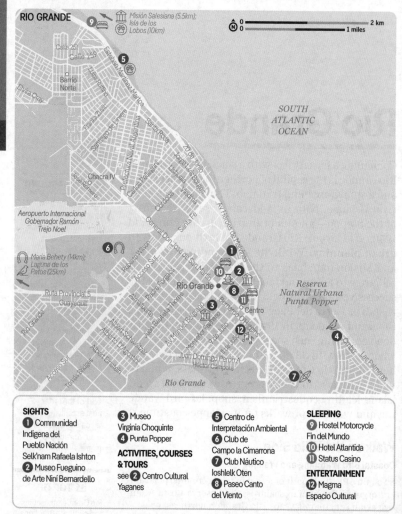

RIO GRANDE

Misión Salesiana (5.5km);
Isla de los Lobos (10km)

SOUTH
ATLANTIC
OCEAN

Aeropuerto Internacional
Gobernador Ramón
Trejo Noel

María Behety (14km);
Laguna de los
Patos (25km)

Ruta Provincial s
Guayaquil

Río Grande

Reserva
Natural Urbana
Punta Popper

Río Grande

SIGHTS
1 Comunidad
Indígena del
Pueblo Nación
Selk'nam Rafaela Ishton
2 Museo Fueguino
de Arte Niní Bernardello

3 Museo
Virginia Choquinte
4 Punta Popper

**ACTIVITIES, COURSES
& TOURS**
see 2 Centro Cultural
Yaganes

5 Centro de
Interpretación Ambiental
6 Club de
Campo la Cimarrona
7 Club Náutico
Ioshlelk Oten
8 Paseo Canto
del Viento

SLEEPING
9 Hostel Motorcycle
Fin del Mundo
10 Hotel Atlántida
11 Status Casino

ENTERTAINMENT
12 Magma
Espacio Cultural

freezes over, but you can take to the ice to skate instead. Horseback riding around this city center nature reserve happens year-round.

Once upon a time it sheltered beachside Selk'nam settlements: today stand dozens of lively shrines to Gauchito Gil at **Cabo Domingo's** base. The ascent and return to the looming bluff's 100m-high summit takes an hour and is best exercised with caution. On a clear day, you can spot Río Chico and **Isla de los Lobos** through a lens. The sea lion island is also accessible on foot, via horseback from **Misión Salesiana** and by kayak from **Club Náutico Ioshlelk Oten**.

WALK LIKE A PENGUIN
For avian enthusiasts a visit to walk among the penguins of Isla Martillo is unmissable. It's situated and owned by **Estancia Harberton** (p460) on the Beagle Channel archipelago, although penguins can occasionally be seen wandering the beaches of the Reserva Costa Atlantica too.

Sea lions, Patagonia

Museums, Myths & Legends
Celebrating the North's Indigenous Culture

Across the towns of Tierra del Fuego tributes trumpet the indigenous history of the archipelago. The Selk'nam, or Ona, roamed the north, Yamanas and Alacalufs the south coast and the Haush the Peninsula Mitre. Disease, displacement and genocide were widely purported to have rendered these peoples extinct after 10,000 years of settlement.

Today, over 400 Selk'nam members are recognized in Río Grande. In Av Belgrano a succinct display with English translations explains the endemic heritage of the region at **Centro de Visitantes Zona Norte**. Look out for traditional Selk'nam basketry workshops with Professor Margarita Maldonado in adjoining **Centro Cultural Yaganes**.

A few minutes' walk away stands the **Communidad Indigena del Pueblo Nación Selk'nam Rafaela Ishton**, the heart of indigenous community activities. Admire the exterior installations of an Ona lodging, guanaco and elder statues, and pink edifice depicting snow-painted trees.

Museo Virginia Choquintel is the north's most prestigious. With text in Spanish, non-speakers can fawn at the

MOONBIRD: FLIGHT OF FANCY

The red knot is endemic to Río Grande: in 1995, one such bird at Cabo Domingo was tagged to learn quite how far it traveled. The findings earned B95 the nickname Moonbird as its lifetime annual coastal Atlantic flightpath between arctic circles equaled the distance to fly to the moon (and almost back). It was last seen in 2013, and sadly its species is suffering a serious decline. The endemic Hudsonian godwit *(Limosa haemastica),* which had nearly disappeared from Tierra del Fuego before the 1998 formation of the Reserva Costa Atlantica, which sweeps from Cabo Nombre down to Rio Ewan, has since been spotted around San Sebastián, home to many rare breeds of geese, some endangered, meandering the farther reaches.

🍸 WHERE TO DRINK IN RIO GRANDE

Doop Disco
Serious club welcoming national acts and partygoers on weekends for late nights under neon lights.

NN
Sleek, black bar set off the main drag with character nooks, a laidback vibe and ranch food.

Queen's
In the bar hub west of Av Belgrano, Queen's has pool, pints and live music.

ENGLAND VS ARGENTINA

Jorge Luis Borges described the dispute as 'a fight between two bald men over a comb'. Across the island's cities you'll see memorials. Around 600km to Tierra del Fuego's east – known in Britain as the Falklands Islands – lies the Malvinas archipelago, settled by, and under the sovereignty of, the United Kingdom for around 200 years. Argentina sought to capture the islands with an invasion on April 2, 1982. After 10 weeks of fighting and several hundred military deaths, Argentina withdrew. With the EU recently recognizing the Spanish name of the Malvinas and monuments such as the Héroes de Malvinas, Museo Malvinas e Islas Atlanticas Sur and the March anniversary events each year, the fracture is still very present.

Misión Salesiana

wall art and late 19th century installations announcing the century-old rose facade. Inside, creative curations celebrate an explosion of items drawn from the region, from the Malvinas War to ceramics of the city's first buildings – including this one – and bird and marine-life skeletons. A third of the sprawling, vaulted space showcases historical statues, artworks and prehistoric finds exploring the Selk'nam legacy.

14km from Río Grande's center, a pedicured arrangement of imposing period white buildings emerges. The **Misión Salesiana** was founded in 1893 by Monsieur Fagnano. Its mission? To evangelize, and later protect, the indigenous population of Tierra del Fuego's north.

An escorted tour through the museum and grounds reveals Ona artifacts, documentary and history alongside taxidermy displays. Students from the agrotechnical school here share homemade delicacies in the farm kitchen. Horseback riding tours from here are unmissable: book ahead.

 WHERE TO STAY IN RIO GRANDE

Hostel Motorcycle Fin del Mundo
Sleep in Harley Davidson–styled bedrooms in this motel along the beachfront Ruta 3. $

Hotel Atlantida
Recipient of a recent shiny new refurb, Atlantida sits close to the waterfront and museums. Great cafe. $$

Status Casino
Excellent location with generous if dated hotel rooms and good views high up. Skip the breakfasts. $$

Arts & Artisanry After Dark
Weekends in Río Grande

The **Museo Fueguino de Arte Niní Bernardello** is a buzzing arts hub and a sweeping, contemporary two-story platform engaging the work of regional artists in rotating exhibitions. On weekend evenings art classes and workshops expand the gallery's seasonal themes, from ecology to gender identity. Afterwards, check the program of **Magma Espacio Cultural**, which hosts performances from contemporary dance to stand-up comedy and live music.

Be sure to stop by **Paseo Canto del Viento** (3–8pm Sat&Sun). This chattering *feria artesanal* has dozens of stalls showcasing artisans and cottage impresarios crafting and selling gifts, food and clothing in the blue building behind Plaza Almirante Brown's Radio Nacional.

Crazy Cabalgatas
Río Grande's Handsome Horseback-Riding Centers

Polish up on gymkhana and polo skills or explore the city's nature on horseback. The epicenter of Tierra del Fuego's gaucho heart and the south Patagonian livestock industry has an array of equestrian propositions for explorations on saddleback.

One of the best-known and loved *estancias* in Tierra del Fuego, despite its founder's nefarious past, **Maria Behety** inhabits a picture-perfect lane of crimson buildings with the world's largest shearing shed. Full-day tours trot to Cabo Domingo and Misión Salesiana, which also has stables offering showjumping and trekking to local nature highlights.

Brush up on riding skills at **Club de Campo la Cimarrona**, set across 40 hectares of land in the center of the city. Classes (Saturdays in winter, weekday evenings during summer) span show jumping, polo and equestrianism. Running for an hour and a half, feeding, grooming, handling and saddlery are incorporated alongside riding. There's a small teahouse for breakfast and lunch.

Signpost with 'Falkland Islands are Argentinian' in Spanish

WHERE TO DINE IN RIO GRANDE

Patio Balto
Sprawling seafront restaurant and bar featuring a disco ceiling, beachfront dome, award-winning burgers and occasional live music. **$$**

Grande Hotel
The restaurant of the city's most upscale hotel draws residents in droves for its fish and *parrilla*. **$$**

Nistro
Set in the upscale outskirts on the Ruta 3, sea views extend the sense of romance. **$$$**

Posada de los Sauces
Welcoming aperitifs and service accompany fantastic fish dishes at this waterfront stalwart. **$**

Chocolatería Mama Flora
Artisanal chocolatiers with a homey tearoom set in one of the city's historic houses. **$**

465

Beyond
Río Grande

Rolling tundra horizons merge with clouds and are punctuated by Tierra del Fuego's oil rigs and mega *estancias*.

GETTING AROUND

The bus station in Río Grande has regular connections to further-flung destinations. A 4WD car is needed to travel to the surrounds beyond the Ruta 3 in winter – in summer they're a pleasure to drive and cycle.

☑ TOP TIP

Most *estancia* accommodations, and the land border between Argentina and Chile at Bella-Vista, are closed during the austral winter (May–October).

Tierra del Fuego's northeast spans a windswept steppe of guanaco-rich subpolar pampa home to huge, handsome *estancias*. Those settled on the inland Río Grande have been reinvented into catch-and-release trout-fishing lodgings. The late-19th-century gold rush that originally attracted settlers to the north, when dust was discovered in the Bahía San Sebastián region, has made way for a profitable oil industry dotting the smudge of low-hanging clouds, arid tundra horizon and subpolar sea. With the Reserva Costa Atlantica protecting the avian life from Cabo Nombre down to Río Ewan, what's left of the former capital of San Sebastián now serves as the border with Chile and land route to Argentina's north.

Lapataia Bay (p469)

Punta Páramo
DISTANCE FROM RIO GRANDE: 2HRS
Black Gold

Driving north of Río Grande along the Reserva Costa Atlantica, past guanaco herds and meandering geese, lies Punta Páramo. 'A huge breakwater jutting out some seven and a half miles like a stone arm around a wide bay' was how the Chilean novelist Francisco Coloane described it.

The constructed, 100m-wide spit shouldering Bahía San Sebastián was commissioned by the newly minted (literally, he produced his own currency from the carats guarded by his private army) Julius Popper, to facilitate the extraction of pay dirt – aka flecks of gold from the coast's black sand. Today, you can explore the breakwater on a treasure hunt for parts of the original rail track used to wheel resources to the mainland, discarded ironworks (though the major furniture is exhibited at Misión Salesiana), giant seashells, the scent of the subantarctic swell, mesmeric panoramas from sea to mainland and beguiling birdlife. Check the tide before attempting to reach the charming fishing *refugio* at Punta Páramo's tip.

Central Interior
DISTANCE FROM RIO GRANDE: 1½HRS
Nice Catch

The Río Grande is where the largest, most athletic sea-run brown trout in the world swim the waters of the 'big river'. World-leading lodges cater to keen anglers on farm estates in small groups under stunning steppe sunsets fading into constellation-laced skies. The Río Grande is rightly famed among anglers and is home to a polished catch-and-release scene. The Kau Tapen Group – who, be warmed, also have bird- and stag-shooting arms – operate the lodges on José Menéndez's former *estancias*, including Maria Behety, Aurelia Lodge and Villa Maria Lodge.

Lago Escondido
(p469)

CAPTURED ON FILM

Among the spate of anti-colonial Westerns released in 2023, *Los Colonos*, depicting the Selk'nam genocide led by José Menéndez, received multiple awards. It followed Chile's 2018 entry to the Academy Awards, *Blanco en Blanco*, which also centered around the hunting of the indigenous people of northern Isla Grande. Skip the movie *Tierra del Fuego,* based around the brutal massacre led by Julian Popper, and instead read the book it's modeled on. Francisco Coloane's excellent short story collection hinges around south Patagonia's short-lived gold rush under the so-called King of Paramo, Popper.

BEST ESTANCIA DAY EXPERIENCES

Las Hijas
Welcoming family-run *estancia* with introductions ranging from an hour's tour of the farm to full days.

Estancia El Roble
Every March, this traditional working *estancia* hosts the Fiesta del Ovejura sheepdog festival across its pastures.

Estancia San Pablo
Horseback ride to the *Desdemona* shipwreck and culminate with a visit to the shearing shed.

End of the Ruta 3

Snaking all the way from Prudhoe Bay in Alaska down through the Americas across two continents, the Pan-American Hwy becomes the Ruta 3 in Buenos Aires, reaching its thrilling finish line in Tierra del Fuego. Cruising past Isla Grande's sensational shifting landscapes, absorbing towns and natural phenomena over 295km is one of the world's most iconic road trip finales: the end of the Ruta 3.

❶ Bahía San Sebastián

You've just crossed over from Punta Delgada via Cerro Sombrero in Chile and exited the border at San Sebastián. Head to the windswept beach opposite, the arm of Punta Páramo fringing the marine horizon. Breathe in the biting sea air and wander among the birds of the Reserva Costa Atlántica – this is their biggest wintering spot on Isla Grande.

The Drive: Head south for an hour; edged by the gray-green waters of the subantarctic sea to your left, oil rigs dot the pampa.

❷ Río Grande

Save money and energy for the island's south by booking a good-value room in the city. Fill up your tank and get some driving tips at Hostel Motorcycle Fin del Mundo. Set on the beachside Ruta 3, it's well-versed at welcoming those navigating their own *Motorcycle Diaries* across the Americas.

The Drive: Career south for an hour and a half. Reaching Tolhuin, continue past the Selk'nam statue announcing the entrance to the town center and take the first right after crossing the Río Turbio.

Lago Fagnano

FREEDOM_WANTED/SHUTTERSTOCK ©

BEYOND RÍO GRANDE TIERRA DEL FUEGO

THE GUIDE

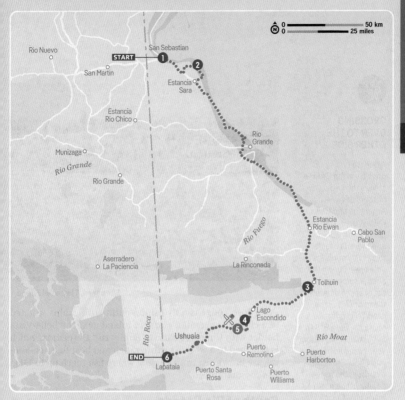

❸ Lago Fagnano

Stretch your legs around the lake and nature reserve and browse the vehicle carcass installations at Camping Hain. Stop for coffee in the center surrounded by walls lined with hundreds of number plates at Raíces Fueguinas, then grab a cake for the ride at La Unión Panadería.

The Drive: Rejoin the Ruta 3 and head south. After around 50km, the snowcapped mountain pass climbs and silver Lago Escondido on your right shimmers in the bowl below the Andes.

❹ Paso Garibaldi

Alight at the only paved mountain pass through the Fuegian Andes to walk up the mirador for panoramic views of the length of Lago Escondido and wide blue expanse of Fagnano beyond the forest bridging the two great lakes.

The Drive: Continue south through the shrug of the mountain pass for around an hour towards the tunnels weaving under the slopes of Cerro Castor.

❺ Museo Moto Cafe 3005

The first of the winter centers is a milestone on the Ruta 3 journey. This immaculate, log cabin Haruwen motorcycle museum is named after its distance from Buenos Aires: 3005km along the Ruta 3. It showcases the stories and vehicles of road trip adventurers before you, including the first person to cross between arctic circles by motorbike; petrolheads can get their passports stamped with the Pan-American Hwy marker here.

The Drive: It's another hour to the national park. Heading west, pass Ushuaia to follow the Ruta 3 as it climbs northwest and pay to enter Parque Nacional Tierra del Fuego.

❻ Lapataia Bay

Follow the end of the Pan-American Hwy through some of the most epic terrain of Argentina – ending with an obligatory snap at the sign announcing the End of the Ruta 3. If you started in Alaska then you've traveled just over 30,000km!

CROSSING OVER TO THE OTHER SIDE

A one- to two-hour drive from Río Grande stands the two borders between Argentina and Chile. Bella-Vista – the quieter entry point and therefore faster to pass through – is only open during the austral summer. It's set at approximately the midpoint of the island's interior along the Ruta B. San Sebastián is the other, year-round entry point into Chile. Crossing over from the former capital of the north leads past Cerro Sombrero, after which a short ferry journey crosses the Magellan Strait to Punta Delgada to continue on to mainland Argentina. Both borders can access Porvenir, capital of Chilean Tierra del Fuego, from where regular boat journeys reach Punta Arenas, with air connections to the rest of the country. Those thinking of cycling should bear in mind that there is 20km between the Chilean and Argentine borders at San Sebastián.

Shepherd, Tierra del Fuego

San Jose Lodge is a fly-fishing outfit with cabins situated in a classic Patagonian *estancia* inland near the Bella-Vista border with Chile. It's close to family-run Despedida, which is attached to a working cattle ranch and host to catch-and-release brown sea trout angling where fish reach up to 15kg. *Asados* guaranteed.

South of Río Grande   DISTANCE FROM RIO GRANDE: 1HR 🚗
Ranch Life

Set across the sprawling steppe upon the lands on which Argentina's sheep industry first flourished, today *estancias* inhabit settlements the size of villages, replete with schools, football pitches and hospitals. Smaller ranches invite travelers to experience this world with welcoming hospitality, agricultural introductions and home cooking converging under starlit skies amid splendid pastoral isolation.

Estancia Las Hijas is among the finest on the island for a farm visit or stay, with tours including a visit to one of the island's few remaining original Selk'nam dwellings close to the ranch, horseback riding and handling of its Romney Marsh sheep.

Estancia Viamonte is another formed by the Bridges family and still run by their descendants today. One of the island's finest, it's set along the east coast south of Río Grande with upscale rooms for bliss and solitude with fantastic home cooking, bird watching along the seashore and hospitality.

The Ruta A is among the most scenic *estancia* routes on the island – Rolito and San Pablo are two of the farms welcoming guests with day tours and overnight stays.

Tolhuin

Lifesize Selk'nam statues salute entrants to a working town of 12,000 settled on seismological marvels gifting its western flank panoramic natural beauty. Gravel streets roamed by wild dogs stretch from the town center to forest lakes and down to the eastern shore of Lago Fagnano, which floats above the plates delineating Antarctica and South America. Tolhuin turned 50 in 2022; new enterprises feel like the town is just beginning to catch on to the tourism that's swept its near neighbor Ushuaia.

Selk'nam art looms large, from the murals emblazoning the tourist office and ubiquitous sawmills to the new sculpture announcing Lago Fagnano, a tribute to Tolhuin's heritage and reserve just outside the city – the first piece of land in Argentina to be officially returned to its indigenous community in 2020. Tolhuin is the folk soul 'heart of the island', as the name translates to in Ona language, where the faces are friendly, the creative current eclectic and the tourism proposition as fresh as the lake air.

GETTING AROUND

Tolhuin has no public transport and the distance between the town's center and the lake is around 4km, so it's best to drive or cycle unless planning to stay around Lago Fagnano. To reach and leave Tolhuin, regular minibuses arrive and depart from behind La Unión Panadería throughout the day for Río Grande and Ushuaia.

☑ TOP TIP

For anyone harboring visions of re-creating the bonfires in the snow that caught the imagination of the first European explorers, at the time of writing there was an island-wide ban on lighting fires, due in part to the devastating inferno that blazed for months through Tolhuin's Reserva Corazón de la Isla throughout the winter of 2022–23, rendering Lagos Yehuin and Chepelmut inaccessible.

Statue, Selk'nam

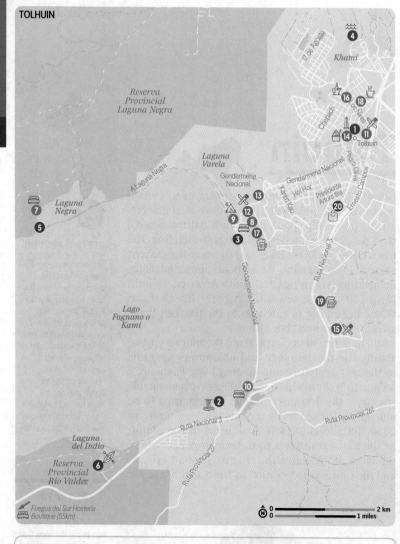

TOLHUIN

T. de Agosto

Khami

Reserva Provincial Laguna Negra

Laguna Varela

A Laguna Negra

Gendarmería Nacional

Gendarmería Nacional

Laguna Negra

Chepach

Xaren Kau

Hol Hol

Pedro Oliva

Tolhuin

Los Ñires

Presidenta Arturo Illia

Ernesto Campos

Lago Fagnano o Kami

Gendarmería Nacional

Ruta Nacional 3

Ruta Nacional 3

Ruta Provincial 261

Laguna del Indio

Reserva Provincial Rio Valdez

Ruta Provincial 77

Fuegos del Sur Hosteria Boutique (55km)

N 0 —————————— 2 km
   0 —————————— 1 miles

SIGHTS
1 Casa de la Cultura
2 Cascada Porfiada
3 Lago Fagnano
4 Lago Khami
5 Laguna Negra

ACTIVITIES, COURSES & TOURS
6 Puero Khami Extremo

SLEEPING
7 Cabañas Laguna Negra
8 Cabañas Mirador del Tolhuin
9 Camping Hain
10 Hosteria Kaiken

EATING
11 El Rincón Mayorista

12 Enriqueta – Proveeduría de Sabores
13 La Ribero del Fagnano
14 La Unión Panaderia
15 Parrilla Rio Turbio

DRINKING & NIGHTLIFE
see 14 Bar e Studio
16 La Antigua
17 Laumann Beer

18 Raíces Fueguinas
19 Rio Turbio Cerveceria

SHOPPING
see 14 Kau Kren Artesanias
see 14 La Aldea de los Yoshi Duendes
20 La Familia

Cycling, Lago Fagnano

Lake Expectations

Exploring the Island's Inland Waterways

Lago Fagnano was formed from the prehistoric glacier that covered much of Isla Grande's south. It sits atop the Magellanes Fault, connecting the South America and Scotia plates, and is one of Argentina's largest lakes, extending above Parque Nacional Tierra del Fuego into Chile. It has great spiritual significance to the indigenous peoples of the island – Hain ceremonies were practiced along its shoreline, commemorated by the new 50th anniversary statue at its head.

Tolhuin's lakeside tourist resort – where *cabañas* are set in the stillness of forest nature, overlooking the water and Southern Andes' peaks – lines the town's west. Surrounded by nature reserves, lagoons, rivers and waterfalls, routes for various walks – taking in everything from bird watching to geology and history – are well signposted from the beach.

Laguna Negra is a dark water lagoon reached by tracing the resort's east coast. You can canoe or ride along the pebble beach fringing the lake towards the snowcapped Andes horizon from the log cabin center of **Cabalgatas Sendero Indio**, where show jumping and polo are taught too.

SKATE EXPECTATIONS

Just north of the city center lies **Lago Khami**. **Complejo del Ecotono** offers natural ice skating here in winter when the lake freezes over and lessons can be booked and skates hired: be sure to ask for and follow the guidance on weather conditions when you visit. Both **Aventura Turismo** and Complejo del Ecotono offer kayaking around Lago Khami's waters during summer. The latter's HQ is like a fairy cabin in the woods, doubling as a carved and knitted crafts emporium from where a trail weaves around lenga forest, peat bogs and facts revealed about the nature of the terrain. Walk it from 10am to noon and 3pm to 5pm.

WHERE TO DRINK

Bar Estudio
Smart and lively bar by established restaurateurs with a class selection of Fuegian gins.

La Morada de el Flaco
Beer, wine, live music, poetry and much more in the purple buildings and domes fronting Lago Fagnano.

La Antigua
Hip, homey hospitality with excellent craft beers. Best to use the tattooist and barber onsite pre-drinks.

THE HAIN CEREMONY

Practiced by all the indigenous peoples of Tierra del Fuego, the Hain ceremony is honored in museums, municipal statues and the names of restaurants, accommodations and even a theater across Isla Grande. The days- or weeks-long initiation ceremony saw adolescent boys learn to fish, hunt and engage in spiritual development under the guidance of community elders who imparted their wisdom in a specially built ceremonial hut. The boys were decorated using body and face paints, as well as costumes made from down and fur, and the rite of passage was accompanied by Hain chants. The anthropologist Anna Chapman documented the phenomenon extensively, with the last known ceremony taking place in 1923.

FREEDOM_WANTED/SHUTTERSTOCK ©

Laguna Negra (p473)

To explore the surrounding waters by kayak, **Puerto Khami Extremo** has canoes for rowing around the **Laguna del Indio** on the southeastern flanks of Lago Fagnano. The Aguas Blancas are also the entry point to **Cascada Porfiada**, which spouts down a rock face. A burgeoning gastronomy and accommodation scene is emerging to meet the growing number of visitors, with a new hotel enclave host to **Fuegos del Sur Hostería Boutique** opened along the southwest of Lago Fagnano's inner shore.

Collectors' Editions
Holistic Showcases

The sprawling warehouse building of **Raíces Fueguinas** opened in 2022 and is an immaculate, gleaming passion project by its collector-owner. It houses everything from taxidermy to kerosene lamps and Disney memorabilia that's showcased across its vast wall-to-wall glass cabinet displays. Be sure to pull up a chair around one of the sparkling glass cabinet tables for coffee or wine and live music.

BEST ARTISANAL BOUTIQUES

La Familia
Gaucho outfitters purveying affordable handmade *estancia* garb, *mate* gourds, jewelry, berets and more.

La Aldea de los Yoshi Duendes
New-age friends or foes will be entranced by the spiritual and folk accoutrements at this unique boutique.

Kau Kren Artesanías
Charming selection of handmade ceramics and adornments from local artisans: catch the crafting live in-store.

In the center, pass by the diminutive **Casa de la Cultura** to admire a garden of creatures carved and sculpted from logs and, inside, Selk'nam figurines. Down by the lake the life-sized rendition of two Hain ceremony participants was strikingly unveiled on the bank of Lago Fagnano to mark the 50th anniversary of the formation of the city.

Continuing north from there along the shoreline, you stumble onto a *Mad Max* set. Oh sorry, our mistake, it's actually **Camping Hain** – a holistic, artful outdoor sculpture park lined by some of the city's 17,000 recycled green glass bottles reimagined as treetops, a woodcutter's track and mini sauna that a guest spent three months building during the pandemic. We clearly weren't the first passersby yearning to explore the part-buried motorbike and helicopter carcasses here or step into one of the Selk'nam wigwams that can be camped in. Signs announce a small entrance fee for a selfie or tour around the site led by the father-and-son creator-owners.

Sabores Superlativos
Authentic Experiential Dining with Soul

If Tolhuin translates to 'heart of the island', then **La Unión Panadería** is the soul of the town. Often cited as 'the best bakery in the world', La Unión meets the superlative with counters of appetizing cream- and chocolate-laced cakes. Visit during the late afternoon to see the convening community in full swing.

For savory food on the move, the specialty delicacies – homemade condiments, handmade knives, superlative wines and oversized cheese – at epicurean emporium **El Rincón Mayorista** demand to adorn *cabañas* and picnics.

A log cabin dining scene has sprung up in the forested fringes of Lago Fagnano. **Enriqueta – Proveeduría de Sabores**, set in an intimate cottage dining room (open from Friday to Sunday, reservations advised) with residencies by celebrated rotating chefs, has been making forays into events around its lakeside forest setting. You don't choose what to eat at **La Ribera del Fagnano** – rather the mother and her children who helm it serve what they've prepared. You can hedge your bets with a coffee here instead. With many *estancias* in close proximity, *asado* is a religion in Tolhuin. **Parrilla Río Turbio** and **La Casona 2**, riverside restaurants off the Ruta 3, are famed for barbecued lamb.

Wash it all down with a draught by **Laumann Beer**. The well-established micro-distillery is set near Lago Fagnano, or head to the newly established **Río Turbio Cervecería** for pints, *parrilla* and live music.

CABAÑA
GOOD TIME

Hostería Kaiken
On the bluff overlooking Lago Fagnano, the town's smartest proposition has contemporary rooms and cabins. **$$**

Cabañas Laguna Negra
Set by the lagoon off Lago Fagnano, cabins set in pristine waterside nature have outdoor hot tubs. **$$**

Camping Hain
Pitch your tent or sleep like a Shelk'nam in the replica huts adorning Lago Fagnano. **$**

Cabañas Khami
Cabañas set on the beach with hydrotherapy overlooking the lake and communal games room. **$$**

Cabañas Mirador del Tolhuin
This well-established hotel has introduced glamping domes complete with log fires onsite for forest bathing. **$$**

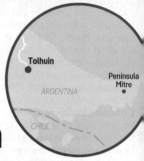

Beyond Tolhuin

As Tierra del Fuego famously has four seasons in an hour, adopt 'onion dressing' by wearing layers you can peel off to suit the climate.

Raw, rugged nature, dramatic mountains, devastating shipwrecks and unexplored pastures. Carve your own journey through some of Isla Grande's most magical domains.

With the beginning of the Fuegian Andes chain and the most easterly point of Tierra del Fuego surrounding it, the geographies beyond Tolhuin unveil some of Isla Grande's most dramatic landscapes and natural phenomena. The Ruta A is the only road to reach the recently protected Península Punta Mitre. It winds through one of Tierra del Fuego's most visually evocative and beautiful terrains, where the north and south of the island meet in a land of fairy-tale *estancias*, itinerant wildlife and dramatic seas, skies, shipwrecks and cliffs. To Tolhuin's west the lake district meets its dramatic climax with the heavenly sight of the Fuegian Andes curling around Lago Escondido – called the hidden lake for its tendency to be shrouded by cloud.

PATRICIA MATIAS GEO/SHUTTERSTOCK ©

Paso Garibaldi

Start your hike with sweeping views from **❶ Paso Garibaldi**, the only paved mountain pass through the Fuegian Andes. Climb the viewing platform for pictures and scenes of clouds suspended below the cradle of the snowcapped peaks with the silver shimmer of Lago Escondido occasionally revealing itself below. The road down starts just to the left of the *mirador*. Follow the interior wall to the right-hand side as it winds down the curling mountain road, past trickling waterfalls and stalactites until you reach its forested base at the edge of **❷ Lago Escondido**.

Explore the abandoned ruins of the former **❸ Hotel Petrel** and *cabañas* and revel in the views of the shimmering, mountain-hugged lake. Follow the shore northeast, passing through the fringing lenga forest, stopping for pastries and *mate* by the **❹ water's edge**, until you see the road bordering the forest begin to climb. Walk up it to follow the **❺ Ruta 3** east for 2km – past the police station on your left, observing the carnage caused by beavers to your right across the highway. Upon reaching the Río Milna, continue over the bridge to visit **❻ La Casona 2** for empanadas and the best spit-roasted Fuegian lamb for miles (open 10am to 3.30pm, closed Mondays).

Well fed, continue east a few hundred meters along the Ruta 3's left-hand side until you see the road leading to the **❼ entrance to the forest** on your left. Enter the woods and follow the signposts for around 5km to **❽ Lago Fagnano**, watching out for silver foxes, otherworldly birds, nothofagus fauna and wild mint until you glimpse water through the clearing – you've reached one of Argentina's largest lakes.

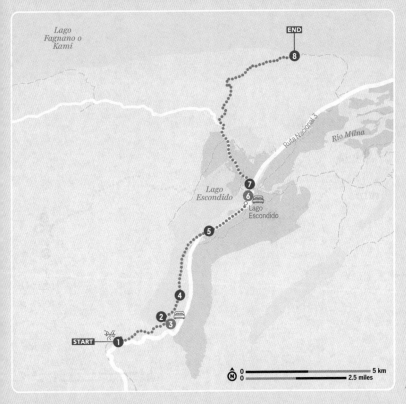

Commencing off the Ruta 3, a small police cabin and billboard marks the **❶ entrance to the Ruta A**. After half an hour you reach the first *estancia* in a picturesque procession. Take coffee at Tepi. The domes in the opposing field are starlit glamping and fly-fishing accommodations **❷ Domos de la Estancia**. Continuing for half an hour, cross the wooden bridge over the river until you reach **❸ Estancia Rolito**. Pre-book at this century-old homestead to tour the farm or stay overnight. During the hour and a half ahead, observe and give way to howling farm dogs, shaggy Hereford cows and glossy mares across the grassland. After passing Estancia Pirinaica follow the sun to Río Ladrillero. Reaching the beach, alight at the sign **❹ Sendero Faro San Pablo**. Walk towards the sea and glance back – the surroundings are a favorite domain of guanaco herds. Follow the path

to ascend the cape to your right. After about 20 minutes you'll reach the listing **❺ lighthouse** at the summit. Look down to the right to survey the *Desdemona* shipwreck. Back on ground level, head south for a couple of minutes past the cape and across the Río San Pablo. All the following roads to the left lead to the *Desdemona*. The cluster of signs at the first turning point towards the entrance via the abandoned Hostería San Pablo. At the next is a fishing hamlet – check for humans before entering, due to guard dogs. Pass the campsites – **❻ Miguel y Silvia** is the only place open for food here in winter: pay for the views rather than the overpriced empanadas – to take the next left onto the beach. Nothing prepares you for the sight of the rusting, listing, looming **❼ Desdemona** – the German cargo ship that ran aground in 1985, the cement it was carrying anchoring it as an icon of the island's seafaring past.

Península Mitre

The Shipwreck Coast

DISTANCE FROM TOLHUIN: **2HRS**

Darwin described Tierra del Fuego's easternmost tip as a 'broken landscape, an unstable amalgamation of loose fragments', when he landed here in 1832. Little explored but much-storied, the Península Mitre is a land of pristine, ruggedly beautiful nature, howling winds and cruel seas. The largest peatland in the world, its 10,000km were designated protected in late 2022 after decades of environmental campaigning.

Leading from Estancia Maria Luisa past Cabo San Pablo on the Ruta A, the only road into the Península Mitre, to its north, and accessed via Estancia Moat along its south, tours leave from Estancia Policarpo on horseback and Ushuaia by car and then on foot. Explore where Captain Cook touched Tierra del Fuego in 1769, iconic shipwrecks on wide sandy beaches, a lot of *refugios,* gauchos, the remnants of the shortlived 19th-century goldmining rush at Bahía Slugett and *estancias* at the end of the world. In Bahía Aguirre stands Biblioteca Peninsula Haush, named after the indigenous population who occupied southeastern Tierra del Fuego. The viral following of the library at the end of the world, opened in 2022 by a photographer who spent three years restoring the house abandoned when attempts to form a town here floundered, keeps it connected with the rest of the world. Apart from the odd itinerant gaucho you won't see a soul but you will experience the land as it appeared to the first explorers: amid a devastating terrain of shipwrecks, penguins, condors, guanaco and lighthouses at the end of the world.

LIGHT FANTASTIC

The nimbus clouds that swirl amid subantarctic mists atop the everchanging landscape of Tierra del Fuego are dramatic and mysterious at any time.

The Haush who once occupied these lands said that the east sky was the most magnificent but treacherous of all above the island. During the austral winter, when sunsets start at 5pm, 3D constellations shine brighter, sunsets glow redder and stars sparkle closer, it's possible to see the Southern Lights from Antarctica emblazoning the subpolar horizon, a psychedelic light show when the landscape becomes a halo of green and pink auroras dancing across the skies.

Desdemona shipwreck

END-OF-THE-WORLD REFUGES

Estancia Maria Luisa
Near the end of the Ruta Complementaria A, this homely *hostelería* has horses for exploring the Península Mitre.

Puesta la Chaira
Part of Estancia Policarpo, this gaucho refuge with ATV adventures is the last manned stay in Península Mitre.

Rancho Ibarra
Near Cabo San Pío, at the southernmost point of Isla Grande, gaucho Luis Andrade welcomes and guides travelers.

MARISA RAINER/SHUTTERSTOCK ©

TOOLKIT

The chapters in this section cover the most important topics you'll need to know about in Argentina. They're full of nuts-and-bolts information and valuable insights to help you understand and navigate Argentina and get the most out of your trip.

Arriving
p482

Getting Around
p483

Money
p484

Accommodations
p485

Family Travel
p486

Health & Safe Travel
p487

Food, Drink & Nightlife
p488

Responsible Travel
p490

LGBTiQ+ Travel
p492

Accessible Travel
p493

Women Travelers
p494

Nuts & Bolts
p495

Language
p496

Arriving

Buenos Aires is the primary port of entry for most travelers visiting Argentina. Most fly in to Aeropuerto Internacional Ministro Pistarini, known as 'Ezeiza', about 35km from town. International flights arrive in Terminal A, and domestic flights in Terminal C. The other international airport, Aeroparque Internacional Jorge Newbery, is about 3km from the city center and only has one terminal.

Visas

Most nationalities can enter Argentina without a visa and stay up to 90 days. This includes nationals from the US, Canada, New Zealand, Australia, Japan, South Korea, and most Western European countries.

Withdrawing Cash

In Ezeiza, ATMs are behind the Starbucks in Terminal A. You might be charged the official exchange rate. Consider other options in the city for better rates.

Onward Ticket

You might be asked to show an onward ticket by both the airline with which you are flying and the Argentine immigration officer. An airplane, ferry or bus ticket out of the country should suffice.

Wi-Fi

There's free wi-fi in both terminals. It's decently fast and can be accessed even outside of Terminal A in the pick-up and drop-off area by McDonald's.

Public Transport from Airport to City Centre

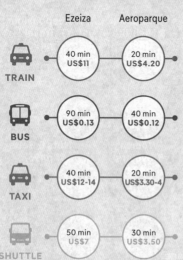

	Ezeiza	Aeroparque
TRAIN	40 min US$11	20 min US$4.20
BUS	90 min US$0.13	40 min US$0.12
TAXI	40 min US$12-14	20 min US$3.30-4
SHUTTLE	50 min US$7	30 min US$3.50

VISA RUNS

If you receive a 90-day visa on arrival and leave the country, there's not a specific number of days you must wait to reenter the country. You will receive another 90 days upon reentrance, even if you come back the next day. Some travelers use Argentina's lack of reentry limit by spending some time in Uruguay during their trip (generally a day trip in Colonia, just across the Río de la Plata), and returning shortly after, thus allowing them to spend longer than 90 days in the country.

Getting Around

Argentina's cheap public transport will be your best option in cities, but if you want to see Patagonia and the wine country, renting a car is the way to go.

TRAVEL COSTS

Rental
From US$32/ day

Petrol
Approx
US$0.49/liter

SUBE card
US$1

Bike rental
US$15/hour

STRIKES

Strikes regularly impact all types of transport in Argentina, especially in Buenos Aires. Even international flights can get rescheduled due to airport strikes. *Paros* (strikes) can be called by members of the public transport workers union, airport workers union and other types of unions. Protests not directly associated with transport also affect traffic conditions since sections of major streets close down to allow for marches, especially in Buenos Aires.

Taxis, Rideshares & Remises

Taxis tend to be cheaper than rideshares, but usually only accept cash. Uber, Cabify and DiDi operate in several cities and accept cash and card. *Remises* (unmarked radio taxis with fixed fares) are another common option, and can be called directly or booked via WhatsApp. *Remises* usually only accept cash.

Car Hire & Fuel

You must be at least 21 and have a valid driver's license to rent a car. If you plan on driving far, get the unlimited kilometer option. Gas is called *nafta*, and attendants fill it for you. Most aggressive wins right of way at unmarked four-way stops.

TIP

For navigating Buenos Aires, download the app Como Llego, which usually has the most accurate travel times.

DRIVING ESSENTIALS

Drive on the right.

Speed limit is 30mph on most city streets and 70mph or more on highways. Limits are marked in km/h.

.08

Blood alcohol limit is 0.08%.

Subte

The Subte is Buenos Aires' subway system and the only subway in the country. To ride it, purchase a Sube card from a Subte station, a *kiosco* or a lottery office, then charge it. The Subte is the quickest transport option on days when there are strikes.

Bus & Train

Both bus and rail travel is cheap in Argentina. The country has an extensive network of local and regional buses. Trains connecting the Buenos Aires Metropolitan Area (AMBA) run frequently, while many cross-regional trains run less frequently, sell out quickly, and usually need to be bought in advance.

Air

The national carrier in Argentina is Aerolíneas Argentinas and offers the majority of domestic flights. Low-cost carriers Flybondi and JetSMART can be cheaper than taking long-distance buses and produce less emissions than Aerolíneas flights. Plan for delays at smaller airports.

Money

CURRENCY: **ARGENTINE PESO (AR$)**

Card vs Cash

More and more businesses are accepting major credit and debit cards (Visa, Mastercard and American Express), but not all do. Cash is still the preferred form of payment, especially for small businesses. Some businesses will give you a 10 % discount if you pay in cash.

Digital Payments

Mercado Pago is the most common form of digital payment, though you must have a DNI to get an account. Apple Pay and Google Wallet have recently arrived here.

Tipping

Most businesses cannot add a tip to a card payment. Carry cash pesos to tip.
Hotel staff and delivery people Give them a few bills.
Restaurants and spas 10% is standard. Note that a *cubierto* charge is not a tip and you should tip on top of this.
Taxis Not expected.

ATMs

ATMs are easily found throughout Argentina. Withdrawal limits can be low, and fees are charged per transaction (in addition to your home bank's fees).

HOW MUCH FOR...

A bus ride
US$0.10

Museum entry
free to US$4

National park entry
free to US$19.50

A Subte ride
US$0.14

HOW TO... Save Some Dollars

Instead of getting cash from an ATM, use a money wire service, like Western Union or MoneyGram, to send yourself pesos to pick up at an agent location within Argentina. The limits are far higher and sometimes the fees are lower than ATMs. Also, these services tend to provide an exchange rate comparable to the MEP rate, while some ATMs use the official exchange rate.

LOCAL TIP

To get the highest rate for your money in Argentina, bring US$100 bills to exchange in person in a *cueva* (unofficial exchange house) for the blue rate.

INFLATION & PARALLEL EXCHANGE RATES

Argentina has a complicated financial history, including the 2001 financial crisis and current dollar controls. This history, coupled with the over 100% annual inflation rate, has led to parallel exchange rates (the official rate, MEP rate, and blue dollar rate) and prices constantly changing to keep up with the rate of inflation. Prior to 2023, tourists could only access the more favorable rates by using wire transfer services and exchanging cash, but now the government allows foreign cards to use the MEP rate, thus giving tourists nearly double their money compared to the official rate.

Accommodations

Estancias

Estancias are large family-owned mansions in the countryside that typically raise cattle and horses. Some are attached to a polo club. They can be visited via day tours, but if you stay the night in one, you'll generally be provided with three meals, horseback rides, and access to any onsite sports facilities. They can also include gaucho equestrian demonstrations and folkloric shows.

Refugios

Refugios (mountain huts) are common in areas where through hiking is popular, like the Lake District, Patagonia and Córdoba. You must register for these before you start your hike. Some provide meals, which also must be booked prior. You can sometimes rent a sleeping bag or towels, but usually only a mattress is provided. Running water and toilets are not guaranteed.

Wineries

In Argentina's wine regions, it's possible to stay at wineries, and sometimes even within the vineyard itself, like in the lofts at Mendoza's Entre Cielos Luxury Wine Hotel & Spa. Some of these accommodations come with tours of the wineries, as well as meals and a tasting, like at Bodega Colomé in Salta.

Hostels & Homestays

Hostels can be found throughout Argentina and range from the more luxurious, with co-working spaces and private rooms, to bare-bones dorm rooms. Homestays are also common, especially for people in immersive Spanish programs, and can sometimes even be booked with meals included. Generally, the Spanish academy will organize placement with a list of vetted candidates offering their homes.

HOW MUCH FOR A NIGHT IN...

An estancia
US$80–US$375

A hostel dorm bed
US$10

A midrange hotel room
US$50–US$90

Camping & Glamping

Wild camping is permitted in Argentina, and you'll find both public and private campgrounds in some cities and throughout the countryside. Glamping is slowly catching on in more touristic areas, ranging from campgrounds using domes as one of their more luxurious offerings, to dedicated glampgrounds in many places like Ushuaia, Bariloche and on the salt flats of Jujuy.

HIGH SEASON & VAT

High season is from late November to the end of February and July. In October through November is when many high schoolers take their class trips in Bariloche, and it can be overrun with teenagers. The coast is most crowded in January and February, with some places only accepting bookings of at least a full week. There is a 21% value-added tourist tax, but if you pay with a foreign card, it should be automatically reimbursed. Even then, the cash rate can sometimes be cheaper, depending on exchange rates.

Family Travel

Argentina is extremely kid-friendly, and safe for families. People take their kids with them everywhere, even if it's to eat dinner at 10pm. Museums and other cultural spaces hold many kid-centric activities, events and creative arts classes. The country's national parks offer nature adventures suitable for the whole family too, from wildlife watching to kid-friendly rock-climbing routes.

Transport Fares in Buenos Aires

Subte Children under four years ride free.

City buses Children under three years ride free.

Trains leaving from Retiro Station Children under three years ride free.

Mar del Plata Train Children under three years ride free. Three to 12 pay half the price of a regular ticket.

Domestic flights with Aerolíneas Argentinas Children under two years ride free; two to 11 pay a reduced fare.

Baby Facilities

- A lightweight pram with thick wheels will be best for navigating uneven streets. Pack a baby carrier as well.
- Many women's bathrooms in malls, tourist areas and airports have diaper-changing stations.
- Most hotels accept children, and fancier ones sometimes offer babysitting.
- Major cities have 24-hour pharmacies.

Eating Out

Kids are welcome in most restaurants in Argentina. The *menù infantil* (children's menu) usually includes pasta, pizza and *milanesa*. If you take your kids to cafes, order them a *submarino* (hot milk with a chocolate bar to stir in).

Bus & Subte Etiquette

If getting on the bus with a stroller, enter from the side door. Passengers with children are entitled to priority seating on the lower level of the bus. Breastfeeding in the open is culturally acceptable.

DÍA DE LAS INFANCIAS

If you can, plan your trip to coincide with Argentina's Childhood Day (Día de las Infancias, formerly Día del Niño), celebrated throughout the country annually on the third Sunday of August. Restaurants, bakeries and candy stores all have promotions geared toward kids (especially chocolate shops). Museums, neighborhood associations and cultural centers host events for kids, many of which are free. Puppet shows, concerts, circus shows, art workshops and plays are just a few of the types of offerings you'll find in the major cities. Buenos Aires' Museo Gardel even hosts a tango music workshop for kids, combining visual art and the bandoneon.

Health & Safe Travel

WILDFIRES

Every province in Argentina has recently experienced wildfires, with 561,165 hectares of land burning. Risk depends on time of year, with the north more vulnerable from the months of July to December, and the south and middle of the country from January through April. Corrientes is one of the provinces that has been most affected by wildfires.

Pickpocketing

Violent crime is not common here, though pickpocketing, especially in crowded tourist areas in Buenos Aires, is. Robbers on motorcycles have been known to snatch phones out of people's hands as they are using them on sidewalks, especially on street corners. If you carry a bag, thread your leg or arm through its straps when seated in public outdoor spaces.

Bird Poop Scam

In Buenos Aires, scammers will squirt people with white gunk, making them think a bird has pooped on them. While one person offers to help the unsuspecting victim and begins to clean them up, another will pickpocket the victim's wallet. If you get squirted, just keep walking, and the scammers will leave you alone.

CANNABIS

Medical cannabis is legal here, and sometimes people smoke it on the streets, though it's illegal to do so.

INFOGRAPHIC HEADER

Black and red flag
Danger, no swimming

Yellow and black flag
Possibly dangerous sea

Light blue flag
Calm or good sea

Black flag
Possible electrical storm. Beach will be evacuated.

White flag
Lost child

Dengue

Dengue, the viral tropical disease that can cause horrible fever and aching joints, has recently been on the rise in Argentina. While cases are still relatively low, they have been reported in 13 provinces as well as Buenos Aires. Check your accommodations for any standing water and dump it out, as the disease is spread by Aedes aegypti mosquitoes.

HEALTH INSURANCE

You do not have to have health insurance to travel to Argentina, and anyone in the country (even tourists) have the right to use its free public healthcare system. However, it can often be more expedient to pay to be attended in one of the private hospitals, rather than waiting to be seen for several hours in the public ones.

Food, Drink & Nightlife

When to Eat

Desayuno (breakfast, 7am to 10am) Generally *tostados* and *mate*

Almuerzo (lunch, 12:30pm to 3pm) Consists of appetizer, main and dessert, or something more casual (like empanadas, pizza or *choripan*)

Merienda (teatime, 5pm to 7pm) Coffee or tea and pastries

Cena (dinner, 9pm to 11pm) Similar number of courses as lunch but with more elaborate dishes

Where to Eat & Drink

Parilla Steakhouse

Panadería Bakery

Confitería Cafes serving light meals

Café Traditional cafes as well as newer specialty coffee shops

Tenedor libre Buffet-style all-you-can-eat restaurant

Heladería Ice-cream shop

Empanadería Empanada shop

Bar de vino Wine bar

Comida por peso Takeaway paid for based on weight

Puerta cerrada Closed-door restaurant.

Pulpería Old-timey general-store-cum-bar.

Pizzería Pizza restaurant.

MENU DECODER

Cubierto Small charge for bread and utensils.

Menú del día or Menú ejecutivo Lunch special, with drink, appetizer, main and desert.

Entrada Appetizer.

Plato principal Main.

Parrilla Used both for 'grill' and 'steakhouse'.

Bife Beef.

Jamón Ham.

Milanesa Breaded cutlets of meat.

Cordero Lamb.

Fideos Pasta.

Postre Dessert.

Agua con gas Sparkling water.

Sifón Spritzer bottle of water.

Agua sin gas Flat mineral water.

Gaseosas Soft drinks.

Vino tinto Red wine.

Vino blanco White wine.

Menù degustación Tasting menu.

Carta de vinos Wine menu.

Cerveza artesanal Craft beer.

Pinta Pint of beer.

Café de especialidad Specialty coffee.

Café con leche Half coffee, half milk.

Cocina sin animales Food without animal products.

Sin TACC Gluten free.

Vegetariano/a Vegetarian.

Vegano/a Vegan.

HOW TO... Order a Steak

First, decide what cut of meat you want. The marbled *ojo de bife* (rib eye) and juicy *bife de chorizo* (sirloin) are two of the most popular, high-quality cuts in the country. Try the lean *lomo* (fillet, tenderloin) if you want something less heavy. Other options include *vacío* (flank steak), *cuadril* (rump steak), and *entraña* (skirt steak). Next, decide how you want it cooked, or just go with the usual: *a punto* (medium to well done). It's not common for a waiter in a steakhouse to ask a patron how they want a steak cooked, unless you're in a restaurant that caters to tourists. If you want your steak rare, request it be cooked *vuelta y vuelta*. For medium rare, say *jugoso* (though it might still come out more medium than medium rare) and for medium well, try *pasado de punto*.

HOW MUCH FOR...

Gourmet dinner
US$30–US$100

Scoop of ice cream
US$1.75

2 Medialunas
US$1

Empanada
US$0.75

Latte at specialty coffee shop
US$1.40–US$2.40

Draft beer
US$1.50–US$2.25

Glass of wine
US$1.5–US$5

HOW TO...
Drink Mate

Yerba mate, or *mate* (pronounced mah-tay) for short, is a tea with about as much caffeine as coffee. Argentina is one of the largest producers and consumers of the tea. The beverage is drunk throughout the country. You'll see people everywhere – in parks, concerts, even offices – armed with carved-out gourds filled with the loose-leaf tea, sipping it through a *bombilla* (filtered straw) with a thermos of hot water close by for easy refills. Generally, it's a shared beverage. Should a friendly Argentine offer you some, follow these protocols if you accept.

The *cebador* (server) will pour hot water to the brim of the gourd and slowly pass it to you. When you accept it, do not say 'thank you'. A *mate* drinker only says 'thank you' on their last turn to signify they don't want more *mate*. Do not move the *bombilla* with your hands! Put your lips on the straw and sip, cautiously at first, as Argentines like their *mate* very hot. Take some time to drink it, but not too much. Holding on to the gourd for too long is considered bad manners. Drink the gourd dry before you pass it back – a partially drunk gourd is yet another faux pas. Always let the *cebador* fill the gourd, should you continue drinking, unless they plunk the thermos down and state it's *auto-servicio* (self-service).

Make Your Own Mate

Make your own *mate* by buying a gourd, bag of *yerba*, thermos and *bombilla* from the supermarket. If your gourd is made of wood or squash, cure it before using it (fill with hot water and *yerba*, then let sit for 24 hours).

GOING OUT

A typical weekend night in Argentina will start around 10pm, when most Argentines go to dinner (even in smaller towns). Dinners can easily last for two hours, especially if you're with a group of loquacious Argentines. Next, people hit the bars, which vary greatly. Craft beer has exploded in the country, and in cities like Buenos Aires, Mar del Plata, Bariloche and La Plata, visiting individual breweries' tap rooms or bars with taps featuring multiple craft breweries is popular. Those wanting something more elegant can go to wine bars or speakeasies (somewhat hidden bars, generally at the back of or under a restaurant that sometimes requires a password). However, the best people-watching is usually in dive bars. You can also buy beer from a *kiosco* (kiosk) and simply walk around, as there's no law against open containers. Others skip the bars and go to cultural events, like theater shows and concerts, and call it an early night, maybe around 1am. People drinking in the bars will stay until 2am (or longer), then head to the club starting around 3am, when the *boliches* (nightclubs) really get going. Most clubs have a relaxed dress code, but some, like those in Palermo in Buenos Aires and Playa Grande in Mar del Plata, have stricter standards. Once in the club, people will dance or watch live music, often using the energy drink Speed as a mixer to help them stay awake until 6am.

Responsible Travel

TOOLKIT

Climate Change & Travel

It's impossible to ignore the impact we have when traveling, and the importance of making changes where we can. Lonely Planet urges all travelers to engage with their travel carbon footprint. There are many carbon calculators online that allow travelers to estimate the carbon emissions generated by their journey; try resurgence.org/resources/carbon-calculator. html. Many airlines and booking sites offer travelers the option of offsetting the impact of greenhouse gas emissions by contributing to climate-friendly initiatives around the world. We continue to offset the carbon footprint of all Lonely Planet staff travel, while recognising this is a mitigation more than a solution.

Carbon-Neutral Rideshares

Rideshare app Cabify operates in Buenos Aires and several other cities. It offsets all of the carbon emissions of its rides by partnering with the energy supplier Genneia, supporting six wind farms between Buenos Aires and Chubut.

Reforest

Trown is an outdoor clothing company that, for every cap it sells, plants a tree in areas that have been affected by forest fires. You can also volunteer to plant trees with them (email voluntarios@trown.com.ar).

Ditch the car and bike the length of Argentina on Ruta National 40, South America's longest road.

Cero Market is a zero-waste chain of stores selling toiletries and dry goods in several cities.

EAT A MEAL OF THE SENSES

Experience both sensory deprivation and heightening at the Teatro Ciego (Blind Theater), a social enterprise that puts on dinner theaters in complete darkness with a troupe made up of blind and partially sighted actors.

WALK THE DOGS

Multiple animal-focused nonprofits, like Gapra Refugio and Ayudacan in Buenos Aires, need volunteer dog walkers to help rescues stretch their legs. Find both via their Facebook pages. Message them directly to organize a time to volunteer.

LEAVE NO TRACE ON THE TRAILS

Trails and campsites, especially in Bariloche, can be littered with toilet paper in the high season, spoiling the experience for other hikers. To help keep the environment pristine, pack out what you take in.

Check Out a Centro Cultural

Centros culturales (cultural centers) can be found throughout the country, putting on talks, concerts and local performance art shows. Oftentimes they highlight subcultures, local art scenes or the heritage of immigrant groups.

Ski at an Indigenous-Run Resort

The Mapuche Puel indigenous community manages Batea Mahuida, an affordable ski resort located at the top of a volcano in Neuquén, where you can cross-country ski, snowboard and ice dive, plus purchase Mapuche handicrafts.

Fund Paleontological Research

Entry to Neuquén's Parque Geo-Paleontológico gives you access to its dinosaur museum and helps to support the working paleontology site on the premises. Want to help dust off bones? It also takes volunteers (@ geoparqueproyectodino).

Donations in Local Arts

Considering financial accessibility, community art projects and performances will sometimes ask for donations, rather than charge for tickets. These are usually the minimum these projects require to keep functioning. Consider giving more, if possible.

In Buenos Aires, visit the significant sights of Argentina's Dirty War (Parque de la Memoria, Plaza de Mayo and Espacio Memoria y Derechos Humanos ex Esma) to learn more about the *desaparecidos* (those disappeared).

Awasi, a low-impact luxury lodge in Misiones, protects 340 hectares of native woodland in Iguazú and Patagonia, which absorb 10,000 tonnes of CO_2 per year, offsetting the lodge's carbon emissions. Find it at awasiguazu. com.

104

In the Global Sustainability Index, Argentina ranks 104th worldwide. Though it has committed to being carbon neutral by 2050, there is a lack of clearly defined policies in place to work towards achieving this goal.

RESOURCES

hpha.org.ar
Build houses with Habitat for Humanity Argentina.

wwoofindependents.org/en/
Volunteer at local farms through WWOOF Argentina.

worldpackers.com
World Packers has many kinds of volunteer opportunities.

LGBTIQ+ Travelers

Argentina is very LGBTIQ+ friendly, and one of the world's top gay destinations. It was the first Latin American country to legalize same-sex marriage, and polls consistently show over 70% of the population accept homosexuality. The LGBTIQ+ community is very visible, with many dedicated queer spaces like clubs, hotels, cafes and *milongas*.

Progressive Legislation

Argentina has enacted several laws to protect and ensure the rights of LGBTIQ+ people, including legalizing same-sex marriage in 2010, and in 2012, passing the gender identity law to allow trans people to legally change their gender without having to go through hormone therapy first. The cities of Buenos Aires and Rosario have further protections to punish discrimination of LGBTIQ+ people. The country has been heralded as a champion of trans rights in particular, with 1% of all public jobs reserved for trans workers.

BUENOS AIRES PRIDE

The Marcha del Orgullo LGBT (Buenos Aires Pride Parade) is held annually in November. It begins in Plaza de Mayo in front of the Casa Rosada and ends at Congreso. The week prior is filled with pride events like concerts, art popups, photography exhibits and more occurring throughout the city for Semana #OrgulloBA (Pride Week).

Queer Grape Harvest Festival

The Vendimia para Todos (Harvest for All) is a queer grape harvesting festival in Mendoza that takes place every year in early March with DJ sets, body painting, aerial acrobatics and drag queen presentations. Check facebook.com/vendimiaparatodosoficial for the lineup. Information tends to be posted last minute.

BALLROOM CULTURE

Vogue balls are on the rise in Argentina, particularly in Buenos Aires, where you can also find voguing classes. Usually, the catwalks feature local queer designers. Socio Ballroom (@socioballroom) is a nonprofit that helps to organize these events in Buenos Aires and spread awareness about accessible medical care.

Gay-Friendly Districts

Buenos Aires has many gay-friendly bars, clubs and cafes throughout the city. Amerika, one of the largest gay clubs in South America, is located in Almagro, and many more of the city's best-known gay-friendly businesses and events are in Palermo and San Telmo. In Córdoba, go to Güemes, and in Puerto Madryn, La Rambla. Mendoza, Rosario and Mar del Plata also have queer scenes.

VOLUNTEER

The Federación Argentina LGBT (FALGBT) works to ensure equal rights for all members of the queer community at the institutional level while also organizing inclusive sports and arts programs. Join their cultural activities by contacting them through their website: falgbt.org.

Accessible Travel

Argentina is not the best-equipped country for providing accessibility support, though it is improving all the time, thanks to both government and grassroots initiatives. Despite the lack of services, you'll find the general population very inclined to help those with accessibility needs.

Iguazù Falls

Iguazù Falls is a highly accessible destination: 90% of the trails are wheelchair-accessible, signs have Braille, and motorized transport is offered for the elderly. Disabled persons enter for free.

Airport

At Ezeiza International Airport, mobility assistance services should be requested through your airline prior to travel. On the tarmac, AmbuLift is available and the airport has wheelchair-accessible bathrooms and elevators.

Accommodation

Buenos Aires, Puerto Madryn, Ushuaia, Calafate, Bariloche, Iguazú and Córdoba are all cities in which you will be able to find wheelchair-accessible hotel rooms. Sometimes the bathrooms can be cramped, though.

TACTILE MAPS

The Recoleta tourist office, Palermo Lakes tourist office and Casa Rosada Museum in Buenos Aires all have tactical maps of the city with Braille and 3D models.

Cobblestone Streets

In the older neighborhoods of Buenos Aires, you'll find cobblestone streets, oftentimes with narrow sidewalks that may be difficult to navigate for wheelchair uses. An exception to this are the wide sidewalks of Recoleta.

Deaf Community Space

The Asociación de Sordomudos de Ayuda Mutua (ASAM, Association of the Deaf and Mute of Mutual Aid) is a nonprofit in Buenos Aires that acts as a meeting space for deaf people and teaches Argentine Sign Language courses.

PUBLIC TRANSPORT

Many Buenos Aires buses have a manual ramp at the back door. Stops for buses are not always accessible for wheelchairs, though. Some Subte stations have elevators, but many are not accessibility-friendly. Several cities, like Córdoba and Neuquén, have some wheelchair-accessible buses, but overall, buses with ramps are not guaranteed in Argentina.

RESOURCES

The city of Buenos Aires keeps an updated English **directory** of its accessible hotels, restaurants, tango venues, and tourist attractions on the government website.

Ok Traslados
is a wheelchair-accessible taxi service that provides rides and tours around Buenos Aires, as well as to the Atlantic coast.

Travel Xperience
is a tour company specializing in leading wheelchair-accessible trips to Argentina and beyond.

⚥ Women Travelers

Argentina can be challenging at times for female travelers. Though it's one of the safer countries in Latin America, and filled with fierce feminists, you'll still encounter its machismo nature in both overt and subtle ways.

What to Wear

Fashion can range from the conservative to lingerie-esque tops. Take your cues from what you see locals wearing, but generally, whatever you want to wear will be fine. It's far more acceptable to not wear a bra here than in North American countries, but you won't see as many people walking around in yoga leggings as you would in those countries either.

Healthcare

Non-applicator tampons and diva cups are readily available in the big cities, as well as sanitary pads. Applicator tampons are not available at all. The morning-after pill is readily accessible, and abortion is legalized up to 14 weeks (more if the life of the pregnant person is in danger). Should you need them, Buenos Aires has excellent gynecologists, but you might need help with translation if your Spanish isn't decent.

Transport

Generally public transport is safe. Be aware that the subway does not run all night, and buses do not run as frequently at night. Taxis are generally fine too, but if you want the quickest, most secure option, rideshares in which you can share your location, such as Uber, Cabify and Didi, will be best. Cabify tends to vet their drivers better. Be aware that there are rare reports of voyeurism on public transport here. Should you find yourself receiving unwanted attention or if someone exposes themselves to you, be loud about your disapproval and tell the driver – other passengers will come to your aid.

Chivalry

It's normal for men to hold doors open for women here, as well as let them enter taxis first. They will also give you the right of way on the sidewalk. However, these chivalrous attitudes do not always translate to paying the bill on dates.

CATCALLING

Catcalling is common in Argentina, especially in Buenos Aires, where you might experience hisses, whistling and *piropos* (pickup lines that are often vulgar). Most women choose to ignore them (which is generally effective and advised), while others address them head-on with a sharp 'No me jodas!' (Don't mess with me!) If you walk with a male companion, catcalling will be a non-issue. If someone is trying to pick you up, and you don't want the attention, very firmly tell them that you are not interested and walk away. They will probably still keep talking, but it's best to walk away and not engage anymore.

ACCOMODATION

Some hostels offer completely female dorms and many hotels, *estancias* and B&Bs that usually cater primarily to couples are happy to accommodate solo female travelers. Should you want something a bit more long-term in Buenos Aires, but only want to rent from or live with other women, the Facebook group BsAs Girlfriends Group has a thread specifically for connecting potential renters to landladies.

Nuts & Bolts

OPENING HOURS

Banks 8am to 3pm or 4pm Monday to Friday and until 1pm Saturday

Bars 8pm or 9pm to 4pm or 6am nightly

Cafes 8am to 8pm daily

Clubs 1am or 2am to between 6am and 8am Friday and Saturday

Restaurants noon to 3:30pm and 8pm to midnight or 1am

Smoking Smoking is banned in all public transportation and public indoor areas, including hospitals, museums and theaters.

Toilets Bidets are common in homes and hotels. Turn them on slowly or you might spray yourself – and the bathroom ceiling.

Tap Water Tap water is safe to drink in Buenos Aires and most of Argentina.

GOOD TO KNOW

Time zone
GMT–3

Country code
+54

Emergency number
911

Population
46,044,703

PUBLIC HOLIDAYS

Argentina has 14 national public holidays. Some businesses and non-essential services may be closed.

New Year's Day January 1

Carnival Monday and Tuesday in February/March – the days before Ash Wednesday

Day of Remembrance for Truth and Justice March 24

Easter Week Days vary in March/April; many businesses close on Thursday and Friday

Malvinas War Veterans Day April 2

Labor Day May 1

Revolution Day May 25

Flag Day June 20

Independence Day July 9

San Martín Memorial Day Third Monday in August

Respect for Cultural Diversity Day Second Monday in October

National Sovereignty Day Fourth Monday in November

Immaculate Conception Day December 8

Christmas December 25

Electricity 220V/50Hz

Weights & Measures

Argentina uses the metric system. Decimal places are indicated by commas, and thousands by points.

Type H
230V/50Hz

Type C
220V/50Hz

Language

TOOLKIT

Spanish is the national language of Argentina, and knowing some very basic phrases is not only courteous but also essential, particularly when navigating through rural areas. That said, a long history of North American tourists has made English the country's unofficial second language.

Basics

Hello. Hola. *o·la*
Goodbye. Adiós. *a·dyos*
Yes. Sí. *see*
No. No. *No*
Please. Por favor. *por fa·vor*
Thank you. Gracias. *gra·syas*
Excuse me. Con permiso. *kon per·mee·so*
Sorry. Perdón. *per·don*
What's your name? ¿Cómo se llama usted? *ko·mo se ya·ma oo·ste*
My name is ... Me llamo ... *me ya·mo ...*
Do you speak English? ¿Habla inglés? *a·bla een·gles*
I don't understand. No entiendo. *no en·tyen·do*

 ## Directions

Where's ...?
¿Dónde está ...? *don·de es·ta ...*
What's the address?
¿Cuál es la dirección? *kwal es la dee·rek·syon*
Could you write it down?
¿Podría escribirlo? *po·dree·a es·kree·beer·lo*
Can you show me (on the map)?
¿Me puede enseñar (en el mapa)? *me pwe·de en·se·nyar (en el ma·pa)*

Signs

Abierto Open
Cerrado Closed
Entrada Entrance
Salida Exit
Servicios/Baños Toilets

 ## Time

What time is it? ¿Qué hora es? *ke o·ra es*
It's (10) o'clock. Son (las diez). *son (las dyes)*
It's half past (one). Es (la una) y media. *es (la oo·na) ee me·dya*
Morning. Mañana. *ma·nya·na*
Afternoon. Tarde. *tar·de*
Evening. Noche. *no·che*
Yesterday. Ayer. *a·yer*
Today. Hoy. *oy*
Tomorrow. Mañana. *ma·nya·na*

 ## Emergencies

Help! ¡Socorro! *so·ko·ro*
Go away! ¡Váyase! *va·ya·se*
I'm ill. Estoy enfermo/a. *es·toy es.toy en.fer.mo/a (m/f)*
I'm lost. Estoy perdido/a. *per·dee·do/a (m/f)*
Call ...! ¡Llame a ...! *ya·me a ...*
A doctor un doctor *oon dok·tor*
The police la policía *la po·lee·see·a*

 ## Eating & Drinking

Can I see the menu, please? ¿Puedo ver el menú, por favor? *pwe·do ver el me·noo, por fa·vor*
What would you recommend?
¿Qué me recomienda? *ke me re·ko·myen·da*
Cheers! ¡Salud! *sa·lood*
That was delicious!
¡Estuvo delicioso! *es·too·vo de·lee·syo·so*
The bill, please. La cuenta, por favor.

NUMBERS

1
uno *oo·no*

2
dos *dos*

3
tres *tres*

4
cuatro *kwa·tro*

5
cinco *seen·ko*

6
seis *seys*

7
siete *sye·te*

8
ocho *o·cho*

9
nueve *nwe·ve*

10
diez *dyes*

DISTINCTIVE SOUNDS

Note that *kh* is a throaty sound (like the 'ch' in the Scottish loch), *v* and *b* are like a soft English 'v' (between a 'v' and a 'b'), and *r* is strongly rolled.

DONATIONS TO ENGLISH
Numerous – you may recognize armada, aficionado, embargo, fiesta, machismo, patio, plaza...

Where the @!*# is it?

Spanish-language and English-language keyboard layouts differ because the two alphabets aren't quite the same. This shouldn't generally be a problem, but for one pesky – all too useful in the age of email – key. The @ ('at') symbol – in Spanish this symbol is called *la arroba* (la a·ro·ba) – isn't necessarily labeled on keyboards or may not be accessed by simply pressing the keys you're used to. Try the F2 key, use an ALT code – or ask for help:

Where's the @ key? *¿Dónde está la arroba?* (don·de es·ta la a·ro·ba)

To Lisp or Not to Lisp

If you're familiar with the sound of European Spanish, you'll notice that Latin Americans don't 'lisp' – ie the European Spanish *th* is pronounced as *s* in Latin America.

Río de la Plata

Spanish in the Río de la Plata region differs from Spain and the rest of the Americas, notably in the use of the informal form of 'you'. Instead of tuteo (the use of tú), Argentines commonly speak with voseo (the use of vos), a relic from 16th-century Spanish requiring slightly different grammar.

SPANISH AROUND THE WORLD

Spanish speakers in Argentina give the language its very own local flavor – the letters ll (pronounced ly or simplified to y in most parts of Latin America) and y are pronounced like the 's' in 'measure' or the 'sh' in 'shut' in Argentina. You'll get used to this very quickly listening to and taking your cues from the locals.

497

STORYBOOK

Our writers delve deep into different aspects of Argentine life

Traditional gaucho outfit, San Antonio de Areco (p304)

BERND ZILLICH/SHUTTERSTOCK ©

A HISTORY OF ARGENTINA IN
15 PLACES

Argentina has lived through war and peace, feast and famine, and frankly there's rarely a dull moment in its rollercoaster history. Geography, ancient fossils, an array of architectural styles and rupestral art reveal the country's past and its people's passions. Here we choose 15 destinations that chart Argentina's journey. By Sorrel Moseley-Williams

THEROPOD FOSSILS IN Parque Provincial Ischigualasto show that life in Argentina existed long before hunter-gatherers such as the Tehuelche left their fingerprints in rock art in Patagonia. For thousands of years, ancient peoples made their mark in this 'land of silver'. Pre-Hispanic communities included the Quilmes – whose dwellings can be seen in Ciudad Sagrada de Quilmes, Tucumán – and the Inca civilization. Archaeological ruins of the latter's *pucará* (Andean fortifications) are visible in the Quebrada de Humahuaca canyon in Jujuy.

From more recent centuries, literature, poetry and music recount who built this vibrant and culturally rich country in words and lyrics that share their writers' passion – or otherwise – for their motherland. In Buenos Aires, calle Caminito in La Boca neighborhood is an excellent example of what the European migration in the 19th century contributed to Argentina. There's an outstanding collection of architecture to enjoy too, such as the brutalist-style theater in La Plata that's an indelible reminder of the 1976–1983 dictatorship. But after a dark past can come triumph and hope. A recent chapter in the country's history was its 2022 World Cup glory, and a lifesize 3D printout of soccer legend Lionel Messi in Caminito commemorates that victory.

1. Parque Provincial Ischigualasto
MOON WALKING IN VALLE DE LA LUNA

The desert valley that is San Juan's Parque Provincial Ischigualasto is also known as Valle de la Luna (valley of the moon) for its remarkable lunar landscape – plus it's the only place on Earth where you can see every stage of the 50.5 million-year Triassic geological period. The park is tucked between two sedimentary mountain ranges, and hiking through it feels like walking on another planet thanks to terrain consisting of red sandstone, volcanic ash and clay rock formations that sport nicknames such as El Gusano (the worm), El Submarino (the submarine) and El Hongo (the mushroom). The park is also home to incredible 180-million-year-old fossils. Truly an otherworldly experience.

For more on Parque Provincial Ischigualasto, see page 296.

2. Museo Municipal Ernesto Bachmann
WHEN DINOSAUR GIANTS RULED PATAGONIA

When dinosaurs ruled Planet Earth, one of the world's largest carnivorous dinosaurs, the Giganotosaurus carolinii, roamed modern-day Patagonia. There are no complete remains of this appropriately named theropod, but estimates reckon it measured up to 13 meters in length and weighed up to 14 tons. Pro and amateur paleontologists alike will be wowed by the Giganotosaurus fossils carefully pieced together at the Museo Municipal Ernesto Bachmann – named for the Argentine dino enthusiast – in Villa El Chocón near Neuquén, an area this behemoth once called home.

For more on Museo Municipal Ernesto Bachmann, see page 385.

3. The Andes
THE MOUNTAINOUS BACKBONE OF ARGENTINA

The Andes mountain range accompanies you every step of the way in the country's west. whether you're traveling to the Salinas Grandes in the north of Salta and Jujuy or the extreme south in Ushuaia. Its formations create vibrant canyons such as the Quebrada de Humahuaca and classic pistes for skiing in Las Leñas; the 8900km-long range also has the southern hemisphere's highest peak – the 6961m Cerro Aconcagua. The backbone of Argentina and the South American continent, this natural border reached its current shape between six and 10 million years ago.

For more on the Andes, see page 390.

Quebrada de Humahuaca (p42)

4. Cueva de las Manos Pintadas
AN ANCIENT CAVE ART GALLERY

In a remote corner of this Patagonian province sits one of the world's oldest art galleries, an extraordinary assemblage of wall paintings believed to have been made between 13,000 and 9500 years ago. The hunter-gatherer Tehuelche people stenciled outlines of human hands here, and depicted images of guanaco and hunting scenes. The hands are painted with natural mineral pigments such as red and purple iron oxides and black manganese oxide and, given their position at the cave's entrance, make for a poignant greeting to this special site.

For more on Cueva de las Manos Pintadas, see page 435.

5. Ciudad Sagrada de Quilmes
THE LAST PRE-COLONIAL BATTLE SITE

The reconstructed Ciudad Sagrada de Quilmes depicts what life was like for a group of the Diaguita people – the Quilmes – who lived in this, the largest pre-Columbian settlement in Argentina. The city thrived during the 12th century, protecting itself with a fortress and two smaller forts in its location on the 2300m Cerro Alto del Rey. A population of 3000 lived in Ciudad Sagrada itself, while a further 10,000 Quilmes lived in the surrounding countryside. A strong and fierce people, they were the last to be conquered by the Spaniards in 1665 – after 135 years of resistance. Visitors can walk around the restored settlement.

For more on Ciudad Sagrada de Quilmes, see page 204.

6. Quebrada de Humahuaca
HOW PRE-HISPANIC COMMUNITIES LIVED

Populated for at least 10,000 years, first by hunter-gatherers and then pre-Hispanic communities, the elevated Quebrada de Humahuaca canyon came into its own during the Inca period. In the early 15th century it was used as a vital trade and communication route between what today is Argentina and Bolivia.

Lying alongside the Río Grande meant communities could easily cultivate crops – corn, potato and quinoa are still grown here. A few *pucará* (Andean fortifications) remain, although most were razed by the

Spanish. A series of small towns, such as Purmamarca, Tilcara and Humahuaca, still prosper.

For more on Quebrada de Humahuaca, see page 42.

7. El Shincal

FAR-REACHING POWER OF THE INCA CIVILIZATION

The strength and reach of the Inca civilization is seen in the province of Catamarca, specifically in the village of Londres, which was believed to have been a key political, religious and military center in the region for a brief period between 1457 and 1536. The 100 or so buildings that form El Shincal de Quimivil archaeological site are particularly prominent, and include a collection of warehouses and a central platform. Many of the ruins are surrounded by shinqui shrubs.

For more on El Shincal, see page 210.

8. Museo de Arqueología de Alta Montaña

INCREDIBLY PRESERVED MUMMIES

Located on Salta's main Plaza 9 de Julio, the Museo de Arqueología de Alta Montaña carefully displays the culture of high-mountain communities in the pre-Hispanic era. The collection's highlights are the Niños Llullaillaco, three mummified children from high-ranking Inca families who were sacrificed on top of the Llullaillaco volcano around 500 years ago. Lightning Girl, the Boy and the Maiden, along with their trousseau holding miniature ceremonial objects, were discovered in 1999, still in exceedingly good condition. The mummies are cryopreserved to mimic their original mountain burial site.

For more on Museo de Arqueología de Alta Montaña, see page 176.

9. San Ignacio Miní

A SUBTROPICAL MISSION COMPLEX

One of 30 mission complexes founded by Jesuit clerics in Argentina, Brazil and Paraguay, San Ignacio Miní, in the northeastern province of Misiones, was built in the baroque style yet also decorated with native motifs. Constructed by the religious order to convert the Guaraní indigenous people, the site includes a stone church with a wooden interior, a hospital and a school. Jesuit missions were often attacked by locals defending their land, meaning the clerics frequently moved around – they made their final base here in the Misiones subtropical rainforest in 1696. San Ignacio Miní is one of the few remaining examples of such complexes in South America, and a beautiful example at that.

For more on San Ignacio Miní, see page 139.

10. Casa de la Independencia

THE ROAD TO POLITICAL FREEDOM

The northwestern province of Tucumán is where Argentina's road to freedom began. Behind the whitewashed walls of a colonial-era building, the Casa de la Independencia is where independence from Spain was declared on July 9, 1816. Politicians continued working here for a further year until given a new home in Buenos Aires. While parts of the casa have been demolished or remodeled over the decades, many original features remain. Thanks to the role the city played, every July 9, San Miguel de Tucumán becomes Argentina's capital – for one day.

For more on Casa de la Independencia, see page 197.

11. Manzano Histórico

WHERE A FREEDOM FIGHTER RESTED

In a corner of Valle de Uco lies Manzano Histórico, a village tucked away at 1700m of altitude in a protected natural reserve whose name was changed to pay tribute to a historically relevant manzano (apple tree). It was under its branches that South America's freedom fighter General José de San Martín – who led the revolution against the Spanish in Argentina in 1812 – is said to have rested with his troops after liberating Chile and Peru 11 years later. The stone-constructed Retorno a la Patria monument created by Luis Perlotti is an artistic focal point, and today, the natural reserve is a gateway to the Andes.

For more on Manzano Histórico, see page 286.

12. Caminito

THE CAPITAL'S MOST COLORFUL STREET

The corrugated zinc facades of the *conventillos* (tenement housing) in Caminito, one of Argentina's most emblematic streets found in La Boca neighborhood, tell part of the country's early migration story. While there were various waves, the late 19th and early 20th centuries saw many Europeans – in

Caminito (p104)

particular those of Genoese descent – make the port their home. Often, working-class families lived under a single roof of the precarious conventillo housing, painted in vibrant primary colors. Today it's an open-air street-museum, home to murals and busts created by renowned artist Benito Quinquela Martín; it was he who gave the barrio of La Boca its artsy reputation in the 1950s, and named Caminito street after a tango.

For more on Caminito, see page 108.

13. Museo Gauchesco Ricardo Güiraldes
THE LIFE OF A GAUCHO LITERARY HERO

It's highly appropriate that a museum dedicated to the life of notable rancher-turned-author Ricardo Güiraldes – whose great gaucho novel *Don Segundo Sombra,* published in 1926, recounts the story of the eponymous cowboy – is located inside an authentic 150-year-old *pulpería*, La Blanqueada. This bar, historically frequented by gauchos, today houses the Museo Gauchesco Ricardo Güiraldes in this authentic cowboy town; the museum also contains a mill and stables as well as a silver collection and equestrian artifacts that cover daily life in the pampas.

For more on Museo Gauchesco Ricardo Güiraldes, see page 308.

14. Teatro Argentino
A REMINDER OF THE DICTATORSHIP

While it's Argentina's second-most prominent opera house (after the Teatro Colón in Buenos Aires), La Plata's Teatro Argentino is the number one symbol of the country's years under military rule between 1976 and 1983.

Originally constructed in Renaissance style in 1887, it was destroyed by fire in 1977.

Though much of it was salvageable, the dictatorship's leaders chose not to rebuild it, seeing the fire as an opportunity to bulldoze the ruins and then create a new cultural space in the brutalist architectural style, favoring concrete and minimalism over classic structures.

For more on Teatro Argentino, see page 330.

15. Lionel Messi statue
WORLD CUP TRIBUTE TO A SOCCER LEGEND

December 18, 2022 is etched in the memory of every single Argentine because it's the day their country won its third World Cup trophy – and soccer player Lionel Messi became a national hero. While a wave of celebratory street art covers walls all over the country, in Caminito, in the capital, a wonderful life-size statue pays tribute to the number 10 player and team captain.

The full-color 3D printout – which took almost 700 hours to print – was unveiled in 2023 to celebrate the player's 36th birthday. It depicts the glorious moment when Messi lifted the cup in Qatar.

For more on the Lionel Messi statue, see page 108.

MEET THE ARGENTINES

You might lose yourself in Argentina's unique landscapes and varied identities, but trust any Argentine you meet to help you find the way. Federico Perelmuter introduces his people.

WE, THE ARGENTINES, come from many places: our country was second only to the United States in total number of immigrants during the 1880–1930 period and first, globally, per capita. By 1914, immigrants comprised one third of the population. Before the wave of mass immigration began, Argentina was sparsely populated after a century of political instability, civil war, and the near eradication of its indigenous people failed to disperse urban concentration around Buenos Aires.

At the government's behest, immigrants arrived, mostly from southern Italy and Spain, but also Jewish migrants from Eastern Europe and other parts of Europe who settled in places like Moisés Ville in Santa Fe. Their influence combined with the existing colonial, indigenous and Afro cultures to transform Argentina into a feverishly cosmopolitan country and made our cities into hubs of cultural diversity. To this day, immigration continues from neighboring countries like Paraguay, Perú and Bolivia, as well as South Korea and China, and in recent years Senegal, Venezuela and Russia.

If anything unites Argentines, it's our wild blend of lifestyles, which suit the country's size and breadth of regions, not to mention our own disparate origins. *Porteños* (people from the city of Buenos Aires) are renowned for our arrogant irony (and rightly resented for our self-centeredness), and should not be confused with *bonaerenses,* from the province of Buenos Aires, many of whom want nothing to do with porteños.

Cordobeses love a party, and their iconic *tonada* (accent) is inimitable; *rosarinos* live by the river Paraná, tributary of the Río de la Plata, and the gateway to Northern Argentina. Wine and mountains make Mendoza's people uniquely wise and jovial, while Tucumán is the country's most densely populated province, Argentina's founding place, and has the best citrus around. *Salteños* and *jujeños,* from Salta and Jujuy, are sometimes made into rivals and are as famous for their spectacular cooking and vistas as for their stubborn friendliness. The list goes on.

Argentina is not renowned for its economic stability or calm political life, though 2023 is our 40th year of continuous democratic rule. But the unpredictable world around us makes Argentines uniquely resilient and solidaristic, willing to lend a hand to anyone who may need it.

In fact, friendship is Argentina's most noble tradition: many Argentines will stick with their childhood friends until their very last days, and form friend groups that spend days and weeks together and often come to resemble families. Argentine friendship is unbreakable, forged in a country where living alone is impossible, where everything can change from one day to the next, where many arrived in search of opportunity. Befriend one of us and you will never walk alone again. Show me who your friends are, and I'll tell you who you are: in Argentina, the answer is simple.

Who & How Many

Of the 46 million Argentines, 3.5 million live in the city of Buenos Aires and 11 million in its metropolitan area. Ninety-two percent of the country's population is urban, but agriculture has always been very important in Argentina, once known as 'the world's granary'.

Pictured clockwise from top left: Gauchos, Cafayate (p183); A football fan in the Argentine national jersey (p512); Drinking mate (p47); A young man in Buenos Aires (p54)

I'M ARGENTINE-ISH

My immediate family was born and raised in Argentina, as was I until the US beckoned. I lived in Philadelphia and New York until graduation, before a swift and long-awaited return home.

I'm Jewish, and my grandparents were the first generation of my family to be born in Argentina: my great-grandparents emigrated from present-day Russia, Moldavia, Poland and Ukraine.

Since then, we have always lived in Buenos Aires: my father's side lived in the early-20th-century working-class immigrant hotspot of Avellaneda, while my father came of age in the quieter neighborhood of Villa del Parque. My mother's family resided in the bustling and energetic working-class neighborhood of Parque Patricios, and later in Almagro. I was born in Villa Crespo, and raised in suburban Pilar.

Buenos Aires, with all its enormity and historic importance, should never be confused for Argentina, nor should a *porteño* like me believe he can tell you everything – Argentina is enormous.

VINTAGES & VINES

After five centuries of history, Argentina's wine industry has developed fast and furiously over the past three decades to become a true world-class player. By Sorrel Moseley-Williams

WINE IS CULTURE. Wine is history. By decree, it's Argentina's national alcoholic beverage, with a story dating back almost 500 years. And, as much as we love uncorking an inviting bottle of Malbec, the great news is that nowadays there is much more to Argentina than that favorite red that's become popular the world over.

Cultivating a Diverse Wine Industry

Savvy winemakers and grape growers have strived to create a diverse wine industry in Argentina, and their vision has paid off. The terroir they traverse is extensive, as are the grape varieties and winemaking styles. While Mendoza remains king in terms of both quality and production, the country's terroir is no longer limited to hugging a small segment of the length of the Andes – it now extends from the high-altitude Valles Calchaquíes in Salta to the steppe-hugged vineyards of Río Negro in northwestern Patagonia.

In a bid to explore and express the vast terrain they have to play with, winemakers are cultivating vineyards ever higher into the mountains, in the likes of the Quebrada de Humahuaca in Jujuy, further south in Patagonia where dinosaurs once roamed, and east towards the Atlantic in the provinces of Buenos Aires and Chubut, to create wines with maritime influence. Argentina has long been the world's fifth-largest wine producer – after France, Italy, Spain and the US – but never have aficionados been so spoiled for choice in terms of what's being produced.

From Mass to Malbec

Argentina's relationship with wine began, as is often the way in the Americas, with the Catholic Jesuits' need to use the sacred grape to create sacramental wine. Some say the first vineyards on the greater continent were in Baja California, Mexico, while others say Peru or Chile. The first vitis vinifera (common grape vine) cultivated in Argentina was in the 16th century in the province of Córdoba. (While it never boomed like Mendoza, today Córdoba is considered one of the country's new wave of viticultural hubs.)

As an industry, Argentine wine wasn't even in the game until given a boost by the vision of Domingo Faustino Sarmiento. The future president of Argentina recruited a

PAY-PRO PHOTOGRAPHY LTD/SHUTTERSTOCK ©

Organic vineyards, Mendoza (p256)

French agronomist to create a wine industry in 1853. Among the Bordeaux vines brought over by Michel Aimé Pouget was the red grape Malbec, today Mendoza's and the country's star grape. Did Pouget know that this underappreciated Bordeaux red – used by Bordeaux oenologists to boost color and tannin – would become Argentina's celebrated variety? Perhaps he saw Mendoza's unexplored potential. Perhaps it was a gamble. But no matter what fueled the decision, more than a century later Malbec propelled Argentine winemaking to international recognition and Argentina has Sarmiento and Pouget to thank for it.

Make it Mendoza

Mendoza Province remains Argentina's winemaking powerhouse, producing approximately 76 percent of all wine and a fifth of all Malbec. While neighboring San Juan Province has made wine since the 17th century and is the country's second-biggest producer, it is only responsible for about 18 percent of wine production. And Salta's Valle Calchaquíes historical wine industry – which includes large bodegas (wineries) such as Colomé (Argentina's oldest continuously operating

bodega, in operation since 1831), El Esteco and Etchart – accounts for a tiny 1.5 percent of all output.

Besides its vast vineyards, many framed by the Andes, the beauty of Mendoza is its terroir diversity, and the key departments of Luján de Cuyo, Maipú and Valle de Uco break down into smaller sub-districts. Out of Luján de Cuyo alone there are many sub-districts – Mayor Drummond, Las Compuertas, Vistalba and Chacras de Coria – meaning it's no longer enough to say 'my favorite wine is from Mendoza'. Today, makers are highly specific about their vintages' origin, and proud to spotlight the differences and identity of these districts.

Despite a grape-growing tradition dating back to the turn of the 20th century, Valle de Uco is Mendoza's current star, producing top-quality wines which are regularly awarded 100 points, the top score denoting perfection that's awarded by the world's most trusted critics. Zuccardi Valle de Uco, Catena Zapata, Per Se and El Enemigo have all taken top marks in recent years, and given the passion and world-class knowhow behind these and other projects, it's a safe bet more vintages will join them.

Where to Visit

Mendoza is Argentina's most developed region when it comes to enotourism, with around 200 bodegas opening their doors for wine tastings, paired lunches and dinners, horseback riding and workshops. Almost all require reservations, so book ahead to avoid disappointment; that said, it is easy to visit on your own if you have adequate transport such as a car or a driver. If you're short on time, an organized tour or a hop-on-hop-off bus will cover at least three bodegas on a day excursion. Top wineries here that offer tastings followed by lunch include award-winning Zuccardi Valle de Uco and Catena Zapata, while more modest bodegas that also offer wining and dining include Mil Suelos, Bodega Lagarde and Riccitelli Wines.

Elsewhere, Cafayate in the Valles Calchaquíes makes for a refreshing alternative to more popular Mendoza, thanks to its small town ambience and the 20 or so traditional wineries in the area. Book tastings at El Porvenir de Cafayate and Estancia Los Cardones. Other, new wine destinations include Trevelin in Chubut Province in Patagonia and the Quebrada de Humahuaca in Jujuy. In the former, it's easy to visit the three wineries – Contra Corriente, Casa Yagüe and Nant y Fall – in the town, while in the latter, stop by Bodega Kindgard, Bodega Fernando Dupont and El Bayeh.

Right on Trend

Argentina has little trouble keeping up with global wine trends and style explorers will relish diving into the buoyant natural wine movement, appreciating organic and biodynamic agricultural practices, wines created under flor (a yeast veil in the Jerez style) and sampling all manner of rosés and skin-contact wines, known as vino naranjo (orange wine). This experimental drive forward is important when it comes to firming up the country's reputation as a world player.

When you visit wineries, a sommelier will guide you through a tasting, starting with the basics of how to taste wine (observe its color, sniff its aromas, then taste in the mouth). Bodegas tend to offer tastings at various price points: the most basic will provide at least three sampler sizes to try. Don't forget to spit if you're driving.

Most sommeliers in Argentina either work in Buenos Aires or Mendoza (though, obviously, they work in restaurants in other parts of the country too) and are respected professionals. Use them as a fountain of knowledge on what's hot, or just come into the cellar: they are well-informed and passionate individuals who take their vocation of sharing Argentine wine with you seriously. It's a dialogue. Let them know what you like and to what extent you're willing to venture further afield, and never be afraid to set a budget. That said, enjoying Argentine vintages at a winery in Argentina will always be much more reasonably priced than back home. When visiting wineries, ask about shipping directly back home, as prices and import taxes depend on the country.

Whether you're sampling by the glass in one of Buenos Aires' fantastic wine bars, devouring a paired tasting menu in Valle de Uco to an Andean backdrop, or uncorking a souvenir in your backyard, the fact is that Argentina offers countless ways to enjoy its vino, so raise a glass to one of the world's most exciting wine countries. ¡Salud!

ARGENTINA HAS LITTLE TROUBLE KEEPING UP WITH GLOBAL WINE TRENDS AND STYLE EXPLORERS WILL RELISH DIVING INTO THE BUOYANT NATURAL WINE MOVEMENT

White wine, Cafayate (p183)

TITONELI FOTOGRAFIAS/SHUTTERSTOCK ©

ICON OF THE PAMPAS

Influencer, muse and antihero: the life, times and future of the gaucho, the greatest living – and longevous – subcultural icon.
By Victoria Gill

IN THE 18TH century, the English dandy was born; a century later, the cowboy corralled the US; and who remembers the Sharpies? Thankfully, not us. None survived more than a few decades. Argentina's gauchos saw them all through and out, today standing as the world's most enduring living subculture.

You'll likely spot bereted *puebleros* (townspeople) sloping through the cobbled lanes of San Antonio de Areco, practicing dance steps for the Malambo competition each September in Laborde, riding into towns across the nation to dazzle the Día de la Tradición or glimpse a poncho-draped arm emptying a *mate* holder from a refugio deep in the Patagonian wilderness.

Gauchos – loosely defined as ranchers or horsemen – draw their closest comparison with the cowboys of the US. It's thought that their title stems from the Quechuan word *huacho,* meaning orphan, given to the solitary 18th-century riders who roamed the pampas, trading and taming the cattle and horses left behind by the conquistadors after the first attempt to build Buenos Aires failed.

Get the Gaucho Look

The gaucho's appearance is as unifying as it is indelible. Originally of mestizo blood, their ponchos, penchants for *mate* and *boleadoras* (weights on cords) are adopted from the ancestral peoples of Argentina; the criollos (Latin Americans of Spanish descent) shared their *facónes* (knives), guitars and Basque berets. Completing the look are bombachas (pantaloons) and chiripas (sashes). You'll most certainly know a gaucho when you see one. Their effects are sold everywhere, from specialist plaza-front boutiques to *ferias artesanales* throughout the land.

The Gaucho Soul

Let's strip away that uniform now to see what simmers beneath. Think of the gaucho's penetrating eyes as his meter for justice; his mouth spouts a waterfall of passion; his shoulders bear the burden of hardship and his spine the weight of loyalty. From his heart bursts the passion for freedom, his touch carries the warm caress of acceptance and protection, and his arms the embrace of loyalty.

Famously solitary and independent, the gaucho's soul is singed by lament. It's no surprise, given the injustices he endured. The first settler wave who commanded the land so freely were later put to work on it when the Spaniards ring-fenced the pampas into *estancias* during the 19th century, enlisting the gauchos' ranching expertise.

Their innate courage, equestrianism and honor made them natural-born cavalrymen and saw them corralled to join the War of Independence to liberate Argentina and heroically succeed. They then threw their support behind the gaucho *caudillo* (army chief) Juan Manuel de Rosas, only to be conscripted to fight on the frontiers and turned against their own, those they'd sought to protect. With independence, loyalty and righteousness running through their backbones, many instead galloped away to live among and defend the

CRISTIAN LAZZARI/GETTY IMAGES ©

Gaucho drinking mate

indigenous, who in turn fled incursions to hide among the gauchos.

The disrepute of the fallen gaucho as a brazen bandit and uncouth outlaw within mainstream Argentine society was cemented. Charles Darwin disagreed. On November 26th, 1833, having spent nearly a year traveling South America, the young biologist noted in his diary: 'The gauchos, or countrymen, are very superior to those who reside in the towns. The gaucho is invariably most obliging, polite, and hospitable: I did not meet with even one instance of rudeness or inhospitality. He is modest, both respecting himself and country, but at the same time a spirited, bold fellow.'

The Art of Gaucho

'And this is my pride: to live as free as the bird that cleaves the sky', proclaims Martin Fierro, the protagonist of Jose Hernandez's epic. Selected for Unesco's Collection of Representative Works of Latin America, the ballad recounts the travels and tribulations of the eponymous fugitive deserter and is the flagbearer of La Literatura Gauchesca.

The 1870–1920 literary movement ascended at the same time as the North American cowboy and saw Buenos Aires writers recount the outcast's dilemma through novels and poems narrated in first-person *cieletos* emulating the languorous rhythm of their protagonists and helping to transform their reputation from bandit to folk hero. The stories also addressed mental health long before millennials seized the sphere. (It's said that there are more psychiatrists than patients in Buenos Aires, the city with the most therapists per capita of anywhere in the world.) In the same period, the stories of the Robin Hood lifestyle and miracle-spinning death of Gauchito Gil captured the nation's imagination.

The Gaucho Today

While Argentina's gaucho population today has dwindled significantly, its sphere of influence hasn't; their spirit and customs infuse and inform the national culture and character. To label a person *gauchito* describes them as kind and helpful, and where did Argentina's favorite cooking style – *asado* (barbecued meat) – start? During long nights idled around a fire under the stars on the livestock-heavy pampas, of course, serenaded by *payadas* (verse to a guitar), the prototype of Argentine folk music.

Year-round festivals across the country draw the furtive gauchos away from *estancias* and *refugios* to trot into towns to demonstrate their horsemanship prowess. The legacy of Gauchito Gil is such that there have been repeated calls to beatify him, with shrines to the folk saint marking roadsides throughout the land.

The modern-day culture is adapting to the times amid its inherent, prototypal *machista* (macho) values. The last few years have seen the rise of the female gaucho. Not content to weave and wash clothes anymore, and with their kith and kin population vastly diminished from their 19th-century heyday, the female gaucho today canters with her brothers and father to work on the *estancia*.

Perhaps most of all with their spirit of freedom, nomadic lifestyle, worldweariness, hedonism, tendency to lay down their heads wherever they find a pillow (or poncho), ties to no one and openness to all, the indefinable gaucho soul defines the spirit of the traveler.

FOOTBALL'S IMPACT ON ARGENTINE LIFE

The sport has a religious-like devotion in a country that has produced some of the greatest players ever. By Federico Perelmuter

FOOTBALL HAS NEVER been a mere pastime in Argentina. It's been a near-religious spectacle for over a century – the sport unites the entire country.

When a major game is on, everything stops, streets empty, and crowds gather around any available TV set and follow every play.

Avenues for Social Life

When football began to professionalize in the early years of the 20th century, the various club teams served as key avenues for social life. Going to see the neighborhood team became a key ritual for integrating the country's sizable immigrant population, especially for working-class men, and football clubs were spaces for socializing among those

Fans celebrating in Buenos Aires after Argentina won the 2022 FIFA World Cup

of similar provenances, from Genoa and other parts of Italy and Spain to Jewish, English and Irish immigrants. For most Argentines, the team they support became a central piece of their identity, almost a birthright, and because teams are often passed down through generations, most families share their allegiances.

The Five Grandes

Though games between rivals (most often determined by geography) are known as *clásicos*, the game between River and Boca is known as the *superclásico*, since they are Argentina's most storied teams and have the largest fanbases.

Two of the other three *grandes*, Independiente and Racing, known as *Diablos Rojos* (Red Devils) and *La Academia* (The Academy) respectively, have stadiums mere blocks from one another in Buenos Aires' working-class urban suburb of Avellaneda.

The final *grande*, San Lorenzo, was founded in the central neighborhood of Almagro, but currently has its stadium in the working-class neighborhood of Bajo Flores.

Each club has its own private mythology, folk heroes and *ídolos* (idols) of bygone eras that adorn the walls, minds and even

Boca Juniors' stadium (p113)

tattooed bodies of its *hinchas* (supporters). Through a century, each team developed a repertoire of chants and songs, sung –often with percussion and wind instrument backing – nearly nonstop throughout a match. Flares and smoke bombs are often present, as are an abundance of homemade flags hung around the stadium to identify the *hinchas'* wide-ranging provenance.

The Game Grows

Though men dominate football in Argentina, women's football has grown rapidly over the past decade and, as of 2019, the first division of women's play is semi-professional. Though *cancha* (stadium) attendance remains mostly male, as stadium violence decreases and social norms shift towards safety for everyone, women and children attend games in greater numbers.

The True No 1 Team in Argentina

Argentina's national team cools the oft-insurmountable divisions of club allegiance. The 2022 Qatar World Cup win, led by the iconic Lionel Messi, poured the entire country into the streets in celebration. Much like the country's prior victories, as hosts in 1978 and led by the mythical Diego Maradona in 1986, every moment of this championship became the stuff of legend.

How to Go to a Game

There's only one way to truly experience the passion and madness of Argentine football culture – go to the *cancha* (stadium) for a game. Though some teams offer online ticket sales, many require in-person purchase on match day.

Stadiums have two broad classes of seating: *populares,* standing seats reserved for the most intense *hinchas,* and seating-room *plateas,* more amenable to those lacking *cancha* experience. Boca and River tickets can prove challenging to obtain, but most other teams (including the remaining grandes) will have tickets available at various price points, both on game day and online.

Be ready for lots of safety checks, and make sure to grab a *paty de cancha* (stadium burger) on your way out after the game. Each game is an unparalleled collective experience, a distinctive expression of Argentine culture that should not be missed, and without which Argentina cannot be understood.

513

AN ARGENTINE ROCKSTAR:
CHARLY GARCÍA

His music bewildered censors, stomped on dictators and spoke for a lost generation of Argentine youth: Charly García and the zeitgeist. By Christine Gilbert

HE HAS AN unlikely look for a rockstar. Tall, lanky and with his trademark half-white, half-brown mustache, Charly García, despite the odds, has been rocking out since the 1960s. Some claim him to be the father of *rock nacional* – Argentina's homegrown Spanish-language version of rock. He's certainly one of the country's most influential musicians. Over the last half-century, his lyrics and melodies have been the soundtrack to some of the most

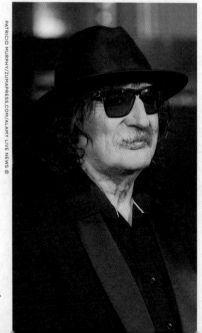

Charly García

traumatic and celebratory moments in Argentina's modern history.

García's Impact on Popular Culture

Every four years, the Quilmes beer company releases a television ad to promote the upcoming FIFA World Cup. In 2022, in the lead-up to the tournament in Qatar, the ad was a lucky premonition of what would eventuate in December. The ad features a series of conversations (that great Argentine pastime) between friends, siblings and co-workers about coincidences between 1986, the last time Argentina won the World Cup, and 2022.

From the more obvious realisation that the Argentine team had the best player in the world in 1986 (Maradona) and again in 2022 (Messi) to more offbeat musings around Jupiter in Pisces and when Robert De Niro has visited Argentina (once in 1986 and again in 2022).

It was funny, deeply sentimental and culturally spot on. For the soundtrack, Quilmes pulled out a classic, 'Hablando a tu corazón' (Talking to Your Heart) written by Charly García and Pedro Aznar in 1986. In the ad, the two musicians pass the baton to young indie-pop stars Bandalos Chinos and Louta, who end the video with their version of the hit.

The catchy ballad was released on García and Aznar's LP *Tango*. And the album title, well, that's no coincidence. Argentines love a heavy dose of nostalgia. You only have to listen to a couple of tangos to realize all that yearning for the homeland, lost loves and mothers is still hanging around in Argentine culture. Charly García deftly wove both musical and lyrical themes from tango throughout much of his discography, and his enduring popularity is due to his uncanny ability to zero in on the zeitgeist.

Garcia Finds His Voice

Starting out as a teenager in the 1960s singing Beatles covers with his band, Walking in Spanish, García went on to form one of the most influential *rock nacional* bands, Sui Generis, with Nito Mestre. One of the first rock bands to enjoy widespread mass appeal, songs like 'Canción para mi muerte' (Song for My Death) managed to speak directly to the generation of young Argentines rebelling against military service and patriarchal institutions. Sui Generis was the voice of the counterculture and heavily influenced by the folklore songs of the *nueva cancion* singers like Mercedes Sosa and Chilean Victor Jara, who tragically disappeared the day after the Chilean coup that disposed of President Allende in 1973.

The times were violent and tumultuous, to say the least. By 1976, the military dictatorship had taken hold in Argentina and in a reflection of the general state of instability, Sui Generis disbanded after two 20,000-strong concerts at Luna Park in Buenos Aires (an art deco beauty which is still the stadium of choice for big shows in BA). Charly started a new band, La máquina de hacer pájaros (The bird-making machine).

And it is here that Charly's genius came to the fore. At a time when young Argentines were being disappeared and any depiction of youth was notably absent in the media, Charly dodged the harsh censorship imposed by the regime by subverting their tropes and writing in allegory and metaphor. In 'Hipercandombe' (1977) Charly sings in the first person to an unknown protagonist, itself a device borrowed from tangos.

His lyrics are poetic and abstract when he tells the audience to cover their faces and long hair, but with hindsight, we know that he is speaking to the heart of the fear and paranoia felt by young people during the military dictatorship, bringing the invisible experience to light. He also sings of the Río de la Plata, Buenos Aires' grand river where the junta dumped many of the bodies of the disappeared. The song is a subversive call to arms as he subtly instructs listeners to change the station if they don't like the song, but ultimately, it tragically foreshadows 1979 when dictator Jorge Rafael Videla defined the disappeared as neither dead or alive. Simply, he told journalists, they are not here.

Dinosaurs Disappear

Towards the end of the dictatorship, after some very dark days, García and the rest of Argentina started to sense a glimmer of hope. In 1981 García released 'No quiero volverme tan loco' (I don't want to be so crazy), a middle-finger salute to the authorities with defiant lyrics about not wanting to be paranoid any longer, it instead being time to let loose. The dictatorship wasn't over, but in 1983, just a month before the fall of the junta after Argentina's defeat on the Islas Malvinas, García released the mighty 'Los dinosaurios' (The dinosaurs) as a solo artist on his 1980s classic album, *Clics Modernos* (Modern Clicks). Never was there a song more in touch with the zeitgeist as Charly sang of the just-about-to-be defunct dictators as extinct – heavy and dead – dinosaurs. With some of the most arresting lyrics ever written, Charly gently plays with grammar to confirm that yes, our friends can disappear, but the dinosaurs will disappear.

Now in his 70s, Charly no longer performs but every day in Buenos Aires is an opportunity to soak up his sounds – be it in a taxi, a bar or in the shops – listen long enough and you'll start to understand his enduring popularity. The stretch of street where he lives in Palermo has been renamed Av Charly García and fans often scribble messages on the building in homage to the icon.

During the early months of 2020 quarantine, García's neighbours even created a 9m×7m mural on their shared rooftop patio of the Oberheim keyboard Charly used to record 'Yendo de la cama al living' (Going from the bed to the living room) – of course, another García stroke of genius when his 1982 song resurfaced as a pandemic anthem.

515

LAUZLA/GETTY IMAGES ©

WILDLIFE IN PATAGONIA

Home to an array of both land animals and marine creatures, Patagonia boasts some of South America's most diverse wildlife.
By Madelaine Triebe

IF YOU'RE LUCKY, there'll be a wildlife welcome party when you touch down in Patagonia. Everything from Magellanic penguins off the Atlantic coast, huge elephant seals brawling on the shores of Península Valdés, gray foxes scurrying over the arid land and guanacos grazing on the steppe call this majestic place home. Further inland, along the Andean Mountain Range, the landscape changes and so do the species, though here on the tree-clad slopes, spotting animals gets trickier. Elusive predators like pumas, who easily disappear among the peaks and hunt at night, and the endangered huemul deer, which live far from civilization, are rare sightings, as is the tiny pudú – the smallest deer in the world hides in the temperate forest along the Andes. Don't forget to look up too and spot the many birds that hover above the steppe and the mountains, including the tong-tailed meadowlark, the iconic Andean condor and the lesser horned owl with its distinct ear tufts.

Patagonia's varied landscapes provide ample opportunities for seeing wildlife, but it often takes patience, timing and a bit of luck. To maximize your chances for specific animals, visit during the right time of year; in season (June to December) you are almost guaranteed to spot southern right whales along the shores of Puerto Madryn and Península Valdés, while from late November through January young chicks with fluffy brown and white plumage run around in the continent's biggest colony of Magellanic penguins in Punta Tombo.

Coastal Patagonia

From the coast of Río Negro down to Tierra del Fuego, the shores along the Atlantic Ocean contain a wealth of animals. Parque Nacional Monte León, around 200km north of Río Gallegos in Santa Cruz Province, protects 40km of coastline and is home to Magellanic penguins, sea lions, guanacos and pumas. A bit further north, trek the coastline of Puerto San Julián and watch the abundant birdlife or go on a boat trip to Bahía San Julián to see more Magellanic penguins – roughly 130,000 of them. Local companies run trips to the bay, taking around two hours and led by marine biologists.

But the most popular place to see wildlife, particularly marine mammals, is Puerto Madryn and Península Valdés. This is where southern right whales migrate to breed – don't be surprised to see young calves jumping out of the water as you walk along the shore in the former, while the latter is also the only place on Earth where orcas have been seen to hunt on land by beaching themselves. Though you'd be extremely lucky to catch this phenomenon, to up your chances book a stay at La Ernestina (p407) where owner and orca specialist Juan Copello will take you on expeditions seeking out these killer whales.

Patagonian Forest and the Andes

You'll find the most intriguing and elusive animals at the foot of the Andes. Pumas exist in healthy numbers along the Andean cordillera, but are rarely seen, along with the endangered huemul and the pudú, a tiny deer with short single-pointed horns and a petite stature measuring not more than 38cm at the shoulder. Flying high above, you might glimpse the emblematic Andean condor – it has the largest wingspan of any bird of prey. Watching them navigate the wind, soaring high up on the Patagonian plateau, never gets old. Brought to Tierra del Fuego, the southernmost point of the Andes, by the Europeans in a futile attempt to establish a fur industry, the introduction of the beaver has had a devastating impact on the natural environment, destroying huge swaths of native forest. Further up, particularly around the Lake District in the northern parts of Patagonia, more introduced species include the red deer and wild boar which inhabit the dense Patagonian forest and grassy mountain slopes; both are also considered by many to be a pest.

Guanacos (p407)

MATT MUNRO/LONELY PLANET ©

Patagonian Steppe

Defined by its grassy semi-desert landscape, the Patagonian Steppe is where you find guanacos – one of four species of llamas found in Argentina – the endemic mara (or Argentine hare) and gray foxes (also known as Patagonian fox and the gray zorro), scurrying around national park entrances looking for discarded food left by tourists. Your best bet for sighting any of these animals is to head to Península Valdés and Punta Tombo – where you also have the chance to see big hairy armadillos and the much smaller pichi armadillos (endemic to Argentina) – or the less-visited Cabo Dos Bahías.

The black-chested buzzard-eagle is a broad-winged bird of prey that can reach a wingspan of 200cm. It is often to be found high in the Alpine forest or hovering over the grassy shrubland on the steppe, hunting for viscachas and other small animals. It's fairly difficult to spot though, as it rarely makes any sounds. Darwin's or the lesser rhea – the classic bird of the steppe – is an ostrich-like flightless big bird with brown plumage and three toes. It's only found on the Patagonian scrublands and the altiplano in South America where it feeds on plants, roots and the occasional lizard.

Environmental Threats

As in many countries around the world, the rift between economic and political interests and the environment and animals is very present in Argentina. Despite a solid network of national parks – most notably Parque Nacional Perito Moreno, Los Glaciares, Los Alerces and Tierra del Fuego – protecting vast areas of wilderness and conserving what is home to Patagonia's precious native wildlife, human intrusion in the region still poses one of the biggest threats to the region's fauna. Plans for hydroelectric dams on the Santa Cruz river would have huge, negative effects on endemic species relying on the surrounding wetlands. Overgrazing by domestic livestock causes erosion in Parque Nacional Los Glaciares. And mining plans in Chubut and deforestation in Tierra del Fuego both contribute to habitat loss at the expense of the region's diverse species. Patagonia and its wildlife face many challenges.

THE HEART OF TANGO IS BEATING

The music of Buenos Aires is living a second golden age after the boom of the '40s. The roots are still alive in the *milongas* and the young musicians' creations. By Diego Jemio

IT DOESN'T MATTER if it was a show for export or a small milonga full of locals – if you've ever seen tango dancing, it will have been the couple's embrace that caught your attention. It is a sensual, intimate and silent gesture. The world stops at that moment before the beginning of the music and the movement. It is one of the most beautiful aspects of this dance.

The History of Tango

As with many other types of music worldwide, it can take time to establish a precise starting point of tango. However, many researchers agree that tango is the offspring of cosmopolitan improvisations on both countries' banks of the Río de la Plata. The sounds came from *candombe*, *milonga*, Cuban habanera and polka, among other music.

These new dance and musical genres emerged in the Río de la Plata in the mid-19th and early 20th centuries, a period known as La Guardia Vieja. The great boom of tango came after a period of hatching and formalization of the music in the 1940s.

In the '40s, the great orchestras were mass consumption. On a walk through Buenos Aires, it was commonplace to hear a teenager whistling a tango on his way home from school. The dances were trendy, and tango was spread by mass media: radio, disco and cinema.

The country was a thriving territory, far from the fierce conflicts of Europe. Tango was the music of that party, which could be heard in cafes, clubs, salons and carnivals. The National Academy of Tango of Argentina defines that stage with one word: exaltation. In addition to popularity, Tango had reached great expressive maturity.

After the '50s, the popularity of tango began to fall. In parallel, the worldwide phenomenon of rock and roll and the local phenomenon of Argentine folklore, driven by the popular nationalist culture promulgated by peronismo, began their methodical ascent. Just when tango seemed to be in terminal decline, a fundamental figure for modern music appeared: Astor Piazzolla.

Traditionalists said that his music was not tango. He countered that it was the contemporary music of Buenos Aires. Radios ignored his records, and only small labels released his recordings. But time has given its verdict. Today, Astor Piazzolla is the most influential tango musician internationally and, undoubtedly, the most interpreted by artists of other genres. It is not surprising because, throughout his life, he was influenced by jazz. And later, he

519

was an inspiration not only for tango musicians but also for rock musicians. The author of 'Libertango', 'Las cuatro estaciones porteñas' and 'Adiós Nonino' died in 1992.

In the last years of the 20th century, so-called electronic tango burst with force, although it later declined, with reference groups such as Malevo, Gotan Project and Bajofondo. At first, the media spoke of electronic tango as a great animator of this musical genre, which had arrived to fan the flame of tango. However, what began as an expansion without a ceiling became something small.

Give Tango a Go

Visitors who want to know what the atmosphere of the popular dances of the 1940s was like can go to Villa Malcom, a tango club founded in 1928, which still offers tango practices in the Villa Crespo neighbourhood.

Tango singers of all ages still gather at El Boliche de Roberto, a bar in the Almagro neighborhood, which opened in 1893. Every night, the musicians relive the ritual of meeting, of singing without a microphone, with a drink in their hands. Those walls are witness to the music of Osvaldo Pugliese and Carlos Gardel, who passed through the place.

Another place where tango lives outside the show lights is Los Laureles in Barracas, almost on the border between the city and the outskirts of Avellaneda. On Thursdays, a meeting of singers is organized, where old glories and the new generations of tango meet. The atmosphere is familiar, and it is a pleasure to spend the evening listening to those heartfelt tangos while, through the window, you can see the streets with the old cobblestones.

Another essential *milonga* for understanding the world of tango is La Viruta

in Palermo, the neighborhood most popular among tourists. Since its inception in the 1990s, this venue has aimed to make the traditional *milonga* codes more flexible. Furthermore, it pioneered offering tango lessons before the formal dance, effectively democratizing the art form.

Similarly, La Catedral de Almagro provides a bohemian atmosphere in a rustic old shed. Alongside tango classes and dancing space, it often hosts other music shows. At Maldita Milonga, in the traditional neighborhood of San Telmo, the worlds of classic and contemporary tango converge. Every Thursday, this venue offers live music and, of course, a *milonga*.

THE TANGO ACTIVITY IN BUENOS AIRES IS SO INTENSE AND DIVERSE TODAY THAT SOME SPECIALISTS AND SCHOLARS SPEAK OF A MOMENT SIMILAR TO THE GOLDEN AGE OF THE DANCE.

The tango activity in Buenos Aires is so intense and diverse today that some specialists and scholars speak of a moment similar to the golden age of tango. 'In the last 20 years, tango has significantly contributed to new sounds, creativity, and the revival of old styles. Today, in the city, you can find orchestras that play just like those from years past and others that explore innovative ideas. Young people dedicated to dancing and playing tango have expanded the repertoire and resurrected songs from bygone eras,' Gabriel Soria, President of Argentina's National Tango Academy, shared in a conversation with this writer.

Why do tourists love tango as much as *porteños* do? It isn't easy to know precisely; perhaps it's because of the connection of that intimate embrace, which is somewhat distant in some cultures. Maybe it's the energy that tango expresses or because it's an excellent way to socialize and make friends. What is certain is that tango is alive and pulsating in this city. Exploring it in the city's bars and *tanguerías* with a curious spirit is a truly worthwhile endeavor.

Dancing the tango, Argentina

INDEX

Map Pages **000**

Map Pages **000**

"Buenos Aires has managed to preserve its ancient traditions and the charming corners of yesteryears."
– DIEGO JEMIO

"The world's most southerly well-populated land is a storied island where the windswept, subpolar pampa makes way for snowcapped mountains, glacial waters and Antarctic wildlife."
– VICTORIA GILL

Mapping data sources:
© Lonely Planet
© OpenStreetMap http://openstreetmap.org/copyright

THIS BOOK

Destination Editor
Alicia Johnson

Production Editor
Graham O'Neill

Book Designer
Virginia Moreno

Cartographer
Julie Dodkins

Assisting Editors
Andrea Dobbin,
Melanie Dankel,

Clifton Wilkinson,
Maja Vatrić

Cover Researcher
Lauren Egan

Thanks Ronan
Abayawickrema,
Imogen Bannister,
Karen Henderson,
Alison Killilea,
Vicky Smith

MIX
Paper from responsible sources
FSC® C021741
www.fsc.org

Paper in this book is certified against the Forest Stewardship Council™ standards. FSC™ promotes environmentally responsible, socially beneficial and economically viable management of the world's forests.

Published by Lonely Planet Global Limited
CRN 554153
13 edition – May 2024
ISBN 9781838696689
© Lonely Planet 2024 Photographs © as indicated 2024
10 9 8 7 6 5 4 3 2 1
Printed in China